A Hardcore Heart

Adventures in a D.I.Y scene

By David Gamage

Published by Earth Island Books
Pickforde Lodge
Pickforde Lane
Ticehurst
East Sussex
TN5 7BN

www.earthislandbooks.com

First published by Earth Island Books 2022

ISBN 9781739647735

Printed and bound by Solopress, Southend.

To my brilliant boys, Carl and Jake –
may you always have adventures and find your own scene

Contents

A Hardcore Heart

Adventures in a D.I.Y scene

By David Gamage

1, Instrumental

Right from the start I want to say that I fully realise that not everyone reading this book will have heard of the bands I talk about. Probably not Rydell or Couch Potatoes, let alone Joeyfat or Come The Spring, nor even BHP fanzine, Ignition or Engineer Records, and certainly not much of the obscurity and minutiae of the hardcore scene that follows. For now, that really doesn't matter as it will all be explained. This book is about a group of friends on tour, the people we met, the bands we played with, the venues we visited and the adventures we had along the way. What follows is a story of enthusiasm and passion, of youthful exuberance and heartfelt belonging, of really building and being part of a scene. It's something that meant the world to us and still does to me, informing much of what I do, the way I look at things and those I call my friends, even to this day. We started out in garages and basements, village halls and pub back rooms, the exact same way as a thousand other bands did, and anyone who's been in a group will be able to relate to this story. My friends and I started a band, and it was a great thing. For us, the destination didn't matter so much, but we wanted the journey to be fun. We went off wandering through hardcore-land and this book is all about what we found.

To set the scene; it was the end of the eighties, the Berlin wall had just fallen as the cold war thawed and Europe was joining back together, but all was not well, and riots would take place at the football or on the streets, over anything from inequality, poverty, or the poll tax. The world could seem an unjust and cruel place, and just like it is now, any negativity would be amplified by the media and brought straight to your door. Students and civilians were being shot during peaceful protests in Tiananmen Square and sex selective abortion was being practised in China. IRA bombs were going off on mainland UK and Ayatollah Khomeni had placed a fatwa on Salman Rushdie for his Satanic Verses. Electronic tagging was introduced in the UK for criminal suspects and permanent gates were erected at the end of Downing Street. Margaret Thatcher was Prime Minister of the UK and George Bush senior had just taken over from Ronald Reagan as President of the US. The Chernobyl nuclear power plant meltdown was still being tidied up and the Exxon Valdez had just run aground in Alaska. Like a tiny sunken needle in the vast Atlantic haystack, the wreckage of the Titanic had been found, although it later turned out that they hadn't even been looking for it, they were searching for a damaged nuclear submarine!

The AIDS epidemic was rife and famine still wracked Africa, but on the plus side we'd had the Live Aid concert and the 'Do they know it's Christmas?' singles so surely all would soon be well. For our musical entertainment, Michael Jackson, George Michael, U2, Madonna and Bros were all in the charts, whilst Back to the Future, Indiana Jones and Batman were showing at the cinema. Coronation Street, Blind Date, Only Fools and Horses and Top of the Pops were all regular TV favourites. This is what we were dealing with on a daily basis.

The expectations and norms of society seemed to be about getting into a lifelong career, as baby boomers kids became yuppies with nine to five jobs based on gathering money and comfort at almost any cost. Everywhere community spirit and altruism seemed to be diminishing, whilst self-interest and greed were on the rise, and if you let yourself, you could sleep-walk into a very grey and mundane existence. I did not want that. I wanted to learn, I wanted to travel, and I wanted something creative to be a big part of my life.

My dad, Peter, was a great man and a good artist. A painter and handyman, he'd found himself working for the NHS in a maintenance job where, although he made many friends, he spent most of his days re-painting dilapidated hospital walls and fixing broken down equipment. To add to our income my mum ran her own hairdressing business, Pamela's, where she spent most of the day setting blue rinses, drinking tea and gossiping with her customers about their lives and all the local characters. My parents both worked hard to look after our family. I have two brothers and a sister. My identical twin brother, Steve, and I both went to the grammar school in Tunbridge Wells, the first in our family to do so, and we did pretty well. I wanted to start work and earn money rather than stay on to do A levels, so I started at an easy office job in town, but immediately knew it wasn't really for me. When my dad suffered a stroke, I left work to help look after him. His art and myriad other interests always inspired me, and he seemed to get better for a while, but when he died, just three days before my eighteenth birthday, I realised how short life was and became even more determined to follow my passions and live my own way.

I'd gotten into rock, then heavy metal, then hardcore and punk rock in my teens, and for now I'd work any dead-end job so that I could buy records or go to a gig whenever I wanted to. Music was already becoming a big part of my life, and I was getting into the social aspects of it too, enjoying the close-knit community. Remember, this was way before the internet or social media, so you had to seek out like-minded individuals locally to build your own scene. No one was going to do it for us, but that was fine. We were young punks, in a very literal, do-it-yourself, underground community kind of way. We went to see every band we could and soon started getting more involved, putting on shows and starting a fanzine. Sure, we all had our friends and favourites, but we supported each other and made every effort we could to help people out and build something special. This was thirty years ago now, but what we'd stumbled onto would shape the way we'd view the world for the rest of our lives. Looking back now, with careers of sorts, mortgages, families and responsibilities, we may seem a little less punk to those that don't know us, certainly less carefree or spontaneous, but I assure you, it's in our blood and we'll always be rebels at heart.

Couch Potatoes would be my first proper band. Before that I'd been in a few rock and punk jam sessions with friends, and most notably a punk rock band called 'The Yobs'. This was when I was about sixteen and my word, we made an awful racket. A few mates, my brother and I had turned the basement beneath my mum's shop, which was actually an old bomb shelter that ran underneath Chandos Road in Tunbridge Wells, into a pretty decent place for parties and for bands to practise in. It was a little bit damp and mouldy, but we attempted to sound-proof it, painted it up and called it 'The Madhouse'. We jammed with whatever instruments we could find. Eventually forming a band of sorts with a few school friends – all punk rock and alternative lifestyle nerds. This was a proper 'old skool' '77 style punk band, with studs and spikey hair, and we wrote songs about nuclear war and the IRA, Margaret Thatcher and John Merrick, all sorts of nonsense. Partly because we were into alternative politics and partly because we couldn't play our instruments very well, The Yobs became a noisy punk band. I played guitar (badly), my bro Steve played the bass (even worse), Adam French, a life-long friend who would later become the bassist of both Couch Potatoes and Rydell, was the singer / shouter and another good friend, Damian Farnes, played the drums (actually pretty well).

We all jokingly called Damian 'Omen' as he was into horror films and dabbling in Satanism, and of course as Damian was the name of the antichrist in the Omen franchise of horror movies. I have to say that Damian was by far the best musician among us back then and he became a great drummer, sure enough going on to play in several punk, metal and goth bands, including Deadlights, Dayglo Buffalo, Purity of Decadence, Drag and Lynching Maria. The only one of those bands to gain much recognition was Purity of Decadence, although that was partly because they were the only goth band for miles around. They had a manager though and recorded a single at the Granary Studios in Tunbridge Wells, which helped them build a decent following and play quite a few good shows up in London. I remember they were in the local papers one time, after the Reverend Michael Banner, a vicar who wrote books about Christian ethics and contemporary moral issues, turned up at one of their gigs at the Forum to see their lead singer, all 6'7" of him in his New Rocks and rubber catsuit, happily passing a bloody pig's heart around the audience. The Rev walked out in disgust, branding Purity of Decadence the work of the devil in his weekly column and they did pretty well from that.

Later, Damian also collaborated with Niall Parker from Age of Reason and Gravity Machine in his early band Order of Azrael after recording Purity of Decadence's first demo with him. It amuses me to tell you that The Omen also worked for a while with a famous Swedish jingles composer too. At one PoD show the ex-tour manager of Duran Duran, who was at the time managing the massively popular Scottish rock band Travis, saw them play and said that Omen was the best drummer she'd seen for years. Clearly his early days in 'The Yobs' had set him up well.

Getting high with The Yobs in The Basement

Damian was also a great illustrator and painter so did all the art for the dodgy live tapes we eventually came up with for The Yobs and any posters or banners we needed too. He developed his style through drawing demons and painting art for RPG sessions, so much so that one of his paintings was used in the Dragon Warriors books. We all thought he'd go on to make a good living from that, but instead, he's currently working for a logistics company as an anti-traffic-warden trying to get their driver's parking fines cancelled.

Anyway, The Yobs wrote songs prolifically as we weren't too worried about the artistry or quality but instead wrote noisy, fun, minute-long blasts of anger, humour, or both. We developed a rough metally punk style and had a couple of practises that turned into mini shows when a bunch of people we knew turned up unexpectedly. We also played at a few parties, sometimes in garages or basements, but usually at our mates houses when their parents were out. More often than not these spontaneous 'gigs' would carry on until we were stopped by the owners returning home or the neighbours freaking out because of the noise. All this was really just a warm-up for the real thing that was coming.

By now I'd been strumming on a guitar for much of my teen years. Initially introduced to it by my next-door neighbour, Nik Neeves, a good friend who'd started jamming with me when I was about fourteen. We'd play football and hang out together, listen to obscure rock bands, and as Nik was having guitar lessons, he decided to try to teach me a few things. Some of it stuck, but as I was into the heavier side of rock music, I'd be hammering away on my crappy guitar, trying to chug along with various crunchy riffs as best I could. Nik, who was and still is a great guitarist, as well as a massive Jimi Hendrix and blues fan, would encourage me to try to add certain subtleties to what I was doing. We'd both be playing along to 70's or 80's rock albums with some attempts sounding better than others. Rainbow, Deep Purple, Led Zeppelin, and then later AC/DC, Iron Maiden, Thin Lizzy and the like. Anything with a good riff. I loved the rock and metal but by now was getting into more noisy punk bands like Discharge, GBH and The Damned. Their songs were easier to play and had an angry energy to them that I really liked.

Nik had a really heavy, solid old Westone Thunder guitar, with an active battery in the back to give the pickups a little more power. He'd play this through a Fender combo amp with a few basic effects and it sounded great. I had a really dodgy Les Paul copy, which I'd bought off a mate for a few quid and promptly covered it in stickers. It didn't really want to stay in tune and it was hard to make it sound any good, plugged into a crappy little Peavey amp. As we played along together though, we'd slowly get better at the riffs and timings, and then start coming up with our own ideas and additions. Nik would have a crack at most of the solos and lead parts, with mixed success in his bluesy style, until I gradually became more dextrous, more confident and a little bit better at it. Although, as many will readily tell you, I'm still learning the guitar even now and thirty years of fretboard gymnastics later, I know my style still has plenty of room for improvement.

Adam bringing the anarchy with The Yobs

As well as all the mainstream rock bands you will have heard of, we tried to jam along with and emulate anything new we could find, from blues guitarists to noisy punk bands and thrash metal, Nik would dig up all sorts of weird stuff and bring it along. There was a US stadium group called Foghat that he was into who had some good riffs, and a really oddball Finnish rock band that he'd insist on playing called Sielun Veljet. They were Scandinavia's answer to the UK's own Sigue Sigue Sputnik, who incidentally, I saw play in the recreation ground clubhouse in St James Park in Tunbridge Wells to about 100 people. This was just as their big hit, 'Love Missile F1-11', was zooming up the charts. It was kind of hair rock and new wave punk, with a touch of Dr and the Medics playing Norman Greenbaum's late 60's psychedelic anthem, 'Spirit in the sky'.

I've travelled to Finland many times since and I know the locals there can be an odd bunch. Nik tells me that Sielun Veljet now have something to do with tractors in their home country and have opened a bar in Helsinki where you sit on barrels or straw bales and eat off tractor engine hoods. I have no idea why, but apparently this became quite popular over there. Anyway, we kept on jamming and got into thrash bands like Metallica, Anthrax, Slayer and Testament, these were followed by Acid Reign, Sabbat, Nuclear Assault and Tankard, and then more crossover bands like DRI, Gang Green, Wehrmacht and SOD. This influenced how I started to play. Fast, chuggy, crunchy riffs that you could develop melodies over the top of or just rock out to. But these guys were listening to hardcore as we know it and this would be the real deal. I'd see the bands names on their t-shirts or thanks lists and check them out. Descendents, Minor Threat, Dag Nasty, Black Flag, SNFU, 7 Seconds, Gorilla Biscuits. I soon found that this was what I'd been looking for, both the music and the message. I was hooked, for life, and delved deeper and further into the hardcore scene. I thank and blame those old HC bands, and Nik, as they really helped me develop what little guitar style I have back in the early days.

Part of the reason Nik had gotten into a load of odd Finnish stuff was that he had been writing to a Finnish pen pal called Helja. She'd been sending him weird things to check out, probably to fend him off, but undeterred he went over to Finland to meet her and came back telling us that she was lovely, definitely the one for him, and that one day they would marry! He was just eighteen at the time but was absolutely earnest about it. Sure enough, they are married now and have a lovely daughter, Erin. They live in Helsinki where Nik gets his native American style tattoos from the guy who inks the Red Hot Chilli Peppers. He still calls me up to talk about new bands and I know he plays heavy metal and early hardcore to anyone who is foolish enough to visit 'Nik's Barber Shop' when in town.

I lived in Royal Tunbridge Wells no less, so not very promising for a punk rock band you'd think, but this is the same town that had spawned The Anti-Nowhere League, had taught Sid Vicious at Sandown Court school, and has since kicked out The Slaves, as well as hundreds of alternative indie bands. The town had already created quite a few great rock bands too, including the old school metal, head-banging goodness that was Deuce.

It was good to have some local inspiration and Deuce were big heroes of mine, especially early on when I was just leaving school and working at my first jobs. Those are the times you really need an evening out. I'd been to see Deuce play so many times over the previous years that I'd lost count, jumping in the back of their tour van, or into a car or minibus heading to some pub or rock club in the depths of London or the southeast of England. I'd met them in JB's, the musical equipment store run by Jonathan Birch, the Anti-Nowhere League's (fourth) drummer, and we'd just got chatting. I went along to see them play at some local pub and loved the atmosphere of it all. It may well have involved a lot of shaggy permed hair for them and clothes so tight that even veins stuck out, but they clearly enjoyed playing and their gigs were always a great night out.

This was the mid to late eighties before Porky, actual name Paul Belton, one of two lead guitarists in the band, went on to form St Hellier. The other guitarist in Deuce, a guy called Mick McGovern, later moved to Somerset and formed another great rock band, called Engine Room. They were both incredible guitarists. Their own songs had a mixture of the bands I was into early on, Thin Lizzy, Iron Maiden, AC/DC and the classic rock of the late 70's too. I remember they covered some great tracks, Bob Seger's 'Rosalie', Golden Earring's 'Radar Love', Mud's 'Tiger Feet' and Deep Purple's 'Black Night'. This might seem cheesy now, but this was great stuff to see played live, especially when you are a teenager just hanging out at the show with your mates. To get to one particularly well hyped Deuce show I actually quit my job, nothing impressive, just stacking shelves at Tesco's, but because they wouldn't let me have an evening off to go and see the band play, I got to say the famous Dead Kennedy's line "Take this job and shove it, I don't work here anymore!"

As much as I was into heavy rock, by this time I was listening to a lot of punk bands too. I liked The Damned, GBH, The Ruts, The Buzzcocks, also Dead Kennedys, Discharge and Circle Jerks, but these bands just didn't seem to play very often, certainly not in the southeast of the UK, and I really wanted to see bands play live. I wanted to go and see bands who could actually play their instruments well, so I gravitated more towards rock acts. When crossover bands like D.R.I, S.O.D. and Gang Green came over to the UK I was there at the Marquee, and later the Astoria, stagediving with my friends. This progressed through well-known US thrash bands like Anthrax, Slayer, Metallica, Sacred Reich, Suicidal Tendencies, Wehrmacht, Death and Testament, and German groups such as Tankard and Kreator, on to their UK counterparts, all of whom had real character and stage presence, but particularly Acid Reign and Sabbat. I even had a gansta rap phase going to see bands like Ice-T, Public Enemy, Gunshot and Credit to the Nation. I'd been 'hanging on the apple core' at Acid Reign shows and noticed them wearing Descendents t-shirts, so thought I'd better check them out. Before long the Descendents became my absolute favourite band, and I was listening to 'I don't want to grow up' and later 'Milo goes to college' on regular rotation. I soon got into Minor Threat, Black Flag and 7 Seconds too, and then loads of more obscure punk and hardcore bands you may not have heard of, unless of course you too are an old school punk rocker like me. These mainly US bands would now be called 'seminal hardcore acts' with a deserved sense of gravity and adulation. The energetic music, the heartfelt lyrics and the general feeling of anger dealt with through honesty, positivity and unity really spoke to me. The music was great, but this went way beyond the music.

All of this paved the way for my first band, Couch Potatoes, a far more dedicated and structured affair than The Yobs. Right from the start we wanted to be a 'proper' band, serious about our music, well-practised, and most of all, out there gigging as much as possible. Soon we'd bought some half decent equipment and found a regular place to practise. Initially this was the garage at my mum and dad's house, which the neighbours absolutely loved, I can tell you. We'd taken some time to learn a few covers first and then gradually wrote some songs of our own. It was really good fun just to play and hang out, and the better we got at it, starting to sound like an actual band, the more fun it became. Soon of course, we wanted to start playing gigs to see how it all went down in the real world.

Now, all the bands I have ever been in have been groups of friends first and musicians second. Whether this has been a good thing or not with regards to our musical output, the jury is still out. But I suppose you'll just have to play one of our many records or come to a show to decide that for yourself. This has always meant that fun and friendship has been a major part of everything I have done in a band, even more than musical ability. This would be a good thing to remember later on, when we were touring around dingy squats and damp clubs across the UK and Europe. It allowed us to see it all as an enjoyable adventure as much as an artistic exercise. I can tell you that it'd be very easy to get on each other's nerves in a bad tour situation if things aren't going well, and I'm not saying that never happened, but it was thankfully very rare and if ever, usually the fault of an outside influence.

All the guys in Couch Potatoes were very close friends. Ian 'Yan' Harland, our vocalist, Adam 'Ads' French, our bassmaster general, and me, on guitar, were all in the same year at school and shared many of the same classes too. More important even than this though was that we all had similar tastes in music and had been hanging out and going to shows together for ages already. The teenage hijinks we three, along with my twin brother Steve, got up to would be plenty enough for another book, but that's not really relevant here and would likely, even now, get us in a lot of trouble. We needed a drummer and roped in a guy called James Booth. Jim was a friend from the year below us at school that we'd gotten to know even better since we'd all left to bounce around in the real world. At this time Jim was going to West Kent College but he never seemed to study much as he'd gotten himself a second-hand drum kit and would be tapping madly on tables and desks, working out rhythms all day long, then going home to practise and perfect them. His total enthusiasm for drumming helped him become

Omen, possessed by the beat

really good remarkably quickly. By this point I'd been playing guitar for a while and Adam had tried singing, but found he was a much better bass guitarist. Yan had the best voice of us all and was brave enough to go for it, so was volunteered as the singer. That was it, we'd formed a band, and started jamming immediately, slowly getting better.

At seventeen I was rolling around in my first car, a burgundy Honda Accord with various shiny chrome parts on it that I'd polish and try to stop falling off. It seemed to be an absolute magnet for the cops, and I lost count how many times they stopped me for seemingly no reason whatsoever. Yan and Adam also had cars, semi-reliable run-arounds that weren't absolute bangers, which was a good job as they lived over in Sevenoaks, about twelve miles away. Jim was a year younger and didn't have a car yet, but lived in a house, called 'Goblins Glen', on the edge of a farmyard that always stunk of cow shit. This was in Hadlow, near Tonbridge, so was kind of on the way between Sevenoaks and Tunbridge Wells which made it easy for pick-ups. At first, we thought we'd practise in one of those stinky farm buildings, far away from anyone, but Jim's dad was home a lot and a right grumpy old turd, so that didn't work out very well at all. This meant that a lot of driving around, picking up equipment and arranging practises ensued, but we all had spare time and were determined to make it work.

Couch Potatoes started practising at my house but that was soon getting serious push back from the neighbours. I don't blame them, we weren't very good to start with, and there was a particularly hard no from an older lady who lived over the road. There's a hilarious photo of us taken by one of my mates, where she's shouting at me and wagging her finger whilst I just stand there, in a Tankard t-shirt, beach shorts, baseball boots and mullet, strumming a star-shaped Ibanez guitar, that I'd probably turned up to eleven. We deserved it, but this still cracks me up. That Ibanez Explorer was actually my third guitar, as the Les Paul copy had its neck snapped clean off in a very energetic moshing session and was replaced by a bright blue Columbus guitar. Basically, a cheap Charvel copy, very heavy metal with a pointed headstock and a whammy bar. I loved it for a while, but it had a fretboard like cheese-wire and didn't sound too great either. I soon managed to kill that too and decided to splash out on the Ibanez. A different league of guitar entirely, but nothing to the Gibsons I use now. Anyway, I apologise unreservedly to the patient and partly deaf residents of Chandos Road and Granville Road in the St James area of Tunbridge Wells.

So, as we were slowly getting better and really didn't want to turn down our amps, and you just can't turn down drums even if you try. Next, we tried to sound-proof both the garage and the basement at my parents' house, eventually finding out that no matter what we did, it was still too loud, so we started looking for other places to rehearse.

First, we tried out this old barn, next to a run-down house right on the edge of town, in what has now become the Tunbridge Wells industrial estate. This place was situated right in the glamorous end where the dump (recycling centre) and sewage farm are. God only knows how we found it or were offered to go there. I think it belonged to a friend of my brothers and they were long-suffering enough to let us make some noise there for a while. It served us pretty well for a few weeks until one fine day an entire gang of gypsies turned up. Some just wandered in the front door without a 'by your leave', others climbed in through the windows that we'd left open as it was a hot day and there were no nearby neighbours. They'd been living in the woods nearby and had heard us playing. I guess they just wanted to hang out. At the time it was a little intimidating though as they had such broken traveller speech it was hard to understand them. We offered them a drink, probably foolishly, so they hung around and began asking us if we knew any Elvis songs, or if we could play any Eagles covers. Ha, we could hardly play our own stuff. It would have been hilarious if it wasn't so scary out there on the edge of the woods, like a scene from Deliverance. If I'd have heard 'He's got a real pretty mouth ain't he?' or anything about squealing like a pig, I would have legged it for sure. Needless to say, we kept on looking for an alternative practise spot.

Next, we were told about a garage space at the back of a pub called The Bull Inn in Brenchley. It was our buddy, Clive Martin, who'd come up with this idea as one of his metaller friends, Pugsy, was working at the bar there and had noticed that it was empty and pretty much unused, so kindly asked for us. We gave that a go a couple of times, with the added benefit of a bar next door, but the pub was in a residential area, so

Practising in the garage and bringing the metal

predictably enough the racket we made was not at all appreciated by the locals and that didn't last too long either.

Then we found the Headway centre, a youth club in town situated near our old school. This may seem like a more obvious choice I hear you saying, but most 'youth clubs' at the time were religious affairs, run by church groups and were fairly strict on what they'd allow. Although we weren't exactly devil-worshipping church-burners we figured our punk band might not really suit them. But luckily for us, Headway was a brain injury charity and quite willing to help special needs kids like us. I don't know why, but as teenagers, with all the noisy music and head banging that was going on, it being a brain injury charity amused us. In any case, the people there were friendly, and we were sure this place would be way better for us to practise at. It turned out that the club was being run by a brummie guy who was really into rock music, so said we could have any evenings that the hall wasn't already rented out on. This was excellent news and we got stuck in. I swear he wanted us to play Slade covers so he could sing along, but when he found we wouldn't, he just closed his office door and put up with our racket with very good-hearted nature. There was also a kettle and vending machine for sweets and snacks, with easy parking right outside the door for moving equipment in and out, and the club was far enough from any houses, right on the edge of a playing field, so that we didn't get bugged about the noise at all. This became our regular slot for the next few months, and later on we'd help do the place up and even put on a few fairly successful shows there to raise money for the club and the charity.

So now we were getting better, writing our own music and all bringing ideas along to the jams, working on the songs until they clicked. Couch Potatoes had a definite direction in mind, inspired by melodic hardcore bands and wanting to be part of the growing UK hardcore scene. Maybe one day we'd make a record, but certainly we wanted the thrill of playing a few really good live shows ourselves. Hopefully our band would get good enough to go out on tour. That was the dream. But for now we were having a lot of fun just hanging out, putting our songs together, and taking the piss out of our host's thick Brummie accent.

We'd started out with a few easy covers by our favourite bands of the time, just to make sure we had the style and structure more or less down. Punky stuff like the Dead Kennedys and Hard-Ons, and then later Descendents when we were good enough to play that sort of thing. The Dents were absolutely our favourite band at the time and you can really hear the influence in any early Couch Potatoes recordings, both in the music and the lyrics. I know everyone strives for absolute originality in their art, but this wasn't our main goal back then. We just wanted to be able to play to a decent standard and had found a style of music we loved and were starting to get good at. This sort of pop-punk was hardly heard of in the UK at that time, late in '89, so we wanted to get out there and let people hear it.

1. Let's Drink Some Beer
2. Bartender
3. Lost Chapter
4. We'll Give It To You
5. We Can Go
6. Have Fun
7. Last Chance
8. Just One Bullet
9. Born To Rock
10. Rabies
11. Voices Carry
12. Sold Out
13. Bedroom Of Doom
14. Bomb
15. Alcohol
Bonus tracks:
16. Thunder"
17. Rub It In Your Face"

Duncan stagediving on the back cover of Gang Green´s live album!

Crushing punks at The Marquee

15

The early covers we played included 'A child and his lawnmower' by the Dead Kennedys, from their '87 album 'Give me convenience or give me death', 'Then I kissed her' originally by the Crystals, then made famous by the Beach Boys, although of course we played our own take on the faster, more heavy and distorted version the Hard-Ons had sung, partly in Arabic, on their 'Hot for your love, baby' '87 album. Don't ask me why. I guess it was just three chords, easy and fun to play. We also played 'Coffs Harbour Blues' and 'Yuppies Suck' by the Hard-Ons too, as all their stuff was really easy to work out. Later, we added 'Suburban home' and 'I'm not a loser' from the Descendents 'Milo goes to college' album, and 'I like food' and 'Hey Hey' from the 'Fat' EP. A while after that we added a few more subtle covers, one of which was 'Only of you' by a new band called Green Day, from their awesome '1000 Hours' EP. I had loads of fun working out and noodling that cool Billie-Joe guitar solo towards the end.

As well as the covers, we were writing our own songs now or trying to at least. The first keeper was called 'No More', we all loved the riff and Yan had come up with some good lyrics. We followed that with some faster bangers, 'Cold Can' and 'Tired' and some more mid-paced riffs in 'Such a bad day', 'I don't think so' and 'The Sound'. We were just starting to get half good so the next thing on our agenda would be to play some shows. That'd be the thing that made it all real.

Nothing was booked yet and getting shows as a new and unheard-of band isn't that easy, so to keep up our inspiration we'd all go and see pop-punk and hardcore bands as much as we could. We'd all be out at gigs every week. There'd be loads of us going along, not just the four of us in Couchies, but all our mates too, piling into cars or occasionally going up to town on the train, headed to any and all decent gigs that came along. I always thought that going to gigs in cars was way better as we could blast music all the way, stop for burgers, and stay out as late as we wanted. Driving your own car back then seemed like a real freedom. I guess it is for any new drivers but there were very few cameras then and we got up to all sorts of nonsense.

I'd saved up for my beaten-up old Honda Accord and thought I'd raised enough but found that as it had a 1600cc engine the insurance on it was almost as much again as the car was worth. Insurance companies were crooks then just as much as they are now. Luckily my dad knew this and was solid gold. He very kindly agreed to match what I'd saved, so thanks to him, I soon had my own transport and was rolling around. He did this for both of my brothers and my sister too, and considering he was a painter / maintenance man at the towns hospital that wasn't an inexpensive gesture. Thanks Dad. The Accord had a burgundy paint job, black roof and lots of chrome. It was a four-seater, but we'd often squeeze in six, or seven, or even eight if we used the boot too, usually deciding then to reward the brave passengers by hammering around car-parks or bridge jumping in it. I'm amazed the axles held out considering the number of times we bounced off down the road at high speed.

Adam diving in

Pigtails and dive fails

Acid Reign at The Marquee

I mentioned before that there were very few traffic or CCTV cameras around at this point and that was a damn good job, or my driving license would have been even more like a bingo card! However, the UK is now one of the most heavily surveilled countries in the world, second only to the US, with an average visit to London catching each person on camera at least 300 times. Back to the car. The old rustbucket had a few dodgy patches on it but ran well and I used to polish all the chrome on it when I was meant to be working. I'd spend ages looking for cassette tapes to play in the stereo and keep a pencil in the dash to wind them on too. One of the biggest issues when driving with your mates at seventeen, even in a fairly well to do suburban backwater like Tunbridge Wells, was dodging any patrolling cop cars who would always come and hassle you. The first year I was driving, and this is even when I was being sensible with just the four of us onboard, all lights on, tyres in good condition, well within the speed limits, and no-one hanging out the windows or roof-surfing, I was still stopped thirty-two times by the police. 32 times! That's in one year. It was never for anything serious, they just liked to hassle kids really. I was in and out of that poxy police station producing my documents on such a regular basis the desk sergeant knew me by name after a while, and that's surely not a good thing. Maybe they were just bored too, certainly that was how it seemed to me. Anyway, once past the cops and at the venues, there were plenty of great shows going on. They were usually packed, never more than about £3 on the door, and always great fun. The absolute sauna that was the Hard-Ons gig at the Fulham Greyhound particularly stands out. They must have thought they were back home on Bondi Beach in Australia. I don't think I've ever been so hot at a show in my life. There were so many good rock venues in London at the time and there seemed to be a gig worth seeing, or even two or three, every weekend.

Some of the best shows I remember from back then were the first All tour of the UK. They were the Descendents but had changed their name to All when their singer, Milo, went off to college. The Descendents were one of the seminal US hardcore bands and their songs managed to strike a chord with me more than most. I guess the lyrics could be a bit nerdish and naïve, mainly about girls, food, and hanging out, but the music was just amazing and there was something about these songs that really sparked empathy. Their early records came out in the eighties whilst Milo Aukerman was the vocalist, with Stephen Egerton on guitar, Karl Alvarez on bass and Bill Stevenson on drums. Then, when they became All, their first singer was Dave Smalley, of DYS, Dag Nasty and later Down By Law. They released the brilliant 'Allroy sez' album and 'Allroy for prez' EP, but by the time they came to the UK for the 'Allroys Revenge' tour Scott Reynolds was now singing and they were starting to get pretty well known. 'Allroy's Revenge' is an amazing record and Scott is one of the best vocalists I've ever heard. He was a massive influence on our singer, Yan, inspiring his own singing and songwriting. I can't remember exactly how we all hooked up but we went with them on pretty much the whole UK tour and just hung out. We got on very well with our shared love of food, music and taking the piss out of everyone and everything. Bill Stevenson stayed at Adam's, our bassist's, one night after they'd played a big show in Norwich at the Uni, and we drove him back with us so he could have a break, just get a shower and some rest. We persuaded him to try mushy peas, which after some initial complaints is now a firm favourite of his on UK trips. After long lie-ins the next day Adam made us all cheese on toast before we headed up to London for the next gig. We also saw them rock Brighton, downstairs in the tiny Basement club (where we would play many times over the next months and years), and Canterbury Uni too, where we went to McDonalds for high cuisine after soundchecks with Bill, Scott and Bug Phace, one of their roadies. We ate trays of cheeseburgers whilst setting the world to rights. "It's very hard to stay healthy when on tour," Bill warned us. But it certainly seemed easy to have fun.

The All show in London on this tour was particularly great and a week or two later I was shocked to see a really poor review of it from some inept music journo (Ian Cheek) who'd clearly just sat at the bar during their set. I'm pretty sure it was in Sounds, the least informed of the three national music mags at the time, the others being NME and Melody Maker. They all seemed to focus on shoegazing indie or grunge and had no clue about hardcore or even pop-punk. It wasn't a terrible review, just not good, and as the world's biggest fans of All / Descendents, it really annoyed us. Enough that we decided to write a letter and send it to the paper's editor.

Our letter simply said:

Ian Cheek is a twat. Your so-called reporter, who thinks that Scott Reynolds can't sing, must be deaf as well as unbelievably fucking stupid. All are the best band there will ever be. Please sack this utter knob-end.

Cheers, Couch Potatoes, Tunbridge Wells.

PS, You can stick all that Manchester stuff up your arse.

PPS, Ian Cheek is a twat.

Of course, we didn't expect to hear back, but unbelievably, in the very next week's issue, they actually published the letter, more or less word for word too! But for some reason, with typical inaccuracy, put Tonbridge instead of Tunbridge Wells as our address.

Yan saw a copy of this issue of Sounds first and came bounding around to show us all, laughing his head off. We were chuffed to bits they'd published it, and I dropped a copy of it to Bill, thinking he'd like it and have a good laugh. He wrote back, saying:

Dave,

I just wanted to say that what you guys wrote to Sounds in reply to their article about us is one of the best things that has ever happened to us.

The British press is notorious for not knowing the first thing about the actual music that they are writing about.

I'm glad you guys had the balls to slam this guy's words down his throat.

This has made me feel that there are people who actually comprehend exactly what we are trying to do – and that feeling doesn't come to me very often.

Take care and thanks,

Bill Stevenson.

As a major fanboy I was stoked and have kept that letter to this day.

Between going to gigs and messing around on my guitar I'd started exchanging a lot of letters with bands, labels, fanzines and promoters. It all seemed very easy and accessible to me. It felt like a friendly scene with a common goal and shared character that seemed to bind everyone together as equals. To my mind that made anything possible, and it was inspiring.

I'd soon be writing to a lot of people in the hardcore scene, exchanging info, sending out Couchies demos for gigs and collecting tracks for Gotham Tapes, a cassette / demo tape label that I'd put together, initially to send compilations to mates, now slowly developing and keeping me busy. I corresponded with quite a few bands and labels, receiving letters and tapes back from most of them, regardless of their size or fame. It just went to show how approachable and down to earth most of these guys were. If you got off your ass it wasn't too hard to put on a gig, run a zine, join a band, or even start a tape or record label. There was a lot of energy and enthusiasm, ideas were shared throughout the scene, so you felt you could just get on with it.

There also seemed to be loads of great shows being put on too, notably down in Brighton at several great venues and also along the coast at The Joiners in Southampton. All of these shows were very D.I.Y. Do It Yourself - Put on by local promoters or collectives of HC fans for the local kids, with flyers handed out and posters stuck everywhere, so despite a few ads in zines, the gigs generally became known about by word of mouth between the regular punters and they started to bring their friends. The whole 'Do It Yourself' ethic pervaded the punk scene from the very beginning and continued even more in the hardcore scene. If what you wanted didn't exist, you'd

Dave –

I just wanted to say that what you guys wrote to sounds (in reply to their article about us) is one of the best things that has ever happened to us.

The British press is notorious for not knowing the first thing about the actual music that they are writing about.

I'm glad you guys had the balls to slam this guy's words down his throat.

This has made me feel that there are people who actually comprehend exactly what we are trying to do. – – And that feeling doesn't come to me very often.

take care –

thanks –

Bill Stevenson

Bill Stevenson's letter

simply get up, go out and make it happen yourself. This sort of thing takes effort, of course, but that's what makes it so great, as what doesn't take effort that is worthwhile?

People were putting on shows, forming bands, writing zines, running record labels and even starting up a few radio stations. Everyone seemed to be doing things in small ways at first that soon became a lot bigger. They'd help each other and share information so there'd always be leaflets, flyers and posters all over for gigs, protests and events. It seemed that there was always something going on. You couldn't be lazy about it, you couldn't really just be a consumer, you had to get involved. It was a great scene to be part of as it welcomed all and looked after and entertained itself, and for such small set-ups there always seemed to be a great band playing somewhere or a party going on.

By now I really wanted to play some shows and we all agreed that Couch Potatoes were as ready as we were ever going to be, so we should just get out there and gig. We were working hard to make contacts with promoters and get some shows booked, but when at last a gig came up it was booked by our friend Macca, the bassist in our favourite local band, the BBMFs. The Beebs were another local band that massively influenced me and were definitely instrumental in my starting Couch Potatoes.

Macca had managed to get an evening for The BBMFs, Couch Potatoes and another new punk band called Deadworld, to play at The Shelley Arms in Nutley, a cool little pub venue deep in the East Sussex countryside with a tolerance for underage drinking. We'd seen loads of bands play there before and were all pretty excited about playing on that stage ourselves, knowing that a lot of our mates would be there to cheer us on, but still more than a little apprehensive about it too.

Deadworld was an anarcho punk band featuring the Marriott brothers, a couple of local punk characters, and would soon change their name to Active Response, as their main goal seemed to be to promote direct action, such as hunt-sabbing and protests. They used punk music as a message and came screaming out of East Grinstead, another home counties commuter town full of bored kids, clad in DM boots and army surplus fatigues, replete with mohawks and attitude. I think this was their debut show too as they didn't have many songs, but they rocked the gig with lots of chuggy punk riffs and shout-along political choruses.

The BBMFs were brilliant. Great guys, talented musicians and damn funny with it, so always a favourite to go and see play. They were a high energy punk band, but in a clever, original and often comical sort of way too. Always incredibly entertaining, as they could actually play their instruments, and I found their melodic style a real inspiration too. The Beebs knew that kids just wanted to have fun at gigs so were never too serious about it all. They'd often open their set (at the Shelley Arms, in the small Sussex village of Nutley), with 'No sleep 'til Nutley', their version of 'No sleep 'til Brooklyn' by the Beastie

The Shelley

Yan and Jim in the Accord

BBMFs demo tape

The BBMFs at The Shelley Arms

Boys. This would be changed to 'No sleep with Kylie' if they were playing elsewhere. Then it'd be into 'Banana milk' and 'Pant mosh' and other songs of theirs that rapidly became local scene classics, despite being a bit silly. They swapped the band name between Big Bastard Mother Fuckers, The BBMFs and The Beebs, and then much later on they would evolve into the only slightly more serious Rudedog.

The vocalist, Alan 'Al' Wilson, would talk a lot in-between songs, cracking jokes, chatting with the audience, and constantly changing hats on stage. For some reason he had a whole trunk of hats and caps to sift through and share, including some animal hoods. He'd bounce around the stage in his lion's head, occasionally roaring or falling over, whilst the rest of the band; Toby 'Toady' Donbroski on guitar, Mark 'Macca' Wilkinson on bass and Owen 'Oders' Ridley on drums, would just keep on playing and hold it all together. Al liked a bit of banter, but they'd just go off into the next song if he chatted for too long. As well as silly hats, Al had spare pants too, big y-fronts that he'd wear outside his camo-shorts and then throw down in front of the stage so that everyone would mosh around them in a circle during one of their songs, called 'Pantmosh'. It was all a bit silly, but everyone seemed to enjoy it and their crowds grew and grew.

The Beebs songs were mainly about simple, funny things; milkshakes, Newkie Brown, Mr Benn, awkward shopping trolleys, superfly hedgehogs, fantastic rabbits called Fraser, John 'tic tac' McCririck, E. R. Pinkus (his pants were stinkers) and generally being pukka geezers. This was 1990 and they were playing driving hardcore with lyrics kind of rapped over the top of it. Their style was way ahead of its time really, and also great fun, often to the point of hilarity. They'd already supported some pretty big punk / HC bands down in Brighton, like The Dickies and False Prophets, and were a tight unit live.

We played with The BBMFs many times early on and every occasion was a good show. They were certainly a big influence on Couch Potatoes and a great example of how to enjoy yourselves on stage and interact with the audience. They were good musicians and prolific songwriters and I still have some of their early demos on cassette. The cover artwork for one of these featured UK cartoon characters Stoppit and TidyUp as straight edge warriors with X's on their hands and baseball bats ready to beat you up if you littered. There was the BBMFs 'Fantastic Potato' demo, also the Thunderbirds inspired 'Beebs are go' and the classic 'Live at the Shelley' on my own Gotham Tapes, a recording of a live show obviously, but which also featured Couch Potatoes, Angus Bagpipe, Beanfeast and Headway too. The Beebs had a track, 'E.R.Pinkus', on a compilation LP with the gross name of Ingrown Toejam, as it was released by Toejam Records. They'd later have a track on the Concoction compilation CD, out on Jamboree Records, called 'I'm a Pukka Geezer (Such a pukka geezer)'.

After a while Macca went to Uni up in Sheffield and Oders wanted to try playing bass, so they brought in Jamie Donbroski, Toby's brother, on drums. Oders on bass didn't really work out though and when Macca came back, Oders left, and they roped in Al's brother Jon on second guitar and became even tighter. Up to this point Jon had been playing in an indie band called The Lawnmower Men, but with him on guitar it really allowed the batshit crazy Toady to start dancing around and rapping even more. Toady soon gave up the guitar just to sing and with two vocalists and everyone jumping around the BBMFs gigs turned into real parties.

Later in the nineties the BBMFs would try to take things a little more seriously, when they changed their name to Rudedog and signed with some guys from Take That and Steps management company, who obviously saw their potential. They spent quite a lot of time recording tracks in expensive studios but unfortunately not much of that work ever saw the light of day. The management couldn't decide on which demo tracks were best or find a profitable enough deal to release them I guess. The band never did fit neatly into a niche. They'd come a long way since singing about 'Trusthouse Forte toilet soap' and blowing up marrows on-stage with crow-scarers at their 50p entrance gigs. They'd even left their mosh pants and big hats behind, stumbling into the right place at the right time, but never taking it seriously enough to make anything of it. That always seemed a real shame to me as those guys could really rock and when they eventually broke up, we persuaded Macca, already a good friend, to join the Rydell line-up.

I have quite a few BBMFs demos and CDs from back then but am pretty sure that the only Rudedog tracks that saw official release was 'Rudedog' on the '97 compilation CD 'Wanted (Brighton)' and their excellent crowd-pleaser 'Give it Away' on the '98 'Unlabel Two' compilation, which also featured 'Try 17' by Rydell, as well as sixteen more tracks by bands who'd played with us at the '3 Days in May' event at the Tunbridge Wells Forum from 22nd to 24th May '98, including Stroppy, Cove and TipaGore. This CD was a giveaway for anyone who attended the shows and my copy still makes it out for an occasional listen.

I asked Macca if they'd released any of the Rudedog tracks more recently and he told me that they eventually put some of their later 'nu metal' style demos up online around 2002/3 and noticed that they were getting quite a few downloads. They checked where the interest was coming from and many of them appeared to be downloads at a US Airforce base, so it seems that Rudedog's rock rap stylings may have sound-tracked part of the Iraq war!

The BBMFs played at the Shelley Arms so many times it was like their home from home and we'd often all go along to hang out and have fun. This was not as easy as it sounds though as the venue was a pub absolutely in the middle of nowhere, with no public transport going to it. It was not even near the beaten track let alone off of it. Most of the crowd were kids who had only recently learnt to drive. They'd make their way from Brighton, Tunbridge Wells, East Grinstead and all the surrounding towns and villages to wheelspin in the carpark and then hang out watching the bands in the pub. The

Shelley seemed special to us, so we all thought it was well worth the effort to get there. When a hundred or so kids were jammed in, all along the bar and in front of the small stage, it made for one hell of an atmosphere at showtime.

Although it became a hardcore mecca for us, The Shelley Arms was actually an old Georgian coaching hotel that became a bit run down and turned into a day-drinkers pub. When our friend Warren took over running the place, he wanted bands to play and turned it into a great rock and indie venue, bringing it back to life in the evenings. It became the starting point for many local bands and soon featured on the indie / alternative touring circuit.

The Shelley had a large bar facing three sides of a lounge full of tables and chairs, with dark red curtained windows and posters all over the walls from the gigs that took place there. To one side was a small room with a pool table and a jukebox, with a door from there that led out into the back garden, which was nothing more than a square of grass with a couple more tables. The stage was small and low, but right in front of the bar and the main focal point of the entire pub. Warren had managed to get a decent p.a. system and a lighting rig hooked up too. He'd also painted the back wall behind the stage black so that bands would hang their banners there when they played. The whole place smelled of beer, crisps and sweat, and if you didn't know better you'd think it was one of those pubs where dreams go to die, but for us it was heaven. As well as The BBMFs I saw Doctor and the Crippens, Metal Duck, Jailcell Recipes, Libido Boyz, Go!, Drive, Sleep, Strength Alone, Beanfeast, Angus Bagpipe, Juice, The Spermbirds, UK Subs, Pseudo Hippies, Understand, Standoff, Sonar Nation and Goober Patrol all play there and most of them rocked the roof off the place The Shelley would also be where Couch Potatoes played our first ever show, and the venue Joeyfat ventured for our first ever gig too.

The Shelley is definitely a venue that means a lot to me, and many who've been there to play or see a gig would agree that it should go down in the annals of punk rock history. Luckily, it is a listed building so they can't knock it down, but they built a Little Chef next to it for a while and then knocked that down for more access, soon turning the car park into a housing estate. What's left of The Shelley Arms Hotel is now a private house which you can still see on the edge of the Ashdown Forest as you drive down the A22 between Wych Cross and Horney Common. It stands proud in its rock 'n' roll history, and important venue and cradle to many bands, now someone's home more or less opposite the Hathi Indian restaurant. Whenever I drive past I'm reminded of all the great shows there; the reckless energy of kids diving off the bar to Jailcell Recipes or Libido Boyz, the madness of Doctor and the Crippens throwing foam cakes or spitting fire in scary costumes, the tightly honed noise of Joeyfat hammering out a manic rhythm with our backs to the audience, or the pure fun of Couch Potatoes jumping around playing Descendents and Green Day covers, and it always, but always, makes me smile.

In a way that is what this book is all about. The people we met and the places we went, what happened and how it made us feel. I can only write about what I know, and I know that this takes a whole scene. Everyone needs to get involved and be part of it. This is in no way a rose-tinted reminiscence, and certainly not some rockstar's ego trip. I'll talk about the bands we played with, the venues that put us on, the records we made and our own small-scale punk-rock adventure. I think the D.I.Y. style and underground scale of what I'm writing about will make this book much more real and interesting to many; as this could be about you, or your girlfriend, or the guy next door. Just starting a band with a few mates and going out to have some fun and play some gigs. There's no stadium shows or private jets, more's the pity, but plenty of insight into the UKHC scene and anecdotes about quite a few of its leading bands. The ups and downs of an unheard-of rock band, on the road. I was caught up in it all and on the inside of a scene that I am still proud to be a part of. What I've learnt is just as important to me now as it was then, and it's been great fun to re-visit everything for this book. I hope you enjoy it too...

Jim and Adam larking about in too much denim at practise

2, The first five

That first Couch Potatoes gig, on a hot sweaty evening in July 1990, was a real game changer. The audience, numbering maybe just seventy-five people and mainly made up of our friends, were all there to have a good evening and see the bands play well, but the four of us were still very nervous. We'd practised over the weeks before, sound-checked earlier that evening, and even double checked the tuning and levels, but I can tell you, we were bricking it. After all, we'd seen a lot of our heroes play at The Shelley and it meant a lot to us, so when we stepped up onto that little stage for the very first time, we were all shaking. Mind you, we were also damn determined to put on a good show and not let ourselves down. I find that solid, thick-minded determination can overcome your nerves every time if you care enough about what you are doing.

I slung on my guitar and checked my gear. The leads were plugged in and the amplifier turned up. I glanced around at my bandmates, they all looked ready, we were good to go. So I strummed my guitar to check it was loud enough and sounding good. I chose a simple A chord and it reverberated around the stage. I love that fat distorted sound of a punk rock guitar. Standing directly in front of your amp on a small stage you'd feel it as much as hear it, vibrating all through your body and into your balls. I looked out at a couple of my mates standing chatting at the bar and casting around recognised plenty of friendly faces. Feeling my confidence rise I was letting the chord gradually turn into feedback. Then, before I could think about it too much, Yan was introducing us; "Hi, we're Couch Potatoes", Jim's counting us in, 2, 3, 4, and off we go.

We had a song called 'No more' about quitting your job and just playing in a band, it had a pretty decent riff, though I say so myself, and Yan had written some good lyrics for it, so we opened with that. I went from being jelly-legged petrified to absolutely elated and buzzing by the time we'd finished that first song. We'd managed to get through it pretty well so now I was grinning like a madman. The adrenaline was loosening me up now and I was starting to relax and enjoy it. Everyone was. Jim was smiling and clicking us in for the next song already. Yan and Adam were bouncing up and down, and our friends were clapping and cheering. I know it was a 'home' crowd, but that first song had gone very well and most of the kids seemed genuinely into it. We ripped straight into the next song. This was going OK.

I was moving around with the music but concentrating on what I was playing so didn't look up at the audience too much initially. At the end of the song I looked out and then around at the guys again and all I could see was smiles. Jim was twirling his drumsticks, wearing his laughable fingerless gloves, Adam was grinning from ear to ear and catching his breath from jumping around so much, and Yan was bouncing up and down on the spot, already introducing the next song. "You know, I've had such a bad day. Just such a bad day" he intoned in some Sloane ranger piss take voice and we ripped into the next song, 'Such a bad day'. We only had seven or eight songs ready for that gig. Just a short set, twenty-five minutes at most, probably less the way we ripped through them, but I can't tell you how much fun it was.

It seemed to me like just seconds later we were finishing the set with our Descendents and Dead Kennedys covers. Then stepping off that low stage, out of the hot lights, sweating and stoked. For our first gig ever we had been pretty tight. It certainly sounded OK and as far as we were all concerned, we'd darn well nailed it. We went to stand with our crew at the bar and soak up a little adulation mixed with a lot of piss-taking so we didn't get too carried away. We were so relieved to have survived that first gig and busy congratulating ourselves, but had been incredibly unprofessional, leaving our gear on the stage. Adam and I both had to go back to unplug and pack up our guitars. Bloody idiots. But we were a bit brain-addled by it all. There was an absolute elation from playing the gig, with a lot of our closest mates there, and really hitting the songs that we'd written and worked on over the previous weeks and months just right. We went down well with the audience too. I've never really been into drugs, but if they can give you a feeling anything like a decent show, I could soon understand being an addict. This was going to become my drug. Playing that gig was a pretty special feeling and one that I'd strive for continually over the next years with all my bands. Couch Potatoes gig one, as far as we were all concerned, was a huge success, and we were hooked. We were all buzzing. And now we could just enjoy it and watch the BBMFs play.

9/8/90 Drive, BBMFs, Couch Potatoes.
The Shelley Arms, Nutley

Over the next weeks we practised hard, adding a few more songs to our short set and tightening up any intros, breakdowns, song ends or joints, so that when we went back to The Shelley again on the 9th August for Couch Potatoes second show we were not just ready but raring to go.

It was a sweltering summer evening and we'd driven out from Tunbridge Wells in three cars full to bursting with friends and equipment to meet up with the BBMFs again. We'd loaded in our gear already but didn't soundcheck as we were all waiting for the headline band, Drive, to show up. We sat in the sun, in the pub garden, drinking and chatting while we waited. This was a Thursday evening in the middle of nowhere but to us this was absolutely the centre of the world.

You have to remember that this was before the internet and getting to hear any new records or checking out new bands was not as easy as you'd think. Certainly not as easy as it is now. Luckily there were a few good punk and hardcore distros that sent tapes, records and zines through the post. We were already big fans of a UK band called Jailcell Recipes, they'd ventured to the southeast a few times to play and we'd got chatting with them at their shows. The band were signed to a record label called First Strike which was run by Alan Woods, a very friendly guy who also owned Alans Records, a punk record and skateboarding mail-order shop based out of Wigan in the northwest. He had some great releases on his label already that really inspired us, and he always had loads of good stock in too if you needed a cool pair of Converse or Vans, some stickers or shirts, and plenty of new records. One of the bands on First Strike was called Drive.

Drive wasn't really a hardcore band. They were more a pop-punk indie band, reminding me of Dinosaur Jr. or Husker Du. The main character of the band was Iain Roche, he was their lead singer and guitarist. Iain would wear his old Godflesh t-shirt with his guitar slung so low I wondered how he ever reached it to play as he drawled his way through the songs in such a lazy but cool manner that you couldn't help but be impressed. Surely this band could not be from Liverpool, they must be from Seattle or Chicago or somewhere cool like that. I imagined this must be what J. Mascis or Kurt Cobain were like on stage, but having never seen either of them live I didn't really know. For just a three-piece group though, Iain on guitar and vocals, with Dan on bass and Jeff on drums, they really managed to put out a solid wall of noise.

When Drive finally turned up for the gig, screeching into the car park late amidst a shower of stones and dust, full of apologies and excuses about not being able to find the place, we helped them load in the drum kit and their big, professional-looking amps and set up for a quick soundcheck. This came together fast and was sounding pretty damn good. Even better than the Beebs equipment we used last time. I was glad of this as Couch Potatoes would be on first and it seemed, thanks to them, that we'd sound great.

The three Drive guys and their roadie sat around drinking with us and the Beebs whilst the crowd gathered. They'd heard the venue was a pretty good place to play from the Jailcells, who'd been here before, but clearly weren't sure until they saw the place filling up with hardcore kids, chatting, laughing, checking out the show posters and looking for records to buy. Luckily Drive had also brought a mate with them to run a small merchandise stall. This merch guy's name was Whitey and he worked with Alan at First Strike, but more importantly he had a box of the band's new single with him, 'No Girls' and I think they'd all gone even before the band had played a note. Most people, including myself, bought the 12" version with all four tracks, and a few people grabbed the limited edition two track 7" version as well, as this had hand drawn cover

Drive, BBMFs and Couchies gig poster

Yan and Jim at The Shelley Arms

art. These records were all short run, so personalised whenever possible and pretty much instant collectors items. It was a small scene, but a lot of heart and creativity went into the art for each release.

Sure enough, this would be another great evening at the Shelley Arms with about a hundred or so people packed into the bar in front of the stage. It was so hot in there that the normally closed and sound-proofed windows near the stage were open so the entire village must have heard the show on that sweaty summer evening. I'll bet this wasn't what they were expecting, but I'm glad to say that all three bands really rocked it, so they'd have been able to listen to a good show. The nervousness of our first gig had completely disappeared for me, and it seemed my fellow Couch Potatoes too, as this set was even better. We threw in an extra cover and the whole thing was definitely tighter and better sounding. The BBMFs played a great set too. They always did, but especially at The Shelley. They'd brought extra hats along and at one point Al had his lions head mask on again and was roaring at the audience before falling off the stage and dancing around. Drive were just as good as we expected them to be. Better even.

They played really cool, catchy songs and were nice guys with it. I'm glad to say that we'd share a stage with them again on at least four or five more occasions, and they just got better and better each time we saw them play.

16/8/90 H.D.Q, Couch Potatoes and Dumptank. The Winchester Club (aka Rumble Club) Tunbridge Wells

We all wanted to play more shows as soon as possible and at different venues, so for Couch Potatoes third gig, about a week later on a hot, stormy Monday evening, we stayed at home in Tunbridge Wells and played our first show at the Winchester Club.

The basement of this 'club' had been recently taken over by a few older school mates of mine and was fast being turned from a dingy and unknown drinking hole into a pretty decent indie music venue. These guys had been promoting shows at various local venues for a while now and I'd been along to quite a few of them. They called their evenings 'The Rumble Club' and had moved around a few local venues. Now they'd stay here and that's how come the Winchester Club gradually changed its name to The Rumble Club. This group of friends included Jason Dormon, (now the main man at The Forum in Tunbridge Wells), Mark Davyd (now the CEO of the Music Venue Trust), Ian Carvell, Stephen Cookson, David Jarvis and Haydn Wood, all of whom had gone to the same school as me in Tunbridge Wells but were a year or two older.

They were more into grunge and indie than hardcore or punk but I'd got chatting at gigs with Jason, who was playing bass in an indie band called Big Pop Trotsky at the time, and Mark, who was playing guitar and singing in a rock band called Chinese Whisper. We shared a lot of political opinions and musical tastes so soon became mates, and this led to me working with them at the Winchester Club on and off for quite a while. I started booking bands and putting on gigs at the venue, with their help learning how to promote all the shows. Sometimes I'd be selling tickets or working security on the door, and often I'd be tending the bar too. I enjoyed it and helped out with all sorts of jobs at various stages of the club's development. This allowed me to witness and play at some of the very best shows ever within the Rumble Club's dark and cramped but atmospheric confines.

Like many small venues it had a vibe about it that really added to the event. You went in through a small single doorway along a short corridor. Inside it was entirely painted black throughout, but with lots of mirrors on the walls that helped to make the space seem large enough for all those people. The place could become pretty claustrophobic when a sold-out show was on. The fans on the ceiling just about kept it at a bearable temperature and if things became too bad we'd just have to open the side doors to let some of the steam and sweat out. There was also a back entrance through the bar, but it was often blocked with barrels and cases of beer, so it was rarely used. It would have been a fire marshal's nightmare. The stage area was in a recess at the front and on the right side as you came in, through the narrow doorway and corridor, there was a little DJ's booth off to one side. The bar ran along the back wall to the left and there were various seating areas in between. Bench seating ran along the entranceway and walls, with more tables and chairs to the right of the stage, as well as left of and in front of the bar. Every inch of space was being used but this still left an area for people to jostle and jump about directly in front of the stage recess itself. The venue could probably hold 150 people at a push with some tables cleared, but just fifty or so made it seem busy, so it was ideal for smaller gigs.

We really wanted to play a hometown show for all our mates and when the opportunity arose we jumped at it. Couch Potatoes first show at The Rumble Club was with H.D.Q., whose name was an abbreviation from their first record, 'Hung, Drawn and Quartered'. They were a well-known band in the UKHC scene at the time and played melodic riffy hardcore in the same sort of vein as Dag Nasty. We would be their main support and another new local band, called Dumptank, would be going on first. We'd put posters up all around town and telephoned all our friends so we knew, or hoped at least, that it was going to be packed. Gary 'Gaz' Smith, the drummer of Dumptank and another of our mates from back at school, had done the same. This was a Monday night after all and as good as H.D.Q were, not many people had heard of them in sleepy Tunbridge Wells. It was just £2.50 on the door and beers were £1.20 a pint. This, as much as our rampant flyering, made sure that the gig was indeed packed and would be a really fun show.

Dumptank were a shouty punk band from the local art college who'd brought quite a few people with them. Their set was a rough and ramshackle affair with lots of stopping and starting, chatting and tuning, but they had a great song called 'No news is good news' and we enjoyed their set. It certainly warmed up the home crowd very well. Unfortunately, I don't think they played many more shows, and this was the only time Couch Potatoes gigged with them.

Couchies went on next, all fired up and raring to go. We'd been listening to H.D.Q.s tracks over the previous weeks, their 'Believe' 7" on Looney Tunes that I'd gotten from Macca of the Beebs, and the albums we'd picked up from Alans distro, 'You Suck!' out on Meantime Records and 'Sinking' out on Positive Records, and we all loved their style of playing. They were very much a UK punk band, with that Mackem / Wearside accent, but also clearly influenced by the same sort of US bands we were into; Descendents, Dag Nasty, 7 Seconds, Government Issue, Minor Threat, Moving Targets, etc. We'd heard their soundcheck and they were tight and powerful, considerably more melodic than we expected too, so we knew they'd be good and we stepped up our game to keep up as best we could. Yan introduced us and we ploughed into our set, playing most of it slightly faster than maybe we should have, all getting a bit excited by the event. It seemed to pass by in a flash.

Couchies being introduced by
the ever-professional compere

Yan and David at The Rumble Club

Couch Potatoes rocking The Rumble Club

Couchies getting intimate with the audience

We'd been practising for ages, so even this early on Couch Potatoes were already getting quite good at rocking out on small stages, bouncing around without knocking each other over or going out of tune too much. That evening there really was a lot of jumping around and singing along from our little crew. Our first hometown show was a definite success and soon people were talking. That was just what we wanted to help us get more gigs.

The highlight of the evening by far was H.D.Q. though. They had come all the way from Sunderland, right up in the northeast of the country, and were starting a short tour to promote their new album, 'Soul Finder', which was just coming out on a fairly new punk rock label in the UK called Full Circle, as well as a larger punk rock label in Germany by the name of Blasting Youth Records, who'd been helping them get tours around Europe. We hadn't heard the new tracks yet but were hoping to pick up a copy of the new album at the gig. I'd been chatting with Dickie, their guitarist, and Golly, their singer, before Couch Potatoes went on and they'd both been really friendly, calming any nerves and saying just enjoy it and have fun. Now they were on stage and about to begin, giving us all the thumbs up. They kicked off with the great guitar riff and powerful drumming of 'Wise Up' and the party began. Plenty more jumping about ensued and this sort of fun would set the tone for all the hardcore shows at the Rumble Club from then on.

All the guys in H.D.Q. went on to lead prolific musical careers, playing in punk and hardcore bands, the most notable of which were Leatherface, who boasted Rob Bewick (bass), Andy Laing (drums) and Dickie Hammond (guitar) at various times. Most Leatherface fans would agree Dickie and Frankie Stubb's powerful duelling melodic guitars were absolutely key to their sound and songwriting. Unfortunately, Richard 'Dickie' Hammond passed away in 2015 aged just fifty.

31/8/90 Surfin Lungs and Couch Potatoes
The Winchester Club (Rumble Club) Tunbridge Wells
That first show in Tunbridge Wells went so well and the club had such a good turn out that just two weeks later they invited us back so that Couch Potatoes could support a popular surf-core band called The Surfin' Lungs.

The Lungs had a new album out, excellently entitled 'The beach will never die' and this show was part of their UK tour to promote it. They'd booked the date themselves with Jason and Mark at the club but they didn't have a tour support, so we got the gig. It must've been hard for promoters to know what sort of band to put on with these guys as they had a fairly unique sound, definitely influenced by The Beach Boys and sixties pop rock, but also touches of The Ramones, Misfits and Blondie too. We had a few good riffs and even a Beach Boys cover in our set, so we got the call.

The Surfin' Lungs turned out to be pretty cool, a four-piece band with two guitarists, one of whom alternated with playing keyboards as well, so a pop band as far as we were concerned, but good guys, nevertheless. It was fun and the show went very well, with sand spread across the stage, surfboard backdrops and another busy night for the club. This was a good result for a Tuesday evening, so in less than a month we'd be back yet again.

21/9/90 Couch Potatoes (No Swervedriver)
The Winchester Club (Rumble Club) Tunbridge Wells

Our third gig at the Winchester Club was on another Tuesday evening, hardly the most buzzing night for a show, but worse now in September as all the kids had gone back to school. We were still keen as mustard and happy to take on more or less any gig, but this one would be with an up-and-coming shoe-gazing indie band from Oxford called Swervedriver. That wasn't really our thing at all, but I guess Jason wanted us to liven things up.

We didn't want dodgy Tuesdays to become our regular slot at the local venue so we'd been all around the town, in fact all the nearby towns too, putting up posters, flyering the record shops, book shops, friendly food stores and bars. Jim (our drummer) would plaster the college refectory and we'd paste any notice boards we could get our sticky mitts on. In fact, we'd stick a poster anywhere we thought might help bring in anyone new to a show. This would later get us in a bit of trouble and cause some upset. But for now, word was spreading and already, just five shows in, we were building quite a decent local following and were pretty confident about the next gig.

Looking back now it amuses me to think of just how self-assured we were. In a couple of months Couch Potatoes had already created a pretty tight and energetic thirty-minute set, that if need be, could be stretched to forty-five minutes with a bit of banter and some more dodgy covers thrown in. We had a set list of sixteen tracks ready for this gig, not bad for what was only our fifth show. It turned out that was a good job, as the main band, Swervedriver, had some van trouble on the way down from Oxford and never showed up, so we'd have to stretch things out.

Yan was already pretty good at crowd interaction, easy enough when it's all your mates, and we'd been practising hard for several months now. As well as that, we'd been to see what felt like hundreds of gigs, although was probably actually around fifty, over the previous three or four years, and we knew pretty much exactly what we wanted our shows to be like, just on a smaller scale. Again, this gig was a good one, certainly great fun for us and we played pretty well, although I bust a couple of strings jumping about and overall it was a fairly low turnout when people heard the headline band weren't showing up. Their loss. We ended up just doing our best to make a good show of it for those who were there, throwing in everything we could play. Hardly the rock 'n' roll ideal we were after yet, but it was still very early days and we all managed to enjoy ourselves.

Adam, Older Budweiser

David, Part Animal, Part Machine

BBMF's at The Shelley

HDQ, BBMFs and
Blockmania poster

Macca being dragged off stage

Al sporting his
lion's head

Dead Kennedy's 'A child and his lawnmower' went down very well; "Some clown in Sacramento was dragged into court. He shot his lawnmower. It disobeyed, it wouldn't start. But might makes right, it's the American way. So they fined him sixty dollars and sent him on his way. You know some people don't take no shit. Maybe if they did, they'd have half a brain left" and so did Descendents 'Suburban home'; "I wanna be stereotyped, I wanna be classified. I want to be a clone. I want a suburban home".

In the end it was pretty good that we were the only band playing, as it meant we could take a little longer over the songs and mess about if needs be too. We had quite a few friends in the audience that night and a couple of them had brought some equipment along to get a basic live recording of us that we might be able to use as a demo tape to help get more shows. I still have a copy of this, a fairly poor-quality live recording of the gig, as the Couch Potatoes set was released on Gotham Tapes as GOT002, the tape label's second release.

Already I wanted to play as creative and constructive a part in the scene as possible, sharing tracks by bands I was into, as well as spreading the punk rock message to anyone that wanted to listen. Plus of course we needed to get a demo tape of some sort out there to help get more shows. So it was about this time that I ended up starting both a hardcore fanzine called BHP and a D.I.Y. tape label called Gotham Tapes. I was a big Detective Comics and Batman fan so that's where the name came from. This was in a genuine and much needed attempt to share information about the small UKHC scene and the bands we knew in it, as well as make new contacts and find new records. The zine was simple, just a black and white, cut and paste, photocopied and hand stapled job, but it did pretty well. All copies of BHP shifting quickly at local gigs, with more copies printed each time. The tape label started with a compilation, basically a punk rock mix tape of local bands I was into and went on from there. We tried to share tracks by any of the bands we were into.

So, the live Couch Potatoes demo tape from this show quickly came out and was copied to be sent to fans and promoters alike. The cassette came with a black and white photocopied paper cover showing a photo from the gig of Yan wearing his beloved 'Allroy for Prez' t-shirt. The sixteen track setlist from the show that night was No more, Such a bad day, I'm not a loser, Suburban home, Cold can, I saw you, Child and his lawnmower, The sound, I like food, Yuppies suck, I don't think so, Coffs harbour blues, Tired, Feedback, What's that noise and Then I kissed her. Nine tracks of our own, of varying ability, and seven sing-a-long covers. Of course, it was not great quality. I'm not sure what we expected from a live recording on old equipment in a tiny rock club. But it did give kids and promoters alike a good idea of the punk rock party they could expect if they booked Couch Potatoes to come and play. We started booking more shows, and I'll tell you about a few more of them...

3, Bucketfulls of sickness and horror

30/9/90 Alice Donut, Sleep and Couch Potatoes
The Richmond, Brighton

Five gigs under our belts now and we were loving it. We already wanted to start playing further afield. This wouldn't be easy, so we'd started making tapes of our tracks, just lo-fi live recordings or practises for now, and sending them out to promoters at rock clubs. I really feel for some of the guys who must've received that racket and those early letters. They must have wondered what the hell had landed on their doorstep. We did know some good promoters though, friendly guys we'd met at shows and just got chatting with. Luckily for us one of the guys we hit it off with was a prolifically busy and enthusiastic punk show promoter from Brighton called Johnny Deathshead.

Now Johnny was a real character. A scruffy and somewhat ripe punker, always clad in his threadbare denim jacket with an Operation Ivy logo scrawled on it in felt tip, ripped jeans covered with patches, spiky hair under a camo baseball cap with Alice Donut daubed in tippex on it, well-worn converse with gaping holes in them, and perpetually soaked in patchouli oil. He usually had the latest records though and always seemed to be putting on great shows. There was no-one he didn't know and most weeks he would be promoting a decent gig well worth going to, usually in some pub or club in Brighton.

Originally, Johnny lived above the fishmongers shop in Uckfield, a small town about half way between Tunbridge Wells and Brighton, and had a band that practised there under the extremely self-confident moniker of The Johnny Deathshead Formation, or JDF for short, when he was feeling modest. This is obviously where his nickname came from, but Johnny's real name was John MacKay. I don't think many people knew that as it seemed that everyone in the punk scene quickly adopted the name of their band or fanzine as their given surname, and sure enough, I was rapidly gaining the less-than-flattering moniker of Dave Potato!

JDF had a decent little following for a while amongst the local old school punkers and heavy metallers, playing the Zap club in Brighton a few times. They also played at a pub in Lewes that regularly put rock bands on too, although rumour had it that they were soon banned from the town after one of them pissed in a church font before the show. Anyway, the band had split up so Johnny was concentrating on putting on shows now, and he was good at it. He even became the manager of the BBMFs for a while, helping get them onto great bills with bands like The Dickies, Spermbirds, Sink, H.D.Q., Shudder To Think, The Libido Boyz and Go! Anyway, Couch Potatoes next show was to be a biggie and it was all courtesy of him.

When we saw Johnny at gigs in Brighton we'd talk about the bands we were into and anything new that was going on. I'd make mix tapes for him and he'd laugh and hand me far more obscure ones with felt tip notes I could barely read scrawled on them, to try and educate me on real hardcore punk bands. My tapes would have stuff like Gorilla Biscuits, 7 Seconds, Dag Nasty, Jawbreaker, SNFU, Operation Ivy or Crimpshrine on them, his would have stuff like G. G. Allin, Angry Samoans, Uniform Choice, False Prophets, Flipper, Bad Brains, Jerrys Kids, Attitude Adjustment, Verbal Abuse, NoMeansNo and would invariably lead me into all sorts of new areas musically.

One of these revelations was when he gave me a tape of the first two Alice Donut albums, 'Donut Comes Alive' and the genius that was 'Bucketfulls of Sickness and Horror in an Otherwise Meaningless Life'. Great album titles I'm sure you'll agree. They also later released albums called 'Revenge Fantasies of the Impotent' and 'The Untidy Suicides of Your Degenerate Children' and their track names were happy little ditties too, try for starters; 'Roaches in the sink' 'Tiny Ugly World', 'My Life Is A Mediocre Piece Of Shit' and possibly the longest song title I have in my collection, 'The son of a disgruntled ex-postal worker reflects on his life while getting stoned in the parking lot of a Winn Dixie listening to Metallica'. They knew how to write a song lyric and give them intriguing titles.

Alice Donut were great. Not a straight forward punk band at all, coming out of the arty college scene in New York, they had influences from garage and indie, and liked to tell stories with their songs, often becoming very theatrical about it. They'd signed to Alternative Tentacles, the record label run by Jello Biafra, the singer of the Dead Kennedys, and that label now had a London office that was bringing them over to play in the UK. I don't know how he managed it, but Johnny was booking the Brighton show and said we could play it. He'd already offered the main support slot to local heroes Sleep, another great band and good bunch of guys that we'd end up playing lots of shows with, but he said that we could go on first to make up the three-band bill. We were stoked.

Big yellow posters started appearing all around town and for weeks before the show you couldn't visit a club, pub or college in the Brighton area, let alone go to another gig, without knowing that Alice Donut, Sleep and Couch Potatoes would be playing at The Richmond. Sure enough, on the evening the place was absolutely heaving, and Johnny met us on the door with a big grin on his face. "This is going to be a good one," he said, and he was right.

There were pretty big bands coming through Brighton most months and the Richmond, with its two hundred plus capacity, was no stranger to them. The venue hosted several good alternative club nights including The Zap and Pressure Point*, bringing loads of touring punk and indie bands, as well as better known artists as diverse as John Lee Hooker and Manic Street Preachers to Bratmobile and The Distillers. The sound guys knew what they were doing and at our soundcheck, with quite a few people already milling around, we were all very pleased to discover that we sounded way bigger and more powerful than ever before.

*The Zap Club moved into its own venue converting two of the Kings Road arches on the Seafront into a performance art space and hosted loads of great bands, including Fugazi. The Pressure Point became the new name of The Richmond later in the 90s and they continued to put on gigs there until the pub was closed in 2009 to become a backpacker's hostel.

All the bands were sharing equipment, borrowing the best backline of amps and all using the same drum kit as it saves time on change overs and keeps the atmosphere going. At this venue there were also proper monitors and a separate stage mix so you could really hear yourself as you played, and it was sounding good. As we were on first, we sound-checked last and barely went through half a song, just enough to get levels and the right balance of sound on-stage. It was enough though and the venue was filling up fast. We didn't really know much about stage craft but we were learning quickly and tonight the band sounded huge so we couldn't wait to play. Adam had saved up and bought himself a new Fender Precision bass and the tone of that thing was just great, really punching through his bass lines. I had repaired my old Les Paul copy. It was dirty and distorted, quite trebly and metallic sounding, covered in stickers and now plugged into a huge Marshall stack. Jim only had to bring his snare drum, bass pedal and the two cracked and warped cymbals he owned, he borrowed the rest of the kit and spent some time getting comfortable with it all, and Yan just brought himself. We were good to go.

When the time came, we climbed onstage and opened the show with the heavy guitar grooves of 'No More' and 'Such a bad day', then sped it up with 'Cold Can' and 'Tired' before going into the DK's cover, as a kind of tribute, and then a few more of ours, playing 'I don't think so' and 'The Sound', before the Descendents cover 'I'm not a loser'. Johnny was standing over by the sound guy now and signalled that we were running out of time, maybe just two more, so we played 'Yuppies Suck' and 'Then I kissed her' to round things off and left the stage to a very warm crowd response considering we were newcomers. The stage at The Richmond was quite high and while we were playing we could see right to the back of the hall. Throughout the set kids were into it and a few were even dancing around in front of us so the place was really warming up now.

Alice Donut, Sleep and Couch
Potatoes poster

ACID RAIN presents :- FROM NEW YORK .....

ALICE DONT

"SINGLE OF THE WEEK" (NME)
"LOUD NASTY AMERICANS" (SOUNDS)
"BUZZCOCKS MEET THE DICKIES" (MRR)
"A STRANGE HYBRID OF THE BUTTHOLE SURFERS, DRI, FALSE PROPHETS + THE DICKIES"

+

S L E E P

AND
THE **COUCH POTATOES**

SLEEP "SUFFOCATE" EP
OUT SOON ON
MEANTIME RECORDS.

£2·50 adv./UB40
£3·00 on Door.

At the
RICHMOND, BRIGHTON
SUN. 30th SEPT. 7·30 p.m.

**Alice Donut, Sleep and Couch
Potatoes flyer**

Alice Donut

Sleep went on next. We'd seen these guys play before, both in Brighton and at The Shelley Arms with the BBMFs, so we already knew they'd be good. They had a fairly similar sound to us, Dischord meets Cruz, meets UK pop-punk, but they'd been at it considerably longer and were a well-polished unit. Allen was a great frontman and Danny, Jamie and Sam all sung backing vocals too, which made it sound great. Harmonies from a hardcore band. Their sound was kind of like 7 Seconds or Dag Nasty, meets H.D.Q. or Exit Condition. I remember they covered 'Young 'til I die' by 7 Seconds and we all sang along. Like us they were influenced by US hardcore but definitely had their own UK punk rock style too.

Meantime Records had put Sleep's new single out, it was a three track 7" which they'd brought to the show and they played through all of the tracks on it; 'Suffocation', 'Who's the Savage?' and 'Sign Language', as well as a bunch of other really good songs that I hadn't heard before. Allen would prowl up and down the stage, wrapping the mic cord around his arms and bouncing up and down, never staying still for a moment. We played several other shows with Sleep but I think this was the best I ever saw them.

By now the place was absolutely packed, everyone had come upstairs from the bar, making the close-windowed music hall very hot and sticky. It was at this point that Alice Donut hit the stage, to much expectation. It was brilliant and chaotic right from their first notes. I was right at the front dancing, singing and sweating along for this one. I wanted them to be as good as the tapes I had heard and they did not disappoint.

This tour was for their new 'Mule' album and pretty much every track on that is a rocker. The urgency of 'Mother of Christ' and 'Mrs Hayes' opened things up with Tom's nasal vocals over the wailing guitars and pounding drums. Then 'Roaches in the sink' and 'Bottom of the Chain' with its plaintive refrain "The head of my company doesn't realise that he's expendable, it would still survive. But I'm the cannon fodder, the grease inside the wheel. I'm the nerve centre, the Achilles heel".

They clattered through the album, only pausing for breath when Ted, the bassist, took over singing for the brilliant and far-sighted 'Tiny Ugly World', with its lyrical truth already apparent then as it definitely is now; "Spotlights gleam across a Star Search nation, a million cries of 'Me' drown out the cruel frustrations of a normal life. It's a different kind of thinking.

A whole new way of telling lies 'til they're true, when you're waiting for the light".

Then they were back at it again with 'J Train Downtown' and 'My severed head', followed by 'Egg', 'Incinerator heart' and the brilliant 'Testosterone gone wild' from 'Bucketfulls of sickness and horror...' this all followed by a rousing singalong of 'My Boyfriend's Back'. This is what it was all about, a really fun, alternative, punk rock party. It was nights like this that we'd formed the band for and certainly what I was hoping for. We hung out late into the night, chatting and drinking with Johnny and the other bands, and a bunch of us ended up at the all-night café around the corner, fuelled by adrenaline and cups of tea, and not heading home until early the next morning.

We really enjoyed that evening and learned a lot from it too. I saw Alice Donut play again at the Steam Inn on Lewes Road in Brighton about two years later, and then again up in London about a year after that at the Mean Fiddler in Harlesden. They rocked it every time. They really were a great live act, and you could see how they went on to play a thousand gigs. These gigs included UK appearances at the Reading Festival in '93 and their final and reputedly 1000th show at the Astoria 2 in London on 25th November '95.

20/10/90 Sleep and Couch Potatoes
Winchester Club (Rumble Club) Tunbridge Wells

After that great show with Alice Donut in Brighton we invited Sleep up to Tunbridge Wells to play with us at the Winchester Club, and after some arrangements it was booked for the 20th of the next month.

The Winchester Club was, of course, named after the club in Minder, an ITV series where Arthur Daley and Terry McCann (played by George Cole and Dennis Waterman respectively) would go to have a few drinks, find out the craic from Dave the barman (Dave Harris, played by Glynn Edwards) and carry out their dodgy deals. Now The Winchester was becoming The Rumble Club, as I mentioned, and starting to be promoted as that by its new tenants. The main guys that ran it were Jason, Mark, Pete and Mike. They were busy booking bands all the time now as well as improving the promotions, bar and sound system. All these guys had gone to the same school as me but were a year or two older, so I knew them more through the music and shows we'd been at since I left, and we'd developed our friendship from there.

They had a lot of helpers at the club, me included, but the main guys booking the bands were Jason Dormon and Mark Davyd. By now they'd had Lush and the Boo Radleys visit to play and the club was getting onto the UK indie tour scene. I was introducing them to a lot of the heavier local bands and hardcore tour promoters were getting in touch too as I was passing on any contacts I found through the band or zine. I'd given Jason a copy of Sleep's 'Suffocation' 7" and now I had their new ten-track album 'Cat and Mouse' out on Meantime Records to play him too. He was into DC style stuff like Fugazi and Embrace so loved it and agreed that we should book them.

Meantime had become quite a well-known label in the UK punk scene having already released albums for H.D.Q., Sofahead, Wat Tyler, Leatherface, Inside Out, Thatcher on Acid and Exit Condition, so the Sleep guys benefitted from the label's contacts and promotions. Through '90 and '91 they played shows with labelmates The Joyce

Sleep and Couchies poster

Live from LA...

CHEMICAL PEOPLE

plus
COUCH POTATOES

MONDAY
NOVEMBER 26

THE DOORS OPEN 8.30. LAST BAND ON STAGE 10.00. TICKETS £3/£3.50

basement

underneath the art college, grand parade, brighton, 0273 683585

UNGRATEFUL FUCKING DEGENERATES

present

HARDCORE
at
THE
basement

underneath the art college, grand parade, brighton, 0273 683585

RAGING BANDS

THE
CHEAPEST
DRINKS IN
TOWN

PAY ON THE DOOR
£3.00 £3.50

DOORS OPEN 8.30. LAST BAND ON STAGE 10.00.

NOVEMBER 1990

WEDNESDAY 7th
Ex Stupids
SINK
plus the new Snuff?
SLEEP

SPECIAL AT THE ZAP
TUESDAY 13th
THRASH DOUBLE BILL
from New York
AGNOSTIC FRONT
plus British Metalcore
M.T.A.

WEDNESDAY 21st
Vinyl Solution artists
JOYCE McKINNEY EXPERIENCE
plus Nuttley idiots
B.B.M.F's

MONDAY 26th
From California
USA Pop Punk
CHEMICAL PEOPLE
plus Lazycore
THE COUCH POTATOES

Flyers for Chemical People and
Couch Potatoes at The Basement

McKinney Experience and Leatherface, as well as with the awesome US 'farmcore' band, Libido Boyz, and later they even had a support slot on Bad Religion's 'Against The Grain' UK tour and all of Quicksand's awesome first UK tour too.

Probably the most melodic band on the label, they could have gone much further but late in '91 they split as Sam, Danny and Jamie all went off to college, leaving Allen to join a Brighton-based Ramones and Misfits style punk band called Frankenslag. This didn't work out too well though and he left after just one show, to be replaced on vocals by our old buddy Johnny Deathshead.

All of Sleep had other musical endeavours later though. Danny and Sam moved to London and formed the great but short-lived band, KnowNothing, with Jamie Owen from Jailcell Recipes. KnowNothing had management who, amongst other things, got them onto the Reading festival line-up and signed them to an offshoot of Capitol Records. They released an album and a couple of singles but unfortunately sunk without a trace. Sam continued to drum with Brighton's long-running metalcore band M.T.A. for many years. Their name was an abbreviation of Mock The Afflicted. He was also in the first line up of Abandon Ship in the early 2000's, as well as more recently appearing again in another short-lived band called Cheap Affects. Danny Leigh went on to write a couple of popular books, The Greatest Gift and The Monsters of Gramercy, and then served as the resident film critic from 2010 to 2017 for the BBC's 'Film Review' programme, co-hosted at the time by Claudia Winkleman who'd taken over from Jonathan Ross.

Our gig together in October '90 at the Rumble Club went very well, with Couch Potatoes and Sleep both playing full-on, energetic and sweaty sets to a very busy and bouncy room. In the conversations afterwards Allen suggested that we get down to Wilbury Road Studios in Brighton to record and he gave me the contact details of Chris Priestly, the producer there, who had just recorded them, and also demos for The Levellers. The next day I gave Chris a call and we booked Couchies in to record our 'Eight Songs' demo early in the new year. This would be our first ever studio recording. We definitely needed something better to send out as a demo to promoters, and maybe even record labels, so we couldn't wait to get into a proper recording studio.

6/11/90 BBMFs, Couch Potatoes, Active Response and Arran Sweaters The Shelley Arms, Nutley

Next month we headed back to The Shelley Arms for another real party show with a load of our furry woodland chums. The BBMFs would headline and be as hilarious and great as ever, Couch Potatoes would play a particularly bouncy rocking set, though I say so myself, and this would be our first show with the new Deadworld band, now called Active Response, and featuring some of our crusty punk buddies from the East Grinstead and Forest Row area.

Active Response were an anarcho punk band and for them it was more about the political message than the music. Their songs were about hunt sabbing and direct action, but the music was pretty basic stuff. We got on well though and this would be the first of several shows together. They were even younger than us and had our good friend Nick Wilkinson on bass guitar. Nick was the younger brother of Mark 'Macca' Wilkinson who played bass for the BBMFs, and would soon be covered in tattoos and sport ever-growing ear-tunnels. The band was fronted by the two Marriott brothers on vocals and guitar, and one of the Ludman brothers on guitar too, with Julian Lea on drums. The Marriott brothers were dedicated punks with mohicans, combat jackets and anti-fascist flyers to hand out at all times. Long after these early shows they continued to make anarcho punk music as 'Burnt Cross' during the mid-2000's, releasing five albums and eleven 7"s over about five years. As far as I am aware they are still life-long punks, probably out putting superglue in butcher's doors or sugar in delivery truck's petrol tanks somewhere.

Everyone there had punk rock and D.I.Y. ideals but this didn't go against the Beebs dancing around in silly hats, or Couch Potatoes singing about food and girls. We all just had different ways of putting alternative views across, some more seriously than others. To me this just showed how inclusive and accepting the hardcore scene was at that time. This gig was just a party really, so we also found time to create a new band to play for the evening. It was kind of a sound-check that turned into a set with a bunch of improvised straight edge covers. We jokingly called ourselves the Arran Sweaters and I played guitar, Macca played bass, with Oders on drums and Al and Toady singing. Everyone was jumping around and joining in. The atmosphere of the entire show at The Shelley was just great, and again we all had to thank Warren, the friendly owner and barman, for putting us on and letting us treat the place like a musical playground.

26/11/90 Chemical People and Couch Potatoes
The Basement, Brighton

We kept on writing new songs, practising, and improving our set. We had a recording session booked and were working hard to find more gigs too. We wanted to keep the impetus on gigging and building up a bigger following, so luckily, towards the end of November, we were booked back down in Brighton for another great show. I don't remember exactly how we got the gig, probably Johnny Deathshead again, but it was Couch Potatoes as the sole support for Chemical People, a great melodic punk rock band from Los Angeles, and we were pretty excited about it.

Couch Potatoes bassist, Adam 'Ads' French, was particularly keen as Chemical People were a Cruz band, their bassist Ed was amazing, and he was a big fan. That is to say they were on Cruz Records, part of Greg Ginn's SST label. Greg Ginn was the guitarist of seminal US hardcore band Black Flag. He'd set up SST when he was just twelve years old, originally to sell radio parts, hence the name that comes from Solid State Tuners, but then later on from about the age of sixteen, he used it to release records for his own band, when no-one else was interested, in the true punk rock D.I.Y. way. His first release was Black Flag's debut EP 'Nervous Breakdown' way back in 1979. The Cruz imprint (part of the SST label) was for the more pop-punk bands and our favourites on the label were All, Big Drill Car and Chemical People. All, basically being the Descendents under a new name with a new singer. My absolute favourite band at this moment in time and a huge influence on Couch Potatoes musical style.

We'd be playing at The Basement, a tiny downstairs rock club on the main drag leading towards the beach and pier in Brighton. We'd seen quite a few good shows there and the place had a really great atmosphere, not taking too many people to fill it up. This was probably a good thing as it was a rainy Monday night when the Chemical People hit town and despite being pretty big in the US, this band were not very well known in the UK yet.

Although quite prolific, with two albums and several singles released already, the Chemical People were something of an acquired taste. It wasn't so much their music as the subject matter that was the issue for some. Both their albums so far had Taija Rae on the cover, a US porn star, and many of the lyrics were decidedly dodgy, 'Walkin' down the street' being a prime example of this. (What's wrong with being sexy? - Spinal Tap). They were kind of like punk rock's answer to Mötley Crüe but could really play. Chemical People were another three-piece band that would surprise you with how much noise they could make live, and we loved it. Dave Nazworthy was singing and drumming, Ed Urlik was on the bass and Jaime Pina was on guitar.

Both Chemical People and Couch Potatoes played really decent powerful sets that went down very well with the small but noisy crowd that night. We'd tried out a new one in the middle of the set. It was slightly slower and intended to give us a welcome breather between the more hectic songs. The new track still had the working title of 'Newun' at that point and Yan had scribbled it on the setlist like that, so it just ended up sticking. It had a short and melodic solo in it that I was very pleased to be allowed to play too. Being a punk band, solos and any form of noodling about or fretboard gymnastics was generally discouraged, but this lead piece was simple and melodic enough. It fitted in well so it stayed in. We were pretty tight that night, and came off the stage pleased with ourselves, but Chemical People went on and were just so much better, so professional, almost automatic, like a well-honed rock music machine. They played tracks from 'So Sexist" and 'Tenfold Hate' as well as their new 'Ask the Angels' 7" which we all grabbed a copy of after the show. Later in the set they played a new track called 'Shit on my dick', with Naz shouting "I got shit on my dick and I can't get it off" and much banter with the Brighton crowd soon ensued about it, but it all went off pretty well in the end.

Two of the Chemical People guys, Naz and Ed later went on to help form the punk rock supergroup Down By Law, with Chris Bagarozzi on guitar and Dave Smalley, formerly

Al (Sleep) joins Al (BBMFs) onstage

Sleep being cool at The Shelley

Yan and Adam rocking through
`Suburban Home´ at The Pagoda

David and Yan working on their
Duke of Edinburgh´s awards

of DYS, Dag Nasty and All, on vocals. But unfortunately, they had both left the band by the time I got to play with DBL whilst in Joeyfat, about three years later. Dave Naz went on to continue celebrating his public love of the female form and has found even greater success in the new millennium as one of the world's leading fetish photographers. He has loads of 'specialist' books out including 'Lust circus', 'Butt babes', 'Girls of seduction' and 'Genderqueer' and has become a fairly well known character in the L.A. skin flick scene, marrying pornstar Ashley Blue in 2009.

15/12/90 Couch Potatoes, Rabeez and Active Response Pagoda Youth Club, Tunbridge Wells

We managed to fit two more shows in that first year. We'd been playing locally at the Rumble Club quite a lot, but it was getting popular now with many more mediocre indie bands and therefore wasn't always available for our gigs. You can overdo even a good thing, so we started looking for other venues to host punk rock parties with our friends and fast growing local fanbase. We'd been practising at the Headway Centre, now being called the Pagoda Youth Club as it looked a bit like an Asian pagoda, and they said they'd be OK with us putting on a show there so long as everyone behaved themselves. This just meant no drunken antics or breaking things really, which seemed reasonable, and we wanted to raise some money for the charity as they'd helped us out with this place to jam. Our drummer, Jim Booth, was studying at West Kent College at the time and had loads of new college friends who wanted to see us play. We'd also met another Kent-based punk band called the Rabeez at a recent gig and they really wanted to play a show with us too. We wanted to make that happen so our tenth show as Couch Potatoes ended up being a punk rock pre-Christmas party and fundraiser at a youth club behind the swimming baths in Tunbridge Wells.

We called up all our mates from near and far, and went out to poster and flyer the town too. When that Saturday came along the place was packed with more fifteen to twenty year olds than it had ever seen as a youth club. It was absolutely heaving, and everyone had to stay inside with the windows and doors all shut, partly due to the cold weather but mainly due to the noise. Yan and I had to nip out to fetch some extra things; guitar leads, plectrums, demo tapes, stuff like that, and when we pulled up again, we could already tell that this was going to be an amazing show.

Our anarcho punk buddies from East Grinstead, Active Response, went on first to warm everyone up and played way better than just a month before, really getting into it and already they had people dancing and jumping about. Then the Rabeez went on. We'd never actually seen them play before but they were very '77 punk in their style with a little hardcore thrown in to bring it up to date. They'd brought quite a few kids with them and it was a good energetic set. When they came off stage I told the singer that we'd get him on another show with us as soon as possible. They seemed good guys and said they'd book us on a few more with them too. Then Couch Potatoes went on and from the start of Adam's bassline intro to 'Child and his lawnmower' it all kicked off.

Kids were jumping off the low stage into each other, then climbing on the p.a. speakers at the side of the stage and jumping off them too, slam dancing into each other and moshing about like loons. In reality there was probably less than 150 people at this show but it seemed like every one of them was just there to let off energy and have fun. Up to that point it must have been the closest thing to a proper hardcore set that Tunbridge Wells had ever seen. And none of these kids were drunk or high either, it wasn't just the straight edge vibe that was starting to pervade the hardcore scene, it was a youth club with no alcohol at the bar, so they were just being themselves and getting into it for what it was. Pure energy and adrenaline, and for me, that made it even better.

Couch Potatoes played for about forty-five minutes, going through every song we had, including all the covers we knew and debuting our latest track, entitled 'Bad Habit'. The lyrics to 'Bad Habit' were taken, verbatim, from an old 'How to play the guitar' book that Yan had found in my bedroom and was taking the piss out of. At the end of our set we played our crowd-pleaser 'Tired' again as an encore. It was a pretty fast number and caused one last big pile-up in front of the stage with Yan shouting "I'm tired of trying to put my point across. It's a worn-out subject and nothing ever changes". Then it was all done, and well before eleven o'clock for early bedtimes too. This was a charity gig at a youth club after all. Afterwards we hung around and helped our Brummie host tidy up, with sweaty shirts and silly grins on all our faces whilst we did it. We definitely planned on playing more shows at this fun new venue.

24/12/90 BBMFs, Couch Potatoes, Rabeez and Active Response The Shelley Arms, Nutley

There was one show left for us to play in that first year and of course it had to be at The Shelley Arms, our self-proclaimed 'home of hardcore'. Warren, the friendly landlord, wanted a big Christmas party so had asked Macca and the BBMFs if they could set something up. Macca called me, and Rob of Active Response, and I suggested we bring the Rabeez along too. It would be a four-band punk rock party, not your normal Monday evening in the middle of nowhere, but then again it was Christmas eve.

I don't remember all the details from that evening. There was a lot of snakebite and black going down. I know it was a good gig, as busy as I'd ever seen the pub, with people dancing up and down the bar, and both Yan and Al falling off the stage a few times then walking around the front of the pub letting various members of the audience grab the microphone and sing along. All the bands were bouncing off the walls and roaming about the pub. It was crowded and the stage was just too small for all that energy. I always feel that the best shows are where there is very little division between the band on stage and the audience, and of course most of our gigs were like that, due to small venues with small stages and small crowds, but at this one in particular you could hardly tell who was who and it was great. Not a bad way to end our first year as a band, and we'd be in the studio to record in the New Year too. That made for a merry punk rock Christmas!

4, Reel to reel and page to page

Recording `Eight songs´ and `Wash´
Wilbury Road Studios, Brighton

Both of Couch Potatoes early demo recordings, 'Eight Songs That Suck' and 'Wash', were recorded at Wilbury Road Studios in Brighton and engineered by Chris Priestly. Chris was into alternative rock and punk style bands and had already recorded The BBMFs, Sleep, MTA and The Levellers, all from Brighton. On our first ever visit to a recording studio we spent the weekend of 26th and 27th January 1991 trying to record what became the '8 songs' demo.

There was cream-coloured carpet all over the walls and floor at Wilbury Road so it was like being trapped inside a musty, furry box. At that time there was no digital equipment in recording studios, not even DAT machines yet, so Chris had these huge spools of half inch Ampex tape on a big reel to reel machine. This was attached to a sixteen-track mixing desk and some big-ass speakers. It was like being trapped in a room with a low budget James Bond baddie and I was waiting for him to start stroking a fluffy white cat whilst the floor opened up and sharks ate us all. Thankfully, that didn't happen, but this equipment meant we had to get the sound just right before he could even start recording. We were adjusting and agreeing on tone, levels, speed, everything, and then we had to play the track bang on, more or less perfect, live in the studio, in one hit. For us scruffy lot of amateurs, that was not easy.

For keeping time there was a metronome and of course you could be clicked in by the engineer, but that was about all the help you were going to get. After a few frustrating goes on his blown out and crackling bass amp, Adam had to play directly into the desk through a DI (direct input socket) which he did not like one bit and the bass sound suffered from it. Some mixing could be done on the desk though and even clever bouncing down of tracks onto shared lines to allow us to add in more options and layers, but drop-ins were very clicky and dangerous so it was best to just avoid anything like that and nail it in one. Our early stuff was hardly prog-rock. We played as if it were a live gig but one where you stopped jumping about and just stood still and concentrated on getting the track just right. A little bit more time and effort could be spent on the vocals if need be, so this meant that Yan could just sit around reading comics, eating crisps and taking the piss out of us for most of the recording session, then stand up and belt out his vocals right at the end.

For the 'Eight songs that suck' demo we recorded 'No more', 'Such a bad day', 'Tired', 'The sound', 'I don't think so', 'Newun', 'Get straight' and 'Cold can'. It was fun to do and came out OK for our first ever attempt. We were well pleased, but then didn't know any better. We all thanked Chris for his skill and patience, and told him we'd book in again for another session in a few months as we were already working on more new songs. We bought the big old Ampex tape reels the tracks were recorded onto, naively thinking we may use them again for a remix or something one day, although they still gather dust in my bedroom somewhere. We also asked Chris to record the tracks onto regular cassettes for us too, so that we could listen to them on our car stereos on the way home and see what they sounded like on normal shitty speakers rather than on his expensive studio monsters. The tracks still sounded pretty good to us, so we were stoked. Listening to our songs on a car stereo in the real world was fun and certainly made it all seem much more real for us. We couldn't wait to share the tracks with people so over the next few weeks this is how many of our friends were forced to hear the very first studio recordings of Couch Potatoes, sitting in parked cars outside their houses or in parks, scoffing burgers and drinking coke, with the tape player turned up way too loud.

Luckily for us our singer, Yan, was also a pretty good artist and really into comic book style illustration. He'd come up with our logo, which was already spray-painted onto our amps and guitar cases through a dodgy card stencil, and also appeared on all our gig posters and flyers. Now he came up with the 'Cold can' artwork and the smiling hardcore kid in a baseball cap that would be plastered all over our new demo tapes and any gig posters from now on. This design even showed up on the back of a few of our fan's leather jackets too. The hand drawn style was more out of necessity than artistic choice as we didn't have computers to create designs, and the black and white artwork meant it was easy and cheap to reproduce on photocopiers at work or at college if need be. It worked out well though as that meant any printing on shirts could be just one colour and that kept costs down.

We started copying cassettes and handing them out. Very soon we couldn't keep up with demand and needed to get a load done by a duplication company, about 200 initially, so Yan had created a sleeve for the cassette. It had all the obvious stuff on it; band name, demo name, tracklist, etc but also my home telephone number to call for gigs. That would please my mum I can tell you. I'd get calls from weirdos at all times of the day and night. Also we made space on the demo cover to thank all our mates and all the bands we'd played with up to this point. That wasn't too many, so it was easy enough. This was our first release of any sort so it was important to us and like the saps we are, we decided to dedicate it to a few key people. Peter Gamage, my dad who had died the previous year, three days before my eighteenth birthday, Bernard French, Adam's dad who had also died while he was just a kid, and Ant Sutcliffe, a close friend of Yan's who had also passed away recently, aged just fifteen. That may not seem a particularly cheery thought, and maybe it didn't fit with the sort of music we played, but I guess it shows how much it meant to us to actually record some of our own songs and start getting them out there.

Our fifty or so home-recorded copies, followed by the 200 duplicated copies all went fast, so then we got another 200 done, and another 300, and then even more. We distributed them as far and wide as we could, through gigs, zines and distros, and we started sending them to friends abroad, promoters, magazines and radio stations. Some even went with letters of introduction with band photos and more of Yan's art to a few larger, well-chosen record labels too. Couch Potatoes meant business and we were keen to see if anyone out in the big wide world was interested at all. It wouldn't have stopped us if they weren't, but amazingly a few smaller punky record labels were into it and we had a few offers come back that we slowly, but excitedly, started to develop.

Partly because of this interest we went back into the Wilbury Road studios to record again with Chris a few months later, when we'd tightened up those original songs and written a couple of better new ones too. The 'Wash' EP, so called because of all the smelly goths, hippies and grunge types we perpetually had to play shows with, was intended for proper release on vinyl by a UK punk label called Retch Records. This second release had another eight tracks on it; 'Lunchbox', 'Why', 'No more', 'I don't think so', 'Newun', 'Tired', 'Bad habit' and 'Lucifer's lunchbox'. Four of those were older songs we'd wanted to re-record, and Lunchbox was an instrumental intro, with Lucifer's lunchbox being a silly backwards version of it created in the studio with guitar solos over it as an outro, so really only two proper new songs, just all better recorded.

We were well pleased with it, but Retch Records were unreliable and soon started to mess us around and delay the release on vinyl. Because of this, 'Wash' was initially only another demo cassette, just slightly better quality than the 'Eight songs that suck' demo. Yan came up with some new art and we all sent out hundreds of these new demos, probably in the low thousands in fact, mainly for free to promoters, radios, zines, labels, etc but also to any fans, and over quite a long period too. Sometimes we asked for fifty pence towards postage and the coins would arrive taped into cardboard so the postie didn't nick them. Later we got carried away and asked for a pound or an S.A.E. and blank cassette to record the demos onto so we could keep it all going and afford to get more copies duplicated later. We worked hard on the promotion of Couch Potatoes and I would send out demos with all of my new BHP fanzines and as well as including tracks wherever I could on Gotham Tapes and any compilations I was working on.

Looking back now these tracks really needed to be heard live at a show and didn't translate as well as we'd hoped in a dodgy studio with none of the live gig ambience or atmosphere, but everything we were doing then was still a learning process and it all helped us massively.

The two early Couch Potatoes demos eventually came out together on one CD entitled '8 songs / wash', first on a self-released demo CD through necessity, and then later properly released by Scene Police Records in Germany. This was meant to be a limited-edition release as we doubted many people would want it, but it also had a seventeenth track on there, a live cover version of 'Hey Hey' by the Descendents taken from one of our shows at the Shelley Arms. The CD actually went down pretty well and we shifted quite a few. I still have a copy somewhere that I dig out occasionally for posterity.

We managed to get a lot of reviews from those early Couch Potatoes demo tapes though and although they were a mixed bag, these reviews definitely helped us get more shows booked. We were mentioned in quite a few scene round-ups and what's on guides too. Richard at Armed With Anger was kind and simply said 'Couch Potatoes are one of several promising up and coming bands from the UK'.

Another one of the larger UKHC zines of the time was called UK Resist. It was run by a couple of political punkers out of Surbiton in Surrey, not really a police-aware hotbed of anarchic dissent, but in fact a well-to-do London suburb where the tv series 'The Good Life' had been set. Despite that, UK Resist built up a decent following and were happy to review demos, zines and live shows as well as records. I used to get a regular copy to check out the gig guide and see what new stock Alans / First Strike Records had coming in. Within issue number four they ran this brief review:

Couch Potatoes – Eight songs that suck – demo cassette.

'Very US influenced melodic hardcore. Touches of Minor Threat and 7 Seconds, though closer to the sound and speed of Bad Religion'.

They didn't really like it, saying later that it was 'pretty basic and straightforward stuff' and as they were generally much more into political punk bands I'm not surprised really. We didn't feel too bad about it though as in that very same issue they slagged off Jailcell Recipes, who were definitely one of the best bands in the UK at the time, and also didn't seem too impressed by new releases from Drive and The Strookas, two more great bands. So we ended up being pretty chuffed with just getting a mention as lots of people saw that review, but we soon came to learn that reviews, good, bad or indifferent, didn't really seem to make much difference to how a record sold or how many people showed up to your shows over the next weeks.

Lots of smaller zines and foreign labels seemed to like these songs though and my post became more and more interesting over the next weeks and months. I was sending out tapes like a crazy man and soon started sending out more copies of my new zine too. In fact, in the very next issue of UK Resist fanzine, number five to be precise, they reviewed

3 SONGS THAT SUCK!

RECORDED AT WILBURY RD STUDIOS 26+JAN '91
ADDITIONAL TAPES GIGS, ETC (0392) 219159

8 SONGS THAT SUCK!

EIGHT SONGS THAT SUCK!!!

1. NO MORE 2. SABD 3. TIRED! 4. THE SOUND 5. I DON'T THINK SO 6. NEW ONE 7. GET STRAIGHT 8. COLD CAN PT. II.

BASS: ADAM
GUITAR: DAVE
DRUMS: JIM
VOCALS: YAN

THANKS + HELLO'S: OPEN (NIK PAUL NIK) RICH KEV ALEX STEVE RIORDAN CHARLIE ROB CLIVE TONE + VIQUE JOHN DUMPTANK BBMF'S ACTIVE RESPONSE HEADLAM SKATING VPL'S JOHN D + ALL IN BRIGHTON WARREN + ALL AT SHELLEY YAN'S GRANDMA R + HIS FAMILY DAVE'S MUM JIM'S FAMILY ADAM'S FAMILY NIK (FINLAND) VAL + MIKE DUNCAN TRUDY THE PIKE PAULA LOUISE DONATELLA WINKEY CHARLOTTE CALVIN + HOBBES ANNE GREGG CHRIS AT WILBURY RD + ALL REAL HARDCORE. ALL.

+ ANYONE WE FORGOT.

DEDICATED TO ANT. SUTCLIFFE BERNARD FRENCH + PETER GAMAGE

Couch Potatoes `Eight Songs´ demo tape

Gotham Tapes covers

the first issue of my BHP zine and said it was "Well worth sellotaping your fifty pence between two bits of card for" and that it "Redresses the balance for Tunbridge Wells after giving the world the Anti-Nowhere League". Ha. I was chuffed with that. I'd have to take it to show JB.

Other great fanzines of the time, a few of which I still have copies of, ran reviews of the very first Couch Potatoes demo too. Two of the better ones in the UKHC scene were 'Vision On' and 'Fear and Loathing'.

Steve Lee of Vision On wrote in issue number two:

Couch Potatoes – Eight songs that suck – demo.

"Eight songs that don't suck at all. Coming across as the bastard offspring of Dag Nasty and Screeching Weasel, this rocks to Tunbridge Wells and back. With Descendents and Hard-Ons thrown into the blender too, you know you can't really go wrong. The faster stuff's really cool (Such A Bad Day and Tired), but then so's the slower stuff. Well worth the asking price".

Vision On then went on to say that you could get the demo from me and gave my address, also mentioning that I was starting a cassette tape label, Gotham Tapes, and I was looking for bands to be on it. Which indeed I was, and I had plenty of interest.

Then Andy Pearson of Fear and Loathing wrote in issue number ten:

Couch Potatoes – Eight songs that suck – demo tape.

"Not a bad little tape if ever I've heard one (and I have, several times). Pop based hardcore with DC leanings. The influences are a bit obvious in places, but it's all done with a great degree of enthusiasm and an excellent sound mix. If you're into checking out new bands this is one to go for"

Then, again, the review gave my home address and how to get the demo from me. Direct and to the point, and clearly effective as we sent out a lot of those tapes!

Steve's great Vision On fanzine went on for at least twenty issues, and Andy's Fear and Loathing fanzine, or FnL as it was known then by the kids, is still produced now. FnL was based out of Canterbury and has been going continuously since the late eighties. After seventy-one issues and twenty-five years of great old school style, printed on paper zines, Andy finally decided to go online with it, but I'm glad to say that the fanzine is still going strong and he is now producing a few printed versions too. As I write this, he has just put out volume 78. He's moved up to Erith now, still in Kent, and

I'd encourage any bands to get in touch at fearandloathingfanzine.com as he loves to review anything new.

UK fanzines and independent labels

Fanzines were massively important in the scene back then. They were the punk rock grapevine. They'd come about in the decades before and there were plenty of punk zines in the late seventies, but they really became an integral part of the UK hardcore scene in the nineties with all sorts of cliques growing up, from crust punk to straight edge. They all had messages and were eager to share them, or at least report and review them. Some of my early favourites and later regular reads were Suspect Device, Armed With Anger, How We Rock, Cloth Ears, Ripping Thrash, Useful Idiot / Dragnet, Garbled, Artcore, Take a Day, Ernie, Noisefest, Riot, No Idea, Hormone Frenzy, Raising Hell, Less Than Brainless, Trinkets and Baubles, Fear and Loathing, Prototype, Gusset, Raising Hell, Gadgie, Vision On, Grim Humour, Synthesis, Warzone, Dead Beat, Zips and Chains, Chemical Warfare, Catalyst, Mass Movement, UK Resist, HAGL (Have a good laugh), Fracture, Trust, Ox, Slug and Lettuce, Lookout, Flipside, Profane Existence, HeartattaCk, MRR / Maximum Rock n Roll and Thrasher mag.

A lot of these early hardcore zine guys and girls went on to play in bands and do other really creative things in the scene too. The editor of Hate Edge, an intensely straight edge zine from up north, played in UKHC bands Unborn and Voorhees. Similarly, the Darkest Hour editor went on to play in Ironside, Hard To Swallow, Iron Monkey and Wartorn. And both the Dark Side editors played in bands, one singing for In Touch, No Way Out, All is Lost, Nailbomb, Neckbrace and Stampin' Ground, and the other playing bass in All is Lost.

Richard Corbridge, who wrote Armed With Anger, a vegan straight edge fanzine, developed it into AWA Records and went on to release some of the most important records in the '90s UK hardcore scene, including incredibly heavy stuff by Voorhees, Dead Wrong, Kito and Stalingrad, as well as the beautiful early emo of Schema's 'Sooner than you think' album and the amazing first 7" by my buddies Understand.

There was also Up Up and Away, a Brighton based zine by Anthony 'Tone' Sylvester who went on to play bass in Fabric and then sing for Turbonegro. It had a cool 'Calvin and Hobbes' style cover so I was immediately into it. Fabric was a great straight edge style hardcore band with members from Brighton and London that we'd play a few shows with in the mid-nineties. I'd met Tone back in the day when he was going out with Vique 'Simba' Martin (who ran a zine called Simba and then went on to work for Revelation Records, and now Pirates Press Records) but they were both into melodic pop-punk back then. They actually introduced me to Green Day. I was into pop-punk too, but also collected DC comics, particularly Batman, and I swapped a few of my stash with Tone for the early Green Day, Crimpshrine and Operation Ivy 7"s out on Lookout Records and never looked back.

Tone and Vique were both soon really into straight edge. While Vique ran Simba zine she wrote columns for many of the other zines of the time too, she was heavily involved in both the early UK straight edge and emo scenes, and then in '98 went off to work for Revelation Records in the USA. Tone helped form Fabric, along with Andrew Hartwell on vocals, Jamie Tilley on guitar (Jamie was also in HC band Long Cold Stare), Kevin Williams on guitar and Chris Turner on drums. Chris is in stoner rock mammoths 'Orange Goblin' now. Fabric had some great releases, put out on their own label Whole Car Records. (Set up with help of Gary Walker who ran Wiiija Records, another UK based label, run out of Rough Trade record shop in Notting Hill, London, with the postcode W11 1JA, giving the record label its name) and also on Vique's Simba Recordings, but later on Machination Records out of Belgium and Doghouse Records out of the US. Their 'Body of water' album, released in '94, is a classic and well worth hunting down. And in fact, their debut EP, Colossus, is incredible too. The review of this release in BHP zine number six read 'The sound is kinda early DC (Embrace, Swiz) meets emo-edge (Lifetime, Admiral) but there's so much more to it. The lyrics are brilliant, subjects covered include the male ego, 'A statue standing proud, we must tear it down', non-communication, 'I cut my throat to speak to you, words spill out, collect in puddles at my feet' and sexism 'She can't close her eyes because she knows you'll be there, and you never go away'. It's all covered with real feeling and emotion. I hope this has sold it to you because it's our 'buy of the month'. And then it had their Whole Car Records contact address so you could order a copy. We obviously liked it.

As I mentioned, I was also working on my own fanzine by now, bursting with things to say and feeling I needed to get even more involved in the scene and become a part of it as best I could, so I'd started BHP zine. It ran for nine issues from '91 through to '95 and as all the old copies are long gone now it was recently collected into book form. The paperback is called 'Punk Faction, BHP '91 to '95', so you can grab a copy on amazon, or better yet find one in a book store and go back in time to see what life was like for an alternative kid before the invention of the internet and instant access to everything and nothing.

BHP, also variably known as British Hardcore Press and Big Hot Potato, gave me a real reason to sit down and chat with a lot of the bands we were later playing shows with, as well as quite a few bands we didn't get to share a stage with too. It also helped me publicise and sell my own band's releases, and those of friends bands too, as well as letting people know about gigs and events, and putting across anything I wanted to say at the time. Bands were usually friendly and happy to chat, even if my questions were bad or their answers were drunken nonsense, and at various shows I sat and spoke with, or sent interviews to, All, Alloy, Angus Bagpipe, Annalise, Civ, Compulsion, Dawson, Decadence Within, Down By Law, Funbug, Garbage, Goober Patrol, Green Day, Hard-Ons, Jailcell Recipes, Jawbreaker, Lifetime, Mr T Experience, No Empathy, Pennywise, Pseudo Hippies, Quicksand, Ramones, Rancid, Riverdales, Samiam, Schema, Shelter,

Shreds, SNFU, Strookas, Sugar and Understand, as well as Daniel Clowes of Eightball Comics and Steven Jesse Bernstein, the spoken word poet on Alternative Tentacles.

Already by the early nineties though, major labels were getting involved and it was a time of real change for the hardcore scene, splitting it into cliques and sub-genres, and making some bands much less likely to openly speak their minds. By the time emo came around and the social media scene on the internet was taking off in the mid-nineties the underground and really D.I.Y. part of the scene seemed pretty much done.

BHP fanzine focused mainly on the bands I was into and the music they were releasing, but this was still a time of punk and politics with the poll tax riots and then the first gulf war, so of course it also had articles within it that the more seriously punk would have approved of. There were pieces on third world debt and hunt saboteuring, animal rights, sexism and vegetarianism, the failure of capitalism, the rise of AIDS and the urgent need, even back then, for environmental activism. It was all there alongside the articles on skateboarding, comics, good eating and going to gigs.

Although I've always been a punk rocker with strong alternative lifestyle views, to me most of this just seemed sensible so I've never felt the need to ram my opinion down anyone's throat. I figured any intelligent person would eventually feel the same way I did, and we'd share opinions on most things, or at least learn about and debate them, so just give people information and they will get there at their own speed. I'm a born optimist, if not a realist. I like sharing knowledge, and as the personal is the political after all, this seemed the scale of things I could positively effect. One person at a time. As I get older though I am not so sure and can't help but feel that we are surrounded by self-serving, short-sighted idiots, certainly running the major media, big business and government at least, but that's a whole other discussion.

Anyway, through these fanzines you'd find a lot of positivity and great information on exciting new bands, their gigs and releases, both local and worldwide. Most of these bands had messages they wanted to get out there too. There was also contact information for distros (mailorder distributors / stores) and record labels that would become regular sources of inspiration and energy. Zines really shared alternative knowledge and brought people together. They were and are a vital part of the scene. I've mentioned First Strike Records a couple of times and I'm pretty sure this is how I found them, from an ad in UK Resist fanzine.

First Strike Records, Wigan
First Strike Records was a really great hardcore label run by Alan Woods out of 'Alan's Records', a punk record and skate mail order shop based in Wigan in the northwest of England. They had so many great releases and were a real inspiration to me and all my friends in the early years of our band and the UKHC scene. We'd buy all the new releases

from them as well as shirts and trainers too, and it was easier to call up these guys and get the stuff sent through the post than to travel up to London and trawl around Carnaby Street, Soho or Camden trying to find stuff. Their records and shirts always arrived on time, safe and sound, and usually with extras thrown in such as stickers and posters. This was something I'd always remember and appreciate, so to this day I copy that practise myself and throw in plenty of extras with any orders we're sending out from Engineer Records, the label that I run now. I ended up setting up an account with Alan and regularly ordering stock for me and my mates. We'd chat about his bands and any tours they had coming up, as well anything new going on in the scene, so much so that when he produced a special 'First Strike crew' t-shirt my name was right there on it. Sad but true, I was well chuffed to have helped him along and have my name on that shirt as a thankyou.

First Strike Records put out some really great releases and were, for a while, one of the most important European hardcore labels. Their records always looked great, the covers were well laid out with a clean graphic identity clearly owing something to larger US labels like Revelation and Dischord. Even the First Strike logo was, no pun intended, striking. At the time, the UKHC scene was in something of a lull following the mid-80's explosion of distinctly British bands like Heresy, The Stupids, Napalm Death, etc but before the rise of bands like Voorhees, Bob Tilton, Spy vs Spy, etc. With the exception of some of Meantime Records output, there just wasn't another label like First Strike at that time. They even pre-date the UK institution that is Boss Tuneage Records by a couple of years. All of which is probably why they called their posthumous 7"s box set 'Punk Rock: The Dark Ages 1989-1991'.

Launching with the largely forgotten Default 7" (check out their later incarnation as Monks of Science for some great angular, melodic hardcore), the label made a statement from day one. The record both looked and sounded great, and clearly stated that the label was going to be one to watch. This was quickly followed by quality, era-defining albums and 7"s by the UK's Jailcell Recipes, Drive and Decadence Within, as well as releases by Majority of One, Chain of Strength, Go! and Libido Boyz from the USA. There was even a live 7" by the fire-breathing, foam-pie throwing, cabbage-detonating loonies that were Doctor and the Crippens.

My absolute favourites on the label were Jailcell Recipes. I'd been to see the Jailcells play many times and they really rocked. This band were definitely a huge inspiration to all the guys in Couch Potatoes. Their first album 'Energy in an empty tank world' was good, but it was very fast and hectic hardcore with slightly muddy production, and I was definitely more into the melodic and better produced 'Poulton Road' EP. Through 'Poulton Road' the band carried on that policy of open and direct contact, as used by the fanzines of the time, and put photos of their houses with their home addresses in Wigan and Liverpool on the back cover of this vinyl release. I thought that was cool. The singer Robbie Reid lived at 154 Poulton Road. Jamie Owen the guitarist lived at 4 Townsfields. Dave Arnold the bassist lived at 36 Mill Street and the drummer, Ian Barwick, lived at 4 Gamford Lane. They'd all hang out in Poulton Road, so that street sign was on the front cover. This was like an old skool Google Earth. Can you imagine any band doing that sort of thing now?

For record collector nerds, like me, the second pressing of the Poulton Road EP was limited to 1063 copies and mine is number 220, on grey vinyl with a fold-over cover. The first pressing was in a glossy pocket sleeve with the band's name on a removable sticker, some of the stickers were black & white, some were orange and black. This was their early stuff, and they were now writing even better songs as the brilliant 'Worn down' 7" would soon show in '91. This featured a great cover of Black Flag's 'Jealous again' as well as their own very positive and hammeringly powerful track, 'Worn down' where Robbie tries desperately to encourage the listener with "Are you breathing all of your breath? Living your life to its full?... Start again, pick it up, try harder and don't be easily pleased." This Jailcell Recipes 'Worn down' 7" vinyl was limited to just 500 copies as a pre-album promotional release and they were all hand numbered. Mine is number 66. I wish there'd been at least 700 and I could've had number 666, but there you go. On the cover of this single there's a great live photo of the band on stage at a show in Belfast. Robbie has just one trainer on and I figured it was just something that happened while he was jumping around on stage or in the crowd, or maybe he was trying to be a bit 'Rollins'. (Henry Rollins, the singer of Black Flag and later The Rollins Band, would often charge around on stage barefoot and wearing very little other than shorts), so I asked him about it one day and Robbie told me "There was a partially paralysed and mentally ill guy called Joey Deacon on Blue Peter in the '80s and they wheeled him out one day for a boat trip. He somehow managed to lose a shoe overboard in the Thames. Being bratty young punk kids, we thought it was funny and took the piss, calling ourselves the one shoe crew". I remember Joey Deacon well and Couch Potatoes doing similar stupid stuff at the time too, so there you go, more humanity and humour in hardcore. It didn't always have to be 'Dead serious.'

This 'Worn down' single was closely followed by the Jailcell Recipes brilliant 'Two Years of Toothache' album, so named as Jamie 'Jailcell' Owen, the band's guitarist and main music writer, refused to visit a dentist all the time he was writing these songs even though he had a rotting tooth and again, they all wanted to take the piss. Although a hugely underrated band at the time, through more or less constant touring they still managed to play with the likes of Fugazi, Bad Brains, Rollins Band, Gorilla Biscuits, Naked Raygun, All, Green Day, Snuff and seven times with Couch Potatoes. Lucky them! In fact, our next couple of shows would be with the Jailcells as part of their tour with Force Fed, another hard-rocking UKHC band.

5, Jailcells, straight edge and

mix tapes

5/3/91 Jailcell Recipes, Force Fed, BBMFs and Couch Potatoes
The Shelley Arms, Nutley
6/3/91 Jailcell Recipes, Force Fed and Couch Potatoes
The Basement, Brighton

Force Fed were a hardcore band from Nottingham. They'd featured ex-members of Heresy, Meatfly and other heavy UK acts in the past but the line up on this tour was Mike Knowlton on vocals, Neil Smith on bass, and the two brothers Nick Clark on guitar and Nigel Clark on drums. They made a noise like an airplane landing and had just recorded at Whitehouse studios with Martin Nichols, a well-known studio and producer in the UKHC scene where both Jailcell Recipes and Couch Potatoes would go to record too, as well as Ripcord, Annalise, Slowdive, Revolver, Bob Tilton and many more. Force Fed had a couple of releases that only the really keen HC kids had heard of, but their new record was an eight-track LP called 'Elounda Sleeps', out on Nottingham's Sycophant Records, and it was great. For these shows they also had a red vinyl 7" out on Sister Records called 'Fast Forward' and this would be a very busy year of touring for them.

Couch Potatoes first gigs back after our studio sessions early in '91 would be with Jailcell Recipes and Force Fed. Although I'd been to see the Jailcells play quite a few times over the last year or two this would be the first I'd get to meet them properly and get to know them. Macca from the Beebs had brought the Jailcells down and put these shows on. The first at The Shelley in Nutley with the BBMFs supporting too, and another in Brighton at The Basement club where we'd played with Chemical People the year before. Each time we played we seemed to get better, I suppose we were inspired by our company, although it could also just have been borrowing their decent-sounding equipment. That said, it did seem to me that we were getting tighter as a band, and we were certainly gaining confidence with every show we played now.

The gig at the Shelley was a cracker, just as we'd expect, and it was good to be back. All the bands played really well in front of a full house. The place went off on one, with everyone bouncing around and singing along like some crazy punk rock karaoke. If you asked any of the Jailcells right now where the centre of the UK punk rock universe in the early nineties was, I'm sure they'd still say The Shelley Arms.

The Jailcells were such nice guys, just incredibly down to earth for all their talent, and we struck up a good friendship, skateboarding and hanging out, chatting about all the bands we were into, particularly All and Descendents. We'd soon see that Robbie was an awesome skater. We'd all have a go in the car parks around Tunbridge Wells where we'd waxed the curbs for grinding - sliding along them on the trucks (axles) of the skateboards - and we had a few drop-offs we could try to jump down too, in warehouse loading bays where they'd chase us out after a while. Although a lot of my mates were pretty good, I was just playing at it really and could barely ollie, so just tended to roll around hanging out. I knew for that sort of thing you have to really commit and the more sensible part of me would much rather play guitar and avoid breaking my wrists or collar bones! These thoughts of self-preservation did not seem to affect Robbie at all, as he hammered along, grinding on curbs, jumping over barriers and off of ramps, zooming around without a care. I swear if he wasn't a singer in a touring band, he could have been a professional skateboarder, he was that good. After a while a few of us, who clearly couldn't keep up, went to get food. We needed milk, for tea and cereal, as the guys were staying with us, and I took Jamie, the Jailcell's guitarist, and Whitey, their roadie, with me to go and get it.

I was driving a battered old Toyota Celica at the time. I'd killed the Honda Accord in a cloud of steam and smoke, then also managed to trash a couple more old jalopies too. I went through cars like people changed their socks, but I was fond of this Celica. It was pretty nippy, had a decent stereo, a sunroof that worked and a two-tone silver and blue paintjob. Grabbing a few groceries ought to have been simple enough but Whitey had a t-shirt on that said 'Christianity. Stop it, it's stupid' in big letters across the front and was wandering around Sainsburys in Royal Tunbridge Wells while the locals looked on, even more disapprovingly than usual. This became doubly awkward as Whitey was happily shoplifting, stuffing his pockets full of vege food, beer and yoghurts as we wandered around the store. He was not subtle about it, so this behaviour, alongside his shirt, was soon attracting unwanted attention. I just wanted to buy the bloody milk and get going.

Let me tell you that the average nosey and judgemental 'Disgusted of Tunbridge Wells' type was not used to noisy northern punk rockers coming down to casually shoplift in their local grocery store. I managed to get them through the check-out relatively unscathed and we left in a rush, driving back to meet up with everyone at our friend Paul's house. The Jailcells were staying in Langton, one of the nicer parts of sunny Tunny, with two of the guys in the Couchies crew. Paul Skinner, the ginger-haired bassist of Angus Bagpipe, and Nick Meggitt, a great skateboarder himself, who'd been the only one of us who could attempt to keep up with Robbie. Heading back in such a rush was definitely a mistake though as Jamie was pretty clumsy and instantly managed to drop a full pint of milk in the passenger seat footwell of my car. It went everywhere and sunk into the carpet, so much so that despite my best efforts I never managed to get all the milk out, so after a couple of days it stunk to high heaven. The stench was so revolting that I ended up having to get rid of that car. Thanks Jamie!

We all piled down to Brighton later for the next gig. All the usual suspects were there, Johnny Deathshead, the guys from Sleep, and also Miles 'Milo' Booker, another Brighton scenester and a good mate of mine. He was a big Couchies fan, so much so that he'd later get roped in to be the singer for a later version of the band, and then become the vocalist for Rydell too. Milo was there that night on a rare date, he was trying to impress a girl from his art college by taking her to a hardcore show. I guess it was cool that he was hanging out with the bands and she certainly seemed to enjoy the show. I think he did OK with her later.

Force Fed had already gone down to Brighton as they wanted to spend the day at the seaside. They met us at the venue and went on after Couch Potatoes, playing a pretty intense and heavy set. Then the Jailcells hit the stage and blasted through most of the songs off 'Two years of toothache' which everyone seemed to love. It was bouncy and melodic stuff, more instantly likeable than their early releases, and seeing it played live in these small venues, full of die-hard fans, none of whom were yet jaded by apathy or too much choice, it was great fun. We all hung out again the next day until the Jailcells headed off along the coast for their next show, at The Joiners, and I headed up to town with Yan and Adam to see Drive play at the Camden Falcon. Even when we didn't have gigs, we'd go along to see as many as possible.

A couple of weeks later we ran into some trouble getting home from a show. I was in a particularly anarchic mood after having been to see the UK Subs play down at The Crypt in Hastings. It was hot and busy as the Subs played through all their rabble-rousing hits. Charlie Harper looked like worn-out leather even then but was a pretty cool guy, chatting to the crowd and engaging in banter. The gig went on until very late and this lateness became a problem as my stinky car was knackered so we'd taken a train down. By now all the trains had gone, leaving me, my brother Steve, and our guitar-playing neighbour Nik, trying to find a way home. We managed to find a cab but knew that late at night the taxi would be ridiculously expensive for such a long journey and we didn't have enough cash. What little we had was already spent on the evening out. This was not ideal, of course, but we needed our beds. When the cab reached Tunbridge Wells we gave the driver an address near enough to where we lived, but a few roads over, close to a load of alleyways and gardens with high fences. When he pulled up we simply jumped out and scarpered, legging it down the passageways and climbing over a couple of barbed-wire fences that we knew how to traverse from a few previous nefarious deeds. The poor sod had no chance of catching us. This was not something I am very proud of, but there you go, we had no money and really needed our beds. Sorry cabbie.

13/4/91 Couch Potatoes, Active Response, Headway and Angus Bagpipe Pagoda Youth Club, Tunbridge Wells

Couch Potatoes had another show coming up at the Headway centre in Tunbridge Wells. The first show at this youth club, now called The Pagoda, had gone down very well so we wanted this one to be just as good and we'd been inviting everyone we knew, including three support bands made up of our friends.

Active Response had played with us before and were really developing their own style now. A sort of crust punk, anarchist vegetarian, animal rights, Crass meets angst-ridden middle class teenagers thing. They were good mates of ours who'd been at a lot of the Shelley Arms shows too and now Nick Wilkinson, Macca from the Beebs brother, had joined the band as bass player alongside Paul Marriot on vocals, Rob Marriot and Tom Ludman on guitars, and the long-haired Julian Lea on drums. Nick used to quip that Julian should have been playing a very different genre of music, maybe something in hair rock with more cowbell and spandex. They'd been rehearsing at Felbridge Village Hall, near East Grinstead, where they were once double-booked with a ballet class of little girls and often had to listen to loads of OAPs complaints about their noise, being asked to turn down more or less constantly by the local bowls club or horticultural society. They had gotten pretty good now though and I remember them playing a great cover of Blitzkrieg Bop at this show. A Ramones cover was quite light-hearted for them, these guys really meant what they had to say and Active Response still had their flyers and leaflets to hand out at the gigs, always on about some sort of activism or protest. They were still heavily involved in direct action and hunt sabbing and had several run ins with the law over the next months and years.

Headway were a straight edge hardcore band. What that meant was that they played a fairly heavy, crunchy style of metallic rock with lyrics over it that reflected the fact that they did not drink or do drugs, were all vegetarians, and generally tried to lead a pretty clean lifestyle. There was quite a bit of jumping around at these shows, and quite a lot of finger-pointing, both literally and figuratively speaking. Although these were really good guys and close friends of ours, when you were straight edge it could be a fairly short hop to frowning at those that weren't, and that's not really an ideal situation for a scene that preached unity.

The straight edge, or SxE bands, were particularly influenced by the current New York Hardcore scene at the time and its bands, including Youth of Today, Gorilla Biscuits, Bold, Burn, Side by Side and Judge. But straight edge as a hardcore movement started way before that with bands like Minor Threat and 7 Seconds singing about needing clear minds to make a positive difference. There was a subculture of no drinking, no drugs, no smoking and no casual sex in the hardcore scene, which later also idealised being vegetarian or vegan too. This may seem to go against all that was rebellious in rock music but you have to remember that this scene wasn't old school punk and certainly

U.F.D present
UK HARDCORE DOUBLE BILL

JAILCELL RECIPES

FORCE FED

plus **COUCH POTATOES**

WEDNESDAY 6th MARCH 1991

THE **BRIGHTON POLYTECHNIC STUDENTS' UNION**

basement

underneath the art college, grand parade, brighton, 0273 683585

TICKETS £3.00 / £3.50 AVAILABLE FROM ROUNDER, UPSTAIRS AT JUBILEE & UNION OFFICE GRAND PARADE. DOORS OPEN 8.30pm LAST BAND ON STAGE 10.00pm.

Flyer for Jailcell Recipes, Force Fed and Couch Potatoes at The Basement in Brighton

Jailcells at The Shelley

73

Jamie Jailcell

Robbie gets some air

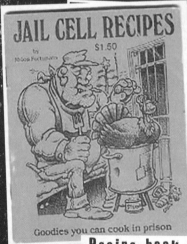

JAIL CELL RECIPES
by
$1.50

Goodies you can cook in prison

Recipe book

Jailcell Recipes

not standard issue heavy rock, this was new hardcore and there were always groups of people looking for better or different reasons to belong.

When Minor Threat* released their 'Filler' EP on Dischord Records way back in '81 it had a track on it called 'Straight edge'. The lyrics went "I'm a person just like you, but I've got better things to do, than sit around and fuck my head, hang out with the living dead, snort white shit up my nose, pass out at the shows. I don't even think about speed, that's something I just don't need, I've got the straight edge. I'm a person just like you, But I've got better things to do, than sit around and smoke dope, 'cause I know I can cope. Laugh at the thought of eating 'ludes, laugh at the thought of sniffing glue. Always gonna keep in touch, never want to use a crutch. I've got the straight edge." That seems a pretty clear message to me and this track is often cited as the start of the SxE sub-genre and the reason it is called straight edge.

On that same record there is another track entitled 'Bottled violence' about idiots getting drunk and going out fighting. You have to remember this later hardcore punk scene was more about alternative lifestyles and finding something you could believe in, not just spitting and spiking up your hair whilst you shouted at authority. Although hardcore is definitely anti idle government and big business, it is also about equality, respect and the sort of abstinences that could be seen as a good thing.

Later, on Minor Threat's brilliant 'Out of step' album in '83, the title track proudly announces "I don't smoke, I don't drink, I don't fuck, but at least I can fucking think!" and that same year on 7 Seconds* 'Committed for Life' EP the chorus of the track 'Drug control' shouts "Drugs make you turn on me, drugs will not set you free". It was fast becoming seen as a real weakness to do drugs in any way, even being a hazard to the survival of the hardcore scene and its in-built positivity. On 7 Seconds superb and unifying '84 album 'The Crew' this point is revisited several times, but particularly in the track 'Straight on' where the lyrics include "Thumbs down to all those drugs you need, because I'll just stay high naturally. Just more false starts, it tears apart, your heart, your head, your soul, your brain. It helps the feeling, eases your pain". Straight edge and anti-drugs were definitely becoming a big part of the hardcore scene.

SEHC was never just about the anti-drugs message though and all the straight edge bands, in common with most hardcore bands, had lyrics about positivity and unity, rallying against prejudice and asking for a commitment to the scene. Youth of Today became the SxE band to follow in the late eighties and everyone had their records and shirts. I was never that into them, much preferring a little more melody in my hardcore, and I'm sure that's why Gorilla Biscuits* became by far my favourite New York style straight edge band when their brilliant and inspiring 'Start Today' album came out in '89. I loved that record and was inspired by it. Every track on this album is a storm of positivity and inspiration, and ought to be standard listening for every teenager out there. Maybe it should even be taught in schools. On the title track, Civ sings "Next time I'll try, for the first time in my life. It won't pass me by. Procrastinate it can wait, I put it off. Let's start today, let's start today" adding "My room's a mess and I can't get dressed, I gotta be out by eight o'clock. Deep inside I know the answer. Well there's no time like the present and I'd like to hang out but who doesn't? I've made enough mistakes for this lifetime now I'm here to make amends".

Another attribute of the straight edger at hardcore shows would often be that they had drawn a large X on the back of their hands. This had come from the entrance markings at all-age shows where younger kids could not be served alcohol at the bar and in doing this the staff could easily see the X's on their hands if they asked. Straight edge kids didn't want to drink alcohol anyway so clearly marked their hands with X's as large and often as they could on purpose to show their commitment to abstinence and the lifestyle they had chosen.

Some kids I knew were part of all this straight-edgeness quietly and for themselves. Others wore it like a fashion with XXX or True 'til death tattoos. There were many SxE band shirts and accessories with this sub-genre of the scene eventually becoming more and more militant and extreme. It was certainly non-mainstream and a big part of hardcore throughout the decade, and in many ways still is very popular with newer bands like Have Heart, Inclination and Year of the Knife carrying the torch, whilst the older bands reform every now and again to tour. Yes, I've seen kids since who had 'Straight edge for life' tattoos and shirts when they were teenagers and in their early twenties, now drinking in the pub or even getting high, but they were young then and part of something bigger, so I wouldn't hold it against them. ("One night doesn't mean the rest of my life", as the Get Up Kids would say). Thirty years is a lifetime for some and life often gets in the way, as we all find when we get older. What's more inspiring is that I knew a bunch of morally strong, straight-edge kids then who still are to this day, and these are some of the most positive and inspiring people I have the good fortune to be close friends with.

All this meant that I was also straight edge for quite a while myself and although I did it mainly just for my own sake, I would occasionally get self-righteous and tell people what I thought of their smoking or drinking. It was the smoking that bugged me really, it still does, as it's more of an invasion of personal space and effects those around you even in moderation. I've never really smoked, so it often irritated me that I'd come out of shows absolutely stinking of it. I welcomed the ban on smoking in public places in 2007 and was surprised to see the government do the right thing for once for people's health, considering how much tax money they made out of it. I'd already had a few of my own issues with alcohol and fighting, but by this time I'd stopped drinking too. That may surprise many people who know me now, as I do enjoy the occasional tipple, but I was also vegetarian for over two years around this time too. This fact might

Couchies backing vocals crew - Jim, Adam, Megs, David, Nick and Paul

Angus Bagpipe at The Shelley

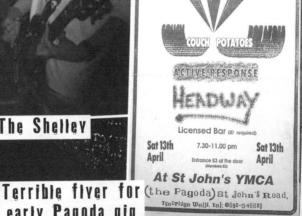

Big Mix

LIVE BAND NIGHT

COUCH POTATOES

ACTIVE RESPONSE

Headway

Licensed Bar (ID required)

Sat 13th April   7.30-11.00 pm   Sat 13th April

Entrance £3 at the door (Members £2)

At St John's YMCA
(the Pagoda) St John's Road,
Tunbridge Wells. Tel: 0892-548882

Terrible flyer for early Pagoda gig

77

Headway

Barry, vocals

Phil, bass

Jamie, drums

Simon, guitar

surprise people the most as I'm such a rotund foodie, but during this period I wrote quite a few articles for PETA and Animal Aid, and I still hold the ideals of animal welfare very strongly.

This show at a local youth club was a good example of the way the hardcore scene could attract all sorts of people and turn them on to all kinds of alternative lifestyles. We were all mates with a common cause, beyond the music, but even in a small town like Tunbridge Wells there were crusty 'dog on a string' cider punks alongside clean-living straight edge types. There were punkers, metallers, skateboarders and pretty much every form of teenage drop out. I'd X up for some shows and took it pretty seriously for a while. Mainly inspired by Gorilla Biscuits 'get up and go' positivity and the love of hardcore unity that 7 Seconds and Minor Threat preached. I'd also listen to, and often act upon, the more direct action advice of punk bands like Conflict or Crass, aimed at stopping hunters, butchers or testing labs, with lyrics suggesting we put "super glue in their locks" and "sugar in the petrol tank means delivery is going nowhere."

The straight edge I saw locally was very anti-drugs and this probably came as much from a middle, or more realistically upper working-class fear of it that had been instilled by parents and school teachers throughout our adolescence. But having 'the edge' was more about self-control and being in a frame of mind that you look after yourself and others, you don't treat anyone like shit or take advantage of them. Just normal things for any decent people, and it was hard to see how an addict could adhere to such high ideals. In the provincial area I lived in around the Southeast of England, I never really saw that much in the way of hard drugs. They were definitely there as I'd often hear from older guys that Tunbridge Wells was a well known stop-off for drugs coming in from the coast and heading up to London. They'd tell me that cocaine, or even heroin, was fairly easy to get hold off, but I hadn't seen it much outside of London and really didn't want to. What we did see a lot of in the 'burbs though was weed. All sorts of it and often in a resin form called red leb that seemed to be prevalent at that time. The people into it pretty much kept themselves to themselves and knowing a few, they seemed quite chilled to me. Punks didn't really hang out with hippies, so that could have been it too.

Anyway, back to the gig and back to the point. Headway were straight edge and the first posi-core band I'd seen play live. They were a new band and very young, but already really rocked. They had a crunchy metallic style to their hardcore with earnest vocals asking listeners to take a stand for a better way. In one track, 'Where to turn', Barry prophetically sings "All around I see corrupted morals, corrupt ideals forged by greed. We must cease before this world burns up around us. It's ignorance feeding the fire." Although initially named Headway, they'd later change the band's name to Strength Alone, quite possibly because of the name of the charity we were all playing for that evening. They were a four-piece comprised of Barry Thirlway on vocals, Simon Goodrick on guitar, Phil Secretan on bass and Jamie Donbroski on drums, hailing from a little Sussex village called Newick. God knows what had spawned them, but we all became good mates, playing and going to many other shows together, and even now, many years later, Simon and Jamie are still both playing alongside me and Macca in Come The Spring and The Atlantic Union Project.

This brings me on to Angus Bagpipe, another group made up of good friends of mine, who'd started up soon after Couch Potatoes and musically seemed to combine the best aspects of hardcore, straight edge and anarcho punk. This would be their first ever show and as their set had been hastily put together, partly to celebrate the birthday of their bassist, Paul Skinner, it was far from polished. But they went for it nevertheless and the crowd always appreciated that. Macca's brother Nick pulled a double duty that evening because as well as playing bass in Active Response he was the singer of Angus Bagpipe. In fact, when he wasn't leaping about with the microphone in his hand, he'd have a go on the guitar in a few Angus songs too. They had an instrumental called 'Monkey Magic' and he'd don this bright white V-shaped Ibanez PR1660 guitar and wield it like a barbarian's axe, getting at least some of the chords right. Wisely though, he left most of the guitar playing to Duncan.

Duncan Morris was another good guy we'd met at the Shelley and saw at most of the Brighton gigs. He played guitar for Angus Bagpipe and was really good at it. He wrote most of their music too and I remember being blown away by some of the guitar lines when I saw them live. They also had Paul Skinner, an energetic ginger-haired kid from Langton Green, who loved 7 Seconds and Gorilla Biscuits and played a fretless Yamaha bass guitar whilst jumping around a lot, and Aegir Morgan - that's an Icelandic name that I soon learnt is pronounced Ire - was on drums holding it all together. I fondly remember one of their songs called 'Peany B', about peanut butter, as both Nick and Dunc were vegetarians and this seemed to be their sandwich of choice.

Other great Angus Bagpipe songs were 'Prisoners', 'Killing Fields' and there was definitely something about a secret squirrel. But by far their best track was 'Crime Squad', and they played it twice this evening, the second time as a well-deserved encore. Not bad for their first ever gig. Nick later told me that although he and Dunc wrote most of the Angus songs, that particular track had been written by Rob Marriot of Active Response. He'd written these angry anti-establishment, anti-corruption lyrics and given them to Duncan who'd added a really crunchy riff with a police siren nee-naw like lead guitar line, and then they'd kind of rapped the lyrics over it. It somehow worked and was always their encore if a show went well, even if they'd already played it in the set. I remember that soon after this Angus Bagpipe won a local 'Battle of the Bands' gig that was judged by the bassist of OMD!

The gig was going great and finally it was Couch Potatoes turn. We couldn't wait to get onstage. We'd been practising and recording but there was really nothing better than this

fun live environment with the great atmosphere created by all of our buddies there. It always brought out the best in us. The stage at the Pagoda though was one of those that could be made up of wooden blocks so that it could be moved and be put away afterwards. That was pretty solid for your average event, but this was a hardcore show and we were all bouncing up and down, with kids jumping up and off it, slamming into it, and sure enough the stage blocks started to move apart and then give way in the middle of our set. A few hasty repairs got us going again but this was how it was going to be now, kind of an Indiana Jones adventure jumping between blocks for the rest of the set.

We played all the tracks from 'Eight songs' and 'Wash', including the new ones 'Bad habit' and 'Why', and we'd added 'Only of you' by Green Day to our repertoire of covers now and this would be the first show we played it at. This was a good song to dance to and enough people there knew it to singalong. It had a simple enough chord progression but also a pretty decent solo for me to have a crack at. This went down pretty well, earning me a clap from the musos in the crowd, and we wrapped things up with the speedy chaos of 'Cold Can' and 'Tired'. I couldn't help think about the Gorilla Biscuits lyric in 'New Direction' that says "I'll tell you stage dives make me feel more alive than coded messages in slowed down songs". It'd been another great show and although I realise that headlining a youth club in Tunbridge Wells is hardly playing Wembley Arena, at that time and that age, the feeling was electric. I'd definitely settle for it and just wanted to play small clubs every night.

*Minor Threat were a massively influential hardcore band from Washington DC. The vocalist, Ian MacKaye, and drummer, Jeff Nelson, started Dischord Records to put out their own and friend's releases. After Minor Threat, Ian MacKaye also played in Embrace and Fugazi. Jeff Nelson also played in Three. The guitarist Lyle Preslar also played in Meatmen and Samhain, and the bassist Brian Baker, who later switched to second guitar when Steve Hansgen joined, also played guitar in Bad Religion.

*7 Seconds were another seminal HC band out of Reno, Nevada, led by the Marvelli brothers, under their stage names of Kevin Seconds (vocals) and Steve Youth (bass), alongside Dan Pozniak (guitar) and Troy Mowatt (drums). Their early releases were on BYO Records, Better Youth Organisation, a label set up by Youth Brigade, another US HC band, and then their own Positive Force Records.

*Gorilla Biscuits were a SxE HC band from New York with releases on Revelation Records, the NY-based label started by Jordan Cooper and Ray Cappo, the vocalist of Youth of Today. (Ray left Revelation to start Equal Vision Records when he formed his Krishna band Shelter). The Gorilla Biscuits vocalist Anthony 'Civ' Civorelli later formed his own band, CIV, and now owns Lotus Tattoo studio. One of the guitarists, Walter Schreifels, also played in Quicksand, Rival Schools, Walking Concert, CIV, Youth of Today and Project X, as well as starting Some Records. The other guitarist, Alex Brown, ran Schism fanzine with Youth of Today guitarist John Porcell and later started a record label of the same name, as well as playing in Project X and Side by Side. The bassist, Arthur 'Arty' Smilios, also played in CIV, Judge, Underdog and Warzone. GB went through a few drummers, including Ernie Parada, George Megasopolis and Sammy Siegler, but it was Luke Abbey who played on 'Start Today', as well as in Judge, Moondog and Warzone.

15/4/91 BBMFs, Couch Potatoes, Brand New Day, Headway and Angus Bagpipe
The Shelley Arms, Nutley

We were still on a high from that show when, just two days later, we headed out to the Shelley Arms again to play another gig with the Beebs, Headway, Angus Bagpipe and a new band called Brand New Day. It was fairly easy to put on four or five band shows, partly because there were so many new young bands starting up, but also because we all shared the same equipment on stage, so it just needed one set up and this saved a lot of time and hassle. Anyone could have a go, so long as they didn't break the gear. As well as all the hardcore kids from Brighton and the Shelley regulars, the place was packed with loads of extra kids from Tunbridge Wells who'd made their way over too. These little local shows were fast becoming brilliant parties and people wanted to be there. All the bands played their hearts out and threw in a few covers as crowd-pleasers, mainly straight edge style hardcore as that seemed to be the flavour at the time, but bands were experimenting with all sorts of stuff and turning it into hardcore. I don't think that Warren, the landlord of the Shelley, had ever seen so many people dancing and singing in that tiny bar.

Angus Bagpipe's set had four good covers that everyone knew. The Spermbirds 'You're not a punk' from their 'Something to prove' album, and Gorilla Biscuits 'Biscuit power', an added track on the re-issue of their self-titled EP, as well as 'Regress no way' and '99 red balloons' by 7 Seconds, from their classic album, 'Walk together, rock together'. Now I realise that '99 red balloons' was originally by the German band Nena, the catchy 'Neunundneunzig rote Luftballons' in their native language, but when 7 Seconds started playing the song, it became a hardcore classic and an anti-war singalong. "Ninety-nine red balloons floating in the summer sky. Panic bells, it's red alert. There's something here from somewhere else. The war machine springs to life, opens up one eager eye. Focusing it on the sky when ninety-nine red balloons go by".

Gotham Tapes

I've mentioned my D.I.Y. tape label a few times and today that idea may seem quaint and naive, even a little OCD as an extension of making mix tapes to share tracks by bands I was into with my mates. But vinyl and CDs were expensive, and this was still more than a decade before MySpace, Facebook, YouTube, Bandcamp, Soundcloud or any of the digital music sharing platforms, so it became very useful to promote demos and tracks of the bands me and my friends were playing in. Gotham Tapes developed through necessity and was the simple predecessor to the record label I would later run. Both Couch Potatoes and then later Joeyfat would benefit from coverage on this tape label (as would Understand, Fabric, Jawbreaker, Moral Crux and many more) and it definitely helped open doors and get us more gigs.

I regularly corresponded with loads of bands from near and far, as well as independent labels, promoters, fanzines, etc. I'd progressed from exchanging one-off mixtapes with my mates to compiling collections of new tracks into a compilation and then duplicating the cassettes for distribution. It was all very low tech, but I'd make up covers and track listings for the tapes and put the band's contact details inside, usually their home phone numbers to help them get gigs. I even started to add catalogue numbers to the releases, GOT001, GOT002 and so on, although the only real distribution available was the postman and me at gigs. It was fun and practical so soon quite a lot of bands got involved, booking shows through these tapes and finding some good new fans too. The experience certainly helped me when I finally came around to setting up a 'proper' record label later.

The first Gotham Tapes release was called Tee Hee and had a rather portly character on its blue card cover, hand drawn by Yan in a Beano or Viz cartoon style, running off with a cake that he'd clearly just nicked. It featured all the good local rock bands we'd played with or seen at shows, as that way it was easy to ask them for tracks. Side one had

BBMFs 'Superfly Hedgehog', Big Pop Trotsky 'Fuck', Couch Potatoes 'Bad Habit', Sleep 'If Only', Active Response 'Wake Up' and Electric Sex Circus 'Prince Albert'. Side two had Headway 'Opinions Voiced', Hybrazil 'Amelia', The Audience 'Grey', Understand 'Shove the Dove', M.T.A 'Ease My Heart' and Sorb 'No Justice'. That would be forty minutes of brand-new music to check out from twelve bands over those twelve tracks.

The second cassette was Couch Potatoes 'Live in Tunbridge Wells', sixteen tracks from the dodgy recording of our forty-minute set at the Rumble Club on 21st September 1990. That was only our fifth show ever so it's a bit ropey, with plenty of shouting and feedback between the songs. The sixteen track setlist from the show that night was; 'No More', 'Such a bad day', 'I'm not a loser', 'Suburban home', 'Cold Can', 'I saw you', 'Child and his lawnmower', 'The Sound', 'I like food', 'Yuppies suck', 'I don't think so', 'Coffs harbour blues', 'Tired', 'Feedback', 'What's that noise' and 'Then I kissed her'.

GOT003 was 'Live at the Shelley', a sixty minute, twenty-five track collection of five track live sets by five bands, Angus Bagpipe, Beanfeast, Headway, Couch Potatoes and The BBMFs. This tape had a printed yellow cover and included some amusing between track banter, plus a lot of cover versions and was surprisingly good quality compared to some other dodgy live recordings of the time. The Angus Bagpipes tracks were 'Monkey Magic', 'Crime Squad', 'You're not a Punk', 'Prisoners' and 'Better Than You'. The Beanfeast (Active Response / Protest) tracks were 'Fight Back', 'Beanfeast', 'Cover Up', 'Nobody Wins' and 'Borders'. The Headway (Strength Alone) tracks were 'Reflections', 'Beliefs', 'Change for the better', 'Proving a Point' and 'Best of Times'. Couch Potatoes tracks were 'Lunchbox', 'Why', 'Newun', 'Tired' and 'Hey Hey', and the BBMFs tracks were 'Fraser the Fantastic Rabbit', 'E. R. Pinkus', 'No Sleep 'Til (That bloke)', 'Superfly Hedgehog' and 'Unbelievable'. This tape really takes me back to the fun gigs at The Shelley Arms and I'm particularly glad I made it. It has more hand-drawn cartoon art on the cover, this time of a hardcore style guitarist in a baseball cap and shorts jumping through the air. Yan drew it from a photo of Paul Skinner, the Angus Bagpipe bassist, which was taken at a gig at the Shelley.

The fourth Gotham Tape was called 'Hello, Bollox and Welcome' in tribute to a Viz character called Roger Mellie, the man on the telly, and sported a cartoon of him on the red and yellow cover. It introduced twenty-five more heavy rock, hardcore and indie bands over sixty minutes with a UK side and a rest of the world side, including all their postal addresses for booking tours / gigs.

'Tout a fait punk' or 'Everything made punk' was the name of the next Gotham Tape, a live radio broadcast by French hardcore band Moral Crux. It had a black on pale green cover and twenty tracks that went on for about sixty minutes. The band were pen-pals of mine and J P Lemarchand, who ran another tape label called Broken Tapes in France, had helped me set it up. The band were friendly enough and wanted to get better known outside of their home country so agreed to put this live recording out through Gotham in the UK as well as JP's Broken Tapes in France. It went down very well and introduced them to a lot of new fans.

Then GOT006 was 'Another' compilation, this time with thirteen bands providing about forty minutes of new music, and including tracks by Older Than Dirt, Headcleaner, The Killrays, Live and Learn, Kotzen and The Blanks, amongst others, again with all their contacts.

There was a short break before we compiled the seventh Gotham release, a collection called 'Eyes Down For God' with a cartoon of the pope drawing bingo balls from a font, and having just drawn the 666 ball. I'm pretty sure this artwork was created by my old mate Austin, a great artist and illustrator, and also the singer in a local band called Head. This one introduced twenty more hardcore and alternative bands with tracks by Pseudo Hippies, Couch Potatoes, Stand Off, Ground, Joeyfat, Youth Fed Up, Wartorn, Nailbomb, Strookas, Moral Crux and Guitar Gangsters on the church side, and on the bingo side tracks by Agent 86, Guttersnipes, Angus Bagpipe, Surf City Rockers, Bembix, M Ways, Portobello Bones, Klaw and Understand.

I'd been chatting with J P again in France about a few ideas and he introduced me to a lot of small indie labels and distros that were now helping us with distribution. The compilations all went down pretty well but the single band releases seemed to be taken more seriously so I wanted to work on more of those. I had new recordings underway, first of Couch Potatoes and later Joeyfat, but I'd been corresponding with plenty of other good bands too, a couple of them very well-known, and the next release would be a real cracker.

About this time Jawbreaker had moved from New York, where they'd been at college, back to the West Coast and were hanging out in the mission district of San Francisco. Unfun had already come out so they were starting to get known, but this was way before Bivouac or 24 Hour Revenge Therapy and all that followed. They played the Gilman Street centre in Berkeley quite a lot and had a good quality recording of a show they did there on 11th August 1990. I'd been corresponding with Adam and Blake from the band, introduced through their friends Noah and Christy. They told me this recording was available and good enough quality to release so it'd be great if we could get it out to more people around the UK and Europe. Absolutely we could, so 'Jawbreaker, live at Gilman Street' became GOT008.

Unsurprisingly, this Jawbreaker live cassette would be by far the most successful tape yet. It had a pink wraparound cover with a photo of a boxer getting punched in the face on the front. The band's set consisted of 'Welcome to our band', 'Gutless', 'Down', 'You're right', 'Softcore', 'Lawn', 'This is big', 'Freebird' and 'Want' on one side and then 'See thru skin', 'Driven', 'Fine day', 'Equalised', 'Shield your eyes' and 'Eye 5' on the other. Just fifteen tracks in all, but going on for nearly an hour.

We followed this with the cassette version of Couch Potatoes new 'Excess All Areas' album. Initially sending it out as a demo to get the new tracks to record labels, hoping to get them released properly on vinyl or CD, and again we sent tapes to promoters to help us book shows, to reviewers at zines and mags, radio stations for airplay and any contacts we could think of. The album had fourteen tracks; 'Lunchbox', 'Impossible easier', 'Part of you', 'Weak', 'Kill it', 'Three', 'Another', 'Bob', 'Hole', 'Why', 'Hooked', 'Take it', 'This morning' and 'Excess' and was a huge step up from our early releases. As we had space left on the sixty-minute cassettes we added ten more tracks to fill it up, using some of the better earlier tracks. (The extra tracks on GOT009 were 'No more', 'I don't think so', 'Newun', 'Tired', 'Bad habit', 'Lucifer's lunchbox', 'Such a bad day', 'The sound', 'Get straight' and 'Cold can part 2'). The artwork was black and white but properly printed, with a fat bloke jumping into a swimming pool on the front cover and pictures of other fat blokes on the inside that were meant to be the four of us in the band. There was also a tracklist, credits and a thanks list, and our contacts, of course. It was this hour long, twenty-four track assault on melodic hardcore that we then sent out to hundreds of people over the next months. We'd duplicate a couple of thousand copies before it eventually came out on CD too.

By this time I'd be playing in a new band called Joeyfat too and we'd made several demo recordings and had live sets of decent quality. We were already sending out some quite professional-looking demos, maybe three or four tracks, packaged with press info for the label, magazine or promoter. We'd been creating a definite artwork style for the band, using various slogans and even designing some t-shirts too, but we needed a tape for fans. For GOT010 we used a live recording of Joeyfat at the Rumble Club on 17th January '92 on one side and our first proper studio recording from 18th March '92 on the other. We called the cassette 'Soup' and the two sides were 'at work' and 'at play'.

The studio 'work' side had the tracks 'Windscreen', 'Tear', 'People come into your house', 'Amusement', 'Piecemeal', 'Spoilt', 'Sugarhead' and 'Simmer down'. The live 'play' side had 'Windscreen', 'Spoilt', 'Tear', 'Amusement', 'Mr Smugfellow', 'Pass the sprouts' and 'Simmer down'. The cover was black and white but had hand-drawn angry girls and monsters on it, as well as our contact details for gigs, of course. I sent a lot of these tapes out over the next months and kept the postie very busy.

Quite some time later two more compilations came out on Gotham Tapes introducing new bands I was into. GOT011 was called 'Lowbrow head tread' and contained tracks by twenty bands including Another Fine Mess, Decadence Within, Nux Vomica, The Shreds, Erase Today and Concrete Idea, as well as '25 Years' by Joeyfat.

GOT012 was called 'All the smiley faces' and featured another twenty-one tracks from fifteen great bands including Wordbug, Fabric, The Strookas and Stand Off, as well as the songs 'Cushion Fed' and 'The day I realised I was god' by Joeyfat and 'Hole' and 'Cold Can part 2' by Couch Potatoes.

Although I'd continue to send out demos for what seemed like forever more, I'd intended that these two comps would be the last Gotham Tapes releases as I was now getting into 'proper' vinyl and CD releases and starting to work with more record labels. Many of these record labels never sent out half as many copies as I had done of these tapes, but they did help me start Ignition, and then Engineer Records, and find production and distribution partners all over the world.

I did however have one more Gotham tape. GOT013 was Couch Potatoes new mini album called 'Mans greatest friend in the windswept heights' and these professionally printed and duplicated cassette versions of it went out all over, while we waited for a label to pick it up for other formats. The tape had a Mongolian yak herder on the cover and contained ten tracks; 'Lost', 'User friendly', 'Kill it', 'Engineer', 'Impossible easier', 'Wall', 'Venue', 'Why', 'Poison me' and 'Never'.

Gotham Tapes covers

Jawbreaker, live at Gilman Street

Live at The Shelley

6, Majority of none

A couple of weeks later we all piled down to The Joiners in Southampton to play a gig with the Beebs and a really energetic new US straight edge band we were all into called 'Majority of One'. We were particularly looking forward to it as The Joiners was a great venue that we'd been to many times before to see loads of great shows, but we'd never played there ourselves yet and we couldn't wait. The guys that ran the punk shows at The Joiners were called the S.T.E. collective and they were some of the coolest and friendliest people we knew in the HC scene. They'd been putting on gigs since '88 and I'd never been to a bad show down there, so it was always worth the trip. The main S.T.E. guys that I knew were Rich Levene, PJ and Rob, as well as Tony and Gaz from Suspect Device, a great fanzine from down that way. They supported local bands just as much as the bigger groups on tour and had their own newsletter to let everyone know what was happening. The S.T.E. in the collective's name stood for Southampton, Totton and Eastleigh, the local boroughs, and some of the regular punters used to like to chant where they were from at the shows just to annoy each other, but it was always fairly good-natured and I thought it was pretty cool that they wanted to represent their area and were proud of it, very much like football fans, it gave the Joiners shows a little bit of that terrace feeling. These guys put on so many great shows and I'm glad to say that Couch Potatoes, Joeyfat and Rydell all played for the S.T.E. collective promoters at The Joiners Arms in sunny Southampton several times and we alwas enjoyed ourselves.

A music journalist named Ged Babey interviewed Rich Levene quite recently for a great piece about the S.T.E. in Louder Than War fanzine for their twenty-fifth anniversary and Rich sent it to me. It talks about the Joiners being the spiritual home of the S.T.E. and the local punk and hardcore scene, and how there were no contracts, guarantees or major label bands. With all the gigs set up directly through the bands themselves, or by friends who were booking tours simply because they were into the music, it all saved a lot of hassle and was done on mutual trust. That was definitely the goal of the scene then and probably should still be even now. Whatever minimal expenses were incurred would be covered by the door money with the remainder, most of it, going straight to the bands. Occasionally a little money was kept aside to cover any future poor turnouts but the S.T.E. was strictly non-profit making. Gig admission was as cheap as possible with concessions for those who were unwaged and the collective always endeavoured to promote an environment that was friendly, fun and free from violence, racism, sexism or homophobia. In the thirty or so shows I saw there, and the ten or so more I played at, I don't remember there ever being any trouble.

Like most promoters the S.T.E. guys used to put up the touring bands after their gigs and feed them a vegetarian or vegan meal. They'd provide a sofa or floor for the bands to sleep on and breakfast in the morning, all for playing the show. In the Louder Than War interview Rich said "We would often head off for work the next morning and leave sleeping punks to let themselves out when they left. Considering the number of people we put up over the years, this caused comparatively few problems. As the S.T.E. house was in a quiet street in Eastleigh, our neighbours became accustomed to strange-looking visitors and vans with foreign plates coming and going at all hours. One German guy, inspired he said by Jack Kerouac, slept in his sleeping bag out on our dewy front lawn. Another time we came home to a kitchen that had kindly been cleaned from top to bottom by our visitors Circus Lupus and Lungfish". Not at all what most people would expect from punk rockers on tour.

Speaking with Rich about some of the shows, he remembered a few more stories, "The U.S. band Downcast had a falling out with their guitarist just weeks into their three-month long '92 European tour. They persuaded him to stay on and complete it, but he was barely speaking to the others and as Southampton was the last date of the tour and they had a cancelled gig before they flew home, the three nights they spent at our house were strange and awkward to say the least. Downcast's last ever gig was in Southampton." Also, Rich soon found that, "Sometimes people were not as we imagined. In 1993, the American band Alloy played a storming gig and afterwards they, along with some visiting Germans and Norwegians stayed at our house. A drunken but friendly discussion about U.S. imperialism was suddenly interrupted when the Alloy drummer stormed out, enraged at criticism of his country, to sleep in the van. At which point a deadpan Rob asked him if he was going to "sleep wrapped in the Stars & Stripes". This did not go down too well. Another time, in 1991, Quicksand, who had roots in New York's straight edge scene, shocked PJ with their predilection for hash hot knives". I guess what goes on tour stays on tour.

The relationship between the Joiners venue and S.T.E. collective as promoters was one that would be repeated, sometimes with even greater, but unfortunately usually far lesser success throughout the UK hardcore scene, including many of the venues we'd play at over the next years including our own Forum in Tunbridge Wells. I always think that the stories from these shows are interesting and well worth hearing so the discussion with Rich continued, "We were always conscious of the notion that we didn't want to come across like just another gig promoter. To this end, the S.T.E. bulletin was very important to us. What started out as a one-sided A5 sheet with details of forthcoming gigs, had by 1992 become a free monthly double-sided, folded A4 mini-fanzine with news, information and columns written by us, with contributions from people within the scene. The columns covered music, politics, opinions and issues that impacted on the punk community. Some people bared their souls, others simply took the piss. But it was also a useful tool when leafleting and promoting other gigs, as people tended to be less likely to throw away something they could read later, rather than a simple flyer. Sometimes people said we were too politically correct, while others felt we weren't radical enough. We were happy to let our benefit gigs for Hunt Sabs, Rape Crisis, Anti-Fascist Action, Zapatistas, striking Liverpool dockers, etc speak for themselves. Occasionally a criticism was levelled that we were cliquey but although we fostered a close-knit scene, we always encouraged people to get involved with us and tried to be friendly and welcoming to newcomers".

Rich continued, "In terms of the calibre of bands we put on probably the 1991-93 period was the heyday of the S.T.E. in most people's eyes. During this time we put on gigs for several bands that would later become huge. In December 1991, Green Day played The Joiners with Jailcell Recipes & Older Than Dirt on their first UK tour to around just 75 people. OTD's singer Mike put them up afterwards at his flat. As it was near my birthday, they dragged me on-stage and sang Happy Birthday to me and somewhere it's all caught on video. Green Day were due to play for us again in 1993 but the gig got cancelled and by the time they returned they were on a major label and massive. Later they were to tell journalists from the music press that the Joiners was one of their best ever gigs, whilst Kerrang! reproduced the poster from our gig in a feature and mocked the fact that the door admission was the 'princely sum' of £3/2.50. NOFX played two S.T.E. gigs in the summers of 1991 & 1992. The gigs were both fantastic but at the second, Rob ended up arguing with Fat Mike from the band over just £20. We'd paid them all the remaining door money of £180, but Fat Mike insisted on £200. Suffice to say we didn't pay them the extra (we didn't have it!) and didn't put them on again. The next night in London, our friend Selina drunkenly heckled them with '£200 you green-haired bastard!' to bemused looks from most people in the crowd!"

I well remember the Alloy, Green Day and NOFX shows at the Joiners myself, having been at all of them, and to see and play with bands like that in such an intimate venue is like chalk and cheese compared to dots on a distant stage at a big festival. But opportunities for such shows would soon be gone as the hardcore scene was changing fast, so Rich then touched on that; "The mainstream success of Nirvana and Green Day in the early to mid 1990s, whilst attracting more people into the scene, also had the effect of pushing a lot of bands out of our mode of operating. Some bands that we had earlier put on; Samiam, Jawbreaker, Understand, etc had now signed major label deals, while others went through commercial booking agencies. I remember one particularly heated telephone conversation with a booker who could not comprehend why we had no intention of doing a gig which involved a contract, a guarantee to pay a ridiculous amount of money and provide the band with a hotel for the night. The NME journo Angela Lewis took a shine to us and reviewed our Baby Harp Seal gig in 1995, where PJ made her pay to get in on the door like everybody else. She used to telephone us regularly for info and sometimes we were honest and helpful, but other times we made up some preposterous tales. Sometimes we were pleasantly surprised though. In 1994, I took a call from a guy who wanted to book a gig for Huggy Bear. Now as this was just after the time when the band had caused a furore on the TV show The Word and the press was full of Riot Grrrl hype, I suggested perhaps it would be better to contact someone else. However, he insisted they were happy to play a D.I.Y. gig and had specifically asked to play an S.T.E. show. We did it and there were no problems. Graham Coxon, of Blur, was going out with one of Huggy Bear at the time and accompanied his girlfriend to the gig, causing one of our regulars, the self-styled 'Queer Rob', to exclaim that he'd have 'decked him' if he'd known someone from Blur was here".

Trying to build a scene around hardcore punk in Tunbridge Wells wasn't too easy, but we had the Rumble Club, soon to become the Forum, also the Pagoda, and a couple of other venue halls and music pubs. We also had London and Brighton both fairly nearby, and lots of colleges and schools we could put posters up in. It was important to have good local bands though that could help build their own fanbase and bring their following along to shows. Couch Potatoes always tried to support any other local bands and help them if possible, with gigs and promotions. In his Louder Than War interview Rich was also asked about this; "We always felt that local bands were vital to the strength of any scene and above all the members of these bands were often our friends. We used the Bulletin to promote what they were up to and we provided contact details and put them on gig bills as often as we could. The two Southampton bands most associated with the S.T.E. were Older Than Dirt and Minute Manifesto, who coincidentally both played seventeen gigs for us. Older Than Dirt were around in the early 90s and as Mike was an S.T.E. founder and one of our oldest friends, it was always special to have them play for us. Minute Manifesto were around at the end of the 90s and as well as featuring our own Rob, had Jamie and Matt who were two of the influx of mid-90s newcomers we nurtured, so likewise it made us proud to see them develop into a band who made internationally renowned records and gigged across the UK." At this point Rich also gave honourable mentions to other south of England hardcore bands; Corporate Grave, Hate That Smile, Watch You Drown, Fusion, Smog, Haywire, Thirst!, Pogrom, Portiswood, Trophy Girls, Good Grief, Chicken Bone Choked, The Zimmer Frames, Disoma and Killjoy.

"As well as the overseas visitors, we built up relationships with some wonderful bands and people from all across the UK. Two bands I have particular fondness for are Harlow's Travis Cut, and Shutdown from the West Country, who played ten and seven S.T.E. gigs respectively. I named my cat Travis Cat as he turned up as a stray just as they left the morning after Travis Cut played their first gig for us in 1994 and they even credited him on the sleeve of one of their singles, how punk is that? Twelve years on Travis is still going strong. Shutdown's gigs here were amazing and I'll always remember the memorial gig they did here for no money after the tragic death of my best friend (S.T.E. co-founder and Thirst! guitarist) Steve Burgess in 1994."

Rich continued, "People always ask what are my favourite S.T.E. nights at the Joiners and I always pin it down to three. In joint second would be Norway's Life... But How To Live It? with Older Than Dirt in 1993. The D.I.Y. punk scene on mainland Europe was always an inspirational example to us, so to see one of the greatest ever bands from the continent here was pure joy. Level pegging with Life... would be the second Joyce McKinney Experience gig in 1990, with my Austrian friends Target of Demand and Brighton's Sleep. As well as being exhilarating musically, it was notable for the textbook way the packed crowd dealt with a troublemaker without ruining the atmosphere of the gig. Incidentally the only other fight I can recall at a Joiners S.T.E. gig was at Born Against in 1992; their singer Sam McPheeters ran out of the venue and when it was all quelled had to be retrieved from sitting in the grounds of the church up the road in St Mary Street. My top S.T.E. gig though would be Richmond, Virginia's Avail in 1995. We knew their records but had no idea how incendiary they were going to be live. Almost from the get-go the place exploded. It was their first gig outside North America and afterwards they told us initially they were apprehensive of the amount of people dancing, as in the States gigs could be very violent. However, when they noticed that there were women stagediving and that people had huge grins on their pig-piling faces they relaxed. They came back for two more S.T.E. gigs but that first one was the stuff of legends. Plus, they always raved about my veggie Shepherd's Pie."

Finally for his Louder Than War interview Ged had asked Rich about festivals in smaller venues; "Inspired by the festivals put on by our friends at the 1 in 12 club, an autonomous punk centre in Bradford, we too did an annual two-day festival at the Joiners from 1996-1999, along with a Christmas all-dayer. Around nine bands - overseas, national & local and of varying punk sub-genres - would play each day and people would travel from all over to attend. The Sundays would often start slowly as people recovered from the excesses of the night before, but overall, the S.T.E. fests were brilliant affairs, with people helping us out with equipment, sleeping places, feeding and putting up visitors."

I mention all this as the S.T.E. were a great example of what gig promoters really should be like and it's probably more important to get a feel for the scene at the time and how it could be when done well, than to talk about specific shows. These anecdotes and stories from Rich shine a light on the positive attitude of the people involved, and as we went on to learn, whilst in Couch Potatoes and all my bands, not all promoters would live up to these examples. This is just one venue and one collective out of hundreds in the UKHC scene, but Green Day, Jailcell Recipes, NOFX, Quicksand, Jawbreaker, Samiam, Lungfish, Alloy, Down By Law, Avail, Majority Of One, Understand, Couch Potatoes, Joeyfat and Rydell all played shows at The Joiners, put on by the S.T.E. collective, so cheers guys.

Before I get back to writing about the gig and the bands we played with on that night in April '91, I'll also just mention another mainstay of the Southampton area hardcore scene and that was Suspect Device fanzine. This great punk fanzine was run and edited by Tony and Gaz, who were always at the shows and always trying to support the bands in the UK scene. They wanted to create something for the punk scene rather than just be consumers, so they told me after being inspired by a copy of 'Damaged' zine, out of punk central that is Dorset. That's when they started their own fanzine back in '84 and have been working on it ever since.

They used Suspect Device to reach out with features and reviews, inform people and connect people, and then later, as it was mainly based around the music, they also decided to produce some recordings too. They, like many small labels at that time, started with some cassettes that could be easily and inexpensively recorded, duplicated and distributed, and I'm proud to say that the fourth one, a compilation called 'Shouting Music' features 'Tired' by Couch Potatoes, as well as great tracks by The BBMFs, Sleep, and many of the better early '90s UK hardcore bands. Tony later told me that the compilation was called 'Shouting Music' as that was what his young niece called the racket / music we all made and listened to at the time.

Tony and Gaz have had plenty of help and contributors over the years and they still keep on producing the fanzine even now. Tony told me, "We keep going because we love it. We still get excited by new music and new bands and feel the need to tell people about it. There have been a few years where it's taken a bit of a back seat as we've both had to deal with family issues, but we've always come back to it, and it will only take a brilliant new release or gig to get a new issue started." The scene dynamics and their personal situations may have changed over the years, as both now have families and Gaz has moved away from Southampton to live in Norfolk, keeping in touch via the internet, but they are working on issue #63 as I write this.

I asked Tony what kept it all going for him; "Like most of us in the scene I think being integrally involved in something and helping to spread the word is a big part of what drove us. And with bands, record labels or fanzines you got to meet so many cool people too. There have been a few stories down the years. Sometimes people are easy to get on with and sometimes not. We interviewed both Target of Demand from Austria, and Sleep from Brighton, on the same night before they both played at The Joiners in Southampton and that was a fun night. I sat on a tour bus outside the George Robey in London one night and interviewed Casey Jones of Ignite. We got on very well and are still friends. Then about a year later I sat on the same tour bus outside the same venue and interviewed Texas Is The Reason, but they were never likely to become friends. They were pleasant enough, but kind of distant. I also interviewed Mike Bullshit from Go! We stood outside The Joiners and spoke mainly about our shared interest in native cultures in the Americas."

Having produced BHP myself, I knew that production of a fanzine, not just the creation and costs, but also getting it out on time could all be an issue. So, I asked Tony about that; "We've had a few printing issues down the years. One time we got the page count wrong for the issue and were left with a blank page, so we created and photocopied an extra page quickly and sat at The Joiners hurriedly sticking it in before the gig started. There was also an earlier issue that had a printing problem that wasn't our fault, but the printers were cool about it and printed us another batch. Gaz kept the first batch as he couldn't bring himself to throw them away and ended up giving them out at Rebellion Festival for free. Gaz said that it was odd to see all these punks sat around reading this old, poorly printed fanzine all over the place."

Much later on, Suspect Device went from cassette tapes sent out with the zine to CDs and vinyl. Quite a few CDs were given away with the zine, and with SD number 38 the 'Knowledge is power 2' compilation CD featured tracks by several Engineer Records bands of the time including Chamberlain, Speedwell, Crosstide and One Last Thing. As well as supporting my record label, the SD guys have reviewed many of the releases by the bands I have played in and seemed to like most of them. It's about supporting the scene and helping people I guess, and I am grateful for it. Tony added that, "The best thing about doing the zine is the friends we've made and the good people who've helped us along the way. But I always find it odd when people remember or recognise me. It happened recently in a record shop in Birmingham, and even more surprisingly, in a record shop in San Francisco when I was there, I heard someone say from behind me, 'Tony?' and I turned around to see Lance Hahn from J Church grinning at me".

All this was part of the reason why Couch Potatoes were so stoked to be playing at The Joiners for the first time. We'd been there many times before to see shows but now we'd get to share the stage that saw all that talent, and work with promoters that brought all that positivity to the scene. We did our best to rock it, and I know BBMFs were great too, but the main thing I remember from that night was the awesome energy of Majority of One. It was raining outside so it wasn't a big crowd at all, but they played as if it were the most important show of their lives and I was just blown away by them.

Majority Of One were a straight edge hardcore band from Toledo, Ohio. I'd first heard of them through First Strike Records and picked up some early vinyl UK releases in time for Alan to get them over on tour. This early on though no-one over here had heard of them yet and they played some pretty small shows to just a handful of hardcore and straight edge kids. Whitey, from Electro Hippies (and also the shoplifting Jailcells roadie), was driving for them and doing their merch store at the gigs. He was clearly having to do his best to keep their spirits up at some of the drearier UK venues. Added to this, their bass player on the first records, Todd Swangstu, didn't want to come over on the tour and left the band just beforehand, so the line-up we saw and played with was; Dirk Hemsath on vocals, Ali Moazed and Chad Scouten on guitars, Doug Walker

on bass and Eric Lemie on drums. To me they all looked like the sort of US jocks you'd see in a John Hughes movie, archetypal sport billies in clean white shirts, khaki cargo shorts and trainers. I thought they looked cool though, especially when they ripped into their hardcore tracks making any grotty metallers in the clubs sit up and take notice, but they were clearly annoyed by the small crowds, and after coming across an ocean to tour in the pouring rain I guess that's fair enough.

Supposedly before their tour hit the UK they had 'lost' a member while in Amsterdam and travelled to the UK without him and played the first couple of UK shows as a four-piece. This has been well documented on various blogs since but presumably the missing guy caught up with them because I'm sure I watched a five-piece band play when we went down to see them for the first time at The Basement in Brighton.

Couch Potatoes, BBMFs and our mates made up more than half of the audience at that gig. A few of the Southampton crew came over too as I remember south coast HC legend Bod being there. He was a good guy, but very tall and bony and I remember always having to dodge his elbows in any mosh. There can't have been more than about twenty-five people in that room when M.O.O. played the Basement. But I tell you, if you didn't bother you missed out as these guys were absolutely great and really rocked it live. They simply believed in what they were doing and when it all kicked off at the shows you could just tell they meant it.

Majority Of One were also probably the first band I'd heard sing songs about the environment too. The title track of their first album 'Think about tomorrow' was a straight-up message about impending environmental disaster, way ahead of its time. And their second album, 'Setting The Pace' had a clear-cut forest burning on the cover. Their music fitted in very well with the crunchy heavy metal-sounding New York Hardcore style of the time, but they were a fair way ahead of that lyrically. Dirk, Ali, Chad and Doug would go on to form another great hardcore band called Transcend, and Majority of One would also make a third album, called '2000 Years of Indecision', in a much grungier style, but still with some good songs on there (check out 'Circle') but by then they sounded like a very different band. Dirk would also be the main man behind one of the most influential labels in nineties hardcore, Doghouse Records.

Doghouse started out like many hardcore labels in a small way releasing Dirk's own bands, Majority of One and Transcend, but then he also started to sign other straight edge bands, Stronghold and Endpoint, and released an Animal Liberation Front compilation called Voice of the Voiceless with Youth of Today, Shelter, Downcast, Outspoken and Worlds Collide all providing tracks. This all helped the label expand and find distribution partners to allow them to reach a wider audience. They later discovered several really important hardcore bands, including Split Lip / Chamberlain, The Get Up Kids and Hot Water Music, three of my favourite bands of all time, and two of which would also have releases on Engineer Records.

Dirk Hemsath also became involved with the Lumberjack and Mordam distributors, so he could distribute and sell his band's records easily in both the US and Europe. Doghouse put out releases by Threadbare, Cable, Omaha, Husking Bee, Favez, River City High, and even one for Fabric, the great emo band from London that my friend Tone Sylvester was in. Another great Doghouse discovery was Joshua, who became an Engineer Records released band later on too. Dirk and I clearly had very similar tastes in music, but he had considerably more luck with his releases. He then went on to sign The All-American Rejects, a massive stroke of good fortune as they sold hundreds of thousands of records. In fact, over 30 years and 150 releases it's reckoned that Doghouse have sold over six million albums and 15 million songs worldwide. That's pretty impressive for a kid playing hardcore songs to small crowds at The Basement and The Joiners on rainy days in April '91.

7, Punk in drublic

9/5/91 Battle of the bands
The Crypt, Hastings

By now I'd gone through a few guitars and needed something decent. I'd swapped my black Les Paul copy for a bright blue Columbus, and then swapped again for an even more metal Ibanez Explorer, a star-shaped monstrosity. That in turn was rested whilst I borrowed my mate Nick's Westone Thunder, but that was a heavy and troublesome lump, a bit like me, so I eventually saved up enough to splash out and get myself a far better guitar. I bought a second-hand Gibson SG.

Now this baby was not an Epiphone copy, this was the real thing and had come to me second-hand from a local rocker via an importer in London's Denmark Street, the home of many a good guitar. The guy I bought it from had done a bit of a custom job done on it, painted black over the usual cherry red colour and replaced all the black plastic tone and volume controls with textured silver knobs. I liked the way it looked and loved the way it sounded. This guitar had a wider neck than I was used too, but much smoother fret wires and I very quickly became used to playing it. It was also way lighter than the guitars I'd been playing before so this meant I could throw it around and jump about even more, so wisely I invested in some locking nuts for the strap too. Most importantly it had those amazing humbucking pickups and just sounded way better than my previous guitars. You could just strum it, walk away, and come back half an hour later and it'd still be playing. It was a dream to play and I was very glad to have it for the upcoming shows. I added a few stickers to the guitar and placed it carefully into its new case, grabbed my bag of leads and a Boss distortion pedal, and jumped in the car with the other Couchies so we could drive down to Hastings for our next gig.

We were on the way to take our own particular brand of pop-punk hardcore to another south coast rock venue. This time it was The Crypt in Hastings where I'd seen the UK Subs play a few weeks earlier. The Crypt was a decent club, we were there for a battle of the bands show, not the sort of gig we'd normally play, but we thought what the heck, it's a gig nonetheless, with other indie, rock and punk bands playing, so why not? We always had fun and we might pick up one or two new fans. On arrival we looked at the poster on the door and none of us had ever heard of any of the bands playing so for a moment we started to wonder if we'd done the right thing. But these are the moments you just push on and all small bands have to go through many of them. They are tests of your resolve. You must remind yourself to enjoy the journey and be glad your mates are there with you. Luckily enough, there was soon a good crowd forming up and by the time we'd sound-checked people were coming in and bustling around. The bar started to fill and the music started to play and we tried to ignore the smell coming from the flooded toilets, the sticky floors and peeling walls, and the junkies lurking in the dark corners.

The Crypt had been an indie music venue for years and was well known to the local punks and metal kids. Throughout its history it would see hundreds of bands. More mainstream acts such as Coldplay, Muse, Ash and Snow Patrol graced its stage, and the club also hosted cult acts like Chas 'n' Dave and Bad Manners, but tonight it would be the turn of Couch Potatoes. We were on in the middle of the bill and rocked our way through the set as best we could, dropping most of the covers as we didn't think anyone would know them and filling the set with more of our own songs now. All the while Yan was cracking jokes and sharing confident banter with the locals who seemed to be enjoying themselves and digging what we did. There was good sound and professional-level stage lighting too, and this was stuff you didn't always get at the pub shows. It turned out to be another fun evening and as we'd borrowed quite a lot of the gear for this show from the other bands, we hung out with them afterwards just drinking and chatting at the bar.

Years later I remember reading an interview in the local paper with Simon and Peter Wilkes, the brothers who had run the club for the last 20 years, when they confirmed that the venue would be forced to close. "The Crypt came into being during the heady days of the punk revolution," they said, "And from that day to this it has been a beacon of light in the darkness of mainstream mediocrity, a sanctuary and breeding ground for new and exciting musical talent and a haven for those people who cherished those things." In the same article the interviewer also asked the sound guy what he thought of the club, and he added; "Most of all though, The Crypt was just a great place to be. Yes, it smelled a bit. Yes, the paint was invariably peeling off the walls, and yes, on occasion we had to do a bit of wading when the drains backed-up and overflowed. But none of that mattered, because a club isn't just its four walls, or its fixtures and fittings, or even the people who run it, it is the people who go there, and The Crypt had absolutely the best crowd you could ever wish for." The sound guy had a good point.

We headed back home just after midnight to get some sleep as the next day we were heading up to London to see Conflict play again and believe me, you need your energy for gigs like that. They had a show at Shoreditch Town Hall and we knew this gig could become a little more involved. The last time I'd been to see Conflict was in Woolwich and it had all kicked off with the cops after they'd come in to shut the show down amidst much slanging and scrapping. We tried to get a bus back across the common and up to a central London railway station from where we could get a train home, but we were kicked off the bus by the police, who'd come on just to hassle us, before we'd even reached Blackheath. They were causing trouble and being a pain in the arse as usual, but there really wasn't much we could do about it so we had to walk from there all the way back to Waterloo station to try to catch the milk train home. On the way there were more fights and trouble pretty much all through the night, not just between the punks and the cops, but also various old herberts and drunken characters all the way up the Old Kent Road. It could be a sea of puke, piss and blood around there so as this was a Friday night we prepared in advance.

The show that night wasn't too bad though, a great gig as ever with Conflict ripping through the 'Ungovernable Force' classics and Colin Conflict, their singer, dragging Steve Ignorant from Crass up onto the stage to sing a few songs with him. Conflict was definitely the best 'old school' punk band I ever saw play live and always hardcore to the max. Reading their lyrics inspires me even now and as they were from London I'm glad to say that we got to see them play quite a few times, even though we did get harassed by the Metropolitan cops at or after more or less every one of their shows. It was just unbelievable what the pigs got away with really. Conflict knew this only too well so amidst all their usual angry fightback lyrics they made space for a track called 'The Arrest' where they calmly advised their fans what to do when they were harassed and arrested, because as it says in another of their tracks 'Force or Service', the rules of the force are the laws of the land.

18/5/91 The BBMFs and Couch Potatoes
The Shelley Arms, Nutley

We were soon headed back to The Shelley Arms to play with our good mates the BBMFs again. These shows were always fun but I was doubly looking forward to this one as I had a new (second-hand) amp to go with my new (second-hand) guitar and I couldn't wait to try them out at a gig. I'd gotten rid of the old Peavey quite early on, swapping that for a Vox AC30 that I'd then blown up as it just couldn't keep up with our noise. Let me tell you now that it is never ideal to be plugged into something electrical when there is smoke and sparks pouring out the back of it! So then I'd bought myself a pretty decent amp called a Crate and used that for a few shows, but it was too small really and certainly not giving me the sound I was after for my SG, so now at last I'd gotten myself a proper amplifier, a Marshall stack. As all rockers all around the world will know, this is the real thing. It was quite an old set-up and had been well-used, but I liked that. I'd bought it from a guy called Porky, who was one of the Deuce guitarists, so it had already seen a lot of action, but he'd kept it properly serviced and in good order. He did a good deal for me and this was a dream piece of kit. I had a JCM 800 100 watt valve amp head, warm and beautiful sounding, sitting on top of a big 4 x 12" Celestion speaker cab. It could shift some serious air, which basically meant it could sound great whilst blowing your ear drums out when just set at five, and I'd have it up to eleven. Well, seven at least. We weren't Spinal Tap after all. My biggest concern, with it being a valve amp, was that no-one should rest their drinks on it, but I had a feeling that this thing could withstand

GENUINE KENTIFORNIAN COUCHCORE

Couch Potatoes DR and Quinch
`Eat plutonium death´ gig poster

AMBUSH BUG PRESENTS.....

GORILLA BISCUITS

THURS
18th APRIL

THE DOME, BOSTON ARMS
JUNCTION RD. N19
OPP. TUFNELL PARK ⊖

£4 / £3·50 (concs)

JAILCELL RECIPES

GOOBER PATROL

TUES 28TH MAY

NO FX (usa)
HAPPY HOUR (germany)
IDENTITY

COUCH POTATOES

ARRIVE EARLY!!!
1st BAND ON 5PM

THE DOME
BOSTON ARMS
JUNCTION RD. N19
OPP. TUFNELL PARK ⊖
£4/£3.50 (concs)

STOP PRESS....STOP PRESS
MAJORITY OF ONE (usa) + ????? + JUICE – THURS MAY 2nd
MOONLIGHT CLUB, WEST HAMPSTEAD

The Astoria in London

The Alternative,
cancelled gig

The Alternative :
SUCTION (tun.wells)
+
COUCH POTATOES (tun.wells)
+
i'm Being GOOD (Brighton)

SAT. 11th JUNE

DOORS OPEN 8·PM – SOOO BE EARLY
PAGODA YOUTH CENTRE
A·K·A· THE ONE NEXT TO THE SWIMMING BATHS
ONLY:
£2·00
Live Music / Lights / BAR 'Till 11pm

drive

BOOKING
Paul Bolton, Concorde, 19erb Merch,
London, W6 7PA.
Tel: 071 603 3353
Fax: 071 602 8822

FIRST STRIKE RECORDS

Drive's First Strike
promo photo

anything. I'd already sprayed our Couch Potatoes logo onto the brass plate backing of it, using a cardboard stencil Yan had made and some white spray paint. It looked cool, it sounded great, and I was dying to try it out live.

Tonight would be ideal as it was just Couch Potatoes and the BBMFs playing, so both bands could rattle on for long sets, with all sorts of covers and messing around thrown in, and it'd just become another big party with our mates. We had noticed a lot of new faces starting to turn up to these shows at the Shelley too. My mum only ever came to see me play once and I think it was this show. She came along with one of her friends and stood at the back, then left as soon as we'd finished playing. I asked her what she thought of it afterwards and she said it sounded like a racket, "a race to the bottom of a lift shaft" I think was the actual phrase she used. But these evenings were never any stress, just great fun, with Warren grinning away at us from behind the bar.

I'd gotten to try out all my new gear and it sounded great. I was glad to play to a friendly home crowd as we had a bunch of shows coming up in London and they always seemed a lot more serious. When we'd gained more experience from touring we'd treat every show exactly the same, but for now we didn't know that. We'd just played another good gig though and sang along to 7 Seconds in the car all the way home.

London venues

There were loads of great music venues in London in the early nineties. Seriously, you could go and see great bands most nights of the week and pay next to nothing to do it as well. There were the bigger metal venues in Charing Cross Road, such as The Marquee, where we'd regularly stage dive to hardcore metal crossover bands like Gang Green, D.R.I, Acid Reign and Sabbat, also occasionally going to see rap acts like Ice-T, most recently on his O.G. 'Original Gangster' tour. I'd seen him locally at the Tonbridge Angel Centre on his previous 'Power' tour, after which all the local chavs decided to have a little riot. That didn't matter much in Tonbridge though, you could burn that town down and it'd still look the same.

The Beastie Boys played at The Marquee on their relaunch tour in '92, and I went to see House of Pain there too, but the show was cancelled after some joker claiming to be from the IRA phoned in a bomb threat. What a prick. I saw Public Enemy at Brixton Academy, Gunshot at the Camden Palais and Credit To The Nation at the New Cross Venue too.

One great Gang Green show at The Marquee particularly sticks out for me. Several carloads of us had gone up and we were all stage diving and moshing around like crazy, just having fun. The band were recording the show for a live record and lots of photos were being taken. There's a really good photo from the show that captured about ten of my close friends in it, either dancing, stagediving or lining up on the stage getting ready to jump, and it turned out that was the photo the band decided to use on the back cover of their new live LP 'Can't Live Without It'. Unfortunately, that was also the gig (and photo) where Duncan, the guitarist of Angus Bagpipe (and later to be the drummer of Rydell), timed a stage dive really badly and managed to break his wrist and give himself concussion! Ouch. He says it was worth it and I have to say that the photo of him launching himself into that dive, resplendent in his Gang Green 'Older Budweiser' t-shirt, does look awesome. No wonder it made it onto the back cover of the album. I'd say this incident may also explain his jazz-tempo drumming later on for Rydell too. I'm very glad to still have a copy of that live Gang Green record to remind me of those great times as unfortunately, and with no respect for the thousands of great nights that had happened there, The Marquee was closed down as a live music venue and is now just part of a crappy pub chain.

There was also the smaller Borderline Club in Charing Cross, where I saw Sense Field, Quicksand and many others play. As well as the biggest rock venue around there, The Astoria. This place was even larger than The Marquee and mainly hosted big metal and rock bands. I saw Suicidal Tendencies, Anthrax, Slayer, Acid Reign, Sabbat, Testament, Flotsam and Jetsam, Kreator, Tankard and quite a few more play there. This was all good until the venue security started getting over-zealous and erected barriers about six feet in front of the stage, forcing kids way back and calming the whole thing down to a spectator sport. We wanted to be part of it so that took away a lot of the fun and really harmed the atmosphere. This venue was also closed, in 2009 for the Crossrail development and demolished, but before that happened there was at least a farewell party show with Get Cape Wear Cape Fly, And You Will Know Us By The Trail Of The Dead and Frank Turner rocking the stage for one last time. Frank later mentions it in his song lyrics for 'Polaroid Picture' with "The only thing certain is that everything changes, and they closed the Astoria, at the end of last summer. The place we earned our pedigrees, scene of our victories, sanctuary in the centre of London".

Bigger bands were playing the Brixton Academy or the Hammersmith Apollo and mid-sized bands often played at the Camden Palais, where we went to the regular rock nights to see great bands like the Doughboys or Gunshot, or the New Cross Venue further south, where we saw All, Snuff, Conflict and many more, then staggered from the Venue, New Cross Inn or Goldsmiths Tavern nearby after drinking too much snakebite and black with the 'Pseudo Hippies'. We'd dance around like idiots to bad indie bands with all the sarf luhnduhn girls, before wandering out late at night to grab some (far from) Perfect Fried Chicken and ribs. Just along the road from there I saw an early Napalm Death gig in the spit and sawdust of the Amersham Arms, which is now a trendy bohemian pub, popular with Goldsmith's students and mid-day drinkers.

Later on, we used to more or less live at the Camden Underworld, between watching or playing shows there and often running Engineer Records distro stalls too. The Camden area of town had a lot of great venue pubs. The Barfly, The Laurel Tree and The Monarch, as well as The (Camden) Falcon, well known in the early '90s as an indie music watering hole and said to be where Blur were signed, although we won't hold that against the place. There was also The Dublin Castle, featuring a hilarious sound guy named Jonathan 'The Ears' Digby who we always used to get into arguments with when we sound-checked there. I remember at one show, for a laugh, we'd tried to get him to raise the level of the hi-hats on stage throughout the set. 'More hi-hat, Ears!' Yan would shout at him after every song. We'd also wander a little further out to see good bands play, sometimes to the Roundhouse or Dingwalls or the Forum. Also the Powerhaus and the Hope and Anchor in Islington, or The Dome in Tufnell Park, and of course the Sir George Robey in Finsbury Park, where, if you could avoid the piss streaming across the toilet floors and the beer-sticky carpets and tables, you could often have a superb night seeing a really great touring band playing on that well-trodden smoky stage to just a few people. London in the '90's seemed a good place for live rock music and we were heading up there next.

28/5/91 NOFX, Happy Hour, Identity and Couch Potatoes
The Boston Arms, London

Tonight had a good chance of being another one of those great nights that we'd look back on and smile, as we were heading up to town to play at The Boston Arms, a small London venue well known for great live music. Couch Potatoes would be supporting the US band NOFX, who had signed to Epitaph Records and were fast becoming massively popular in the punk, hardcore and ska-core scene, so this was likely to be a very well attended show.

I'd been sending out loads of Couch Potatoes demo tapes and having conversations with gig promoters, some of whom were more friendly than others, but luckily for me one of the good guys was Aidan Taylor. He'd put on a lot of good shows in London and liked our demo tape. He also played guitar in a band called Juice so knew well enough what it was like to need a few decent shows but how hard it could be to get them. Aidan seemed to know everyone in the London HC scene and kindly said he'd try to hook us up with some gigs.

I'd also been bugging an American girl called Christy Colcord who seemed to know all the US bands and labels well. She was trying to set up Lookout Records in the UK and also doing some pr work for a new label at the time entitled Epitaph Records. I knew the record label was owned by Brett Gurewitz, one of the guitarists in Bad Religion, and they'd just set up a branch in London and were looking to promote and possibly sign some new bands. This was an exciting prospect, although to say the least a long shot for an unheard-of UK hardcore band like us. Epitaph were already being courted by Sony and must've been doing pretty well as they seemed to have lots of money to spend on promoting their bands. Nevertheless, I persevered and after a while found out that

Christy was friends with Aidan too. It all came together from that, and thanks to these guys, Couch Potatoes managed to get one of the support slots for the NOFX show in London.

We headed straight up to town after work but got caught up in the traffic and didn't get to the venue until about 7.30pm. It was already packed as we loaded our gear in and we had the shortest sound check on record. It didn't really matter as we were sharing most of the equipment, very common at hardcore shows as it saved a lot of time with change-overs and so long as the first band sound-checked properly you should all sound good enough. We could pretty much just turn up, plug in and be good to go. This show was important to us though and the venue was filling up fast, so we did just take a moment to check our levels and tuning, and get it all sounding about right before we kicked off. If something was off the soundman would hopefully make adjustments as we played, but we didn't want to let Aidan down after putting us on, and we certainly did not want to suck either. This was our first London show after all. The crowd was ready, so we'd better be.

What a show. Our first London gig and we were supporting NOFX. Now that's not too shabby. Alright, they had Happy Hour from Germany touring with them and Aidan had also originally promised the show to Identity, a great UK pop-punk band, so we were going on first out of four bands, but he'd still got us onto the bill and that was pretty great. To see all four bands play it would cost you just four pounds on the door. Three pounds fifty for concessions in fact, so quite a few punkers brought their UB40's and students showed their union IDs. The place was rammed now. We only had twenty minutes to play so just enough time for six or seven songs if we blasted through them. So we did. Hitting the stage just after 8pm we hammered through our best songs, and it went pretty damn well. Yan, Adam and I bounced around while Jim did his best to keep us all in time. This was a London show so of course some people were still drinking outside when we went on and others steadfastly ignored us at the bar, but quite a few were into it, and more and more people crowded into the room as we played. We came off the stage sweaty and elated, having given a decent account of ourselves, and Aidan mentioned that several of our audience were gig promoters too. Double bonus. Now we could just enjoy the rest of the show.

Identity had come down from the Midlands to play their simple three chord pop punk in a very Green Day or Ramones style. They were way better at it than most and possessed a real stage presence too. They had a five track 7" EP on Fourth Dimension Records called 'Some kind of fun' and were soon signed to a larger record label, Damaged Goods, to release their great 'Yeah, about time too!' album. I'm glad to say that we'd play with them again quite a few more times and always had good fun. They later changed their name to Funbug and released a 7" on Lookout Records, so we'd see them again and play with them on the Green Day tour too.

I didn't pay as much attention to Happy Hour as I should have, as I was chatting with Aidan, Christy and the other promoters, but they played ska-core and shouted out song titles like 'Make it to the show' and 'Late night take out' and at one point went into a cover of 'Warriors of Genghis Khan', the song made famous on tv by the parody heavy metal band Bad News, featuring Vim Fuego, Den Dennis, Colin Grigson and Spider Webb, better known as Ade Edmondson, Nigel Planer, Rik Mayall and Pete Richardson from The Comic Strip Presents. It was great fun, and the place was getting hyped up and ready for NOFX to come on.

For anyone that doesn't know, NOFX are a punk band from Los Angeles, California that formed back in the '80s and became very popular in the '90s, pretty much from '91 onwards when their third album, 'Ribbed', came out on Epitaph Records and they really started taking off. Around that time El Hefe (real name Aaron Abeyta), a guitarist and trumpet player, joined Fat Mike (real name Michael Burkett), their bassist and vocalist, Eric Melvin, their guitarist, and Erik Sandin, their drummer, to form the band's current and long-standing line-up. This was the band we would support tonight, and later at the White Horse too.

When NOFX finally hit the small stage after fighting their way through the packed crowd, predictably, it all kicked off. Pints were spilled as people danced all around the room and kids dived into the crowd off the side-tables and speakers. I'd heard a few NOFX tracks on mixtapes and was keen to see them live. They could certainly bring it, playing a kind of high-speed energetic ska-core punk and seeming to enjoy all sorts of onstage antics. Fat Mike, the bassist, would try to sing whilst the two guitarists, one of whom (El Hefe) played a trumpet in a few songs, both jumped about like mad men and tried to knock him over. At one point the small stage was packed with people, it seemed an entire brass band had joined them, all rocking and swaying around. I didn't know the band well enough to pick out tracks at that time, but it was a well-honed wall of noise and a really energetic show. We all left the gig very sweaty and a bit bruised, but with big smiles on our faces. Definitely a good way to spend a Tuesday evening in old London town.

30/5/91 Couch Potatoes and Headway
Rumours Bar, Eastbourne
A couple of days later we were down in Eastbourne to play a small rock club called Rumours with our straight edge pals Headway. The show had been booked by the guys who ran the punk fanzine down there and we had a bunch of chums with us for the evening. We all wandered along to the pier between soundcheck and playing and sat on the beach with ice-creams. It was like being old people on holiday. The show was good fun but there weren't too many regulars on a Thursday night at a rock club in Eastbourne so we played to less than fifty people and headed back home. It was just one of those evenings. A bit of a come-down after the packed sweaty show with NOFX just

two nights before, but that was often how it went. We did meet the guys from Less Than Brainless fanzine though and did a quick interview that appeared in their next issue alongside Jailcell Recipes, Cowboy Killers, Sink, Fudgetunnel, Exit Condition, Citizen Fish, MTA and Thrilled Skinny. We'd go back and play at Rumours a couple more times, ever the gluttons for punishment and always desperate for shows, but it was never a huge success as a music venue, so closed down, becoming a vegan café that probably has more straight-edgers there now than ever before.

21/6/91 Drive and Couch Potatoes
The Rumble Club, Tunbridge Wells

It had only been two months since we played a show to our home crowd in Tunbridge Wells, but that seemed quite a while to us, and a lot had gone on since the last Pagoda gig. We actually had another one booked, a fundraising party on Saturday 11th June with new local boys Suction and I'm Being Good from Brighton supporting us at the youth club, but we were asked to cancel it by the Rumble Club guys, getting ever more territorial and business-like in their promotions, and instead play a show for them. This would be better, as it'd been about eight months since our last Rumble Club show, and we were just glad to have a good gig booked in and coming up fast.

I'd been speaking with Alan at First Strike and Iain from Drive and we'd agreed for them to play in Tunbridge Wells the next time they went out on tour. Drive had been busy, playing a load of shows and then recording a Peel Session, basically a live music session recorded for John Peel's BBC Radio 1 show. These Peel sessions were pretty much an early prototype for what has become 'BBC introduces' and the 'Live Lounge' now, but much more focused on indie bands and recording them live in the studio. This was a big thing really, not only because Radio 1 has a lot of listeners, but also because John Peel had decent taste and the bands he recorded, although often obscure indie, metal or hardcore, often went on to become very well known. The better-known Peel sessions artists include The Cure, The Smiths, The Fall, Joy Division, New Order, Killing Joke, The Ruts, The Slits, Pulp, Smashing Pumpkins and Thin Lizzy. The Margrave of the Marshes loved extreme music and regularly had the likes of Napalm Death, Bolt Thrower, Carcass and Extreme Noise Terror in for sessions, often recording what many fans consider to be the definitive versions of their songs. Plus, John Peel would regularly invite UK punk and hardcore bands in to record a session. Some of these included Broccoli (twice), Hooton 3 Car, Bob Tilton, Exit Condition, Goober Patrol, HDQ and Joeyfat. He also played tracks he liked on his radio show to introduce new bands, one of whom was Rydell.

Ever eager to play, we had quite a few shows coming up, and this one with Drive would be a great way to kick them all off. This time they arrived early, and we all had time to soundcheck and get the equipment warmed up and the stage set, before sitting at the bar drinking and then strolling around The Pantiles, the more pleasant and historic end of Tunbridge Wells. While we were out the club filled up, more or less to capacity, and when we came back it was nearly time to go on. Tonight, it would be just Couch Potatoes and Drive playing, and Drive had a bunch of new songs to try out. It was great to just enjoy a local gig with all our friends there and then have the added bonus of not needing to go far to get a shower and jump in bed when it was all over.

Drive went on to record and release two more EP's in '91, 'Greasegun' and 'Go out, be happy'. These, along with 'No Girls', made up their first full CD, an eight-track release called 'Greasegirls', which they quickly followed up with a full album entitled 'Out Freakage' in '92. This record was produced by Frankie Stubbs of Leatherface and my copy of the album must have been one of the first 500 because it came with a 7" of cover versions too. The 7" contained the Descendents 'My world' and Minuteman's 'This ain't no picnic'. It is a cracking piece of vinyl and very rare now. Couch Potatoes would play with Drive again, and so would my next band Joeyfat, before they went on to play shows with The Lemonheads, Fugazi, The Dickies, Leatherface and Mega City 4 amongst others, before eventually calling it quits.

In 2007, to coincide with Boss Tuneage records releasing their complete discography CD, Drive reformed for a handful of shows, including Liverpool, London and a few in Japan. The London show was at the tiny basement Buffalo Bar in Islington. Drive were on fine form especially considering it had been fifteen years since their last gig and they'd told me that they'd only practised twice since. Their bassist, Dan Pie, said he hadn't even picked up his bass guitar since '93!

Iain Roche later played in the wonderful but short-lived BUZZorHOWL with Dave Arnold from Jailcell Recipes. They released two split 7"s in 2014 and then sadly disappeared. They were massively under the radar and first I'd heard of them was when Milo, the later Couch Potatoes and Rydell vocalist, suggested I check them out. By then they'd already broken up! Milo said "Listen to BUZZorHOWL's 'Fuel', the key change into the first chorus will send a shiver down your back". Damn, he was right.

8, A Green Day
Christmas party

27/6/91 Paradox UK, Juice, Couch Potatoes and Angus Bagpipe
The Shelley Arms, Nutley
28/6/91 Jailcell Recipes, Paradox UK, Juice and Couch Potatoes
The White Horse, Hampstead, London
29/6/91 Jailcell Recipes, Paradox UK and Couch Potatoes
The Rumble Club, Tunbridge Wells

The gigs we'd been playing and the demo cassettes we'd been sending out were starting to have an effect now and I was in conversations with quite a few decent promoters and even a couple of smaller punk rock record labels. One of the labels that showed an interest in Couch Potatoes was the endearingly titled Retch Records, a punk label out of Merseyside who'd recently signed Juice and also had Paradox UK, Blitz and Self Destruct on the books.

Juice was Aidan Taylor's band and they sounded a bit like Minor Threat or Murphy's Law and played quite a few shows around London. Paradox UK, Blitz and Self Destruct were all punk / Oi old school style bands and all from up north. It may not have been the ideal label for us, but it was a start and we were happy that anyone wanted to help us out with a release. I'd been speaking with Spike, who ran the label, and it turned out that he was also the singer of Paradox UK and they wanted to go on a UK tour. After a few more calls and letters we hooked it up and ended up playing three dates in a row with them so he could check us out live. It was part of a larger tour they were booking and we had the Monday, Tuesday and Wednesday nights in the southeast, which for most bands may have been tricky, but luckily for us we had lots of good local venues and a decent following by now for an audience too. Looking back, I guess Spike just wanted to get a few shows for his band outside of the northwest, but for whatever reason it was still worthwhile and we'd arranged for a few other good bands like the Jailcells, Angus Bagpipe and Juice to join us on the shows.

The first Paradox UK and Couch Potatoes show was with Juice and Angus Bagpipe at the Shelley Arms on 27th June '91. The second with Juice and Jailcell Recipes at the White Horse in Hampstead, London on the 28th, and the third at the Rumble Club in

Tunbridge Wells, with Jailcell Recipes on the 29th. They all went pretty well but had a lot more of a '77 punk feeling to the gigs than we were used too. This involved a lot of spitting and swearing, from both the band and the crowd, and also a hell of a lot of feedback from Ales, the Paradox UK guitarist. He came up with all sorts of theatricals on stage and would then ruthlessly try to shift their records to every person at the shows. I don't blame them for that though, you had to cover your costs and neither records nor petrol were cheap. They had three vinyl releases out already, a 7", a 12" and a split LP with a band called 'Mere Dead Men', all out on Retch, Spike's own label, and they'd brought a load of these records with them on the tour. I did ask about their unique style over a drink at one of the gigs and their drummer, Si, described it as "A cacophony of kick arse!"

Sure enough, after hanging out together on that mini tour and seeing us play at those three shows, Spike did indeed offer to release an album for us on Retch Records and said that it would come out on vinyl too, which was what we really wanted. We were excited about this and Yan spent quite some time working on artwork ideas whilst Adam and Jim helped me contact even more promoters, radios and zines to get a release tour booked and ready. But for some reason the record kept getting delayed and never seemed to see the light of day. It was very frustrating, as you can imagine, but this was the first of many similar let downs and we soon became so used to it that we never celebrated a release until it was actually in our hands. In the end it turned out that Couch Potatoes would only ever have compilation tracks released on Retch Records. The first of which was 'Bad Habit' on a vinyl compilation LP in '92 called 'Get Yourself A Crash Helmet And A Bit Of Tax You Can Go Anywhere You Like Even In The Daytime'. It had a rather dull green cover taken up by the overly wordy title, but the album did have fourteen tracks, seven on each side, including 'Fundamental' by Juice and 'El Salvador' by Dr & The Crippens. Couch Potatoes 'Bad habit' was sandwiched between tracks by Threshold Shift and Shock Treatment on the B-side.

Then there was also 'Such a bad day' on a CD compilation called 'Life sucks - Get a crash helmet' that came out early in '93 as the label's first CD release. Spike clearly had some fetish about crash helmets going on but I didn't ask him. This CD featured eighteen tracks including decent ones by Another Fine Mess, Contempt, Erase Today, The Insane, Sanity Assassins and Threshold Shift. Spike carried on with Retch Records signing The Varukers, English Dogs, Distortion and The Instigators, and he also started singing for Blitzkrieg too.

We'd made many new contacts by now and over the next months started to get offers rolling in from all across the world. At first just punkers making tapes like me, but then vinyl and CD compilations too. We soon had 'Bad Habit' on another UK LP, 'Tired' and 'Cold Can' on French vinyl and CD comps, 'Why' on a US compilation and we hoped our own vinyl releases would follow soon. We wanted to get back into the studio and have something better to send out to radios and reviewers. We also wanted to get out there and play more gigs too.

17/7/91 BBMFs, Couch Potatoes, Headway, Beanfeast and Angus Bagpipe The Shelley Arms, Nutley

Our next gig was booked by Macca, the Beebs bassist, as he was back from Sheffield University for the summer and wanted to put on a couple of shows to celebrate. The first of which would be a five-band classic at our spiritual home, The Shelley Arms. He called and booked Couch Potatoes and then Headway, Angus Bagpipe and Beanfeast too.

Beanfeast was basically the Active Response guys, but Nick had left to concentrate on Angus Bagpipe with Duncan, Paul and Aegir, and in the meantime the Marriott's had gone to college in Brighton, met a few new friends, changed their band's name and become even more punk, if that was possible. They now had brightly coloured Mohicans and lots of militant vegetarian songs. I hadn't seen them play as Beanfeast yet so was looking forward to it. All the bands got on so well, I knew this show was going to be fun.

BBMFs and Couch Potatoes tended to get to the Shelley shows early, partly as we brought all the gear, but then we could sit in the garden talking and drinking whilst we waited for everyone to arrive. The other bands weren't coming from far away, Headway from Newick, Angus Bagpipe from Forest Row and Beanfeast from East Grinstead. Nick turned up in a hideous beige Metro he called Biscuit Power. It'd gotten smashed up in several minor crashes so he'd painted a huge Angus Bagpipe logo on its tartan bonnet with cartoon punker faces scrawled around the wings. That old rust-bucket barely went, but he thought it looked cool. At one point three of the Angus Bagpipe guys all drove Mini Metros and they'd try to park them in a line at gigs, it was like a really shite version of The Italian Job. Anyway, when Nick climbed out of his car, we saw that he had a smelly old Paradox UK t-shirt on. He was soon at pains to explain that he'd just moved in with his girlfriend, Addie, and unbeknownst to him she decided to tidy all his old t-shirts into the bin so now this was all he had!

The Headway guys turned up next in their slightly cleaner cars, with their considerably cleaner clothes. Champion sweatshirts, baseball caps and NYHC straight edge band t-shirts, they were probably the heaviest band of the lot of us but looked as if they were off to a sports dinner or maybe to play golf. Headway would change their name to Strength Alone and then get a little more melodic, sounding a bit like later Turning Point. They would soon sign to Helene and Ian's Subjugation Records based up in Darlington. Their great 'Never Enough' 7" record was the very first solo band release on that label, after an animal rights compilation featuring various European straight edge bands, and it sold out fast. I still have my copy, and quite a few other Subjugation records too, as the label brought the UKHC scene loads of great releases by bands like

Bob Tilton, Tribute, Baby Harp Seal, Month of Birthdays, Schema, Beacon, Spy vs Spy, Pylon and Stapleton.

Every car that turned up that evening was packed with our mates and it made for another busy, sweaty, noisy and fun hardcore party. We'd been writing new songs and agreed that we should try them out for the first time at this 'friendly' show, so this evening would be the first time we played 'Impossible Easier', 'Another' and 'Kill It' live, all of which would later make it onto Couch Potatoes 'Excess All Areas' album.

The BBMFs had a second guitarist now, Al's brother Jon, who could really play, and Jamie Donbroksi, Toby's brother, had taken over from Oders on drums now too, so they had a bunch of new songs to play. 'Fraser the fantastic rabbit' and 'Superfly Hedgehog' were two of them, and Al and Tobes jumped around and messed about even more than ever.

As great as this show was, the next that Macca had arranged for August was even better, as that was the first time I'd seen the Libido Boyz play. They'd come all the way from Mankato, in Minnesota, USA to play their 'farmcore' for us in the UK. They were in Europe courtesy of Alan at First Strike, and in Nutley courtesy of Macca and the Beebs. That was their only show in the southeast and with no Brighton or Southampton gig booked loads of people came up from the south coast to see it. I bought one of their blue and yellow Libido Boyz OPGU t-shirts and the tour 7", 'Childhood Memories', and then picked up their brilliant 'Hiding Away' album too, full of incredible songs with great lyrics. (First Strike had put the album out with two slightly different coloured covers and three different coloured vinyls, blue, yellow and green. The Childhood Memories 7" EP had two versions too, one on First Strike and one on Red Decibel, both different colours and with different B-side tracks. Being a nerd, I have both. I also have their great but rare 'It's all so obvious' 7" EP too). I remember being absolutely blown away by the Libido Boyz and becoming really encouraged to make our shows even better and travel further afield to play. We ended up playing a lot of shows all over the place that summer and improving our new songs as we went.

17/8/91 Spitfire and Couch Potatoes
The Rumble Club, Tunbridge Wells
20/8/91 Big Pop Trotsky and Couch Potatoes
Rumours Bar, Eastbourne

As well as our travels further afield, we played a couple more local shows later that summer which I remember for different reasons. The first was at the Rumble Club with Spitfire. This was not the US metalcore band of that name with releases on Goodfellow Records, this was a ropey indie band from Brighton with a couple of club DJs who went on to get themselves in the news by handing out backstage passes to girls they figured were their groupies and then generally getting up to no good, really dodgy sexist stuff they later claimed were 'just jokes' when it all came out. Not all bands were good guys and we were finding that out in all sorts of ways.

We also made another ill-advised trip down to Rumours in Eastbourne to support another Tunbridge Wells based band, called Big Pop Trotsky, who had developed quite a following in the indie scene. A typically artsy Tunbridge Wellsian name for an indie band, but I'd seen them play before and they were pretty good as well as being nice guys. They had a vinyl 12" out called 'Wry Smile' and although it was a bit mellow I'd still included one of their songs on the first Gotham tapes compilation. I knew Jason, the bassist, very well from the Rumble Club and we wanted to support them, as he supported us. We'd been hanging out, putting on a few shows together at the club and about this time he had asked if I wanted to write some new music together too. We'd set up this show for a trip out and it seemed that we would be playing to a decent crowd this time, partly made up of travelling fans and partly drunken holidaymakers who were clearly bored out of their brains and fancied seeing some rock bands in the evening. Both bands went down very well and I started hanging out more with Jason and writing music for a new band we'd later form called 'Joeyfat'.

6/9/91 Jailcell Recipes, Decline and Couch Potatoes
The Rumble Club, Tunbridge Wells
7/9/91 Jailcell Recipes, Decline and Couch Potatoes
The Joiners, Southampton

Just two weeks later our buddies in Jailcell Recipes came back down south and between hanging out, skateboarding and trying to learn some rock classics on a piano, we played a couple more shows together. This was the start of another tour they were doing around the UK, this time with a Leeds band called Decline. The Jailcells were definitely one of the hardest working bands I knew and were well respected throughout the scene because of it. They played a lot of shows and always gave everything on stage, regardless of the venue or size of the crowd.

Decline were good too and had toured around the UK several times before. I'd seen them play on the Go! tour and had met Paul, the drummer, and Julian, the guitarist. Now they had Mark 'Whitey' Wightman, the First Strike roadie and merch guy, and also the original drummer of Electro Hippies, playing bass guitar for them. They had a new 7" release called 'Lost Again' that'd just come out on their own label, Blind Records, so were on tour promoting that. We had the good fortune to play two very busy shows with them, first at the Rumble Club in Tunbridge Wells to a packed and energetic local crowd, and then another well received gig at The Joiners in Southampton for the S.T.E. It's always a good gig there. These were proper hardcore shows with a lot of energy and we loved them.

After one of these shows I was chatting with Jamie Jailcell again and he was telling me about Karl Alvarez, the All bassist, being such a good guy and a great cartoon artist.

IT'S ALL SO OBVIOUS

7" singles

INSPECTOR 12

FROM MINNEAPOLIS - USA

LIBIDO BOYZ

WAT TYLER   THE BBMFs

SHELLEY ARMS
£2 19TH MARCH

OFGU ACROSS THE SEA
LIBIDO BOYZ
EUROPEAN TOUR 1990

Poster for Libido Boyz,
Wat Tyler and The
BBMFs at The Shelley

JAILCELL RECIPES

Clapping For A Shambles

FINALLY A RELEASE THAT DOES THIS GREAT BAND JUSTICE!!!!

It's all here... Unreleased tracks that equal if not surpass their
previous releases. Live recordings of their best material that
annhilates their studio counterparts ternate studio versions,
humour, guitar solos, and inbetween song 'banter'

THIS WILL BE THE BEST CD THESE GUYS NEVER RELEASED...
UNTIL NOW!!!!!!!! (Available late 2002/early 2003)

IN AT THE DEEP END RECORDS
www.inatthedeepend....

IATDE Jailcell's flyer

LIBIDO BOYZ

HIDING AWAY
Album cover

Jamie told me that Karl had drawn the 'Two Years of Toothache' album artwork for them after they'd played a few shows together. I was impressed and a little jealous that they had the bassist of All drawing album art for them. Also, Dave Arnold, the Jailcell's bassist, was talking about their favourite shows and venues, and said that his top four venues to play in the UK were; The Shelley Arms in Nutley, The Rumble Club in Tunbridge Wells, The Den in Wigan and Planet X in Liverpool, in that order. No small praise for the local scenes we'd helped create and coming from a band that'd toured the country several times, they should know. They wanted to get us up to The Den in Wigan or maybe Planet X in Liverpool to play soon.

I was still spending a lot of time sending out demo tapes, trying to get us onto compilations, benefit releases, radio shows and gigs as much as I could. I was also regularly chasing zines for reviews, interviews and any coverage really. Being in an unsigned band is not very glamorous and it can certainly be hard work. We didn't see the band that way though, it was our passion and our creative outlet. So I kept on at every contact I could find and it was slowly starting to pay off. Couch Potatoes were getting more reviews, more interviews and more gigs. Yan and I had just completed an interview with Rich Corbridge for the second issue of his Armed with Anger fanzine and Couch Potatoes would appear alongside Downcast and Disaster in this popular UKHC fanzine. It would cost just £2 but also had a vinyl 7" (a Wartorn / Nailbomb split), as well as a bunch of stickers and a button badge with it. That was value and it was good to see others in the scene who shared our energy for getting the music and the message out there, almost despite any cost or workload involved.

This zine and split 7" was another important step in rebuilding the UKHC scene. Even if the bands were not yet at their best, the whole package meant something. Wartorn had Rich Corbridge on bass, Nailbomb had Heath who would go on to front Neckbrace and then become the first singer for Stampin' Ground with Ian Glasper and co. Both the fanzine and record were well put together and packaged by someone who clearly cared a lot about what they released. Rich quickly followed this with the Consolidation compilation 7" which some would say was ground zero for the new 90's UKHC scene. It featured a good mix of bands from the north and south, who played a variety of styles. They were all new bands and it felt like a resurgence of the scene was starting to happen. To reinforce this, AWA had included a list of contacts in the booklet full of bands, labels, promoters and distros. After this, Subjugation records really found their sound too, with Bob Tilton and Tribute, and soon other labels such as Caught Offside and Kwyjibo Records were following suit.

We spent the autumn sending out demos, playing shows and writing new songs for what we hoped would soon be our first album. We also went to see a lot of gigs too and I think it was just after the Doughboys 'Happy Accidents' show at the Camden Palais, (now known as Koko), that we heard from the Jailcells that they'd be back on tour again soon and wanted to play a few more shows with us. This time we'd be supporting an even bigger band with them, Green Day.

Now don't get me wrong, as soon as Lookout released their first couple of singles, Green Day started to become well known in the hardcore / pop-punk scene. But for now, they were still relatively unheard of. Both their '1000 hours' and 'Slappy' 7" EPs were catchy as hell pop-punk records and there was already something special about these guys. You could tell they were destined for bigger things. It wasn't just the timing, or quality of what they did, it was also the character. It all came together in one package. They were in the right place at the right time, but they backed that up with a lot of talent and hard work too. The Beatles of pop-punk maybe, but deservedly so.

Green Day were on Lookout Records, Lawrence 'Larry' Livermore's Berkeley, California based label that also boasted Operation Ivy (the predecessors of Rancid), Crimpshrine and The Mr T Experience (or MTX). Lookout went on to release loads of great records by often times massively underrated bands such as Screeching Weasel, Avail, Tilt, The Queers, The Riverdales, The Donnas, Fifteen and Pinhead Gunpowder. The latter a great side project of Billie-Joe Armstrong's that also featured Aaron Elliott, editor of the excellent alternative bay area Cometbus fanzine, as well as Bill Schneider and Jason White from Monsula too.

Larry had formed the label back in the late eighties, partly to release records for his own band, The Lookouts, that featured a very young Tre Cool on drums. The label was well-liked by Maximum Rock n Roll (MRR), a popular hardcore punk radio show and fanzine, and also had a great local venue for all the bands to play in the Gilman Street Project. Lookout also hooked up decent US and European distribution and support from Mordam, a big rock and alternative music label and distributor so their bands had very good coverage. The scene was set and I remember first hearing Green Day when I swapped some DC Batman comics for some new vinyl releases with a couple of hardcore friends of mine - Vique 'Simba' Martin (later of Revelation Records) and Tone Sylvester (later of Fabric, Turbonegro). I still have those first pressings of Green Day, Operation Ivy and Crimpshrine in my collection and they are still some of my favourite records. Thanks guys.

Christy Colcord, who we'd met at the NOFX show in London, was bringing Green Day over to Europe for several weeks through her Mullethead tours. Christy was a great promoter and supporter of the alternative scene. She had moved from the Bay Area to London, along with another girl called Mary Jane Weatherbee, to try to set up a Lookout Records office in Europe. Sadly, this didn't get much further than a well-stocked distro for Lookout releases and also New York's Vermiform records (Born Against, Heroin, Econochrist, Moss Icon, etc), but she did become more involved in tour booking and was responsible for bringing the Mr T Experience over soon after the first Green Day tour too. She helped Jawbreaker, as well as Green Day, and other well-known bands, get their first UK and European shows, and along with Aidan was hugely influential in the scene at the time. She ended up moving to Amsterdam for a while before heading back to the States and has more recently been involved in the filming of a documentary about the East Bay Punk scene called 'Turn it around'.

I'd met Christy thanks to Aidan at the NOFX show, so knew that she was involved in booking tours, video-making and the promotion of bands and labels. As I mentioned, she was heavily influential in the rise of some of our favourite bands, including Green Day and Jawbreaker, and the spread of some of the most well-known pop-punk / hardcore labels of the time too, including Lookout Records. Luckily for us, she knew and trusted our good promoter buddy Aidan Taylor in London and he was often kind enough to offer us some decent gigs. Christy asked Aidan about the best venues and supports for the UK leg of the first Green Day tour and gave him the shows to promote. This would not have been as easy as it sounds at the time, as although the incredible 39 Smooth album was out now and many of us had it on such regular play that the vinyl was wearing thin, Green Day were still relative unknowns beyond the tight knit hardcore scene. I'd have to say that some in the heavier scene found them just too saccharin with their pop-punk love songs. 'It's just not punk or hardcore enough!'

I hassled Aidan a lot and he'd seen us play often enough to know we'd put on a good show and warm people up well. He'd already given us some decent support slots and I'd been to see his band, Juice, play a few times up in town too, so we'd become close. Both Aidan and Christy had seen Couch Potatoes play with NOFX in London of course, so when the UK tour was booked it was Green Day headlining, with Jailcell Recipes as main support, and Couch Potatoes, Goober Patrol, Wat Tyler and a few lucky others sharing the support slots at various shows on different nights. We were excited about it to say the least. This would be a great way to celebrate Christmas this year!

We went to see most of the shows on that first Green Day UK tour and they rocked every venue, promoting their brand new 'Kerplunk' album. After seeing them live they fast became everyone's favourite pop-punk band. They brought a great show and really rocked live, night after night. They were very hard-working, even then, and this UK stint was just a two-week section of an eight-week-long European tour. They played at The Rails in London, at a show put on by Lawrence of Fluffy Bunny Records, with an anarcho punk band from Somerset called Thatcher On Acid, (most of whom went on to form Schwartzeneggar with Steve Ignorant of Crass), then the Joiners in Southampton for the S.T.E., where Billie-Joe fell off the quite high stage, jumping around so much during the set, but luckily didn't injure himself badly. Christy and Mary-Jane were running a merch stall and they had copies of the new record, so Billie-Joe stopped between songs towards the end of their set at The Joiners to give a copy to Rich Levene as it was his birthday. They also played two great shows with us at the Rumble Club in

Poster for the first Green Day
Christmas gig at The Rumble Club

Front row of the packed-in
crowd at Green Day

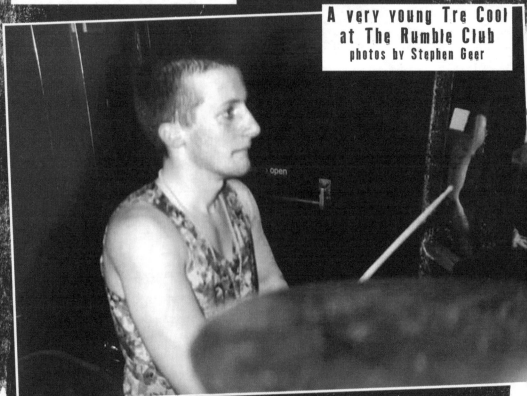

A very young Tre Cool
at The Rumble Club
photos by Stephen Geer

Tunbridge Wells (we managed to squeeze an extra gig in for them on Christmas Eve as they figured they'd have a day off!), as well as more gigs at TJ's in Newport, The Cockpit in Leeds, where they played for over two hours, The Cricketers in Wigan, where they famously re-enacted the Nativity for Christmas with Sean from Wat Tyler charging around dressed as an Easter Bunny knocking beers out of people's hands shouting 'be straight edge' at them, even though he clearly wasn't. Then they went over and played the Attic in Dublin and Richardson's in Belfast, where Tre is rumoured to have taken a dump in the middle of a bowling green on his way to the show. Lovely. They were all young punks then, slightly younger even than us, with Tre the youngest at just nineteen. In fact, it was his 19th birthday on the first night of the UK tour.

18/12/91 Green Day, Jailcell Recipes and Couch Potatoes
The Rumble Club, Tunbridge Wells
24/12/91 Green Day, Couch Potatoes and Angus Bagpipe
The Rumble Club, Tunbridge Wells

Green Day was / is Billie-Joe Armstrong on guitar and vocals, Mike Dirnt on bass and Tre Cool on drums. (Although very early on they had a different drummer, and either Dr Frank of MTX or one of the guys from Pinhead Gunpowder joins them on second guitar for some shows now too). They were in Europe and the UK for the first time, to promote their second album on Lookout Records, called Kerplunk! This is now a classic record that everybody knows and sings along too, but back then it was still a new thing of wonder and amazement. They were going to be touring in the UK with Jailcell Recipes, and Couch Potatoes would get to play at a couple of the shows. This was going to be fun!

We saw them at The Joiners in Southampton and were blown away, we couldn't wait for the show at the Rumble Club in Tunbridge Wells. It would be on a Wednesday evening but that wouldn't matter, Couch Potatoes would be supporting and we knew it was going to be absolutely mental. But it didn't start that way. Billie-Joe had disappeared, wandering off to look around the town. He was gone for quite some time and the promoters started to get worried and went out to find him. When he eventually came back it turned out that he'd just been walking around the Pantiles and was now telling us how much he liked the town, and how rich we must all be as what amazing houses we all had. I suggested showing him Showfields, Ramslye, High Brooms or Sherwood, all run-down council estates.

He disappeared at soundcheck which meant that Yan and I got to jam for him (on vocals and guitar respectively) with Mike and Tre, playing through a couple of tracks. We knew 'Only of you' as we covered it at some shows, and we'd recently worked out 'At the library' too. This little soundcheck was fun but nerve-wracking. It made our night even before the show had started. We were all using Jailcell Recipes backline and drums and it sounded powerful as hell in that small room.

Luckily, Billie-Joe came back in with Christy and Aidan, and took over to sound-check properly, grinning at us for having a go and apologising to Mike and Tre. It sounded great and there was still time, so they went out to grab some dinner. All apart from Tre, who went upstairs into the other bar (that wasn't being used) and fell asleep on the pool table up there. He slept through the Jailcell Recipes and Couch Potatoes soundchecks. We were still tuning-up and messing around as the doors were opened and the crowds started coming in.

Goober Patrol, a great band out of Norwich who we'd get to play with later, were meant to be playing this show too. Aidan had invited them and we'd put their name on the posters, but for some reason they couldn't make it. They played other shows on that first tour, as did Wat Tyler, and we got to see a few of them.

The doors were open now and the place was filling up fast. No-one tell health and safety but however many people the Rumble club was meant to hold, it certainly held a lot more than that on this night. When one person started jumping up and down everyone had to. There were kids jumping off seats and the bar, and it was a big party right from the get-go.

A friend of ours, Leigh, was down from nursing college in south London with a load of her friends. They were all trainee nurses who really wanted to party and let off steam. Pretty much all of Jim's college friends had finally made it along to this gig, after hearing what a good show it should be, and all our usual crew were there too. When it was time, we pushed our way on stage and played the best set we could in front of our home crowd. It was all a bit hectic as we bounced through a half-hour set, warming everyone up and trying to build the excitement. We could hardly play our Green Day cover, but we finished with a couple of new ones just for fun, 'Six Pack' by Black Flag and 'Warriors of Genghis Khan' by Bad News, possibly inspired by Happy Hour. Both of these had plenty of drunken singalong accompaniment. I managed to bust a string in that last one and we came off stage sweaty, smiling and looking forward to the rest of the show.

Then it was time for the Jailcell Recipes. They went on and were as brilliant as ever. 'Smiles' was a particular highlight. Robbie was constantly jumping around and leading the mosh pit, Jamie was manic on the guitar, despite having a bad cold, and Dave was solid as hell on bass as usual, but he needed to be even more so, as their regular drummer Ian was away travelling in Europe so they had Drive's drummer, Jeff, standing in. This didn't seem to slow them down or phase them at all though. They rocked. By now the walls were running with sweat and condensation, and this was before Green Day even managed to push their way onto the small stage.

When Green Day started with 'I was there' it all kicked off at another level. The venue was tiny so by the time they got to 'Don't blame me' people were climbing on top of each other, dancing and jumping around, and the low ceiling was gradually being kicked in by crowd-surfers. A few more songs in and they started to slow it down a little and during 'Christie Road', which they dedicated to Christy Colcord for bringing them over, Billie Joe asked everyone to sit down and chill for a moment. There wasn't really room for everyone to sit but we tried and he then slithered through, around and over the crowd as best he could, kind of like a sweaty punk-rock snake, whilst the drums and bass carried on playing. When he finally made it back to the stage and grabbed his guitar it all kicked off again. That evening Mike did not stop bouncing up and down, but he never missed a note, and Tre was grinning like a madman throughout the entire set. I'm sure they'd seen it all before at larger US shows, but they really seemed to be getting a kick out of this intimate UK gig.

At one point Billie-Joe was wearing a dress, a little floral number with a tie on over the top of it. I'm not sure why or where it came from. It was very hot inside the Rumble Club. The amount of people dancing and the low ceilings made it worse. By now Paul, our mate who played bass for Angus Bagpipe, was so out of it with heat exhaustion that he fainted and was being passed around on top of the crowd. Probably not the best thing for him. At the abrupt end of the next song Billie-Joe stopped to check that he was alright, luckily, he was and people passed him across their heads to the bar at the back where they dumped some ice on him and gave him a drink. Paul was fine and back dancing a couple of songs later, and in fact he'd be back to play a show with us all in just a few days too.

No-one there wanted that show to end, but when it finally did, way after it was meant to, we all sat drinking and talking about the gig and asking the Green Day and Jailcell Recipes guys about their plans for the tour. Robbie had his girlfriend Kate with him at the shows so was stoked about that, and Dave had hired a camera to film some footage on the tour too. Mike and Billie-Joe were telling us how much they loved the UK and Europe, and saying there was a lot more dancing at shows and more good-natured fun. This was about the time that the doorman for this evenings show, who just happened to be Animal, the singer of the Anti-Nowhere League, was getting into a fight outside with some drunken gypsys!

The Green Day guys also thought that everyone seemed so much more politically aware on this side of the pond too. They joked that they may just move over here. We discussed the stories behind some of their songs, 'Christie Road', the great new track 'Welcome to Paradise', the love songs '2000 light years' and 'At the library'. It was interesting to get an insight. Then someone asked Billie-Joe why he was wearing a dress this evening; he said that it just seemed more acceptable over here, so why not? Something as simple as that would definitely be a problem in the US he said. Mike added that when he and Billie-Joe had kissed during 'Disappearing Boy' at a show in Florida a couple of months earlier there was total silence, about 450 people just standing still, mouths open and staring. We spoke some more about the tour and where they were going as Christy and Aidan joined us. They said that they had help from a lady called Julia in Germany, and a guy called Jose Antonio in Spain, and between the four of them they'd put the whole tour together. The Green Day guys were all having the holiday of a lifetime. Tre was still celebrating his birthday. They were doing what they loved and looking at it all as a great adventure, they seemed genuinely pleased and thankful for it all.

The tour was going well and the next day we all headed up to London for the show. It turned out that Green Day had planned a few days off for Christmas so we arranged to meet back up in Tunbridge Wells for a Christmas Eve party. The Jailcells guys unfortunately couldn't join us as they had to be back home. It turned out that this would be our last show with them as they broke up in April '92 after just a few more shows, the last of which was in Dublin. This always seemed very sad to me. They were at their best at this point and always great guys to share a stage with. There are still several great unreleased Jailcell Recipes tracks from those days, some of which were meant to be coming out on a release by In At The Deep End Records, amusingly titled 'Clapping For A Shambles', but that never seemed to see the light of day. I've been chasing Jamie and Dave for the masters as I'd love to put those unreleased Jailcell's tracks out on Engineer Records even now.

More happily, Aidan and Green Day were well up for the extra show and a Christmas eve party, so we roped in our buddies Angus Bagpipe as support and arranged to do it all again a few days later. So, on Christmas Eve, Tuesday 24th December '91, Green Day and Couch Potatoes played at The Rumble Club again. Angus Bagpipe went on first and were great. They were clearly excited about the gig and rose to the occasion, playing all their catchy hits and singalong covers and getting the party started in great style. Couch Potatoes played for a little longer than the previous show, throwing in a few more covers too and playing with a confidence that a year of great shows had brought us. We'd spoken with Green Day about it and even played our cover of 'Only of you' as a tribute. Then Green Day went on, the three of them easily managing to fill that tiny stage area and knowing pretty much everyone there had bought their album just the week before, they played through a sweaty set of requests while we all bounced off the walls.

Even though there weren't as many people packed in this evening as the previous gig, some having to be with their families on Christmas Eve of course, the 150 or so who attended were treated to another unforgettable evening. Green Day were having a very successful Kerplunk! release tour but this set included a short rendition of the Nativity Play, where the promoter Aidan, who was a nurse by day at a London hospital, specifically a midwife, was roped in to look after baby Jesus, whilst the chaos continued all around him. This was a truly great fun gig, and one hell of a Christmas party. I doubt Tunbridge Wells has seen such a dancing pile up of kids since and it's a good job the damaged ceiling of the club was not yet repaired, or they would have kicked it in all over again. Even after the music had stopped this was a late night of drinking and fun, and a superb high for us all to end the year on.

Green Day setlist from December '91 Kerplunk UK tour.

I Was There
Don't Leave Me
Only of You
409 in Your Coffeemaker
At the Library
Welcome to Paradise
Christie Road
Disappearing Boy
Going to Pasalacqua
80
16
Paper Lanterns
One for the Razorbacks
Dominated Love Slave
2000 Light Years Away
1000 Hours
The Judge's Daughter
Road to Acceptance"
(into Van Morrison's 'Brown Eyed Girl')
One of my lies
Dry Ice

Adam, Couch Potatoes, catching some air

9, It's all one word

All I wanted to do was write more music and play more gigs all the time now. I was bursting with ideas and energy. All of Couch Potatoes were inspired by what we'd achieved in '91 so we went into '92 determined to record an album and keep things rolling. The 'Eight Songs' and 'Wash' demo cassettes were doing ok and going out all over the place, but we were already writing the new songs for our 'Excess All Areas' album, which would also give us the 'Brad' EP on Born to Booze Records in Germany and the 'In Bed With' EP on Weird Records in the UK. These recordings, alongside more gigs, including some European trips, and about twenty compilation and benefit tracks, would keep us busy throughout the year. But constantly being able to play shows was going to prove tricky for Couch Potatoes as our singer Yan was heading off to university in Birmingham. Sometime later our bassist Adam, who already had a fairly full-on day job for the Royal Mail, would join the South London pop-punksters Pseudo Hippies too, but for now though, we were as busy as ever.

Around the time we were writing these new tracks for Couch Potatoes upcoming album I'd also spent some time hanging out with Jason, from the Rumble Club, and writing some music with him. We'd become pretty good friends after his band, Big Pop Trotsky, had broken up, and he had lots of ideas down on eight-track tape. He was into indie and grunge, but most of these new ideas were way heavier, as he was now getting into the quirkier side of hardcore too. He'd been using a drum machine and his knackered old bass guitar and Fender Stratocaster to get these rough ideas down. They were mainly based around rhythms rather than riffs, but there was some good stuff there. He wanted me to see what I thought and add some guitar lines, so had invited me around to have a listen. This was to his flat just off Upper Grosvenor Road in Tunbridge Wells and when I got there, I found that the entire room was overflowing with all sorts of musical paraphernalia. Stacks of vinyl records and tapes, musical instruments and recording equipment all over the place. There was a mattress on the floor and a bong in the corner, a few clothes and some weights next to that, but everything else in his bedsit was to do with music. I loved it, although I had to tread over it all carefully just to be able to move around the place.

Compared to the pop-punk and hardcore I was into, his early ideas sounded avant-garde to me, mixing indie, grunge and reggae, so we started jamming together and the tracks soon coalesced, becoming darker, heavier and much tighter, taking on a new energy, like a kind of Sub Pop meets Alternative Tentacles and Dischord. I'd play guitar and he'd play bass with a drum machine keeping time for us while we built the structure of the songs. This wasn't how I was used to doing things. With Couch Potatoes we'd just turn up with riffs and ideas and jam them out. This was much more disciplined, and we'd record everything, then listen back, making changes and improvements as we went. Jason was really into getting the rhythms just right, making them as odd and interesting as possible. We'd try to put all sorts of ideas into each track and often use weird time signatures. By the time we had five or six ideas that we thought were good enough down on tape, we'd decided to rope in the perpetually tapping Jim, the drummer of Couch Potatoes, and the ridiculously tall and thin Matt, a vocalist friend of Jason's who had also been the singer of Big Pop Trotsky. Now we had the makings of a new band and if we created a set, we could fill in any dates that Couch Potatoes were offered but couldn't play for any reason. That meant to me that I'd be much closer to my dream of constantly playing gigs.

This happened gradually over a few months, but when we decided that we were going to form a band and play shows then of course, we needed a name. Initially we couldn't decide between The Joeys or The Fat, so we ended up with a compromise that we all thought worked and was just weird enough, Joeyfat. It was purposely obscure and impossible to pigeonhole, just as we intended to be, so we were pleased with it.

Jason and I worked on the songs some more and they came together quite quickly. His early ideas down on tape became the basis for 'Windscreen', 'Sugarhead', 'Piecemeal' and 'Tear', four tracks that just needed decent guitar lines added. Then we wrote together the ideas for 'Simmer down', 'Pass the sprouts', 'People come into your house', 'Spoilt', 'Mr Smugfellow', 'Amusement', and a few others as our musical writing partnership really got going. These tracks didn't actually have names yet, they were waiting for Matt to add his weird and wonderful lyrics, but musically they were ready to rock. Very soon we had a whole set of new songs. We had strong ideas about what we wanted this band to sound like and plenty of time to achieve it, so we made the most of that. He'd play me obscure indie, reggae and grunge, I'd play him upbeat hardcore, punk and rock, and we'd eventually meet somewhere in the middle. What came out was sounding pretty good to us.

We had created some complicated riffs and some tracks that were more about rhythms and time changes than melodies. Jim was a constant tapper, a drummer who was always working on beats and fills, drumming away with his fingers on desks and anything around him, usually when he was meant to be working, so, despite upsetting the neighbours and anyone within earshot, we set up a kit and he brought the drum machine ideas to life pretty quickly, improving the whole thing and making it way more real. Matt was already a confident frontman and fancied himself a writer too, so the oddball and meandering lyrics he penned for these new tracks started off left of centre and then just became weirder and weirder as we went on. His voice and influences were more depressed Smiths, or Shudder To Think, crossed with his own lunatic megalomania rather than hardcore or punk, but that, along with his tall gangly frame and the menacing way he'd wander around the stage, twisting himself and preaching, would soon help Joeyfat stand out from the average band. We created an effective and possibly even unique mix of indie and hardcore.

Considering that Couch Potatoes were still gigging a lot and had built a decent following by now, plus Jim could plaster the West Kent College refectory with posters for every local show we played, and Jason, along with a bunch of his mates, was running the Rumble Club, we stood a pretty good chance of getting some gigs and getting a crowd along to see us. Add to that the fact that between us we knew most of the alternative gig promoters in the UK, we should be able to get rolling and keep busy. And sure enough, that's exactly what we did.

There were now plenty of new places to practise in Tunbridge Wells too and we had the time to focus on each track and craft them a little more. That was a good job as these tracks were a bit more involved than just four chord pop-punk. I loved the music I was playing with Couch Potatoes, the spontaneous energy of it, the catchy chord progressions, and I'd always be into that. But this gave me the opportunity to try something different. I kept working on both, writing the 'Excess' tracks for Couch Potatoes and working on these new tracks for Joeyfat. Jim and I would attend practises with both bands and by the time I'd booked Joeyfat our first shows, at the friendly Shelley Arms and our home turf of The Rumble Club, along with Angus Bagpipe, The Pseudo Hippies and Protest, we were ready and raring to go.

16/1/92 Angus Bagpipe, Pseudo Hippies, Protest and Joeyfat The Shelley Arms, Nutley
17/1/92 Angus Bagpipe, Pseudo Hippies, Joeyfat and Protest The Rumble Club, Tunbridge Wells

As it was with most shows, this day, or evening at least, couldn't come fast enough for me. I was chomping at the bit and wanted to get going. I couldn't wait to start gigging and show off the new tracks we'd written and rehearsed. Joeyfat's first gig was on Thursday 16th January at The Shelley Arms in Nutley, the little rock 'n' roll venue in East Sussex. It's good to start off with a friendly 'home' show so it was one of two local gigs we'd booked together to get us started. The second would be the next night, Friday 17th at The Rumble Club in Tunbridge Wells, which had only just recovered from the recent sweaty assaults that were the Green Day and Couch Potatoes shows.

Our starting line-up was Matt Cole on vocals and guitar, me on guitar, Jason Dormon on bass and Jim Booth on drums. We'd practised hard and were more than ready to gig. I still have videos of these first two Joeyfat shows and it surprises me even now how tight we were, right from the start. This never faltered throughout our shows. They could be fun and hectic and sweaty and energetic, but discipline and rhythm seemed to be the watchwords for us. I always enjoyed writing guitar riffs and came up with some crazy ones for Joeyfat, although Jason and Jim would still manage to work out tight rhythms with bass lines and beats for them. It was a very different thing to Couchies, much more restricted in some ways, but trying to break new ground in others. It was great fun and certainly helped me develop as a musician. Right from our first set I thought we had some pretty decent songs.

Both these first Joeyfat shows were with our friends and local band buddies, Angus Bagpipe, Pseudo Hippies and Protest. Angus would have headlined as they'd played the most shows up to this point and were a very solid live unit now. Protest was basically Beanfeast / Active Response but they'd changed their name again and became even more political. They now had a guy named Adrian Tarrant on bass and continued down the anarcho punk route.

The Pseudo Hippies were a great bunch of pop-punkers from South London. We'd kept on bumping into them all through the year before at Doughboys, Hard-Ons, Descendents and various other shows and the band they'd now formed was somewhere between the Misfits, Ramones and Screeching Weasel. Kris, the singer and guitarist, had a Green Day shirt he'd made himself with a smiley flowerpot on it and a battered Fender Telecaster. Tom played the bass and Danny tried to break the drums. They'd started out as this three-piece and were writing songs about girls. Initially they only knew a few chords and kept to simple song patterns, but they became good fast and put their catchy songs together so well that the Pseudos were always great fun to see live and sing along with, just getting better and better each time.

These two shows were benefit gigs for the Last Chance animal sanctuary. The fundraisers went well as we had good crowds, getting us off to a very good start and introducing Joeyfat to the local alternative scene. We opened our set with 'Windscreen', basically me just hammering out an A chord, major to minor, and jumping about, so nice and easy to get things started. Then we went on with 'Spoilt' and 'Tear', then the slightly more complex 'Amusement', 'Mr Smugfellow' and 'Pass the sprouts'. We finished up our own songs with the heavy Nirvanaesque 'Simmer Down'. Already seven tracks of our own and then two covers, to close our first ever gig. It was a while ago, but I'm certain of this setlist as I watched back the live tapes for this book. We preferred to play our own stuff, but threw in a couple of covers, 'Only of you' by Green Day for the hardcore kids as I was pretty good at the solo, and 'Egg' by Alice Donut for the more indie / grunge kids as it was more in our style, and both just for the sake of a party really. It was a decent set and we went down pretty well. I was stoked. We played that same set the next night at the Rumble Club too.

14/2/92 Angus Bagpipe, Pseudo Hippies, Understand and Joeyfat Rumours Bar, Eastbourne

Joeyfat practised hard and wrote new songs almost constantly, with me, Jason and Jim honing the music into tight circuitous rumbles, whilst Matt went off on one with his storytelling lyrics. A few weeks later, we had our next show booked, down at The Rumours rock bar in Eastbourne, with Angus Bagpipe and Pseudo Hippies again, but this time Understand would join us too.

Between songs Matt would wander around saying things like "It's all one word", a reference to our band's name, "Hairy Hatman", a reference to an alphabet learning poster on the wall where we practised, or "Stay home and read a book", just because he thought that was cool. Meanwhile we all tune up and click in for the next racket. The show was fun and good enough, but not a blinder, with just the bands and our mates there who'd travelled with us to watch us play. But seeing Understand rock so hard at this gig inspired us all.

I'd already seen Understand play some of their very first shows in '91. They were all great musicians and good guys too. The first time I'd seen them was with the Pseudo Hippies in London, but since then they'd been playing various sports clubs and bars all across south east England. Understand, like Couch Potatoes and later Joeyfat, would go almost anywhere to play a gig. They'd been over to the Rumble Club and the Shelley to see us play too. So by November '91, the day after a very hot and sweaty Hard-Ons gig in London, we'd booked them onto a show with Bassinger at the Rumble Club in Tunbridge Wells. It was £3 entry and £1 a pint and it was a busy evening. I loved their heavy hardcore groove, kind of Fugazi meets Quicksand, and although we'd spoken before, I took the opportunity to interview them for BHP fanzine. We discussed hardcore and straight edge, bands that influenced them, and the local scene around Southend, where they came from. They told us funny stories about Vulture Squadron, a psychobilly band, and Nuclear Anarchy, a '77 style punk band, and said that Stand Off were the only other band really worth checking out from their neck of the woods.

I had the Understand demo tapes and particularly liked a track called 'Shove the dove', which they called 'STD' for short, but I always thought that was a bit of an unfortunate name. I was into their early stuff and started corresponding with them, putting this 'STD' track onto a compilation tape. We became good mates, playing lots of shows together and hanging out at gigs or sometimes meeting up for late night film showings at Thurrock Cinema. They rocked every time I saw them, and very soon they'd written all new songs and managed to get signed to a decent-sized record label. This meant they could practise in their own space, write and record whenever they liked, and because of this they quickly became even better.

Understand's first proper release was a self-titled three track 7" on Richard Corbridge's Armed With Anger record label, with a limited release mainly in the UK. But soon they recorded their 'Bored Games' EP with well-known HC producer Don Fury, famed for his previous work with bands such as Youth of Today, Gorilla Biscuits, Shelter, Inside Out, Agnostic Front, Born Against, Quicksand, Into Another and Farside. This would be released on Equal Vision Records*, the label founded by Ray Cappo, the singer of Youth of Today, Shelter and later, Better Than A Thousand. This release would be more widely available in the US too, leading to tours there.

*Equal Vision Records would be taken over by Cappo's friend Steve Reddy in '93 and see him expand the label to include releases for bands as diverse as Converge, Bane, American Nightmare, As Friends Rust, BoySetsFire, Copper, Saves The Day, Coheed & Cambria, Liars Academy, Alexisonfire and Jonah Matranga.

Understand signed with EastWest Records (part of Atlantic Records, and now Warner Music Group), and went on to even greater success with their awesome full album, entitled 'Burning Bushes and Burning Bridges' which they then promoted with a tour in the USA supporting Helmet. 'Burning Bushes and Burning Bridges' is a powerful rock album that I still love and listen to often now. It shows one of the UK's best bands off at their very best. Produced by Chris Sheldon, who'd become known for his work on Therapy?'s 'Troublegum', the album features eleven great tracks, including the songs 'Fleeced and Felched' about being ripped-off by costly service stations whilst on tour, 'The Rudeness we Encounter', a plea for the return to the old-fashioned English concept of politeness, and 'Southend', a tribute to the group's seaside hometown. 'Southend' became their best-known single with a great video filmed on Southend pier, the longest pleasure pier in the world, and was broadcast often on the Raw Power rock video show at the time.

Understand was made up of Dom Anderson (vocals), John Hannon (guitar – and later trumpet), Rob Coleman (guitar – 'six positive strings'), Stuart Quinnell ('Stu Q' - bass) and Andy Shepherd (drums – 'veggie beats') and they all jumped around like bouncing beans while they played. Several of the band had been in Stand Off, whose other members later went on to form a new band called Above All, and most of them had continued Stand Off's 'straight edge' creed of abstinence from drink and drugs. Although Understand weren't actually a straight edge band it was very much in that genre and they were clearly influenced by American bands such as Quicksand and Helmet, although they'd developed and added their own style too, in my opinion far surpassing many of the bands that had originally influenced them.

The show we played together at Rumours would be the first of many and as Understand developed as a band they'd have more amusing stories about bizarre parties their record label would throw, attending them alongside artists as diverse as Tori Amos and the Cheeky Girls.

Understand never really received the acclaim they deserved but went on to keep working within the music industry. Dom (their vocalist) became the tour manager for

Muse, and married Kari DeLonge, sister of Blink 182's Tom DeLonge. Rob (one of the guitarists) became the lighting technician for Iron Maiden. Andy played as a session drummer for various bands and Stu played bass for The Wonderstuff for a few years. John (their other guitarist) played the trumpet in a jazz band called Liberez and was also in Stirling and Woe. John also ran a great recording studio, Mushroom / No Recording, where he patiently and expertly recorded albums with Hell is for Heroes, Hundred Reasons, Rydell, and many more. Tragically, our good friend and scene stalwart, John the Hat, aka JazzJohn, passed away from a heart attack in 2021. RIP. I fondly remember him as a great guitarist, a key part of the UK music scene and most of all, a genuinely lovely human being.

2/3/92 Strength Alone, Angus Bagpipe, Joeyfat and Standoff
The Shelley Arms, Nutley
9/3/92 The Atomic Vicars, Cravola Earthworm and Joeyfat
The Shelley Arms, Nutley
12/3/92 Spermbirds and Joeyfat
The Rumble Club, Tunbridge Wells
19/3/92 Understand and Joeyfat
L.S.E. (London School of Economics), London

About a month later we'd play with Standoff, the other Southend band. They were booking a Standoff, Understand and Voorhees UK tour and wanted a few warm-up shows beforehand. Hallam from Standoff had been speaking with Simon from Strength Alone and he booked Joeyfat and Angus Bagpipe to complete a line-up for a gig at The Shelley. It was a great show, incredibly energetic and with a very straight edge vibe to it. Joeyfat being the odd band out there, but we held our own, adding a couple more tracks into our set. 'Sugarhead', 'Piecemeal' and 'People come into your house', came in and the covers came out. For me, the best band at the gig that night was Strength Alone.

Strength Alone was the new name of Headway, the noisy SEHC band that had played with Couch Potatoes four or five times already in the previous year, and we'd spent some time talking nonsense with them at shows and playing crazy golf down in Brighton. They were very young but had already become a really good band and had quite a few stories and gigs under their belts. Jamie, their drummer, told me about the day they had to bunk out of school to get up to London in time to support Sick Of It All, and Simon, their guitarist, told me about a time they were nearly all run over by GBH in their tour van, when they played with them at the Zap Club in Brighton.

They'd just come back from playing what must have been the first hardcore show ever to be put on at Leeds University. It was with Jailcell Recipes, Downfall (a predecessor of Bob Tilton), Voorhees, In Touch and Wartorn so must have been a very heavy affair. Strength Alone were going down well in the UK hardcore scene as one of the only posi-core bands at the time and it was good to see. They had very powerful music, of course,

Nick and Angus Bagpipe
at The Shelley Arms

Looking out from the stage

Barry, Strength Alone

Simon, Strength Alone,

08:03

Understand at The George Robey

Understand

Understand at The Shelley

Understand opening for Farside at the Duchess of York in Leeds, Dec. '92

but also such positive lyrics that they inspired a lot of people. Helene from Subjugation Records mentioned the gig in her excellent blog and said that she and her friends Claire, Ian and Tom managed to put the show on by setting up a student's 'University Hardcore Society' so they were able to use the room and p.a. They charged just £2 / £2.50 on the door for six bands and gave all the profits they made to Rape Crisis.

Strength Alone came back from that having signed to Subjugation Records for their first EP and played the tracks 'Never enough', 'Opinions voiced', 'Where to turn' and 'Best of times' from that record at the show, along with a few demo tracks and some covers that everyone sang along to. Strength Alone's 'Never Enough' 7" release was one of the very first on Subjugation Records, the great record label run by Helene Keller and Ian Simpson that brought the UKHC scene releases by Ironside, Bob Tilton, Tribute, Baby Harp Seal, Month of Birthdays, Schema, Beacon, Spy vs Spy, Pylon, Stapleton, Imbiss, Friends Unseen and Nathaniel Green.

The singer of Strength Alone, Barry Thirlway, played guitar for a while in a short-lived band called '33' along with, amongst others, Tony Sylvester of Fabric and Turbonegro. And although Strength Alone broke up before recording another record, both Simon (guitarist) and Jamie (drummer) played with me and Macca (Rydell and BBMFs) in Come The Spring and our new band The Atlantic Union Project. We've all played a lot of shows together and released quite a few records.

Always keeping busy, Joeyfat played again at The Shelley just a few days later as Warren, the owner, bar keeper, toilet cleaner, promoter and general dogsbody, had asked us to make up the numbers on an indie night. It was cool how we could play a full-on jump-around, finger-pointing, noisy, sweaty, hardcore gig one night and then a mellow indie affair just a few days later. We were flexible like that, straddling the scenes, and just wanting to play gigs. We'd bring the noise either way and put on the best show we could. It was a pleasant drive over the forest from Tunbridge Wells to Nutley so we were always good to go. This would be an indie rock sort of evening as the other bands playing were The Atomic Vicars and Crayola Earthworm.

The Atomic Vicars were down from London with Tim Briffa singing and playing guitar. He went on to be in 'My Drug Hell'. They had a single out called 'Garden Party' on Voltone Records and had brought a few copies to shift that night. Also on the bill were the Crayola Earthworm guys, up from Eastbourne and pretty good in a low-fi kind of way. I was impressed by both bands, to me they were original sounding and almost orchestral. They would have made good indie film soundtrack music. Seeing good new bands always inspired me.

Joeyfat didn't have a single out yet, just a live demo cassette of our first show that I was sending to promoters to try get us gigs, so we really needed to get into the studio.

I was writing songs for both Couch Potatoes and Joeyfat and wanted to book studio time for each as soon as possible. This basically meant as soon as we could afford it and make the time. I hoped it'd be soon as I figured that we'd get more gigs if we had some decent recordings.

Our next show came up fast though as we'd brought another pretty big hardcore band to Tunbridge Wells to play within the tight confines of the Rumble Club. Couch Potatoes were meant to be playing but for some reason couldn't, so Joeyfat got the gig, with all the ensuing chaos. There was a full house, and we played a tight and ultra-disciplined set to a good response. I was pleased, but we were soon made to look a little pedestrian when the headline band kicked off. This time it was a German hardcore punk band, The Spermbirds. I'd been to see them play the night before at The Shelley for my birthday party so knew well what to expect. They'd rocked that small pub, supported by our buddies Angus Bagpipe, who were even brave enough to roll out their own Spermbirds cover on the night, 'You're not a punk', much to the amusement of the band!

These guys really had a lot of energy and like most German bands I'd seen, could play very well with loads of technical ability. Even though they were all crammed into that small stage area they were bouncing off the black painted mirrored walls and really rocking out. I'd later come to find this to be the norm on many of our German tours, with great bands used to playing on tiny stages and still managing to put on brilliant shows.

The Spermbirds singer, Lee Hollis, was an American, an ex G.I, so all their songs were sung in English and in fact, all of the band spoke perfect English too, even if it was with an MTV American accent. This would be another thing I'd find to be the norm on our later German tours. We'd make laughable attempts at the local languages, but almost everyone in Europe spoke English anyway! The band's English lyrics had clearly helped them progress and gain wider popularity in the scene outside of Germany, but then so too did their intelligent and ironic song-writing and brilliant musicianship.

'You're not a punk' was the Spermbird's big hit and most skaters and hardcore kids knew it. Another of their songs that became a well-known anthem within the hardcore scene was 'My god rides a skateboard', both of these tracks came from their 'Something to prove' album, out on We Bite Records. The cover of this album had a cartoon aardvark on it named Cerebus. Apparently, this character was created by a Canadian comic book author and illustrator called Dave Sim, and although the band had not asked his permission to use the artwork, luckily for them he liked their music and let them carry on, not suing them for using it. In fact, he helped them out by mentioning the band in his later comics too.

This gig at the Rumble Club with Joeyfat was part of a tour promoting their new album called 'Eating Glass'. It was an absolute barnstormer of a record, released on Armin Hofmann's X-Mist Records label, and featuring more sarcastic lyrics and punk rock hits, including 'You're only as good as your last war' and 'Waiting for the bomb to drop'. (They followed this with more albums; Joe, Shit for sale, Family values and Get off the stage, a double album live recording of their last gig, on 15th October '95 at the Kammgarn Club in Kaiserslautern, although they have since reformed and even have a new album out, called Go to hell then turn left, jointly released by Rookie Records in Germany and Boss Tuneage in the UK).

They had another big album early on called 'Common Thread', which came out on X-Mist Records and Dead Eye Productions in Germany, but was also released in the UK on Full Circle, a record label out of Huddersfield that had put out H.D.Q's 'Soul Finder' album and Sink's 'Drainpipe Jane' EP. Spermbird's brilliant 'Common Thread' album was also later re-released by Rookie Records, part of the big German distro Flight 13, from whom we would buy loads of Ignition / Engineer Records distro stock, and later sell our own records all across Europe through them too. Engineer Records worked with Flight 13 distro alongside Aston Stephen's Boss Tuneage label, another criminally underrated but superb UK record label with over 400 releases and home at the time to such great UK bands as Goober Patrol, Shutdown, Annalise and Wordbug. All of whom we would also go on to play shows with.

Anyway, that Joeyfat and Spermbirds gig was a bit of a classic in my eyes and I was still buzzing from it a week later when we were booked to play another cracking show. This time with our mates Understand up at the London School of Economics.

The LSE had a really decent sound system and stage, and we were looking forward to playing there, chatting about it and making plans as we drove up the A21. I'd seen some great bands there before but tonight it was our turn to go and rock the students. We'd been practising hard and just the day before had recorded a new demo with eight tracks on it to send out. I'd soon start mailing my lists of promoters, labels, zines, reviewers, radios, and anyone else I could think of. The tracks we'd recorded for this demo were; 'Windscreen', 'Tear', 'People come into your house', 'Amusement', 'Piecemeal', 'Spoilt', 'Sugarhead' and 'Simmer Down' and that would be pretty much the set we'd play at the show tonight, those tracks, in that order.

The place was packed, and the sound was powerful, so although we'd have to say so ourselves, both Joeyfat and Understand really rocked it that night. The students all seemed to enjoy the show and quite a few came up to us afterwards to grab the tapes and stickers that we'd brought along. The promoters were making encouraging comments too and hoped that we'd be back to play again soon. I hoped so too. This was all great fun.

27/3/92 Drive, Thin Gypsy Thieves and Joeyfat
The Rumble Club, Tunbridge Wells
29/3/92 Drive, Joeyfat and Pseudo Hippies
Rumours Bar, Eastbourne

As an additional bonus of Joeyfat making lots of new fans in and around London we were starting to get some really good press reviews too. We wanted to keep that rolling, of course, so I went back to sending out demos and booking gigs. Later that month, our mates from Liverpool, Drive, were coming down to play again and between Iain in the band and Alan at First Strike I'd managed to get us onto two of their tour shows. They'd already seen Couchies pop-punk hardcore and it'd be interesting to see what they'd make of Joeyfat's slightly more off-beat style.

We'd have to share support at the first gig with another northern indie rock band called Thin Gypsy Thieves. They had a new release out on Yellow Moon Records, and it wasn't really my sort of thing, but Jason had already booked them for that night at the Rumble Club so the show became a three band evening, with them on in between Joeyfat and Drive. It was still a very fun gig and we shared a few drinks and stories with Iain, Dan and Jeff afterwards. They spoke mainly about how their tour for the new 'Out Freakage' album was going, as well as the Peel session they'd just recorded too. They were having fun and doing well, and Alan was supporting them with any releases they wanted on First Strike. That must have been lovely for them, and I was a little jealous, but then they were a great band and thoroughly deserved the success and coverage they were now getting.

There would be another Drive and Joeyfat gig just two days later in Eastbourne at the Rumours Club and quite a few people made the journey down with us. Our buddies Pseudo Hippies were coming along too and this was going to be more of a punk rock party. A convoy of cars headed down the A22 from London and Tunbridge Wells that evening, blasting hardcore as we went to the seaside. It was probably the best show I'd see at that venue, and after much excess we all wound our way back home, looking out for cop cars all the way.

15/4/92 Land of Nod and Joeyfat
The Shelley Arms, Nutley

At this time neither Jim nor I had proper jobs, although we'd both been in and out of several, but not enjoyed them or stuck around. Jim still had college and I was focused on the bands. We spent most of our spare time going to gigs and writing new music. I was still coming up with new guitar riffs for both Couch Potatoes and Joeyfat, and we'd all get together to jam them through, working out any extra parts that were needed over two or three rehearsals every week. This meant that new songs came together fast and we honed everything we had. We all wanted to get back into the studio and we all wanted to play more gigs. But that said, our next outing was a slightly odd indie evening that I just chalked up to experience.

A band called 'Land of Nod' were booked at the Shelley and Warren needed a support band who could bring a few people in. We agreed to do it, always eager for a live practise session, but when we got there soon found that we needed to load in all our gear as Land of Nod were a two-piece instrumental ambient guitar band, comprising of just a guitarist and bassist, with a pre-programmed drum machine and keyboard. I wish Warren had told us this before as we hadn't brought all our equipment. Luckily, we managed to borrow a drum kit from Aegir of Angus Bagpipe, as he lived locally, and we set up and sound-checked our wall of noise. The gig was OK, with their older fans not quite knowing what to make of Joeyfat, and ours drinking politely and listening to them. I guess that's not too bad for a Wednesday evening in the middle of nowhere. The Land of Nod guys, Ant and Dave, turned out to be pretty cool and we shared some drinks at the bar. Clearly their ambient style struck a chord with some people as one of their tracks was later used as the theme tune for the Tour De France on TV.

Leeds Uni gig flyer

GBH gig ticket

10, Excess All Areas

I'd been writing music with Adam, Jim and Yan for Couch Potatoes for about two years now and over the last few months I'd say we'd really hit our stride. We'd written an entirely new set and most of these songs would become our 'Excess All Areas' album. We needed to get back into the studio soon, and we also wanted to play more gigs to try these songs out.

Now I was enjoying writing and playing the new music with Jason, Jim and Matt in Joeyfat, but this had a very different energy to Couchies, so with the exception of one or two pre-booked indie nights out, Jim and I went back to playing melodic hardcore all through the spring of '92, when we had studio time booked to record an album at last.

We were very glad to be embarking on a run of pop-core shows arranged by our south London buddies Pseudo Hippies. We'd played a few times with the Pseudo Hippies before and had become good mates, often meeting up at The Venue in South London for raucous evenings out. We'd play all around the southeast for the rest of that month, mostly with the Pseudo Hippies, from London to Brighton, Canterbury to Southampton, and we fitted in two more local shows in Tunbridge Wells at the Rumble Club too, to see what our local following made of the new set. These shows were on back-to-back Friday nights (17th and 24th April '92) and both were packed, so people clearly weren't getting bored of us. I can only assume that Jason and Mark must have had a cancellation on the second evening, and we jumped in again. With able support from our good mates the Pseudo Hippies, all these shows turned into pop-punk parties.

Kris, the Pseudo's singer and guitarist told me that they had met and formed at Christ the King sixth form college in Charlton sometime late '90 or early '91. They'd started out trying to play heavy metal but soon realised that their musical limitations would make them a very bad metal band, but luckily at that time they were discovering the Misfits and Ramones and fell into three chord pop punk instead. The band's name was a nod to the Manchester scene. Tom, their bassist, who'd later switch to guitar when Adam joined, came up with the name after a few too many beers in the pub one night and it just stuck. The Pseudo's first gig was a new band night at the Woolwich Tramshed to which about a hundred of their fellow sixth form friends showed up to shout encouragement. Vic Reeves, the UK comedian, was in the crowd too, having just finished a show around the corner, and he told them after their set that he enjoyed their version of 'Rockaway Beach', their Ramones cover. They'd been playing pop-punk shows around London ever since, gradually getting better at it and now venturing further afield.

It wasn't long after this gig at the Tramshed that we first met. When I asked Kris what he remembered for this book, he said "We bumped into you guys at a Hard-Ons gig in London, at The Venue in New Cross, and you (Dave) pretty much changed the direction of our lives, at least musically. The tapes we would receive from you would feed our curiosity and thirst for pop punk. Early Green Day, Samiam, Mr T Experience, Down by Law, Fugazi, Dag Nasty, All. The list went on and on. You also linked us into the UKHC scene, and we got to know so many great people and bands who we swapped gigs with. The Shreds, Understand, Funbug, Another Fine Mess, Angus Bagpipe, Breaker, Toast, Reverse and many names I've sadly forgotten. We shared great days of five-hour van rides and sleeping on floors all across the country. We recorded a bunch of demos and somehow over the course of two years released two records and played countless gigs".

It seemed to me that the Pseudo Hippies had new tracks and a fresh demo tape every few months. They'd send me them to review in BHP zine and I'd run contact ads for them too, trying to help them get gigs. These ads would use their new demos artwork, always some cartoonish drawing that Kris had done. They stood out and looked cool, and the Pseudo's were soon picking up even more shows.

We'd established that the new set was good, and it was definitely time for us to get back into the studio. In May '92 Couch Potatoes were booked in to record again and these tracks would become the 'Excess All Areas' album. The recording session would be engineered by a very hairy guy named George Althus at his werewolf's lair called The Posthouse Studios tucked away in East Peckham. This studio was a step up from our last sessions at Wilbury Road in Brighton but still used analogue tapes and bounced tracks across limited recording space. It had very little in the way of gadgets or effects, although this time we did have larger rooms to mess around in and twenty-four tracks on the mixing desk to fill up with our noise.

The studio was built into an old post office and wasn't too far from where we lived so it made the recording a lot easier for us. This was a good thing as we wanted to take a little more time over this release. The studio had its own kitchen, and parking right outside too, so this was a luxury for us. Although there were still a few quirks turning up as we went along. I believe for some reason Yan had to sing from within a small bathroom rather than in the live room where the drums and guitar amps were all set up, and this, it has since been pointed out to me, could possibly be the reason for the unique and slightly desperate nature of his vocals on 'Excess', as he tried to bounce around whilst avoiding the toilet. It often gets a bit odd in studios when the engineer is trying to get the right sounds into the desk. The important thing though was that we had more time to make this record, an entire week in fact to get everything down for what later became a fourteen-track album, which George then helped us mix and produce over a few more days in June.

We couldn't wait to get the masters back and play these new tracks to all our crew. Friends, girlfriends, families. Hell, I'd have stopped strangers in the street and made them listen to these new recordings quite happily. And sometimes I did. This record sounded a thousand times better than the demos and the songs were way more developed too. I'd hope so after two years of Couch Potatoes gigging and writing, but this is a record I still listen to every now and again and am very proud of to this day. And why not? There are some great guitar riffs on there!

Couch Potatoes new record would be entitled 'Excess All Areas' and this would become our first album and proper full release. It had good artwork too, although still in black and white, mainly of fat guys going for a swim or sitting on chairs. Yan had taken the time to create some ideas for decent cover artwork with his new-fangled computer software, then he'd passed it to Sam Archer, a skateboarder mate of ours who was pretty good at layout, having practised on a few record covers as his dad worked for London Records. We thanked all our mates and the bands that we'd played with on the inner sleeve notes, all of whom were cool and most of them loaned us their gear, and importantly we also took the time to thank Calvin and Hobbes, Chinese restaurants, Andrea Clarke (a glamour girl of the time that we all had a thing for) and The Count from Sesame Street, who we'd sampled on 'Three', one of the new tracks.

'Excess All Areas' contains the tracks 'Lunchbox', 'Impossible easier', 'Part of you', 'Weak', 'Kill it', 'Three', 'Another', 'Bob', 'Hole', 'Why', 'Hooked', 'Take it', 'This morning' and 'Excess'. As you can see, Yan was not known for his wordy song titles. He'd often come up with lyrics, and song titles, at the very last moment, just before a gig or a recording session. The overall sound was very much Dag Nasty meets Descendents but with many other influences thrown in and this album would get some great reviews. We'd send out, trade and sell, first hundreds, then thousands of copies, initially on cassettes, then later on CDs too.

(The CD album contained the fourteen tracks we recorded with George at The Posthouse, but on cassette we added ten more unlisted tracks to fill up the space. These were; 'No more', 'I don't think so', 'Newun', 'Tired', 'Bad habit', 'Lucifer's lunchbox', 'Such a bad day', 'The sound', 'Get straight', and 'Cold can part 2' all from earlier recordings we'd done with Chris Priestley at Wilbury Road).

The promised Retch Records release never came about, but maybe that was a good thing as several other labels including Weird, Born to Booze, Panx and Food Not Bombs all wanted to release EPs, all of which we did over the next months. We self-released the

Couch Potatoes
record covers

full album at first, as soon as possible to get copies out there to promoters, fanzines, radios and record labels. Later the record would have a full release on Scene Police Records in Germany, followed by Engineer Records in the UK and US, as well as licensed copies in Japan and around the world. Over the years 'Excess All Areas' saw several more pressings and most recently, in 2015, Aston Stephens issued a full re-release of the album on CD on his Boss Tuneage record label. Between that and streaming on digital channels this album has shifted thousands of copies and is still available now. These songs certainly kept me and all the Couch Potatoes busy for the next few months, posting out copies, answering interviews and playing more shows.

To celebrate this recording our next show was to be another big punk rock party for all our local fans with Couch Potatoes headlining a four-band bill including the Pseudo Hippies, Angus Bagpipe and Joeyfat at a larger venue in Tunbridge Wells called The Watson Hall. This would take place on the Saturday after the recordings, on 16th May '92.

The Watson Hall was a big place in Langton Green, one of the posher parts of Tunbridge Wells, and we'd hired it out so we could fit more people into the show. It was about three or four times larger than the Rumble Club and we intended to cram it full. Of course, this venue has now been knocked down and turned into yet another suburban housing estate, but for this evening we'd turned it into quite a cool rock venue. Arriving early to plaster it in posters, set up a record stall, arrange the bar, and of course, set up our equipment. We'd hired a decent sound system and lights from JB's music store in town.

Jonathan Birch, or JB as he was known to everyone, was the drummer of the Anti-Nowhere League through the late eighties in their hair-metal meets punk phase and he played on their 'Perfect Crime' and 'Fuck around the clock' releases. He also ran the musical equipment shop in town where we all bought our gear and his store was a great place to advertise shows and meet other musicians. Many of the guys noodling around in there were just rock wannabees of course, but some could genuinely play. There were a pair of brothers I met there, Andy and Alistair, one of whom was a drummer and the other a guitarist, both so good that they gave lessons. I had a few jams with them when I needed to work out a tricky solo for a cover or learn some new style and they were just incredibly talented, playing anything by ear and going on to be session musicians with Elton John, Roger Daltrey and other massive names.

Anyway, we'd all been putting up posters, in JB's and everywhere else, and telling everyone about this show for weeks and we knew that a lot of our friends were coming along to this one. Both Couch Potatoes and Joeyfat were going to play, so Jim and I would have a very busy evening, and we'd also invited Angus Bagpipe over to rock the joint, and Pseudo Hippies came down from south London with their infectious brand of pop-punk too.

Nick from Angus Bagpipe had managed to slice his hand open though, almost losing the end of his finger in a rather foolhardy 'careless chef playing with a meat slicer' incident, so he had to play this show with a splint and bandage on his finger and just sing. They were still great as Duncan played most of the lead guitar riffs anyway and this soon became the new set up for Angus Bagpipe with Nick just singing and leaving the music to Duncan, Paul and Aegir.

All the bands played great sets that evening and I remember having so much fun. Our local crew was all there. Shout outs to Sam, Lee, Bomber, Paddy, Benji, Paul, Megs, my bro Steve, Adam's bro Paul, all our girlfriends, and plenty of local punks and rockers too. Annoyingly I don't have any photos from the show, this being long before mobiles and no-one thinking to bring a camera. Doh! I certainly wish I could bottle that sort of atmosphere though and share it when we needed it, maybe on duller nights that would occasionally follow. This was one of the gigs that made all the practising and effort seem well worthwhile.

Excess All Areas flyer

11, Amateur psychiatry

23/5/92 World and Joeyfat
The Shelley Arms, Nutley
4/6/92 NOFX, Rorschach and Joeyfat
The White Horse, Hampstead, London

As busy as I'd been over the last couple of months with Couch Potatoes, I was keen to keep Joeyfat rolling along too, so we embarked on another run of shows. Not long after the Watson Hall gig, we headed out to our local haunt The Shelley, on 23rd May, to play with another more or less unheard-of indie band. We did this sort of thing a lot as there were plenty of dodgy grunge and indie groups around at the time and some of the band looked at it like a live practise. That annoyed me though as I figured we should be playing every show full on. To achieve that live energy it really helps if you believe in what you are doing. It comes across in the atmosphere every time. I always wanted us to play like we meant it. I figured that even if we picked up just one or two new fans at each gig then it was worth it. It shouldn't matter if there were twenty people there, or two hundred, or two thousand. It's all good and I wanted us to play the songs like we wrote them, with full energy and commitment. We usually did.

Jason and I had been working on two more new tracks and gave the music tapes to Matt to come up with the lyrics. The latest new ones became the chuggy groove of 'Cushion fed' and the modestly titled 'The day I realised I was god'.

'The day I realised I was god' had a rather long-winded guitar intro and some off-beat timing but we all really liked it and this track would become our first single. We were pleased with both of the new songs and wanted to try them out live as soon as possible. Especially as my promoter buddy Aidan had hooked us up with another really good show in London that was coming up soon, with NOFX and Rorschach. That would be a full on hardcore punkathon and I didn't want us to be out of our depth. I didn't think we would be, but it's good to be sure, so any gigs or practises were welcome.

The show at The Shelley Arms was as great as ever, even though a lot of the regulars that would come to see Couchies or BBMFs were not about, mainly due to college exams. There was a whole new bunch of indie kids at the pub and even a few metallers that had started following Joeyfat to shows, so we were never short of an audience for our antics. This only encouraged Matt even more, whose entertaining stage presence was getting increasingly theatrical and a little narcissistic. We had several different demo tapes going out then which had been receiving quite a few positive reviews. We were just chuffed to see some good press building up about our band. Matt had seen some of the demo requests coming in to me, some from the media asking for tracks by Joey fat, (two words), and one even for Joy phat, so now he had taken to screaming "it's just one word" throughout much of our set. When we played gigs, Jason would often stand with his back to the audience now, playing in tight rhythmical circles with Jim to hold the chaos together, but this left just me and Matt facing the often bemused audience.

Several of the Joeyfat tracks were quite complex and Matt's guitar playing could often leave something to be desired, so for a while now he'd dropped the guitar and concentrated on singing so I was the only guitarist in Joeyfat. The riffs and rhythms we were developing often had layers so it was around this time that I suggested we get another guitarist in. I had in mind that Aidan Taylor, the London promoter and guitarist of Juice, would be a good idea. He was not only a friend but also a good guitarist. Certainly much better than Matt, who was happy to concentrate on his vocals anyway. Also, Aidan was into Fugazi and quirky indie bands, as well as full on hardcore, so an ideal addition to my way of thinking. Plus of course, he knew more or less every venue in the UK and most of the touring bands too, so the sooner he joined us the better as far as I was concerned. I called him and made the offer and he agreed. It would take some time and practising to bring him up to speed though, as there were a lot of songs to learn. I'd keep on writing new music with Jason, but when we came up with proper second guitar riffs now, we would record them on an eight-track and send them to Aidan too. He would come down from London to Tunbridge Wells for practises with us and pretty soon we would be rocking our Joeyfat live set as a five-piece. Creating a scary wall of noise just as we intended and inflicting it upon anyone who came to see us play from then on*.

Most people think Rorschach was a psychiatrist who came up with a series of ink blot tests to be able to tell if you unconsciously wanted to eat, rape or kill people. If you are into '80s DC comics like me, you'll also be reminded of the anti-hero of the same name from the Watchmen graphic novel by Alan Moore and Dave Gibbons. But in this case, Rorschach was a seriously heavy metalcore band seeping out of the bowels of New Jersey who we'd soon be playing with. Rorschach had an album out called 'Remain Sedate' on Vermiform (the label owned by Sam McPheeters, the singer of Born Against) and an EP called 'Needlepack' on Wardance Records. We'd play with them on a Thursday night at The White Horse in Hampstead with NOFX, and by this time they were already writing tracks for their big album 'Protestant' for Gern Blandsten Records, the label their vocalist, Charles Maggio, set up himself.

The Rorschach guys were initially a bit stand-offish and scary, so we didn't really speak much with them, not knowing much of their stuff and only really having heard of them from hilarious blasts of noise that my friend and big Couchies fan, Milo used to play to me occasionally. Their music was angry, brutal, and what most people not into hardcore would definitely call noise. They were 'of the moment' and had something to say, so they said it with as much force as they could muster. I respected that and was a little in awe of it.

We borrowed their equipment to save space on stage and sound-checked, so now the guitarists, Nick and Keith, were friendly enough, and the drummer, Andrew Gormley, who went on to play in Shai Hulud, was chatting with Jim, quite OK with the fact that he'd turned up with just a snare, a pedal and two cracked cymbals.

Joeyfat went on first, playing to a busy room, and we were tight, powerful and angular. But then Rorschach went on and just hammered through such an intense set that it made our grooving rhythms feel a bit like elevator music in comparison. Both they and NOFX were on big European tours so they hadn't come to London to mess around. Even now, years later, you can still hear them, with just a quick clip sound-blasted like Van Halen is in Back to the Future, in Zero Dark Thirty, the film about killing Bin Laden. They use a clip from 'Pavlov's Dogs', the opening track from 'Remain Sedate', to torture the suspected terrorists. It would definitely work.

The evening's interesting mix of hardcore styles continued with NOFX. Their skate-punk ska-core songs always brought a party to the show, and they were on form tonight, crammed into that small venue, jumping around the stage and cracking gags between their short, fast, blasting songs. By now NOFX were pretty big and had come along with a whole entourage including a brass section that could barely fit on the stage. It was hot, sweaty and crowded, and as much as I enjoyed the show it seemed to go on for a long time. I was glad when it finally finished, and we packed our gear back into our cars and said thanks to Aidan and the London crew for the gig.

*Years later, whilst writing up my notes for this book, I asked Aidan how he got into punk, formed his band Juice, and became a promoter. Also, what he remembered about first joining Joeyfat.

"How did I get there? Punk kids often started with metal. I had made the less travelled path of progressing from 80's indie, through to noisier stuff like Sonic Youth, Buttholes Surfers, Dinosaur Jr, and the very early stages of grunge. Then I discovered the hardcore/punk roots of these bands, and thus intrigued and enthused, I headed for the same, but considerably rougher, mosh pit comradery of gigs by Fugazi, NoMeansNo, Bad Brains, Youth of Today, Gorilla Biscuits, DOA. Whatever was going on.

"I took less interest in the weekly music press, and started reading Maximum Rock 'n' Roll. I'd always gone to a lot of gigs, usually on my own or maybe with a handful of friends. Suddenly I had a whole new bunch of mates who played in bands, did fanzines, ran record labels, or knew this great US band who were playing at the Fulham Greyhound next week. Ah, so this was a 'scene'.

"Sometime in 1989 I took my full nine months of guitar playing experience, did the punk thing and formed a band. We were called Juice. Very average. Not shit. OK. Good second demo. Dan the singer had a mate who fancied himself as a bit of a promoter and could get free nights at the uber-grot venues of The George Robey and Lady Owen Arms. We all had friends in bands who were happy to knock out a thirty-minute set and loads of their mates would provide a decent crowd.

"Some folk in the nascent London hardcore scene also had bands (Long Cold Stare, Insight, Harmony As One) and it wasn't long before I focused on promoting these sorts of groups, as well as new pals from further afield, such as Couch Potatoes, BBMFs, Understand, plus Norfolk's Goober Patrol and Southampton's Older Than Dirt.

"The first time Samiam played London, at the George Robey, it wasn't really terribly well attended; and it was empty enough for me to be intrigued by a woman at the front who clearly knew the band and their music, but few others in the crowd. It turned out Christy Colcord was from Florida, via Massachusetts, and had washed up in the Bristol cider punk / Bugs and Drugs zine scene. She was now organising tours for US bands in the UK. Did I want to put any of her bands on in London? Yes, I fucking did, primarily seeing potential decent support slots for my own mostly overlooked group.

"The initial reality wasn't that glamourous. I was offered a date to put on The Asexuals, from Canada. A band no one had really heard of, and were unlikely to, given the tour date offered of December 26th. I showed them a good time by spending £15 of my own money buying them all a hot meal from Starburger and chucking them most of the door money from the 45 punters that weren't nursing Xmas hangovers at their parents houses.

"In the early 90's, small North American bands realised they could tour in the European D.I.Y. punk scene, and make enough money on the mainland to subsidise frequently loss-making trips to the UK, for both them and me. Many came and went, some still remembered, others forgotten, a few even active now. Sons Of Ishmael, Mr T Experience, Quicksand, MDC, Samiam, Rorschach, Gorilla Biscuits, Christ On A Crutch, Go!, Cringer, Econochrist, J Church, Born Against, Sick Of It All, Farside, Alloy, Jawbreaker, Artless. Maybe some I've forgotten. Very few made any money, but none ever pissed and moaned about it, except NOFX. They moaned.

"Christy had moved to our chaotic house in London, soon to be joined by her pal Mary-Jane and started booking full European tours. I found myself with a list of friendly people in random places like Wigan, Newport, Stoke, Southampton, Bradford, Scotland and Eire to call up and arrange dates for the bands, using some iffy US military 'calling card' that gave us free calls. We used a phone box a mile from our gaff, for fear of being traced by the CIA.

We also took on the short-lived and ill-fated responsibility of running Lookout Records (Europe). Green Day were only vaguely on my radar as a pretty competent young pop-punk band on Lookout, however the response from many mates when I told them they were going to tour made me realise we may be onto something. One of the most thrilled was Dave Gamage. Like anyone from the scene in a band, I'd given Dave's group, Couch Potatoes, a support or two on London gigs. I'd also travelled down to his hometown of Tunbridge Wells a few times too, enjoying some fairly messy weekends.

"Despite all this, the offers weren't exactly rolling in from anyone wanting to put out anything by Juice, cue Spike and Retch Records. He was an enthusiastic sort, but fair to say not very well connected. He promised us a great gig in Preston so we dutifully drove up from London to play to six people in the back bar of an 'old man' pub, only to be interrupted by the landlady after the second song, complaining loudly "I told 'im, no 'eavy metal on Friday night!" A 12" EP eventually came out, recorded by a young Paul Tipler, who went on to have a decent career as an indie producer. The highlight of the session was Genesis P. Orridge (poet, songwriter and lead-singer of Throbbing Gristle) popping into the control room. I suspect most copies ended up in landfill, however my friend James Sherry did spot a copy in a record shop a few years ago with the sticker proclaiming, 'includes members of Joeyfat, who toured with Green Day'. Desperate measures!

"I'd gone to see a gig with Dave's new band playing. This new one had a few members of a somewhat underwhelming local indie-rock act, so I wasn't planning to be wowed. A soundcheck of two songs, and I was declaring to anyone that would listen that Joeyfat were the best new band in Britain!

"A few months later, with frontman Matt deciding that he didn't want to sing and play guitar, and Juice having finished, I was invited onboard. I loved the fact they were miles from any generic sound, with shades of newer DC bands like Shudder To Think as well as Fugazi, plus post-hardcore geniuses Slint, and melodic stuff like Jawbreaker, and a unique vocal from a more odd British lineage.

"It was a step up from playing generic punk/hardcore to having learn parts in 13/8 time. I put in the hours, as it felt thrilling to be part of something so different and progressive. I'd ride my little East German 125 cc motorbike the 75km down to Tunbridge Wells, where we rehearsed in an odd community space that I think may have doubled as a playgroup. A strange place for a strange band. I could see my promoter credentials were as much of a requirement as being able to plug in a guitar.

"I didn't take that long to tire of the rigmarole of promoting gigs and tours. The arse-ache of crusties and nutjobs that came along with the decent sorts, and the time consuming flyering and organising shit while living in a Hackney squat, while working full time as a nurse.

Joeyfat slowly drifted into a different orbit, their angular edges at odds with the hardcore orthodoxy and I submitted to let other indie-orientated D.I.Y. promoters do the job. Meanwhile Christy and Mary Jane had moved to Amsterdam, UK immigration having decided they had outstayed their welcome.

"My twelve-year-old is just starting to learn guitar, eight years before I even picked one up. He chose a Green Day song as something to learn. I told him to stop learning other people's songs. It's not fucking punk. Make your own up instead. Look where it might lead you."

12/6/92 Identity, Joeyfat and Pseudo Hippies
The Rumble Club, Tunbridge Wells
9/7/92 Blood on the Trax, Joeyfat, Slambamsam and Bluff
The Victoria Hall, Tunbridge Wells

About a week or so later we'd have another chance to prove ourselves and try out a few new songs in a longer set. We had another show booked at the Rumble Club in Tunbridge Wells, with our noisy three chord pop-punk buddies the Pseudo Hippies and Identity.

Identity were a pop-punk three-piece from the Midlands who, soon after this gig but hopefully not because of it, changed their name to Funbug. Couch Potatoes had played with them before and we knew that they were great at rocking out three catchy chords live and having good fun doing it. They'd signed to Ian's Damaged Goods label and he'd managed to get them on quite a few good gigs, including one at the Bull and Gate in Kentish Town with an early Manic Street Preachers. This gig was just £3 on the door for three bands, the other being our mate Aiden's band, Juice. Anyway, Identity had an album out called 'Yeah, about time too!' and Ian said that it was called this because it took them just a couple of weeks to record it, but over a year to sort out the cover artwork and name, and he got bored of waiting for it. Watching them and Pseudo Hippies play was like being at a UK version of a Green Day, Misfits or Ramones show. Very enjoyable with lots of energy, melody and harmonious singing, but nothing that was going to tax you too much musically. Joeyfat went on in the middle of them and stood out like a sore thumb.

We kept on practising and gigging, playing a few smaller party-type shows as well as another gig at The Watson Hall, and in between these I'd go out, usually with the Couchies crew, to see hardcore bands play in Brighton or London. One particularly good show I saw was on the 7th July at the Robey in London, with Mr T Experience, on their great Milk Milk Lemonade tour, supported by Alloy (ex-Dag Nasty), That's It (ex-Government Issue) and Goober Patrol. Now that's a pretty decent four band special for about three pounds fifty on the door!

Soon we would get to play to our largest home audience yet at the Victoria Hall in Southborough. This was a huge venue by our standards as it held over 600 people and had seen shows by bands like Fleetwood Mac and Deuce, my old local metal heroes. It has of course been knocked down now to make way for some boring council offices and high-density flats. But back then it was a great place to play with a big stage, a full sound and light rig and even a proper back-stage area where we could prepare for the gig and pretend to be rock stars.

For a while before this show we'd created posters and stuck them up everywhere. Initially in record shops such as Talisman and Sounds, and music stores like JB's, but also in cafes, pubs, clubs, shops, and anywhere that couldn't move itself out of the way of our paste pots and flyers quickly enough! This was way easier back then, with far fewer cameras and much less 'giving a shit'. Jim was still at West Kent College in Tonbridge, the next town over, where it was widely believed that everyone had webbed feet and an extra head under their shirts. But the college had a refectory with a notice board which he could plaster with posters so all his student mates would come along. We chased everyone up. This was no 'too cool for school' London or Brighton hardcore show, this was a local rock night, and the tickets were selling well. This may have been due, at least partly, to the other bands playing; Blood on the Trax, Slambamsam and Bluff.

You probably haven't heard of any of these bands. Blood on the trax were not a Dylan covers band as the name might suggest. Nor were SlamBamSam a child's board game. And Bluff, well they weren't a broad rounded cliff edge or a straight-face at poker either. These bands were more metal or alt-rock than indie, and that always drew a bigger and more determined crowd around our way. So, although you may never have heard of them they had a pretty good following back then. The local press and radio had been called and a cameraman was even dispatched to the gig by one of the papers. We eyed their army of fans in the same way a fat lad looks at cake. They would be ours.

When the big night finally came, the place was indeed busy and the packed bar was doing a roaring trade. We were on third and had a tight set planned. I seem to remember it all going a bit Spinal Tap. Not that Jason was stuck inside a pod, or any dwarves danced around a mini Stonehenge, nothing like that. But there were plenty of lights, effects and even smoke. The drums were on a riser, a raised block at the back of the stage, so everyone could clearly see Jim's fingerless leather gloves when he twirled his sticks and laugh at him along with us. Matt was wandering around wearing eye-liner long before it was emo or acceptable to do so and it had all gotten a bit strange as Jason and I had opted for wearing dresses for this evenings show. I don't remember if it was our idea or something that had been suggested to us by the odd girlfriends we had at the time, but I had a flowery little number on that I'd had to rip at the shoulder just to get it to fit and must have looked lovely. Just what everyone wanted to see. But anyway, when the time came, we strolled onstage and off we went on the hard-rock roller-coaster, playing our hearts out to a very busy room of happy faces.

My lovely wife Louise, tells me that she was there that evening, attending one of the first shows she'd ever been to and absolutely loved it. Having been persuaded by a friend of hers that Joeyfat were great and well worth going along to see. She'd really enjoyed herself, being out late on a school night and I do remember a very pretty girl with bright pink hair standing out in the audience. She would have been very young though, so the less said the better.

22/7/92 Understand, Strength Alone and Joeyfat
The Shelley Arms, Nutley
23/7/92 The Pigkeeper's Daughter and Joeyfat
Kings Hall, Herne Bay

Later that month we were back at the Shelley for a brilliant energetic jump-around SEHC type of show with the excellent and heavy Strength Alone and the equally excellent and bouncy Understand. It was always a good show with those guys and always a good gig at that venue. The very next day we travelled over to Herne Bay for a busy show at the Kings Hall, a big venue where I saw an incredibly energetic Fugazi show, possibly the loudest gig I'd ever been to. This time it was to play with a band called The Pigkeeper's Daughter, but unfortunately, they were a bit shite. I've later found out their name came from some dodgy seventies skin flick. We'd all had ice-creams and fish 'n' chips on the beach, making the best of it, and The Kings Hall had a big stage and great sound, so we rocked out and gained some really great reviews in the press soon after.

A couple of days later, Mark and Jason were putting on Midway Still at the Rumble Club and I'd managed to get my mates The Strookas on the bill as support. We'd played too many local shows recently so would be supporting Midway Still and Bivouac the next day up at the Powerhaus in Islington, so I'd got them on instead. They were chuffed about it as they were big fans of Midway Still and Dave, the Strookas guitarist, had their 'I Won't Try' record and kept on playing it. Midway Still had also recently been on the front pages of several music papers. Melody Maker and NME were popular reads at the time, and I think Sounds was still going too. Of course, if a band were becoming quite well known within the music press it always added a little more excitement to the proceedings.

The Strookas were from over Maidstone way and were part of the predominately 60's influenced Medway music scene, playing gigs in Kent and London, but mainly in punky Sheerness and at Churchills in Chatham. John Edwards, the drummer and vocalist, told me they'd played at Churchills nineteen times up to that point, so were very glad to be playing somewhere else. They hadn't played in Tunbridge Wells before, but had heard there was a good hardcore scene, probably through the various zines and gig guides. I remember that 'Your Mornings Will be Brighter' was an indispensable two-sheet news and gig guide at the time, created by Richard Murrill, based in Folkestone and distributed all over Kent. I'd been sending Rich gig info for a while as he was another great promoter that we had befriended hoping for gigs. He'd list our shows and help us out a lot later.

We played quite a few shows with The Strookas and became good mates. John, their singing drummer, told me, "The Rumble Club sounded exciting and a little dangerous to sceneless wandering minstrels like the Strookas. The Club was situated in the Winchester pub at the bottom end of Tunbridge Wells and as you entered, the bar was on the left and the stage, or band playing area as there was no real stage to speak of, to the right, so it was real 'white of the eyes' stuff with the audience right next to the band. Definitely not for the faint-hearted. I also remember quite a few mirrors and a lot of black paint. After lugging our gear in and a quick soundcheck we found a table and bought some drinks. I remember talking with a few people who were clearly into good bands there, so reeled off some of our influences; Husker Du, Jawbreaker, Samiam, Dinosaur Jr, etc. There was a real buzz of excitement about the place as it began to fill up, I couldn't decide whether it was always like this or just because Midway Still were playing, it was certainly nothing to do with us. We played our slot and it went pretty well." Dave Bloomfield, the Strookas guitarist, added that just the weekend before they'd been into Red Studios with their fresh-faced new bassist Tony O'Rourke. They'd just recorded ten songs that would become their first album, 'Deaf by Dawn', so they knew those songs inside out and were playing them good and tight. That meant the timing of this gig couldn't have been better for them.

John continued, "People seemed to enjoy us, or maybe they were just being polite. It's not easy to tell in Tunbridge Wells, so after playing we melted back into the crowd. We were looking forward to seeing Midway Still and after a while they got up to play, but before they started, one of them kindly announced that 'the Strookas were the best fucking band they'd

The Strookas at The Rumble Club

The Victoria Hall, Southborough

Kings Hall, Herne Bay

seen in ages' or words to that effect. This took me quite by surprise and I could only assume that they'd seen some pretty diabolical bands recently We just put it down to the excellent job the sound guys on the PA did, which was soon confirmed when Midway Still started playing. They sounded magnificent and I reckoned any reasonably tight, fast rock band would be a joy to hear through the p.a. in this Club."

I remember that both The Strookas and Midway Still went down a storm and the club was packed that evening, as it was on most 'indie' or 'rock' evenings now, with people at the bar and along the walls standing on chairs, shouting and clapping. The Rumble Club was a cool place to play. After the show people were asking John where he got his 'Bazooka Joe, he likes a blow' t-shirt from and hassling Dave and Tony for demo tapes or a copy of their 'Summer to fall' 7" vinyl.

John also said, "After Midway Still had stopped playing we all had friendly words with each other and telephone numbers were exchanged. All sorts of good things led from that night. The Strookas arranged several more support slots with Midway Still, and we also got to share some gigs with Joeyfat and Couch Potatoes, and play the Rumble Club a few more times too. Also later, when the successor to the Rumble Club, The Forum, opened up we were kindly invited to play with the Couch Potatoes supporting the pre-massive, but still amazing, Green Day. That was another evening in Tunbridge Wells to remember."

Dave added, "After that gig the Midway Still bassist, Jan Konopka, passed our new ten track 'Deaf by Dawn' demo to Wiz from Mega City Four when they were touring together. Wiz loved the tape and called me at home to discuss the recording of it and suggest some gigs together. We later supported MC4 at the Clapham Grand."

The Midway Still guys also passed on The Strookas name to Sean Forbes from Wat Tyler as he was organising a compilation CD called 'The Best Punk Rock in England, Son' to be released in Japan on a label called Snuffy Smile Records. The Strookas, Midway Still and Couch Potatoes all had tracks featured on this CD, alongside other great UKHC and punk bands of the time including Goober Patrol, Shutdown, China Drum, Exit Condition, Guns 'n' Wankers, Hooton 3 Car, Travis Cut, Cowboy Killers, Funbug, Wact, Chopper, Skimmer and Your Mum. Sean made some good choices there and most of these were bands that Couch Potatoes or Joeyfat would play gigs with too.

Some years later, largely due to this CD, Kei Dohdoh from Fixing A Hole Records in Japan contacted The Strookas and ended up releasing three albums for them on his label. The Strookas also have a great album called 'What you want to hear' on Engineer Records too. Later, their new band Tonota 80, would have two albums released on Engineer Records, called 'Killer sands and beating hearts' and 'Everybody's famous'. All this stemming from that first gig at the Rumble Club with the help and goodwill from the people involved in the scene. "It's a good job," said John later when I mentioned this to him "Because The Strookas would have been far too lazy arsed to get any of it in motion ourselves."

29/7/92 Midway Still, Bivouac and Joeyfat
The Powerhaus, Islington, London

The next day Joeyfat headed up to London to play with Midway Still at the Powerhaus in Islington. This was a big indie venue of the day, run by the Mean Fiddler group who put on loads of good shows. I'd been there quite a few times and was excited to be playing such a well-known alternative rock venue. Even though it was midweek I figured that this would be a busy one thanks to the bands we were supporting. This would also be our first show with Aidan playing second guitar with us and we were all looking forward to that additional level of noise.

The other Kent band, Midway Still, were friendly enough guys. Paul, the singer and guitarist, Jan, the bassist, and Declan, the drummer, were letting us use most of their equipment which saved a lot of hassle, so we were very grateful and promised not to destroy it. They had a couple of singles out and had also recorded a Peel session, but now they had a new album to promote called 'Dial Square' on Roughneck Recordings and were playing loads of gigs. Roughneck was a subsidiary of Fire Records, the label that'd signed The Lemonheads for the UK, and they seemed to be supporting them well with shows and promotions. Later they'd record a great second album, called 'Life's too long' which would be produced by Frankie Stubbs of Leatherface.

The other band playing that night was Bivouac, a rocking grunge style three-piece. They were a new band and quite possibly took their name from the awesome Jawbreaker album released earlier that year. They'd already been signed by Elemental Records, part of Workers Playtime / One Little Indian, and had a brand-new EP to promote.

All three bands played great sets and went down very well with the decent-sized crowd that had come along. There were so many indie shows going on in London that it was quite usual to play to much less than 100 people, many of them standing unimpressed at the bar. Or maybe that was just us! But this show was seen by quite a few more than that, including a few music industry types and I for one was buzzing afterwards, hoping we might get a decent review in one of the big music mags or a few more gigs booked by any of the promoters that'd been there.

This was our only gig with Bivouac so I'll just add a note here about them. After an album and several more EPs on Elemental they were signed by Geffen. Geffen, under DGC Records, was the major label that signed Nirvana and released 'Nevermind' in '91, still their biggest selling album to date. They've also released records by Jawbreaker, Jimmy Eat World, Blink 182, Dashboard Confessional, Rise Against, Girls Against Boys and Enter Shikari. This major label is now even more 'major' as it is owned, alongside A&M and Interscope, by Universal Music Group.

Bivouac signing to such a big label as Geffen led to an album called 'Full Size Boy' and some big tours, taking them a long way from their hometown of Derby. Around this time their drummer, Antony Hodgkinson, became well known for his dancing on stage at labelmates Nirvana's last UK show, the '92 Reading festival. Known as 'Tony the Interpretative Dancer', he was on stage with them and on the video of the show, with 'God is gay' written across his chest. Staying in touch with Dave Grohl, after Kurt's death in '94, he also danced at the first Foo Fighters UK shows.

Paul Yeadon, the singer and guitarist, later said in an interview with Louder Than War fanzine about being on Geffen/DGC, "We lost heart. We were mis-managed, robbed and lied to by idiots. We gave up." But he also added, "I remember we played Reading one year with the tent overflowing, people jumping from the supports and singing along, it was amazing! There were a lot of great gigs, tours with Therapy?, Jacob's Mouse, Seaweed, The Jesus Lizard. Bob Mould asked us to support Sugar at the Brixton Academy and we played our arses off. I remember having a drink with Bob and Greg Norton afterwards, big heroes of mine. We played The Foo Fighters' first UK show, flew back from the USA to do it, jet-lagged and drunk. We always loved playing live".

He added, "We used to keep a Filofax with all our gigs in it. But our van was broken into and it was stolen in Seattle. We were up to 580 gigs in just three years, we played a lot." And back home, "We did a few sessions for Mark and Lard, which were always a blast. I'm still super proud of the Peel sessions we did, to be part of that musical legacy is a great privilege."

The band disbanded when the major label dropped them but Yeadon went on to play in other bands including Pitchshifter and The Wireless Stores. Their bassist, Granville Marsden, still runs the Bivouac YouTube channel and occasionally puts up unreleased or live tracks.

31/7/92 Crayola Earthworm and Joeyfat
The 101 Club, East Grinstead

Just two days after our trip to the Powerhaus we headed over to East Grinstead to play at the 101 Club with a band called Crayola Earthworm. They'd invited us after a show we played with them at The Shelley a few months before.

The 101 Club hosted regular live music on the top floor of a big old coaching inn called The Dorset Arms. It's quite famous locally for live music, good food, and being haunted, and is set within the old town part of East Grinstead High Street. I'm glad to say that this venue is still there and still putting on bands, but it was always a nightmare getting our gear into the place. You could try to go in through the front door, through the bar and up the stairs, but then be dodging people all the way and turning some awkward corners with heavy equipment on the narrow stairways. Or there was an outside metal fire escape at the back of the building going up precipitously from the car park. This stairway went up three or four floors and seemed like a lot more when carrying heavy amps or awkward drum kits. Once up there and you'd caught your breath, the room was cool enough; dark, sound-proofed and atmospheric, with a giant glitter ball in the middle of the ceiling that always made it feel like an Abba concert when the lights came on, no matter how hardcore the bands were.

Crayola Earthworm were a weird sort of lo-fi noise band, some would say indie, or even grunge, but they were odder than that with a very tall, hairy bassist who sung for them. He looked a bit like Dave Grohl of Nirvana and Foo Fighters but only if he'd been a tramp living on the streets for a few years. They were odd but nice guys and I remember some good shows with them at that venue. It was close enough for regulars from the Rumble Club or the Shelley Arms to easily get to, and even for kids to travel from Brighton or London, but there were also lots of local musos who were there for the regular nights to check out any new bands. The stage area was OK, a bit crammed into the corner, but the sound was good and we always got paid, petrol money at least and sometimes more, so I hoped we'd play there again despite the crazy stairs.

Joeyfat sticker

12, Blagging it (Stamp my feet, hold my breath)

Joeyfat didn't look or sound particularly punk, but the attitude was there. We were definitely part of the 'alternative' scene and ended up sharing the stage with a lot of very political bands. One of these was Blaggers ITA.

The Blaggers ITA were an anarchist punk band, both in the political sense and the musical sense. Matty, their main vocalist and a real character, had originally been in Complete Control, an old Oi! band, and he was joined by Christie, their second vocalist who'd rap rather than sing. They shouted about anti-fascist action, left-wing politics and the topical news of the day, reminding me a lot of our old mates in Beanfeast. They were backed up by a group of musicians that could always fill up any stage and constantly seemed to be expanding from the usual rock band holy trinity of guitar, bass and drums into brass sections and sampling keyboards too. They made quite a noise and had a strong message to deliver. So much so that shows with them often kicked off with fights between the left-wing ultra-liberal punk supporters and any right-wing Blood and Honour* types that were foolish enough to show up looking for trouble.

*Blood and Honour were a right-wing neo-nazi coalition originating from the skinhead music scene. Originally formed around the band Skrewdriver and their followers and named after one of their tracks / the motto of the Hitler Youth movement. In the late eighties and early nineties, they'd often turn up at gigs and start fights. Their co-founder, Ian Stuart Donaldson, the vocalist of Skrewdriver, died in a car-crash in '93.

I'd seen the Blaggers play a couple of times, having been introduced to them by Aidan at some London shows, and I also had a couple of their releases, the latest being a mini-LP called 'Blagamuffin', on Words of Warning Records, a punk label out of Bristol. For this show they also had a new 7" single to sell, entitled 'The way we operate', it was just out on Fluffy Bunny Records. Fluffy Bunny was a London label run by Lawrence, one of the main punk rock promoters in town, he was keen to do a release for Joeyfat too, but it just never seemed to come around. Although he did later release great records for China Drum, Wordbug and Travis Cut.

This would be Joeyfat's first gig with the Blaggers, at The Square in Harlow, a soulless 'new town' in Essex. The Square was well known as an alternative music venue for those travelling outside of London, and had gigs run by enthusiastic, independent promoters, but it also suffered badly from poor sound and the venue itself being a characterless box of a building in a town full of characterless boxy buildings. I always thought that if there was ever a zombie apocalypse, with people being eaten alive whilst trash blew down empty streets, this is the sort of place it would happen. Certainly, it'd make a good backdrop for a horror film, if boring urban is what you were after.

Thankfully though, when we got inside, the audience did not reflect the venue and we ended up having a rocking show. We got on very well with the Blaggers, arranging to play together again in London as soon as possible. This was set up for us by Aidan at The White Horse in Hampstead for the 10th September and it was at this show that we finally got around to making a live recording of Joeyfat as a five-piece.

19/8/92 BBMFs, Joeyfat and Nux Vomica
The Joiners, Southampton
20/8/92 The Strookas and Joeyfat
The Stick O' Rock, Bethnal Green, London
22/8/92 Sonar Nation, Joeyfat and Jesus Wept
The Kings Head, Fulham, London.

All through that summer we were busy playing gigs, constantly going out to play with anyone who asked us. Amongst those shows I remember good ones with the BBMFs and Nux Vomica, playing their first ever gig at the Joiners in Southampton for the STE collective. The Strookas, and new local nutters, Sonar Nation.

Nux Vomica were a new band featuring Allen and Sam from Sleep, as well as Stevie Snax, the bassist from The Stupids, a hugely popular skate-core band. They were a lot more rough and ready than Sleep's melodic singalongs but as far as I'm aware didn't stick around long enough to make any recordings. The BBMFs were as great as ever and we all played at the STE's 38th show. The flyer had Chris Bald of Faith from the 'Banned in DC' book on it.

Another good show was with our Husker Du and Dinosaur Jr sounding mates The Strookas at the Stick O' Rock in Bethnal Green, a pub that was owned by Steve Bruce, the drummer of Cock Sparrer, and another venue that became famous for live music in London.

Yet another good gig for us up in town was at The Kings Head in Fulham, a big red brick pub that looked like a Scottish baron's castle, where we were playing with Jesus Wept and Sonar Nation. I remember Sonar Nation particularly fondly. They were another Kent

WED. AUG. 19TH

BBMFs Popular Return!

JOEYFAT Tunbridge Wells!

NUX VOMICA Ex Sleep/Stupids!

The Joiners

St Marys St STE 38!

Southampton

£3.00/2.50

8pm Stalls & Hardcore Tunes!

Access - 1 Step   Come Early!

Poster for BBMFs, Joeyfat and
Nux Vomica at The Joiners

Sonar Nation

The White Horse, Hampstead

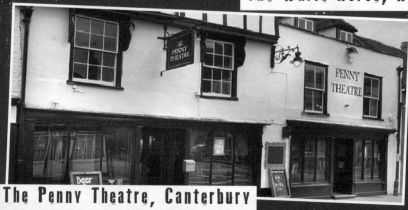

The Penny Theatre, Canterbury

based band, a five-piece who wrote and performed a fairly original and very powerful style of hardcore with an intensity that reminded me of The Rollins Band. They were always loud, almost too loud, arguing with the soundmen at every show about it, and I loved watching their lead guitarist, Simon Clatworthy, try to strangle his guitar. He never stopped jumping around while they played. He and I got on very well and we'd book quite a few shows together.

Sonar Nation had been playing a lot around Kent, mainly in the Maidstone area where they came from, but were now starting to get shows in London and further afield. They put on a good show and deserved the gigs. Shaun Tucker, the vocalist, would always wear his dirty baseball cap and an old t-shirt with a pistol on it. He'd sing his heart out at every show. Simon Clatworthy was the mad lead guitarist, often rolling about on the floor or jumping off of speakers whilst he played, always with his silly woolly bobble hat on, no matter how hot the temperature. And he'd do this in a pub in front of twenty people just as happily as at a big hall with hundreds there too. Then there was Phil Clarke on rhythm guitar keeping it solid, G A Frame, their big hairy bassist, and Jamie Emery, their excellent drummer. Sonar Nation were a good band and massively underrated. I'm very glad that we played so many shows with them.

They'd just recorded and self-released a 12" vinyl EP called 'Surge DT' on their own TMSY Records and the three tracks on it, 'Some place, not home', 'Master plan' and 'Hate photo' were great chunks of power rock, influenced by grunge, hardcore and metal. I still have my copy. It has an ugly bright green cover with dodgy computer handwriting on it and a hand drawn image of a devil monster that looks more like an angry mole. It looks odd to say the least, even a bit amateur, and could in fact be entered into the competition for worst record cover of all time, but trust me, if you see it, get it. It's a diamond in the rough.

They later released another 12" EP called 'Thoughts on anyone' and then two 7" singles, 'Sleepthick voices' (which I also have in my nerdy record collection) and 'Thrill me, said the thinker'. Eventually, in '95 they released a full album on Abstract Records called 'Cylinders in blue', before joining Joeyfat on Tunbridge Wells own indie and post-rock oddities label, Unlabel, for an EP called 'Dirty hands and wishes'. Sonar Nation were a very good band that should have been much bigger, and who clearly can't shake the bug as they have now reformed and are playing again. Go and see them if you can.

1/9/92 Gravity and Joeyfat
Xpose Club, Penny Theatre, Canterbury
10/9/92 Blaggers ITA and Joeyfat
The White Horse, Hampstead, London

I'd continually send out Joeyfat demos and get us gigs, and this meant we received more press, and that got us onto even more 'indie circuit' type shows. Some were better than others, of course. One good indie club night was the Xpose in Canterbury, usually held at the Penny Theatre. They put on some well-known indie bands before they'd ever been heard of, including Radiohead and Reef, and we ended up playing for them quite a few times. Our first trip would be to support a band called Gravity. They were an accomplished Brit-pop type of thing that no-one seems to have heard of, but I remember as actually being pretty good. Whenever we went over to Canterbury we'd try to arrive early and wander around the town, checking out the records, comics and skate shops there, before grabbing a burger and usually playing a great gig. We went back quite a few times to a few different venues.

Next week we headed up to town to play with the Blaggers again, this time at The White Horse in Hampstead. We played to a packed house as the Blaggers were getting pretty big by then, both in the press and literally; The Blaggers I.T.A. had swollen to nine people in the band. They were writing songs for and preparing to record their third album for Words of Warning. It would be called 'United Colours of Blaggers ITA', after the Benetton advertisements you'd see everywhere on TV and billboards, and would come out early in '93. I remember a lot of people had a copy of it and you'd see it for sale in all the punk distros at London shows. This release even made it into the indie charts and almost unbelievably there were rumours going around that the band had started to negotiate a deal with EMI of all labels!

Sure enough later that year they did sign to the major label and were promptly labelled sell-outs by most of the punk scene. Including their fellow anarcho punks Chumbawamba, who later themselves signed to EMI for their '97 single 'Tubthumping', the major label reps must have been pissing themselves at that! Despite this, the band argued that using corporate money to spread their political message to more people was a great thing, an operative working 'on the inside' as it were. They made videos for the next two tracks to be released, 'Stress' and 'Oxygen,' and also appeared on Channel 4's 'The Word' playing 'Abandon Ship'. Blaggers ITA (the ITA stood for In The Area) also placed ads in the national music press promoting direct anti-fascist action and reputedly passed on some of their tour funds to aid left-wing political groups.

In the summer of '93 the Blaggers went on their biggest tour yet as main supports for the Manic Street Preachers and it was at one of these shows that frontman Matty 'Blagg' Roberts punched a Melody Maker writer, Dave Simpson, in the face after comments about his alleged fascist past. No trial took place, and the court hearing was dismissed, but the incident led to the cancellation of festival slots including Reading and Glastonbury, and a boycott of the band by the mainstream music press, eventually leading to EMI dropping them. After that the next music press coverage the Blaggers would get would be about Matty's drug habit, and then again in February 2000, when he tragically died after overdosing on heroin.

13, Unlucky for some

17/9/92 Sofahead, Gan, Couch Potatoes and Pseudo Hippies
The Rumble Club, Tunbridge Wells
18/9/92 Pseudo Hippies, Strookas and Couch Potatoes
The Playpen, Greenwich, London
19/9/92 Couch Potatoes and Pseudo Hippies
The Lord Nelson, Clacton
21/9/92 Couch Potatoes and Pseudo Hippies
The Shelley Arms, Nutley
23/9/92 Goober Patrol, Couch Potatoes and Pseudo Hippies
The Joiners, Southampton
24/9/92 Couch Potatoes and Pseudo Hippies
The 101 Club, East Grinstead (Final show with original Couchies
line-up)

We were out playing shows constantly around this time and had another run coming up for Couch Potatoes. The Pseudo Hippies had helped book the gigs and would play them all with us as they had a great new demo tape doing the rounds called 'Zum Gali Gali'. It had five incredibly catchy pop-punk tunes on it. 'The Na Na Song', 'Bubblegum', 'Why'd you leave?', 'Hey you!' and 'A.P.L.S'. The first four of these ended up being their first vinyl release, a self-titled EP on Nasty Vinyl from Germany. This 7" came with a bright green cover, their large hand drawn logo was on the front with the tracklist, contact info and a photo of the three of them and their cat on the back. Underneath the band photo it said, 'Dan hits the drums, Tom gets pissed a lot, Kris does the rest and Mopsy plays lead triangle'. They had a few boxes of these and wanted to book a southeast England tourette to help shift them. The first show would be in TW at the Rumble Club supporting Sofahead and Gan. It was a pleasant evening and we all sat outside waiting to play, chatting with people as they turned up.

Gan were a UK hardcore band on SMR Records out of Darlington, the same label Sofahead were on initially, as well as Calamity Jane, Yardstick and Hellkrusher. They had a new album out entitled 'Do that again' and had brought some CDs and LPs to sell at the show.

Sofahead had come down from Darlington to play at the Rumble Club as part of a UK tour and had brought Gan down from the north with them. Both bands played tuneful punky rock music but Sofahead in particular had great vocal harmonies. By this time

Sofahead already had two albums out, 'Pre-Marital Yodelling' and 'What A Predicament', both titles being Laurel and Hardy references, and both released on Ian Armstrong's Meantime Records label. Ian happened to be the bassist in Sofahead, and he played alongside singer Claire Sykes (Chapman nowadays, she married Tom), guitarist James 'Wal' Wallis and drummer Matt 'Woody' Woodward, who was later in Kito. They'd previously had Andrew Laing from H.D.Q. on drums for the recordings, but he wasn't at the show as he'd joined Leatherface by that time.

Sofahead played melodic punk with humorous and insightful lyrics, both personal and political, so crossed over several genres and went down very well with the Tunbridge Wells indie kids and punk rockers alike. It was a good show and I'm pretty sure Kris from the Pseudo Hippies tried to hit on Claire before the evening was out, and although he was rebuffed on that evening, he generally had a pretty good hit rate. I don't remember for sure if they played it at this show, but Sofahead did a great cover of Tasmin Archer's 'Sleeping satellite', it was a favourite of Milo's at the time and you should check it out. The track appeared a year or two later on a Snuffy Smile compilation CD called 'The best punk rock in England, man' alongside Snuff, Chocolate, Annalise, Another Fine Mess and a bunch of others.

Sofahead reformed for a one-off show at the Underworld in 2007 along with an also briefly reformed Wat Tyler and the original three-piece line up of Snuff, performing together for the first time in years under the name Pot Kettle Black. And, for any gigging hardcore bands reading this, Ian Armstrong still runs Hidden Talent Booking Agency and books shows.

The Pseudo Hippies had booked us in to rock The Playpen in Greenwich the next day and had roped in The Strookas too. Adam, Yan, Jim and I headed up to town early to meet Kris, Dan and Tom at Café Sol, a great Mexican restaurant we'd often go to in Greenwich and a place that Kris and Adam loved so much they later wrote a song about it on their first record as Wact. We hung out there for quite a while and lost track of time, causing us to arrive at the Playpen late for a soundcheck. Luckily Dave, John and Tony of The Strookas had already set their gear up and checked it, so we were all good to go.

The Strookas played a great set with songs from their 'Summer to fall' EP and 'Deaf by dawn' LP as well as a load of new ones too. What they did was very much in the style of Husker Du, Radio Birdman, Dinosaur Jr or Descendents and I always enjoyed seeing them play. Then Couch Potatoes blasted through all the tracks from our new 'Excess All Areas' album and finished with Descendents and Green Day covers just for fun.

A pretty decent crowd had gathered at the pub and for a London audience they were being a lot more appreciative and paying more attention than normal. This was mainly

STE COLLECTIVE

Forthcoming S.T.E. Events At The Joiners:-

Monday September 7th:- M.D.C./OLDER THAN DIRT/HAYWIRE.

Millions of Dead Cops, Multi Death Corporations, Metal Devil Cokes, Millions of Damn Christians, or quite simply M.D.C., this legendary political hardcore outfit from San Francisco (via Texas), visit the Joiners as part of an extra week of U.K. dates, tagged onto the end of their European tour. Showing our age, some of us S.T.E. people remember seeing them open for the Dead Kennedys, at the University back in 1982 (!) + in London in '87, when folkie Michelle Shocked joined them on stage!! Older Than Dirt play their 1st S.T.E. gig in a while, in the wake of their great EP garnering a rave review in Maximum Rock 'N' Roll (making two of the playlists!!) + days before heading off to Ireland for 5 shows. This should be a night to remember...

Wednesday September 23rd:- GOOBER PATROL/COUCH POTATOES/PSEUDO HIPPIES.

A feast of melodic hardcore!! Opening for The Mr T Experience here last month, the Goobers showed they'd lost none of their humour, or fine tunes. Tunbridge Wells boys the Couch Potatoes, make their 3rd appearance at the Joiners (1st for the S.T.E.), with a new album om its way. The Pseudo Hippies hail from London, promoting a new demo which Tony compared to the Hard-Ons, in 'Suspect Device'. All/Descendents/Cruz t-shirts are compulsory for this one (hee hee!!)!!

"Passivity = Compliance" – Rites Of Spring 1985.

Norwegians Onward who were due to play here on August 19th, unfortunately had to cancel their U.K. tour, because their singer was unable to get the time off - plans are afoot for a possible December visit. In response to the last bulletin's appeal for donations, those fine 'Suspect Device' chaps, have made their next issue + compilation tape S.T.E. benefits!! What can we say other than it's much appreciated + if anyone else wishes to contribute, then please go ahead. Thanks to everyone everywhere who continues to support us...love + greetings...Rich/S.T.E Collective...c/o 15 Sparrow Sq, Eastleigh, Southampton, SO5 3LB...(0703) 617522 (after 6pm)...

Raging South Coast!...Raging South Coast!...Raging South Coast!

The S.T.E. (Southampton, Totton + Eastleigh) Collective was born during Summer '88 (although all of us have been actively involved with the punk/hard-core scene since the early '80's). We are a non-profit making + non-hierarchal co-op + we only work with bands/individuals we feel some sort of affinity with - no commercial agencies or contracts. The S.T.E. is made up of individuals, we don't all think the same but share a common thread - those time-honoured principles of trust, honesty + a sense of community SPIRIT. The emphasis is on COMMUNICATION + the gigs being FUN - something we will protect at any cost. New ideas + volunteers with enthusiasm are more than welcome, so please get in touch!!

£3/2.50 (Unwaged) Goober Patrol...£4/3.50 M.D.C...

Doors Open 8pm...Record/Fanzine Stalls...Friendly Atmosphere!!...

The Joiners Arms, St Marys Street, Southampton, The Raging South Coast!

Watch Out For...One By One...Farside...Green Day...Shutdown...
Exit Condition...Decline + Life...But How To Live It?

because it was a local show for The Pseudo Hippies and by the time they staggered, more than half drunk, to the stage the place was heaving with all their mates. They rocked through every song they knew, and Kris led a singalong that even had the bar staff joining in. It was brilliant fun, a real pop-core party. We all loved nights like that.

Over the following days Couchies and Pseudos played at The Lord Nelson in Clacton, where we were told we were much too loud about five times, before eventually having the plug pulled on us by the barman a couple of songs before the end of the set. Bastard! There was a cool little live review in a local punk zine we saw afterwards that said, "Couch Potatoes played melodic hardcore, not unlike Green Day, and rocked my world until they had to stop".

We also took the Pseudo's with us to the Shelley Arms in Nutley, our spiritual home, then The Joiners in Southampton, a place we all loved and where the brilliant Goober Patrol would be playing with us too. Then onto the 101 Club in East Grinstead, up those steep steps and under the glitterball. They were all good fun gigs with decent audiences and I'm very glad that they were too as it turned out that the last show on this mini-tour, Thursday 24th September '92 at the 101 Club, would be the final show for the original line-up of Couch Potatoes as Yan went off to university in Birmingham again. As low key as these gigs may sound, I could have happily carried on playing shows like this with these great guys forever. It's sad that this was Couch Potatoes last show with the original line-up, but it was a great way to send Yan off to college. Those were brilliant days that I will always cherish and remember.

Pseudo Hippies

Playpen flyers

14, Lard as nails

Just days after those Couch Potatoes shows Jim and I started gigging again with Joeyfat. The first two shows were with those lunatics in Goober Patrol. They were down from Norwich and always looking for fun. Couchies had played with them a few times before and I had their first album, called 'Truck Off!', on Boss Tuneage Records. Although it wasn't brilliantly produced some of the songs, like 'Timothy', 'She knows' and 'Shadows and reflections' still stood up very well. I was keen to hear the new songs from their 'Dutch Ovens' album (also on Boss Tuneage, the album's name being a reference to farting under the duvet cover) that these shows were part of a tour to promote, and sure enough, there was more silliness with songs like 'Paddington Bear' and 'Don't give up your day job'. This album would be more of their catchy pop-punk, just slightly better recorded.

The Goobers were often likened to other UK pop-punk acts of the time like Snuff and the Senseless Things, but they reminded me much more of US bands, or our buddies in the BBMFs with their on-stage antics, or the Pseudo Hippies with their perpetual drunkenness. When the Goobers played it was usually a party and these two shows were really fun, although I expect they preferred Couchies pop-punk mayhem to Joeyfat and Sonar Nation's more serious indie-rock.

Simon and Stuart Sandall were brothers, on guitar and drums respectively, and both sang in a weirdly effective East Anglian country lilt, with Ian Clithero on bass guitar making up their initial noisy trio. They'd all gone to school together and were clearly good mates first and a band second, just like Couch Potatoes. They were all vegetarians, in fact Ian was vegan, but they were far from straight edge, perpetually propping up the bars at shows. I interviewed them for BHP zine just after the 'Truck Off' album came out and they told me that although they played lots of gigs in Norwich, mainly at the Arts Centre there where they'd already played with The Lemonheads, Mega City 4 and Tad, they preferred going out of town to play as they liked to try out new chippies. I instantly liked them.

These guys were nearly as silly on-stage as the BBMFs, and even worse in interviews. The parting information given by Ian at one interview, as he called Stu and Si the 'Divvy

Brothers' and wouldn't let them speak, was "Look both ways before you cross the road. Always wash your hands before a meal. Never go out without telling a grown-up where you are going. Always check your change after making a purchase of chips or beer as some shops make mistakes. Unplug all electrical appliances before retiring to bed. Try to have the correct fare when travelling on public transport. Never walk into a public house wearing a badge that says 'I'm not sexist, but if she's offering I'd give her one' as it may offend the bar staff. Always buy a large portion of chips. Never say bugger in front of your mum. Always be kind and helpful to those less fortunate than you. Never buy a bible on Sunday, it's illegal to do so. Always get a grown up to help if you are using sharp implements. Never stick your hand in a pot of boiling water. Always check strangers' identity cards before allowing them into your house. Never use a wire brush to scratch your bum. And buy our piggin' album."

The Goobers would turn up to venues in baseball caps and shorts, and to hear them chatter you'd think they were lost farmers, country bumpkins that'd taken a wrong turn on the way to the market. But they knew that and played up to it, letting their performances on stage do the talking and then people could buy them a beer at the bar afterwards.

As the band developed, Tim Snelson joined on second guitar to bolster the sound and when Ian left, probably due to an inflamed liver, one of their road crew, Tom Blyth, took over on bass guitar. This four-piece line up was pretty solid for years and I'd expect them to still be dragging their asses around pubs and clubs, looking for free beer and new chippies to try out even now. But eventually Tom left to join the Toy Dolls, along with Duncan from Snuff on drums, and they've been on the bill at some huge punk festivals playing more silly songs, including their own version of 'Nellie the elephant'.

I played with the Goobers quite a few times with my different bands, most memorably at the big Green Day and Hot Water Music shows in London, where they'd play great sets, singing songs about Spiderman, then walk around drunkenly soaking up the adulation. They also supported Samiam, All / Descendents, Rich Kids on LSD, NOFX and Mr T Experience (who they released a split record with, helping to get them a John Peel session when he heard it) so I wasn't surprised when they signed to Fat Wreck Chords, leading to tours in the US.

Fat Wreck Chords was the record label started by Fat Mike of NOFX and when Goober Patrol's third album, 'Vacation', came out on it in '96 they went over to play a big tour in the US with Tilt. Tilt was another great Bay-Area pop-punk band, initially on Lookout Records, then on Fat Wrecks, who were a little bit different as they had a great female singer in Cinder Block. The original brightly dyed red-haired songstress and I'm sure who Hayley Williams of Paramore modelled herself on. They also got to hang out more with MTX and Green Day, Rancid and NOFX, and no doubt ate lots of burgers and drank loads of crappy beer too. They'd have loved that!

All this led to another album on Fat Wrecks called 'The Unbearable Lightness of Being Drunk' and the Goobers had more releases on Them's Good Records, Fixing A Hole Records, Snuffy Smile, Hulk Rakorz, Lost and Found, and Punk as Duck Records too. Their most recent release is out on Tunbridge Wells' very own Bomber Music. They also toured the States again with Diesel Boy, and then went to Canada with Down By Law and The Bouncing Souls, the lucky sods. Expect to find them drunk or dead at the end of a bar near you soon.

1/10/92 Dog Day, Joeyfat and Ugly Beat
The Sir George Robey, Finsbury Park, London

Thursday 1st October '92 was a rainy day with not much going on, but we were off to town again, this time to play at the George Robey. Aidan could pretty much walk there from his flat, but the rest of Joeyfat were driving up from Tunbridge Wells in two cars with a couple of mates and our guitars. Although I'd been to the Robey many times before to see gigs, this would be the first time I'd play there, and as it turned out, the first of many. The Sir George Robey Inn was a large venue pub on Seven Sisters Road in Finsbury Park, north London, more or less opposite a large church that had once been the Rainbow Theatre where the Ramones and the Damned had both played, and Thin Lizzy and Iron Maiden had both recorded live videos. The Robey was your archetypal London music pub, so much so that it appeared in Irvine Welsh's 'Trainspotting', when Sick Boy and Begbie visit, and is also the basis of The Harry Lauder tavern in Nick Hornby's 'Fever Pitch'. Just to confuse the issue, The Robey would later become known as the Finsbury Park Powerhaus when the Mean Fiddler music group took it over, but the Powerhaus we knew at the time was in Islington and we'd played there before.

When we arrived we soon found that this place was smoke stained and piss smelling, a real rockers dive and pretty much what we expected. It was covered in posters for gigs, with beer on the floor, a fairly small stage in the corner and a grumpy soundman. This was all standard issue for London pub shows. Loads of well-known bands had played there before and it was amazing they all fitted in, but The Robey always seemed to produce great shows and this one would be a classic, at least as far as Joeyfat were concerned.

We played between two grunge-influenced indie bands, as any bands outside of the hardcore scene seemed to be at that time, one called Dog Day and another called Ugly Beat.

We'd been practising a lot and getting the set tight with the double guitar attack now that Aidan had joined the band. The songs were sounding even better than before as the sometimes intertwining, sometimes offset guitars suited the texture and atmosphere we were trying to achieve with our music. It also allowed Matt more freedom on stage and his vocal stylings and banter became increasingly left-field and entertaining. He was a very good front man, charismatic and endearing, and Joeyfat were a tight unit behind him. We could go from pin-drop to powerhouse, one moment to the next. Even though I say so myself, we played a great set that night and absolutely blew the other bands away.

There was a review of the gig in the New Musical Express the following week that really just focused on Joeyfat. It was written by an NME journalist and reviewer named Simon Williams and it captured what we were trying to do surprisingly well. It said:

Joeyfat, London, Finsbury Park, George Robey.

"Joeyfat, it's all one word, it's all one word!" So says singer Matt, strolling around the stage as if he blinkin' well owned it. And so he should, as after all the man is (seemingly) nine feet tall, with mercilessly cropped hair and hence just a suggestion of pathological violence.

Without wishing to labour the point this man is positively elongated. He could challenge tower blocks to a fight and win. But if this suggests a discomforting goliath, more awkward than a three-legged donkey who's just been caught shoplifting, the vocalist turns the prejudice with consummate ease. Persistently stroking his stomach helps, grinning to himself is also an advantage, and gracefully leading the Joeyfat pack into Hardcoreland is most certainly the cake underneath the icing.

While the vast majority of UK bands peering across the Atlantic have opted for the slack plaid passion of the grunge brigade (see Bivouac, Edsel Auctioneer, et al), Joeyfat have burrowed deeper into the American turf and emerged with a sound that demands the term 'lethal' and then punches it in the face.

Taking their cue from Fugazi, the Tunbridge Wells five-piece go for the jugular with a jagged edge of sound that confronts as much as it comforts; a tense guitar assault that leaves the senses all wondering and wobbly.

'People' and 'Windscreen' set the scene perfectly, abrupt titles backed up by equally economic hardcore touches. Where so many in their position are thrashing around in search of some kind of Nirvana, Joeyfat aren't afraid to strip down to freak out, to leave holes that compatriots fill with pure bluster.

Jeez, if they were any more disciplined we'd be calling in the vice squad for fear of their propriety. Joeyfat: Lard as nails."

I was pretty chuffed when I saw this review and went to show the rest of the guys. This journalist seemed to actually get it, and there it was, printed in the mainstream music

JOEYFAT
LONDON FINSBURY PARK GEORGE ROBEY

"JOEYFAT — IT'S all one word, it's all one word . . ." So says singer Matt, strolling around the stage as if he blinkin' well owned it. And so he should — after all, the man is (seemingly) nine feet tall, with mercilessly cropped hair and hence just a suggestion of pathological violence.

Without wishing to labour the point, this man is . . . positively *elongated*. He could challenge tower blocks to a fight. And win. But if this suggests a discomforting Goliath, more awkward than a three legged donkey who's just been caught shoplifting, the vocalist turns the prejudice with consummate ease. Persistently stroking his stomach helps; constantly grinning to himself is also an advantage; and gracefully leading the Joeyfat pack into Hardcoreland is most certainly the cake underneath the icing.

While the vast majority of UK bands peering across the Atlantic have opted for the slack plaid passion of the grunge brigade (see Bivouac, Edsel Auctioneer et al), Joeyfat have burrowed deeper into the American turf and emerged with a sound that demands the term 'lethal', and then punches it in the face.

Taking their cue from Fugazi, the Tunbridge Wells five-piece go for the jugular with a jagged edge of sound that confronts as much as it comforts; a tense guitar assault that leaves the senses all wondering and wobbly.

'People' and 'Windscreen' set the scene perfectly, abrupt titles backed up by equally economic hardcore touches. Where so many in their position are thrashing around in search of some kind of Nirvana, Joeyfat aren't afraid to strip down to freak out; to leave holes which compatriots fill with pure bluster.

Jeez, if they were any more disciplined we'd be calling in the Vice Squad for fear of their propriety.

Joeyfat: lard as nails.

Simon Williams

Local band Joeyfat playing to a packed audience at The Chalybeate Forum

And the band played on ...

ABOUT 150 people had to be turned away as crowds packed into the The Chalybeate Forum, the new music and arts centre on Tunbridge Wells common, on its opening night last month.

Headlining on the night were London band Four Heads in a Fish Tank, supported by Jocyfat. The following evening saw local band Code performing.

Mark Davyd, one of the four founders of the centre, said: "It couldn't have been any better. It was a superb opening evening.

"It was packed on both nights and there were no problems at all.

"We had to close the doors just before 9pm on Friday and at about 9.30pm on Saturday because of the amount of people."

The Forum, off London Road, has a film club on Tuesday nights, jazz on Wednesdays and rhythm and blues is on Thursdays. Fridays and Saturdays are rock and pop nights. Mark said he wanted to hear from classical and folk musicians to play on Monday nights, and someone to run comedy evenings on Sundays.

Anyone seeking further information can contact The Chalybeate Forum on 0892 530411.

Joeyfat reviews

press. It just so happened that the reviewer, Simon Williams, would go on to create the well-known and successful indie record label Fierce Panda, so naturally he'd later put out a Joeyfat record, amongst plenty of other great releases.

8/10/92 Joeyfat and Uru
The 101 Club, East Grinstead
13/10/92 Headcleaner, Scissormen and Joeyfat
The Expose Club, Canterbury
22/10/92 Malchiks, Joeyfat, Rife and Live on sky
The 101 Club, East Grinstead
25/10/92 Joeyfat and Cathode Nation
Nottingham University, Nottingham
31/10/92 Joeyfat, Head and Bits of this
The Rumble Club, Tunbridge Wells (The last show we played at the Rumble Club).

Over the next weeks and months there'd be more good reviews in the press and I'd start sending copies of these out to promoters along with our demo tapes. Both me and Aidan were working on getting shows for Joeyfat, and with Couch Potatoes on hiatus we'd pick up any offered to them too, so for the next months we played a hell of a lot.

I remember quite a few good shows in various clubs and universities, playing with a pretty wide range of bands. On the 8th October we played with a band called Uru at 101 Club in East Grinstead. That was on the same day that Rage Against The Machine played their first ever UK show at the Town and Country Club in Kentish Town, London. RATM came back to play the Borderline, Underworld and ULU in quick succession on that tour too.

Then on the 13th we went back to the Expose Club at The Penny Theatre in Canterbury to play with two more up and coming UK indie bands, Headcleaner and Scissormen, at an Eve Recordings special.

Headcleaner were a three-piece with a noisy French drummer, a dreadlocked guitarist and a shaven-headed bassist (called Pid) who both sung. They had a new record out, artily titled 'Au Fou' (meaning the fool, or to indulge in buffoonery) and played a terrible single from it entitled 'Anal Turnip'.

Scissormen were a four-piece with stripey shirts and dodgy hair, and they too had a new record out, called 'Nitwit?' (Yes, with the question mark, I guess they were asking people what they thought of them – and I'm sure the answer on many occasions was 'not good'). They sounded a bit like Mudhoney. Both bands were going for a UK version of the SubPop thing but coming up a bit short.

Then on the 22nd we were back at the 101 Club for a four-band show with three more or less unheard of grunge / indie bands, called the Malchiks, Rife and Live On Sky. We knew Live On Sky from gigs at The Shelley Arms and the singer used to wear his grungy Lemonheads 'Lick' shirt at every gig, and that was pretty much what they sounded like too.

On the 25th we went up to Nottingham University to play with another dodgy indie rock band called Cathode Nation. That was a long day, but a gig was a gig and Joeyfat usually went down pretty well at all the student shows we played.

We had a couple of days off, but as ALL were over on their Percolater tour, me, Adam, and some of the Couchies crew, went to three of those shows to hang out with them. They were still playing all the classics from 'Allroy's Revenge' and 'Allroy Saves' so that was really great. They played the University in Canterbury, The Underworld in Camden, London, and the Arts Centre in Norwich where, of course, the local heroes Goober Patrol were the main support.

Then on the 31st Joeyfat came back to our hometown venue, the Rumble Club in Tunbridge Wells, to play a show with two more indie bands, Bits Of This and Head. Head was our friend Austin's band, a local alternative character with a huge quiff who used to hang out at all the shows and also illustrated the Gotham Tapes and BHP fanzine covers for me in his spare time. Milo (the singer of Rydell) would join Head later on guitar for a while. The whole show was weird though. All through the Joeyfat set Paul, the Angus Bagpipe bassist, was sat on the edge of the stage making toast and handing it out to people in the audience. I'm not sure if this was meant to be 'performance art' and or just 'a show and a meal' but it seemed odd to me. The gig on the 31st October '92 would be important though as it was the last show we played at the Rumble Club. In total the Rumble Club ran from '88 to '92 and saw some awesome gigs. Then, in January '93, we all moved to The Forum, a public toilet and brass rubbing centre that had been re-purposed as a new live music venue. It was just across the road on the common.

26/11/92 The Strookas and Joeyfat
Fairholt House, City Polytechnic, London

There was a bunch of good hardcore shows to go and see all through November, the best of which were on the SNFU tour. SNFU were one of my favourite bands and they'd recently reformed and come all the way from Canada to tour in the UK and Europe, playing sets of skate-core punk rock songs from their brilliant albums 'And no one else wanted to play', 'If you swear you'll catch no fish' and 'Better than a stick in the eye'. The energy at these shows was intense. The band would constantly be jumping about, the singer Chi Pig rolling around, the crowd singing along, and always in intimate little clubs where the band and the audience would just mingle.

The band's name, SNFU, was variously said to stand for 'Society's no fucking use', 'Straight, not fucked up', 'Situation normal, fouled up' and my favourite, 'Satan needs fresh underwear'. I saw them play at the Expose Club in Canterbury, which unfortunately was almost empty that night, The Boat Race in Cambridge, which was absolutely rammed and where we hung out with the band and went for burgers, and the Underworld in London, where my shiny new Vans hi-tops that Steve and Adam had brought me back from a recent trip to the US, got stomped all over in the hectic mosh. Every sweaty night filled me with inspiration again for the punk / hardcore scene. Even nursing a sore head from being bashed on the bonce so many times by Chi's plastic leg prop during 'Where's my legs?' I was thinking about new songs and what to do with the band next.

There were more Joeyfat shows through November too and later in the month, on the 26th, we'd be up at the London City Polytechnic for another student show, courtesy of John from The Strookas, who worked at the student's union there. This venue had a stage with a porthole window facing out onto Whitechapel High Street at the back, but to get up to this stage you had to carry all your gear up six flights of steps. If you were lucky the goods lift worked but we were told that people often got stuck in it between floors and sure enough, that day it was 'out of order'. The venue had a very low ceiling but a decent size dance floor with a big, loud P.A. Another saving grace was its brilliant cafe at the back. It was named Mandelas, not surprisingly at the time, and an ANC supporters plaque behind the counter that normally read 'the struggle is my life' had been changed by some wag to read 'the struggle is my pizza.' John had told us that club nights there could be great and he'd tried to open up a Sunday Night Comedy Club whilst he was there. It eventually bombed but quite a few of the alternative comedians he booked went on to be big. That night, Joeyfat and The Strookas arrived to bring the students some noisy alt-rock.

The Brighton scene

In December too there were good gigs to hang out at. The best of these was the Alice Donut show in Brighton at The Dome in New Road on 4th December where they were supported by a bunch of weirdos called Swine Herd. This show was put on by Mark and Illuminati promotions. Mark, like Johnny Deathshead and Pete MTA before him, as well as Buzz Punker Bunker after him, was one of the top gig promoters based in Brighton. But he was a bit of a mystery to us. I think he lived in Shoreham or Worthing, somewhere out of town along the coast, and he only ever appeared at his own shows. Somehow, he had become the go-to guy for any middle to large sized hardcore or punk bands on tour wanting a south coast show. I was chatting with Milo about the Brighton scene in the '90s and other Illuminati shows that sprung to mind were:

Fugazi at the University of Sussex. This was circa 'Red Medicine', so around '95, and for reasons unknown the show was booked in some giant hall at the Falmer campus way out of town. Unfortunately, it was during Freshers Week so all these eighteen-year-olds who'd just left home were losing their minds. I can remember seeing rugby shirted bozos in the pit, waving full pints aloft whilst trying to grab each other in headlocks. It was weird.

DOA at the Pavillion Theatre. This was a huge and very fancy venue but there was literally only twenty-five people there. Some of them, like us, had gone to see the support band, Decadence Within. This was during a bit of a drought for hardcore gigs in Brighton, post-Basement gigs but pre-Buzz gigs. The promoter must have lost a lot of money that night.

Snuff at the Steam Inn. Again, during the mid-90's HC drought years, but it seemed that everyone came out for this gig. Snuff started with their cover of 'I think We're Alone Now' and within about five seconds all these dreadlocked crusties invaded the stage, grabbed the mic and started bellowing the lyrics, gang vocal style. Funnily enough, by the end of the song the microphone was missing, and the soundman was having a fit. Snuff seemed none too happy with what was happening either (at this point they were on Fat Wreck Chords and had become something of professional band) and they spent a lot of time discussing whether to continue playing or not, during which time the microphone was 'found' and nearly all of the crusties had passed out on the floor in front of the stage.

Agnostic Front at the Zap club. The Zap was a big club under the arches right on Brighton seafront and usually reserved for the bigger acts. I remember seeing Henry Rollins there and a few metal bands that came through. This show remains the one and only time that either I or Milo had seen Agnostic Front and it was weird, not so much because Pete MTA put it on so his band, Mock The Afflicted, played as support and went on playing forever, taking up all the time, but because due to some issue at immigration the AF vocalist Roger Miret was not allowed into the country. That meant that their roadie ended up singing for the whole UK tour. He wasn't a bad singer / shouter, but he kept on reminding the audience that they were from 'Noo-Yawk-Cideee!' in a thick NY accent.

Then there was Rancid at The Beachcomber Club / Fishermen's. This was a big old pub on Brighton seafront, and I think the only show I ever saw there. Certainly it was the most violent show I have ever been to. I loved Operation Ivy and was more or less an instant fan of Rancid too so couldn't wait to see them play when they came to Brighton. This was Rancid's first visit to the UK not long after the release of their debut album, so they kicked off with 'The Bottle', went into 'Rejected' and pretty much played most of that great punky 'Rancid' album. They'd attracted a huge crowd of punks and skinheads and clearly there was some beef because right from the get-go there was fighting in and around the pit. The show was stopped several times and Tim Armstrong,

Rancid's guitarist and singer, kept trying to get everyone to calm down, but every time the fights just started again. The songs we did get to hear were great, all about unity and supporting the scene, but I reckon that maybe we had about half of the set they intended to play that night.

Thankfully, later in the nineties another Brighton scenester called Buzz started putting on loads of mid-sized bands at smaller venues so there were plenty of good gigs to go to or play at again. He also set up a great record store, called Punker Bunker, in the independent shopping area known as The Lanes in Brighton. Punker Bunker was a small store underneath a mod clothing shop, and he put on occasional punk and ska gigs there too. These promotions became known as 'Just One Life' and they put on loads of great hardcore shows, mainly at the smaller venues like The Free Butt and The Albert. We went to loads of these and played at quite a few too, with great bands like Blue Tip, Kerosene 454, Tristeza, Farewell Bend, Sparkmarker and The Marshes.

5/1/93 Alloy and Joeyfat
The Penny Theatre, Canterbury
6/1/93 Alloy, Joeyfat and Suck
TJ's, Newport, South Wales
7/1/93 Alloy, Joeyfat and Your Mum
The Sir George Robey, Finsbury Park, London
8/1/93 Alloy and Joeyfat
The Duchess of York, Leeds

Unlike the previous year's parties we had a quiet Christmas and New Year this time and Joeyfat's first shows back in '93 would be a four date mini-tour with the US band Alloy.

We'd honed our art now and had a pretty tight and intense live set. The reviews had been good and our demo tapes were moving like hot cakes at a fat man convention. Now, early in '93 we had the chance to support Vic Bondi's new band, Alloy, on their UK tour. We knew this would be fun.

Vic Bondi was, and still is, a bit of a punk scenester. Originally from Chicago he was the singer of Articles of Faith, a political punk band with three guitarists from back in the eighties, both of whose EP releases would be produced by Husker Du's Bob Mould and gain AoF quite some acclaim, allowing them to tour all across the States. But when the band broke up he moved to Boston to become a professor of history at the University of Massachusetts.

Always being a prolific songwriter with something to say he'd later go on to form other bands, including Jones Very, Alloy, Report Suspicious Activity (with J Robbins of Jawbox and Darren Zentek & Erik Denno of Kerosene 454), Weatherman (with Tom Morello of Rage Against The Machine) and Dead Ending, the band he still plays in back home in Chicago, with Nate Gluck, (Ex-Ensign, Nora and The Fire Still Burns), Jeff Dean, (Ex-The Story So Far), and Derek Grant, (Ex-Alkaline Trio and Walls of Jericho). Vic would also be featured in various punk / alt-rock documentaries such as 'American Hardcore' and 'You Weren't There'.

Alloy had become well-known in Europe pretty fast as the band also featured Pat Mahoney, Roger Marbury and Colin Sears, all ex-Dag Nasty, and their first album 'Eliminate' was out on Bitzcore, a popular German hardcore label at the time. They were in Europe to promote their second album, imaginatively titled 'Alloy', but packed with classic hardcore punk songs. They really knew how to produce intelligent lyrics and powerful music. This was the first of two great Alloy albums released on Engine Records, 'Alloy' and 'Paper Thin Front'.

We were stoked to be playing with these guys and we headed over to Canterbury for our first show with them at The Penny Theatre. This was an awesome venue to play, and we'd been there many times before. The Americans were clearly impressed by the history of the town and the venue, so we sat at the bar with them discussing the local history as much as politics or music.

The Penny Theatre was an ancient old venue, originally known as the Alexandra Music Hall, it had been in operation since the mid-1700s and the entire inside, stage, seats, stalls, balconies, was all painted light blue. It was reputedly haunted, even cursed, and this rumour came to the fore again as recently as 1998 when the infamous reggae / ska singer Judge Dread died in the theatre from a heart attack as he walked off the stage. According to The Times his last reported words were: "Let's hear it for the band!" When he collapsed, the audience at first thought that this was part of the act. An off-duty paramedic in the crowd realised that it wasn't and attempted resuscitation, but shortly afterwards Dread was pronounced dead. This created another headline to go alongside his addition in the Guinness Book of World Records as the artist with the most songs banned from BBC airplay.

I'm glad to say that there were no deaths on stage that night though, with both Alloy and Joeyfat playing pretty intense sets to a good crowd. I remember the local zine editors, Andy of Fear n Loathing and Andrea of Cloth Ears, both being there to interview Alloy too. It was a pretty late night, which wasn't ideal as the four shows we had booked were all quite far apart and would mean some long days travelling. The next gig being all the way over at TJ's in Newport, South Wales.

It was a long drive over to TJ's the next day, but as we were borrowing most of Alloy's backline, we made it over in a couple of cars in relative comfort. We found the nightclub in Clarence Place and as we'd arrived first went off to get some burgers. By the time we got back Alloy's van was there and they were loading in, so we went over to help.

TJ's was another famous rock music venue. It'd been going since '85 and named from the initials of the owner, John Sicolo, and his late partner, Trilby Tucker. Trilby and John, so TJ's. After a while the place even advertised itself as 'The Legendary TJ's' and I have to say that I wish I'd grabbed one of the posters that was adorning the outside walls, announcing our show that evening.

TJ's is also known as the place where a presumably drunk and high Kurt Cobain proposed to Courtney Love. This was back in '92 and he hadn't lived to regret it yet. It is also where local heroes Catatonia filmed the video to their single 'Mulder and Scully' (Localish, they were from Cardiff). It'd seen a lot of cool rock bands play there already and would see more, including Iron Maiden, Muse, Descendents, The Mighty Mighty Bosstones, Misfits, NOFX, Green Day, The Offspring, Lagwagon, Bouncing Souls, The Vandals, The Ataris, Lost Prophets, (more local heroes from down the road in Pontypridd who became massively popular until the singer, Ian Watkins, managed to get himself sentenced to 35 years for child sex offences. He should have stuck to sheep!) and other local (Blackwood) faves, Manic Street Preachers. Also, of course, a load of overrated shite had played there too, including Primal Scream, The Stone Roses and Oasis.

We waited ages and finally went on very late that night, but it was another great show so well worth it. In fact, I still have a live recording of that TJ's gig on cassette so although I had to wind it up with a pencil to check, I know the exact setlist of both bands that night. Considering how late the shows at TJ's kicked off we both played quite long and intense sets. Joeyfat opened with a new track we'd been working on called 'Lemon King' then played 'The day I realised I was god', which would soon be our new single, followed by 'Windscreen' with its constant strumming in 'A', then 'Spoilt', 'Simmer Down' 'Resolve', another fairly new one, 'Cushion Fed' 'Sugarhead', 'Piecemeal', 'Amusement', '25 Years' and 'People come into your house'. Alloy went on soon after us, keen to get on with it, and opened with 'Unafraid' then played 'An advertisement', 'Forever', 'Without', 'Homicide', 'Run', 'Concrete valentine', 'Hard reign', 'All eyes', 'Iron minds', and finished up with 'Alloy' and 'Eliminate'. It all went down very well with the Newport locals.

As the headline act the Alloy guys had a place to stay with the promoters, but we said our thankyous and goodbyes and started on our way home, leaving Newport past the massive scrapyard and ironworks about three in the morning, heading back towards London and Tunbridge Wells beyond, speeding all the way and getting back just in time to grab a few hours in bed before it all started again.

The next day though I awoke bright eyed and bushy tailed as I knew we were heading up to town to play at The Robey, where this time we'd be supported by a new band called Your Mum. They were a London punk band who sounded very much like Snuff, this is partly because they had Simon Wells, the original guitarist of Snuff, playing drums for them, and Laurent 'Loz' Wong, also known as 'Short term memory Loz', from the later reincarnation of Snuff, in the band too. This could have been their first gig in fact, but they were already very good and had brought quite few mates along. Sean of Rugger Bugger Discs was at the show too, I remember as Milo sold him a Couch Potatoes 7", and this may even have been where he agreed to do the Your Mum releases for them. Rugger Bugger was a great UK punk label with releases by Snuff, Guns 'n' Wankers, Wat Tyler, Leatherface, Broccoli and loads of others. Anyway, they warmed things up nicely with the crowd really enjoying themselves, before we had to go on and disapprove them of their fun. Alloy rocked out and it was another good show, with only a fifty-minute drive home too, speeding along in a battered Toyota Carina estate, even though the bonnet had blown up a few days earlier and was now being held down by bungee cables.

The next morning we braved the M25 again, overtook tractors on our way up the M11, then swerved between lorries on the A1 as we headed towards yet another venerable old pub and music venue. This one, the Duchess of York on Vicar Lane in Leeds, was another that was famous for live bands and rock music. Those that had played there included Nirvana, Green Day, Fugazi, Alice Donut, The Lemonheads, All, Superchunk, Naked Raygun, Verbal Assault, Rancid, China Drum, Snuff, Senseless Things, Goober Patrol, J. Church, Wat Tyler, Millencolin, Girls Against Boys, Tad, Melvins, D.R.I, Corrosion of Conformity, D.O.A, Acid Reign, Lawnmower Deth, Xentrix, Tankard, Muse, Radiohead, Coldplay, Pulp, Suede and Travis, as well as some filler they'd let in too like Oasis, Blur, The Verve, The Wedding Present, Inspiral Carpets and Hole.

The promoter at the Duchess was a guy called John Keenen and he'd been putting punk bands on there since the late '70s. We were stoked to be playing in such a cool venue. The hardcore scene in Leeds had always been pretty good and sure enough this was another great crowd. Playing as main support to US bands when they were over was becoming our main thing and it served us well, usually providing us with good audiences and rarely any hassle with equipment. The local bands warmed things up and we got to go on just before the main act and do our thing before people became bored or tired. It was great, and sure enough, so was this show and we even got paid enough to cover our petrol home.

The Duchess of York closed in March 2000 with Chumbawamba playing the final show. Another great live rock circuit venue closed, never to be seen again. Now it has become a Hugo Boss store. There won't be much left soon for touring bands, can the last person to leave please switch off the lights and turn off the amps?

14/1/93 Joeyfat, Suck Henry and Attichead
The Dome, Tufnell Park, London
15/1/93 Foreheads in a Fishtank and Joeyfat
The Forum, Tunbridge Wells (First ever gig at The Forum)
16/1/93 Joeyfat, Sonar Nation and Purple Slime
Bottoms Club, Folkestone
20/1/93 Artless and Joeyfat
Saks, Southend

We only had a couple of days off after the Alloy tour but started practising again for the next shows. Aidan had booked us to headline an indie bill at The Dome in Tufnell Park. This was another great venue where we'd later play a great show with Green Day, and I also saw a reformed Gorilla Biscuits there a few years later too. At this show we'd have two indie bands supporting us.

First on was Suck Henry, quite possibly an instruction to a smiling vacuum cleaner, and they had a pretty British-Chinese girl singing over their indie noise. Her name was Michelle Yee-Chong and she'd previously been in a band with Lil from Household Name Records called Creaming Jesus that sounded a bit like Die Cheerleader. Suck Henry had a new EP called 'So Depraved' out on Kill City Records and they were trying to shift a few copies of the clear vinyl from a small stall at the side of the stage.

Then it was Attichead's turn. These guys were another indie rock band that I'd first heard on a Liquid Noise compilation that our Liverpudlian buddy's Drive were also on. That album also featured an early Boo Radleys track from before they signed to Creation, but most of the bands on there were cardboard cut-out meandering indie rubbish. I always found it interesting to see if these new indie 'studio bands' could pull it off live. Usually, they couldn't.

Joeyfat could and we rocked out. Playing in London was becoming like a hometown show for us now, partly thanks to Aidan's constant booking and promotions, but also as there were quite a few friendly faces in the crowd to cheer us on. I saw several good reviews of this show in the indie zines over the next weeks and months.

The very next day we would be playing the first ever show at the newly opened Forum in Tunbridge Wells. This sizable, detached building on the common in the middle of town had been a public convenience since 1939, and then more recently seen use as a brass rubbing centre. It wasn't the most likely of music venues, but through hard work and sheer determination a group of us had turned it around, sorted it out and now it was ready to rock. Joeyfat were the first band to grace that new stage and we'd play on it many times afterwards, as would all the bands I've played in since. Twenty-five years later they put up one of those round blue plaques outside on the club wall mentioning us and celebrating the venue's first show.

Joeyfat at The Forum

Joeyfat at The White Horse

TUNBRIDGE WELLS FORUM

joeyfat

were the first band on stage.
They performed 'Piecemeal' here
at 8:48 pm on 17th January 1993
Forum founder member
Jason Dormon
played the bass guitar

ESTABLISHED 1993

Our blue plaque

Joeyfat at The White Horse
photos by Jan Paulson

The Dome, Tufnell Park,
London

TJ's, Newport

We went on stage just before 9pm in front of an absolutely full house and opened our set with 'Piecemeal'. It was a good evening and great to be playing back in our hometown to a load of our mates. We bounced around and had a great old time christening that new venue. Even though we weren't headlining a lot of people had come to see us and celebrate the opening of the new club, it was a party and a really fun show. We ended up getting cheered for an encore and stopped briefly to tune up before launching into it, but Matt seemed to be getting upset at something and started moaning at us to hurry up and just play. Someone in the crowd flicked a lit cigarette at him (you could still smoke inside pubs and clubs then) and he reprimanded them with "A cigarette, how very big and clever of you" before going off on a rant about who should and shouldn't take credit for the creation and opening of the new venue. This was not ideal, so we launched into our encore quickly.

The headline act that night were Foreheads in a Fishtank. They were good. Art rockers out of Southend, they rolled and rocked along in kind of an early indie version of what would later become math rock or post-punk. They had a self-released single out called 'Happy Shopper' that was later banned for using the chain store's logo without permission. They also had a single called 'I want to masturbate at Castle Donnington' and another track called 'British Telecom Suck'. Their first album, 'Buttocks', was a big hit with John Peel and their discordant, noisy, awkwardness went down very well with the Tunbridge Wells indie kids who had turned out to see Joeyfat that evening.

Looking back now it seemed that Matt's vocals in the Joeyfat songs were getting weirder and weirder, and it could be that bands like this were partly his inspiration. By the time FIAF signed to Some Bizarre Records for their second album, 'Yeah baby, wow', they had songs called 'Bodily functions', 'Sea Cow', 'Master Butcher' and my favourite, 'Hotel Lobby (Pianist's guide to seduction)'.

There was a great piece soon after in our local paper, the Kent & Sussex Courier, under the headline 'And the band played on...' with a large photo of Joeyfat on stage, it read 'About 150 people had to be turned away as crowds packed into The Chalybeate Forum, the new music and arts centre on Tunbridge Wells common, on its opening night last month. Headlining on the night were London band Foreheads in a Fishtank, supported by Joeyfat. The following evening saw local band Code performing. Mark Davyd, one of the four founders of the centre, said, "It couldn't have been any better, it was a superb opening evening. It was packed on both nights and there were no problems at all." He added, "We had to close the doors just before 9pm on Friday and about 9.30pm on Saturday because of the amount of people."

That was Friday night and on Saturday we headed over to Folkestone to play at Richard Murrill's Bottoms Club. Richard was another local scenester and promoter who also ran the Kent what's on guide called 'Your mornings will be brighter'. I'd been chatting with him for a while about Couch Potatoes and now Joeyfat, and he'd finally gotten around to booking us at one of his shows. We got on well and this would be the first of many times we played for him.

The club was situated in the basement of The Carlton Hotel on the Leas, the clifftop seafront at Folkestone. It was a cosy little venue with a good bar and if you were lucky, you could park right outside and then walk one block into town for some food after sound-checking.

Our good buddies Sonar Nation also played this gig. We hadn't seen them since the previous year's shows and I hoped we'd play more gigs with them. I got on very well with Shaun, the singer, and Simon, the slightly insane guitarist, and they always put on a good show and brought a few mates with them. They were still pushing their 'Surge DT' 12'' and had a new 7" called 'Sleepthick voices' for this gig.

There was also another band on this evening called Purple Slime but I'm afraid I don't remember much about them, just that it was another fun gig. We thanked Richard for putting us on and hoped we could come back and play again soon.

We rounded off this run of shows with a gig in Southend. I'd been speaking with the Understand guys and they'd helped me contact some local promoters, managing to get us on as support for the US band Artless when they came over on tour and played a venue called Saks.

The venue was more like a sports bar than a rock club and although Joeyfat played a good set I seem to remember feeling as if we just weren't quite 'punk' enough for the evening. It was an odd one. There were a lot of people at the show, a few punk-looking kids but mainly skater types, and all the guys from Understand and Stand Off were there too. I wasn't sure why they weren't playing. Maybe they knew something we didn't.

Artless were an American punk rock band, fronted by Mykel Board, and they blasted through what seemed like hundreds of short noisy punk songs. Mykel was an outspoken scenester who wrote a regular column for MRR (Maximum Rock n Roll) and had reviewed our demos in the mag. His band, Artless, had been around for ages now and had a new collection of all their short, sharp songs together on one CD called 'Plugged'. It had twenty-seven songs on it, most of which they played at this gig, with fun titles like 'The joy of anal sex' and 'Ugly people with fancy hairdos'.

15, The day I realised
I was God

Recording the `God´ EP

Back in the Wells the new Forum venue had a great sound desk and some good recording equipment in place so we'd started practising regularly there and wanted to make full use of all the gear. On the 1st February '93 we made a decent quality live recording of four new Joeyfat tracks. This was not just a new demo to send out but more a test of the tracks to help us decide which to record for our long-awaited debut single when we finally got into a proper studio with an engineer, which we'd optimistically booked for a month or so later. First, at the Forum, we recorded 'Cushion Fed', 'The day I realised I was god', '25 Years' and 'Lemon king'. All good tracks but we decided that '25 years' and 'Lemon king' still needed a little more work, so improved them later, and agreed that 'God' would be our first single, backed up by 'Cushion fed' and maybe one other if there was space on the vinyl.

A few days after seeing Rage Against The Machine at the ULU in London on 19/2/93 we finally got into the studio proper to record our first single. We had a couple of days booked over the weekend at Recent Studios, under the railway arches in Leyton, London, with Charlie Mackintosh as the sound engineer. Charlie was a good guy and really knew what he was doing with the sound desk, but I couldn't help but feel he'd be more at home with a pop or dance band. He certainly had his hands full recording all our noise and trying out all our ideas whilst the trains passed noisily overhead every few minutes. Nevertheless, we managed to record four good tracks in just one day, so had a whole day left for mixing and mastering. Joeyfat's first vinyl record would contain 'The day I realised I was god' as the A-side with 'Windscreen' and 'Cushion fed' on the B-side. We'd also recorded 'Sugarhead' at that session too, but it was too long to fit on the vinyl as well, so was just used on our demos with the other tracks.

By now we'd developed quite a strong art style for Joeyfat, with stylised and stark black and white artwork from our demo tapes and t-shirts sporting our logo and band phrases, backed up by menacing stick figure characters and hand drawn bugs and people. This art idea had been taken on by a friend of ours, Ros, and she agreed to provide the artwork for the new 7" single too. She already had a good idea of the sort of art we wanted for the record so got cracking on it, whilst Matt sat down to write the insert sheet text too. We thought this'd just be his lyrics but it turned out to be another one of his interesting ramblings, all of which helped form the band's unique identity.

The outside sleeve had 'Joeyfat, god ep' handwritten on it surrounded by lots of angry faces and the inside of the sleeve had this little story; 'At seven each evening I take a table at the Man's Man Bar. The host winks his eye and appeals to no-one but himself and the tawdry beer flies who perch carefully on their stools searching eagerly for something to be sick over. I have replaced the sheets on the bed with those of a quality newspaper. The pages have yellowed in appreciation of the length of my stay. I have had just one dream, in which I save a berry-faced man from drowning in a vast pool. A woman (his wife?) dismisses my thoughts of weary heroism. 'He won't thank you, he would've been better off dead'. The telephone rings incessantly, just well-wishers about their daily chores. I wish I could change my number – it is forbidden. How I yearn for a letter, unsolicited, with just a matter-of-fact description of the sender and a diagram. A detail of the human tongue and its taste centres would be ideal. O restless hope, the scourge of the cynic! An excerpt - A letter from Club Dowdy'.

This was followed by the record's tracklist and credits, of course, and the JOE001 catalogue number from the new Something Cool record label, that Pete Hoare, Dave Jarvis and I decided to start to put this EP out and make it more 'official' than our usual demos. We also added our contact addresses, Pete's for the label and mine for the band.

Then we decided to add an insert too, this comprised of a sheet of bug art by Ros with another note from Matt, or M. Edward Cole, as he was now calling himself, on one side and a thanks list on the other, replete with a curse at anyone we'd left out and a parting line of 'Our regards to your good taste!'.

Matt's latest missive read; 'From my position on the boundary I can see a small boy wearing a t-shirt. It bears the legend 'Kick butt', a testament to the high-fiving, bully-boy, glutton-era. Yes, they start young, the litanies of American advertising campaigns etched indelibly on their foreheads. This generation knows that everyone can be anyone, a hero in the arena and in the bedroom, a sports car with the chequered flag tied proudly to its bumper. They want you to talk, say something, anything, and repeat yourself please. But there is no patience, the people they know (and especially those they don't) are boring and lifeless because they can't talk fast enough or in the right case. All at once we are a nation eschewing flair whose goal it is to be a Jack Russell snapping at the heels of the thoroughbred. I refuse. I would rather be the horse'.

The first fifty or so copies also had hand drawn art on the centre labels too, most featuring odd-looking flowers and insects, with one or two smiley faces and an Allroy on one. All this I think is just as interesting as the lyrics themselves which never did find their way onto the insert. The vinyl was a simple black pressing but in the run-out grooves on one side we had etched 'There are some people I'm afraid...' and on the other side 'that aren't able to cope.'

17/3/93 Homage Freaks and Joeyfat
The Richmond, Brighton
9/4/93 Homage Freaks and Joeyfat
The Falcon, Camden, London

So Joeyfat had become a very solid unit and we were wound tight as a spring now, with M Edward Cole on vocals, me and Aidan Taylor on guitars, Jason Dormon on bass and James Booth on drums. We had our new single, humbly entitled 'The day I realised I was God', several demo tapes (which we just numbered rather than named) and a new t-shirt too, which had manga style characters on it proclaiming that Joeyfat is all 'just one word'. These shirts were designed by my skateboarding chum Sam Archer, who went on to design logos and record covers for quite a few artists, including drum 'n' bass pioneer Goldie.

We were getting booked for gigs a lot now, not just with hardcore bands but with indie bands too. We could have been playing shows almost every night, but not all the band and Jason in particular, were up for that. Jason and Matt started to pick and choose which gigs we would play and that meant we had to let a few promoters down. Not ideal at all, as any band will tell you. Despite this, our next couple of shows were with another of those early nineties indie bands that the press got behind as they saw some promise that the audiences in the clubs, myself included, just didn't see.

The Homage Freaks were three hairy guys with dreadlocks and one shaven-headed guy tagging along. They were a fairly noisy indie rock band in a similar vein to Swervedriver or The Scissormen but a bit punkier than either of those. They had live demo tapes from gigs at the Robey and the New Cross Venue, and were in and out of the UK music press a lot but never quite seemed to get a handle on anything before breaking up. We played with them first at The Richmond, down in Brighton on a rainy Wednesday night, and then again, a couple of weeks later, up in London at the Camden Falcon on a busy Friday night. They played what seemed to me to be exactly the same set both nights, even with the same breaks and comments between songs, and for me these evenings couldn't end soon enough.

16/4/93 Guns `N´ Wankers, Your Mum and Joeyfat
White Horse, Hampstead, London

We were back up in town the next weekend for a pop-punk Friday evening at the White Horse in Hampstead. Aidan had booked this one with two bands made up partly of ex-Snuff members; Your Mum, who we'd played with on the Alloy tour a couple of months earlier, and the brand-new Guns 'n' Wankers. As they were all local boys, we knew it was going to be a good crowd.

I'd bought a well-worn but cool looking second-hand van from some surfer dude. I didn't pay much for it as it had already done some serious mileage and was more than a bit knackered, although I was of course assured it was reliable. The van was for us to use for touring, and I was in the middle of doing it up. It seemed fairly sound mechanically, or at least so I thought, as in fact it had already done over two hundred thousand miles so didn't exactly need running in. Most of what I was doing was paintwork and getting the inside ready for a band on tour with all our equipment. We called it 'The Beast' as it was massive and battleship grey. The Beast was a long wheel-based Ford Transit in that slightly older squarer seventies shape with big headlights and a massive windscreen perpetually covered in squashed bugs. It had back doors that were padlocked shut but it also had a side door, and room inside for all our gear. We loaded in amps, drums, guitar cases, and various bags, and it still had room for all of us, quite a few of our mates, plus a sink, a cooker, four bunk beds (two that folded out from the walls and two with cupboards underneath), and plenty of wall space for stickers and posters. It was like a teenager's bedroom on wheels. We all headed up to town in that, initially bouncing off a few curbs and swerving around a bit on the way, but I soon got used to it and we all arrived safely enough.

This was the only time we played with Guns 'n' Wankers and you could hear their influences from both Snuff and The Wildhearts. They were a sing-a-long three chord pop-punk band with loads of great melodies and reminded me of my mates, The Strookas and The Pseudo Hippies. The band consisted of Duncan Redmonds on guitar, Joolz Dean on bass and Patrice Walters on drums, and all three of them sung. They'd go on to release EPs on Sean's Rugger Bugger Discs and later Fat Mike's Fat Wreck Chords. That evening was a big party, and I was happily reminded again of why we did what we did.

23/4/93 Joeyfat and Dune Buggy Attack
The Forum, Tunbridge Wells

The next weekend we were back home in sunny tunny for a show at the Forum with pop-punk kids 'Dune Buggy Attack'. They hadn't brought many people with them, but it didn't matter as the place was packed with all our mates to see us play and pick up copies of the new single we'd been telling them all about. There were quite a few photos taken at this show that capture what a party it was. I still have one of the original gig posters too, which was a stylised drawing of the Joker, pointing a shotgun at the reader and saying "Joeyfat – There are many I'm afraid, that just will not be able to cope". Obviously it had the gig details on it too, and a note at the foot that said 'It's still all one word!'

The Dune Buggy Attack guys were cool and put on a good show, but only had a few compilation tapes with them, featuring a track of theirs called 'Making love to a chair'. They knew of Couch Potatoes and had our demos so went away with new Joeyfat records and tapes too. Later they'd be on one of the Snakebite City compilations

JOEYFAT

god e.P

ROS 13

the strookas

The Strookas doing their impression of Only Fools and Horses

`Deaf By Dawn´ album cover

Joeyfat at The Forum,
Aidan, Matt and David

Aidan with his `Lamey` amp

alongside '90's pop-punkers China Drum, The Shreds, Who Moved The Ground? and Apocalypse Babies.

Joeyfat's shows were still mainly around London and the Southeast but our new EP was out now and we were starting to see plenty of good comments about the record, and our live shows, both in the alternative scene fanzines and the more mainstream music press alike.

Kris Beltrami reviewed the new 'God' EP and said that it was 'Unique sounding hardcore with varied and interesting vocals, and powerful but restrained music in a kind of Shudder To Think or Fugazi sort of way. A very competent release' and Sean Adams at Drowned in Sound said 'Joeyfat prove that they're so enduring for one reason: They fucking rule live'. Even NME had something to say about our shows, 'Joeyfat add rapier wit, nagging chords and a clownish cunning of their own... Therein begins a hardcore show more evil than most'. It was good to see these positive reactions in the music press.

2/5/93 Green Day, Funbug and Joeyfat
The Dome, Tufnell Park, London

The weekend after that we had devised a great way to spend a Sunday, well, that is Aidan had. Along with a bit of help from Christy and Mary-Jane, he'd sorted it for us to head up to London and play with our mates Green Day again. By now Green Day were becoming very popular by alternative scene standards and this show would be at The Dome in Tufnell Park. A five hundred capacity London venue known for putting on decent touring rock, punk, indie and metal bands. It had a large room upstairs and a slightly smaller one downstairs, where we'd be playing. It'd turn out to be a very busy evening indeed, but it started out quietly enough with an easy trip up to town, a good soundcheck, and then everyone just hanging out. First in Green Day's tour van, and then in ours as we actually had more space and beds too, which they loved as no one had been letting them get any rest. They were knackered from all the travelling and crashed out.

They were still the same excited and energetic young punks we'd played shows with the year before, but now they'd bought Tre a clean shirt, had some better equipment and grown their hair a little longer. Billie-Joe had short dreadlocks and Mike had grown long curtains and had to keep flicking his hair out of his eyes. Somewhere I have a great photo of all three of them lying in the back of our van, grinning at us. I gotta dig that out.

That evening Joeyfat would be the first band on, then our chums Identity, who had now changed their name to Funbug, then Green Day. I wouldn't say we were nervous but there was a little feeling of expectation in the air, mainly I think as Aidan had a lot of his mates coming along and we didn't want to be crap in front of them. The sound on stage was awesome though and we'd been playing every week for ages now, so we figured we'd be ok.

I went back out to our van and sat down to do a quick interview with Green Day for my BHP zine, which turned into a chat about their shows in Spain from the week before with a band called 'Trip Inside', and then went on about the customs hassles they had when Billie-Joe and Tre had said they were on holiday, but unknowingly Mike had said that they were working, so they all got bollocked and threatened with being booted out of the country before the tour had even started. Luckily Christy Colcord managed to smooth it all over and now here they were.

The Kerplunk album was out and doing very well, most people at the gig knew every word so we figured it'd be a sing-a-long show, but they'd already written quite a few of the tracks for what would become 'Dookie', and knew they would be leaving Lookout and signing to Warner Brothers. They'd already signed in fact, they just hadn't recorded anything for Warners yet. I asked them about that and although Billie-Joe said jokingly that they'd signed their lives away in return for a stack of Bugs Bunny stuffed animals, they all seemed quite excited about the fact they could get their music out to more people and tour even more. They promised everyone there that it'd be fine, they were no sell-outs. Then suggested we went looking for beers and to see if the crowd was building up yet.

Going back into the Dome we got our hands stamped at the door along with everyone else. The entry price for the evening was the princely sum of four pounds so we didn't want to have to pay that. Once back inside we saw that Funbug were at the bar so went over for a drink with them to calm any nerves. They were good guys and always had a few jokes or stories, especially Jason, the singer and guitarist. He'd set up his amp and was happy for me to use it. They were the first band I'd seen use Marshall amp heads through Orange speakers, creating a fat sound that I loved. His Marshall was painted in luminous pink and green, and sat on this big old style orange cab. It sounded great at sound-check, a really big guitar sound that I tried to emulate from that moment on.

Funbug were the only UK band to sign with Lookout Records. Their first EP, since the Identity album on Damaged Goods, was called 'Tezbinetop' and those four catchy pop-punk ditties on it were enough to secure them the release and then this support. They deserved it though, they were a great band and always put on a good show. Their songs were deceptively simple, GCD three chord progressions, but with memorable hooks and that big guitar sound. They reminded me of Snuff, or Senseless Things, or Mega City Four, but also of our pop-punk mates Pseudo Hippies too. These self-deprecating lads from Redditch in the West Midlands were basically the closest thing England had to Green Day or MTX and they'd later brag themselves that they were the best 'third rate punk band ever'.

GREEN DAY

POPCORE GODS FROM the USA!!

+

JOEYFAT

+ **THE STROOKAS**

THE FORUM

THE PURPOSE-BUILT VENUE
ON T.W. COMMON OPPOSITE THE PANTILES

TUNBRIDGE WELLS

MONDAY
3 rd of MAY
8 pm

Flyer for Green Day, Joeyfat and
The Strookas at The Forum

A while after the 'Tezbinetop' EP on Lookout they released a fourteen-track album called 'Spunkier' on Golf Records. Golf was an offshoot label of Plastichead Distribution and mainly put out imports as re-releases, but also had a few great original releases for some of the more successful UKHC bands like Shutdown, Snuff and King Prawn. The UK releases of US bands they distributed included Samiam, The Get Up Kids, Jimmy Eat World, Chamberlain, Down By Law, As Friends Rust, 7 Seconds, No Use For A Name and Less Than Jake. This was great as later on we could get hold of these easily in the UK at sensible cost for Engineer Records distribution and shifted hundreds of them.

Funbug later had all their recordings, twenty-eight tracks, collected together onto one compilation CD called 'I Still Smile At You' and released by Fixing A Hole Records in Japan. This great label run by Kei Dohdoh seemed to specialise in good UK pop-punk and still does. They have released records for our gigging mates Drive, Wact, The Strookas and Goober Patrol, as well as Pylon, The Shreds, Skimmer, Broccoli and Vanilla Pod too.

Anyway, it was time for the show to get started and for Joeyfat to go on. The place was packed as we climbed on stage. I plugged the lead into my trusty Gibson SG guitar and strumming, turned up the volume on the ridiculously coloured amp. It felt as good as it sounded. This would be fun. Matt and Aidan were grinning wildly at faces in the crowd. Jason and Jim were watching each other as they always did, and then Jim clicked us in. 1,2, 1,2,3,4, and off we went. I remember it as one of the best shows Joeyfat ever played. All three bands were brilliant that night. I'll paraphrase from one of the reviews of the evening; "Joeyfat seem to be improving every time I see them! Their style is distinctive hardcore, but restrained in that Fugazi, Shudder To Think kind of way. Singer Matt is still the hero, very intense, jumping, clapping, twisting, his vocal style is distinctive, and the words seem deeply personal. Joeyfat are getting better and better and deserve more attention, but will the bassist ever turn around and face the audience are the words on everyone's lips". The reviewer added, "Green Day play perfect pop-punk, they are the best in their class. It's a rougher, rawer sound live than their clean smooth sounding recent LP (Kerplunk) and Billie-Joe's voice is pretty wonderful through it all. Green Day are at their best live. It's good fun, friendly and swelteringly hot, but we don't care, Green Day cheer us all up no end".

After the sweaty, fun show the Green Day guys headed back to Aidan's to eat, wash and get some sleep, and the Funbug guys headed back home. We had The Strookas as support for the very next day, when Green Day would come back down to Tunbridge Wells to play with us at the newly opened Forum.

3/5/93 Green Day, Joeyfat and The Strookas
The Forum, Tunbridge Wells
I still have posters from this gig as it had been pretty well promoted at the local colleges and schools over the previous few weeks, but it was on a Monday evening, a school

night, so ended up being fairly poorly attended for what really was another classic show and one that everyone locally now seems to think they were at. Maybe one hundred people at most saw this gig, where Green Day played through all of 'Kerplunk' and much of what would soon become their ten million-selling 'Dookie' album. It was another cracking evening that made me so glad to be in a band. Most of the audience were our mates and we had even more time on stage than the previous night. The Forum stage was high enough so that everyone could see, and we had all our own equipment already set up as we regularly practised there now, so the mix was exactly how we wanted it and sounded awesome.

All three bands played really good sets. The Strookas started off a little nervously but soon got into it and rocked out, probably the best I'd seen them up to that point. Then we went on and played a couple of newer songs that we'd been working on, 'My life as a counter-puncher' and 'Perfumery Incendiary', a particular favourite of mine and a track that made it onto the 'Unwilling Astronaut' album a few years later, alongside 'Piecemeal' and 'The day I realised I was god', both of which we also played that evening.

Green Day were absolutely brilliant though, just the three of them managing to fill the stage, jumping around, getting everyone to clap and sing along, turning the gig into pop-punk paradise. Starting with '2000 Light Years Away', dedicating 'Christie Road' to Christy Colcord again, stopping, starting and teaching everyone the chorus to 'Welcome to Paradise', blasting through older hits like 'At The Library', 'Paper Lanterns' and 'Disappearing Boy', also 'Only of you' (which we decided not to cover this time!) It was just a superb show. Practically a Green Day 'greatest hits' set. I wish all our gigs were like this one.

I'd always loved the 'Slappy' and '1000 hours' EPs and knew pretty much every note of the '39 Smooth' album too, thinking that it could hardly be bettered for sickly sweet pop-punk love songs, but 'Kerplunk' stepped it up another gear. Green Day's music was maturing even if they weren't. Mike told me that after their last US tour, when they released 'Kerplunk', its first pressing sold out of all ten thousand copies instantly and became by far the biggest selling release on Lookout Records. Lawrence didn't know what to do and had to get more copies pressed fast and bring in more people to help with packing and shipping. It was just such a massive release for a small independent label. When 'Kerplunk' was re-released later, on Reprise and Epitaph, it went on to sell over four million copies.

Tre said that they wanted to call the new album 'Liquid Dookie' after all getting diarrhoea on their last tour, but Warner's didn't think much of that, so it was shortened to just 'Dookie'. Other than that small concession the band were pretty intent that nothing would change them going forward, despite being on a major label. The next year when 'Dookie' was released pop-punk pretty much took over from grunge as the mainstream alt-rock style on the radio.

The next day after the Forum show, Green Day were heading back up to London to hang out with Christy and Aidan and celebrate Mike's 21st birthday. Then they were all going up to Wigan to play at The Cricketers with our mates Jailcell Recipes. I wanted to go with them but couldn't because we had more awesome gigs booked. Joeyfat had been offered the support slot on the first three shows of Down By Law's UK tour and I'd jumped at that. But of course, it started the very next day.

16, Breaking the beast

4/5/93 Down By Law and Joeyfat
The Joiners, Southampton
5/5/93 Down by Law, Joeyfat and Your Mum
The Underworld, Camden, London
6/5/93 Down by Law, Joeyfat and The Park
The Richmond, Brighton

Joeyfat were booked to play on Tuesday, Wednesday and Thursday with Down By Law at the Joiners, Underworld and Richmond respectively. I think we could have played more of the tour, and I'd have loved to, certainly over the weekend too, but Jason had to be back to work at The Forum and Aidan had to be at the hospital in London (he was a nurse) so we couldn't really head up north. This was a shame as Samiam were playing some of the later dates too and they were another one of my favourite bands. It was unavoidable though and I was just stoked that we were getting offered so many good shows. I cleaned the sweat off my guitar from the previous night, helped load our gear into The Beast and we all headed towards Southampton to see Rich and our STE collective mates at The Joiners.

From my house in Tunbridge Wells to the doors of The Joiners in Southampton was exactly 100 miles. I'd been there so many times before to see shows and had measured the trip on my car's mileometer. We could go around the M25 and down the M3, but we usually went down the A26 and then along the coast on the A27, sometimes stopping to pick up more people or grab some fish and chips in Brighton. It took the best part of two hours in the van and during that time we'd have to repeatedly re-tape the tax disc to the windscreen when it fell off, try to get cassettes to play in the dodgy dashboard stereo, hoping they didn't get stuck, again, and between songs annoy each other with whatever the latest nonsense we could think of was. It was my van, so I commandeered the stereo and we had Pegboy on for this trip. 'Three Chord Monte' and 'Strong Reaction' on a loop. They are great records to drive to, or dance around to, or come to that, just sit around and listen to. When we finally arrived at The Joiners there was already a van squeezed down the side of the pub with its doors open, and there was Dave Smalley, along with the rest of Down By Law, loading in equipment.

We said our hello's to the STE guys, and also Tony and Gaz, running the Suspect Device stall, and helped load in, quickly finding out that all we needed to have brought with us was our amp heads, snare and cymbals. In one way this was great as it meant easier set up and less to carry, but in another way it wasn't such good news as it also meant not having the sound we were used to at practises for the show, as well as having to worry all night about the rest of our gear getting stolen from the van. This wasn't such an issue at The Joiners though as we could pull our van in tight at the side of the venue when everyone was in. The community there was pretty solid, so our gear was safe. Also, the DBL tour equipment was really good and as they were fine with us using it, we got chatting to the band as they set up for soundcheck.

It wasn't the 'Down By Law' and 'Blue' line-up I was expecting, with Chris Bagarozzi (ex-Clawhammer), on guitar and Ed Urlik and Dave Naz (the two Chemical People guys) as the rhythm section. It was Dave Smalley, singing, of course, but with Mark Philips from That's It on guitar, Pat Hoed from Left Insane on bass and a very young Hunter Oswald on drums. Hunter was just nineteen and had moved out to L.A. to join Down By Law. He was clearly loving every moment of it. They were all friendly enough and we got on very well, sharing equipment and a few beers over the next three gigs. But maybe they didn't get on so well themselves as the line-up changed again after this tour and before DBL recorded their next release, in '94 for Epitaph Records, their great album 'PunkRockAcademyFightSong'.

This would be the STE collective's forty-seventh show and there were flyers all around for it with a picture of some cops dragging some poor sod off for a beating. The flyer read; Tuesday May 4th, Down By Law from USA, Ex-Dag Nasty, All and DYS! Joeyfat the UK's best new band! Joiners, St Mary's Street, Southampton. 8pm, come early. Stalls and hardcore tunes. £3.50 on the door, or £3 for UB40s and students. That was very generous of them I thought – the part about the UK's best new band. We'd better live up to it. There was no local support tonight, as was normal at STE shows, just us and Down By Law, but that gave us plenty of time to rock.

We played a set of some newer tracks including 'My life as a counterpuncher', 'Perfumery Incendiary', 'Lemon King' and '25 Years' as well as our older faves, 'The day I realised I was god', 'Cushion Fed' 'Piecemeal' and 'People come into your house', then finished with our cover of Alice Donut's 'Egg' followed by a thumping version of 'Simmer Down'. We could have played for longer but that was a tight ten-track set that we, and everyone I spoke with there at least, seemed to really enjoy. Now we could pack our guitars away and just concentrate on watching Down By Law.

Down By Law played a great set with all the best songs from their first two albums, plus a couple of covers thrown in too, one of which was a crunchy, rocky version of the Proclaimers '500 miles' which made it onto their next record. It was a great gig and I was already looking forward to the next one as we thanked everyone, packed up and headed home.

The journey back was a long one though with The Beast making some interesting noises and conking out on us several times along the south coast. Sometime just after Brighton, and during 'The Best of R.E.M' with all the good stuff from the IRS Records years, the normally reliable Beast started to smoke and make really odd noises. By the time we'd reached Lewes, just along the coast, the van was over-heating and clearly knackered. I pulled into a garage just through the Cuilfail Tunnel and lifted up the smoking and steaming bonnet to have a poke around, but with none of us being very mechanically minded, this didn't get us too far.

We didn't have AA cover or anything like that and we couldn't get a tow until the morning. It was late but I called around and luckily my brother answered. He came out to grab us and save the day. First he dropped Milo off in Barcombe with most of the merch and gear, then we managed to fit seven people into his old Merc, running it almost on the axles all the way back to Tunbridge Wells. I'd parked The Beast at the back of the lot, well out of the way and the garage were cool with it, which was a good job, as it took me two days to arrange to get the van back to a garage in Tunbridge Wells, where it ended up having to have a replacement engine, which took me another week or so to find from a scrapyard. I'd need to get the beastie back up and running in time for our next trip out, but for the next couple of shows I had to borrow my mum's car.

The next day we were all meeting again up in London at The Underworld. This was a great venue that I'd seen bands play at many times before, but this would be the first time we'd play there. It was a rock club in the basement of The World's End pub in Camden High Street and was well known by punkers and metallers alike. It held about 500 people and was on the tour circuit for any mid-sized alternative rock bands. We were stoked to be playing there.

Parking was a bugger though, it always was around Camden, so I pulled over to let the guys jump out with most of our gear then drove around the one-way system looking for a place to park. By the time I'd found one and then wandered back, guitar case in one hand and bag of leads, pedals and demo tapes in the other, they were already waiting for me to soundcheck.

The Underworld had a cosy little backstage area where the bands could hang out and drink. Quite a few zines were turning up to interview Dave Smalley and DBL, and there wasn't much room back there so we left them to it and went to find our mates out the front. The place was filling up already and I saw a few of my buddies at the bar, Kris and Dan from Pseudo Hippies, Adam and Yan from Couchies. I went to chat with them and seeing my 'Underworld, All Access' pass they took the piss out of me for being a 'rockstar'.

Usually at HC shows you just get a hand stamp or a felt tip cross drawn on your hand, but at The Underworld they gave the band these little blue passes, stickers that you

Flyer for Down By Law and Joeyfat at The Joiners

could put on your jacket or shirt. I wasn't used to that yet and being such an uncool nerd, I was chuffed with it and wandered around with the pass stuck to my shirt, on full display for most of the evening. I probably still have it kicking around here somewhere.

This was another fun show with really good on-stage sound, but a bit muddy out the front I was told later. Your Mum were great and rocked through more of their Snuff-esque melodic punk rock, and Down By Law played a great set with the new songs 'Last Brigade' and 'Break the walls' particularly growing on me, as well as some older tracks like 'Dreams away' and their Outlets cover 'Best Friends' standing out too. It was a bit of a singalong evening. I loved it.

We had one more show of this little midweek adventure with Down By Law left to play, and it turned out to be the best of the bunch. It was at The Richmond in Brighton and the place was packed. Another great venue with good sound, lights and stage. I could really get used to this, playing with really good bands, to decent audiences, night after night, it all seemed so easy and fun. I wanted to support larger touring bands all the time. It was all very rock 'n' roll.

Most of the Brighton crew were at this show, and there were hardcore kids from all around the southeast. It was great to see so many friendly faces. I didn't really see the support band, The Park, as I was sitting with Milo while he interviewed Dave Smalley for BHP zine. Dave was talking about the tour, how they'd gone through Germany and Holland before they reached the UK, and how well it was all going. He loved how much the people in the UK and Europe cared about the music and the scene, and said that to him it felt like coming home. They went on to discuss DBL signing to Epitaph, the music they were listening to, new records they planned, skating, travelling, wanting to make a positive difference, all sorts of interesting stuff, but then Jim came over to get me as now it was time for Joeyfat to play.

We rocked out as best we could, although I swear the stage lights guys was chasing me around with a particularly blinding and hot spotlight for most of the set. Trying to blind or melt me before we could finish. In spite of his efforts, it was a pretty slick set. We were very well practised by now. Then Down By Law went on and played the best set I'd seen yet, ending it with a couple of extra covers, including a great version of 'That's when I reach for my revolver' by Mission of Burma. Not wanting the evening to end we grabbed some burgers and drinks, when we'd packed the gear up, and just hung out chatting. We ended up going back to the house DBL were staying at with the promoter, somewhere up near Seven Dials, and added a few more questions to the BHP interview from our earlier conversation. By this time everyone had left apart from me and Milo, so we said our goodbyes before piling into the car and heading home through the night.

We took a couple of days off after this busy run of shows, but I did meet up with Jim and Jason again at the Forum in TW the next Friday as Samiam and Goober Patrol were playing. I was a big fan of Samiam and had booked them in as they were touring Europe to promote their brilliant 'Billy' album. This had been released at the end of the previous year on New Red Archives and almost everyone I knew could sing along word for word.

New Red Archives was the label set up by UK Subs guitarist Nicky Garrett when he moved out to New York in '87, but he'd moved over to the west coast and set up in California, Samiam's home state, by '90 and signed Samiam along with No Use For A Name, Christ on a Crutch, Anti-Flag, Corrupted Ideals, Swinging Utters and the brilliant Canadian emo band, Two Line Filler. Check out their 'Listener' album from '95.

It was great to see such a good band play in our home town. We all hung out for a while afterwards and I tried to interview the Samiam bassist, Martin Brohm, for my BHP zine, but the Goobers were charging about and up to no good, so as often happened with interviews after shows, he was tired and on a bit of a come down from the gig, so didn't really have much to say.

21/5/93 Joeyfat and N.F.L.
The New Moon Club, Pigalle, Paris, France
I was still perpetually chasing up record labels, fanzines, radio stations, promoters and other bands, sending them tapes, asking for shows, reviews, airplay, tracks on

Joeyfat in Paris

Joeyfat in Paris

David

Jim

compilations, anything really, just seeing if we could work together or help each other, and it didn't really matter to me where they were. I would happily correspond with kids in the hardcore scene all over the world, but especially in Europe as we were all very keen to play some shows there sometime in the near future, and living in the southeast of the UK, this shouldn't be too difficult for us logistically either.

I was exchanging a lot of demo tapes with French bands and labels, some were more helpful than others. One guy, J P Lemarchand, ran a little cassette label called Broken Tapes, and he put out some great compilations that included Couch Potatoes tracks, before eventually helping me with a couple of Gotham Tapes releases too. He introduced me to the great band Moral Crux, for whom we later did a joint release of a live radio broadcast gig, and he also helped me with the live Jawbreaker tape we put out on Gotham and Broken Tapes later too.

Another good guy, Frederic Brasselet, played in a band called N.F.L. and kept going on about us doing some shows together. He was based in Paris and his band, N.F.L., which stood for Nice Fucking Life I believe, were pretty good and knew a lot of the rock clubs there. I wasn't sure anything would come of it, but I sent him a bunch of Joeyfat demo tapes and some copies of the new single and a few weeks later he'd got us both a gig at the New Moon Club in Paris. It was a one-off show on a Friday night, but he said we could all stay at his place for the weekend, so we thought why not. I bought a ferry ticket from Newhaven to Dieppe, and we all jumped into the newly repaired Beast and got rolling.

The New Moon club was in Pigalle, the red-light district of Paris, and was situated more or less opposite the famous Moulin Rouge, the Red Windmill burlesque club. This rock club was at 66 rue Pigalle, just off Place Pigalle to be precise, where we eventually found it after about a three-hour drive from Dieppe and met up with a broadly grinning Fred and the rest of the N.F.L. crew. It turned out that all the clubs in this area were burlesque or strip clubs, but the New Moon was actually very well known for alternative rock bands and Fred told us that it'd seen loads of famous punk acts grace its stage, most of whom were French bands I'd never heard of as he reeled them off. But this was apparently their equivalent to the Marquee, or Roxy, or CBGB. The place was a strip club downstairs, called the Narcisse, already full of seedy looking guys at the bar, smoking and talking, or slouched in big red velvet chairs whilst the girls danced around poles on stage.

There was a narrow set of stairs to the side that we loaded all our gear up and came into this awesome rock club with a low stage at the front keeping you close to the crowd, a long bar, blood red walls with a few arty posters and looking up, the entire ceiling was covered in amazing artwork. It was a huge painting of black angels against a silver sky. It was very cool. We were offered free beer, as much as we could drink, and one of the promoters went off to get a load of pizzas while we set up and sound checked. The N.F.L. guys were loving it, they'd wanted to play here for a while and were telling us, in perfect

English with a French accent, that they'd invited all their mates and although it was quite an expensive door price for a punk rock show they hoped it would be full tonight. We did too.

The rock shows at The New Moon started quite late on Friday nights but I guess that meant there was plenty of time for the punters to go and get dinner, then get drunk or high, before turning up to the club. It was weird to be playing a punk rock show above a strip club. I felt like we ought to at least be a glam-rock or metal band. You could hear the dodgy beats of pop music seeping through the floor from the striptease acts below and the clash of cultures felt a little weird to me. But we were fed, had some more drinks, and were soon having a good laugh with Fred, his bandmates and their girlfriends. None of whom seemed at all conflicted about it.

The place was soon packed, and it was time for N.F.L. to go onstage. They were good, playing melodic punk songs with catchy choruses and the odd guitar solo thrown in, as I think they wanted to be a rock band really. There was a lot of banter between the songs, some in French and some in English, and the crowd seemed to love it, singing along, clapping and shouting. I was excited for it to be our turn to play, and when it finally was, Aidan and I turned the Marshalls up another notch or two, just for good measure and to drown out the stripper's music.

We had plenty of time on-stage and made the best of it, blasting through a strong and slick set. Matt was wandering around holding his head and crooning over the noise we all made, with me and Aidan rocking out either side of him over the heavy rhythms. Jason as usual was playing the bass with his back to the audience, but playing as well as ever and in perfect time with Jim's clever beats. We'd put some serious texture and power into our sets, and this was a good show. Maybe not the jump around sweaty party a straightforward pop-punk band like Couch Potatoes might have brought, but certainly an energetic rock set with plenty of clever hooks and time-changes to impress the musos in the audience. It seemed to go down very well with this more varied, artsy and challenging crowd.

There was no rush to pack up or leave afterwards and the club continued playing heavy rock into the early hours whilst we drank and chatted with the locals. A couple of girls from a French indie rock magazine were trying to interview Matt and Jason, but that was an amusing clash of languages that eventually involved one of the N.F.L. guys as a translator to get the subtleties of what M. Edward Cole had to say over to them. The rest of us were drinking and sorting sleeping arrangements for when we made it back to Fred's.

As I'd later find out, it was commonplace to bring the party back to the promoter's or band's house after the shows in Europe. This meant that sleep was a rare and wonderful thing on tour. This was just a long weekend, but it'd be no different. So as much as I

Joeyfat at The New Moon Club, Paris

On the ferry at Dieppe

appreciated the places to stay and shower, I'd often end up sleeping in the van on tour, in the cold with the equipment, just to get some rest between driving and playing. Not tonight though. At about 3am it was all outside for photographs and exchanging t-shirts, and then all back to Fred's for coffee or beer, depending on your intention. About 4am I found a comfy couch and didn't get up to shower until nearly lunchtime, scoffing croissants and jam with scalding coffee. Then we all went into the centre of town again to do the tourist thing. I still have plenty of embarrassing, or some may say romantic, photos of Joeyfat and N.F.L. in Paris, wandering down the Seine or going up the Eiffel Tower. It's best they remain unseen. We thanked Fred and the N.F.L. guys for their hospitality and headed back to Blighty.

The thing about being in an artier rock band like Joeyfat is that people who got into it, partly encouraged I'm sure by Matt's flowery word-smithery, would write some quite arty, interesting, left-field things about us. Not meaning to be pretentious really, just creative, and often bringing with them a little more depth and character. We liked that a lot, well, most of it, and I still find these reviews and articles more intriguing than the usual short, sharp, shock report in punk terms. It's nice when people say kind things about you, but it's hard to tell where the facts leave off and the poetry and prose begin. Joeyfat were quite happy to describe our own style of music as "Sprout-tending and slugbubbery" or some other such nonsense in an attempt to minimise the pigeon-holing that is commonplace in music reporting. You can't blame the reviewers, as often to review something is to compare it to similar stuff so that people can judge for themselves if they'd like it or not. It was just harder for them to find similar stuff to Joeyfat, and I'm proud of that. As our singer once boasted in an interview, "Joeyfat's aims are to please ourselves and keep being selfish in front of as many people as possible."

Years later, when I was no longer in the band, Joeyfat would split, then reform, then split again, then reform into some kind of alt-music collective with hundreds of members and go through all kinds of weird changes, but there were still kind words being written about Joeyfat. Some of which is true, and much of which is interesting. Around the year 2000 a line-up featuring Jim, Jason and Matt, got back together to play a series of shows to promote the release of 'The Unwilling Astronaut', a sixteen-track collection of studio, live and session tracks spanning the years '91 to '96. Now this is a good album with several tracks on there that I am particularly proud of to this day, so if you don't have it let me suggest that you hunt one down. It was released by Unlabel in a slipcase CD format with the cover artwork of an astronaut floating through space put onto promo postcards at the time too. It can still be found online quite easily.

Unlabel is a Tunbridge Wells based indie record label, originally set up by Phil Avey, who was working with Jason Dormon and the Forum guys, to promote Joeyfat and other localish Tunbridge Wells bands, trying to help bolster the local 'scene'. In fact, there was already a strong punk and alternative rock scene in and around Tunbridge Wells, and had been for a few years, but it was getting more indie, so as grunge and indie, and then pop-punk, became the mainstream, they wanted to take advantage of that and build on it. A great thing about the D.I.Y. culture of the alternative scene is that if a label didn't sign your band, you could just release it yourselves or even set up your own record label. I helped do that on several occasions.

Unlabel did so in a more successful manner than most, with its first release in '96 of Joeyfat's 7" 'Gin rummy for beginners' slowly followed, nearly two years later, by the compilation CD 'Two' featuring tracks by Joeyfat's offshoot band Unhome with 'Par Avion', as well as Rydell's track 'Try 17', Rudedog's 'Give it away', Cove's 'Westward ho!' and fourteen more. The label now has well over one hundred releases out and is still going strong, running a local festival, called Unfest, at the Forum and venues around Tunbridge Wells each year.

After a few years the day to day running of the label was taken over by a hard-working guy named John Bamfield, and although it is very much in Matt's style, it would've been either him, or maybe Phil Avey, that wrote this press release for The Unwilling Astronaut, Joeyfat's first CD album, that finally came out in 2000, a full seven years after we, the original line-up of the band, had broken up;

Unlabel album release: Joeyfat `The Unwilling Astronaut´ CD
Release date: End of May (2000)
Live launch: Saturday 3rd June. Camden Monarch, London.

'A music industry whore writes; Joeyfat make me very, very angry on just about every level you can think of. When first confronted by the hideous five-headed hydra of alternative rock I was forced to point out to its parents that they had accidentally given birth to a beast with no talent whatsoever. The various heads would fix their gaze upon me, smile, and then wink, as if to say exactly. From the lanky bastard Jamie Theakston lookalike singer to the drummer who insisted on hitting the side of his toms, the whole motley crew seemed to delight in antagonising the crap out of A, the audience, and more specifically B, me. At certain points in what you might loosely want to call their career I began to think that option B was the only reason they didn't give up. Their maudlin anthems to an unhappy childhood were set to the kind of art-rock guitar neck noodling that gives music shop assistants a bad name and every song seemed to be in the (off) key of E. Unable to get them to realise quite how awful they were, I took to hanging around at the back of their shows shouting 'prog rock!' and 'Where's the Rock Wakeman?' whilst patting myself on the back at my own witticisms. This made me somewhat of a pariah amongst their fans who all seemed to be the kind of trainspotting, anorak-wearing musos who wouldn't be out of place at a 'What's the best plectrum?' convention. For some reason I've never been able to fathom it appeared to cheer the boys up. Driven to despair by their unwillingness to join the ranks of the unemployed

Joeyfat
the unwilling astronaut

un005

imminent...

www.unlabel.net

Joeyfat

ALBUM:
The Unwilling Astronaut
RELEASE DATE:
End of May
LIVE:
London Camden Monarch
SAT JUNE 3rd

"A Music Industry Whore Writes"

Joeyfat make me very, very angry on just about every level you can think of.

When first confronted by the hideous, five-headed hydra of alternative rock, I was forced to point out to its parents that they had accidentally given birth to a beast with NO TALENT WHATSOEVER. The various heads would fix their gaze upon me, smile, and then wink as if to say "exactly". From the lanky bastard Jamie Theakston lookalike singer to the drummer who insisted on hitting the side of his toms, the whole motley crew seemed to delight in antagonising the crap out of A) the audience and more specifically, B) me. At certain points in what you might loosely want to call their "career", I began to think that option B was the only reason they didn't give up. Their maudlin anthems to an unhappy childhood were set to the kind of art-rock guitar neck noodling that gives music shop assistants a bad name and every song seemed to be in the (off) key of E. Unable to get them to realise quite how awful they were, I took to hanging around at the back of their shows shouting "prog rock!" and "where's Rick Wakeman?!" whilst patting myself on the back at my own witticisms. Whilst this made me somewhat of a pariah amongst their "fans", who all seemed to be the kind of train-spotting, anorak-wearing musos who wouldn't be out of place at a "What's the Best Plectrum? Convention", for some reason I have never been able to fathom, it appeared to cheer the boys up. Driven to despair by their unwillingness to join the ranks of the unemployed and save my ears, I even took to complimenting them as a form of reverse psychology. M.Edward would fix me with an innocent stare and say "Why, thank you".

Well time moves on and, as much as it pains me to say it, when you listen to this album you probably won't be able to hear what used to annoy me so much. There's a reason for this. Somewhere along the way, this tiny, irritating little band who just wouldn't play the game appear to have become some sort of benchmark for everything that's good in alternative British music. Quite frankly, I am fucking appalled. I am haunted by their collective smug faces mouthing the words "Told You So" in nightmares, and the waking world is bloated with pale imitations spewing their half-arsed attempt at "Joeyfatness" out of my radio. If they knew how to play the game properly they probably would have sued for plagiarism by now. Even worse, when they sent me this compilation back-catalogue so that I would spit venom in its general direction and pour witty bile over the very idea of its release, I actually find that they make me burst out laughing and I can hum all the songs. Curses. In the Millennium where mediocrity is a virtue, ladies and gentlemen, I give you Joeyfat; irritating, painful, hateful and awkward.

Sociopaths to a man. I kind of miss 'em

www.unlabel.net

Album press release

and save my ears, I even took to complimenting them as a form of reverse psychology. M.Edward would fix me with an innocent stare and say 'Why, thank you'.

Well time moves on and, as much as it pains me to say it, when you listen to this album you probably won't be able to hear what used to annoy me so much. There's a reason for this. Somewhere along the way this tiny, irritating little band who just wouldn't play the game appear to have become some sort of benchmark for everything that's good in alternative British music. Quite frankly I am fucking appalled. I am haunted by their collective smug faces mouthing the words 'Told you so' in nightmares, and the waking world is bloated with pale imitations spewing their half-arsed attempts at 'Joeyfatness' out of my radio. If they knew how to play the game properly they probably would have sued for plagiarism by now. Even worse, when they sent me this compilation back-catalogue so that I could spit venom in its general direction and pour witty bile over the very idea of its release, I actually find that they make me burst out laughing and I can hum all the songs. Curses. In the millennium where mediocrity is a virtue, ladies and gentlemen, I give you Joeyfat; irritating, painful, hateful and awkward. Sociopaths to a man. I kind of miss them.'

As well as 'The Unwilling Astronaut' Joeyfat would go on to release other albums; 'Ye Bloody Flux' was another collection of older tracks, with me playing guitar on the first seven of them. That came out a year or so later on Unlabel and was a limited edition of just 200 CDs that came in hand-numbered brown paper bags like a desperate alcoholic's fix. Then 'The House of the Fat' in 2003 and the double LP 'Suit of Lights' ten years later in 2013, again both on Unlabel.

As well as our first EP, 'The day I realised I was god', there was also 'Little big man' on Fierce Panda and Love Train Records in '95, and 'Gin rummy for beginners' on Unlabel in '96. There was a split 7" with a band called Part Chimp on Awkward Silence Recordings in 2004, as well as many compilation tracks, live recordings and demos. That's quite prolific for a band whose own frontman said in one of his countless wordy interviews about Joeyfat, that we "Formed in a haze of spite and self-righteousness, armed with a love of their own peculiar talents and a distaste for music careerists. We don't tour, have no schedule for releases and don't have ambitions to go down in the pantheon of rock history, sell millions of records, or have rockumentaries and hagiographies based on them. We're aware that at best that sounds like an excuse for failure, at worst a euphemism for hopelessness, but Joeyfat aren't like other bands or groups or whatever you call them. I know you've heard that a lot, but it's true."

Joeyfat certainly built up a small but devoted following, including the late John Peel, and later recorded a live Peel session for BBC Radio 1 in July 2003 at the Maida Vale studio as part of the 'Two minute men 2' gig with five bands playing ten minute sessions each. The other bands on that evening were Bilge Pump, Charlottefield,

Twinkie and I'm Being Good. It seemed that the skewed spoken word meanderings over knotweed tangled, dozen riffs per song guitars and circuit-bent percussive compositions seemed to appeal to quite a few people, and over time we all played our part and brought something to the mix.

It was great to be so creative and beloved by the indie press. It was around this period though that the newly opened Forum was starting to take up quite a lot of Jason's time and he seemed unwilling to tour very much. We were offered some more great shows, mainly through Aidan, but he or Matt would often turn them down or not be able to make the dates. This would start to get annoying for me as it was losing us many opportunities.

Quicksand had released their incredible 'Slip' album in February and I remember the sandpaper flyers and promo sheets going around the scene, with the great review 'Recommendations are higher than Frank Bough - 9/10 Indiecator' printed on them. We were offered the support slot in London on their UK tour and Jim and I, being big fans, really wanted to play the show but Jason didn't feel up to it. There was a lot of good music about though and soon enough Sense Field were over to play at The Borderline in London. They were another of my favourite bands at the time, they still are, and they had a brilliant new record out on Revelation Records. We were offered the Borderline support, but again, couldn't play it for some obscure reason. I was gutted and getting wound up by this, but thought we'd sort it soon and get back on track. I went along to the gig anyway and was very glad I did, as it was awesome.

19/6/93 Long Haired Lovers, Joeyfat, Green Divide and MMV The State Hall, Heathfield

Nevertheless, over the next weeks we started rehearsing again and writing more new songs for Joeyfat. We thought that the sets we'd played with Alloy, Green Day and Down By Law were pretty damn good but we all wanted to record again so needed a few new ideas. Jason had been working on his eight-track and we all came together to jam in the practise room at the Forum. This wasn't quite how we'd done it before, but it seemed to be working OK and we could make rough recordings at the practise that Aidan could take back to London if need be and Matt could take away and work on his lyrics.

We also had a show booked at the State Hall in Heathfield which was fairly local so all our mates could come along. It would be a 'Battle of the bands' indie night type of thing with three other bands, the Long-Haired Lovers, Green Divide and MMV. A bit of a come down from our recent dates, but a gig is a gig and at least we were playing one, so as usual I was looking forward to it.

The State Hall was one of those large event halls that could just as easily be hired by a church group or a wedding party as it could by an indie band for a music night, but the promoters had done a lot of work and had posters up everywhere. The show was on a Saturday night and tickets had sold very well. I wasn't expecting there to be cake and balloons, but it could still be a good gig.

We took a little convoy from Tunbridge Wells over to Heathfield, with me in The Beast with the equipment and some of the crew, and the other guys in three cars, with as many friends and girlfriends as we could pack in. There was quite a lot of activity going on as we pulled up in Station Road outside the hall, with the other bands already there and loading in equipment. It seemed to us there may be too many drum kits and amps already so we left our stuff in the van initially and went in to see what we could borrow and share on stage to save time in changeovers. When the bands all knew each other this seemed eminently sensible and never a problem, we'd just make Jim promise not to break the snare drum or eat the cymbals and we were usually good to go. But sure enough, this time we didn't know any of these bands and they didn't know us, so it didn't go too well. The first band in had set up all their gear already and were waiting for the sound guy to finish rigging the p.a. so they could start an endless soundcheck of their one good song. The rest of us all stood around wondering what equipment to bring in and where to fit it on the stage. The stage, by the way, was a moveable one that had been rigged from large wooden blocks and looked like it was ready for a vegetable judging competition rather than a rock gig. The stands for the heavy p.a. speakers were holding it together at each end so it looked solid enough, but then the lighting rig was added and ended up so low that it wouldn't be so much a case of Matt hitting his head on it, as strangling himself or knocking out a tooth.

After a while it was eventually all sorted out and we sound-checked. It was decided that the first band would go on last, as they had the most hair, and equipment, and seemed to know the promoter the best. One of their songs was an indie pop version of the Rupert the Bear theme tune, so now we'd all heard it twenty-seven times it was well and truly stuck in our heads. "Rupert. Rupert the bear, everyone sing his name. Rupert. Rupert the bear, everyone come and join (in), with all of his games". I hoped they had other songs too. Then we would go on, third out of four, and before us the other two bands, who were still arguing about the running order with the promoter. We'd each play half-hour sets with fifteen-minute changeovers in-between, so that meant we had to wait until 10pm to go on. Considering we'd been asked to be there at 6pm for soundchecks this was turning into quite a long day. Pretty standard though for gigging bands unfortunately.

The place was filling up now, mainly with kids from the local schools and colleges. There isn't much to do in Heathfield and a gig there was a rare and special thing, so it seemed everyone was making the effort to come out. A few more of our buddies showed up, and disappointed by the lack of cake at this party, we went for a walk around town to grab some food.

By the time we'd come back the place was almost full. The local bands clearly had all their mates there and we could pick out a few more friendly faces too so this might be pretty good after all. This was a party gig so when it was finally time we just went for it. No subtlety or new tracks to try out here, we just blasted out our favourites and a few covers in quick order. During 'The day I realised I was god' Matt decided that he would walk amongst his people and went for a stroll off the stage and around the hall through the crowd. You could see him wandering about banging the wireless mic and clapping his hands between lines and rubbing his stomach whilst he sang. He towered head and shoulders above most of the kids so he wasn't hard to spot, even when he reached the back of the hall. We were chuckling at his antics and enjoying ourselves, and by the time we reached the second bouncy chuggy part of 'God' we were all jumping up and down on the stage in time with the rhythm. "Wrap around, wrap around me, those arms you have, wrap them around me" and before he could get to "I grab my coat, I put it on, I built myself a spiritual platform. I was raised, I was healed, I went home, I had a good idea" we all went crashing through the stage.

The drums didn't fall down so the racket didn't stop totally and Matt kept singing for another line or two. It must have been pretty funny. There was a lot of screaming feedback and interesting notes as me, Aidan and Jason rolled about on the floor. The sound guys and promoters pushed the stage back together as quickly as possible, so we climbed back up and carried on from where we left off. Click, click of Jim's drumsticks and off we went again. "In an envelope clutched to my heart I held some holy things, one lock of my beautiful hair, a finger on a ring. I dug myself a shallow grave and laid myself therein, saying look no further, look no further, I am him". There was no real damage done, it just added to the theatre of the whole thing. But the stage was a bit ropey after that and we had to take it easier for what was left of the set. Matt wasn't too happy about our set turning into a comedy act though and started barking things at the crowd like "Demand your money back". I still thought it was fun but 'Demand your money back' turned out to be the opening line of a gig review that I saw about the show in Spiel fanzine later.

We had a few more practises after that, working on some new songs, but that turned out to be the last gig I played with Joeyfat. About two weeks later, early in July, the same week I'd been up to town to see NOFX at the Powerhaus and then J-Church and Econochrist at the Robey, I received a telephone call at home from Matt saying that the band had decided they didn't think I should be part of it anymore. What the hell? This came as a bit of a shock to me! He said maybe my heart wasn't in it and maybe I wanted to do something more hardcore. Now this came out of the blue, I can tell you. I loved playing in Joeyfat, but I was pissed off about this and wasn't going to stay if they didn't want me. They clearly had something else in mind. We didn't discuss it, although maybe we should have. At the time I just felt incredibly let down, especially by Jim who I'd played well over a hundred shows with, but also by Aidan who I'd invited to join the band, and Jason who I'd written most of the music with. I was shocked. I didn't see it coming at all. It really annoyed and upset me at the time, and it still does a bit if I think about it. But there you go. Things happen for a reason. People change and can be strange, but life goes on. Joeyfat was losing its energy and now its guitarist too. I would just have to come up with something else.

"It takes a little piece of love just to hold it all together and one big idea."

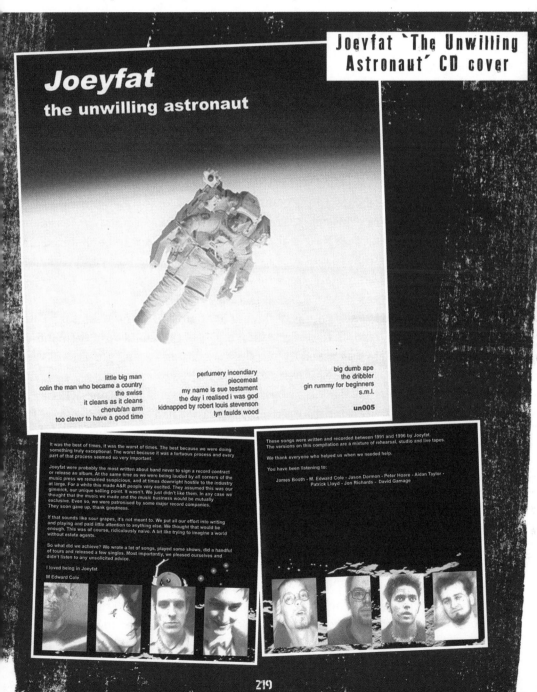

Joeyfat 'The Unwilling Astronaut' CD cover

Joeyfat
the unwilling astronaut

little big man
colin the man who became a country
the swiss
it cleans as it cleans
cherub/an arm
too clever to have a good time

perfumery incendiary
piecemeal
my name is sue testament
the day i realised i was god
kidnapped by robert louis stevenson
lyn faulds wood

big dumb ape
the dribbler
gin rummy for beginners
s.m.l.

un005

It was the best of times, it was the worst of times. The best because we were doing something truly exceptional. The worst because it was a fortuous process and every part of that process seemed so very important.

Joeyfat were probably the most written about band never to sign a record contract or release an album. At the same time as we were being lauded by all corners of the music press we remained suspicious, and at times downright hostile to the industry at large. For a while this made A&R people very excited. They assumed this was our gimmick, our unique selling point. It wasn't. We just didn't like them. In any case we thought that the music we made and the music business would be mutually exclusive. Even so, we were patronised by some major record companies. They soon gave up, thank goodness.

If that sounds like sour grapes, it's not meant to. We put all our effort into writing and playing and paid little attention to anything else. We thought that would be enough. This was of course, ridiculously naive. A bit like trying to imagine a world without estate agents.

So what did we achieve? We wrote a lot of songs, played some shows, did a handful of tours and released a few singles. Most importantly, we pleased ourselves and didn't listen to any unsolicited advice.

I loved being in Joeyfat

M Edward Cole

These songs were written and recorded between 1991 and 1996 by Joeyfat. The versions on this compilation are a mixture of rehearsal, studio and live tapes.

We thank everyone who helped us when we needed help.

You have been listening to:

James Booth · M. Edward Cole · Jason Dormon · Peter Hoare · Aidan Taylor · Patrick Lloyd · Jon Richards · David Gamage

17, We have the technology to rebuild him!

I had a job in a record store at this time, nothing too serious, so I could play or go to gigs whenever I wanted. Even though I wouldn't be playing any gigs for a while now, and understandably wasn't in a rush to hang out at the Forum either, I was still going to shows in London or Brighton with a lot of my old band mates. A few of them were coming back from Uni now and those that had been there all along, like Adam, the Couchies bassist, and now Milo, who would soon become the new Couch Potatoes singer, were always up for going to see a show or just hanging out. We'd be listening to Minor Threat, 7 Seconds and Gorilla Biscuits, or Samiam, Descendents, SNFU and Dag Nasty, and it was impossible not to be inspired and energised listening to that sort of music. I had plenty of song ideas and riffs, and wanted to get a band going again, but who with?

Adam had joined the Pseudo Hippies, playing bass guitar for them, so that Tom, their old bassist, could switch to second guitar and beef the sound up at their shows. I think originally Adam was asked to join the Pseudos on second guitar, but then Tom managed to somehow lose his bass. So as Adam already had a well-worn Fender Precision and was very good on it, he became the new bassist and Tom switched to guitar, borrowing a Telecaster from Kris initially. They had a gig coming up at the Bull and Gate in Kentish Town, supporting China Drum, and wanted us all to go along.

Milo was playing in a new band called Head, with Austin and a few other Tunbridge Wells scene characters. You couldn't even really call it a band, it was very heavy art noise with some screaming over it, but they'd wangled their way onto the show as first support, in a slot they intended to try to fill with just one very long song. I thought that was very brave for a London gig. Somehow, I got dragged into this to play second guitar and try to bring some structure and experience to it all. I wasn't keen at all, but I did want to help my mates and to continue being creative wherever possible, so reluctantly agreed that I would join in if they needed me. I'd be at the gig anyway and had done this sort of impromptu thing a few times before at various shows and parties, standing in on guitar for jams and just freestyling it.

I was chatting with Milo about all this, and he remembered the downtime period for me, before we started the new incarnation of Couch Potatoes, far better than I did. I think I'd blanked a lot of it out of my mind, probably because I felt so depressed about my bandmates letting me down. Or maybe I just wanted a break, although that was highly unlikely as I loved being in a band and playing gigs. Either way, the notes he later sent me explain it well, and along with the Pseudo's German tour notes I wrote soon after for a tour report in BHP zine, this will give you an insight, for what it's worth, into the origins and reforming of Couch Potatoes.

Milo began, "Well, I was in a band called Shortfall. It was just a weekly get-together to bash out a few cover versions for fun. None of us had ever been in a band before or played any gigs. There was my friend, Simon Fox, who had taught me the basic guitar chords on his acoustic guitar. He had some chops and was definitely the most proficient musician amongst us. Also, Gareth and Scott on bass and drums respectively, who were some guys that Simon knew through work. We all had the cheapest equipment money could buy, although Simon's Westone guitar had previously belonged to Toby from the BBMFs before he treated himself to a beautiful Gordon Smith (which would later be played by Mark 'Macca' Wilkinson for a while when he first joined Rydell).

"We played an L7 song, we played a Snuff song, we played a Who song, we would try to work out a version of whatever someone knew the chords to. We also had a couple of original ideas that were a little post-hardcore sounding. I really wanted the band to play gigs and become part of the scene but Gareth and Scott were just not interested. So much so that when I actually got us onto the bill for a show at the Shelley Arms they just vanished. They never called to apologise before or after the day of the gig, and were never heard from again! I have no idea what they do now, but I'm guessing it's not musical. Importantly though, I still went along to the Shelley that evening, and that was the first night I spoke with Dave.

"Dave and I became fast friends and to say we spent a ridiculous amount of time with each other over the next decade or so would be a huge understatement! He gave me cassettes of both Joeyfat's demo and Couch Potatoes 'Excess All Areas'. I loved them both, but for a while was absolutely spellbound by how good 'Excess' was. Some nights it was a case of should I go to sleep or listen to 'Excess' one more time?

"The music was great, but it was the vocals that really did it for me. It's still hard to describe how they affect me, but there's a desperation in Yan's delivery of those lyrics. It's sung straight from the heart and Yan sounds utterly sincere in every syllable. He switches between an almost monotone harmony, where he hangs on the notes just that bit longer than his range should allow, which gives it such a sorrowful feel, then shifts up a gear to more of an angry, snappy bark in exactly all the right places. And those moments when his voice cracks still break my heart to this day. For a perfect example of this I would direct you to 'Weak' where his opening line is 'Why am I not what I want to be?', seemingly shouted up at the sky in the desperate hours of night in a voice wracked with pain and desperation. You just have to wonder what brought him or Dave so low for them to write these lines. Even the album's more light-hearted moments like 'Three' have Yan sounding angry and mad at the world. 'Excess All Areas' is a damaged pop-punk classic that sits perfectly between similarly themed albums like Samiam's masterpiece 'Billy' and All's divisive 'Allroy Saves'.

"A few months later, Simon and I tried again with a new band. I had been spending more time in Tunbridge Wells, both in the final days of the Rumble Club and during the birth of the Forum and had come to know a lot of cool new people. Again, I wanted to be in a band that was part of a scene, although now there seemed to be less of a local scene to be part of. It seemed to me that the closing of the Rumble Club also signalled the end of many bands. Couch Potatoes seemed to go on hiatus after their summer tour of venues around the South, as with Yan away in Birmingham at university the band had been a lot less active. Surprisingly to me, I clearly remember Dave suggesting at some point not long after we'd met that I could play second guitar in Couch Potatoes, which may be why I thought of it as a hiatus at that time. Also, Angus Bagpipe seemed to have called it a day, and the BBMFs played fewer gigs, mainly as Mark too was away at university in Sheffield. Only Joeyfat, Dave's other band, seemed to be representing Tunbridge Wells at all. It was definitely a bleak time after what had been a thriving scene for a few years.

"But I met a girl involved in the local scene called Claire Lloyd (Dave's girlfriend at the time) who played the bass, and actually owned a bass guitar, and also knew a drummer, so that was perfect. The next day I was introduced to a fifteen-year-old Dan Kingdon during his school lunch break. He had been drumming in a church band on a donated drum kit and had a few lessons from the previous drummer there. He was super enthusiastic about forming a band almost as soon as we met, so I booked a practise on a Saturday afternoon at the Forum, which was actually still under construction, but they said we could use the back room for a tenner.

"The final piece in this short-lived puzzle was a singer. Randomly the night before the practise I ran into Duncan Morris, the guitarist from Angus Bagpipe, at a gig and after telling him about the new band he volunteered to come to the practise and sing. This jam proved to be a lot of work for very little reward. First of all, I had to go pick up Simon, he lived the other side of Lewes in the opposite direction to Tunbridge Wells. After dropping him and his amp off at the Forum I then turned around and drove back to Broadwater Down, on the southern end of town to pick up Dan and his drums. After dropping him off at the Forum I had to drive almost to Southborough in crawling Saturday afternoon traffic to pick up Claire, then crawl back across town to the Forum. Luckily Duncan arrived under his own steam. Finally ready and set up, Simon and I ran through the ideas we had, which

Quicksand sandpaper promo for `Slip' album

were really just a couple of Quicksandesque verses and choruses. Claire and Dan quickly joined in and got into the groove of things but Duncan, who had turned up with the lyric insert of the Turning Point album to use as makeshift vocal lines, must have had something different in mind as he said that he was going out for bit and never returned!

"The rest of us stopped after a while to go to a café, but on the way out a few of the guys who were there painting the new Forum assured us that it was sounding pretty good. We wanted to rehearse every Saturday, but the following week Claire decided, for reasons unknown, she didn't want to be in the band. That's when I asked former Angus Bagpipe bassist Paul Skinner if he would like to play with us, but that didn't go so well either. First of all, he didn't actually own a bass guitar. I have no idea why as I assume he had one when Angus Bagpipe were gigging, so I asked Claire if we could borrow hers and it meant I had the long drives and logistical nightmares again. Then, when Simon, Dan and I had set up and run through the song idea we had, Paul said 'I'm not sure about all that, it sounds like an intro or something but not really a song', suggested we scrap everything and decided we should sound more like Sonic Youth. He was in that 'I'm over hardcore' phase, but to make music anything like Sonic Youth you'd have to be able to freestyle whilst staying on the same wavelength as your bandmates, something we clearly were not going to be able to do at this stage. We spent a couple of hours jamming ideas but everything that started to sound any good was dismissed by Paul. It just wasn't working so I put my guitar down and went for a walk, hoping that perhaps by the time I came back they would have found a groove. But no such luck, so that attempt at a band ended too.

223

"Luckily for me though, a month or two later, I was recruited to play bass in Head, a group of random musicians from the Tunbridge Wells area pulled together to provide improvisational musical backing for the insane antics of a local character called Austin. The idea was that Head would be able to get up and play whenever the Forum needed a support slot filled, provided enough of its members were present at the show. I was asked the night before the gig if I wanted to play bass and immediately said yes, despite not having a bass guitar, nor ever playing the bass, or having ever actually performed on stage in front of an audience before, none of which I mentioned at the time. The following day at a very brief soundcheck I met the two other guys who would be playing, a drummer and guitarist from a Kent band called Powerhouse (whose names, I'm sorry to say, escape me now). They gave me a bass, showed me the root notes to play and said just keep playing that until the whole thing falls apart.

"We came on stage to a busy Saturday night crowd at the Forum, the drummer started with a roll and we launched into some super heavy Rollins Band / Swans / Killdozer style riffing while Austin, wearing nothing but a very small pair of shorts, started rolling around screaming his head off and generally going mental. It didn't really cross my mind that I was playing an actual gig for the first time, let alone with musicians I'd only just met, or playing an instrument I'd never even held before, it all felt very natural and I wasn't even nervous. We destroyed that riff for about ten minutes, gradually breaking it down until Austin was collapsed on the stage having screamed himself hoarse.

"After that Austin had all sorts of grand ideas for Head, like more guitarists, he wanted at least three, and getting a cheap used guitar for every gig and smashing it to pieces as part of his act. Neither of these things actually happened but about a month later we were playing again. This time I'd be on rhythm guitar and a girl called Polly would be playing the bass. That was an improvement as I actually owned a guitar and Polly was a good bassist who'd played in a local indie band called Repeater. Again, with no rehearsal whatsoever, Head played hard and heavy, just the same one riff as before though.

"Not long after this gig Head were asked to support South London pop-punkers The Pseudo Hippies on a Sunday night at the Bull & Gate in Kentish Town. This was a couple of weeks before they headed off on their European tour. This may have been set up by Dave as I had only met two of the Pseudo Hippies by then, but he was going to be driving them on tour and asked if I wanted to come along and roadie for them. Despite having a couple of weeks notice to actually prepare for this gig I had a lot of trouble getting in touch with the Powerhouse guys. I tried calling both of them for several days and when I finally got hold of the drummer he didn't sound particularly excited and said that neither he or the guitarist could make that date. Damn. It's possible, looking back now, that the idea of actually planning a Head gig and travelling up to London to play it went against the original intention of the band, and I guess that might've been why those guys didn't want to do it. But we needed a drummer urgently, so I called Dan Kingdon to ask him and, with the same enthusiasm he showed the last time, he said he was in. I felt bad as Dan said he'd enjoyed our first attempt and was wondering if I would call again. He was still only sixteen years old.

"We really needed a solid lead guitarist, but asking Dave was not immediately obvious to me. Not long before this he had unexpectedly and unceremoniously been told by the other members of Joeyfat that they no longer wanted him in the band. It made no sense to anyone at the time, least of all Dave, as the band was doing so well and really seemed to be going places. I remember him calling me after they'd told him, and he seemed completely bewildered by their decision and understandably very angry after all the work he had put into the band from day one. However, when I asked him if he wanted to play guitar in a new band that had a gig booked, but no songs and no rehearsals, I was pleasantly surprised when he said "Yeah, why not?""

"That Bull & Gate gig was the first time I stood on a stage with Dave, but I would continue to share a stage with him for the next ten years or so. It was also Dan Kingdon's first time playing a gig with a band that wasn't in a church! I'm not certain if we all spoke about forming a new Couch Potatoes band that evening, but I do remember that Dan got hold of a copy of 'Excess All Areas' and started drumming along to it, learning all the tracks as fast as he could. Now it must be stressed, the drumming on 'Excess' is fantastic. Jim's hi-hat and ride cymbal work is exquisite. Seriously, playing that fast and getting that much detail in, being that precise without going all jazzy was no mean feat. Just listen to 'Kill It' as an example. The fact that Dan studied this and very quickly became an awesome, fast drummer himself clearly owes something to his predecessor's skills. The three or four songs from 'Excess' that we played initially as the new Couch Potatoes were always great fun, due in no small part to how driving that drumming was. In fact, once we got going, I think Dan played those songs even faster than Jim had.

"So, for a while it was just Dave, Dan and me. We'd hang out and jam ideas in the garage at Dan's parent's house. This didn't last too long as Dan's parents got a lot of complaints from the neighbours, but we made the most if it while we could. Dave would play the guitar and Dan would drum whilst I sang along, initially without a mic, working out ideas. I became the singer because one day Dave just said to me that I was going to sing in the band, I was always singing along loudly to music in the car without any shame so that probably had something to do with it. Singers were hard to come by, he said, and he thought I'd be good at it.

"We went on the Pseudo Hippies German tour and started jamming a few Couchies songs with them at soundchecks. This was Dave and Adam, of course, but with the Pseudos drummer, also called Dan, drumming, and me trying out my singing on a couple of songs, mainly 'Why' from 'Excess'. By the last few dates of the tour, we were going on first as support band, or even having a go during the Pseudos set. It was fun and we knew we had to get a band going. This is partly why it became a reformation of Couch Potatoes.

"That autumn, when we got back, Dave and I were working together and regularly 'borrowing' CDs and videos from a terrible record store chain in town. We spent most of our time there just chatting with anyone that came in who looked remotely 'alternative'. We met a lot of good people that way and this added to our later crowds at local shows immensely. Around Christmas time, a skater guy we had never seen before came in and asked if we had the new All album, 'Breaking Things'. Sadly, we didn't, but Dave was so astonished that someone locally liked All and we didn't already know them, that they got talking and he ended up asking him if he wanted to join the band. Dan Pullin, who at this time had never played an instrument, said yes and immediately started getting guitar lessons from Dave. He bought an extremely angular, bright red guitar from Dan K and practised hard, getting good pretty fast. He learnt more in a few weeks than I'd learned in a few years. Thinking about it now, I'm not sure why Dave didn't ask him to play bass, as that's what we really needed, but I think maybe he was hoping Adam would come back and play bass for us. The problem was that Adam was already busy gigging with Pseudo Hippies, and then Wact, so we needed to find someone else. Luckily, it wasn't long before Dan P suggested his friend Paul Smith, who could not only play the bass like a demon, but also lived on a farm with an empty garage where we could set up all our gear and get rocking. So that's what we did, and the second entity of Couch Potatoes was born."

15.8.93 China Drum, Pseudo Hippies and Head
The Bull & Gate, Kentish Town, London

The Pseudo Hippies were always a good live band, but as a four-piece with Adam on bass they became a much better group and their shows improved constantly. Each time I went to see them they'd honed a track or added something new to the set and they were rapidly becoming one of the best pop-punk bands in the UK. By the time we saw them at the Bull & Gate they were just brilliant. And so were the band they were supporting, China Drum.

Head went on first and we just made a racket for about ten minutes whilst Austin screamed a lot, but then both the Pseudos and the Drum played great sets of melodic pop-core, mainly their own stuff, but with a few covers thrown in too. Both bands playing like their lives depended on it and with China Drum in particular, having come all the way down from the far northeast just for this show, changing up the tempo and treating us to some fast but surprisingly melodic punk.

China Drum were another pop-punk three-piece, very much in the vein of early Green Day, but with a singing drummer, Adam Lee, and two brothers, Bill and Dave McQueen, who played the guitar and bass respectively and sung really harmonious backing vocals. They'd been sending out self-released demos for some time now, usually high-quality CDs with colourful press sheets, and they were getting a lot of attention from promoters, labels and fanzines alike. I was really into them and had written reviews in BHP fanzine several times. They were just releasing a CD EP called 'Simple' and were speaking with Lawrence at Fluffy Bunny, as well as Simon and Ellie at Fierce Panda, about releases too. They'd eventually sign to Mantra, an offshoot of Beggars Banquet, and put out some great albums. I'd urge you to track them down, their best release being the first full album, titled 'Goosefair'. The Drum also played as support to Green Day when they came back over in '94 and you can see Mike Dirnt, Green Day's bassist, proudly wearing his China Drum t-shirt in the video for 'When I come around'.

The Pseudo Hippies were also picking up a lot of interest within the pop-punk scene. Their singer and lead guitarist, Kris Beltrami, would send out demo tapes and correspond with as many zines, bands and radio stations as possible. I had several of their demos, full of poptastic Ramones-style singalong tunes and covered with drawings of smiley beer bottles, flowerpots, rainbows and stick-figure people, all dancing around in some kind of happy Pseudomania. It was a similar style of artwork to that used inside Green Day's 'Kerplunk' release and it could easily be put onto merchandise such as stickers and t-shirts. They had a new release out called 'Girlfriend' and were speaking with Aston about releasing something on his Boss Tuneage record label. Kris and I would share contacts and help each other out as much as we could. Partly because of this co-operation, both the Pseudos and Couch Potatoes demos were getting good radio airplay in Europe and our tracks started to find their way onto obscure euro-punk compilations and benefits. One of his demo mailings, first to Isleif at Bad Taste Records, and then to Matze, the guitarist of a band called The Dipsomanics, soon turned into the offer of a German tour.

Kris had developed this offer through their correspondence and by September '93 the Pseudos were booked to play a two-week tour all around Germany. He'd asked if I could drive them in The Beast and as I had nothing better to do right now, I said why not. They had some merchandise prepared to sell at the shows, so I invited Milo along to run the stall and help out. I needed a holiday and figured this trip would be fun. Six teenage and early-twenties idiots travelling around Europe, just hanging out, drinking beer, playing gigs and messing about. We had some laughs and the Pseudos played some really good shows. I learnt a lot on that trip, even though Adam and I were the oldest there at a stately 22, and although it was far from a serious tour, we took loads of photos and scribbled down a few notes for a 'Pseudo Hippies German tour report' to go into any fanzines that wanted it when we came back. Part of it ended up going into BHP #7 as an article entitled 'Travels with the tall people' and another part of it went into BHP #9 as a comedy piece called 'Playing a gig at a squat in Germany'. Neither of these reports were entirely serious but instead focused on taking the piss out of characters and situations that arose on the Pseudo Hippies tour. Looking back on it now, what I remember the most is all the incredibly friendly and enthusiastic people we met everywhere we went and their beautiful country.

18, Fahren und Überleben

in Deutschland

15/9/93 to 3/10/93 Pseudo Hippies and Dipsomaniacs German tour.
Although I'd played quite a few shows around the UK by now I'd only had one brief trip
abroad, to France with Joeyfat, and what I really wanted to do was tour in Europe with
a band. Ideally it would have been a tour all around Europe with my own band, but even
driving for my friends the Pseudos seemed like a fun adventure and I agreed, saying
that I had nothing better to do at the time, but secretly being quite excited and looking
forward to it. I invited Milo along too, figuring there was plenty of space in the van and
he could run the merch stall. I thought we'd all have a good laugh and a bit of a holiday.
We learned soon enough though that touring with a band was nowhere near as
glamorous as it sounded. It was kind of like a big camping trip but with very little sleep
and lots of musical equipment to carry around. You'd sleep rough, if you slept at all,
and you'd eat badly most of the time, whilst putting up with all manner of irritants, just
for the experience and to be able to say that you'd done it.

We spent quite a lot of time getting the rusting hulk of a tour van that we called 'The
Beast' ready. That meant Milo and I gaffa-taping over rust holes and securing loose
wing-mirrors, adding oil and a GB sticker, then upping the insurance coverage at no
small cost, and loading whatever clothes, equipment and merchandise we could find
on board. These technicalities were at the top end of our abilities, and they all had to
be achieved before we could set off, early the next morning. Now mornings were never
my favourite part of the day. Definitely not a strong point. But this morning we had to
round up the Pseudo Hippies in South London, which was about as easy as wrangling
startled cats.

Wisely we'd headed over to Adam's first, the bass-master general was helping us get
things organised and we'd slept at his place the night before so we could discuss our
plans and start out early. We drove into London up the A20, past the graffiti and broken
windows, deftly avoiding the speed cameras and hurtling around the roundabout
where The Terrifying World of Leather now stands, so fast we almost rolled the van.
We hammered through the more built-up areas as quickly as we could and picked up
Kris, the Pseudos singer and guitarist, from his house in Lewisham. Then headed over

to Blackheath to meet Dan, the drummer, at his house, where we all waited for the last guy, Tom, their other guitarist, to show up. He was late and when he finally arrived it was to a hail of abuse, with a girl on one arm and a six pack of Stella in the other.

We had to get out of town and head over to Harwich as fast as we could to catch the 10.45 ferry to the Hook of Holland. Reaching speeds I didn't think that old bus could achieve, we just made it and the ensuing ferry crossing was full of youthful over-excited antics. The Pseudo Hippies all had beer for breakfast and were getting increasingly rowdy. Dan decided to de-staple one of the porno mags he'd brought along and fling it at some guy in a sheepskin coat on the deck below, showering him in 'special interest' photography and shouting an insult before legging it. It amazes me that we weren't jettisoned overboard by the passengers and crew, but we made it across and were up in Amsterdam by the evening where the drunken antics continued, and if anything, accelerated. It struck me now why Milo and I had been asked to join the away party. Not simply as red-jumpered cannon fodder to Kris as Captain James T Kirk, but also as tolerant non-drinkers. Both of us were straight-edgers at the time, we were the ideal chaperones to these alcohol addled idiots. Obviously, I had the van too, but it had 352,011 miles already on the clock when we left and was on its second engine. It was fifty-fifty at best that we'd be making it home in the same transport we set out in.

The Pseudos had been drinking since that morning and could now freely indulge in all sorts of shenanigans, so we checked out a few cafes and clubs in Amsterdam and it became a long red night. I crashed for a while on one of the bunks in the van about 3am and when they'd all arrived back later, exhausted, we started driving towards Germany. Stopping at a garage in the morning somewhere near München Gladbach, which Tom woke up in time to rename Drünken Gladbach, we filled the van up with petrol and ourselves up with cheese rolls and chocolate milk, then pressed on. The Pseudos first gig of the tour was going to be tonight in Neuss, at the Geschwrister Scholl Haus, and we wanted to find it early and get set up.

The venue was a kind of youth club and it seemed to be commonplace in Germany that the Jugendzentrums were used as venues for gigs. This was partly as it avoided any age restrictions at pubs and clubs, but also partly as the youth centres were given money by the government to provide entertainment for the kids. They could then pay this money to the touring bands and it worked out very well. There was plenty of food, plenty of drink and lots of happy faces. All the local kids came along to see the rock bands so there was always a decent audience and the band got paid too. This struck me as simple genius and something that is carried out all over Europe, but for some reason not in the UK, where bands slog it to a grubby pub and are lucky to get fifty quid for petrol money. Every night of this tour and certainly all those that followed, the minimum guarantee was about £200 and as much beer or fizzy pop as we could drink.

The Geschwrister Scholl Haus had a carved wooden totem pole and a large skate ramp outside where we sat in the sun chatting with the older guy in charge, who Dan cracked was no doubt fornicating with all the younger children as part of some cult. He did invite us into a back room, but only to feed us complimentary pizzas and show us where we could make tea and coffee. There was a home-made pool table too, complete with fishing rod cues, as well as table football, which they called kicker or fuschball, and were all so good at we figured it must be the national sport.

I'd gone to sit outside on the skate ramp in the evening sun with a bottle of Fanta and this was when a rusting old orange VW camper van pulled up and out jumped five real characters. Kris had arranged the tour through Andreas Isleif, the owner of the Pseudo Hippies new label, Bad Taste Records, and they'd organised it all with the help of the band that would be supporting them throughout the trip and providing a lot of the equipment and local knowledge, the Dipsomaniacs. This, of course, was them. We'd never actually met before but were sure they'd all be diamond geezers, as Dan would say, and they were.

Isleif came bowling over first in a black and red stripey jumper looking like a punk rock Dennis the Menace. He was shaking everyone's hands and saying 'Just call me Isleif, there are too many Andreas in Germany'. Then Matze, the Dipsos guitarist, came over too. He was wearing some crazy tight jeans with a bum bag threaded through the belt loops. Yes, a bum bag as a belt, and he wasn't even an aging American tourist. He had a big friendly smile and introduced the band as 'Matze guitar, Marco vocals, Thomas drums and Marco the short bass'. Brilliant, both Marco's were the same size. Isleif, who would be the tour manager, had brought along hundreds of records to sell, hoping to make extra money at the shows, but we were disappointed to see that none of them were the new Pseudo Hippies tour single they'd been expecting. This would be a split 7" with the Dipsomaniacs with two tracks by each band to sell on the tour. This did not please Kris and it all went a bit Spinal Tap for a moment, but Isleif promised him that the records were at the pressing plant and on the way. He assured us that they would join us all soon with some other friends bringing them to a later show.

We helped move all the gear in and sat around drinking and talking while the bands sound-checked. It was sounding great and there was plenty of space to set up the merchandise stalls at one side of the hall, Isleif with three tables of records in boxes, all punk and metal, and Milo with a table of Pseudo Hippies tapes, records and t-shirts. We'd gaffa tape shirts and tour posters to the wall behind the stalls too and it looked pretty good, almost professional. The tour posters read 'Bad Taste Records present Pseudo Hippies aus London mit Dipsomaniacs aus Bremen on tour'. All the show dates and venues followed and there was a picture of a scary clown drinking a beer.

The youth club was filling up well now, not just with all the local kids, but also quite a few punkers in leather jackets and hardcore shirts. Isleif and Milo started to do a brisk

Underway and well on the way!

Before...

Pseudo Hippies
skatecore

...After

Travelling in style

trade on the record stalls and the Dipsomaniacs, who hadn't stopped chatting with us since they arrived, got ready to go onstage. We hadn't heard them play before and were pleasantly surprised by their set. They were great, technically very able (like all German bands), massively energetic and very good at getting the crowd going. They were basically the ideal support band. They played a rather thrashy punky beer-induced metal-hardcore, not unlike some other bands I was into at the time like Gang Green, Tankard and Wehrmacht.

The Dipsomaniacs had great songs, one called 'We want chips', another that was 'Walk like a dog'. One called 'Cancer in my head', which Marco informed us was off their new single, 'Growing up', but shouted "Don't worry, we ain't gonna, so long as you save the teddy" and pointed towards Isleif's stall. Isleif held up their 7" EP. It had a teddy bear on the cover with a chainsaw being held to its neck. Then there was 'Tractor blues' and 'We drink 'til we fall' at which point Marco the short downed yet another bottle of pilsner on stage, and then 'If you ever' which had the classic chorus of "If you ever see me with a moustache, put a shotgun to my head". They finished their set with a ripping cover of the Elvis hit 'You're the devil in disguise'. These guys were great musicians and really good fun. I was very glad that they could rock as I'd have to sit through it for the next fourteen nights!

The Pseudo Hippies would have to step up their game as headliners, and they did. The poptastic foursome played out of their skins, a great set full of catchy three-chord singalongs, much improved now by extra guitar melodies and an even tighter rhythm section too. Opening with 'Hey you' and 'Bubblegum', then their newest track 'The girl at the deli counter', they worked their way through every song they knew and threw in some Ramones covers too, that went down very well. Everyone was dancing and it was getting very hot, so Tom and Kris decided to take their shirts off, much to the delight of many of the crowd, boys and girls alike. They played 'Pretty girl', my favourite track off their older 'Okki Tokki Unga' demo tape that I'd had on in the van on the way over, then 'Dumped again' and 'Why'd you leave?' It was good fun pop-punk, all pumped up for the tour.

The music finished fairly early, around 10.30pm, probably because of the noise limits in this residential area, but everyone hung around. The Pseudos answered the interview questions of two or three fanzine editors and everyone sat around drinking and chatting. Milo pointed out that no matter how hot it became in that sauna, with everyone sweating in their t-shirts, Isleif kept both his jumper and leather jacket on. He also mentioned that Isleif's first words to him that evening, for no apparent reason, but whilst selling records and shirts to an army of girls after the show, were "You like young girls then, yes?"

It was a really great gig and the guys were buzzing, only brought down when we were told that we couldn't all sleep at the youth club that night so had to head back to Matze's house, which was near Bremen, about 200 miles away. It was nearly midnight now and the drive would take around three hours. Tom, Dan and all of the Dipsos were steaming drunk by now so didn't care. They grabbed a load more beers and we climbed into our vans. We followed Matze and his smoking orange VW north up the Autobahn.

The next morning, we awoke to find that Tom had fallen asleep drunkenly against the radiator and had woken up burnt with what looked like alien eggs growing on his arms. We threw him in the shower at Matze's beautiful home and then headed to the supermarket to grab some supplies. We found that the supermarket was closed for lunch, an interesting business model, and they'd left a delivery of stock, in this case beer, in crates outside too. We stole a few cases and went over to pick up the rest of the Dipsos from a club surrounded by rusty motorbikes and rocker types where they'd been having lunch. It looked like a real-life version of a Dumpy's Rusty Nuts album cover. Then we all headed up towards Hamburg and on to Husum, a coastal town about 160 miles further north and near the Danish border. Milo decided to have a go at driving and it was dead scary. He looked straight forward but moved his arms up and down, a bit like the way Postman Pat drives, but this was on a four-lane autobahn with big trucks everywhere. I went and hid in the back of the van where I might survive a crash better.

After a heated Castle Belmont tournament on Adam's GameBoy, to take our minds off of Milo's driving, we finally arrived, at about 5.30pm, at The Speicher. This was a large hall, or literally 'Store', that had been turned into a club, sitting on a rather picturesque dock. We all loaded the gear in, set up and sound-checked, where we soon found that the soundman's favourite phrase was 'More high-hat!' The Pseudos would repeat that ad nauseam for the rest of the tour at every soundcheck. The promoter had arranged enough vegetarian spaghetti bolognese for at least twenty people so we all filled up and sat around waiting for the evening to begin. The Pseudos and Dipsos were already drinking again, Isleif was setting up his record stall, and Milo was meant to be too, but he'd been distracted by a green-haired girl he'd met. She was called Mariella and was from Flensburg, a maritime and brewery town nearby, where she studied English at the local college. I'd cracked up when I saw him sidle up to her and try the classic chat-up line, "What sort of wanker mics a hi-hat but not a bass drum?" but it'd seemed to work and now they were deep in conversation, so I was left minding the merch table.

The Speicher filled up quickly and the guys all played another great gig. The merchandising was ruthlessly swift too, up until this guy with a terrible perm kept on asking "What is this crazy pop-punk you speak of?" He'd clearly only ever heard Saxon or the Scorpions. We got bored of dealing with drunks and even the personas Milo and I had adopted for the evening of Juan and Jose, the new ministers for Latin guitar-based rock on a trade mission out of Brussels, had become dull so we decided to pack up and sometime after midnight about twenty five people piled into The Beast and we all went, almost riding on the axles, to check out a nearby nightclub called the Dornbusch. This club was absolutely in the middle of nowhere but seemed to be attended by everyone in northern Germany. They were playing cheesy euro pop, but it was packed. Matze hilariously informed us that we, "Should not go with the girls behind the bars, as you don't know where they've been" and then, "You know, I am thinking that you guys know what it is to party, yes" before falling into a couch near the end of the bar and dribbling in his sleep. By about 4.30am we'd all had enough and I went to round everyone up, but couldn't find Kris. He turned up at last, out in The Beast, but he was not alone and the van was actually rocking.

We headed back with Carsten, the promoter, to his house to crash out and when we got there Kris checked out the dump-plate toiletry that seemed so commonplace in German bathrooms. He then grabbed the 'super white' by the sink to clean his teeth, saying it tasted like grit and salt, before realising he was brushing his teeth with tiling grout. We didn't get much rest before Isleif, wearing a marvellous fluorescent pink and green jumper now, woke us and said we had to get rolling again.

That evening's gig was to be on an island just off the northwest coast of Germany called Sylt. It was only about eighty miles away, right on the Danish border, but there was no direct route and you had to get a train across a causeway so it'd take a while. We thanked Carsten for the show and drove north again, stopping only to piss and marvel at Isleif's jumper, until we reached the railway station at Niebull where we'd catch the train that would take us and our vans onto the island itself. The fare for each truck to cross over to the island and back on this drive on / off transporter type of rattler was 200 deutschmarks, about £80, and that seemed a bit steep. Although Westerland, the main town on Sylt, was only about two and a half miles away, it was over sand flats and there was no road, so we decided to load all the gear into the Dipsos orange camper and leave The Beast behind. The rest of us crossed on foot via the passenger train to save some more cash and managed to get into an argument with a grumpy Monty Python lookalike ticket inspector on the way.

Westerland and Sylt Island would be hosting the world windsurfing finals in another week or so, and I mentioned to Isleif that it would've been cool if the Pseudos could have played at that, but he said it was a big money event and they were lucky to be allowed onto the island to play at all as a punk band. We wandered down to the big wide beach on this windy and overcast day and there were very few people about but quite a lot of seals basking on the sand bars. There was a beach guard on duty though, who came over to say that we needed tickets for access to the sand and was clearly not liking the look of our crew. So we went back into town and bought some postcards. We were practising our German vocabulary in the shops, with Dan trying to order a Coke, surely the most internationally recognised brand in the world, and still ending up with a chocolate milkshake. Then Milo wanted one too but kept insisting upon a geschmekt, or flavour shake.

Meanwhile, the Dipsomaniacs, whose band name meant drunkards or alcoholics, and who had been repeatedly reminding us that they lived to drink beer and that Bremen, their hometown, was the hardest drinking town in the whole world, had gone off to find a pub to hang out in. They soon found they weren't very welcome in any of the bars along the beachfront so we decided to head to the gig venue, where Isleif assured us that there would be cases of beer in the band's rider. The venue was another youth club, or Jugendzentrum, but they all seemed to have plenty of beer. Once again when we arrived there, we found that everyone was very friendly and delighted to see us. They helped us carry all the gear in and the place smelled great as they'd prepared another spag bol dinner, this time with loads of cream and garlic. It also turned out that this club had a back room we could use with comfy sofas, a good pool table, a TV and a pile of Nintendo games. Peter, the blonde-haired blue-eyed promoter, seemed especially friendly and had set up extra cushions and couches for us to crash on over-night after the gig. He seemed cool to me, but he particularly worried Dan when he said, "If you need anything during the night just scream for me and I'll come".

During a leisurely sound-check I noticed Matze trying to fix the p.a. by coating the leads and sockets with Kontackt, so basically spraying water onto electrical cables. I managed to stop that before he killed himself and then went over to help Milo set up the Pseudos merch stall and get ready to sell the shirts and records with him. Once again, he'd been distracted, this time by a redhaired girl wearing leopard skin pants so tight they must have been painted on, very high heels and loads of make-up. It turned out that she was called Sarah and they sat together most of the evening making necklaces out of plastic beads that she had brought along. Later, ever full of entertainment, Sarah started showing us all magic tricks and someone cracked a line about wanting to have a go at breaking her secret ring. A magician's term, I believe.

There seemed to be a lot of weird people on Sylt Island and they all turned up to the show. It made for a pretty odd but still good fun gig. There was a lot of bopping around and at one point mid-set Milo came rushing into the stage-front throng doing some crazy flailing dance. He spun all around the room with several of the Germans for about thirty seconds and then came grinning back behind the stall to sell records. Afterwards most of the crowd headed home but a few hardcore dropouts hung around and that's when the drunken nude pool tournament began. It was both a tricky, and at times, ugly game as the pissed combatants had to lean right over the table to make their shots. After two cues and the light over the table had been broken, and so much beer had been spilt over the baize that the balls would no longer roll, Tom decided to climb up onto the table and douse himself in Sambuca, setting light to his own nipples and then pubes. He was quite a hairy fellow and his smouldering pubes sent him rushing to the showers, with our host Peter not far behind.

A shirtless Hippie

Couch Potatoes
somewhere in Germany

Here be monsters

The Dipsos had drunk their bodyweight in beer and were challenging Dan, Adam and Isleif to drinking games, whilst Matze, in a drunken stupor, kept pointing at Kris' toothbrush and repeatedly asking, "What do you call this tooth tool?" When he fell asleep, he was covered in shaving foam and had his eyebrows shaved off for his trouble. Without his eyebrows he looked ill and startled for the rest of the tour. Things settled down around 4am when Peter had wisely decided to lock everyone in the back room so we couldn't wreck anything else. It was hard to sleep so we tried to write a few postcards home. One of them from Tom read; 'Dear Mum and Dad, having a kraut snogging, trouser dropping, pill popping, fans are bopping, good old time. I've lost my passport, keys and pants. I'm currently residing with a burly sailor called Bernard in Amsterdam. Have nurtured a long at the back and acquired a taste for spandex. If you see Danny say hello. Just set fire to my groota. All my love, T'. It was addressed to Mum and Dad, my house, Blackheathish sort of, SN3 7DP, and it still arrived!

We woke up at lunchtime and took much-needed showers, despite seeing a weird chemical warning notice on the doors. We went for another wander around town in t-shirts and shorts, despite the fact that everyone else on the island was in Arctic survival gear. The crusty old bastard on beach duty would not allow us back on the beach, saying we were too noisy and drunk yesterday, so after a hail of abuse to him we said our goodbyes to the lovely island of Sylt and headed back across the sand flats. But not before Peter had invited himself back to visit us all when he came to England early next year. Thankfully, that's another story.

The Dipsos had a day off so drove back to Bremen, probably to get some sleep, and we drove down to Hamburg for the Pseudos next show. Kris had asked Isleif if there was any way they could play the Kaiserkeller, made famous by the Beatles of course, as he was a big fan. Somehow Isleif had managed it but said that they'd have to support another band who were playing there that evening. It was only The Mighty Mighty Bosstones! The Bosstones were a great ska-core band, and we were all excited to be seeing them play.

The roads back south were swarming with millions of bugs. Not just your normal late summer abattoir of insects on the windscreen, but it seemed to us like crazy biblical plague proportion type stuff. The wipers were working hard but were not very effective at the best of times, so we had to pull over at a service station and wait for the weirdness to pass. It was probably just as well, as although so far The Beast had been holding up to my constant thrashing of it, it had now developed a strange knocking noise from under the hood and I was getting a little worried so wanted to investigate. While I topped up the oil and water and fiddled about cluelessly under the bonnet, Adam went into the toilettenkabinen and as he opened the door a green and white budgerigar flew out. This was pretty odd we thought. Did one of the truck drivers take it in there along with all the porn?

We grabbed some more 'Funny-Frisch' paprika crisps and 'Kakaotrunk' chocolate milk and headed into Hamburg, but took a wrong turn through the tunnel and ended up in the docks. Somehow, I managed to cross over a freight customs line too and we were stopped by a tall man in green overalls who asked us if we had any tea, coffee or spirits in the van. We said no, just beer and guitars, but he didn't believe us so came on board and searched about, pulling faces at all the smells and sounds he encountered. It was getting ripe in there. He soon climbed back out and gave us directions to the Reeperbahn, where the Kaiserkeller was, and we headed there. At the venue we were met outside by the promoter and told that the show had been cancelled as Dicky Barrett, the Bosstones singer, had a throat complaint. This sucked. Milo cracked some gag about how Dicky sounded like he had a throat problem all the time but it didn't go down well. The guy on the door said they were giving refunds so no bands would play that night, but they would have a club evening instead and we were welcome to go in for free to that. But right then we were starving and wanted to go and find some food.

We wandered around the Reeperbahn and found it to be a total scheissloch. Plenty of deeply unattractive huren hanging around outside shops that all seemed to be called crazy something. There was Crazy Jeans, Crazy Leather, Crazy Gun World, and of course, Crazy Sexy Girls. We saw a poster for a Helloween show, they were a bad but local hair-metal band and were playing just up the road in a rock club that had previously hosted Bad Brains, Morbid Angel, Dio and the Scorpions. We went to have a look and a guy tried to sell us tickets, but we didn't really fancy it, so instead grabbed some burgers and falafel and headed back to the KK club, as the Kaiserkeller was now known.

In the UK at the door of a rock club you'd usually get a cross marked on your hand with a felt tip pen, or maybe an ink stamp at best. In Germany all the clubs seemed to have special door passes so kids could get in and out. At the KK Club the door pass was a condom. Now that was definitely something practical in the Reeperbahn area, but not as cool as the 'What do you want the DJ to play?' cards we were given a few nights before at the Dornbusch. Inside the club there was a long bar with laser lights beaming down every few feet onto ashtrays, so when you went to order a beer it looked like you'd been transported, beamed aboard the enterprise. The club was playing Rage Against The Machine loud, blasting a mix of rock and dance music, and had a games area in the corner with kicker and air hockey too. We ended up chatting with a bunch of girls who looked like Heathers and challenging them to a few games. It was fun and some of the guys actually got better at the games as they became increasingly drunk. We left early and drove south out of town looking for somewhere quiet to sleep that would smell less. We ended up kipping in some woods near a village called Tottensen, with all of us in the van, the four Pseudo's in the bunks, Milo in a sleeping bag on the floor, and me across the front seats on a large plank of wood under some blankets. It wasn't the best night's sleep I've ever had but, apart from Dan's quacking, it wasn't too bad.

In the morning we washed with bottled water and cleaned our teeth out in the open air. Kris disappeared into the woods for a while and I do not like to think of what he did. We visited a small bakery in the village for breakfast and bought twenty-four rolls with a load of cheese and ham, and some big bags of doughnuts and apple turnovers. We scoffed this lot and drove into a park where we stopped next to a big fallen tree across a field. Most of the afternoon was taken up with pillow fighting across that tree trunk, patching our wounds and making space in the back of the van, mainly by throwing out empty beer cases. Milo and I had to re-arrange the entire van as the guys had been bringing back all the left-over beers from their rider after every show, even somehow finding extras. With all the merch and equipment, packing the back of the van was like a giant game of Jenga.

Late in the afternoon we drove back to the sinkhole that was Hamburg and met the Dipsos at the Marquee Club. It was smaller than the one in London's Charing Cross Road and the posters outside told us that it had recently seen shows by Sheer Terror, Extreme Noise Terror and Citizen Fish. No doubt all calm and melodic affairs. Isleif led us all in. He was wearing some new tartan bondage trousers covered in chains and zips. That kind of thing had long died out in the UK but was still considered everyday punk attire in Germany. He also had on an old, and I mean old, UK Subs T-shirt. It was a bit smelly and stained and full of moth-holes, but he said it was one of his favourites. He nearly wet himself when I told him about Couch Potatoes supporting them in the UK. Most interesting though was that he was carrying a couple of large brown boxes. Could these finally be the new vinyl the Pseudo Hippies were waiting for? We all followed him expectantly over to a table inside where he opened the boxes with the large penknife he kept on his belt. Sure enough it was the new Pseudo Hippies / Dipsomaniacs tour split 7" EP. Called 'Sex on legs' and with a bright neon pink cover it had two tracks by each band. 'Girl at the deli counter' and 'Dumped again' by the Pseudos and 'Catastrophe' and 'Muss das sein?' (Does it have to be that way?) by the Dipsos. It was a joint release between Isleif's Bad Taste Records and Hohnie's Nasty Vinyl. A widely grinning Isleif had brought the bands one hundred copies each to sell on the tour and was receiving many slaps on the back. It was a good job too and just in time as the Pseudos were almost out of their first single by now and the Dipsos were low on their 'Growing up' EP too. Both bands had some tapes and t-shirts left but Milo needed more to sell and these new EPs would go like hotcakes.

It was quite a thing for a band to have a record out, an actual vinyl record. Remember this was before CDs were very commonplace and way, way before digital made it simple for any old Tom, Dick or Fritz to get a release out just like that. It was even cooler to get something brand new delivered on the tour. These new records really meant something, and all the Pseudos and Dipsos were clearly in heaven. They were caressing the vinyl, checking the aesthetics of the cover, and definitely looking forward to rocking out again that evening so everyone there would be blown away by them and then buy the record. For just one quid any new fans would have something to remember the show by and play over and over again on a shitty sounding, constantly jumping turntable in their bedroom, probably until it was scratched or worn out or broken by a mate tripping over on it. This was what it was all about. They'd wanted to leave a mark in Germany with all these kids and now they were stoked to have the new record. These EPs were meant to help cover the cost of the tour, but the Pseudos didn't care about that anymore, they were a proper band now with a couple of records out and they were on tour! Who cared about costs now. I could see them thinking 'Right, let's stay at a five-star hotel, throw the television through the window and drive a Rolls Royce into the pool. Fuck it, this is the life. No going back to work now'. It was enough to make you forget about sleeping on hard, piss-soaked floors or in the back of smelly, freezing vans. If only we had a record player to play it on right now. But my record player was about six hundred miles away.

Inside the Marquee Club in Hamburg, it seemed claustrophobically small, very dark and the purple painted walls were plastered with posters for shows by rock bands that even we had never heard of. The stage was just about big enough for the bands to cram onto without tripping over their equipment and the lights were red hot and shone directly into the eyes of anyone who looked out from the stage. We had some time so I helped with the sound-check and was jamming a bit on the guitar with Adam on bass and Dan on drums, then Milo came over and tried to remember the words to some of the old Couchies songs and covers. He knew 'Why' and that was handy, being one of the easiest to sing and play. We jammed it out for a while and it started to sound OK.

Meanwhile Tom was trying to chat up the bartender for free tequilas, despite already having free beers. He and Dan were such archetypal sarf luhnduhn geezers and always up to something. Later Adam got chatting to a punker girl from England called Miriam. She was short, very blonde and not at all unattractive, but quite stroppy about something. She explained that she had come over to Germany about two months ago to work with a friend at a new computer firm's office where they received support request calls from English-speaking businesses here, but they had fallen out and now she had no job and no place to stay. She said she couldn't go home as there were issues with her parents too and she was even considering going on the streets in the Reeperbahn and that was why she was in the area tonight, hoping to meet a pimp. It sounded like a disastrous idea to me, and probably a bullshit sob story, but just in case, Adam asked her to stay and watch the show and they spent the evening chatting about punk bands. By the end of the evening, she had decided that she would form a new band with him and they would be called 'Piss off', the first song was already underway and it would be excellently titled 'Cows with tits'. It all seemed to be going well with lots of smiling and dancing during the Pseudos set but by the time they'd finished playing Miriam had disappeared, along with some of our sandwiches and beers. I don't know what Adam expected, but we didn't see her again.

It turned out to be another good show in that crowded little club, and afterwards, when they'd finished what was left of the three crates of beer for the bands, Tom and Dan also led a charge on tequila slammers. The bottle was labelled 'Deathshead Tequila, poisonous' and there was a skull on it. That didn't put them off at all though, and Tom had soon won himself an extra free shot by being the best customer all night. It was when he tried to shag a blow-up sheep (that someone had brought to the gig, like you do) that things started to get really messy and we were obliged to carry him out to the van to sleep it off. We went back in as we were all meant to stay downstairs at the club that night, but the Dipsos had already grabbed the only decent spots, putting their sleeping bags like holiday beach towels on the unbroken couches and beds, and the place stank like shit anyway. We decided to head back out to the van to look after Tom and try to get some peace.

I drove through the night as it was quicker and easier to cross the big distances when the autobahns were empty. The Beast could go pretty fast if pushed properly, but once up to speed and rolling along she was not big on slowing down again in a hurry, so less traffic was a good idea. I would drive for a few hours and the others would try to sleep, nestled in the belly of The Beast as we hurtled along, often at nearly 100mph in that rusty old transit. Surviving the night-time journeys between gigs and not thinking too much about the clanking danger that surrounded them was quite possibly a contributing factor in all the drunkenness, but I was determined to look after them all and get them safely to the next venue. The nights wore on and I'd end up listening quietly to German folk and country stations on the radio as I zoomed past the night-time scenery between stops to piss or fuel up.

We did stop that night, at a service station near Hanover. Kris and I went inside for some food and drinks, as well as the usual piss and a wash, and when we came back Tom was awake but clearly still very drunk. He was chasing Adam, Dan and Milo around the car park with his strides around his ankles trying to piss on them. When he realised that he just wasn't going to catch them like that he started trying to jump over a large metal link fence instead. He was only wearing his jeans and one trainer now so was cutting his stomach up pretty badly, but didn't seem to feel it. Kris and I pulled him back down and put him in the van again, but a few moments later he was at it once more, staggering out then running at the fence time and time again. He eventually fell over and more or less knocked himself out. We threw him back in the beast and continued on our way, eventually stopping to rest and get some sleep in Hamelin, the pied piper's town. We were awoken in the morning by noisy binmen banging around, and then shortly after that some angry Turks telling us we couldn't park where we were and we'd have to move on. Naturally a slanging match then ensued so I couldn't really ask them for directions to Minden where the next gig would be.

We eventually found Minden and the next venue, the FKK, or Freie Kunst & Kulture (Free art and culture). It was just about the largest building in town, but it was hard to find the road to get access to it. The place looked like the bombed-out remains of a railway stockyard or warehouse, and it certainly seemed like a Second World War target factory that just hadn't been repaired or knocked down. Instead it had been covered in graffiti and loomed large in front of us, grey-brown in colour with one doorway up some concrete steps and seemingly every window broken. This old factory had clearly been squatted in by hippies and punks for some time as they'd turned it into an alternative arts centre, and when we pulled up more and more of them started to appear and come over to greet us. They seemed happy to see us and were looking forward to the show, but none of them seemed to know what was going on. Luckily, Isleif and the Dipsos arrived then too. We could hear Matze's VW camper approaching before we saw it and it was sounding bad. It was blowing smoke as it came up the street, but I was just glad they were there and could help us sort out what was going on.

We eventually found out that the stage the bands were going to be playing on that evening was on the fifth floor and sure enough, the only lift in the place had long since been broken so we had to get some of the locals to help us shift all the gear upstairs. There were dogs running about getting in the way and it all looked like a scene from Mad Max to me. The characters that offered to help grabbed the lightest things they could and led the way, asking if they could get free records or a beer in return. We eventually made it up some jagged and piss-soaked concrete stairs, past a few very dangerous-looking holes in the floor, past what we were told were 'living areas' to the 'music area'. Sure enough, there was a large stage across the end of this room and quite a few people milling about, some standing by a mixing desk and looking like they might know what was going on. Of this entire five-storey factory only this one small area was really able to be used. Everywhere else seemed to be swimming in piss and had things scurrying over piles of rags, that could have been bodies for all we knew. In one room there was a band practising that sounded like Discharge on speed. One of these guys saw the face I'd pulled and shouted at me, "Hey, we don't like melody, we like noise. Extreme Noise Terror, Chaos UK, you know it's true". Then he played an imaginary air guitar with such gusto that he nearly fell back down the stairs. Bloody idiot.

It was only at this point the promoter, who they laughingly called 'the chief organiser', finally showed up, just about the time all the work was done. He was wearing army surplus fatigues with a smelly brown jumper full of holes. He had muddy boots on and a heavy bullet belt with various things hanging off of it on strings. He also had a rolled up woolly hat on, in the height of summer, over some very dirty dreadlocks. He had a mate with him too, in shorts and sandals, but with a 1983 Discharge tour shirt on, with the sleeves and much of the sides cut off so you could see his body piercings and bad tattoos. They both stunk of sweat and patchouli oil, and the necklaces they wore were possibly fashioned from home-made beads or even their own teeth. They told us that the support band they had booked, the Y-Fronts, couldn't make it now, but they'd arranged some local bands to go on first to warm the party up. They wondered if they could borrow our gear and have a quick practise?

The first of these support bands consisted of just a drummer and a guitarist, who shouted occasionally into a large orange microphone. The guitarist had both of our guitar amps turned up to a deafening ten, and I'm sure it would have been eleven if he could have found a way. Both Matze and Tom were glaring at him and he clearly had no idea how close to death he was. The next support band seemed to materialise out of the crowd and consist of four bassists, six drummers, two guitarists and many dogs, but apparently no singers or tunes. It all sounded like a banshee gargling glass whilst listening to Napalm Death, or as Couchies had been labelled once before, a band who'd been pushed down a lift shaft and were racing to finish the song before the impact. That sudden death might well have become the case if they didn't turn down a bit and treat the equipment with a little more respect. To top it off we were then told, 'There may well be a political activist coming to give a speech tonight if we are really lucky'. FFS.

Thankfully a slightly less smelly punker that Isleif knew had now turned up and took over the mixing desk, seeming to know a little more about what he was doing and what should be going on. Both the Pseudos and Dipsos sensed that it was now time to sound-check properly and raced over to save their equipment from any further abuse. Milo and I were trying to set up the record stall, between the bar that only seemed to serve home-made cider or the local equivalent of special brew, and a table with a couple of friendly anarcho punks selling their gegen everything patches and badges; gegen rassismus, gegen sexismus, gegen faschisten, gegen sauberkeit for sure. We just about got that sorted and ready when the girl behind the bar offered us all some vegetarian stew. That was excellent news, I was starving as usual, but I'm sure it was chilli. It was way hotter than any normal stew, and I'm also sure it had sausage in it and quite possibly rat too. It was certainly not veggie as advertised. We ate some anyway as we hadn't eaten all day and had lost all ideas of self-preservation. I for one was getting a serious hunger headache. It was around this time that Adam and Dan decided that Milo and I should join them onstage tonight and go through the old Couch Potatoes song 'Why', as well as the Beach Boys cover 'Then I kissed her'. We'd been messing around with them the night before so had another quick sound-check practise and they sounded alright. Hell, why not, we couldn't be any worse than the support bands.

It was getting dark outside now and the whole place was starting to fill up with already drunken punks, spitting, swearing and jumping on one another. The first of the support bands climbed on stage, having acquired a couple more members, and began punishing the drums, the amps and everyone's ears. We were hanging out with Isleif at the merchandise stall when this guy in a bright orange tracksuit came over and genuinely said, "Hey, what is this vinyl? It rapes our mother earth of oil!" I wasn't sure if he was serious or not so suggested in kind that maybe he'd prefer a tenth-generation poor quality ferric cassette, ideally sent by a pen-pal from the eastern bloc using a waxed-over re-used stamp so that neither the government nor the post-office made any money off the back of the proletariat? He looked at me blankly. So Isleif said to him,

"What are you, an arsehole?" and to this he replied, "No, I am guitarist. We will play next." And he did.

There were so many characters and stories from this one evening alone. There was one idiot who'd been slam dancing to the support bands and tried to swap his mosh-broken records for some new ones. Then another older guy, with ridiculously thick glasses like the bottoms of bottles, came over to tell us that if we gave him a free t-shirt he could get us a show at a 10,000 seat stadium nearby. Milo told him that the Pseudos had no interest in supporting the Spin Doctors in front of 10,000 tightly-trousered hippies so he'd better jog on. About this time of the evening that pungent and poisonous chili stew came back to visit me and I needed das toiletten urgently. The problem was that the 'bathroom' had no working lights, no lock, no flush and a wooden pallet for a door. You could see right through the door and had to put your feet up on it to keep it closed when you saw anyone approaching. It sure was a classy joint.

It felt like two in the morning when the Pseudo Hippies finally hit the stage. Half asleep and blinded by the weed smoke, they still rocked it though and put on a good show. Most people cheered, quite a few danced and one huge bloke at the front in a cop killer t-shirt kept on shouting 'fuck off' at them after every song, but was clapping and grinning wildly at the same time. We didn't know whether to throw him out of a window or join in. About halfway through the set Tom and Kris decided they wanted to get some more beers so Milo and I joined Adam and Dan on stage to play the Couch Potatoes songs. It was great fun and went down very well. Milo was smiling his head off and I was reminded just how much I enjoyed all this. Then the Pseudos tried to wrap things up with the last few songs of their set, but were cheered on for two more encores. They played a couple of songs again and threw in some covers that everyone knew and danced like crazy to. Right at the end, the mad, shouting, grinning 'fuck off' guy charged over to Kris to tell him that he loved him and he wouldn't stop hugging him. The Dipsos had already decided they didn't want to stay at this place and were loading the gear out down the steps as fast as they could. All the ugly girls were trying to get the Pseudos to stay at the squat with them for the night, but we needed to get out of there and would be far happier just sleeping in the van again.

Merchandising Milo was on the case as ever and did brisk business for as long as he could, but Isleif and I were looking for the promoter, hoping to get paid and leave. The guy we'd been told was the 'chief organiser' was nowhere to be seen now and we really needed some money for petrol and food. I picked the most likely candidate and hassled him. He saw me coming and said, "Hey, my friends, I am very sorry but there is no money. It was an anti-fascist benefit for our comrades tonight." I had a strong suspicion that the comrades in question were him and his mates and I wanted to shake this fucker out of his skin. "But you can stay and sleep on the floor, or we can party all night and smash many things." It was looking bleak, but that sort of thing could happen. There were never any guarantees on this tour and we accepted that. Isleif and his sound-guy mate had other ideas though. They sneaked into what they figured was the chief organiser's room, as it was the least piss-drenched in the place, and grabbed some money they found in a tin under his pillow, they also nabbed the two records in his entire collection they thought were worth having too. Then, for good measure, Isleif told us that he took a dump in his bed and replaced the already dirty, wet and stained covers. Lovely. Now it was definitely time to leave.

We hastily departed for another long night drive right down to the south of Germany to a town called Donauworth in Bavaria. During this mammoth road trip, I went through hell with my new inside-out stew stomach whilst the others tried to sleep. We crossed rivers and bridges, skirted mountains and forests, went around several awkward road-works diversions and passed a few crashes too. We even met Saxon at a service station near Kassel. They were on their 'Wheels of steel' or 'Fists of fury' tour and had a massive tour bus full of permed hair and tarty heavy metal girls. The journey was about three hundred and fifty miles and took us all night, about six hours. The guys tried to sleep, and mostly did, which was amazing as I blasted every tape and often had the windows down trying to stay awake. Around 8am we reached our goal, or at least a garage carpark in Donauworth, where I crashed out and slept until lunchtime. We were eventually thrown out by the garage workers there when we tried to wash in their toilets. Then we went for a lunch of chips, salad and bread, all smothered in mayo, at a roadside cafe and met a friendly local in a Subaru who suggested we follow him so he could show us where the venue was. It was a coin toss if we'd arrive at the gig venue or end up butchered in some woods, but we made it.

Tonight's gig would be at the Schellen Bergastadte Café, a really cool music bar up on the hillside overlooking the town. It was still early though so there was no one to meet us yet, and we drove into a meadow down by the river to laze around and try to fix a few minor problems with The Beast. We picnicked and wrote postcards and threw things into the Danube and at each other. We were bitten by mosquitoes, probably attracted by our over-ripe tour fragrance and Kris even found himself a stone shaped like a turd which he was determined to keep. We returned to the venue around 6pm and met Toxic Walls, the support band, and Fratz, the drunken promoter. The Walls seemed like good guys and were total metalheads, all very hairy apart from the singer who was the spitting image of Data from Star Trek Next Generation. Fratz brought over a fax that had been waiting for us from Matze and the Dipsos, informing us all that they would not be coming tonight as their camper van had broken down amidst torrents of flame and smoke. It didn't sound too good, and we were now on our own.

We sat in the café with Fratz and the Walls, looking at the amazing view and pondering the situation whilst we ate a meal of salad soaked in oil and flour, with veggie cheese-burgers and plenty of beer and Fanta. The Toxic Walls had come all the way from

Hannover but luckily had brought with them all the extra equipment we needed to play the show and Fratz promised to help us out on the southern part of the tour if the Dipsos couldn't make it to any more of the gigs. After all, he told us, "I am an ace tour manager and close personal friend of Wizo. You know, Wizo, the MTV stars. 'All that she wants' you know?" and he started to sing. "She's going to get you. All that she wants is another baby, she's gone tomorrow, yeah. All that she wants..." you know?

Wizo, pronounced Veeso, were riding high in the German and Scandinavian pop charts at that time with their version of Ace of Base's hit 'All that she wants'. They were even receiving airplay on MTV with a truly terrible video that they had made themselves, playing air guitar to the backing tune whilst running around inside what looked like a public toilet. They were on Hulk Records out of Regensburg, the same label as the Toxic Walls, and were really not very good at all. They were seriously popular with the punks and metallers in Germany though, so amazingly later went on to release an album called 'Uuaarrgh' on Fat Wreck Chords.

It was a beautiful warm evening, and the gig went ahead in great spirits. The Walls rocked out in a very heavy hardcore way, with stand-out songs called 'Get awake', 'No mercy', 'Freedom is coming' and 'Stone cold'. There was some anti-nazi chat, about not being afraid and all sticking together as one, too. The Pseudos decided to take things less seriously and just two songs in stripped off down to their underpants on stage. This was now becoming a feature of their set, partly because of the heat, partly through drunkenness and partly because they'd challenged each other to see just how far they could go. Tonight, Kris had prepared, he'd changed his pants for new ones so played in just them and his trainers. Tom had borrowed a young girl's vest from a washing line and wore that. Being on tour with the Pseudos was like a drunken pop-punk version of Benny Hill. After the show we ended up at some guy's flea-ridden pad, sharing floor space with an over-friendly dog and about ten locals trying to get drunk with the one remaining bottle of wine. About four in the morning, they started some party games and that's when I headed out to the van to get some sleep.

The next day was a Friday and we were hoping for even busier gigs over the weekend. Adam, who'd been awoken by the dog licking his face, came to tell us that we were all being offered boiled eggs for breakfast by some guy that none of us had met before. I scoffed the eggs and some cereal then washed in a bathroom where there was a picture of the Pope holding a condom hanging on the wall. Then we all drove in convoy over to Fratz's house in Regensburg, about 80 miles to the east, to find that it was full of his punk friends and they were all waiting for us to hang out. We ended up watching videos and playing with his mad little kitten before a quick visit into town, so that Kris and Tom could buy some new strings and plectrums. Then we all went on a meandering peregrination for about twenty miles north to the venue for that evening's show, at the Burglendenfeld Jurgenzentrum, where we met the promoter, Maia. She was very friendly and welcomed us all, then led us to the backstage area and fed us pasta with mushroom sauce and gave us as much free beer as the bands could handle, which believe me, was a lot.

The Burglendenfeld Jurgenzentrum was another of these cool youth clubs that put on bands for the kids. It had 'Cool kids join the Juz' painted on the wall outside and the posters inside listed all the upcoming events and had writing on them that roughly translated as 'Good music, good drink and people that are a little different. Everyone knows a disco or pub that puts everything on the visitors, minimum consumption, expensive drinks. This is not the case here. Everyone can get involved here. You are welcome.' I loved it, such a cool sentiment and atmosphere.

That night's show was very well attended and superb fun. The Toxics didn't quite hit their stride like the night before and broke a lot of strings, but the Pseudos really rocked and encouraged a lot of frenzied dancing. At one point, Klausi, the Toxic's bassist, shouted something like, "Look at their lungs, they are so splendid", pointing at Kris' bare chest, and then later tried to chat up Adam, calling him "a bass god". Milo and I joined them on stage again for a couple of Couchies tracks, keeping most of our clothes on, and the Pseudos kept on playing for as long as they were able. "We don't need money, we are punk rock!" exclaimed Fratz later as he threw another empty bottle over his shoulder at the ensuing aftershow party in the club backroom. Smashing glass in a place like this seemed a bit out of order to me, so I grabbed a broom and after a quick rock 'n' roll sweep up we jumped in The Beast and followed the lovely Maia back to her place. Her place just happened to be hidden in the mountains in the middle of the most beautiful Heidi style countryside we had ever seen. When we arrived, Kris grabbed the only spare bed and started demanding hot water, not just hot mind you, boiling, for his pot noodles. I wanted to sleep inside in the warm tonight, so bagsied a big comfortable-looking sofa. The others grabbed what they could and ended up sleeping head to toe, but everyone was inside tonight and in relative comfort.

I could hear the birds singing when I woke up and it seemed a long way away from some of the previous nights, but then I heard one of the guys taking all the hot water in the shower, so I had to get up quickly and wash. It was well worth the effort though as Maia had laid on a sumptuous breakfast for us all. It was a feast of fresh bread and cheese, jam, cereals, milk, tea and other delicious munchies (known as knabbereien in German, I found out). Then she let us play with Gandhi, her dog, and we all took a photo sitting together on the steps in her garden. We really didn't want to go, but unfortunately had to leave at some point, so we hid some money for her under a pillow and piled back into the van for the next leg of our journey. We were near the Czech border right now and not too far from Austria either, and it was beautiful, but I had to drive all the way back west across Germany to Offenburg, about 250 miles away on the French border. It'd only take about four hours if the traffic wasn't bad, but I figured we'd better get started.

After yet another fun road trip we all arrived safely at Der Kessel Club and parked up as nearby as possible. Known as The Boiler, it was Offenburg's 'Unselfish Institute, run by young people for young people', or at least that's what it said on the Pseudo Hippies tour poster outside. It was a cool venue right in the middle of town. A solid-looking bunker right underneath the rathaus, or town hall. We went inside and met the promoters for this evening's entertainment: Imund, a total babe, and Steve, a punker with an afro, both of whom turned out to be absolutely lovely people, and not only because they provided us with the biggest pizzas we had ever seen! There were five pizzas, each the size of a large coffee table. All that yummy melted cheese goodness. Mmm. It was great.

The inside of the club was a large cavern and tunnel complex, totally covered in colourful graffiti art, whose artist's main theme seemed to be monsters heads. Making a hideous noise on the stage right now was a bunch of talentless crusties called 'Ugly Noise Kick'. They were sweating profusely and making one hell of a racket, living up to their name. But at least it meant that they had brought most of the gear we'd need and we didn't have to lug all of ours in from the van.

The Pseudos were in no rush for a soundcheck and fortunately for us we'd arrived in town at just the right time as there was a huge beer festival going on in the main square nearby and it was like something out of National Lampoon's European Vacation. There were hundreds of people just milling about getting drunk and listening to the local oompah bands. They had the world's biggest frying pans filled to the brim with sauerkraut and giant bratwurst. We wandered around, soaking up the atmosphere, and Tom bought some wine and then met some friendly locals to share it with, before hilariously posting his postcards home into a dirt box for dog poop which he clearly mistook for a postbox.

By the time we returned to The Kessel it was packed and for some reason the floor was covered in peanut shells. The sound engineer said he was going to record the Pseudos show and I'm pretty sure Kris still has a copy. When the noisy support band had finished, the temporarily formed Couch Potatoes went on first to warm things up properly. Then the Pseudos hit the stage and absolutely killed it. By this time on the tour, they had become a very tight unit. All the young skater kids were dancing around in their Bad Religion shirts and loving the pop-punk party. We all had places to sleep for the night at the club afterwards, and it was absolutely pitch-black inside with the lights turned off. People were falling over each other in the dark looking for couches to sleep on or getting up to go for a wee. Tom and Dan treated us to a drunken rendition of 'Blue Moon' and would not shut up, so after a while a couple of us headed out to the bunks in the van to try to get some sleep. We soon found that we were lying under what must've been the loudest bells in all of Germany, and then it started to rain really hard too, pattering like a machine-gun on the Transit's metal roof.

The bells woke us early, but that did mean we had time for a hearty breakfast of Honig Schmeckt (Honey Smacks) before visiting the local swimming baths. The Schwimmbader was crammed full of rather hirsute Germans in tiny briefs, and one very fat guy who insisted on diving from the highest creaking springboard he could reach and creating a tidal wave that went right over us. "He likes his diving board does fat boy," said Dan. Adam managed to lose his locker key, but luckily for him Imund found it by searching the whole pool underwater. While she was looking Tom had busted the locker in anyway, but in return for Imund's good deed, her boyfriend Steve spent ages sucking her toes at the edge of the pool, of course wearing just his speedos. We said our goodbyes and left them to it, heading into an Italian restaurant for lunch, scoffing a mixture of pasta, pizza and chips. In the afternoon we drove to Strasbourg, just over the border in France, to check out the old town. The border was the Rhine, but it was easy to cross as they had thought to build a bridge. We parked next to a car with its windows smashed as it had already been broken into, figuring it couldn't happen twice in the same place, then had a wander about, before driving back into Germany and right across to Heilbronn before stopping for a Chinese at the Phuq-Wah. They wouldn't let us stay in the restaurant, so we ate take-away in the truck and then pressed on to the outskirts of Nuremberg where we slept in the van in a layby.

We were woken up by a huge juggernaut hurtling past and just missing us by inches. Tom started going on about the Grim Reaper and how in Eastern Europe they put sickles over their relative's bodies to stop them from rising from the dead, and Dan was now comparing the tour to being trapped in hell with Isleif as the devil. The rest of us were trying to ignore them and searching for clean clothes. We went for a walk to stretch our legs and there was an acorn fight during which Tom was hit in the nuts, by a nut, and now he had three. Then we departed for St Peters in the centre of Nürnberg to try to find the venue for that night's gig, the Kunst Verein. On arrival Adam took one look and informed us that Kunst Verein apparently meant open sewer. It actually meant 'Art Association'.

There was no one here to meet us yet so we parked outside 'Sexy World', wondering where the 'Crazy' had gone, and went shopping, eventually ending up in a Burger King. Milo went into one of the town's numerous bakeries (every shop in Germany either being a bakery or a chemist it seemed), where he met an attractive young lady behind the counter. She decided to serve him before the massive queue that was waiting. "She obviously fancied me," he said. When we returned to the club it was starting to fill up with punkers.

We met Regurgitated, the new support band now that Toxic Walls had headed home. They were another Bad Taste Records artist. They played heavy hardcore and had a short set of powerful songs, one memorably entitled 'Death Assurance' and they finished off with a Chain of Strength cover. Couchies played 'Why' in the middle of the

Pseudos set again, and they rocked out so brilliantly they were cheered on to play no less than three encores by the packed crowd. The gig was such a party and now all the Pseudo Hippies records were sold out and Milo only had four t-shirts left. We followed Thorsten, the Regurgitated drummer, back to his house where Milo and I listened to some of his record collection, 7 Seconds, Born Against, Citizens Arrest and SFA, whilst everyone else got drunk and stoned. Tom, Dan and Kris fell into the shower on top of each other, ripping the curtain down and knocking over the shelves in the process. Thorsten didn't seem to mind and helped us practise our amusing German insults so there were lots of comments about anteaters and aardvarks (Armaisenbeer und Erdvaken), elephants and bus-drivers (Elephanten und Buschvalen) and hospitals and heads (Krankenhausen und Kopfe) but none of it was very useful in day-to-day conversation. We were sleeping in Regurgitated's practise room at Thorsten's house so there were loads of extra mattresses for sound proofing that we could crash out on. Dan threw some at Milo and a massive bedding fight wrecked the whole place before we finally got some sleep.

We woke around eleven, showered and ate breakfast whilst listening to the new Quicksand album with Thorsten and Ollie. They showed us some great local zines and hardcore books, including one on Dischord and the DC scene with loads of great photos. They were good guys and easy to hang out with, but unfortunately, we had to leave for the next show and get up to Reutlingen in the rain.

The venue for tonight's Pseudo Hippies show was another youth club, this one was called the Bastille and was again covered in graffiti. We arrived to find it full of mid-80s style breakdancers, wearing kneepads and helmets, and dancing around whilst asking us things like "Do you still go to the Hippodrome to breakdance?" We thought maybe we had stepped into a time machine. Milo tried to sell one of them his old Public Enemy t-shirt but they weren't having it and shuffled off when they saw it was going to be a punk-rock night. The promoters had arranged a meal of veggie stew and rice for us, and we all had a pool and kicker tournament while we waited for the support bands to show up.

The two other bands playing were Herb Garden, who'd come all the way from Bristol and were just starting their tour, and a French band, whose name I can't remember but were bloody terrible. The makeshift Couchies played a couple of songs again and the Pseudos were brilliant. Possibly their best show yet. Milo sold out of everything Pseudo Hippies apart from their new single, which was also going fast. Everyone was hanging around and there were so many people sleeping at the club that night that we decided to leave, so the band could try to kip in the van while I drove. The promoter gave us 200 deutschmarks extra and thanked the Pseudos for a great show. Then we headed north towards Stuttgart, where we stopped briefly for petrol and supplies, then drove on through the rainy night for another four hours, covering about 250 miles and ending up sleeping in a garage car park near Kassel.

Outside Maia's with Gandhi

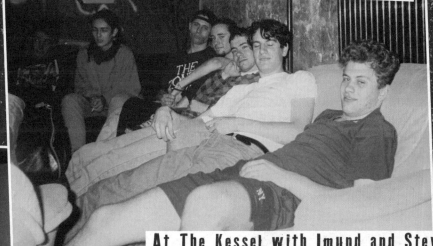

At The Kessel with Imund and Steve

Isleif and Milo at the merch table,
Tom and Danny drinking again

Milo with `Magic Sarah`

Adam and David

Outside the Becks Brewery in Bremen

Dan, Matze (Dipsomanics), Kris, Tom and Adam

We woke to bright sunshine and washed in the garage before driving for another couple of hours up to Hannover. The autobahn was treacherous that day and we passed by several bad smashes. We headed into the town centre and found a cool record shop where Adam bought 'Shreen' by All, and Milo bought 'Holy Name' by 108, each for just £3. Then, as the Pseudos had the evening off, we drove to the Flohtzircus to see Shelter, a Hare Krishna straight edge band with ex-members of Youth of Today and Judge. Milo and I were fans and wanted to see them play, and I wanted to interview Ray and Porcell, their singer and guitarist, for BHP zine too. Shelter had just released their new LP 'Attaining the supreme' on Equal Vision Records and were on tour in Europe but not coming to the UK so this would be our only chance to catch up with them.

They were supported by WWK, a fast and heavy German hardcore band who broke a lot of strings throughout their set and sung angry political songs about fun subjects like beast men and brain death. In stark contrast, when Shelter came out they were surrounded by krishna monks in orange robes chanting and dancing their way through the large crowd to the stage. When they started playing it all kicked off with kids charging about, slamming into each other and stage diving like crazy. It really was an amazing set. I loved it, but noticed that Tom and Dan were more interested in trying to chat up the barmaids. After the show, when Ray Cappo was walking around the venue trying to sell his book to the kids, Tom went over and had a stand-up argument with him about religion. Just as it seemed to be about to come to blows, we went and broke it up.

Soon after the gig had ended, Isleif arrived in an old yellow Fiat to show us the way back to his house in Springe, about twenty miles away. I was speaking with John Porcell, the Shelter guitarist, at this point and trying to interview him for BHP zine, so was in no rush to leave. But we wrapped it up quickly and headed out.

We were low on petrol so stopped after a while to fill up on the way back, and found that the crazy Isleif actually lived around the back of this garage. His back door opened onto the forecourt so he used it as his personal 24/7 shop. Inside his house was awesome, it was just about the most punk-rock place I had ever been. Every room was covered with hundreds of gig posters, and stacked high with records, videos and creepy crawlies. The bathroom alone had tour posters from Gorilla Biscuits and Bad Religion alongside a Married With Children poster (of Kelly Bundy, of course) and hundreds of hardcore zines. We checked it all out while he chose records to play, but I was knackered and fell asleep on the floor listening to the very strange melodies of some old French punk band.

We didn't wake up until the afternoon but couldn't shower as none of the taps seemed to work. Isleif hadn't warned us about this, he didn't wash so he didn't care, so we spent the day smelling whilst we checked out his extensive record collection. We listened to Samiam and then ventured into town for a snack, where we spotted a couple of Nazi skinheads. We went over to have 'an educational conversation' with them, but they saw us coming and did a runner as we approached.

In the evening we were invited to a party by the people from Zap and Plastic Population fanzines. The Pseudos sat around getting drunk and answering a couple of interviews for the zines, but some annoying blonde geezer keep telling them dumb shit like "You are not punks, you do not have green mohicans" so we headed back to Isleif's to get some more sleep.

We were woken early by a couple of his friends turning up to listen to terrible east German thrash bands at a very high volume. One of them, a fat geezer called '76 because he was meant to have met Sid Vicious, seemed to be eating all the food in the house. By the time we were ready to compete for it, it was all gone, so we decided to go out for a sit-down Chinese, blowing what little cash we had left from the merchandise sales. It was delicious though.

Late that afternoon we drove to the Nasty Vinyl headquarters to meet up with Krafpe and Hohnie. These guys had put out the first Pseudo Hippies vinyl and Kris wanted to have a party with them. We ended up at Krapfe's house, a big place made almost entirely out of marble, and it seemed he ran some kind of funeral parlour and gravestone engraving company at the front and a punk rock emporium out of the back. He had shelves and shelves of records, including all the rare ones collectors really wanted but couldn't find. Milo was in heaven searching through them all.

Later we drove with them over to Hohnie's house. He was in a punk band called the Pissed Spitzels and they had set up a pretty decent practise studio at his place where they intended to have a free for all jam session type of gig now. People turned up and started playing and drinking and it was fun. The Spitzels played a few old '77 style punk songs that seemed to mainly be about spending the night in a cornfield or getting drunk on a beach. There was one song called 'I'm in love with your underwear' that they all seemed to particularly enjoy. No wonder they got on with the Pseudo Hippies so well. The makeshift Couch Potatoes played a couple of requests, including our version of 'Then I kissed her' and the Pseudo Hippies jammed Ramones covers and had a go at any punk songs people would shout out, some more successfully than others. Even the Dipsos turned up later on, Matze had managed to get the VW camper repaired and going again, so they joined the Pseudos for a couple of songs. It was a great party that went on very late.

Most people were still crashed out at Hohnie's the next morning but Milo and I were up and went with Krapfe to get breakfast and grab a few records from his mailorder distro. We tried to pay him but he insisted on giving them to us, saying he had enough to spare, he was such a diamond geezer. We said our goodbyes and followed Matze up to Bremen, about 100 miles away, stopping off in town to take a few photos outside the Becks Brewery in front of the largest amount of beer in the world. We also stopped off at a supermarket to spend our last deutschmarks on more beer, chocolate milk and a few presents for people back home. There were now fourteen crates of beer in the truck with us along with all the band's equipment, and despite packing it with our bedding The Beast was clinking as I drove along.

The venue for the final gig of the tour in the Dipsomaniac's hometown of Bremen was massive. It had a great p.a. system with two engineers on the soundboard, a lighting rig, smoke machines and a highly polished floor which was great for sliding up and down on if you got bored during the soundchecks. The Dipsos had been busy promoting the show and were expecting a good turnout. The first band on were called the Aldheim Strudel Experience. They dressed up as terrorists with guns and masks, and made a god-awful racket. Then the Pseudos played another pop-tastic set, with a brief interlude for the Couchies, and finally the Dipsomaniacs blasted through a great set with everyone singing and dancing along. At the end Kris and Tom joined them onstage for a couple of covers to finish things off, swapping instruments and sharing the mics. It was great fun and very good to see the final show of the tour absolutely packed too.

Everyone was on such a high after that and didn't want the evening to stop, so Matze and his girlfriend took us and a load of their mates to a big pub near the railway station that stayed open all night. There Kris exchanged the last remaining Pseudo Hippies t-shirt for the last Dipsos one, that said 'Don't take me serious when I'm delirious' on it. It summed them up perfectly. Milo and Isleif swore to become 'brothers in merchandising', but before that could happen we had to leave or we'd miss the ferry back home. I still had to drive us nearly three hundred miles across Germany and Holland to the ferry port and it had started raining again. We said our goodbyes and thankyous and hit the road. It took a while, but The Beast got us all home eventually, with the milometer reading 382,101 by the time I'd dropped everyone off and reached my house, meaning that we'd covered well over 3000 miles on this great Pseudo Hippies tour. It was a fun trip for sure, but man, I needed my bed.

19, Keep the hardcore flame burning

As soon as we'd arrived home from that adventure with the Pseudo Hippies, Milo and I started working on new song ideas with Dan Kingdon, and the two new guys, Dan and Paul. We were all keen to get going and now had the basis of a five-piece band, with Dan Pullin on second guitar, Paul Smith on finger-bass, Dan K drumming, me on guitar and Milo singing. We were getting along famously already and what we all lacked in musical ability we made up for in enthusiasm. I couldn't bring myself to play any Joeyfat songs, but everyone wanted to try a few Couch Potatoes songs from the 'Excess All Areas' release, so we started out there and were soon writing new tracks together. The first few attempts were a little rough and got booted to the curb, but we came up with the makings of a few new songs, practised a lot and started to develop into a half-decent band. Most of the tracks we were working on were slower and mellower than what I'd been used to, although curiously the super heavy riff that became 'Lost' was one of the first we all agreed on and enjoyed playing.

We also went along to loads of shows to keep up our inspiration, first the weird mix that was Compulsion supporting Credit to the Nation at the New Cross Venue, then the brilliant and bouncy Understand and Bob Tilton at the Camden Falcon, and then a long trip up to Bradford for the hardcore festival at the 1 in 12 Club. This was followed by a visit to the Playpen in Deptford, South London, where Milo and I joined the Pseudos on stage again to play the Couchies song 'Why'. A couple of weeks later we saw two pre-Christmas Rancid shows, one at the Tufnell Park Dome in London and the other at the Fishermens in Brighton. At the latter of these two I saw the most fights I have ever seen break out at a punk show. I watched the chaos from the sidelines, glad not to be involved, while Milo interviewed Matt Freeman, the Rancid (and Operation Ivy) bassist, for BHP zine.

In January I went up to The Venue in New Cross, London, with Adam, Milo, Dee Woods and Chris 'Hair Mare' to see Conflict and remind myself what punk was all about. It was a good show and always fun to see them, but I think only Colin, the singer, and Paco (RIP), the drummer, were from the original line-up. They'd gone a bit metal and had the oxymoron of hundreds of kids wearing leather jackets screaming A.L.F. slogans.

All through February and March we jammed together and started to develop the new tracks. Starting with 'Why', the track we'd played on the Pseudos tour, adding in a couple of other 'Excess All Areas' tracks ('Impossible Easier' and 'Kill It') and some attempts at covers, and then writing our own new tracks that would become part of 'Mans greatest friend...' It takes a while to get in sync with new musicians and our early tracks, even the first record which we rushed out to use as a demo to help us get shows, were not as good as they could have been. We had the songs down, but the recording was rushed and turned out a bit messy. I was just glad to be playing in a band again and these new guys were good fun to hang out with. All young and excited to be in the band, always coming up with ideas and practising hard. Amongst the first couple of new Couch Potatoes tracks were 'Lost' and then 'Venue', followed by 'User Friendly' and 'Wall', but the whole of the new ten-track release we'd record in June came together through the spring.

Getting shows booked was going to be a little more tricky for now, partly as the scene was quieter at this time than it'd been for the previous couple of years, but also partly as I didn't want to play the Forum in Tunbridge Wells again just yet, and we'd lost most of our London shows for now through Aidan too. The Brighton scene, our usual fall back, was pretty dead with most of the bands broken up and even the Shelley seemed to be dying down with Macca away at University and Warren taking more of a backseat with new owners coming in. It didn't look good for gigs. That said, Couch Potatoes 'Excess All Areas' release was still getting good reviews in punk fanzines and a lot of people had that tape. The latest review I'd seen was in Prototype zine, which said "Genuine Kentifornian Couchcore - This is beautifully played poppy hardcore packed with hooks and melody. It reminds me of Samiam at their best. Perhaps this sort of thing has been done before, but this group makes the music seem as relevant and powerful as it ever was. 'Impossible easier' stands out as a brilliant piece of hardcore. I'm glad to see that the US no longer has the monopoly on worthwhile HC groups. This is definitely worth purchasing." As well as that 'Three' and 'Impossible easier' were getting airplay on a few radio stations and various Couchies 'Excess' tracks were appearing on compilations too, most of them tapes but also some CDs and vinyl. It all helped keep our name known in the hardcore scene and maybe we could build on that.

2/4/94 Splodgenessabounds, Sperm Ov Doom, Belinda Carbuncle, Couch Potatoes and Trauma.
The Racehill, Brighton

Late in March, Milo, Adam and I were up at The Powerhaus in London to see All play. It was a great show and we hung out with the band for a while afterwards. I interviewed Bill Stevenson for my BHP zine and we chatted about their tour. We also bumped into a few of the guys from the Brighton scene. One of whom was Allen, the singer of Sleep, who was currently playing bass for a new band called Frankenslag. He suggested we play a show at The Racehill Inn a few days later.

Some of the local thrash punk bands had been playing regularly at this shabby old drinking pub called the Racehill. It stood on the corner of Lewes Road, the main drag into Brighton down to the seafront, and was just over the road from the skate park. The current batch of Brighton's punk lunatics and crusty drop-outs would invite all their friends along and have a laugh. The few big shows were being put on by Mark and Illuminanti, and we weren't ready for that yet. There was still no sign of Buzz and his smaller 'Just One Life' shows at the Free Butt and Albert, so this was the new Couch Potatoes first opportunity to play a gig and it was great of them to invite us.

Milo was the only one of the band who'd been to any of the shows at The Racehill before, so he warned us about what to expect; a grubby venue, unfriendly staff, small drunken crowds and dodgy sound. It turned out that he wasn't wrong, but we didn't care, we all really wanted to play. Even though this would be Paul and Dan P's first ever gig, there was very little nervousness amongst us. We were excited and ready to go. It also helped our nerves that Trauma, the first band on, were so out of it they could barely play and staggered through a short but noisy set, mostly made up of feedback and shouting. We couldn't be worse than that.

Trauma were a bunch of Nausea-loving crusty peace punks who could rarely finish a song, let alone a set. In a previous life their front man, Alex Ray, had been a big Sid Vicious fan. Milo used to see him walking in Haywards Heath, Lewes or Brighton, always with his dyed black hair spiked up and wearing bondage trousers, a bullet belt and his painted leather jacket. He went around like that for years, but then as this little scene started up around the Racehill he'd reinvented himself to become a dreadlocked crust punk and joined Trauma. Milo had told me about one time (at band camp), when he and Dee Woods, (another very '77 punk mate of ours who owned the biggest collection of crepe soled tiger skin brothel creepers and non-decommissioned army surplus you'd ever seen), went with Trauma in their van to see them play a gig in Hastings. They'd all met up at Alex's flat first, where he happened to have a full pub bar set up, with optics, beer towels and ashtrays, no doubt all nicked, and the Trauma boys were all sitting around getting drunk and high before even setting off for the show. They were in such a state they could barely walk, let alone play, and tonight seemed to be a repeat of that.

The noise died out as they shuffled off the stage and now it was our turn. As the sober professionals Couch Potatoes were, we figured we could match that and maybe even improve upon it, and we gave it a damn good go. Our set wasn't perfect by a long shot, with Dan K breaking a drumstick right at the start of the first song and having to grab a replacement whilst keeping time, but even that was done with a big grin on his face. Dan P, Paul, Milo and me were all rocking around the little stage and by the second, or maybe third song, we'd definitely won the crowd over and everyone seemed to be having fun. There may have been a few tuning issues in the final song as Milo and I bumped into each other and my guitar headstock hit the wall, but generally it didn't sound too bad. We only had seven songs ready for this show so it was a short sharp shock and that could be effective. We were all buzzing by the time we'd finished our set.

There were five bands playing that night and that was only because three others; Nux Vomica, Colour Burst and Coalition, had all dropped out! Each band went on and played for about twenty minutes and just had fun. The next band up, Belinda Carbuncle, were a three piece from Canterbury. The drummer was called Slick Nick Lovestick and both the guitarists were called Slim. Slim Paul on bass and Slim Steve on guitar. They all had a go at singing over their noisy two-minute bursts of energy. Their songs seemed to mainly be about animals, with titles like 'The Elephant Love Song', 'The Polar Bear Song' and 'The Frog Song'.

They were followed by S.O.D. or Sperm Ov Doom, a very metally punk band whose drummer, Ghoti, was the brother of one of the guys in Demented Are Go, a massively popular rockabilly band at the time. They messed around a lot on stage and seemed to have very few songs. The vocalist, Scoffa, would talk a bit, swear a lot, and then introduce the next song; This one's called 'Fuck your wars!'

We'd packed our guitars and equipment safely away by now as the drunk punks were dancing around, spilling beer and falling about to anything. It didn't make much difference in that pub as it couldn't have gotten any messier or more beer soaked. We were sitting at the edge of the bar, having a steward's enquiry about our set, waiting for the evening's main attraction to come on and finish things up. This would be Splodgenessabounds. These guys were a punk band down from London who had a big hit a decade or so earlier with a song called 'Two pints of lager and a packet of crisps please'. That song reached number seven in the UK singles charts in 1980 and should have got them onto Top of the Pops, but of all the shit luck for them, the BBC were on strike that week. They did make it onto TotP with their next single though, a terrible cover of the Rolf Harris song 'Two Little Boys' and they were on the cover of Smash Hits magazine too. They'd imploded and reformed a few times and were now having another go. They may not have been the world's greatest musicians, but it made for an entertaining Saturday night in Brighton. It must have been something of a culture shock for Dan K and Paul, both of whom were only seventeen at the time and had never been to a real punk gig. But they were still grinning, and we were all totally on a buzz from having played our first show.

Splodgenessabounds would go on to record more releases, including Christmas songs, one of which, entitled 'You've got to have a dream' was released on the Black Hole Records 'Cashing in on Christmas' compilation, and was about Cliff Richard dying on Christmas day. Max Splodge, their vocalist, would join the Angelic Upstarts and in the 2003 book 'One Hit Wonders', by Chris Welch (a Melody Maker journalist) and Duncan

Soar, he is quoted as summing up the band; "One night I rushed into The Crown in Chislehurst waving a pound note, trying to buy two pints of lager and a packet of crisps. The bell rang and the bloke wouldn't serve me. The next day I put down a drum track and bass line and just shouted, 'Two pints of lager and a packet of crisps please.' Mike Reid played it on Radio 1 and it started selling 17,000 copies a day!"

Splodgenessabounds still tour, but over the past twenty years there have been seven deaths of band members, mainly from heart attacks and liver failures, including Roger Rodent, their original bassist, also known as Roger Over and Out, who died in 2002. Other alumni include Miles Runt Flat (guitar) who became stage manager of the Astoria in London, Winston Forbes (keyboards) and Pat Thetic (guitar) who are both now electricians, Whiffy Archer, who played paper and comb, now runs a naked bungee jumping firm and Baby Greensleeves, their first vocalist, who is now a bingo caller in Thames Ditton.

16/4/94 Couch Potatoes, Sonar Nation and 18th Dye
Bottoms Club, Folkstone

Our second show as the new Couch Potatoes was just two weeks later and was far more like what we'd been hoping for musically. I'd been speaking with Richard Murrill, a good guy to know in the local music scene as he produced the newsletter 'Your Mornings Will Be Brighter' which listed all the alternative gigs happening in Kent, and he'd now started putting on gigs too. Rich was a big Couchies fan from before, and when I told him that we were back again with a new line-up he booked us straight onto his next show at the Bottoms Club in Folkestone. It would be Sonar Nation, our Fugazi style buddies from Maidstone, and us, supporting a new band from Berlin called 18th Dye.

We headed over to Folkestone early and it's a good job we did as all the roads leading into town were snarled up. The Channel Tunnel had just been completed, after six years of work, and it was due to be officially opened the next week so all the last-minute preparations were underway and the town was crowded and chaotic.

Couch Potatoes played the same set as we had the previous week at the Racehill, but we took our time over it, and this time Dan K didn't break any drumsticks. Dan P had swapped from the Ibanez he was borrowing for the first show to a brand new Epiphone SG he'd just bought, and everyone seemed a lot more comfortable. The sound was way better too, so we could all hear ourselves and each other properly on stage, something that always helps. Our set was tight and pretty musical, we were definitely improving, if not yet totally accomplished.

Sonar Nation went on after us and were, as usual, absolutely brilliant. They are in my opinion one of the great forgotten bands from Kent, in fact from the UK underground scene for that matter. A totally underrated band who should be very well known. They could play a great mix of alt-rock styles, always painfully intense live, with some fantastically memorable songs and were just good blokes to boot. I loved their first two self-released EPs and I was glad they released 12"s instead of 7"s as they sounded so much better on the turntable, although the cover art of the first record, 'Surge D.T.' really may be the worst cover art of any record ever. But live Sonar Nation had such a dark, brooding sound that just crept around them then exploded in emotion. Tonight, they played tracks from their new 'Thoughts on anyone' EP and their classic 'Surge D T' EP with 'Some place, not home' sounding like Fugazi's 'Two beats off', 'Master Plan' also very Fugazi in style and 'Hate Photo', one of their best tracks and a real high point of their live set, building up the tension like The Rollins Band at their best. They were inspiring to watch and had honed their craft.

I was chatting with Richard, the promoter, about 18th Dye and he was telling me about their first album, 'Done', which he'd been sent as a demo and loved, so he'd booked them. No-one in the UK had heard them yet really. When they wandered onto the small basement stage, following the two noisy five-piece bands that had filled it before them, people were still talking and drinking, so Rich, ever the compere, went over to announce them on the mic. "OK Folkstone, pay attention. This is 18th Dye, all the way from Berlin."

18th Dye were a three-piece and made a kind of artsy indie rock noise that still wasn't very commonplace at the time. This was not the bland, shoe-gazing nonsense of the UK indie chart bands of the late eighties and early nineties either, this was far more adept musically, cleverer, and more experimental, and clearly more alternative too. In parts they reminded me of a mellower Superchunk, but they were more indie than that, sort of lo-fi emo predecessors. Both the guitarist, Sebastian Buttrich, and the bassist, Heike Radeker, would sing. And to hear their textured songs with both male and female vocals over the complex guitar lines and Piet Bendtsen's drumming was in stark contrast to the previous Saturday night. So much more subtlety and texture were involved and this particularly influenced Milo. We both picked up copies of their new EP 'Crayon'. Milo bought the 12" mini-album version and I settled for the CD. This EP was released on the Danish record label, Cloudland, although it would also be re-released later in the US on Matador Records. As good as this record and their later releases are (check out 'Tribute to a bus' on Che Records, recorded and mixed by Steve Albini), they were definitely at their best live and it was awesome to see them play in that little basement club in Folkestone.

Early Couch Potatoes releases and reviews

Over the next two months, the five of us could most often be found in Paul's garage working on new Couchies songs, but when we weren't rehearsing, we would be writing to promoters, fanzines, radio stations and record labels, or else going to gigs to speak with them directly. I had loads of copies of 'Excess All Areas' and '8 songs / Wash' on cassette and was still sending them out all over the place, and by now there were quite a few Couch Potatoes vinyl releases out there as well.

The Panx vinyl zine #11 had just come out with 'Tired' by Couch Potatoes leading off tracks by Blanks 77, Wounded Knee, Eight Ball, Lamento and Public Lost, all good hardcore bands from around the world on this popular series of EPs from J.P in France, the guy who used to run Broken Tapes and now ran Panx. This was actually JP's sixteenth release on vinyl and he was sending loads of copies all over Europe. Although the EP only had a black and white fold-over cover, the record itself was heavy black vinyl and had a cool mini-zine with it, packed with artwork, information and pictures of each band inside. The Couch Potatoes page in Panx #11 had our logo and photos of us playing at the Rumble Club with Adam; Basse, Dave; Guitare, Jim; Batterie and Yan; Chant, written underneath as well our contact details and the lyrics to 'Tired'. This was a classic song of teenage angst and frustration at so many things, but put over in a fast, powerful, hardcore way. Yan had simply written; "I'm tired of trying to put my point across. It's a worn-out subject and there's nothing left to say. The ability to think, I frustrate myself and find no answers. No one's listening and life goes on the same. I'm tired. So tired!" but it was shouted angrily, a song of lethal intent and change, not at all about giving up.

We ended up doing two vinyl releases with Panx and there's still a few copies kicking around on Discogs. But interestingly, for hardcore and emo nerds like me, the third Panx vinyl zine, his sixth 7" release back in '89, is the one to look out for and is very sought after now as it features an early track called 'Mirror' by emo pioneers Moss Icon.

We kept on sending demo tapes and corresponding with obscure punk rock labels so next we managed to get onto the Nowhere Street 7". This was a four-band compilation on Andorra Records out of Montebello, California. It had a pink and black cover featuring a drawing of some old punker standing in the road underneath a streetlamp, next to a trash can and a car that had been broken into. It had been drawn by an artist called Keith Rosson and looked pretty desolate. Even the houses had broken windows. There were green and white flyers from the bands inside, and the back cover had the usual track-listing and recording details, but also some tour posters from the bands involved along the foot too. I was glad to see that they'd used a gig flyer from a show we'd played with the Pseudo Hippies at the Playpen in London as ours. The Couch Potatoes track on this record was 'Why', the one we'd rekindled and played on the Pseudos' German tour. The pressing of this 'Nowhere Street' EP was limited to just 499 copies, and I still have number fifteen in my collection. I saw a great review for this release in a fanzine that proudly stated, "Vendabait have two tracks, 'Token prejudice' and 'I'm a jerk' and play fast snotty punk with a vocalist who sounds like he's been recorded at the wrong speed. The Couch Potatoes track 'Why' is excellent, quality pop-punk like Big Drill Car with a cool guitar sound. The Cheese Doodles play 'How much

The new Couch Potatoes

Dan K, Milo, David, Dan P, Paul

M LODY·MAK R

COURT IN THE ACT

FEBRUARY 19, 1994 75p ....

FEBRUARY 19, 1994 75p

IN THE AREA

IAN WATSON trawls his net around the uncharted waters of KENT, and discovers some very strange fish indeed

Kent's healthiest guitar scene, however, is based in Tonbridge Wells, where the indigenous hardcore acts have taken American West Coast influences so much to heart that they're known locally as "Kentifornian". Leading lights are undoubtedly JOEY FAT, who also run one of Kent's only purpose-built venues, The Forum, although kindred spirits SONAR NATION, DOG UGLY, SEEP and THE COUCH POTATOES help to keep the hardcore flame burning.

As well as bands, there are a number of fanzines who have a hand in shaping the Kent underground, most notable A NEW ENGLAND and the countywide newsletter YOUR MORNINGS WILL BE BRIGHTER. Both of these are produced by Richard Morrill, a Folkstone-based enthusiast who also puts on

hardcore acts have taken American West Coast influences so much to heart that they're known locally as "Kentifornian". THE COUCH POTATOES help to keep the hardcore flame burning.

Kentifornian Couchcore

Courier, June 3, 1994

LEISURE

Live music venue opens

A NEW venue for live music is to open next week in Tunbridge Wells at St John's Youth Centre, next to the town's swimming pool.

The Alternative Club is to be an irregular event hosted by the YMCA and local music lovers.

Shows are to be run by young people for young people, and although anyone is welcome to attend, the bands performing will mainly consist of young local talent. It is hoped that The Alternative will provide an option for occasional entertainment in addition to the town's established clubs and pubs.

The Youth Club intends to showcase all genres of music and is open to suggestions and any offers of support. The first show, on Saturday June 11, will be a hardcore/indie night, featuring local bands **Torque**, **Couch Potatoes** and **I'm Being Good**.

Torque caused quite a stir recently with their brand of grunge rock at a

Battle of the Bands gig and are tipped for bigger things. Couch Potatoes, who hail from Tunbridge Wells, have toured throughout the UK and Europe with bands such as Green Day, No FX and Chemical People. Couch Potatoes will be appearing to promote their new EP and will be in the studio again soon.

The warm-up is provided by I'm Being Good from Brighton, who recently supported Unsane.

People are advised to arrive early on Saturday June 11. The doors open at 8pm and proceeds of the £2 on-the-door admission price will go to the youth centre and towards funding further events.

A banner is being made by various YMCA classes and there will be a PA, lighting rig and video equipment on the night, also a soft drinks bar until 11pm. The support of the local young people is necessary to keep these events running and anyone interested in helping out with The Alternative should contact Phil on 0892 548823 or Keith on 0892 542209.

Couch Potatoes, the band will play at The Alternative's first night

Pop bands to play in massive laser show

A charismatic debut from Hungry Horse

HUNGRY Horse are a new four-piece outfit from Tunbridge Wells who look set to figure prominently on the local music scene.

An accomplished, if tentative, debut set at the Royal

do you care?', a good punky tuneful number, and the Pseudo Hippies track 'Bubblegum' perfectly sums up poppy Ramones style punk."

All of this coverage was built up on the back of the earlier Couch Potatoes recordings, of course, mainly using 'Excess All Areas' tracks, and as we were now playing a mixture of 'Excess' tracks and new songs, we were happy to make full use of this and keep building on it.

The next record to come out would be the first full vinyl release for Couch Potatoes. A proper vinyl EP of our own and not just compilation tracks or tapes. The record was entitled 'In bed with... the Couch Potatoes' and came out on Weird Records, a cool little punk and hardcore label based out of Balderton, near Newark in Nottinghamshire. Weird Records was run by a great guy I'd been corresponding with for a while called Ian Weird, although I'm sure that wasn't his real surname, but we only ever knew him as that. When 'Excess All Areas' came out I'd sent him a copy and he loved it. At the time we were thinking it'd already be coming out as a vinyl album on Retch Records so he offered to do an EP instead using four tracks from the release. Now we'd finally gotten around to it and for 'In bed with...' we chose 'Kill It' and 'Three' as the A-side, with the B-side as 'Impossible Easier' and 'Weak'. The cover used artwork from the 'Excess All Areas' release, but with one of the big fat guys printed in black on magenta paper. This was only the third release on Weird Records, but Ian would go on to produce over forty punk and hardcore records, including some for The Varukers, Mere Dead Men, Screaming Willies, and another one for Couch Potatoes later too.

Around the same time, we had another EP planned with a German label called Born To Booze / A-Wat Records. This label was run by another good guy and Couchies fan I'd been writing to called Andreas Focker. He was based out of Borken in Germany and would later help arrange a great tour for us over there. For now, he wanted to put out a record for us on his label and that became the 'Brad' EP. The full title of this EP was 'Oh Brad, why are you such a jerk?' and it had hand-drawn Warhol style artwork by our bassist, Paul Smith, of a girl crying into her pillow. This was printed in black on a bright yellow cover and looked very effective. We chose 'Part of you' and 'Another' as the A-side tracks with 'Bob' and 'Hole' as the B-side, again, all recorded by the original Couch Potatoes line-up for the 'Excess All Areas' album. The two sides of this record had smiley and sad faces on the centre labels. The back cover had the usual track-listing and contact details on there, but I'd sappily sneaked an extra thanks on there with a '4 Kelly' written in the lower right artwork, as she was my girlfriend at the time. The inside notes on the sleeve featured Mr Greedy with an excerpt from a Mr Men book that said; "At the ice cream stall Mr Greedy met a friend. A little lady who was rather fond of her food and as plump as Mr Greedy. If not plumper. It was Little Miss Plump. "Would you like an ice cream?" Mr Greedy asked her. "One indeed. I'll have six please," smiled Miss Plump. Six large, soft, strawberry ices with lots of cherries on top! Greedy girl. When it was time to go home all the Mr Men climbed into a coach, but the coach wouldn't start. Oh dear, said the driver, the engine has broken down." As you can see, we'd gone for silly rather than political, as was in keeping with our earlier pop-punk style. There was also a flyer that went out with all these EPs for the Shock Treatment LP, another release on the same label.

Thanks to Ian and Andreas we had copies of both these 'Brad' and 'In Bed with...' vinyl EPs, as well as the 'Excess' cassettes, for sale at all of our shows. We'd bring along whatever new compilations we had tracks on too and had screen-printed a few 'Excess All Areas fat guy' and 'Mr Greedy' Couch Potatoes t-shirts too. Our merchandise stall for gigs was starting to look half decent.

Very soon the track 'Such a bad day' from 'Eight Songs' was on another UK compilation CD, and then the song 'Another' from 'Excess All Areas' was on a Japanese comp CD called 'World Hardcore'. This came out on Discrete Records and I have one copy left of this beautiful CD and booklet in my collection. All the other bands on it are just so incredibly heavy but the Japanese label guy loved the track and really wanted to use it. 'Another' was soon out on a compilation LP too, this time with Samiam and Rise in the US. Then our track 'Wall' came out on an angry French punk compilation CD called 'Crises'.

Not long after that JP was back in touch too and wanted to use 'Cold Can' on another of his French Panx compilations. This one was #23 and called 'Court Metrage', meaning 'Short film' and had a purple cover with the bands across it in film negative style. The 7" EP played at 33rpm and featured no less that sixteen bands providing a track each. All the tracks on this EP had to be less than one minute in duration to fit on. This was classic hardcore. Short, fast, loud and angry. As well as Couch Potatoes, the 'Court Metrage' EP also had blasts by Kwik Way (USA), Beyond Description (Japan), Six Feet Over (France), No Fraud (USA), Watch You Drown (UK), Post Mortem (USA) and Youth Gone Mad (USA) with us on the A-side, and Rats Of Unusual Size (USA), F.Y.P. (USA), Masturbates Motel (Sweden), Sockeye (USA), Besmet (The Netherlands), Blanks 77 (USA), P.U.S. (UK) and Sea Monkeys (USA) on the B-side.

There were loads of cassette compilations doing the rounds and many of these had Couch Potatoes tracks on them too. These tapes were on stalls at many of the HC gigs and quite a few went out with fanzines, turning up all over the place and helping us find a lot of new fans. One tape that went out with Jolt fanzine, created by a kid called Sean up in Yorkshire, had a pop-punk compilation that featured Couch Potatoes, Pseudo Hippies, The Shreds, Another Fine Mess, Chicken Bone Choked, Kids and Flags, and the brilliantly named Specky and the Poo Shakers.

There was some radio airplay, mainly alternative rock and college stations, and quite a few interviews and reviews from our mailouts too. They weren't all great of course, but it was good to see the coverage and Couch Potatoes were slowly becoming known again all around the hardcore scene.

Maximum Rock 'n' Roll (MRR) was a big HC scene fanzine at the time, it still is in fact, and they reviewed our 'In bed with...' EP saying "Catchy midtempo punk, Big Drill Car type guitar playing but much more direct. It's melodic much the same way Samiam is. They are more D.I.Y. oriented then either of those two bands though. It comes with issue five of God Damn Weirdos Zine. It didn't knock me out, but it didn't put me to sleep either, they're probably good live". This review was by a guy called O.P. and he'd listed it with the Weird Records contact details suggesting readers get in touch and order a copy.

Organ zine #33 said "More home-made power-pop punk" and Arnie zine #5 said "Genuine Kentifornian couchcore with influences from the Descendents and Green Day. Pretty tight with some nice breaks". Radio Turmoil in the USA, a hardcore and punk station, were playing 'Three' regularly and we did a short interview on air. Tony Suspect reviewed 'In bed with...' in Suspect Device #19 saying "Four slices of hardcore tuneage from Kent's All, um, I mean Couch Potatoes. 'Kill it' is the favourite around here, although 'Three' has some cool guitar, and is that really Sesame Street's count sampled at the end? Cool! 'Impossible easier' is a nice little fast number and 'Weak' is just so catchy. The Couch Potatoes seem to have fallen into Joeyfat's shadow, which is a shame because they have the potential to be much better".

Fallen zine also reviewed 'In Bed With...' and said "This four-track single contains songs from the 'Excess All Areas' LP and it grew on me second or third time around. Fuzzy sounding pop-punk rather similar in style to All or Big Drill Car. Roughish production but good fun. The best song is probably 'Impossible Easier' and they sound like they are enjoying themselves, so why not join them?".

A.H. and Downtime fanzines received copies of the 'Brad...' EP, Downtime simply stating "Couch Potatoes are Kent's most cult fat band" and A.H's review was also short and to the point, "Couch Potatoes are Tunbridge Wells finest hardcore band. Since the '8 songs' demo they've just kept improving. Listen to the new record and see for yourself".

In Terrorizer, a glossy heavy metal magazine of the time, they had a 'Hardcore Holocaust' section where they'd discuss the hardcore scene and review new releases. The writer of the column, Ian Glasper, who was also the bassist of Decadence Within and Stampin' Ground, was discussing a great new release by our west country mates Wordbug and then went on to say that, "both musically and geographically Couch Potatoes, who hail from the wasteland of Tunbridge Wells, were not a million miles away from them. They released an EP on Weird Records a while back and now they have a track on a shit-hot six-band compilation EP on France's Panx Records, alongside the likes of Eightball and Wounded Knee, and another song on the 'Nowhere Street' compilation 7" EP on Andorra Records out of California. The Couchies long overdue album might get released one day soon too."

Even Melody Maker chimed in, "Hardcore acts have taken American west coast influences so much to heart that they're known locally as Kentifornian. The Couch Potatoes help to keep the hardcore flame burning." This was a strapline from an article in Melody Maker of February '94, from a piece called 'In the area' written by Ian Watson about alternative music from Kent, and it went on to say that, "Kent's healthiest guitar scene is based in Tunbridge Wells, where the indigenous hardcore acts have taken American west coast influences so much to heart they're known locally as Kentifornian. The leading lights are undoubtably Joeyfat, who also run one of Kent's only purpose-built venues, The Forum, although kindred spirits Sonar Nation, Dog Ugly, Seep and Couch Potatoes help to keep the hardcore flame burning." Ian also added, "As well as the bands there are a number of fanzines that have a hand in shaping the Kent underground. Most notably 'A New England' and the newsletter 'Your mornings will be brighter'. Both of these produced by Richard Murrill, a Folkestone based enthusiast who also puts on shows." It was great to see a well-deserved shout out for Rich.

Couch Potatoes were interviewed by Richard Corbridge for the second issue of his great hardcore scene zine 'Armed With Anger' where we discussed why the band formed, where the name came from and also what influenced us, before a more general discussion about the UK and US hardcore scenes and then a little about Couch Potatoes lyrics.

In 'Kent band' fanzine #19 the editor announced the upcoming 'Excess All Areas' tour by saying, "Unfortunately this summer has been a little lame recently, not really weather to drive your convertible to the beach and drink Coca-Cola, but we mustn't let it get us down because there's always something new and exciting over the horizon. This month I'm talking about a Couch Potatoes tour and their new LP 'Excess all areas'." He went on to say, "Tunbridge Wells based Couch Potatoes have been turning normally boring gigs into parties for a while now, but only recently recorded the fourteen-track album for Vice Records. The tour is a warm-up confined to the south-east to promote the album locally before their UK/European tour early next year." and went on to list all the tour dates and ticket contacts.

Whacked zine was incredibly enthusiastic when they received the demo tape for the new album and said "Excess All Areas' is the debut elpee by the bunch of fat lazy gits known as Couch Potatoes and easily the best Hardcore, and I use the word liberally(?), record ever released by a British band. Forget the (others), this is the album of the year. Make no mistake about it. There are a bucket load of potential singles here, the phenomenally catchy 'Bob', 'Hole', 'Part of you', 'Another' and yes, this word has been used before, the utter classic – 'Three'. Every single song is honed to murder. No fillers here mate, just perfectly crafted, riffy pop-core gems. This album, in my opinion, is on the same level as 'Nevermind' as it has the ability to appeal to indie pop kids, punks, thrashers, in fact bridge a whole spectrum of music listeners. Get it, buy it, steal it, tape it, hear it now!" Bloody hell! I must remember to send him that fiver I promised him for a good review.

We also did an interview with A H Zine for their very first issue. They started out with, "Tunbridge Wells finest melodic hardcore band are the Couch Potatoes. Since their 'Eight songs that suck' demo they've just kept on improving, just listen to the new album and see for yourself." Then their editor Austin asked us some pretty standard questions, which I can summarise to give you an idea of these small zine interviews that we were doing so many of. He'd ask about how the band got together and the Tunbridge Wells scene, to which we said it's great, we played loads of gigs and nowhere compares to it as there's loads of good people and lots of them are in bands which keeps it very creative. He'd ask if we played outside of Tunbridge Wells a lot and we said we did and some places were good, such as the Joiners in Southampton, but others sucked and it depended on the people mainly, but we all enjoyed playing anywhere and we'd love to play more. We told him that playing live was great and such fun, and also that the atmosphere was usually pretty good at our gigs. Then he asked about our favourite UK bands and we'd shout out the Jailcells, Understand, the Pseudo Hippies, Sonar Nation, BBMFs, Strookas and Funbug. He also asked about the bands we'd played with, so we bragged a little and mentioned Alice Donut, Chemical People, Jailcell Recipes (again), Down By Law, Alloy, NOFX and Green Day.

These interviews usually shared a lot of the same questions, but we were always glad to do them. Austin asked about our influences and Yan told him that lyrically he was influenced just by stuff he liked, so girls, food, bed and that sort of thing. I also mentioned the bands that influenced our music and included All, Descendents, Samiam, Big Drill Car, Green Day, MTX, 7 Seconds, Gorilla Biscuits, SNFU, Crimpshrine and Minor Threat. Austin also asked if we funded the new LP ourselves, or if it was paid for by a record label and we told him about Retch Records telling us to go in and record the album and they would fund it and release it, but then basically just fucking us over and letting us down, so we ended up paying for it all ourselves. Just over £600, so we were all skint now. He also asked about the band's name, and we gave the usual answer that we are all Couch Potatoes, quite literally, so we thought why not. We closed this chat with some comments about the new record coming out soon and if anyone wanted a cassette copy of 'Excess all areas' it was just £1.50 post-paid. We gave the contact address and my phone number for him to print too, which helped us shift a few more records and get a gig or two as well. All pretty standard stuff which we did time and time again over the year. It all helps, but must get very boring for bigger bands.

Soon after that, in their 3rd June issue, our local newspaper the Kent and Sussex Courier, ran an article headlined, 'Live music venue opens', which read;

"A new venue for live music is to open next week in Tunbridge Wells at St John's youth centre next to the town swimming pool. The Alternative Club is planned to be an irregular event hosted by the YMCA and local music lovers. Shows are to be run by young people for young people and although anyone is welcome to attend the bands performing will mainly consist of local young talent. It is hoped that the Alternative will provide an option for occasional entertainment in addition to the towns established clubs and pubs.

The first show, on Saturday, June 11, will be a hardcore/indie night featuring local bands Torque, Couch Potatoes and I'm Being Good. Torque caused quite a stir recently with their brand of grunge rock at the Battle of the bands gig and are tipped for bigger things. Couch Potatoes, who hail from Tunbridge Wells, have toured throughout the UK and supported bands such as Green Day, NOFX and Chemical People. They will be appearing to promote their new EP and will be back in the studio again soon. The warm-up is provided by I'm Being Good from Brighton, who recently supported Unsane.

People are advised to arrive early as the doors will open at 8pm and proceeds of the £2 on the door admission price will go to the youth centre towards funding further events".

There were contacts for the Alternative Club with their telephone number so people could book tickets and the article had a photo of the new Couch Potatoes line-up, standing on a bridge and looking thoughtful, positioned just above another article about some cheesy boy band that would visit the town soon. Clearly, we'd hit the big time. But we did need a local show in front of our home-crowd to let everyone know we were back.

11/6/94 Torque, Couch Potatoes and The Strookas
The Alternative Club, Pagoda Youth Centre, Tunbridge Wells

Couch Potatoes first show back in Tunbridge Wells had to be a good one and we hoped, very well attended. So as soon as we'd agreed the date with the youth centre, who were now calling the gigs at their Pagoda where we practised 'The Alternative Club' and wanting to make them regular nights, we went out flyering and sticking up posters with our usual abundant enthusiasm. We put posters up all over town, including (possibly rather foolishly), all around the area surrounding the Forum, a venue which pretty much had the monopoly on live music in Tunbridge Wells now. They clearly felt strongly about this affront because although we finished pasting posters around midnight, the very next morning as Dan K walked to catering college around 8am, somebody had already been out and slapped 'Cancelled' stickers on many of our posters. We thought this was a bit out of order and so it provoked another trip out the following night with even more posters that were worded in some complicated and clever way that even if a 'cancelled' sticker was stuck on them it would still be clear that the gig was going ahead. What ensued was a kind of local 'poster-gate' scandal that got blown out of all proportion with the council and police getting involved. It didn't help that I had fallen out with the Forum guys after the Joeyfat split and hadn't fixed that yet. I would eventually repair that situation but hadn't yet. For now, we just wanted to play somewhere else in town and I guess they didn't like that. We had to advertise the gig and let people know, but this all became a bit of a pain and most of the billboards in town looked a right mess.

Our enthusiasm was such that we'd walk around town handing out flyers and demo tapes to anyone who looked remotely alternative. We clearly had too much time on our hands. This exuberance even included us wandering into pubs and approaching anyone who looked like they might have been vaguely interested in live music, as well as flyering the schools and colleges. Dan and Paul were still at school so it was easy for them to hand out flyers there to all their mates. Usually word of mouth was enough for a local show for Couch Potatoes to be busy, but we were unsure so wanted to keep on pushing.

I tried to book semi-local bands that might bring a few people along with them too. They had to be far enough away to have a different crowd, but close enough to bring them with them. I invited Torque, from the Medway area in Kent and I'm Being Good, from Brighton in Sussex, hedging my bets as Tunbridge Wells sits right on the border of the two counties. They'd been writing about this gig in the local papers so we were getting quite a lot of coverage. For some reason a few days before the show I'm Being Good decided to pull out, so we replaced them with our mates The Strookas as we knew they'd be good.

All the bands arrived early that Saturday to get everything set up and soundcheck, but as the youth club was right next to the playing fields, we ended up having a quick kick around first. Someone booted the ball into a tree and as he shook the trunk to recover it an overhanging branch fell down and pierced the Torque drummer's cheek. There was a lot of blood and Mik had to go to hospital to have it stitched, but gamely came back to play the show in time for their headline set.

Torque were a five-piece hardcore band with a grooving style, heavily influenced by the likes of Quicksand and Helmet. The band consisted of Mal Irvine on vocals, Simon Cruickshank and Roly Mutter on guitars, Stef Dallney on bass and the hero of the day, Mik Gaffney on drums. They played a lot around the southeast and had supported Unsane, Reef and Dub War. They had moments of Soundgarden or Tool thrown into their hardcore stylings and were a pretty decent unit live, always bringing a good few people along to see them play too. Their enthusiastic vocalist Mal was very theatrical on stage and often brought his own pedal-operated strobe light to the shows for the heaviest parts. In one song there was a section where he'd repeatedly shriek "Where were you?!" and stomp on the strobe for effect, but that would then partially blind all the people at the front, and at one very sweaty show in Maidstone it even caused him to pass out! They rocked tonight though. Putting on a great show for the packed audience, getting rousing cheers from the sweaty young crowd and being dragged back on for an encore.

The Strookas had us all singing along to their brand of Husker Du and Dinosaur Jr influenced pop-core. I particularly enjoyed the tracks 'Some kind of wonderful' and 'My sister Dolly' and I know they were blown away by how good the response at this new club was for them.

Couch Potatoes rocked out with our own Descendents and Samiam influenced sound. And though I say so myself, it was pretty damn good for any band's third gig. We were back up and running. The Alternative club's friendly staff video-taped the show and it was hilarious to watch it back afterwards and see all of Paul and Dan's school mates going bananas at the front and dancing around.

This gig had certainly been a fun way to let everyone know that we were back, and we also managed to raise a few pounds for the youth centre too. I felt bad about Mik's injury though and even years later, when I'd see him working in Richards Records in Canterbury, or drumming for Kent Oi legends, The Last Resort, he still had that scar on his cheek.

20, Man's greatest friend...

I chased promoters for more gigs and labels for any interest. The larger US labels never seemed that keen, wanting bands that were already well known and selling lots of records, so they had little work to do and even less financial risk. But quite a few of the smaller UK and European labels were interested and that was where we were more likely to get support for a release. Luckily a couple of them had written back to us.

Amongst these smaller independent labels, I'd been chasing several in Germany about possible tours and releases for Couch Potatoes. The most interested guys at that point were Hohnie at Nasty Vinyl, the Pseudo Hippies' label, and Andreas at Born to Booze, the label that'd recently put out Couch Potatoes' 'Brad' EP. Hohnie and Andreas were working together now and had jointly signed a Dutch punk-rock band from Arnhem called The Harries. They were releasing an album for them and arranging a tour, supporting an American punk band called The Broken Toys. This tour would bring them all to the UK for a couple of shows in London, both of which we would be support at. I suspect they originally wanted the Pseudo Hippies to play these shows, as they were from London and would have been a better match musically, but the Pseudos had just broken up so Couch Potatoes were given the slots instead.

The Pseudo Hippies had spilt-up because they'd run out of steam creatively. After the brilliant German tour in September '93 they'd written more new songs and I thought they'd go on to release an album and make it onto bigger tours. They did book a tour around Ireland supporting Ash in February '94 and played to some big audiences, just before Ash had their big hit with 'Girl from mars' so were still in pubs and clubs mainly. It must have worn them down or caused an argument as they split up pretty much as soon as they returned. Kris said he wasn't enjoying it as much, and then Tom moved to Australia for a year so that put an end to that. However, in July '94, Matze from the Dipsomaniacs came over to London for a few days and I know Kris, Dan and Adam reconvened to meet him for a major drinking session. They decided to give it another go and advertised for a second guitarist, finding a like-minded pop-punkster and life-long friend in Dave Fritz, a Canadian living in London at the time. This is when they reformed under the new name of Wact.

In any case, Couch Potatoes started working with Nasty Vinyl and Born to Booze Records and were offered these shows instead. The first Couch Potatoes show with The Harries and Broken Toys was at The Playpen in Deptford on a Monday and the second at The Dublin Castle in Camden on Thursday the same week. Neither were busy, but both turned out to be fun shows to play.

The Playpen was a grubby little music club at the back of The White Swan pub on Blackheath Road in Greenwich, South London, and we ended up playing there quite a lot. We saw loads of shows there, more often than not after a trip to the nearby Café Sol Mexican restaurant. We'd fill up on good food and bad beer at the Café, then head to the Playpen for the gigs. I used to love the place as it always had a great atmosphere and a decent turn out of local rockers to cheer or heckle the bands.

The Dublin Castle was another London pub with a back room famous for all the bands that had played there. It was covered in posters and steeped in musical history, but it never seemed quite so much fun as the Playpen to me, probably because of its miserable regulars. A bunch of old Irish blokes would sit at the bar in stained suits, smoking and moaning to each other, and they seemed to be there almost every time we'd visit. The venue also employed a very grumpy soundman, named Jonathan 'The Ears' Digby, who we always managed to get into arguments with, and because of that we often had shit sound. Luckily 'The Ears' wasn't at this show, so the sound was good for all three bands.

Couch Potatoes played most of what would soon become our 'Windswept heights' record, The Harries sang songs about first kisses and being a teenager in love, and The Broken Toys threw themselves around whilst shouting about taking Prozac or having a hangover. It was all good fun and great practise for us as we'd be in the recording studio just two days later.

Recording Couch Potatoes 'Man's greatest friend in the windswept heights'

We spent the weekend recording ten tracks for the new Couch Potatoes demo that would become our mini-album, 'Mans greatest friend in the windswept heights'. For all the guys other than me it was their first time in a recording studio, and we'd gone back to the Posthouse Studios in East Peckham, as much for ease and locality as anything. George Althus, who'd recorded 'Excess All Areas' with us, wasn't there any more unfortunately, but instead we worked with Chris Priestley, another very good engineer. He helped us a lot as we got to grips with those new tracks and slowed us down a little when it was needed, as we tried to just bang through the tracks more or less as we would do live. It was very hot in that studio though and although we started out keen, eager to get the tracks down, we soon became hangry, so had to break for food and drinks to save us beating the shit out of each other. When we came back later and hit it again, refuelled and refreshed, it was way better. Or at least that's what Chris seemed to think, repeatedly saying "Now that's more like it".

couch potatoes

MAN'S GREATEST FRIEND IN THE WINDSWEPT HEIGHTS   E.N.A.

`Man´s Greatest Friend´ cassette artwork

We had a few ups and downs at that session, with tuning, timing, and Milo constantly swilling hot drinks as he thought that helped him nail the vocal lines. But generally, it ran smoothly. No-one wanted to waste time and after just two days we had all ten tracks in the bag. One of them, 'Never', was brand new and completely written from scratch, including lyrics, whilst we were in the studio.

A couple of days later we bunked off work, college or school and went back to the Posthouse to help Chris mix the tracks over one more day. On reflection, maybe we should have spent more time on the mix, but there you go. We were keen to get some tracks out that had been recorded by the new line-up as soon as possible. These songs initially became a demo for record labels, radios and promoters, and then soon came out with artwork and a cover as the 'Windswept heights' mini-album. First on Gotham Tapes, before seeing full release on CD through various labels.

There was a picture of a fur-covered Mongolian holding a yak on the front cover that we'd pilfered from a geography textbook one of the guys had for school. The book had provided a caption underneath the photo about yaks being 'Mans greatest friend in the windswept heights' so that's where the release's name came from, Dan Pullin's idea I believe. There's also a great photo of us playing a show at the Shelley Arms, you can see all five of us in it, a rare thing for live band shots. It was taken by Sarah Blackburn, Dan P's girlfriend at the time. Inside the release it said 'All tracks recorded and mixed at the Posthouse Studios on 18th, 19th and 23rd June '94. Engineered and produced by Couch Potatoes and Chris Priestley' and there's a thanks list too that included all our mates, the bands we'd played with and any promoters who'd helped us, plus the mahogany clackers (Milo's favourite pimp shoes) and the blokes at the back (from The Shelley Arms). The tracklist was 'Lost', 'User friendly', 'Kill it', 'Engineer', 'Impossible easier', 'Wall', 'Venue', 'Why', 'Poison me' and 'Never'. Only ten tracks, spanning just twenty-five minutes, but all of them would serve us well, ending up on various vinyl EPs and compilation releases several times over.

Reviews of Couch Potatoes `Man´s greatest friend in the windswept heights´

Ripping Thrash - Good stuff here by this Kent band. This is their third release, with good quality sound. Quite a bit different from their early EP on Weird Records, which was the last time I heard them. They've progressed quite a bit and found their own style of intricate melodic hardcore, but influences such as Jawbreaker and Samiam continue to shine through. A thoughtful and interesting album.

How We Rock - Ten songs with shouted, anguished and sung vocals with the music ranging from tuneful melodic to slow rockin' to more up-tempo stuff. reminds me of mid-80's DC hardcore in places with the melody and back-ups. Scream meets Jawbreaker. Pretty cool.

TDG zine – I've heard it once and already like it so it must be good. Sounds vaguely Fugazi-ish to me. Really lively, it had me and a few friends bouncing off the walls of my abode. Yep, we like this one, and the bloke who does the vocals isn't half bad.... he sings OK too.

Smile - This offers ten great chunks of melodic hardcore that you just might like. Buy it.

Terrorizer - I guess you could call this emo-core but that's not the be all and end all of it, because this is uncomfortable and disconcerting in parts, the lilting 'Engineer', for example. I'm not that sold on the production, but the songs shine through nonetheless.

30/6/94 Couch Potatoes
The Shelley Arms, Nutley

To celebrate our first recording with the new Couch Potatoes line-up I'd booked us a show at The Shelley Arms, an obvious choice for me and Milo as playing there meant a lot to us, but the venue was a shadow of its former self and in fact it closed down for good soon after. This gig was midweek, and during the '94 World Cup, which was disastrous for England, so shouldn't really have mattered in regard to our turn-out, but nevertheless beyond the band and bar staff there were maybe just ten people there, two of whom were, inexplicably under the circumstances, Jim and Jason from Joeyfat (I hadn't quite gotten over being booted out of Joeyfat yet, but I'm glad to say we did make up and are all chums again now. Life's too short.) There was also a group of another four lads hanging out at the back of the bar who really seemed to be enjoying the show and having fun despite the tumbleweed blowing around the venue. They became known as 'the blokes at the back' so we gave them a shout out in the thanks list for the 'Windswept heights' release. It was a terrible gig, just a practise with an audience really, but that happened occasionally. They can't all be good ones.

8/7/94 Squrgully, Couch Potatoes, 75% Dandruff and D:baser
The Angel Centre, Tonbridge

After that poor show at The Shelley, we needed to bounce back with a big party gig as soon as possible, so thankfully our bassist Paul had been setting up a show with all the bands from his school, Mascalls in Paddock Wood. They'd booked a night at the Angel Centre in Tonbridge, a big local venue that held at least three hundred people and would often see indie chart bands like Carter the Unstoppable Sex Machine and Ned's Atomic Dustbin playing there. Paul had got us on the bill with three bands we'd never heard of, but of course, we were still keen to play. All the bands were from Paul's school and he was even roped in to play in another one (75% Dandruff) too, with his good friend Rob Stubbings on guitar. (Much later Paul and Rob would go on to be in a great Split Lip style emo-core band called The Glory Scene. They'd later change their name to The Mockingbird Nightmare and release a split CD on Engineer Records with Saboteur and Red Light Green Light). It was a busy gig with a young and diverse audience that night. Just what we needed and really good fun. We jumped around that big old stage and encouraged as much rowdiness as we could. It cheered us all up no end, like only playing a great gig really can.

Soon after this we all went to see Down By Law on their 'PunkRockAcademyFightSong' tour at the Concorde in Brighton. It was a sweltering night and a great show, so afterwards we'd all hung out, and I spoke for ages with Dave Smalley, turning some of our conversation into an interview that was included in #8 of BHP zine. The DBL band line-up had changed again, with a new guitarist and bassist. Dave told me that Pat, the old bassist who was so cool to us when we played those shows together, was now a roadie for Sepultura. He was very positive about the resurgence of hardcore music that was going on around then, probably as they were now on their third album for Epitaph, and he shared all sorts of tour stories. One of them was about Down By Law recording their new album in the same studio (A&M Studios in Hollywood, California) that the Rolling Stones were using at the time. They'd bumped into the Stones in the corridor and said Hi, but when DBL were playing for the recording, after having to turn everything up to get feedback and the right sound for '1944', one of the punkier songs on the album, the Stones had called through to complain and ask them to turn it down. Dave seemed pretty pleased with that, and why not?

20/8/94 Iconoclast, Couch Potatoes, Bob Tilton and Above All The Dublin Castle, Camden, London

With a killer hardcore line-up like this I have no idea why the promoter booked the show at this venue. We always tried to be positive about any gigs, but as usual when we got there and walked in, there was already a gang of miserable old bastards all along the bar, talking shit and not paying any attention to the bands. To add to this, it'd been a long trip and the toilets were some of the worst ever with no paper, no locks, no working taps, and about an inch of water on the floor. Also, 'The Ears' was there again to fuck up the sound. Despite its positive history as a live music venue, there was now a dodgy pay-to-play policy some nights at The Castle where'd they'd just round up any three bands who needed a gig and hope they'd bring a crowd. This was not what we were into and possibly what was annoying the sound guy and the regulars too. Tonight's show would not be like that though.

During the soundcheck, our singer somehow managed to annoy the sound man, Johnathan 'The Ears' Digby (we'd noticed he had that written on his backpack now too!) I think by simply gesturing at him to turn something up in a way he took offence to, Milo had managed to piss him off, so he basically buried his vocals so far below the music during our set that he couldn't be heard, even with his shouting, unless you were standing right at the front. Some of the guys from Torque who happened to be in the crowd pointed it out to us, and Milo had to ask the sound guy very politely in front of everyone if he could turn him up again, but by then we were halfway through our set.

It was just one of those evenings. The sound for Above All wasn't very good either and although it had improved in time for the normally superb Bob Tilton, even they weren't up to their usual brilliant standards tonight. I can't remember for sure if it was this show, or another one we saw soon after around the corner at The Laurel Tree, that a few songs into their set the Bob Tilton guitarist threw himself into the drum kit and although it looked pretty cool, he really hurt himself, actually managing to break his leg! Finally, Iconoclast went on, five blokes in glasses who seemed to hate each other and mostly played with their backs to the audience. Their music was good but the feeling just wasn't there, and when Milo spoke with the drummer after the gig, he told him he was "mostly listening to Santana these days." Sure enough, Iconoclast broke up straight after this tour.

Couch Potatoes at The Dublin Castle

31/8/94 Neckbrace, Above All and Couch Potatoes
Saks, Southend

We'd been chatting with the guys from Above All at the previous week's show and they'd offered us the support with them for Neckbrace at Saks in Southend. This was a cool little sports bar with a live music room in the basement. I'd played there before with Joeyfat when we supported Artless, and knew that a hardcore show like that would get good support from all the Understand and Stand Off crew, so we jumped at the chance.

Hallam and Tony, who had both been in Stand Off, were now both in Above All. Later they would be joined by Dan Carter from Beacon, before he formed A, and also Ben Doyle, before he went on to join Hundred Reasons. We didn't know it at the time, but Above All were something of an early UKHC supergroup. If you get a chance check out their massively powerful three track 7" 'Blood of ages' on Sure Hand Records. They also had a great track called 'Saviour' on a flexi-disc that went out with issue fourteen of How We Rock fanzine, and they went on to sign to Roadrunner Records and release a great album called 'Domain'. Neckbrace were an extremely heavy hardcore band from the north of England, with Heath Crosby from Nailbomb screaming for them. He'd later be the first singer for Stampin' Ground too. As far as I know they only ever released one self-titled EP and it came out on No Cruelty Records. Both of these bands were pretty full-on hard-line vegan straight-edgers and although we rocked it as hard as we could, by now Couch Potatoes were getting more melodic and must have seemed an odd choice to support them really. The audience much preferring the two noisier bands. Standing watching us, bobbing around and clapping when we finished songs, but then jumping about and going mad to the next bands.

The gig became a bit chaotic later. In fact, I'm pretty sure that Stand Off, who were all there in the crowd, did a short guest set at this show too, as their 7" on Crucial Response, brilliantly entitled 'Worthless is the unity bought at the expense of truth', was just out and they played that along with a cover of Project X's 'Straight Edge Revenge' with some local nutcase on guest vocals managing to get most of the words wrong. Milo and I were standing with the Understand guys and they all seemed to be loving it, laughing their asses off and singing along. Maybe it was just me. We'd played a mixed bag of gigs lately and needed something different. We'd have the long drive home from Southend to discuss it.

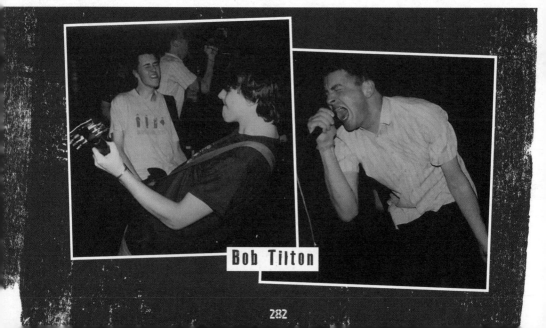

Bob Tilton

21, Another German adventure

Rolling back from Southend in the Beast we all agreed that we needed a change of scenery and a solid run of shows to really bring things together for the band. We were happy enough with the 'Windswept heights...' tracks but knew we could do better and as we started to click, we were writing new tracks with more of an upbeat Samiam meets Lifetime kind of style to them that we were all happier with. Anyone can form a band but being any good takes time and practise. We had the ideas and enthusiasm in buckets, but we needed more gigs to hone our songs and stage presence. We all really wanted to play outside of the UK too, to tour in Europe was a bit of a dream. Milo and I had a small taste of that with the Pseudo Hippies and we knew some promoters that would be positive about Couch Potatoes coming over. We all wanted an adventure and I'd been working on getting us one.

Thanks mainly to Andreas at Born to Booze Records the new Couch Potatoes soon had our chance. He and I had been corresponding about possible gigs and releases, he already had 'Excess all areas' and now I'd sent across 'Man's greatest friend in the windswept heights' too. Andreas told me that he was now calling his label A-Wat Records, (instead of Born To Booze) a great relief to Milo and me, with our current straight-edge sensibilities, and that he wanted to arrange more punk and hardcore tours. He asked if we'd like to get over to Europe and play some shows there and I wanted to hug the guy. Of course we did! It was just what we needed.

Andreas and I had discussed a short tour before but up to this point I wasn't sure the band was ready, just not tight enough yet. There was also the concern about the guys getting out of school and college, or Milo and I getting out of work, but that was usually easier in the summer. We'd just somehow missed the boat so far or had clashing gigs on in the UK, but these were the last days of the summer holidays now and if we went for it, we could just fit in ten or so shows. Luckily for us Andreas was keen and said he'd deal with it all, even print up the tour posters and send them out to the venues, we just needed to book the tickets and get over.

5/9/94 Couch Potatoes and Charlie Don't Surf
The Clockwork Club, Leuven, Belgium.

Getting a good run of gigs together always seemed easier for us in Europe than in the UK. This would be more of an adventure too and certainly more profitable, usually with larger crowds and better organised venues. For this tour Andreas had managed to book us eleven shows over fourteen days and said he'd join us at the second gig, in Bocholt, and accompany us around for the rest. We had to get ourselves over to Leuven in Belgium for the first show and find the Clockwork Club. That sounded easy enough, so we all piled into the beast, which had been off the road for a few months as I couldn't afford to tax or insure her. She'd been stored at a farm where Riley, one of Dan P's mates lived and we occasionally went to practise. Knowing this tour was coming up I'd gotten her back and had the old monster M.O.T'd and serviced. The beast was behaving and running soundly, so we headed off in high spirits, but somehow the bonnet catch got broken on the way to the ferry and we spent the entire tour with a couple of bungee cords strapped across the hood. There were leaks and creaks developing too, so we crossed our fingers.

It was just the band in the van this time, the five of us along with our musical equipment stacked at the back and a bunch of Couch Potatoes merchandise we'd managed to get together in time for the tour stuffed under the bunk beds. We had the 'Brad' and 'In bed with' vinyl 7"s, 'Excess All Areas' and the new 'Windswept Heights' cassettes, and a bunch of t-shirts too as we knew they'd sell well. We had a couple of designs with the usual Couch Potatoes logo on, the one we'd used on the tour posters and 'Excess all areas', but the main shirt design we had with us was a new one with 'Quality is our recipe', the Wendy's burger restaurant logo on it. These shirts had 'Couchies' on the breast in the restaurant's font, with a large circle on the back saying 'Biggreendescenedalliam' around a cartoon of the Wendy's girl with pigtails. They were mainly white shirts with red and blue print, and we had about two hundred of them in all sizes.

For the uninitiated or those that care, 'Bigreendescendalliam' was a comment that Tony Sylvester, a friend, hardcore scenester, Fabric bassist and Turbonegro singer, made to us when describing the sound and influences of the original Couch Potatoes. The Big being taken from Big Drill Car, the Green from Green Day, Descend from Descendents, All being, of course, from ALL and the iam from Samiam. We were flattered by this summing up and thought it was genius so unashamedly made good use of it.

As we bowled across Belgium it started to pour with such torrential rain that we soon had water streaming in through the seals and running down the inside of the windscreen. We could barely see where we were going so had to pull over and make repairs. Dan K, our ever-inventive drummer, grabbed his trusty gaffa tape and plastered it all over any joints or leaks, mainly around the windscreen, but in several other places too, and those repairs stayed on and held for years. Well, the rest of the van's life in any case. We were often grateful on tour for the amazing 'fix all' power of gaffa tape.

We hammered onwards, through the storm, past Brussels and into the centre of Leuven, eventually finding the Clockwork Club and parking up right outside. We were quickly greeted by Gert, the friendly promoter. He was wearing a 'Charlie Don't Surf' shirt, a local band who'd be supporting us tonight. Gert led us through the ground floor café bar,

Andreas sleeping in the belly of the beast

Couch Potatoes at the Innocent, Hengelo

Couch Potatoes at The Clockwork Club, Leuven

't Vervolg, which meant 'to be continued', down into a cellar where the bands would play. This was the Clockwork Club with its big orange sign. This venue was very much like the German punker-bunker places we'd seen on the Pseudo Hippies tour and had a large Clockwork Orange character in a bowler hat painted on the far wall with clock hands coming out of one of his eyes. The venue was already filling up with kids, mostly in Bad Religion and NOFX t-shirts, and although we hadn't arrived that late it seemed like they'd been there waiting for us for a while. The punk rock party atmosphere was already in full swing, and we all felt like this would be a good show.

The support band, Charlie Don't Surf, were already set up and ready to go, so that made it very easy for us, just bringing in the minimum gear through the rain and soundchecking quickly. Dan P, Paul, Dan K and I jammed and quickly sorted the levels both we and the sound guy were happy with, whilst Milo set up a little merchandise stall, laying out the records and tapes across a table, with a lamp to light them, and then sticking a few t-shirts up on the wall behind him with our precious multi-use gaffa tape.

There was a very low ceiling in the Clockwork and quite a few coloured lights, mainly orange, lighting up the small room so the place heated up fast. Even before the support band went on and did a great job of getting everyone going. By the time we played it was boiling in that club. We were rocking around at the front of a small low stage with kids dancing right next to us so Milo decided to go for a walk through and around them whilst he was singing. I joined in after a while, trying not to get my guitar lead stamped on or knocked out as I wandered about, hammering on my sticker covered, black SG and sweating into my new Batman shirt.

We played everything we could, some of it twice, and then sold a load of records and shirts. This was a great start to the tour and gave us the confidence we all needed. (We had, however, gone into this tour without working out a definite set or even writing down a setlist so we were a little unprepared in that respect. We had quite a few songs to choose from so on the drive to the next show there was a discussion in the back of the van between Milo, Paul and the two Dans about what song followed what best, which shouldn't be played next to each other because of similarities, or difficulties, and they eventually came up with their preferred set list which we all stuck to for pretty much the rest of the tour. No more shouting out ideas or deciding between songs needed and we could have a slow track between a few faster ones to give us a quick breather or even a moment to tune up. We were so professional).

We were all hanging out after the show, drinking and chatting, and we ended up spending the night there. Kris, another one of the guys who ran the café / bar along with the promoter, Gert, let us drink and eat as much as we wanted as part of our rider. This was always a big bonus for Couch Potatoes. We liked to live up to our name after all. Dan K and I ended up staying downstairs in the club all night with a couple of the locals, but Milo, Paul and Dan P went upstairs and settled down in an empty room on the top floor to try to get some sleep. This room had just one double mattress on the floor and even though they had sleeping bags, apparently it was freezing and creaky, with dust and cobwebs everywhere. "It was like staying in a bloody haunted house" Milo said in the morning.

6/9/94 Couch Potatoes
The Blauerbock, Bocholt, Germany

The next day we thanked Kris and Gert for the show and their hospitality, and then headed out of Leuven and Belgium, across the corner of Holland and on into Germany to a town called Bocholt. It was only about one hundred and fifty miles away, but it took us three long hours and involved more skidding around in the rain as well as a quick pit-stop for some chocolate milk.

Although I tended to do most of the driving to gigs, certainly with the beast as she could be fun to handle in the wind and rain on the autobahns, the ever-enthusiastic Dan K took over for me on a lot of this tour. He didn't have a full UK license yet but as we were abroad felt this was a good chance to practise. None of us fancied dying in a multi-car pile-up, but figured he didn't either, so we crossed ourselves and let him crack on. Dan drove hundreds of miles on this trip, all around strange lands with wobbly steering and loud distractions. When he got back his driving instructor figured it was still too soon to put in for his driving test, but he figured driving a Metro around Tunbridge Wells would be comparatively easy after this and was right, passing first time, with the guy commenting that it seemed like he'd been driving for ages.

Anyway, we made it safely to Bocholt, a pretty little town, typically German looking with quite a few surviving half-timbered medieval style buildings. We drove around and found the club, noticing that it had gone for a picture of Marilyn Monroe above the door, rather than a blue goat or deer, as the name suggested. We went inside and were immediately offered beers and Fanta by the friendly owners, who even helped us load all the equipment in. Eventually Andreas arrived, I'd met him before, briefly on the Pseudo Hippies tour and he was a friendly enough guy, but as we soon found out on this trip, he seemed to be perpetually sleepy. This may have been drugs but was more likely just that he was quite a lot older than us, a tall, dark-haired punker, who definitely enjoyed our music, but I think became tired-out by our youthful antics after a while. We set up and sound-checked before going to get some dinner, then later played a pretty decent show but to only around fifty or so people. We were told we'd be back at this venue again later in the tour so most people would come along on that night instead.

Afterwards we followed Andreas back to his house, which turned out to be a tiny top floor flat that he shared with his girlfriend, so only Milo and Dan K crashed on the floor in his living room, whilst Dan P, Paul and I went back out to sleep in the van. It was cold but we were used to it and the beast had comfortable bunk beds.

Outside The AK47 in Dusseldorf

Couch Potatoes `Eat Plutonium Death´ Euro Tour poster

7/9/94 Couch Potatoes and supports
The AK47, Dusseldorf, Germany

We had a lazy morning at Andreas flat where he showed us loads of ads he'd placed and reviews he'd received for Couch Potatoes 'Brad' EP in German fanzines in advance of this tour. Most of the reviews were good with the usual 'UK version of US style pop-punk' comments but one reference I liked in particular compared my guitar playing to Stuart Adamson of Big Country. He was an early hero of mine and I'd been to see them play a few times, even once when they came to Tunbridge Wells, so I was chuffed about that.

Andreas told us, whilst dribbling milk and cereal down his chin, that today we would be playing a 'proper punk show' and that sounded ominous to me, having seen some of the German punk squats. But he insisted that the AK47 in Dusseldorf was a cool venue that we would all love. It was only about an hour away so even leaving late we arrived in plenty of time. Driving into Kiefernstrasse later that afternoon we saw that the entire street was covered in colourful graffiti and punk rock murals. Andreas told us that every house was squatted by punks and anarchists, and he thought that this was the coolest neighbourhood in the city by far. We parked up and wandered around, snapping a few photos, including a couple that Andreas took of us all so we could use them as band shots on new releases and for fanzine interviews during the tour. It was a cool looking place and reminded me a little of a more colourful version of the 1 in 12 Club in Bradford.

Dan Pullin was sitting on top of an old fridge with Milo taking photos of him when Andreas came bowling over to us with the club promoter, a large blond guy called Olli, in a Dead Kennedys t-shirt. He offered us inside for some veggie food and said we could set up whenever we wanted, but there would be three local support bands so there was no rush. He already had a copy of 'Brad' from Andreas and said he loved it. He was a big Descendents fan and thought we'd go down really well with the local crowd. I hoped so. Inside the club every inch of wall space was covered in graffiti too and behind the low stage there was a massive red star with AK47 written either side of it and a red machine gun underneath. There was a decent looking p.a. and a big lighting rig too, and even though the place stunk of beer and weed, we knew the sound would be good for tonight's show. We all had some of the veggie stew they had bubbling away in a huge communal pot, but unfortunately for Milo, he went to make use of the toilet cubicle, fashioned out of pallets which you could see right through, sitting pretty much in the middle of the live room, just as they opened the doors and the venue started to fill up.

It was a good show though, with plenty of punkers and local hardcore kids, not all of whom played in the support bands, and many of which were bouncing around and really enjoying themselves. I didn't manage to grab one of the show posters before they were all taken, and annoyingly I can't remember the names of the support bands that evening, but they were a good mixture of hardcore, political and pop-punk. We went on late and rocked out. The sound on-stage was great and this gig was by far the best we'd played so far. We were mainly playing tracks from 'Windswept heights' with a few from 'Excess' but we threw in a few covers too, just for crowd recognition and participation. By now we'd also started writing new songs in a more chiming Samiam sort of style too, for what would eventually become our 'Outweighed' album. The first of these new songs was 'Sunset' and we wanted to give it a go this evening, but Milo didn't have the lyrics ready yet. He'd decided though that it sounded a bit like a Monsula song he knew, so for this show and a couple on the tour afterwards, he sung the lyrics to 'Two' over it. There weren't many lyrics and it worked quite well. When he eventually came up with the lyrics for 'Sunset' they were also inspired by this tour, as the song was about a girl we'd stay with after our show in Siegen. Milo said, "She told me that she was going to be moving away to another area for school and for some reason it made me profoundly sad that she had to leave her group of friends and this really cool scene. We'd got to spend some time with those people after the gig and get to know them. So, I wrote the words on our next epic drive and had them sorted for shows by the end of the tour."

By the end of our show at the AK47 the walls were running with sweat and the floor was covered in beer. The place was filled with noisy punk rockers who just did not seem to want to leave. Everyone sat around smoking and drinking, and Andreas had done very well with sales of Couch Potatoes merch and records from his punk rock distro stall too. The party looked set to continue all night, but we didn't really fancy trying to sleep there amongst it all, so we loaded out the gear and started a long drive south, ending up sleeping in the van somewhere near Frankfurt.

9/9/94 Couch Potatoes and Louis Paleur
The Kessel, Offenburg, Germany

In the morning we grabbed some breakfast from a petrol station and continued our drive down to Offenburg. This was way down in the south, past Baden Baden and Strasbourg, and on the edge of the Black Forest. Milo and I had been here before, the previous year on the Pseudo's tour, and being a nerd, I was keen to visit Staufenberg castle on the way if we had time. We managed to hit some huge traffic jams on the autobahns though and I was getting knackered, so Paul took over the driving for a while. Andreas was already fast asleep in one of the bunks and I tried to get some rest too, but that was about the time the two Dan's decided to wrap tea towels around their heads and goof around like terrorists, hanging out of the side door as we drove along, waving pretend guns at other drivers and coming up with all kinds of crazy reasons for their jihad. Milo took a photo of this, and we used it later on the lyric sheet insert of our 'Square' EP.

It took us a while to get to Offenburg and when we finally hit town we made straight for The Kessel. We parked the beast and stretched out on the pavement outside the venue, we were all just so pleased to be there. There was a bunch of skateboarders hanging around in the square outside again and we were sitting watching them when Steve, the promoter, came over to greet us. Steve and Imund were lovely people and had put the show on last year too, but in the interim they had broken up and Steve looked considerably less jolly, although he told us that Imund would be coming to the show tonight to see us. We all went inside hoping for some massive pizzas and Fanta again but found that the support band had already eaten most of our rider and were now wiping what was left of it over the p.a. and microphones. Fucking tossers.

The support band for tonight's gig were French. They were called Louis Paleur and believe me when I say that they were a very strange assortment of oddballs. The bass player thought he was Jimi Hendrix so dressed and looked very much like him, but of course could not play like him at all. The singer was a hippy who never seemed to wear any shoes and presumably because of that, had incredibly dirty feet. Both the guitarists dressed like stereotypical French fishermen or farmers with thick striped Breton style shirts on. Only their drummer seemed remotely normal to us, and he was the only one able to speak very much English too. He asked Dan K if he could borrow his drums almost immediately on seeing him walk in. They were a sort of rock covers band and they suggested, in all seriousness, that they would play for an hour, and then we could play, and then they would go back on and play for another two hours. We thought they were joking, but that is in fact exactly what they did! They were characters alright and after the long drive they were soon getting under our skin. Dan P in particular was absolutely seething about the time they were taking over their soundcheck and how they were treating our amps. While we were killing time before the gig he was constantly banging on about them and what an affront they were, saying stuff like "Look at him, walking around with no shoes on eating crisps." It's funny now, but at the time I think he came close to murdering a couple of those silly fuckers.

The show was another good one though with plenty of dancing and audience interaction. I wasn't sure if the packed crowd were there to see Louis Paleur or Couch Potatoes, but it didn't matter, working out well as they all seemed to enjoy our set. Afterwards Steve said that we didn't have to stay at the club that night but could come back with him to his parents' house where there was more space and obviously, less gallic idiots. We were only too glad to go with him, leaving soon after we'd finished our set, with Dan grabbing his drum stool and leaving an old beer crate on its side there instead. Always a handy standby. We really didn't want to stick around to endure their second two-hour set, which I know is very bad manners of a band, but really, they sucked. It was a good decision. Steve's parents' house was luxurious. Just heaven compared to what we were used to, with plenty of hot water as well as soft pillows, mattresses and warm duvets. We all managed to shower and get a good night's sleep, returning us back to our normally chipper selves.

10/9/94 Couch Potatoes and Carpe Diem
V.E.B, Siegen, Germany
The next morning, we thanked Steve for the show and his mum for the breakfast then headed out to tidy up the Beast and refuel before grabbing the rest of our gear and starting the long drive back north. We were heading up to Siegen, a beautiful old university town in

the hills about fifty miles east of Cologne, to a venue called the V.E.B. This was a far snappier title than its full name of Volkseigener Betrieb Politik, Kunst und Unterhaltung, which meant State owned company for Politics, Art and Entertainment. It was a massive orange building with all the usual anti-fascist graffiti outside and the VEB logo, a large red sickle crossed over a cocktail glass, painted high up on the brick chimney. The venue was organised by the local collective, kind of like a giant Joiners run by the S.T.E. but with a much larger concert hall, two practise rooms for bands and a café too. We were stoked to learn that Gorilla Biscuits had played there just recently, and we couldn't wait to get on that stage.

It turned out to be one of the best shows of the tour, with two hundred or so people there who all seemed intent on having fun. The university kids had been promoting the gig with the tour posters Andreas had sent and it had been mentioned on a local radio show too, where they'd played a couple of our songs. All this certainly cheered Dan P up after the previous night's shenanigans. He met some friendly skateboarders outside and went for a roll around with them to burn off some energy, while Dan K and I did our best to answer an interview with the guys from the local A-ttacke fanzine. We met Carpe Diem, a great hardcore band who sounded a bit like Life But How To Live It, and when I mentioned that I thought 'Seize the day' was a cool name for a band to their singer, she seemed surprised that we even knew what their name meant. They turned out to be an ideal support band and everyone at the gig was really friendly and into it. Couch Potatoes played the best set we had up to that point, Andreas sold loads of records and shirts, and the whole show really rocked. The atmosphere of the place definitely helped and this is what gigs should always be like.

Afterwards we stayed at the house of a girl who had made her bed out of cardboard. I wish I could remember her name. She was some kind of architecture student and had carefully designed the bed to be load bearing. It was a very impressive structure, but I'm pretty heavy so I decided not to jump on it. We had a day off the next day so stayed there, in Siegen, for a while and that girl turned out to be the inspiration for Milo's lyrics for the song 'Sunset' on our 'Outweighed' album. As I mentioned before, he'd been singing a Monsula lyric to the music up until then but soon wrote some proper words of his own and started singing those.

The next day Dan P and Milo went to a massive indoor skatepark with a bunch of kids who we'd met at the show the night before, whilst the rest of us just hung out and took it easy. Later, Milo went into Cologne with the skater kids to see Rain Like The Sound Of Trains play. He was stoked about it as RLTSOT featured Bobby Sullivan from Soulside, Dug Birdzell from Beefeater and Pete Chramiec from Verbal Assault, three bands that he loved. It was the last gig of their tour and turned out to be their last ever show, as they broke up after getting back home to DC. Milo nicked a poster from the gig which he cherished for a while, before giving it to a buddy, Dan Docwra, who reportedly now has it framed on his wall.

Rain Like The Sound
Of Trains flyer

Square 7" cover photo
taken outside Andreas
parents house

The JKC in Troisdorf

Couch Potatoes Bigreendescendallaiam t-shirt

We later reconnected with one of those kids we were hanging out with in Siegen, Marc Treude, during one of Rydell's many trips to Germany, and he became a labelmate too as he sang in a band called For The Day who released a great album named 'Love isn't brains, children' on Scene Police and Rockstar Records in the early 2000s.

We played a party-type gig the next evening, an impromptu affair at someone's house, and it must've been nearby as Milo was still hanging around with 'Sunset' girl and Dan P was still skating about. He was encouraging Paul and Dan K to have a go too, which I don't think I approved of, thinking that having the drummer and bassist break their arms in the middle of a tour wouldn't be too clever an idea. We also spent quite a lot of time just sitting around playing records and drinking, and I went for an aimless drive too, initially to get some Cacao Trunk chocolate milk that I was a big fan of, but then just ended up rolling about and checking out some of the local scenery along the Sieg river. It is a truly beautiful area.

13/9/94 Couch Potatoes and Tequila Girls
The Blauerbock, Bocholt, Germany
We eventually headed back up to The Blauerbock in Bocholt to play our second show of the tour there, for which Andreas promised there would be a much bigger crowd, partially as that was the day everyone was expecting us to play there as it was on the tour posters and also partially as he'd booked another touring band to play with us on the same night. This was Tequila Girls, a Swedish band with releases on a Polish label who'd helped them arrange the tour. They were a folk punk band, none of whom were girls and in fact I never saw them drink any tequila either. They were pretty damn good though, jumping around with their guitars and mandolins, and singing songs about dolphins with the blues, toxic unicorns and going mad on mescaline. Their lead guitarist wore a kilt and skateboarding knee pads so that he could do knee bombs across the stage. They really warmed the place up as you can imagine, and the evening gig turned into a party.

We stayed at Andreas parents' house afterwards. I think he'd realised his flat wasn't big enough for us all, but he was also missing his girlfriend. He dropped us off at this fancy house and disappeared, but his parents were cool and must have been used to that sort of thing as they had some spare rooms ready for us and there was plenty of space. They let us all take much needed showers in the morning too. After a leisurely breakfast, we had a kick-around in the road outside. Dan Kingdon always took a football everywhere he went, and that's when Andreas and his girlfriend showed up again. They took a photo of the band in a five-a-side football team pose. We thought it was hilarious and used the picture on the cover of our next 7", the 'Square' EP, that would come out on Weird Records.

14/9/94 Couch Potatoes
Dschungel, Dusseldorf, Germany
Andreas said thanks to his parents and kissed his girlfriend goodbye, then we all piled into the Beast and drove back down the Rhine Valley to Dusseldorf where we eventually found

Dschungel, or the Jungle club. This was a weird venue that looked like it usually hosted strippers and saw lots of fights. There were plastic plants and fake gold everywhere and the guy we met running it was wearing a suit. That was the first time we'd seen that at a punk or rock venue. He told us that there were no other bands playing tonight and we had beer, but no food and no place to stay. Smashing. Milo had developed a cold so was feeling rough and getting grumpy. He decided to head straight out and get some hot food. He ended up wandering around in the rain before finding a cheap Indian and getting some hot curry in an attempt to sort himself out and clear his pipes so he'd be able to sing. The rest of us loaded our gear in and took our time sound-checking, as so far there wasn't anyone there apart from us and the soundman. We had some spare time so honed our version of 'Safe', a super-fast Dag Nasty cover we'd been working on.

We needed to befriend someone if we wanted to have a wash and somewhere to sleep tonight, but this was not one of the better shows and I don't think even twenty people turned up to see us. The guys from the AK47 clearly not wanting to venture across town to Dschungel. Luckily for us, there was a bloke at the show who we got chatting to who used to live in Tonbridge, the next town over from sunny Tunny Wells. He was living in Dusseldorf now with his German girlfriend and was a pretty decent bloke as I recall, but we had to turn on as much charm as possible for him to decide he wanted to put up a smelly punk rock band for the night. Astonishingly he agreed, I think on his girlfriend's insistence, and they took us all back to a big flat where we could wash and share some warmer floor space. Some of us bunked down in the living room and some of us went back out to the van. Paul took some floorspace that had been offered in the bedroom, but as soon as the lights went out our hosts started making all sorts of noises that indicated they were getting it on, and Paul came bouncing out of there in his sleeping bag, grumbling, "They're fucking in there, I can't sleep through that." We were awoken in the morning and offered breakfast by our friendly host, only to be totally put off by his hairy-armpitted girlfriend eating raw mince for hers.

15/9/94 Couch Potatoes and Tequila Girls
Remise, Lemgo, Germany

We had to leave early anyway, as it was starting to dawn on me that Andreas had maybe never seen a map before. For the next show we had to drive several hours east across Germany, well past Bielefeld, to a small town in the countryside called Lemgo. This would take us a good three hours in the Beast, and somewhere past Dortmund we stopped in a small town to fuel up, play some pool, and grab a pizza and pasta buffet. While Paul, Dan and I were sitting outside, chatting and scoffing, a couple of Nazi-looking fellows drove past giving us the eye. They must have pulled up and come back, maybe seeing the GB sticker on our van, because a few minutes later as we were climbing back into the Beast, they came charging around the corner, shouting abuse at us and clearly intent on trouble. I grabbed the handy tyre jack we kept in the side-door panel and went straight at them with it. Figuring offence may be better than defence in this situation. Luckily, they scarpered a bit sharpish, and we got out of Dodge before there was any serious trouble.

We were playing at a venue called the Remise, meaning Discount, that evening. It turned out to be an old two-storey abbey building that had been totally refurbished, white-washed and re-purposed into an adult education centre for arts and music. It stood all alone in the middle of some fields on the edge of town, but as we pulled up there were already quite a few people milling about and the promoter came over to greet us. She knew Andreas and said that she had some music students who were going to record the show tonight, if that was OK by us. They would be running the sound desk, lights and everything else, and were really looking forward to it.

We piled over to help the students set things up, and were soon all sat down to a dinner of sausages, chips and salad with them. Loads of kids were arriving so we knew it was going to be a lot better than the shambles of the previous evening. The Tequila Girls were going to be joining us again too, and they were good fun. I asked Andreas why we didn't simply play with them again yesterday, but he said they travelled too far east to play in some folk club, and he couldn't be bothered to go that far. Nice. He slept through most of the journeys, so I didn't see what the problem was, but we didn't get into it. We still had three more shows of this tour to go, and I was grateful that he'd got us there.

Very soon the Tequila Girls turned up, piling out of their van to join us for dinner and then soundchecks. It all sounded great tonight with the guitars booming around that big old room until the crowd started arriving and soaking up some of the noise. The Tequilas treated us to more Swedish folk punk songs, and I still have a tape of them kicking around somewhere, so although it's not my normal 'go to' music I can tell you there were good tracks called 'We will rise', another called 'Harbour of ghouls' and one called 'Serial Killer' too.

Couch Potatoes banged through fifteen tracks in about forty-five minutes with a little bit of banter from Milo and me in between. I know that for sure as I still have the tape the music students gave us after the show, and we later used this live gig recording for one side of a Couch Potatoes release on Dragnet Records called 'Stampbox'. Our setlist was made up of tracks from either 'Excess', 'Windswept heights' or 'Outweighed', plus a silly short song that Dan K came up with for fun. No covers at all, although Dan later came up with a thrash cover version of 'No Limits' by 2 Unlimited on this tour. I think he fancied the singer, and we kept hearing it in the dodgy German clubs we played.

NB: For diehard Couch Potatoes fans, yes both of you, the silly song, 'Bit Rich' was an extremely short track, the sole lyric of which was 'Bit Rich' and took as long to play as it did to say. The inspiration for the song / set interlude was that Dan K had been very amused by a remark made by Chris Priestley, the engineer who'd recorded us at The Posthouse.

After starting one of our troublesome cars up, Chris sniffed and commented in a voice reminiscent of a Harry Enfield character, "Bit rich, been pissing in the tank?" Quite why that might have been the case is anyone's guess, but he said it so matter-of-factly that it just sounded like something that was normal to him. It soon became a band saying for anything that wasn't quite right.

16/9/94 Couch Potatoes and X-Men
Jugendkulture Cafe, Troisdorf, Germany

We started heading back towards home with our next show in Troisdorf, this was in the Ruhrpark area of Germany where most of our shows seemed to be, in an industrial town between Cologne and Bonn. The venue was another one of those youth clubs that regularly put bands on to entertain the kids. This one even looked like a school, but with a large JKC, for Jugend Kulture Cafe (Youth Culture Café) spray-painted above the double doors. The walls were all scrawled with the 'gegen everything' slogans we'd come to expect, and the doorway was plastered with Couch Potatoes tour posters that Andreas had produced. It looked cool, a big blue Couch Potatoes logo on top of a grey background with a DR and Quinch from 2000AD on it, saying 'Be there or eat plutonium death!' Then all the gig details, with support bands, dates, costs, etc and the A-wat and Born to Booze logos on it too. These were big posters and we'd been seeing plenty of them around, but this was the first chance I had to grab a couple, so I went and hid them in the van.

We piled inside and there was already a decent-sounding hardcore band set up and playing. This was the X-Men, a local straight-edge band who would be supporting us tonight. They'd already set up all the gear and it was sounding great, so they were having a practise. The X-Men came over to greet us and eat veggie stew when they'd finished the song. We all got on well, and they told us that they'd invited all the hardcore kids from this and the surrounding towns so it should be a busy night. Sure enough, it was a busy show with a very friendly hardcore energy. Both bands played long sets, and Couchies sold out of our t-shirts and vinyl so just had a few tapes left.

This gig had to be finished before eleven so afterwards the X-Men took us to get some chocolate milk, and then we helped them pack their gear away again into their practise room, which was a barn in the middle of nowhere. We didn't have many photos of the shows as we were all on stage playing, and Andreas never seemed to be awake enough to remember, but we took a couple of photos hanging out with those guys in their practise barn. It looked like a comfortable place to crash, but they said we couldn't and instead the X-Men's singer made a few calls and arranged for us all to stay at his girlfriend's house. He led us over to her place and we all crashed there. I don't even think she'd been at the show that evening, but she still welcomed us in and let us crash, which was great right up until the point where she insisted on blasting bloody Pearl Jam at us most of the night to 'help her sleep'.

17/9/94 Couch Potatoes and X-Men
Innocent, Hengelo, Holland

The next morning the X-Men guys came over to collect us and took us all shopping in Troisdorf. Milo bought a red beret from an army surplus store as he thought the singer of the X-Men looked cool wearing one. Clearly, he was fried and it was time to go home. We had one more show to play and that would be an afternoon matinee at the Innocent Club in Hengelo, just over the border in Holland, so we drove in convoy up there as fast as we could. Couch Potatoes in the Beast, the X-Men in their van followed by a car full of their friends, and Andreas in a car with his girlfriend and some more mates. It didn't take long to get there, and we could see that this was a cool venue. There were already punks and rockers hanging around outside, and although from the front it looked like a regular bar or café, down the side it had a parking area for tour vans and a big colourful anarchist mural leading to a back garden and side entrance to the stage for loading in.

Inside, the whole place was full of gig posters and hardcore band stickers. The columns either side of the stage were so covered in layers of stickers that they were almost padded by them. There were even posters on the ceiling, and we noticed that on the wall behind the bar there was a sign that said, 'Het huis van hardcore', The home of hardcore. The stage had an Innocent logo backdrop with a large skull and crossbones painted on it, and both the X-Men and Andreas clearly knew the guys that ran the place well. They'd been here a few times before, and the promoters came straight over to greet us all.

The venue was buzzing and that was impressive considering it was still broad daylight outside and not long after lunchtime. When first X-Men and then Couch Potatoes hit the stage, we gave it our all. We were jumping around and making the most of the last show of the tour. Dan P broke a few strings and Dan K dropped a few sticks, but no one cared, and it was all great fun. Someone took a few photos of the show, and I have a great but blurry one of me playing guitar, wearing a burgundy Farside shirt that I loved, surrounded by Dutch punks. It was one of those shows you just didn't want to end. We used a couple of photos from this show on the back cover artwork of our 'Square' 7" EP.

Afterwards we shared a few drinks and sold what was left of our merchandise, signing quite a few shirts with marker pens on large-breasted ladies who were already wearing them. That was a fun experience that didn't get old. We certainly could have stayed there a lot longer, hanging out and having fun, and I know Milo wanted to as he was chatting with a couple of girls when we dragged him out as we were all ready to go. We thanked Andreas for the adventure and said our goodbyes to everyone there, leaving them drinking and lighting up a BBQ. We didn't want to go, but we had a ferry to catch and work to get back to, so we jumped into the van, turned up a tape, and headed home.

22, A square, a stampbox and a lot of gigs

24/9/94 > 3/10/94 Couch Potatoes and Torque
Bottoms, Folkstone. Quigleys, Maidstone. Collision Club, Chatham. etc

We had a couple of days off to wash and relax but were then back out on the road again for a bunch of shows around the rock venues and pubs of London and the southeast with our noisy mates from Maidstone, Torque. Mal had booked these shows and they were all close enough to home that we could get back to our own beds every night and still be able to get to work or college the next day if need be too. We started out playing a show for Richard Murrill over at Bottoms, the basement club in Folkestone on the Leas cliff-top where we'd played our second ever show with the new line-up. Then we went on to Quigleys in Maidstone, a big biker boozer with sawdust on the floor and hells angels lurking in the shadows, heckling and throwing newkie brown bottles at you if you weren't any good. Luckily this was Torque's local and by now we had become pretty good. Then it was on to some dives in London that Roly and Simon from Torque knew and had hooked up gigs at, The Cartoon in Croydon, The Bull and Gate in Kentish Town and the Ruskin Arms in East Ham, where Iron Maiden started out, and where I'd been to see my childhood rock heroes Deuce play a few times. We finished up this little Thames and Medway area tourette at the Collision Club in Chatham, another new venue for us, but one that had been going a while as a heavy metal club in the back of The Ash Tree pub, where the rockers fought the local chavs most Monday nights and we'd seen Sonar Nation play a few times. Torque and Couch Potatoes rocked our socks off at the Collision and were still all home to bed by midnight.

12/10/94 Travis Cut, Machines in Motion and Couch Potatoes
The Joiners, Southampton

We all wanted to play more gigs, but there were a few issues starting to crop up now around time off work or college. We'd just have to work around this, like all independent bands do, we couldn't really just be out playing anywhere at any time. We had to choose our shows more carefully, but the next we jumped at. Rich Levene had invited us back to play for the S.T.E. collective at The Joiners Arms in Southampton.

I say invited us back, although both the previous incarnation of Couch Potatoes and Joeyfat had played at the Joiners, none of the new guys had ever played there and this would be Couchies first visit in nearly two years (The last show I'd played there in fact, being my fifth time on stage at the Joiners, was back in May '93 when Joeyfat were there with Down By Law). Anyway, this show on Saturday would be the S.T.E.'s seventy-seventh, and we'd support Travis Cut and Machines In Motion.

Travis Cut were a melodic punk band from the Essex side of London who mixed the catchy style of The Buzzcocks with American hardcore influences from bands like Husker Du and Naked Raygun. They'd already played some great shows, supporting D.O.A. and Huggy Bear, and now had a new 7" on Incoming Records called 'Waking hours'. This would be the first of a prolific run of EPs and albums on Damaged Goods, Karma, Them's Good, Firefly, Fluffy Bunny, Speedowax, JSNTGM, Snuffy Smile, Fear N Loathing, and even one on Tony & Gaz's own label for their fanzine Suspect Device. They made a lot of noise for a three-piece band but kept it just on the melodic side of hardcore, and reminded me of China Drum and Idlewild.

Machines In Motion were a new band formed from of the ashes of Watch You Drown, another three-piece of pop-punkers who were on the 'Court Metrage' EP with Couch Potatoes that J.P released on Panx Records. They were from Hampshire, so locals to the Joiners. Their new band was named after a song by Killing Joke's Malicious Damage labelmates Red Beat. The show was great and well attended, as they usually were at The Joiners, and I still have a flyer from the evening's pop-punk extravaganza featuring the black and white artwork from Embrace's brilliant self-titled album on Dischord.

Shortly after this Joiners show we had another, up north, well in the Midlands, but it didn't go so well. The day before, I'd been driving Milo, Dan K and most of our equipment in a heavily overloaded work Astra to meet Paul and Dan P for practise. There was a humpback bridge on the road near Paul's in Laddingford, and for some reason I decided it would be best to take it at high speed. With the car full of drums and guitars we took off, landed hard and bounced down the road for some distance. I managed not to bin it, but totally screwed the suspension and caused Milo some minor drum-stand related injuries. This was not ideal as the Beast was being serviced and that meant that we'd all have to cram into Dan P's well maintained but very small Renault to get to the gig the next day. The next day was unseasonably hot, so on the way Dan P came up with a game where we wound up the windows, put his heater on full and saw who would pass out first. Great fun for all the family and obviously more funny than dangerous. By the time we reached the show we were dehydrated, knackered and not in the best of spirits. We played the show anyway, of course, but it wasn't one of our best, and as we finished the last song of the set Milo said, "Well, that could have gone better," at which point Dan K threw his drum

SAT. NOV.12TH

travis cut

MACHINES IN MOTION

CouchPotatoes

The Joiners

StMarys St

Southampton

3.00/2.50

STE 77

8pm

Access 1 Step

STE 77 gig flyer with Travis Cut at The Joiners

couch potatoes

Square EP

Square EP

Side 1
Wall
Why

Side 2
Never
Lost

couch potatoes

Square EP

WALL
It's like the hardest wall
that you can imagine,
and it always starts with
I've been thinking about this.
Sometimes it's the tone of voice that sounds like it's
the end of the world.
And it could be, and it could be.

This is the last time
I'm gonna fall
People say they'll catch me
I still hit the wall.

It's like the greatest height
that you could slip from,
and it's a decision
you'll have to live with.
Freefalling through it with you, it's not the experience
that intoxicates,
and it should be.

Did you see them, did they make you smile?
Went to see them, you were gone for a while.
Spent an hour or two, away from me,
You no longer like what you see.

Released by
Weird Records
61 London Road
Badderton,
Notts NG2...

...in touch with us at:
... Road
... Wells
TN1 2NY
Couch Potatoes

couch
potatoes
are:

dan:
percussion

milles:
voice

daniel:
guitar

paul:
fingerbass

dave:
guitar +
vocals

Write to our records
for advice. Couch Potatoes
message...

couch potatoes

couch potatoes : Stampbox
Live tracks recorded in Germany 15.9.94

Thanks to Benno at Ox...

Stampbox

Stampbox

Side 1 Live in Germany '94

1. Lost
2. User Friendly
3. Wall
4. Another
5. Kill R
6. Bit Rich
7. Why
8. Venue

9. Easter
10. Never
11. Part of You
12. Engineer
13. Impossible Lover
14. Sonnet
15. Poison Me

Side 2: Studio

1. Lost
2. User Friendly
3. Kill R
4. Engineer
5. Impossible Lover
6. Wall
7. Venue
8. Why
9. Poison Me

10. Never
11. Bad Day
12. Newett
13. Tired
14. Market
15. This Morning
16. Hey Hey (live)

couch
potatoes
are:

dan:
percussion

milles:
voice

daniel:
guitar

paul:
fingerbass

dave:
guitar +
vocals

`Stampbox´ cassette cover

304

peddle at him. It narrowly missed Milo and the sound-desk, and smashed into the wall, breaking. We couldn't afford a new one for a while, so Dan K repaired it with gaffa tape and had to use it like that for the next few shows. As you can imagine, that made for a fun journey home.

Stampbox

Soon after this fun show we received some good news from Benny at Dragnet Records, a small but cool indie rock label that had grown out of an alternative fanzine (Useful Idiot), based in Presteigne in Wales. He was putting out the new Couch Potatoes 'User Friendly' 7" for us and this vinyl EP would feature tracks from the 'Mans greatest friends in the windswept heights'. This had 'User friendly', 'Venue' and 'Impossible easier' on the U-side, with 'Kill it' and 'Poison me' on the F-side. There was a picture of a blonde girl with pigtails on the front cover and us lot on the back, with a photo taken on tour outside of the AK47 in Dusseldorf, where we're propping up a graffiti covered wall with Dan K in particular striking a silly pose. This 7" was still in the works though, so while we waited Benny had now received the first copies of a new cassette he was putting out for us too, so was calling to say that they were in the post and on the way.

This tape was called 'Stampbox' and had a crashed space rocket on the front cover which was printed on multiple coloured covers. I have green and red kicking around here somewhere, but I think there were quite a few. The first side was a decent live recording of our show at the Remise Club in Lemgo, Germany on 15/9/94 with a fifteen track setlist and the second side was made up of studio tracks from our previous singles and demos, followed by a live version of the Descendents song 'Hey hey'.

The inside of the cassette cover had a photo of Couch Potatoes on our recent European trip with us all standing next to another graffitied wall. It listed the band members and then there was an explanation of the crashed rocket artwork we'd used on the front cover, taken from an old seventies sci-fi art book, that said, "One of the scientists on Eden, crazed with terror, sought to escape the inescapable by launching one of the emergency craft, only to hurtle out of control into the rocky hillside." It was a neat little release and we used it as our demo for a while, adding it to our merch stall for gigs too.

Benny pushed Stampbox in his own Dragnet zine saying, "Now the Kentifornian Hardcoreists have Stampbox and it's a tasty follow up to Excess All Areas. Live songs recorded on a recent jaunt across Germany with new songs and reworkings of crowd pleasers. If you like punky power pop like All or Green Day then you'll be into this."

Square

Later in October, Dan P and I headed up to London to see Jawbreaker play at the Monarch. We'd tried to see them play before when they were over last time, but Blake's throat had been so badly strained he'd developed nodules that needed operating on and the show was cancelled. Jawbreaker were, and still are, one of my favourite bands so I was keen to finally see them play live. This tour was for their '24 Hour Revenge Therapy' album that had come out on Tupelo Recordings, and they played tracks mainly from that and a couple from 'Bivouac' too, including my fanboy favourite, 'Chesterfield King'. It was a sweaty, packed show but seemed to be over way too soon and afterwards Jawbreaker were immediately mobbed by fans and the press. I did manage to get a few questions in for BHP zine, but they didn't seem to want to say much, possibly as they were already discussing signing with Geffen Records to record and release 'Dear You' and, as awesome a record as that is, releasing it on such a major label was never going to go down well with their punk fanbase.

It was around this time that Couch Potatoes new 'Square' EP was released on Weird Records based out of Newark in Nottinghamshire. I'd been corresponding with Ian again and am forever indebted to him that he was so into the band and so supportive. He loved 'Excess All Areas' and was pleased with how the 'In Bed With...' EP (Weird003) had done. Now he wanted to put out a new Couch Potatoes release and we had chosen what we thought were four of the better songs from 'Mans greatest friend in the windswept heights'. This became the 'Square' EP, (Weird006). This 7" had 'Wall' and 'Why' on the A-side, with 'Never' and 'Lost' on the B-side. The artwork featured what we thought was a hilarious photo of the band as a five-a-side football team on the front cover, that was taken outside Andreas's parent's house, and some live photos from our gig at the Innocent Club in Hengelo along with the track-list and our contacts on the back cover.

There was an insert with the EP too, which had the lyrics to 'Wall' on top of a photo we'd taken whilst messing about inside the van on one of the long road-trips during the tour. It's hard to tell looking at it now, but that's Dan Kingdon (drummer) and Dan Pullin (guitarist) with clothes wrapped around their heads like some crazy mujahidins. We thought it was amusing at the time and figured it was as good as anything to use for a background photo.

"It's like the heaviest weight that you can imagine, and it always starts with, 'I've been thinking about this'. Something in their tone of voice that sounds like it's the end of the world. And it could be. It could be."

A cheery extract from 'Wall' by Couch Potatoes, lyrics by Miles Booker.

We'd already started writing the songs that would become our 'Outweighed' album now and although it was taking time to develop, our style was changing and we were evolving musically. This may have been in no small part due to Milo's influence, and not just with his lyrics, most of which were in an abstract way about girls, relationships and personal situations. When we wrote 'Excess All Areas' you could legitimately say that we were just a band doing a decent job of sounding like the Descendents, but by the time we were writing 'Outweighed' there were many more influences on our music, including bands like

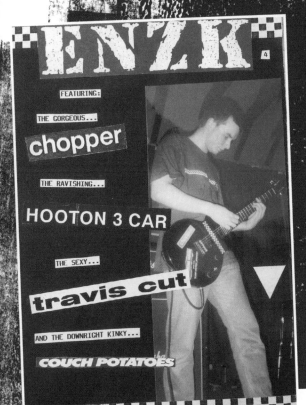

ENZK

FEATURING:

THE GORGEOUS...

chopper

THE RAVISHING...

HOOTON 3 CAR

THE SEXY...

travis cut

AND THE DOWNRIGHT KINKY...

COUCH POTATOES

ENZK fanzine cover

The Railway Inn, Winchester

St John's Tavern, Archway

Flappers Bar, Worthing

The Square, Harlow

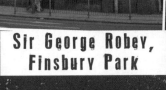

Sir George Robey, Finsbury Park

Leo's Red Lion, Gravesend

Samiam, Jawbreaker, Lifetime, Farside, Quicksand and Split Lip. It was beginning to come together, so we spent the next few weeks practising and writing new songs.

9/12/94 Wordbug, Couch Potatoes and Naked I
The Newmarket Inn, Great Torrington
10/12/94 Blaggers I.T.A. Couch Potatoes and Scum of Toytown
The Cavern, Exeter

In December we headed west to Devon for a couple of shows with Wordbug. I'd been corresponding with Martin Edmunds, Wordbug's singer, for a while now and he'd introduced me to some promoters and venues to help us book gigs in the southwest.

The first of these gigs was at The Newmarket Inn in Great Torrington. From outside it looked like a typical drinking pub, the sort you'd find in the high street of any out of the way town, but once inside we could see that it hosted bands regularly and had more going on. There was a bar at the front and a stage at the back, with gig posters everywhere. We played in the function room out the back, that looked like a village hall had been tagged onto the pub. There was no stage to speak of, although we didn't mind that. This venue was famous for putting on rock bands and was one of the venues that Muse came up through. We were playing there with Wordbug and another local band called Naked I.

I'd had Wordbug's 'Losing It All' album on Aston Stephens Boss Tuneage label for quite a while, and had just bought their new 'Die / Waiting' 7" too. They were a great melodic hardcore band that could always write a good tune, 'Mirror' and 'Dog Skinned Alive' were two of my favourites. We played quite a few shows with them, both as Wordbug and then later when they became Annalise too. For this gig I'm pretty sure they had John Tripe on guitar, he'd replaced Steve Craig, with Martin Edmunds on vocals, David Goodchild on bass and Adrian Stroud on the drums. Their bassist David also helped run The Cavern Club in Exeter, so had hooked us up with a gig for the next day, working alongside the other promoters at the Cavern collective known as Hometown Atrocities.

Hometown Atrocities was the Exeter-based punk collective that put on shows wherever they could, to bring hardcore bands to the town. Their first show was at the Art College and featured skate ramps next to the bar, which must have been excellent fun. Others were held at local pubs. One at The Printers Pie saw the landlady pull the plug halfway through a Cowboy Killers set. The collective put on plenty of gigs before moving to The Cavern, including shows for Fugazi, Verbal Assault, Sink, Victims Family, Senseless Things, and a band called Headless Chickens, who had Thom Yorke on guitar. Thom went to the art college in Exeter and was involved with the Hometown Atrocities collective himself before forming Radiohead.

For this weekend we'd booked an apartment to stay at in Dartmouth, a town on the coast nearby, to save crashing on the promoters' floors or in the other band houses as we usually had to. I'd been to Dartmouth before on holiday so had it all lined up, a couple of nights comfort on our seaside trip in a place I already knew. That'd make a change from sleeping on floors or grubby couches, and had to be better than all sharing one noisy club room with everyone's feet and farts. We could stay there on the Friday and Saturday nights after the shows, and then had back home on Sunday after eating some chips by the sea like civilised people.

We were wandering around Dartmouth on Saturday with plenty of time before we had to head over to Exeter for the gig. Milo and I grabbed some pasties and sat eating them in the park by the harbour, dodging the ever-hungry seagulls, but Dan K, Dan P and Paul had come up with a plan. Knowing Milo would want to wash after the show, they'd bought buckets of crabs from the local kids, who'd been fishing for them with bacon fat off the harbour wall outside the apartment, and they'd filled up both the bath and the sink with them before we left. When we finally arrived back, late that night, tired and sweaty, Milo went to take a bath, but it was filled with snapping crabs, swimming about in the murky water and impatient at having been left there all day. He was none too pleased, and chaos ensued while he chased the rest of us about with various sweaty items of clothing and one of the larger grabby crustaceans. (When he calmed down we put the crabs back in the river)

Anyway, The Cavern was a great venue. The bare brick walls were covered in gig posters and the low ceiling was painted black, seemingly holding in the heat and atmosphere from all the gigs. There was a good sound system and a decent stage too, and in some ways, it reminded me of the old Rumble Club in Tunbridge Wells, although this well-known Exeter rock venue was considerably larger. The Cavern would host Samiam, Hundred Reasons, Converge, Strike Anywhere, UK Subs, Napalm Death, Fugazi, Idlewild, Muse, Biffy Clyro, Coldplay and The Cranberries, as well as the Couch Potatoes a couple of times too.

Tonight's show was with The Blaggers I.T.A. who I hadn't seen since the Joeyfat gigs. Matty and the crew had come down from London, so there was at least seven of them on the stage at any given moment belting out their political punk songs. They had plenty of Anti-Fascist Action literature and shirts to sell, and were still pushing their Words of Warning releases and bootlegs too. They had now signed to Parlophone though, an offshoot of E.M.I, so they were also perpetually defending themselves in the scene fanzines and larger media too, saying it was easier to work from the inside to spread their message and take the money to make better use of it. They'd released the 'Bad Karma' album and been on TV now, on The Word on Channel 4, with their new single 'Abandon Ship', so the show was very busy.

Besides Couch Potatoes they'd have another support too. A noisy punk band called Scum of Toytown who were labelmates of the Blaggers on Words Of Warning Records. They had a 7" out called 'Destruction of both houses of parliament by fire' that included songs titled 'Work, rest and riot', 'Jackboot crusade' and 'Different drum'. John Thurlow, the guitarist, had been in both Chelsea and Chron Gen so it was a very 'punk' evening. Couch Potatoes played our melodic hardcore in-between these two and, although we were used to playing with punkier bands, I realised now why the Wordbug guys let us have this one and didn't play themselves.

Walking around Exeter before the show, just killing time, we'd picked up the latest (December '94) edition of Terrorizer magazine, and in the Hardcore Holocaust section there was a review of the new Couch Potatoes album. It included a decent photo of the band and said "Couch Potatoes have sold over 2000 copies of the 'Excess All Areas' demo through some concerted gigging and self-publicising. In June they recorded ten new songs which are now available as a cassette album called 'Man's greatest friend in the windswept heights'. I guess you could call this emo-core but that's not the be all and end all of it, because this is uncomfortable and disconcerting in parts, the lilting 'Engineer' for example. The production is bassy and thick, maybe too soft around the edges, however the songs shine through nonetheless." Not too bad a review for a metal mag and they'd suggested people wrote to us and asked about BHP zine as well.

There were several fanzines at the gig that night but they were all there to speak with the Blaggers. We saw a couple of live reviews of the show a while afterwards though, with one we liked that simply said "Couch Potatoes play poppy buzzsaw punk in the vein of NOFX, Pennywise and Green Day. Definitely one for the shorts and baseball cap brigade".

13/2/95 Amalgamation, Couch Potatoes and 4 Silvermen
Flappers Bar, Worthing
16/2/95 Who Moved the Ground? and Couch Potatoes
The Lord Nelson, Clacton

On a cold day in February, we headed down to Worthing to the old Norfolk Hotel on the sea front. This venue was now known as the Flappers Club and had been brightly painted in red and white with a large art deco female statuette above the door in the '20s Flapper style, with a big golden Flappers logo and electric guitars painted either side of it, right above the canvas awning that covered the main entrance. Even by rock club standards this was not very tasteful. We'd be playing with Amalgamation, a HC band that veered between mellow indie and screaming chaos. And also 4 Silvermen, a more grunge style band. It wasn't a bad show, with an audience of maybe 60 or 70 disinterested rockers, and we played a lot of the new tracks we were working on for 'Outweighed' live for the first time.

We were soon heading back to the stormy seaside, this time to Clacton-on-Sea in Essex to play at The Lord Nelson again. The Lord Nelson was one of only two venues to host regular rock nights in the area, the other being the Rocking Horse, so it usually had decent turnouts. The last time Couchies were there with the Pseudo Hippies, the landlord had decided that it was all a bit too much and pulled the plug on us about three songs from the end of our set. Hopefully this wouldn't happen again. It was a good venue with plenty of space in front of the stage, before the archways all around that opened into more drinking areas, which meant that the regulars, and usually a good crowd for the rock nights, could watch the band from three sides. I'm sure that added to the atmosphere when bigger bands played, and today we were supporting Who Moved The Ground? so were hoping for a busy show.

Who Moved the Ground? were from Farnborough in Hampshire and sounded very much like Mega City Four or the Senseless Things. They reminded me a lot of The Strookas. Their singer and guitarist was called Rich Savage, with Sid Stovold on lead guitar, Les Green on bass and Chris Redmond on drums, and they were a very hairy bunch with more than their fair share of dreadlocks. I had a copy of their first EP, a 7" on Icarus Records called 'Barneydancing', which for some reason played at 45rpm on one side and 33rpm on the other. They had two other EPs out on Icarus Records, a label based out of Bracknell in Berkshire. One was called 'The Chase / What's That?' that came out in '94, and the other was 'Good Question' that was released in '95. They had a few copies of 'The Chase' 7" for sale at the show and were telling us about a tour they'd recently played, travelling through France, Belgium, Germany and Poland, as well as a gig they'd just played in Windsor with a new band called Oasis that had about five hundred people turn up. Tonight's show was pretty good, although there definitely weren't 500 people, maybe 120, and WMTG? rocked it. They went on to appear on a late-night ITV Battle of the Bands contest, hosted by Jools Holland and judged by Bob Geldof, and release a fourth EP, 'If Pleasure Was Illegal' on London's Riot / Clone label.

8/4/95 Couch Potatoes (Record shop in-store show)
Shake Some Action, Croydon

There was a great alternative record shop in Croydon, South London called Shake Some Action that we'd go up and visit to pick up new releases. James McCabe, the affable indie kid who ran it, decided that he wanted to start putting on bands on Saturday afternoons as showcases for the store. Initially this started with acoustic and stripped-down versions of the bands, but as he found the neighbouring shops didn't really mind the noise for maybe an hour maximum, these in-store shows became full on, full band sets.

We'd turn up around 1pm and load our gear in, pushing an old sofa and some record stands James had there out of the way, and set up against the right-hand wall, close to the front window. If we were lucky, we'd have a very quick check of levels to make sure the p.a. was working ok, during which time people would stare at us through the window. Then you'd go over and check out some records, maybe buy a few and chat with James about whatever new stuff he had coming in and what the last problems with the mics were. Then, when it was time to go on and the shop had filled up, you'd squeeze your way back over to the makeshift stage area and get ready to start, having to be very careful not to knock your guitar out of tune on the big red column that was right in the middle of the playing area. I'd strum a chord and Dan K would bang on the snare drum so that the few hardcore and indie kids that had been hanging around could gather. They'd just about fit in, maybe thirty or so of them, and would cram all along the other wall up to the counter, where most of the new records were. At around 2pm we'd kick off and hope that we'd get to play for half an hour, or even forty-five minutes, before having to stop. It was cramped and a bit like being goldfish in a bowl when people watched through the shop window, but we always enjoyed these shows.

Couch Potatoes played there several times, as did Rydell, and many more artists as they toured through and had a record to promote on a spare afternoon. These included J Church, Wat Tyler, Schwartzeneggar, Broccoli, Toast (the local Croydon heroes), and later just before the shop was closed down, Dweeb (Kris from Pseudo Hippies and Wact last band). Even Dee Dee Ramone played a few songs at Shake Some Action when he was in town promoting his 'Poison Heart' autobiography and signing a few books there. If you want to search for them, you can find a couple of videos on YouTube of great songs being played in those cramped confines by cool bands like Joe 90, Twofold and Blocko.

13/4/95 Another Fine Mess, Couch Potatoes and The Strookas St John's Tavern, Archway, London

We were practising at Paul's parent's farm, where we had our gear permanently set up now and were writing all the new songs. We had a whole new live set and an entire album ready to record. We wanted to get into the studio soon but would still fit in gigs whenever we could. Our next was at the St John's Tavern with Another Fine Mess and The Strookas. This rock pub was another great London music venue that is no longer available as it's been turned into a restaurant now. And as much as I like food, I find this annoying. Couch Potatoes played the St John's Tavern three times and always enjoyed good gigs there. It was a large solid-looking and standalone drinking pub in Junction Road, Archway, North London and had a long bar room with a barrelled ceiling where the bands would play. The promoter was called Slim Chance and he booked several shows for us there and all around London, as well as introducing us to the M-80s and many other bands.

Slim was an old punk and you could tell he'd been about. He put on shows at the Archway Tavern for years and founded the Dirty Water Club in the Wild Western Rooms, the wild west themed back room there, which is where we'd play. It had a wagon wheel hanging from the ceiling and some huge bull horns on the wall at the back of the stage. After a while,

Slim moved the club up the road to the Boston Arms, where we'd played back in '91 with NOFX. One of the artists that played for Slim at the St John's Tavern most months was Billy Childish, under his various guises but mostly in Thee Headcoats. It was the Archway Tavern where they first played their song 'We hate the fucking NME' to an NME journalist who'd turned up to see them called Johnny Cigarettes.

Our indie chums The Strookas had travelled from Maidstone, and the hard-working pop-punksters of Another Fine Mess had travelled all the way from Worcester for this gig. AFM sounded like a west country accented Ramones, or even Pseudo Hippies, and had already supported a lot of old style punk bands including The Buzzcocks, The Stranglers, UK Subs, 999, The Vibrators and GBH. I had an AFM cassette called 'All Messed Up' and the new CD, 'Million Smiles', that came out on Dropzone. 'Smile' was a very good song, and 'I remember you', but I thought their catchiest guitar riff and best sing-a-long was a track called 'Hilary'. They're definitely a band to check out and play in the car when you're heading to the beach in the summertime.

27/4/95 Understand, Couch Potatoes and Torque
The Sir George Robey, Finsbury Park, London
1/5/95 Gink, Couch Potatoes and Headspurt
The Sir George Robey, Finsbury Park, London

We were back in town two weeks later to play at the Robey again, one of London's classic rock music pubs. I'd seen loads of gigs there and Joeyfat had played this venue twice, including the show that would be reviewed in the NME, but this would be the first time that Couch Potatoes would thrash about on that stage. The first of four visits by us in just a year, as it goes. On the 27th April we played a stormer there with our mates in Understand and Torque, and then just a week later on the 1st May we were back to play again, this time with Gink and a new indie band called Headspurt.

The Understand show was something of a rarity as they had been laying low while they wrote and recorded their new album for East/West Records. For a 'major label band' this was something of a low-key gig, just a one-off to test the new songs which most people had not heard yet. They were ridiculously tight and well-rehearsed. They had all grown their hair long, except John (Hannon, one of the guitarists), who'd taken to wearing flat caps all the time by then. It was very much the second coming of Understand. The myth most of the scene believed at the time was that they were living large on East/West's money, but in fact they almost all had to work during this period to keep things ticking over. They did have their own permanent practise space set up now though and, regardless of how they found the time or financed it, they had clearly been honing to perfection all the songs that would make up their magnificent 'Burning bushes and burning bridges' album. This was an outstanding gig and Understand were now one hell of a band to see playing in a small venue like that.

Gink were a pop-punk three-piece from south London that I'd seen rock the Playpen a few times before. Their band was comprised of two brothers, Steve and Gary Wall, on guitar and bass respectively, and a drummer called Graham. They had two 7" singles out on a new label with the great moniker of Potential Ashtray Records. Potential Ashtray also released Shutdown's brilliant 'Sheltered Homes' 7", and singles for Gaunt and the Campus Tramps too. A little while after this show, between the Pseudo Hippies splitting and Wact forming, Kris Beltrami stood in on second guitar for Gink at a few shows too.

Headspurt, who later changed their name to Unfold, was David S. Blanco's first band and I'm pretty sure this was their first show. Blanco was a very good artist and illustrator, and luckily for us, a big fan of Couch Potatoes and then later Rydell too. He designed some of our artwork for t-shirts and flyers and then later created the original cover art for the Rydell / Hot Water Music split 7". The first pressing of which features a photo of his girlfriend smoking a cigarette over a montage of a London street. I loved that HWM split art and still have the original bromide proof of it hanging on my wall at home. Blanco also created the equally stylish, layered and colourful artwork of the bench by the lake for the Rydell / Sunfactor / Babies Three split CD too.

Unfold became a regular feature on the London hardcore scene for a couple of years and evolved a lot as a band. We played with them several times, both around town and down at the Railway Inn in Winchester too. All the members went on to further musical endeavours, with Blanco notably playing in a band called Carver, with Davey and Simon from Schema. More recently he has been running his own art and design company, as well as a small indie record label called Blank Editions, that has released music for Thurston Moore of Sonic Youth and Douglas Hart of the Jesus & Mary Chain amongst others.

12/6/95 Couch Potatoes, Hub and Arden
The Railway Inn, Winchester

This would be the first of many visits to the Railway Inn in Winchester, a large white and pale blue pub on the corner of St Paul's Hill, a main road through town and right next to the railway station. The venue had friendly bar staff, and we'd try to arrive early so that we could play a few frames of pool before setting up. We'd go down this little passageway at the side of the bar and come into the large back room that they called the Barn, and then later Platform One, where the bands would play. There was a good sound system and lighting rig across a low stage that all five of us Couch Potatoes could easily fit on. The room was painted black, and sound proofed as best they could, with posters for various dodgy rock bands all around it and a small bar right at the back. It could probably hold around one hundred and fifty people at a push and would usually have a decent local crowd on the regular rock and indie nights. We got on well with the promoters and the staff so played there often, usually meeting up with the Southampton scene guys at the shows.

On this visit we'd play with two hairy indie bands, Hub and Arden, both playing their own versions of pop-punk meets grunge. They'd brought all their mates along, about 100 skater kids, and the place was packed. I remember it being a good show but wanted some more detail to scribble in here, so I dropped a line to Milo to see if he remembered it better. He sent me this section of a fanzine interview he'd given as his reply. "I liked that place, we played there seven or eight times, as Couch Potatoes and later Rydell, but my enduring memory of the Railway will always be a Couch Potatoes show; the place was packed with both Southampton scenesters and skateboarder types, a great atmosphere and everyone was having fun. We finished our set with a cover of Dag Nasty's 'Safe', a song we had worked out to record for a Dag Nasty tribute compilation. The original version of the song features a classic Brian Baker guitar solo which David could mimic exactly. On this particular night he jumped into the crowd mid-solo and promptly disappeared as he skidded around on the floor but he did not miss a note and was hoisted back up on stage by the moshers." So there you go, clearly another good night of professional musicianship.

14/6/95 Toast, Couch Potatoes and Staplegun St John's Tavern, Archway, London

Two days later we'd be back in London to play at the St John's Tavern for Slim again, this time with two more pop-punk hardcore bands, Toast and Staplegun. Toast had just released their first 7" EP on Crackle Records. It was called 'Smart kids... dumb music' and contained four short snotty songs about being sick, and then being sick some more. These four guys, Spencer, Steve, Roland and Jon, were from the Purley and Croydon area of south London and we'd met them at Shake Some Action. Spencer and Jon had originally been in some industrial noise gothic band, but had now formed Toast and were playing pop-punk in the style of Bad Religion or Screeching Weasel.

Toast had started to play loads of gigs, first around London, and then further afield too. They'd put out more great EPs, 'Songs for losers' and 'Back to the barrooms' on Ian's London-based punk label Damaged Goods and also 'Come dancing with Toast' on Dave and Becky's Leeds-based Crackle Records. Damaged Goods was already well established, but over the next year or two Crackle also became a prolific label in the UK pop-punk scene with releases for Chopper, Skimmer and Crocodile God.

This was a great pop-punk party of a gig with a lot of our Kent and London mates there, and this line-up couldn't help but remind me of the Mr T Experience lyric from 'More than toast' on their 'Our Bodies Our Selves' album. "You said you loved me more than toast, but less than a staplegun".

17/6/95 The Banned and Couch Potatoes The Red Lion, Gravesend

That Saturday we'd also make our first visit to Leo's Red Lion in Gravesend, an infamous biker pub and rock music venue hidden away on a road leading into an industrial estate and looking out over the Thames estuary. This place had seen all the old metal and punk bands play there, from Iron Maiden to UK Subs, and had a huge main stage and music room, with a couple of smaller halls and bars attached. It was your everyday painted black and covered in posters type of rock venue but also had a big roaring lion on the back wall behind the stage. Couch Potatoes first show there was with a punk band called The Banned and the place was packed full of rockers and punks getting drunk and dancing around. The only real drama of the evening, beyond a couple of broken guitar strings and dropped beer glasses, was that my cute but needy ex-girlfriend Kelly, had come along and bumped into my new girlfriend, Bernice, a fiery air-stewardess. That chance meeting didn't go too well, and I spent most of the evening trying to referee their tetchy conversations and then get the hell out of there before it erupted into violence in the ladies' room.

23/6/95 M-80s and Couch Potatoes
The Square, Harlow

The following Friday we played The Square in Harlow with the M-80s. Slim had set this one up for us with Adam, one of the four guys that ran the venue and put bands on there. As I mentioned before, when Joeyfat had played The Square with The Blaggers, I could easily imagine Daleks rolling down the streets of Harlow in a particularly dark episode of Doctor Who, or even blood-thirsty brain-eating zombies roaming the place in a world-ending apocalypse with no-one really noticing or caring about it. The venue was similarly ugly, a new-looking square pub with lots of glass, in the middle of a council estate. But its saving grace was that it was run by local musos who really wanted to help bands and provide a good venue, so you just had to love and support it. The Square could hold over two hundred punters and hosted regular live music, so saw a wide range of well-known bands tread its stage, from the energetic excitement of Rancid or Enter Shikari, to the sleep-inducing dullness of Coldplay, as well as the skanking ska of the Beat or the teenage dirt-baggery of Wheatus. Tonight 'The Only Alternative' club would be graced by Couch Potatoes and M-80s.

The M-80s were an American garage rock band who'd come over to stay in the UK for a while. Or so I thought. What I later found out was that Slim had invited them over and said he'd try to book them a three-week UK tour. It ended up that he actually only managed to get three shows booked for them, two of which were on consecutive days, so the day after they played with us in Harlow they had to get up to Scotland on a National Express coach! Anyway, although originally from Norfolk, Virginia, the M-80s were currently staying in London with Slim, the St John's Tavern promoter, and at this point were happy to play whatever occasional shows that he could book them on, intending to travel there on public transport and just turn up with guitars and a snare drum. Knowing this, we'd brought all the gear and had already set up and sound-checked and were now sitting in the bar drinking by the time they arrived. They'd join us and crack us up with their latest stories of chaotic lock-ins, fighting and drinking in London with Slim. There was Eddie, Witt Drawls, Big Rob and Rusty Floyd, such American country style names, plus they actually had a mate called Roachfarmer too. They already had quite a few records out on smaller garage labels in the States and were pushing a few copies of their 'In a Fury' album on Get Hip as well as the M-80's collection on Reid Recordings at shows, whilst looking for a new UK label to record an album for. They were ahead of their time really, as they sounded like a much better version of the Strokes or the Hives, and it turned out they'd have more luck in Germany. So they went over there on tour soon after this show and released a split record with a band called the Swinging Neckbreakers on Screaming Apple Records out of Cologne. Anyway, we all had a good show at The Square that night, but for all I know the M-80s are still playing gigs around Germany, or maybe back home in Virginia, or maybe even still stuck in London somewhere with Slim!

26/6/95 Policy of 3, Malva and Couch Potatoes
The Joiners, Southampton

The long weekend was followed by a happy Monday as we all piled into the Beast and headed down to the ever-friendly and fun Joiners in Southampton to see all our buddies there. Rich and the S.T.E. guys had invited us to support Policy of 3 and Malva at what would be the collective's 88th show. Our melodic hardcore was getting more emo in its style, but that genre didn't really exist yet and it was certainly a gradual development, and looking back it's clear that we were influenced both by bands we played shows with as well as bands we listened to. I'd say that Policy of 3 were one of the first emocore bands, and they were certainly influential in that style, even if they didn't think so themselves.

Their great 'American Woodworking' 7" had just come out on Old Glory Records, a small but perfectly formed hardcore label based in Brattleboro, Vermont, that had previously released Avail and Iconoclast records, as well as the Policy of 3 album, 'Dead Dog Summer'. Playing live this New Jersey four-piece would build from quieter melodic parts to some seriously heavy climaxes with passionate and angry vocals shouted over them. You can get a complete anthology double CD from Ebullition, the brilliant hardcore record label run by Kent McClard, the same guy who ran HeartattaCk zine. HeartattaCk was without doubt one of the best fanzines in the hardcore scene, with fifty issues between '94 and 2006. And Ebullition, along with No Idea, Revelation and Deep Elm, was one of the first labels who worked with Engineer Records, the record label I'd later set up, to supply us with distro stock for stalls at gigs and mail-order when we started up.

This tour had been jointly organised by Richard Corbridge of Armed With Anger and Helene and Ian of Subjugation Records. It was great to have people like that bringing such good bands over to play in the UK. We were stoked that Couch Potatoes would be playing with them and happy to be opening up the evening to a good crowd for this one, especially considering the S.T.E. had another gig coming up in just three day's time. We played a quick half-hour set, mainly of new tracks that would end up on 'Outweighed' and it went down well. Then Malva rocked out. They were from Leverkusen in Germany and played some pretty great original-sounding hardcore. Check out their songs 'Deus ex Machina' or 'My

break-even point' from their self-titled EP, or the track 'Mister club nobody' that was featured on the Ambala Sweet Centre compilation 7", it remains one of the most intense explosions of emotional hardcore ever recorded. They had a cassette and 7" with them to sell, the self-titled tape had just four tracks on it with a brown kraft paper cover. There was a leaf on the front and a small space station on the inside and it looked like it'd been hand produced. This noisy five-piece also had a great 7" called 'Life is no picnic' (Das leben ist kein picknick) on the German label Equality Records and Milo bought a copy of it at the gig. I wanted the Policy of 3 record but didn't want to carry it around during the show, and by the end of the evening they'd sold out and only had a few t-shirts left. That turned out to be a good thing though as they didn't stay long on this tour. Unfortunately their car was broken into, and a lot of their stuff was stolen.

8/7/95 Couch Potatoes
Shake Some Action, Croydon.
17/7/95 Couch Potatoes and Concrete Parachutes
Railway Inn, Winchester
19/7/95 Couch Potatoes, Beacon and Unfold
St John's Tavern, Archway, London
20/7/95 Couch Potatoes
The George IV, Brixton, London

Early in July we went back to Shake Some Action in Croydon to play another in-store show for James and drop off some copies of our 'Square' EP for him that we'd forgotten to take with us the last time we were there. We were rocking around the shop but had a bit of a disaster as the mic cord was not very long, and during a particularly energetic moment Milo danced off across the floor and rather than the mic cord simply coming out of the p.a. he managed to pull it in such a way that it broke the pin off in the jack socket, basically killing the vocals about two songs into the set. A record-buying session backed by improvised instrumentals ensued.

Then we headed down to the Railway Inn in Winchester again for another good gig on Platform One, this time with a noisy metal punk band called the Concrete Parachutes. This gig was followed by two more up in London, the first a rocking show for Slim at the St John's Tavern, with two new UKHC bands, Beacon and Unfold, supporting us. Both bands were very noisy and damn good, playing an interesting new style of hardcore, they didn't seem to have many songs yet but were happy to blast everyone with feedback to fill in any gaps.

Unfold was the new name of Headspurt, Davey Blanco's band, and they were just getting better and better. Beacon were a three-piece with two Dans and a Martin. One of the Dans was Daniel P. Carter who'd also join Above All and go on to play bass in A and then guitar in the Bloodhound Gang, as well as write for various metal mags and host the BBC Radio 1 Rock Show. This was their very first show and they played a sort of DC-style post hardcore. They'd later add a second guitarist and go a bit more metal. Although they didn't have a demo tape yet they would make some waves and eventually record with Rob Coleman, one of the guitarists of Understand, at the Maple Rooms studio in Southend. This would produce three tracks for their 'Still photographs from one motion picture' 7" on Subjugation Records and two more tracks for their split release with Tribute on Spread Records, both released in '97. Later still, after Fabric split up, their singer Andy Hartwell briefly joined Beacon on vocals too, although I never saw this incarnation play live.

The second of these two London shows was a disastrous trip to a new club at The George IV in Brixton, south London. This was Couch Potatoes first gig at this venue, and it wasn't too long before this that Brixton was still a serious no-go area in London. By this time though it was already turning into a cultural and musical hotspot, and this place was meant to be one of the venues leading the way, so we were keen to play.

The club at the George IV, that was currently a new regular night for rock and punk bands, was just called the music bar but would soon develop into Basement Jaxx. It was in another big old London drinking pub, a solid Victorian building located on the corner of Brixton Hill and Waterworks Road, three storeys high with a large round tower on the front corner and just down the road from where Robert David Jones, aka pop superstar David Bowie, was born back in '47.

We parked up and shifted the gear inside as quickly as possible, worrying about our van and if it'd still be there when we came back later, but going in anyway through the front bar, trying to dodge the grumpy barman and meeting the more friendly sound guy in the back room, sitting in his little DJ booth next to the small stage. This place had a good p.a. and looked ideal for some pretty intimate gigs. We sound-checked and the long-haired promoter finally arrived. We grabbed some drinks and waited for everyone to show up. We waited and waited, but the crowd didn't show up. No one came. No one!

Eventually we plugged in and played through our Dag Nasty cover as a practise and that was it. What an absolute waste of time. While we were packing up, the promoter obviously realised how pissed off we were and decided to do a runner, but Dan K noticed and chased him down the road. Dan was fast, he caught up and pretty much rugby tackled him, taking the promoter's legs out from under him so he went crashing into a wall. Dan demanded some petrol money for this colossal waste of our time, he produced twenty quid and limped off. Because of this nightmare it was the only time we ever 'played' there, but we did venture back to Brixton later to play a few shows at the Windmill over the road. I'd have loved to have gone back to the George IV music club to play a proper show or even just watch some bands there, but unfortunately that's not possible as this venue has been closed down now, like many others, and turned into a Tesco Express.

23, Outweighed, Scene Police and a Frisbee.

Recording Couch Potatoes `Outweighed´ album

It was time to get into the studio and record a proper album. I'd been trying to get us into The White House recording studio ever since the Jailcell Recipes had told us about it. The engineer there, Martin Nichols, seemed like the right guy to record us as he had already worked with several of our friends' bands including the Jailcells, Drive, Decline, Force Fed, Shutdown and Decadence Within, and all their records sounded great so we really wanted to give his studio a go. (Martin would also record with other bands from the hardcore scene such as Annalise, Million Dead, Bob Tilton and Stampin' Ground at the White House later too. He even recorded some early EPs for Revolver and Slowdive, a couple of mainstream indie bands that Milo and Dan P. were into).

I'd eventually managed to book us in for a long weekend, so we crammed ourselves and all our equipment into two cars (I was now driving a crappy Vauxhall as The Beast was off the road again needing more work) and headed over expectantly to the recording studio in Weston-Super-Mare on the Somerset coast, about a forty-minute drive south of Bristol.

We left early but it took us a while to get there, and then we had trouble finding the place. When we eventually did, Martin came out to greet us and show us all inside. He had the studio set up at his house in the hills overlooking the bay below. It was a great location. Inside, the studio had a good-sized live room where we could all play together, banging the songs out more or less live, and he'd said we could all sleep in there too if we wanted – which saved on B&B or hotel rooms, so we could spend all our money on recording and food. As well as the main live room, he also had separate areas where we could overdub, or re-record guitar parts or vocals alone if we needed to and then mix them in later. The control room had the largest mixing desk we'd ever seen, with 24 tracks and loads of extra equipment, but it still relied on the old analogue reel to reel AMEX tapes to record onto.

We always took our amps to gigs and studios, to get the right sound, and on this occasion, we had to take our full drum kit too. On arrival though, Dan K. noticed that he had forgotten to pack the two clamps that slotted into the top of his kick drum to hold his two rack toms in place. For a while there was talk of going to a nearby music shop to buy the parts and enquiries were made by phone. But ultimately, we managed to cannibalise a couple of old cymbal stands using string, gaffa tape and some old drumsticks to fashion something, Heath Robinson style, that would hold the two toms in place. We were so impressed with our handywork that we took a few photos of this contraption. Throughout the recording there was some concern that the drums would just fall apart. Dan K certainly did like to whack them hard and repeatedly at high speed, throughout most of our songs, but miraculously it all held together. Dan K didn't have a drum stool either, so he used an old, orange-painted, wooden chair from our bassist Paul's garage, which he'd brought along for the session at The White House too. It was certainly a professional looking set-up.

To his credit, if Martin was wondering what he'd let himself in for, he didn't say anything to us. He just calmy helped us solve any issues. This meant we eventually got everything set up and sounding good, so then we started jamming through a few of the songs, just to reassure Martin, and ourselves, that we were a proper band, not just a travelling clown circus. But by now we were getting hungry, so all went down into the town to grab some Chinese. Full up and greased up we got going again, and would carry on recording late into the night.

These songs were a little more complex than 'Windswept heights' and we had loads of new ideas for guitar lines and vocal effects that we wanted to try out. Luckily for us, Martin was a great engineer and helped us achieve a result over the next two days that stands up pretty well to anyone's listening judgement even now. It was a hardcore punk record after all, so we were happy for it to be a little rough around the edges.

Over the course of that weekend, we recorded the eleven tracks that would become Couch Potatoes 'Outweighed' album. When you put the CD into the stereo now it says fourteen tracks, but that's because we added our cover of Dag Nasty's 'Safe', to make up the twelve tracks you see listed on the CD cover, but then there was also an unlisted first track, which was a sample, and an extra 'hidden' track at the end, which was a load of older tracks by the first Couchies line-up, added on to make up the space available on the CD. We at least liked to give value to our fans.

Our version of 'Safe', a cover of the great Dag Nasty track from their debut 'Can I Say' album on Dischord Records, was recorded for a Dag Nasty tribute compilation album called 'Her Head's On Fire' that came out jointly on two Belgian record labels, Foolsday and Battle Records, in '95. As well as Couch Potatoes, this awesome little compilation CD also featured Dag Nasty cover versions by Annalise, Horace Pinker, Hooton 3 Car, Amazing Tails, Gomaz, Tempo Zero, Thirst!, Serpico, Eversor, Alkaloid, Loomis, The Unknown, Wardance, Innerface, Slug Bug and In Bloom. All eighteen tracks were taken from Dag Nasty's first four albums and re-worked in each band's own style as a tribute. The cover artwork had an image of a woman, holding a baby, with her head on fire and the track-listing was next to the Dag Nasty flame logo on the back, where it also proudly proclaimed that the CD pressing was limited to a thousand copies and had absolutely no copyright agreement at all. I still have a copy, but they are hard to find nowadays.

Anyway, the next two days in the studio flew by and the recording went very well, with plenty of hectic drumming by Dan K and impressively frenetic finger-bass playing by Paul. Dan's P's guitar work too was incredibly accomplished for a guy who'd only been playing for a year or so. Milo's voice still had that gravelly edge we all liked, but was way stronger now than it had been before. We kept it all slightly rough around the edges, with feedback and guitar slides, all recorded more or less live. It made for a fun session and Martin was doing a rough mix as we went along. At the end of the session, we took this rough mix with us on cassette to listen to in the cars. Then we gave Martin a couple of CDs to listen to, to give him an idea of the final mix we were after. I remember leaving him Farside's 'Rigged' and Samiam's 'Clumsy', but there may have been others too, as for a guy who'd recorded so many hardcore bands, he didn't seem to know much about any of our influences.

The following weekend, Milo, Dan P and I went back down to The White House to help Martin mix the album. Several times during this process we would insist on getting a cassette tape of the songs as they were finished and taking them outside to listen back to on the car stereo. In this way we figured we were checking that they still sounded good on a cheap car stereo and not just on top quality professional studio speakers. I think this behaviour annoyed Martin a bit, but again he was cool about it. I think this stemmed from our experience with 'Man's Greatest Friend...' which sounded good to us in the recording studio but turned out a bit weak and below par on cassette when we listened back afterwards. We did not want that to happen again.

All that said, we had limited studio time so still had to rush the mixing. We were happy with the outcome at the time, and it was all that we could afford anyway. To us it sounded great, and this album was certainly a step up from 'Man's greatest friend in the windswept heights'. We thanked Martin for his excellent work, and he made us a final couple of cassette copies to take in the car. As we drove home, we pressed play and turned up the volume.

The 'Outweighed' album started with a sample that we'd taken directly from an old flexi-disc Milo had found in his Grandad's record collection. It was a plummy voice saying "This record is given free with the April 1967 issue of Practical Wireless. On this record you can hear the faults. You can read how to cure them in the series of articles

Couch Potatoes `Outweighed´ CD cover and Scene Police ads

'Preparing radio sets' now starting in Practical Wireless. For comparison purposes the first recording is a fault-free sample of the test track." Then my guitar riff comes in, followed by Dan's frantic drumming and very quickly away we all go.

Then Milo's singing 'Mathematical type', the opening track; "Every day I sit at my desk, I type up people's dreams, dream by dream I am learning, a connoisseur, this is my calling. Remember it, write it down, in your dream bible. I can't sleep at night, I'm on the roof at 3am, no sleep 'til the sky's blue, the thought of dreamers dreaming. I'm not the mathematical type, I've got my own dream..." which the more literary readers of you will recognise as being lifted pretty much wholesale from Sylvia Plath's short story 'Johnny Panic and the Bible of Dreams'. Even on the car's dodgy stereo it sounded good to us.

The recording had captured the energy and urgency of the songs. The first couple of tracks rattle past as they are pretty fast. 'Grip' with its great refrain, "Is it worth it, all of these motherfuckers on the streets? They'll disappear, they don't matter," then 'Tidemark' with its feedback intro and Milo's poetic chorus of "Windows open on a fine day, you can hear the leaves falling, sounds like waves on the rocks or maybe the ribs of a wrecked ship." I've always found this one uplifting to listen to.

Then we go into the slower 'Poison me', which is basically an anti-smoking tirade, followed by the heart-breaking 'Sunset' about the German girl Milo hung out with in Siegen on our tour who had to move away from all her friends and such a cool scene. Then it's 'Surround', an angry track about bullying, followed by a new and much better recording of the slow-burning 'Lost', with its chuggy breakdown / build up section that was always a favourite of ours to play live and go mad to.

This was followed by the fast fingers Freddie bass intro for 'Slightest interest', then came the oldest track on the album, 'Wall' and the mellow story of 'Ice house' with its opening lines of, "Sitting in a car at night, it's so dark outside, Sitting outside her house, too scared to touch. See that glow in the sky out there, she said to me, see that glow in the sky, that's London," which Milo tells me is about the glow of London seen from Tunbridge Wells in the night sky. This mellow moment was followed by a fight put to music, the Quicksand-esque manic-depressive power of 'Easter', with jagged guitars and Milo shouting, "I've been here before, I nearly didn't return."

About four in the morning, as we were driving home listening to these tracks, we passed a car that was on fire. Maybe it was a sign. It was just burning by the side of the motorway with no other people or cars anywhere nearby to be seen. I guess it had been stolen, joy-ridden and dumped by some horrific urchins, but it seemed surreal and somehow suitable. This scene still pops into my mind when I hear some of these tracks to this day.

These eleven tracks made up our new demo and we started sending them out more or less immediately. We created a cover, using a photo cut from a Thrasher magazine, of a skateboarder ollieing over some railings. We very quickly shifted a lot of these tapes, sending many to promoters, reviewers, radio stations, fanzines, etc and receiving a lot of encouraging press. We could copy and produce the tapes inexpensively and we needed them to sell at our gigs too. We also made some Couch Potatoes stickers to go with them using the same 'Outweighed' skateboarder artwork and we'd hand them out at gigs too, so very soon most of the pubs and music venues of London and the Southeast were adorned with them.

We also harassed record labels with enthusiastic letters and press sheets about the band and all our exciting achievements so far, as bands often do with their new recordings hoping for proper releases. We'd just spent a long time writing these songs and now finally had a good quality recording of them so we'd dish them out to anyone who would listen. At the time those songs were stuck in our heads and on re-play constantly.

On top of that any artist's latest work is invariably their favourite, if not their best. As a band you're only as good as your latest gig or certainly your latest record, so we sent loads of tapes out to the larger alternative labels, like Epitaph, hoping for a good outcome. We had a few polite replies and some small encouragement, but in general were met with a wall of silence from the larger labels. It was annoying at the time, but these guys receive hundreds of demos every week (probably thousands now you can just send a link!) Added to that, around this time the large 'alternative' labels were becoming big business and were only really interested in signing a 'sure thing'. Bands like Green Day and Jawbreaker were very good for sure, but they also already had a big following and that meant for any label that they were a safe bet. This 'no risk' mentality followed suit into some smaller labels and distributors too. It wasn't about breaking new bands or finding good new music, so much as it was about making money. Sad but true, and I guess just good business on their part.

We knew that we could get the album released by any number of smaller record labels that we'd already worked with, but that wasn't initially our goal. We wanted a bigger label that could afford to send us out on tour all the time, with bigger bands, and help arrange promotions that we couldn't afford, such as more recordings and tours, releases on listening posts in HMV and Tower Records, and maybe even making videos, or running ads in the big rock and metal magazines. Now we're getting carried away! Otherwise, we may just as well do it all ourselves, keeping control of things artistically and managing the output in that age honoured punk D.I.Y. way. So, for the time being, that's what we did.

Scene Police Records

I'd also been speaking a lot with two good friends of mine, Dennis Merklinghaus and Emre Aktas, about starting a record label of our own. Dennis and Emre ran a great and very popular hardcore fanzine called Interpol Times and they'd interviewed Couch Potatoes and reviewed several of our releases, so we'd all gotten talking and soon became fast friends. I'd been corresponding with Emre first, as he lived in Surbiton, Surrey, in the UK, and I'd sent him 'Excess All Areas' a while back, but now sent the new demos, telling him that we were working on a brand new album and it would be ready soon. Emre introduced me to Dennis, who lived over in Bonn, Germany and we all got talking.

It turned out that Emre and Dennis were already kicking around an idea for a record label, originally to be called 'Satan as my co-pilot', but this name was changed to Scene Police when Sabbel, a friend of theirs and the singer of Tumult, a German power-violence hardcore band and bunch of utter lunatics from the Bonn / Cologne area, remembered a cover on an Interpol Times zine, #6 or #7, about cleaning up the scene and the name 'Scene Police' was born. Their first release was going to be a Tumult 7", but this never happened as Dennis and Emre both went off to Istanbul for a couple of months, and while they were gone Tumult's 'Heroic Bloodshed' EP came out on Defiance Records instead.

It was when they came back that Emre suggested to Dennis that they could put out Couch Potatoes new 'Outweighed' album as Scene Police's first release. I sent them tapes over and they were into it. They knew a lot of people in the HC punk scene and had a real D.I.Y. mentality right from the start. Through their Interpol Times fanzine contacts they would be able to set up trades with other record labels quickly to get the new releases out into the world. It was a great opportunity and the way we wanted to do things, so we all agreed to work together.

The Couch Potatoes 'Outweighed' CD was released on Scene Police Records early in '96 as SCP001, the label's very first release. It still had the image of the skateboarder on the front cover, but now in a sepia-coloured tone, with a bunch of kids with buckets on their heads on the back cover along with the track listing.

To use up the extra time we had available on the CD we added a version of 'Safe', our Dag Nasty cover, as a listed track, and then also added a hidden track, which included 'Part of You', 'Weak', 'Kill It', 'Three', 'Another', 'Bob', 'Hole' and 'Why' from our '92 release 'Excess All Areas'. Overall, the CD version contained 21 tracks so was pretty good value for all the new pop-punk punters we hoped to find across Europe. The album would give a decent account of where the band were at when this album came out too. You can hear the influences on it from more melodic US hardcore bands of the time like Samiam, Lifetime and even Quicksand, but underlying that it is definitely a UKHC release, and one that I am still very proud of. We felt it was an important release at the time, and with benefit of hindsight now, I'm glad to say that it seems quite a few people shared this opinion.

The CD came in a jewel case with inside photo artwork of my Gibson SG guitar leaning against my Marshall JCM800 amplifier and Celestion cab. This photo was taken by Milo at The White House studio, saying at the time that he thought it would look good on a record sleeve. There was also a fold out lyric sheet covered with band photos and on the first page it had a picture of a whirlwind tearing across a field with our thanks list, various credits and record label details underneath. And 1 DM / 50p of every sale went to Food Not Bombs.

Obviously, I was stoked to have this release out, we all were, but Dennis, Emre and I wanted to work on others too and develop the record label as soon as possible. I got more involved and helped out as much as I could, chipping in for some more releases and helping promote and distribute them as much as possible. We'd all work together and share contacts and the workload. I'd be travelling in Germany a lot over the next few years, both with the band and with my new job at a pan-European publishing company, so I'd often visit Dennis at the Scene Police HQ on Humboldt Strasse in Bonn and stay with him for a while, hanging out in his place full of comics and records, and picking up the latest releases. We'd go for Chinese or falafels and discuss bands, records, zines, politics, gigs and skateboarding, all sorts of HC stuff. I loved it.

The Scene Police label was active from early '96 to late 2002 and although we started slowly, we'd build things up with partners and distributors, eventually producing forty great hardcore releases, with most of those records coming out between '98 and 2001. Revolution Inside, an alternative record label and distributor that also opened a short-lived record store in Bonn, would be our first distribution partner, before Dennis found larger German independent distributors, such as Flight 13, getting involved from '99 onwards, and then Green Hell carrying the releases too.

As well as having great bands, Scene Police always strived for good quality design and packaging for all the releases too, constantly pressing multi-coloured vinyl with special covers, giving the fans of the bands something cool to look at and read, as well as listen to. A lot of these records were, and still are, a record collector's dream and I'm sure they will be cherished by their owners for years to come.

Looking ahead, from '97 onwards, I was mainly focusing on what Rydell were up to so if we needed tours, Dennis was massively helpful with gigs and contacts in Germany and Emre in the UK. It was fun and worked very well. We'd all meet up at shows, often with some of the guys from the bands we'd helped put releases out for too. The hardcore scene in Germany in the late '90's was superb, way bigger and more active than it was in the UK, so as well as putting out records we gigged over there a lot, playing to some great audiences and making many good friends. But more on that later...

Here's a list of the Scene Police Records releases with some extra information on vinyl pressings and special notes where I thought it might be of interest to other OCD record collector nerds like myself:

SCP001 Couch Potatoes 'Outweighed' CD
SCP002 Hot Water Music / Rydell split 7" Six pressings, different covers, different vinyl (from fifth pressing with Ignition / Engineer)
SCP003 April 'April' 7" (with Bastardized and Alveran Records) first press clear, green, orange and black vinyl, second press blue, brown and green vinyl.
SCP004 Pressgang 'Self Destroyed 7" (with Bloodlink)
SCP005 Impact 'Winchester Per Un Massacro' 7" (with Revolution Inside) red & black vinyl
SCP006 Wilbur Cobb 'I eat punks like you for breakfast!' 7" (with Nova and Farewell) First press blue, green and black vinyl, second press red and white vinyl
SCP007 Rydell / Sunfactor / The Babies Three tour split CD
SCP008 The Sharpshooters / Lickity Split split 7" (with Torque Recs) white and black vinyl
SCP009 Creutzfeldt self-titled 7" (with Bastardized) loads of different colours
SCP010 Hunter Gatherer / Rydell tour split CD
SCP011 Tupamaros 'Our modern paest' CD (with Music Is My Heroin)
SCP012 The Babies Three 'A hole where my heart should be' LP pink and blue, yellow with red splatter and black vinyl versions
SCP013 Oddballs Band 'Shit explosion' CD (with Weird Science)
SCP014 Winchester 73 'Sein wechselgeld ist blei' 7" 'His change is lead' (Arizona Terror) black and brown vinyl (with Weird Science)
SCP015 Tupamaros 'Beyond the bias' 10" & CD 400 black, 200 clear, 200 green, 100 blue 100 red and black vinyl with 'Scene Police is watching you' in the run-out grooves.
SCP016 Bitchin' self-titled 7" (with No Idea) 300 red, 700 black
SCP017 Colt self-titled LP 400 black, 100 blue (CD on Monostar Records)
SCP018 Wasted 'Down and out' LP & CD (with Combat Rock Industry) clear red and black
SCP019 Hunter Gatherer 'Low standards for high fives' CD (with Ignition / Engineer)
SCP020 p.u.m.a. self-titled 10" (with Liasons Dangereuses) 200 black, 200 green and black and 100 pink vinyl with an eight-page insert
SCP021 Stalingrad 'Abandonment' 10" bronze, white, khaki, brown and black vinyl, 'Scene Police will eat your babies' in the run-out grooves.
SCP022 Craving 'Comparable? Traces!' 7" pink, green, white and black vinyl. 'Scene Police is watching you' in the run-out grooves.
SCP023 Lack 'Blues Moderne: Danois Explosifs' CD
SCP024 Landscape 'Positive punk power' LP & CD white and black vinyl, anarchism booklet and 'Positive Political Powerful' in the run-out grooves
SCP025 Strike Anywhere 'Underground Europe 2001' 7" (Genoa Benefit EP, five pressings, six different vinyl)
SCP026 Winchester 73 'Weihwasser Joe In: Fauste, Bohnen, Funf Kanonen' 7" 'Holy

Water Joe in: Fists, beans, five cannons' (with Weird Science) on brown and red splatter vinyl.

SCP027 Last Years Diary 'self-titled' 7" (with Ignition / Engineer) 400 white 100 red splatter

SCP028 Children Of Fall 'Ignition for poor hearts' LP & CD 200 hand-numbered tour vinyl.

SCP029 Craving 'Fans will shit their pants' dbl LP & CD gatefold sleeve and lyric sheet silver pressing on cover

SCP030 For The Day 'Love isn't brains, children' LP & CD (with Rockstar and Weird Science) different coloured vinyl

SCP031 Colt 'Marek' LP 313 black and 321 yellow vinyl

SCP032.5 Pageninetynine 'Document #8' 12" (with Electric Human Project and Robotic Empire) 1000 copies with embossed gatefold sleeve and twelve-page booklet.

SCP033 Peace Of Mind 'Values between 0 and 1' LP& CD different coloured vinyl

SCP034 The Assistant 'We'll make the roads by walking' LP transparent blue vinyl

SCP035 My Own Lies / Wilbur Cobb split 5" vinyl (with Flowerviolence) two pressings

SCP036 Forstella Ford 'Quietus' CD (LP with Level Plane)

SCP037 Araki 'Ikara' Dbl LP & CD (with Black Star Foundation)

SCP038 Tiger Lou 'Gone drifting' 7" (with Black Star Foundation) different coloured vinyl

SCP039 Forstella Ford 'Well versed in deception' LP & CD (with One Day Savior) different coloured vinyl

SCP040 Yaphet Kotto 'European tour' 12" 119 on grey marble, 800 on white vinyl.

I loved being a part of Scene Police Records and remember it fondly, although from '99 onwards it was almost entirely run by Dennis and Emre, as I'd created my own Ignition / Engineer Records label so concentrated mainly on that and was much less involved. I'd re-release three of those Scene Police records as joint releases on Ignition / Engineer Records too. These would be the Hot Water Music / Rydell split 7", the Hunter Gatherer 'Low standards for high fives' CD and the Last Year's Diary 7", partly to help me get the new label up and running, partly as we'd sold out of copies and needed to repress more of each record, and partly because these were my favourite releases at the time, and the bands that we were playing shows with the most.

For posterity, I'd like to re-release the Hunter Gatherer / Rydell CD and the Rydell / Sunfactor / Babies Three CD on Engineer Records too, as it's been twenty years since those tours now. Crikey, time flies. I'd better have another chat with Dennis and Emre about it. Of course, all the Scene Police releases are well worth checking out. My favourites are Hunter Gatherer, Tupamaros, The Babies Three, For The Day, Last Year's Diary, Bitchin' and obviously, Couch Potatoes and Rydell. But check out the Converge-style chaos of April, the laid back down-tuned mellowness of Colt, the piledriving riffs of Craving or the spazzed out sounds of Forstella Ford and you'll see what a great hardcore label it was.

Reviews of Couch Potatoes `Outweighed´ album

HeartattaCk #19 - Punk rock from England which could easily pass for punk rock from the US. These guys have studied their Jawbreaker records very closely and exhibit a much finer more experienced sense of melody than most bands playing their game. In some vague sense they remind me of Les Thugs which totally lets the sun shine in on my books. Recorded in '95 with some lesser bonus tracks lumped in on the end from '92, hence the length of the CD. (56 mins, 14 tracks*). The cover art is of the high design environment. A percentage from copies sold goes to Food Not Bombs. Definitely several notches above what I had anticipated.

Smitten - Most of this is on the more aggressive side of pop-punk, tuneful yet emotion packed. There are some really fine moments, like 'Sunset', 'Slightest Interest', the quite poppy 'Wall', but especially storming is the Quicksand-y 'Poison Me'.

Only A Phase #2 – Melodic mid-tempo punk-rock with some heavy DC influences. The singer sounds like a very good mixture of Guy Picciotto (Fugazi) and Jason Beebout (Samiam). Somehow they remind me of Horace Pinker and they also do an awesome Dag Nasty cover. Very good bass player, perfect sound for such a record, cool lyrics, all in all an excellent example for 'Punk Rawk' of the better kind. The CD contains a bonus track with their '92 eight song demo and comes in a very beautiful package.

Plot – Reminds me strongly of early Split Lip and Lifetime. Fifty-six minutes of cool melodies from England. It's a ripper.

Interpol Times – Beautiful, emotional hardcore packed with those melodies you're looking for, in the vein of Samiam, Lifetime and that old DC sound. Comes with a cover version of Dag Nasty's 'Safe'.

Punk Bombe #22 - Very well, some of this sounds like the divine Leatherface, even if the music is not quite as varied. The outstanding singer makes up for this with his budweiser-voiced voice(?!). The band info never got to me somehow and since I have never heard anything from this English band before, I simply assume this is their debut disc. It's very interesting in any case, partly because of the traditional punk structures, but maybe the big hits are missing somehow, but this disc still ranks well above the average.

Maximum Rock n Roll #182 – The Couch Potatoes play in a style somewhere between old Samiam and The Doughboys. Good, snappy, slightly sappy and pained songs that work in a melodic cathartic sort of way. They aren't quite as memorable as their obvious influences, but still power along admirably. The production is a little thin, but the music still comes through. Worth taking a chance on. (BG).

Anvil #3 – This is older material from the current Rydell from England. Quite original, independent, melodic emo with a tendency to be weird and tricky though, which is a bit too much for me in the long run. Nonetheless not a bad album. If you like bands like Quicksand, you should definitely try this out. 14 tracks, 56 mins.

Couch Potatoes / Wact split EP - Frisbee

We also had another release that came out around this time, before the CD version of 'Outweighed' in fact, and that was a split 7" EP with our buddies Wact, that we called 'Frisbee'.

The Pseudo Hippies had reformed under the name of Wact and had been into Sound Advice studios in Greenwich to record a bunch of tracks with their new line-up. The band was still Kris, Dan and Adam, but with Dave Fritz on guitar now instead of Tom. They'd chosen 'Punk rock gurl' and 'Down at Café Sol' to record and had Geoff Woolley engineering them. The new tracks sounded great, so Adam and Kris were keen to put them out and get gigging again.

Couch Potatoes had the new tracks we'd recorded for 'Outweighed' at The White House, but only had them on cassette for now, as this was still before the Scene Police CD came out. We wanted a couple of tracks available on vinyl and thought a split EP would be a good idea.

Making the most of it, Wact decided to call their side of the EP 'Punk rock sucks' and Couch Potatoes, possibly foolishly for misuse in later reviews, went for 'Frisbee'. We chose the tracks 'Sunset' and 'Tidemark' and probably then should have contacted Ian at Weird Records, Hohnie at Nasty Vinyl, or Andreas at Born to Booze, but instead, excited to get the tracks out there, decided to release it ourselves. Having had some experience with the short-lived Something Cool label on our self-release of Joeyfat's 'God' EP, we had the contacts and felt confident enough. No doubt influenced by the recent release of Tarantino's 'Pulp Fiction' movie, we came up with our own imprint, calling the label Get the Gimp Records. The label's logo featured a blow torch and a pair of pliers, and we went ahead with pressing 1000 7" EPs ourselves. These arrived in plain white sleeves, but Adam's brother Paul was a printer, so he helped us sort the covers. We sent a few of these new split EPs out to fanzines and promoters but sold most of the copies at our shows. We had a mixed bag of press for this record, but here's a couple of reviews from fanzines at the time:

How We Rock - A cracker of a split ep here if you ask me. the Couchies play some cool melodic hardcore that's memorable and well executed. Basically, it's catchy as fuck. It's energetic and Miles has a pretty cool voice. There's some cool breaks and tempo changes, but there's no let up and it all flows through pretty damn smoothly. I hope to see these live soon.

Smitten - Couch Potatoes are sounding amazing these days. Powerful emo-punk from them meets ska-tinged poppy pop-punk from Wact.

Land Of Treason - Couch Potatoes have come a long way since their early releases, like a whole new band. I hate to have to constantly make comparisons with American bands, but these two tracks really do remind me of early Samiam and Pegboy. God, their first song is so damn catchy it's driving me nuts. Good jump-around-a-room-at-a-party-music.

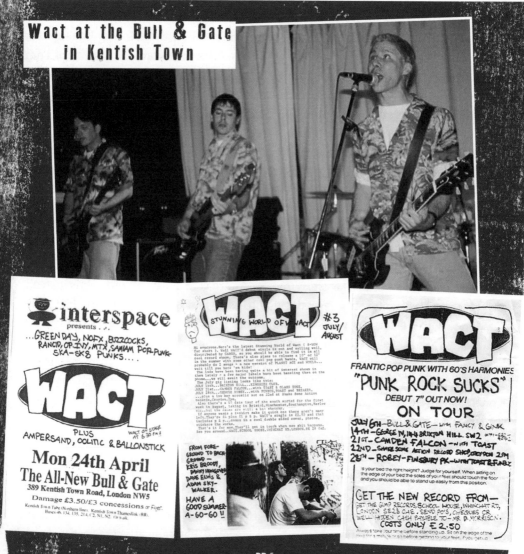

COUCH POTATOES

FRISBEE

COUCH POTATOES ARE DAVID (GUITAR + VOCALS), DANIEL (GUITAR), MILES (VOCALS), PAUL (FINGERBASS) AND DAN (DRUMS). TRACKS ARE SUNSET AND TIDEMARK BY COUCH POTATOES. RECORDED AND MIXED AT THE WHITE HOUSE. ENGINEERED AND PRODUCED BY MARTIN NICHOLS AND COUCH POTATOES. WRITE TO US AT 1 CHANDOS ROAD, TUNBRIDGE WELLS, KENT, TN1 2NY, UK. CATALOGUE NUMBER IS GTG 001 "GET THE GIMP RECORDS.

WACT

PUNK ROCK SUCKS

WACT.45 RPM.PUNK ROCK GURL.2·38.
(KRIS).DOWN AT CAFE SOL.2·20.(WACT)
WACT ARE L TO R : DAVE,VOX,GTR.KRIS,VOX,GTR.
ADAM,BASS,DAN,DRUMS.
RECORDED & MIXED AT SOUND ADVICE
16 TRK.GREENWICH.5TH & 19TH MARCH '95.
BY GEOFF WOOLLEY & WACT (C)95.
ARTWORK.KRIS.PHOTOS.LARA.WACT.

FOR INFO,FREE MAIL LIST,STICKERS OR SHIRTS
WRITE US AT:WACT HQ.SCHOOL HOUSE,
WHINCHAT RD,LONDON,SE28 OAE,UK.
BOOKINGS:KRIS.0181 690 5163.

Couch Potatoes / Wact split 7"   **"PUNK ROCK SUCKS"**
"GET THE GIMP RECORDS" 001

24, Back on the road

We never wanted to stop gigging and would fit in as many shows as possible, happy to play at any venues that would have us, but trying to play with bands that we were really into at the time, and that was definitely the case for the next couple of shows.

The Princess Charlotte was an old-fashioned pub on the main road into Leicester and looking at it you'd probably just want to keep on going, but we had a show to play so needed to stop. That wasn't as easy as it sounds as the pub was right on a busy corner just after some traffic lights opposite the university. Traffic was flying by and there were double yellow lines all the way in front of the pub followed by a row of iron railings too. This was not an easy place to stop, and unloading all our equipment here would be like going through a bloody obstacle course with guided missiles coming at you. We drove on past and got lost in town for a while before making our way back and finding a side street with a back way into a small car park. The brick walls were painted blue and red and there were a few hardcore kids hanging around, some of whom turned out to be in the other bands we would be playing with, Tribute and Schema, and they helped us load the gear in and introduced us to the promoter, Andy, who promptly offered us all drinks.

Once inside, it was pretty cool and you could see why it was one of 'the' venues to play on the alternative music circuit. The Charlotte had a long bar all down one side and a simple low stage, but with a quality sound and light rig and plenty of space for people to watch the bands. Back in the day, The Clash, The Damned, The Buzzcocks, all the greats had played here. More recently NOFX, Offspring and Rancid had been here too, and so had plenty of the Britpop and indie crowd.

Tribute had already set up most of their gear, so we filled in any gaps with our equipment and were soon ready to soundcheck. Tribute and Schema were both new bands and they all seemed very friendly. We'd heard a few tracks on demo tapes and read good things about them in a couple of fanzines so were looking forward to playing this show.

They were both fairly local bands, and they had clearly invited loads of their mates along to the gig, many of whom had already turned up and were sitting around watching us soundcheck, running through a few songs so that the soundman could get the levels just right. Couch Potatoes were meant to be headlining, but we all discussed it and

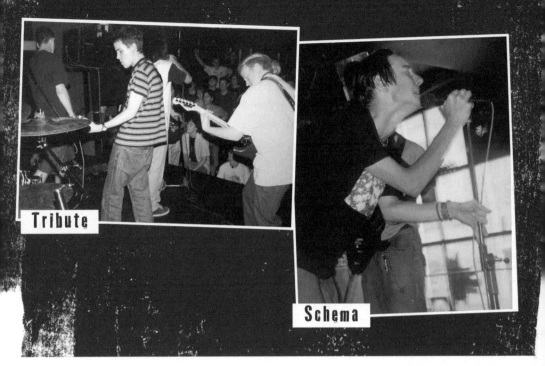

Tribute

Schema

agreed that we should go on in the middle. The other bands were cool about it and this was our favourite place to play on a bill. More importantly, and as all the bands acknowledged, it guaranteed that a mainly local crowd hung around until the end of the gig so that the 'out of town' band still had a good audience, even if they didn't know you, or worse still, didn't particularly like your band's music. We hoped that wouldn't be the case and figured all three bands had a similar emo / post-punk style, but it just seemed wise.

Although I'd only heard Tribute's three-track cassette that Subjugation Records had put out, I was already really into their music. They'd recorded it at Backstage studios with Andy Sneap, the amazing lead guitarist of thrash metal band Sabbat and one of my early heroes, so I figured they'd be good live too and sure enough they were awesome. They'd gone from a four-piece band early on to a five-piece now, and filled the stage with a clever and controlled noise. They were gigging a lot and although they didn't have many tracks recorded, they fed them out over the next months, with 'Names in concrete' and 'Rye grass' on a 7" and 'Distant... relational' on a flexi disc that I received along with a copy of Nick Royle's 'How we rock' fanzine, both released by Subjugation that year. They followed these with the two track 'Torch songs' 7" on Day After Records in '96 and a track called 'Hitherto' on a split 7" with Beacon in '97 on Spread Records. Tribute was Karl Broome singing, with Chay Lawrence and Jon Cannon on guitars, John Watson on bass and Mark Hutchinson on drums. They came from Spalding in Lincolnshire, only about fifty miles away from tonight's show, and John, the bassist, told me that there wasn't much to do there, so they spent a lot of time practising and writing songs. They were stoked to be gigging and putting records out, and they certainly seemed to enjoy the show.

Schema were the local boys, from Bushby in Leicester, about five miles down the road from the venue, and I'm guessing we mainly had them to thank for the crowd that was building up already. They were another band who so far I'd only heard three tracks from, on a self-released demo cassette sent to BHP for review by their singer, Davey. But those three tracks; 'Forget me not', 'Prairie fires' and 'Flies and honey' were beautiful. The artwork on the cassette had caught my eye, the cool old woodblock printed image looked like Ned Kelly in his outback armour, with a helmet and six-shooter, but it also had a Celtic-style stamp with a deer on it and Schema written in an olde worlde way. These guys had recorded with Andy Sneap at Backstage too and would soon be signed by Helene and Ian to Subjugation Records and deservedly so. Subjugation released Schema's self-titled debut 7" in '96 featuring just two tracks, 'Double sun, darkhills' and the brilliant 'Penny dreadful', then Richard Corbridge released their 'Sooner than you think' collection CD on his Armed With Anger Records in '97 and that one's still on regular rotation in my stereo.

It was a great gig for all three bands; noisy, busy and fun, so we didn't mind the one-hundred-and-fifty-mile trip back home in the early hours at all. We just had to negotiate that bloody corner first.

8/8/95 Annalise, Couch Potatoes and Wact
The Joiners, Southampton
9/8/95 Annalise, Couch Potatoes and Wact
Railway Inn, Winchester
10/8/95 Annalise, Couch Potatoes and Filter
Panama Jax, Paignton
11/8/95 Couch Potatoes and Easy Lover
The Cavern, Exeter
14/8/95 Annalise, Couch Potatoes and Wact
The Square, Harlow

Next week we were heading west, off on a mini-tourette. I'd arranged five shows with Martin Edmunds (of Annalise) and Kris Beltrami (of Wact) and their bands would play on the three-band pop-punk bills alongside us.

The first show would be at one of our regular haunts, The Joiners in Southampton, playing the S.T.E.'s ninetieth show with our mates Wact (ex-Pseudo Hippies) and Annalise (ex-Wordbug). This show was busy for a Tuesday night and as usual, had good sound, so everyone there was blasted with an upbeat melding of melody and power. All three bands then headed over to The Railway Inn in Winchester for the next evening and plenty of the same faces were in the crowd again, so something must have gone right.

TUE.AUG.8TH

annal!se   Exeter

COUCH POTATOES
Tunbridge Wells

WACT   London

The Joiners   STE 90

St Marys St

Southampton

3.00/2.50

8pm   Access 1 Step

Poster for the pop-punk extravaganza of Annalise,
Couch Potatoes and Wact at the Joiners

We'd arrived in Winchester early and had wandered around town for a while before sitting on the cathedral steps, eating burgers like a bunch of scruffy tourists. Then we went to The Railway and were pleased to see loads of our posters for the gig pasted up outside. The promoters usually sorted the posters for shows themselves, but just in case we had plenty of designs for geeky gig flyers, mostly with pictures of skaters on them, but some with political stuff, police or Russian workers, and we'd sent a few along ahead of time. There was one with the Wendy's-based logo saying 'Couchies - Quality is our recipe', another had 'Genuine Kentifornian Couchcore' in the Budweiser logo style and another featured a drawing of DR and Quinch, the 2000AD characters, saying 'Be there or eat plutonium death'. All had 'Couch Potatoes, Annalise and Wact - playing here tonight!' written large across them. We played pool and listened to '70's heavy metal on the jukebox while we waited for the other bands to turn up.

Wact piled in with a few boxes of the new Couch Potatoes / Wact split 7" for us to sell at the gigs. They had a load of new material already and had also reworked some of the old Pseudos tracks too, if it was possible giving the songs an even more catchy sing-a-long edge. They'd called the band Wact after a Fiendz album of the same name. They were a pop-tastic unit alright and tonight's gig would show that, but unfortunately their shooting star had a short trajectory and the band came to an end in October '95. Their final show was a barn-stormer with Toast in Brixton, but their new guitarist and singer of just one year, Dave Fritz, had to return to Canada to finish his studies when his UK visa ran out, so that was the end of that.

This wasn't so bad for Dave though. He'd marry his childhood sweetheart the very next year as soon as he'd finished his university course. He'd also join other pop-punk bands and continue writing music, starting with Trigger, soon after his return, but most notably in Junior Achiever with Gene Champagne in 2003. Gene was formerly the drummer in Canadian band The Killjoys who were big in the '90s and released three albums for Warner Bros. Both Junior Achiever, and his next band, Ramona, would have releases on Engineer Records, and Dave still writes great pop-punk tunes, his current studio project is called Droids Osaka.

Wact would have other records coming out after they broke up too, including a split flexi-disc release with Birmingham's pop-punksters Skimmer, that was included with issue #4 of Smitten fanzine, as well as a great, nineteen-track collection CD, called Anthology, on Japan's Fixing A Hole Records (most of this recorded at the 'Sound Advice' session where they recorded the tracks for the Wact / Couch Potatoes split EP).

A short while later, Adam would re-join Couch Potatoes, when Paul went off travelling, and then become the bassist of Rydell. Kris would later go on to form another new band, a more mainstream guitar and synth-pop outfit called Dweeb. They signed to Blanco Y Negro, an imprint of Warner Brothers and MCA publishing. Dweeb would release a great pop album called 'Turn you on'. The promo campaign for this album would be punctuated by plenty of singles and EPs, including a split with Mogwai on Che Records and more Dweeb releases for Fierce Panda and Damaged Goods too.

Annalise turned up to the show last, too late for the pool tournament but in time to play their set to a decent crowd that had come out that night. They rocked it again. Their shows were always full of energy and enthusiasm and this one would be no different. Annalise, named after an airheaded blonde character from the TV show Neighbours, had it all, driving bass lines, clever riffs and really infectious harmonies. They were clearly influenced by some of the more popular US bands and were just as good as them too, but they still remained very English sounding, with Martin never afraid to sing in his broad west country accent. We played quite a few shows with them and they were always good fun.

Although at the time they still had some Wordbug merchandise to shift, Annalise were just about to put out their first release, the 'Fettered' EP on Snuffy Smile and Out of Order Records. They'd soon add to this and build up a serious catalogue of releases over the next few years. There were three albums on their own Pigdog Records; 'Something's got to give', 'Our story goes like this' and 'Versus everything', before they signed to Var Thelin's Gainesville, Florida-based No Idea Records and put out 'Here's to hope'. In true punk / hardcore style they also had many EPs and split releases too, including one with The Tone on Suspect Device Records, one with J Church on Beat Bedsit Records and my favourite, with Gunmoll, on Boss Tuneage Records, which is surely a contender for the thickest piece of vinyl ever pressed. If you include the compilation CDs too, there must be at least twenty records with Annalise tracks on them kicking around. They were prolific alright, but always quality too.

We'd be heading further west to Annalise's neck of the woods to play shows at a couple of Devon venues next. The first would be at Panama Jax, in the seaside vacation town of Paignton. This venue was a nightclub that put on regular rock shows too. It seemed badly run-down to us, with the ramshackle building a bit out of place in this town full of neon arcades and holidaymakers. But it did have a big colourful parrot painted on the sign outside and a decent queue of people waiting to get in, so we hoped the gig wouldn't be too bad. A local rock band called Filter went on first and were pretty damn good. Filter's guitarist Ben Norton later moved to London and played in the screamo bands Soon The Darkness and Narwhal. By the time Couch Potatoes wandered on stage to rock out, the place was already busy, hot and sweaty. We had a good show and a late night, ending up crashing out with a few drunkards at one of the local houses.

The next day we got up late and had an easy afternoon scoffing chips by the seaside, followed by a short road trip with some of our new buddies in tow for another show at The Cavern in Exeter. For some reason Annalise weren't playing and the support band they'd booked didn't show up. It seemed a waste to just have one band playing for everyone on a Friday night so we took a while over sound-check and came up with our new heavy-metal alter-ego band, Easy Lover. Now that may sound like a Phil Collins tribute act to you, but what we had in mind was more of a bluesy biker rock piss-take band, something like Motley Crue or Zodiac Mindwarp or some other glam-rock nonsense, replete with motorbikes, flames and leather-clad female dancers on stage with us. What actually happened was that we made a god-awful racket for about five minutes, attempting a couple of thrash metal covers, and then gave up and all had a bundle at the front of stage.

We survived it and apart from a little bit of good-natured heckling later, went back on and played a proper set of Couch-core for nearly an hour, earning us a generally good reaction from all the rockers. We'd had another good evening at the Cavern, but driving back that night from Devon to Kent, the head gasket went on Dan P's car and he had to be towed home, making for another long night and quite an expensive trip. We all played the last show of this little tourette back east, patched-up and tuned-up at The Square in Harlow. Both Wact and Annalise came along to rock out with us again and it was another busy gig with a lot of good people having a fun evening. We just loved playing these pop-punk hardcore gigs, and despite any amount of sleep-deprivation or car-trouble, it would take a lot to wear us down.

6/9/95 Goober Patrol, Couch Potatoes and Chocolate
The Boat Race, Cambridge

The promoters of this show were Isaac and Sally, they called themselves Spread and ran a really good distro and label under the same name. They'd put up a lot of posters around Cambridge and done a great job of promoting the show. The posters were bright yellow with a cartoon manga girl on them saying 'Ok skate punk, make my day' and announcing the three bands; 'Goober Patrol, signed to Fat Wreck Chords, Couch Potatoes, awesome Kentifornian couchcore, and Chocolate, Ipswich style hardcore, Ex-Stupids & Sink. Just three pounds, Wednesday 6th September, doors open at 8pm'. The poster also said that there'd be 'records, zines and friendly people at The Boat Race, East Road, Cambridge'. It even had the pubs telephone number on there too.

We'd seen a few shows at The Boat Race before, including the awesome SNFU gig where I'd been repeatedly whacked over the head with a doll leg, but hadn't actually played there ourselves yet so were excited for this one. We'd be seeing our mates the Goobers too, so we knew it'd be a chip-eating, beer-swilling tractor-driving pop-punk party. Goober Patrol had just put out a split record with The Mr T Experience, a great band from the San Francisco Bay Area who were on Lookout Records, the same label as Green Day and Operation Ivy. MTX's early album 'Making things with light' was a big favourite of mine when it came out and the band had become very popular since. I was blown away that the Goobers had a split record with them, and to be honest, a little

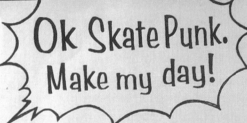

SPREAD presents...

**Ok Skate Punk.
Make my day!**

Goober
Patrol

<<signed to Fat Wreck Chords,   need i say more>>

Couch
Potatoes

<<awesome Kentifornian Couchcore!>>

&
Chocolate

<<Ipswich style hardcore. Ex-Stupids, Sink etc etc>>

Wed **6**th Sept   **3** pounds

doors
8pm

There will be records,
'zines and friendly people.

boat race east rd, cambridge, 01223-570063

Poster for Goobers, Couchies and Chocolate
at The Boat Race in Cambridge

The Joiners, Southampton

The Forum, Tunbridge Wells

The Cavern, Exeter

The Charlotte, Leicester

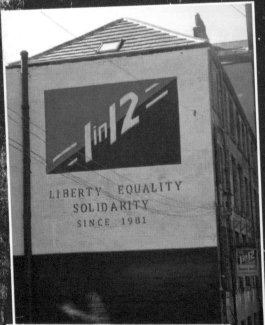

The 1 in 12 Club, Bradford

The Boat Race, Cambridge

jealous. Chatting with Simon about it at the bar, he told me that they'd started working on a new 'proper album' too, with more political punk shout-a-longs on it rather than their comedy yokel sing-a-longs. This turned out to be 'Extended Vacation', which would be released originally on Them's Good Records, based out of Corby in the rust belt of Northamptonshire, but also helped them get signed to Fat Wreck Chords for a re-release in the US, with the album coming out simply as 'Vacation' on Fat Mike of NOFX's own record label early in '96 on CD, LP and cassette.

The Goober's 'Vacation' album was reviewed in the very first issue of Fracture, probably the UK's biggest punk and hardcore fanzine of the nineties, by a guy called Russell Remains, one of the zines two main writers, and this is what he had to say about it:

Goober Patrol 'Extended Vacation' CD / 27:08

Ooh, ouch, just when you didn't expect it, Norfolk's yokel-punks renowned for their catchy singalong pop-punk come along with 9 tracks of raging political punk that surely kick my ass. 'Course it's still loaded with hooks but the singalongs have been replaced by shoutalongs railing against authority and apathy. Add on top of this that the GOOBERS still have the best comedy rural accents you're ever likely to hear, and you're onto one hell of a good thing. (RR) Them's Good, PO Box 8, Corby, Northamptonshire, NN17 2XZ, UK'.

There was another discussion going on at the bar soon after our soundcheck that seemed to be about whether Suffolk or Norfolk produced better punk bands. This was because the other band playing this evening would be Chocolate, a new band hailing from Ipswich, but who boasted ex-members of several well-known pop-punk skate-core bands. Ed Wenn, aka Ed Shred, had played guitar in both Sink and Big Ray before forming Chocolate along with John Ruscoe, also of Sink, Simon Finbow, and Wolfie Retard, the ex-bassist of The Stupids (a very popular band with skateboarders in the late '80s), Perfect Daze and Lovejunk.

These guys had a new record out on Out Of Step Records and sung about even sillier nonsense than the Goobers. They played a set that evening that included the songs 'Butt Hickey' and 'Working for an idiot', as well as 'Dumb fuck', 'Stupid jerk' and a cover of the Angry Samoans 'Stupid motherfucker'. They could certainly play though, swapping instruments at one point to prove the point, and they could certainly swear a lot too, but they didn't take it all too seriously and were good fun to see play live.

I'd walked into the back room of the venue to grab my guitar before we played, and upon seeing the Goobers all laying on the floor drinking cans of beer, I announced that we were going to be playing a set of Motörhead covers and were taking requests, to which one of them replied in a drunken yokel slur, "Oh, anything off Bomber will do for me, thanks."

16/9/95 Ampersand, Couch Potatoes, Skydive and Cynical Smile
The Sir George Robey, Finsbury Park, London

We spent the next couple of days travelling up to London. Milo, Dan P and I went to see Shelter play at the Camden Underworld on the 15th, and then on 16th we all met up to play at The Robey again. This would be our fifth gig at this well-known alternative music venue and we always seemed to have good nights playing there. It was a melodic hardcore kind of evening with the other bands, Cynical Smile, Skydive and Ampersand, all playing good sets. I mainly remember the show for it being Paul's last show with us though. (Or what we thought would be, we actually got him back to play a hometown Christmas show with us too so he could bow out properly). Our bassist had decided he wanted to do some travelling before going away to college, so had booked himself open-ended flights for the following week and was off to see the world, starting with Peru, I think. We wished him all the best but wanted to continue playing the 'Outweighed' tracks and promoting the new album, so as Wact had split around the same time, we asked Adam to re-join Couch Potatoes and spent the next weeks jamming the songs with him.

6/11/95 Tribute and Couch Potatoes
The Sir George Robey, Finsbury Park, London
12/11/95 Couch Potatoes, Bob Tilton and UnderClass
1 in 12 Club, Bradford

It didn't take long for Adam to get up to speed on all the new Couchies songs, but during those weeks the Dag Nasty CD compilation called 'Her heads on fire' came out, and several other punk and hardcore collections confirmed tracks on them too. Soon enough we were ready to rock again, and our first gig back was another up at The George Robey, this time with the brilliant Tribute.

Tribute had their 'Rye Grass' 7" out on Subjugation Records and were gaining a cult following in the scene. Rightly so, as they just got better and better live, having improved massively even from our last show with them, a few months before at The Charlotte in Leicester.

We also played about a week later with the equally great Bob Tilton, up at the 1 in 12 Club in Bradford, West Yorkshire. It was a long trip up there for us but always worth the journey, and as the gig was on a Sunday we had nothing better to do. The 1 in 12 was a great punk venue, very much in the style of the German collectives we'd played at on tour. Located in a big old factory building, solidly made from the local brown stone and dominating the narrow and sloping Albion Street, the 1 in 12 was run by its anarchist membership predominantly to sustain an alternative social scene for the locals. They'd put on regular punk and hardcore shows, including the Means To An End annual punk festival. They'd also help locals with benefit claims and get involved in social campaigning based on anarchist principles, including May Day parades and workers activities, as well as encouraging political protests and direct action. The 'not for profit' club had opened in '81 during a period of high unemployment and social unrest in the area, and its name had in fact come from a statistic in a government benefit fraud investigation of the time, which claimed that '1 in 12 claimants were actively defrauding the state'.

As we pulled up, we saw the big red and black anarchist flag that the club used as the background for their 1 in 12 logo. This giant flag mural decorated the entire side wall of the building, facing up the road, and sign-written underneath, in black on the white-washed wall, was the phrase 'Liberty, Equality, Solidarity since 1981'. The colourful paint job continued all down the side of the building too, with graffiti and murals all along the ground floor which seemed to get added to each time we visited.

We'd been up here a few times before to see shows, and knew that the gigs took place on the first floor, we also knew that the narrow doorway and stone steps would be hell to get equipment up, being very tight. Luckily this gig was an all-dayer, so we could avoid the hassle of trying to lug our amps and kit through steep narrow passageways to get set up, or to have to travel in several cars (as I'd now sold our beloved Beast. She'd broken down yet again and I just couldn't afford to get her fixed this time). We'd arranged with the promoters and other bands just to borrow the backline that was there. That way, as we were coming the furthest, we could all travel up in one car and just bring our guitars and amp heads.

It was never easy to park near the 1 in 12, but once we'd found a place and got inside, up the narrow stairway, the club opened out into large rooms with plenty of people milling about. There was a decent p.a. and lighting rig with a big dancefloor in front of the stage, where people were already sitting around the edges drinking. There was usually a friendly crowd at the 1 in 12 and sure enough, a few people came over to say hi. We dumped our guitars by the stage, ready for soundcheck, and headed over to the smallish bar at the back of the gig-floor and the little record distro stall set up on two tables next to it, where we added our new merchandise too. The club's larger member's bar was upstairs, along with the toilets and a veggie café called Ma Brench's, with a jukebox full of punk rock 7"s and a pool table in the corner. There were quite a few casualties hanging around up here, still nursing hangovers from the previous night. (The Club has since expanded and added an anarchist library, opened by in '96 by Albert Meltzer, a writer and co-founder of the anarchist newspaper Black Flag, as well as rehearsal rooms for bands, and even a children's play area).

At this gig we'd be playing in between UnderClass and Bob Tilton. UnderClass had travelled over the Pennines from the Liverpool / Manchester area and brought quite a few mates with them. They were incredibly noisy, raging in a metallic hardcore kind of way and damn good at it too. Up to that point I hadn't heard of them and was quite blown away. This would be our only show with UnderClass. I'm not sure if they played many and that's a shame. At that point the hardcore five-piece didn't have any records out, just a copied demo cassette, but within a year they'd have three vinyl 7" EPs to push.

The first was a split with the Bradford hardcore band Stalingrad, most of whom were at the gig. It came out on Stalingrad's label, Caught Offside Records, featuring three tracks by Stalingrad and four by UnderClass, including 'A futile attempt at persuasion' and 'Shit Sandwich (Hold the bread)'. This EP quickly sold out and had to be repressed. In the meantime, their self-titled 7" EP came out jointly on two Brighton-based record labels, Refusenik and Tadpole. This 'UnderClass' EP had seven tracks packed onto it, including 'Economics at work in South America' and 'A brief moment of clarity' whose cheery lyrics reminded us of the dual futility and importance of what we all did, playing in bands; "This is irrelevant, this band is irrelevant, this sound is unimportant, these clothes are unimportant, this band is irrelevant, it's my life."

UnderClass had another split release, this time with Nottingham-based noise merchants Hard To Swallow, where they packed in another five short blasts of anger and energy, including 'Testosterone (the missing link)' with the go-lucky sing-a-long of, "Meathead motherfucker spawned on damp locker room floor, why don't you flex your amoeba sized brain?" They certainly had a way with words. I loved them. This EP was called 'Praise God and pass the ammunition' and was released by the Wallasey-based metal hardcore label Days of Fury, the same label that boasted releases by Stampin' Ground and Knuckledust. The cover had screen printed artwork of a Nazi sowing crosses into a field instead of seeds, which was taken from a Spanish Civil War propaganda poster. They'd also have a track, entitled 'A tribute to Frank Worthington', on Caught Offside's 'Strictly Ballroom' compilation 7" in '97, alongside Voorhees, Des Man Diablo, Hard To Swallow, Wat Tyler, Marker and Suffer, but unfortunately by that time the band had broken up.

Couch Potatoes went on after UnderClass and before Bob Tilton at the 1 in 12, not an easy place to play and not an easy act to follow, but we rocked the place as best we could and got a decent response. We were becoming old hands at it by now. I for one still felt the intense enjoyment of playing shows and I was confident about what we did, so never really had any nerves about gigs. I always just enjoyed them.

Then Bob Tilton went on. We'd played with them before, at one of their early gigs at the Dublin Castle in London with Iconoclast and they'd been good then. Now they were just an awesome live act. Playing in a band is personal artistry, not a competition, but you can't help judge your work against your peers sometimes, and these guys were leading the way. I looked on them as an inspiration and a reminder that we 'could do better'.

They were signed to Subjugation Records, Helene and Ian's vital UK HC label based up in Darlington, that had started with our mates Strength Alone's first release and since then built up a considerable following in the scene with bands like Ironside, Baby Harp Seal, Bob Tilton and Tribute. Subjugation would also go on to release records by Schema, Spy Versus Spy, Month of Birthdays, Imbiss, Beacon, Pylon and Stapleton, making it undoubtedly one of the most important labels in UK hardcore in the late Nineties.

Bob Tilton's first release was 'Wake me when it's springtime again', a four track 7" EP recorded in '94 with Andy Sneap at Backstage studios in Nottingham. It had beautiful artwork that looked hand produced, as all the Subjugation releases did, with well-designed lyric sheets and flyers for the label's other releases inside. "Moth to flame, listen close, you'll hear me breaking. Let me sleep this winter, it may take some time, just wake me when it's springtime again." But by the time of the gig at the 1 in 12, they also had the brilliant 'Songs of penknife and pocket watch' 7" out and were already being hailed as the UK's Fugazi, possibly due to the singer's vocal style. Although musically they were a hardcore band, they had various textures and an earnestness about them that many would label "emo". Their press coverage would soon be accelerated by a Peel session, an 'On' feature in NME and the release of their new album 'Crescent'.

'Crescent' came out as a vinyl LP in '96 on Subjugation Records. The 12" contained just nine tracks and lasted almost exactly thirty minutes. It was Bob Tilton's first album and saw them continue to grow in popularity within the tight knit hardcore scene. The original line-up of Simon Feirn, vocals, Neil Johnson and Chay Lawrence, guitars, Mark Simms, bass, and Allan Gainey, drums carried on gigging across genres with all sorts of indie and alternative bands, both in the UK and Europe. But it wasn't until Southern Records got involved in '99 and re-issued 'Crescent' on CD, along with the promotion and distribution of their new album 'The leading hotels of the world' that they really gained more widespread popularity.

'The leading hotels of the world' came out on LP first, and then CD, jointly on Southern and Sousaphon Recordings. Southern was a record label initially based around a recording studio in London, but it had expanded to become a busy record distributor too, taking on various sub-labels and supplier roles. Sousaphon was Bob Tilton's own imprint and only used for this release. By the time these nine new tracks came out, Chay had left the band and Ralph Hamilton had replaced him on second guitar. The album's title track 'The leading hotels of the world' was also released on coloured 12" vinyl and CD by Genet Records, a prolific Belgian record label established by Bruno Vandevyvere and Kathy Dejonghe in '92 and heavily involved in the annual hardcore bash in Ypres called Ieperfest. This release was a split EP with the Belgian band Reiziger, who had themselves developed from another well-known hardcore / punk band, Kosjer D, but had since adopted a more emo / indie style.

15/12/95 Couch Potatoes and Aggressor
The Forum, Tunbridge Wells

We wanted to finish the year with a big local show for all our crew, but that wouldn't be as easy to set up as it sounds. I hadn't played The Forum in Tunbridge Wells since the Joeyfat shows, at the venue's opening early in '93, and then with Green Day and a few others that year. Then we'd broken up and fallen out. The Forum was the only mid-sized music venue in town now. It was pretty much play there or don't play at all. Since the main promoter there was Jason, Joeyfat's bassist, and we'd had all that 'postergate' hassle too when we'd put on shows elsewhere in town, it wasn't easy. I didn't need all that and I certainly didn't want my new band members suffering any hassle because of me, so I'd buried the hatchet, doing my best to patch things up. Most of the other guys in Couch Potatoes went to the Forum occasionally to see bands play, and I guess they'd been speaking with the other promoters and staff there too about our new band. It'd been nearly three years since the venue's opening night gig and even a year and a half since Couch Potatoes last show in town at the Pagoda youth club. We all agreed that was far too long. It was time for us to play there again, but they still didn't seem to want to do us any favours.

The venue had started putting on bands all nights of the week, but were having trouble filling all the slots. I'd suggested a few more alternative acts that were touring to them and hooked up a couple of shows for some friends bands there. Then we started talking about Couch Potatoes coming back to play at The Forum. Initially we'd been offered an empty Monday night slot to fill, but that turned out to be the date we played the Robey with Tribute so we couldn't do it anyway. Now we asked for an end of year / Christmas gig for all our local fans, and they finally agreed we could play on a Friday night, but we had to accept whatever support band they booked (as they had a list of local bands they'd promised Friday and Saturday night supports they were working through) and we had to fill the place up to make it worth their while. That seemed a bit harsh, but we played with all sorts of bands all the time, and we were sure we could fill the venue. It holds about two hundred and fifty people if they're all standing, but we had a lot of local support, and it was time to remind people that we were the local hardcore crew.

So, on 15th December, the penultimate Friday before Chrimbo, Couch Potatoes were booked in to play our hometown again. The support band would be a metal-core outfit called Aggressor who turned up with loads of flash equipment and were happy for us to use it. Dan got to sit on a comfortable drum stool, and we all had stacks of speaker cabs for our amps to blast through. The soundcheck sounded awesome as the venue had a new mixing desk built up on a platform above the bar to save space, allowing real control of the band's sound, both on the stage through wedge monitors and out in front of it through the massive sound system speakers. We had a few mates with us acting as roadies and helping set up, including my bro, Steve, and Adam's bro, Paul. They'd laid out a small distro stall on a table at the back, with Couchies 7"s, CDs and shirts on it and now we just had to hope that all the calls we'd made and posters we'd stuck up over the previous weeks had been effective.

About 8pm they opened the doors and the place started to fill as we went out to grab some burgers. By the time we came back, the venue was almost full and there was still a load of people hanging around outside. I was relieved to see this. Jim, the old Couchies and Joeyfat drummer, was taking tickets in the little cubicle by the doorway that night, and as we came back in to get our hands stamped, he stopped me to say that this was the busiest he'd seen the club for some time. That felt good and now we just had to make sure we rocked.

Both the Dans were bumping into loads of people from their college, and all of us met up with mates we'd invited, many of whom hadn't seen us play for over a year. Paul, our previous bassist, had come home for Christmas and brought along a bunch of his friends too. We'd wanted him to have a 'proper' last gig with us, a hometown send-off, so this would be it. Adam, our bass-master general, was as cool as ever about it, standing down for the evening so Paul could play this gig. Quite a few of our chums from other local bands had come along with their girlfriends too, and there was a real party atmosphere developing as the support band went on. Aggressor played metal-core in a style somewhere between later D.R.I. and Broken Bones, but with a few too many clever effects for my liking. They were technically very good, but never quite seemed to hold the attention of this chatty audience. Now it was our turn.

Climbing on stage around 10pm, we started our set with loud feedback and then burst into 'Tidemark' as soon as Dan K nodded he was ready, with Milo screaming, "Nobody taught me to swim, I should have sunk like a stone," that was followed immediately with the fast chugging of 'Mathematical type'. We were jumping around, falling about on the stage, and the crowd in front of us were doing the same, then bouncing up and down to the bass line in 'Grip' a few moments later. This was fun. We rattled through most of the 'Outweighed' album tracks and then Adam joined us again for a couple of sing-a-long covers and older songs too. We had to be done by eleven o'clock but that gave us plenty of time, even for some jokes and banter from Milo. We finished the set with 'Easter' and it's rousing, "This is my come back. Again, again, and again," and then just had time for a pretty much instant encore of 'Safe'.

I couldn't help feeling that we'd achieved something that evening, locally at least. We needed it to be a good show and luckily everything came together. Sometimes that happened and that time I was very glad it did. We packed up our guitars and we stepped back off the stage, grinning and ready to accept whatever small adulation came our way. That was a good way to end the year.

25, Mr Greedy has left the building

**22/2/96 Couch Potatoes and Rife
The Forum, Tunbridge Wells
23/2/96 Couch Potatoes and The Strookas
The Cardinal's Cap, Canterbury**

I started the new year with a lot of travelling, some of it personal and some of it for my new job, but all of it I turned into holidays whenever I could. I went on my first trip to Canada, somewhere I'd always wanted to visit, going snowboarding and skidooing around Quebec, watching ice hockey in Montreal and eating 'poutine', chips smothered with gravy and cheese, and 'beaver tails', big, hot, flat, sugary cinnamon doughnuts, both of which I loved, at the Fete de Neiges. This would soon become an annual affair for me. Then I went on jaunts around Italy, the USA, Singapore and Malaysia, followed by Sweden and then Italy again, and this was all in the first six months of the year. I'd have trips in France, Belgium, Holland, Germany and Finland later that year too, so fitting in shows became a bit more awkward and something of an art form, with the band playing lots of one-offs or long weekends.

Couch Potatoes first show this year was back at the Forum in TW, where we played another busy gig supported by local indie band Rife. The pre-show highlight was me and Paul Skinner (the old Angus Bagpipe bassist) throwing out some scum-sucking oxygen-thief who was trying to sell drugs in the club. Once outside, it all got a bit lairy and he decided he wanted a fight. That was fine by me, which he soon realised and legged it. We ended up chasing him into a nearby garage, where he grabbed the metal air pump and was swinging it around his head, threatening us with it just as the cops turned up. I'm never glad to see them, but it did save us from having to kill that idiot.

The next evening, we were playing with our mates The Strookas over at The Cardinal's Cap in Canterbury. The Cap was a cool little pub venue that had started putting bands on every Friday and Saturday night, and was fast taking over as the place to play in Canterbury rather than the Penny Theatre. Situated on the corner of Rosemary Lane and Castle Street, the main pedestrian road through the city, it was an ancient and tiny place where the bands shared the tight confines with the regulars and the gig-goers, and you just couldn't help but bump into each other. This made it all better in some way, the punk D.I.Y. spirit was there in abundance and the atmosphere was electric, somehow adding to the music. The bar staff didn't seem to care about anyone's age or how loud we turned up the amps, people were bouncing around, singing along and dancing, and we loved this sort of audience interaction.

We'd travelled across Kent in a convoy of cars packed with a load of our mates who regularly came along to see us play. One of them was Simon Laslett, another guy I'd met back when I was still working in the record store in Tunbridge Wells, and he had been trying to start his own band for a while. It was this evening that he told us that they were finally ready to play, so we'd try to hook them up some gigs with us. Our next run of five shows would include three with Simon's new band, Tartan, supporting us. I dropped him a line to ask what he remembered of the time and he wrote back to me with this...

"When I walked into my work experience placement at a branch of Sam Goody in Tunbridge Wells I hadn't yet thought about, let alone started, a band. By the time I'd finished working there, it was all I wanted to do! My friends and I had been into 'big' indie for a while, the usual early '90s stuff like Carter, Ned's, PWEI, and we'd been to a few shows at local leisure centres and big London venues. Then we discovered that our hometown, Tunbridge Wells, actually had a venue of its own, The Forum. That was it. We were there every weekend, watching anyone and everyone. We couldn't believe that good bands played in Tunbridge Wells, and even more surprisingly, there were bands actually from Tunbridge Wells too! Good bands, like Joeyfat. I picked up their 'God' 7" and absolutely loved it. I was hooked."

Back to the record shop. "I was chatting to the guy looking after me, David, about the music I was into. He said, "Joeyfat? Yeah, I was in Joeyfat. I played on that seven inch." My tiny brain popped. David spent the week telling me tales of touring, which bands were cool and which were pricks, playing me albums I'd never heard, and about his band, Couch Potatoes. Looking back, that week pretty much changed my life. Not bad for a last-minute work placement when I couldn't think of anything I wanted to do. I liked music, so a record shop, right? It turned out I was damn right. Within a few weeks, we went to watch the Couchies play with The Strookas at the Pagoda youth club in Tunbridge Wells. It was a totally D.I.Y. show and brilliant fun. I bought tapes and records by both bands. I was in, 100%."

This was 1994. Pre-internet. "I spent months writing letters to Dave and he sent me tapes of stuff he thought I'd like. Texas is the Reason, Samiam, Lifetime and Jawbreaker stood out. He was pretty much bang on the button. He also sent copies of his fanzine BHP and offered advice on starting our fledgling band, Tartan. Having a local venue meant we had a target as a band, and we played our first show there at a birthday party, with me singing, Matt on bass, James and Nikolai on guitars and Greg on drums. It was terrifying and we were absolutely horrific. Greg soon bailed and, out of necessity, I moved to drums. I'd never played the drums and Matt was still learning the bass, so it took months for us to write some songs that, with a struggle, we could actually play.

"The Forum had a showcase on Monday evenings for new bands, so we started there. It was a 'Battle of the bands' type thing and we'd usually finish last by quite a margin. For some reason, maybe because we were cheap, usually free in fact, and we didn't cause any trouble, we were added to the bill at a bank holiday all-dayer, and thrown on to open things up at lunchtime. Despite being awful and staggering through our half hour set in about seventeen minutes due to nerves, it was amazing to be playing to a crowd. Even if that crowd was left nonplussed at best. I have no idea if Dave had seen us by then, or whether it was purely us writing to him still, but somehow, probably because he's the kindest man in the world, he ended up offering us some shows with the Couch Potatoes. Actual, proper shows. Including gigs outside of Tunbridge Wells. This was literally our dream. I think they were pretty much spread over about a week and a half as well. In our heads this was a tour, damn it.

"We started off in Tunbridge Wells, of course. Baby steps. We were supporting the Couch Potatoes, playing at The Forum again, so recorded this show. In between our songs, the only sound you can hear are the five Couch Potatoes clapping us and other people talking. So, a strong start then. The next stop was Brighton a couple of days later. An actual, proper gig, in Brighton! We'd never been to the Freebutt before, but had a small car loaded with all four of us and our equipment and were trying to find it. We'd gotten properly lost. Luckily, sitting at the lights in a row of traffic, we realised we were right behind Miles and managed to follow him to the venue. I can still remember the terror of walking into the Freebutt for our first proper D.I.Y. show. As the opening band, we were going to be using the headlining band's equipment. Tonight's headliners were Medulla Nocte. Their drum kit was set up on top of a pool table that had been covered with sheets of wood, with some beer crates to step up onto it. I noticed that the drummer of Medulla Nocte was huge, literally a giant, and I had to use his kit. I could barely play it, and there was no way I was going to change any of his set up. He seemed like a nice enough guy, but he could have squashed me with one hand. Anyway, we played, no one threw anything and, most importantly, I didn't break any of his drums. We hung out, watched Couchies rock the place and were amazed that we were somehow on the same bill as Medulla Nocte, who were incredibly heavy.

"A few days later we were supporting the Couch Potatoes again, at The Cardinal's Cap over in Canterbury. In the car on the way there, I convinced everyone we were third on the bill supporting Samiam and Couch Potatoes at a 1500 capacity venue. The terror on everyone's face was hilarious. This turned into real terror when we arrived at the venue though. There were broken pool cues, smashed windows and lots of bikers. We did not

Couch Potatoes and Milo losing it
at the Gravity Club in Kingston

1. HORACE PINKER one to two
2. ANNALISE fall
3. TEMPO ZERO s.f.s.
4. GOMAZ-IO wig out at denko's
5. AMAZING TAILS circles
6. EVERSOR the godfather
7. ALKALOID values here
8. HOOTON 3 CAR under your influence
9. LOOMIS when i move
10. THE UNKNOWN dag nasty
11. SERPICO million days
12. COUCH POTATOES safe
13. WARDANCE we went wrong
14. AMAZING TAILS simple minds
15. INNERFACE under your influence
16. THIRST! trouble is
17. SLUG BUG values here
18. IN BLOOM dear mrs. touma

COMPILED AT CCR STUDIOS, ZULTE
LIMITED EDITION OF 1000 COPIES
ABSOLUTELY NO COPYRIGHT
96

c/o DE LEERSNIJDER WIM
KREKELSTRAAT 13
8770 INGELMUNSTER
BELGIUM

c/o DECONINCK STEFAAN
PONTZINESTRAAT 2
8700 TIELT
BELGIUM

`Her Head's On Fire`, Dag Nasty comp CD cover

Tartan

The Cardinal's Cap, Canterbury

have the songs to pull this off. We left our gear with the Couchies while they set up, and we went off for a skate around Canterbury, trying to think how we could re-work our songs into biker anthems and practise dodging pint glasses. Later, as we got ready to start, a crowd of leather jackets looked to be surrounding us. We took deep breaths and just went for it. After some heckling, I think Nik had to sing some of 'Firestarter', but honestly, this was one of the most fun shows we ever played. There was even dancing. I loved the Cardinal's Cap and it became my local when I moved to Canterbury a few years later.

"Without the Couch Potatoes, I doubt we'd ever have managed to play a show outside of Tunbridge Wells and this was such great fun. Even when Nik and I were confronted at a house party by a member of a local band called Suction, who was furious about a review of his band in BHP and knew we were friends with Dave. It was still definitely worth it."

16/3/96 Couch Potatoes and Tartan
The Forum, Tunbridge Wells
23/3/96 Medulla Nocte, Couch Potatoes and Tartan
The Freebutt, Brighton
26/3/96 Goober Patrol and Couch Potatoes
Gravity Club, Bacchus Bar, Kingston
28/3/96 Couch Potatoes and Somehow
Railway Inn, Winchester
30/3/96 Couch Potatoes and Tartan
Cardinal's Cap, Canterbury

Taking our mates Tartan with us on those few early shows and watching them grow in confidence was great. We'd play with them quite a lot over the next months and years, both Couch Potatoes and then later Rydell, when they changed their band's name to Odd Most Odd. They had a great song, called 'Tartan Trousers', that was always their set closer. Simon told me it was the first song they ever wrote, but they probably never bettered it. For a while they also played a Menswear cover, 'Daydreamer', at twice the speed of the original, which they used to shout at us to play between songs, so for a laugh we did one time.

The Medulla Nocte show we played was the first ever Just One Life show in Brighton, promoted by Buz who went on to promote so many great gigs. I remember there was some drunk punk with a mohawk who kept on heckling Tartan when they played, and I really wanted them to tell him to fuck off, but they never did and by the time they'd finished playing and we went on, he'd passed out next to the stage.

Between the shows with Tartan as support, we also fitted in a trip up to Kingston to play at the Gravity rock club in the Bacchus Bar, a lively basement club underneath a squat brick building in Union Street. It was covered in graffiti and lit by coloured neon lights. The sort of place once inside you had no idea what time it was or where you were, you just had to be there and enjoy it. The sound was awesome in this little club, bouncing off the ceiling and walls and all around the small room, it needed a full house to soak it all up. I went over to the bar to get a drink and noticed the staff had written a sign that said, "Say Please, you cunts!" I always did.

We were playing a rock night with the Goobers that had been set up by a guy called Mark, a new promoter who worked at Banquet Records in Kingston, the bright blue indie record shop whose motto was 'More than your local record store'. As well as putting on shows, Mark had started up Gravitate Records, which later morphed into Gravity DIP Records as a spin-off from those club nights. He released loads of good records, including some by Pylon, Stapleton, Douglas, Twofold, Capdown, Tellison, Spy Versus Spy and even Understand, their final, post-major release, which was a split CD with local heroes JetPak. He would later run a music management company linked to the Beggars Banquet chain and manage Hundred Reasons when they went on to sign to Columbia (the oldest record label in the world, and now part of Sony) and tour the world.

We were hanging out with my good chum and Scene Police counterpart Emre Aktas at this show. He lived in Kingston so, between him and Mark, they hooked us up with plenty more shows at Bacchus / Gravity / Dionysus, The Peel, The Fighting Cocks and other local punk and rock venues. This gig was a goodie with Couch Potatoes and Goober Patrol really on form. We set up a Scene Police stall and shifted a lot of records and CDs that night too.

After that, we went down to The Railway Inn in Winchester again, to headline a rock night there supported by a band called Somehow. They were pretty good and had brought a lot of mates with them. The promoters at the venue had done a good job too, with lots of posters and notices in local gig guides, so there were plenty of familiar faces as well as new ones there to see us play. We were handing out demo tapes and selling a few records, speaking with everyone we could. Amongst the punters that night we got chatting with a very young Frank Turner, getting into hardcore and alternative music way back then, before he'd even formed his first band, Kneejerk.

Then it was back over to The Cap for another Canterbury classic with our boys Tartan. The place was packed with punks and rockers, and they seemed a bit nervous about the show. They'd disappeared off skateboarding and hadn't come back by the time they were meant to go on stage. I doubted they'd bottled it, but we started getting ready to go on early just in case. Sure enough though, they all came bowling back in a few minutes later and went straight on, rocking the place despite a few drunken hecklers. That was another fun gig.

13/4/96 Couch Potatoes and Acab
Shake Some Action, Croydon
20/4/96 Couch Potatoes and The Banned
The Red Lion, Gravesend

In April, we played at Shake Some Action again, the great little alternative record shop in Croydon that was run by James McCabe. We'd asked about sending him some of the new Couch Potatoes records to sell in the shop, so he'd offered us a gig and said just bring them with you. We always liked playing the Saturday matinees there, grabbing a few records then going for a Chinese on the way back afterwards. It worked out very well, appealing to both the rockers and the record collector nerds in us. This time we'd have a support band too, some locals called Acab. Their name stood for All Coppers Are Bastards! and they only had about four songs, so it didn't take very long. We played through most of 'Outweighed' and as no-one had come in to stop us yet, we finished with a couple of covers. I had to make sure I didn't get too carried away, bouncing around into Adam, Dan and Milo, as that bloody big column was still right in the middle of where we had to play.

The following weekend, we made another visit to the rock dive and bikers bar that was The Red Lion, down by the river in Gravesend, for a re-run of an earlier gig we'd played there with The Banned. They'd invited us back to Leo's (Red Lion) and brought all their mates along, so soon enough this became another loud and raucous party show, with plenty of singing and dancing. For some reason, the stage was full of inflatable dinosaurs so, soon into our set, they were all being knocked around in the air above the audience. There was beer splashing and dinosaurs bouncing, and I had the impression this crowd could have had fun at a funeral.

27/5/96 Couch Potatoes and others
The Forum, Tunbridge Wells
(Bank holiday festival - last Couchies show)

About a month later, we had another gig booked at The Forum in Tunbridge Wells. This turned out to be the final Couch Potatoes show. We'd been having trouble finding places to practise since Paul had left as we couldn't use his dad's farm anymore, and we were getting grief about the noise from most places we went now. The 'Outweighed' album and various EPs were out and doing ok, but getting good shows was still tricky, and both of the Dans seemed to be losing interest. Dan K, because he knew he'd be going to uni after the summer, and Dan P because he'd started a new job and was working hard on that, so didn't have much spare time. To be fair, I'd been busy at work too and so had Adam, and this meant we didn't have many new songs, or any tour planned for the summer, as we should have done by then. All of this was not helping the band's creativity, and I think we all needed a break.

I was still chasing up a few compilation releases that we'd sent tracks to and seeing what shows we could get on, as I wanted to keep things together at least until the summer. Scene Police were pushing the album, and maybe Dennis could have booked us a tour, but for some reason we didn't ask him or Andreas. We'd been offered decent shows in Brighton and London earlier in the month, but I had to go over to Italy so couldn't play them, and that wasn't ideal. We did go up to town to see Sense Field play on the 21st though. I was a massive fan of the band and regularly listened to both their self-titled album and 'Killed for less' too. I had a particularly comfortable, dark blue 'Killed for less' t-shirt that I'd wear all the time, and I loved their intricate twin guitar work. Now they had a new album, 'Building', out on Revelation Records and were coming over to the UK, so we went and saw them in London and were soon inspired again, but maybe wanting to try something new. This would have been around the time that Milo, Adam and I started thinking of a new, more emo style band, that would become Rydell.

The Forum wanted to start a new festival over the May Day Bank Holiday weekend. This would initially be an all-dayer, but would grow to cover two, and eventually all three days and include more venues until it became the annual Unfest that they run now. We'd been invited to play the first of them along with a load of other local bands. We played fairly early in the evening to a half-full venue, as most people were sitting outside in the sun. A bunch of our mates were there though, and the Tartan boys, who'd played earlier in the day, so we packed up and went over the road to the Pantiles to grab a curry. Never realising we had just played the last Couch Potatoes gig.

In late June we went to see some Understand shows, and I think it was coming back from one of those that we all agreed to call it quits with Couchies and maybe try something different. Dan P was busy and travelling more now with his new job as a polished plasterer, and Dan K would soon go off to study at Cardiff University where he'd start their UWIC frisbee team. Ever the optimist, I'd booked us into The White House to record again with Martin in August, but we had written nothing new to record so I cancelled that. Adam, Milo and I all agreed to take a summer break, but we knew that at some point we'd need to find a new drummer and get rolling again. Despite all the ups and downs, playing in a band was in our blood.

26, Switched On with the Rhythm Kings

Late in September I went up to the Astoria in London to see NOFX play and met up with a few friends, including Kris Beltrami, the singer and guitarist of Wact and Pseudo Hippies, who was telling me all about the new band he had started, a simple three-piece pop outfit called Dweeb. He'd been working on even poppier versions of some of his older tracks in a studio he'd set up in his bedroom at home, and now he'd involved his sister Lara and a friend from London called John Stanley. This new band created mainstream pop, a sort of indie dance music, and things were starting to take off for them. Kris was using a drum machine to avoid the difficult problem of finding a decent skin-basher. Despite all standing out like 'Animal' in the muppets, when you actually needed one, drummers could be as rare to find as rocking horse shit.

We wanted to get rolling again so we needed a drummer. The first person we asked was Simon Laslett from Tartan. He remembered this when he wrote to me, saying; "Dave and Miles told us they were stopping Couch Potatoes and starting a new band. I was gutted. They were one of my favourite bands, and not just because they were letting us play gigs with them. 'Outweighed' is an absolute classic album. They told us this new band was going to be different. A more mellow thing, more like Cap'n Jazz (I nodded knowledgably, making a note to go and listen to Cap'n Jazz as I'd never heard them). And by the way, did I want to drum for them? Ah. Oh. Shit. Our band was one thing. We'd changed our name to Odd Most Odd by now, a Pigeon Street thing, to try to get people to forget they'd seen us before when we were awful. But basically, it was still just four school friends who got together on a Wednesday night, driving all the equipment to a scout hut in a borrowed cheese delivery van that stank. We'd rig the electricity meter and practise all evening before going to the local pub, and then go looking for ghosts in Matt's haunted house. It was just for shits and giggles. Just a bit of fun. But playing in an actual, proper band? Could I do that? And that was the thing, I didn't think I could. We'd been playing a few shows and I didn't seem to be getting any better at it. What if I joined this new band and just stunk up the place? I thought it over for ages, before going back around to Dave's and saying no. I felt bad for dragging my feet on it, but I did not want to let them down and just had no confidence I could do it. God, I wish I had. Rydell were amazing."

That was a shame, but fine and maybe wise on Simon's part. We all had other stuff going on in our lives too, so were in no desperate rush. I'd moved into my first house and was trying to do it up when I wasn't at work. I was also working with the Scene Police guys, still promoting Couch Potatoes and 'Outweighed', and helping push their Interpol Times zine. I wrote a few articles for some other fanzines too, but had stopped my own BHP zine now, about halfway through the tenth issue, which never came out. I'd been into Criminal Records to sell them most of the remaining Couchies merchandise and all the distro and review stock I had as I needed the money. We were still going to gigs, an expense I deemed absolutely necessary, and all went up to London on 24th October to see a band I loved, Split Lip, play their first ever show in the UK at The Monarch in Camden. Split Lip had recently changed their name to Chamberlain and they'd be supported by our mates Understand at this great gig. They'd just brought out a new album, called 'Fate's got a driver', which is in my opinion one of the greatest records of all time. Its mix of beauty and power didn't really sound like anything else I'd heard at the time. This album showed how a band could develop their sound but remain true to their ideals. It was an inspiring show and I for one was keen to get rocking again.

There wasn't a lot of progress until late November when Milo, Adam and I went to see the BBMFs play at The Steam Inn on Lewes Road in Brighton. We still hadn't found a drummer and we were more or less ready to ask anyone. The Beebs had played early, so we were all sat around a table with them when Duncan Morris, the old Angus Bagpipe guitarist, came over to join us. He'd been away to uni but had just moved back home. We mentioned we were looking for a drummer and Dunc immediately said he'd do it, adding that there had been a drum kit in the house he lived in whilst at uni in London and he'd been bashing around on it, teaching himself how to play. How great was that? After months of looking for a drummer, asking everyone we knew and even some people we didn't, we'd managed to find an old mate who was actually enthusiastic about drumming in a band with us! We discussed our plans over a few more drinks, and Dunc went out the very next day and bought a drum kit from an ad he'd seen in his local paper. He clearly meant business, which was a great sign for us.

Duncan lived in Forest Row, a small town in the Ashdown Forest in Sussex, about halfway between my house and Milo's, and he found a cool little place for us to practise in there. It was a prefab building on the edge of a recreation ground that was currently being used as a youth club and special needs school classroom, and many would say that suited us fine. The Forest Row Youth Centre was a large mobile building that had been plonked down on some scrubby land between a pub and a small park. It was hardly insulated and not at all sound-proofed, but no-one really lived within earshot, so we were ok so long as we kept all the windows closed. It was used in the evenings for various events in the village, like AA meetings or adult education classes, but was still available on a couple of evenings and most weekends. Dunc's mum worked at the local school and she'd hooked it up for Angus Bagpipe to use initially, so now we took it over for practises. We checked it out in December and had a freezing cold practise in the snow, then from early '97 onwards we were booking it up twice a week and jamming new ideas.

We'd been listening to new bands like The Promise Ring, Cap'n Jazz (Milo's influence for the tambourine playing he brought into a few early songs), Texas is the Reason, Sense Field and Split Lip / Chamberlain. Also, Braid, Samuel, Ashes and Sunny Day Real Estate. We were going for the more indie side of post-hardcore, for sure. Very soon, and crucially, we'd get into The Get Up Kids too. This was key as we'd been floundering around a bit, not quite able to nail the new sound we wanted, then Duncan played us a new record he'd bought on a trip up to London. It was the third Get Up Kids 7", Woodson / Second Place, on Doghouse Records and it all just fell into place. Cue the handclaps, bouncy basslines, middle-eights with delicate chugging and jangly second guitar over the top, with plenty of clever drum fills too. Now we were getting somewhere. We'd add to this style later, of course, especially influenced by gigging with Hot Water Music, but for now these post-hardcore American bands would be our inspiration for a more mellow and textured version of hardcore that we wanted to develop.

It took a while to find anything like the sound we were after. Milo had a lot of indie ideas, Adam was a pop-punk kid, and I was still into hardcore at heart, whereas Duncan seemed to listen to anything from straight-edge metal-core to jazz. We mixed all the influences in and tried to develop our own sound. Musically speaking, Adam and I were pretty solid, but Duncan was a guitarist really and drumming is not easy, so it took us a while to get to a point where we were happy that it was tight enough. Dunc started putting in little jazz fills on the hi-hat or cymbals, sometimes they'd work, but sometimes he'd go out of time on the snare or bass drum. At these points he'd get frustrated and maybe pick up a guitar to start playing instead, so we'd be back without a drummer for a few minutes until he calmed down and was ready to go again. We had a second guitar kicking around all the time, as Milo decided he wanted to play as well as sing. Nothing too technical, but he'd fill in some barre chords on the more powerful parts of the tracks and add little flourishes. This was needed right from the start, and the second guitar added a lot of texture. Fair enough, but singing and playing isn't the easiest thing either, like scratching your head and rubbing your stomach, so this would all take some practising. Milo would play guitar on some tracks, and play the tambourine on others. Not something you'd often see in a punk band, so brave on his part I'd say. It worked well, and was certainly different to any band I'd seen in the scene at the time. We slowly improved, developing a sound and a few tracks; 'Across three parks', 'Empty' and 'Don't mean a thing' were three of the earliest, and versions of these would make it onto our first demo, 'Switched on'.

All had come back over to the UK early in '97 and toured as The Descendents. Adam and I had been to see them in London, Leeds and Canterbury, and spoke with a few of the promoters at the shows. One of the guys we bumped into at the Dents show at Canterbury University was Richard Murrill, the guy who wrote the 'Your mornings will be brighter' gig guide for Kent, and who had put on shows for both Joeyfat and Couch Potatoes at the Bottoms Club in Folkestone. We told him about our new band and I promised to send him a demo tape when we were ready. Soon enough though, Rich phoned me and asked if we were ready yet and wanted to play a gig. Fuck it, I was ready, so I asked the guys...

26/4/97 Lever, Uncool Frank and Rydell Bottoms Club, Folkstone

I'd come back from a trip to Chicago the week before the first Rydell show. I'd brought us all work-wear shirts, the US style with the guy's name and the company embroidered into them, or on patches above the pockets. These were second-hand originals, hard-wearing brands like Dickies and Carhart, which you could pick up in the US for about three bucks each in a thrift store, but couldn't find over here for love nor money. I dunno why but it seemed the thing at the time, certainly with the US post-punk bands we were into, and I'd brought a bunch of them, enough for everyone, and even managed to find myself one that had the name 'Punk' on it. We got together to practise one evening that week, working on the five or six songs we had and I handed them out. On Saturday, we all met up and headed over to Bottoms in Folkestone to play our first ever Rydell show, supporting Lever and Uncool Frank. We'd only told a handful of our closest mates as we wanted to keep it on the down low for now. This could be a disaster, after all.

Uncool Frank were from the Folkestone area and had been going for a while. I'd seen them play before at Leo's Red Lion and The Harp and they usually brought a pretty good crowd. They mixed punk with folk and thrashy metal and liked to piss around a lot on stage. Lever was basically Torque, or rather Torque's new band, as two of the guys had left and been replaced, and now they'd gotten even heavier and grungier in style. They sounded like Helmet or Quicksand, but with a lot of Soundgarden or even Tool thrown in too. All these guys were good musicians, but the style of what they were doing seemed quite a way away from what we were about to play, so it'd be interesting to see how it all went down.

We'd arrived early but spent most of the evening playing pool and drinking acidic Coke while we waited for the other bands to soundcheck. Richard, the promoter, came over to tell us that we couldn't be too loud tonight or the hotel owner above the club had threatened to pull the plug. This sort of crap seemed to be happening a lot at shows, and there was a fast turnover of smaller venues around Kent having trouble with landlords or neighbours. In fact, Rich stopped putting on gigs at Bottoms soon after this, and instead started up comedy evenings, under the banner of Lonestar Comedy. I think early on we could even have played one of those shows. We were funny enough. He is still involved in the music scene, but is now also a director of Folkestone Football Club, spending much of his time producing their programmes and running events for them.

I asked Milo what he remembered about the first Rydell gig; "Rydell had only been a band for about three months or so, meaning Duncan had only been drumming for a very short time and I had only been 'playing' the guitar as long. I recall someone offered us a show, possibly because they had booked Couch Potatoes before, and we talked about it but weren't sure if we should play yet, mainly because we only had about five songs. We decided that, as it was relatively out of the way in Folkestone, it would be good to try out the songs we had in front of people. That sounds odd now, but keep in mind that, A) Rydell was quite a departure from Couch Potatoes, B) the sound we were playing had not yet been tagged emo, and there was no scene of similar bands yet, and C) while it may seem ridiculous to think that we thought a 'low key' gig would be ok to 'test' our new material, you must remember that we had our eyes on the prize with Rydell. I remember sending tracks from the first demo to John Peel and Creation Records, as well as playing some major label showcase gigs up in town. Couch Potatoes had gone out on quite a high and there was definitely a buzz about our new band, so we thought maybe it could go somewhere." Ahh, our naive enthusiasm.

"The gig itself was absolutely full of weirdos. It must be something about Kent. The club was busier than we expected but I was not nervous at all, in fact I think we were all quite excited to play this new 'style' to people. We all wore work-shirts with gas station attendant names embroidered on them. The songs we had at that point were 'Across Three Parks', 'Empty', 'Don't Mean a Thing' and 'An Event' which definitely had a certain sound, and I think it's fair to say that we were pioneering something new and different within the context of the HC scene. I was glad that the show went pretty well."

The Tartan guys, now calling themselves Odd Most Odd, had come along to our first show, and Simon mentioned this in his letter too, saying; "Dave let us know when Rydell were playing their first gig, at Bottoms in Folkestone. We were all super curious to see what they were going to be like. Couchies had been so good. I drew the short straw and when lost again on the way I had to ask for directions at a petrol station, "Excuse me, I'm looking for Bottoms." We found it though and spent most of the night playing pool. Rydell played and it was so good. A bit messy by their usual standards, even a bit shambolic as they tuned up and chose which song to play next, but amazing. There was just something about those songs. It was hardcore, but different, and with Milo on guitar too. We all went away that night desperate to dump our entire set and write all new stuff, which we hoped would sound quite a lot like Rydell!"

It wasn't a particularly polished set, but we survived our first show as Rydell and had something to build on. We were away.

16/5/97 Snug, Stroppy and Rydell
The Forum, Tunbridge Wells
25/5/97 Rydell, Odd Most Odd and more
Unfest, The Forum, Tunbridge Wells
28/5/97 Konstrukt, Rydell and Minute Manifesto
The Joiners, Southampton

We kept on writing new songs and developing our sound, managing to fit in three more gigs throughout May. The first two were in Tunbridge Wells, of course, at The Forum. I'd patched things up with the old Joeyfat and Forum guys by then I'm glad to say. Jason and Jim had been along to a few Couchies shows, Aidan stayed up in town, and I rarely saw Matt at gigs. I think they were interested to see what Rydell sounded like and happy to book us to play, figuring that it was better we play at the Forum than look for alternative local venues again. Also, although Jason Dormon and Mark Davyd were still the main guys at the Forum, keeping hold of the booking diary, there were also many other people involved, helping run the gigs on various nights, so more promoters to speak with about bookings on a day-to-day basis now. The club was getting very popular and mixing its busy Friday and Saturday indie circuit nights with various new band evenings and one-off shows reflecting different genres, comedy, poetry, and all sorts.

Rydell's first gig in Tunbridge Wells was on a busy Friday night with two other bands that both sounded like Green Day, and would have been perfect bands for Couch Potatoes to play with five years earlier. The show went very well, packed with a lot of our mates who wanted to hear what the new band sounded like. We were tighter than in Folkestone and had a couple more songs too, so were invited back again the very next weekend, on the Sunday of a weekend long festival, an early Unfest, with loads of other bands playing, including our buddies in Odd Most Odd.

Just three days later, our next gig was down at The Joiners, another favourite venue of ours that felt like a friendly hometown-gig, where we'd play in between the heavy-ass Austrian hardcore band Konstrukt and the debut set of a new Southampton band, called Minute Manifesto. It was a rainy Wednesday night for the S.T.E.'s 120th gig. Rich Levene, one of the main S.T.E. guys, wrote about it; "This show was a real landmark. The first gig of our very own Minute Manifesto. As well as Rob Callen on bass in his first gigging band since Thirst! three years previous, they had Sweet Matt on drums. Matt had sung in Kill-Joy but drumming in a fast hardcore band seemed much more his forte. Joining that pair in the initial Minute Manifesto line-up were Jamie 'Festo' Goddard on vocals and Dingo Valaitis, AKA Romsey Matt, on guitar. Jamie and Matt had been part of the generation of pop-punk kids who'd come into the scene around '94, soon became good friends of ours and we'd nurture them into our more hardcore ways. They'd develop into a decent band with time (and play the most S.T.E. gigs of any band) but you wouldn't necessarily have known it from this auspicious debut - Dingo's 'banjo core' guitar sound in particular prompted soundman Chris London to confide to me

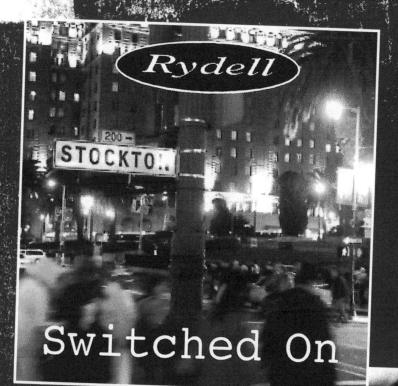

Switched On

Recorded by *Rydell* and Charlie at Recent
Studios in London.
Rydell are: Miles, David, Adam & Duncan.
Cover Design & Photo's: Fleece Napier
Contact: 3 Underhill Lane, Maresfield,
Sussex, TN22 3AY. UK

Switched on	3.12
Streetlight orange	2.26
Empty	2.26
Honeywell shirt	2.35
Across 3 parks	2.55
Don't mean a thing	2.27
Lost under your sky	2.35

'Switched On' demo CD

Rhythm kings

Recorded by Rydell and Charlie at Recent
Studios in London.
Rydell are: Miles, David, Adam & Duncan.
_____ & stylist: Fleece Napier
_____ Photos: Dennis
_____ Lane,
_____ TN22 3AY. UK

Rydell

Rhythm kings

Hey Neve Campbell
Home
You take forever
Across three parks
Try 17
Time of our time
An event
Dont mean a thing

`Rhythm Kings´ demo CD

that someone should teach him how to play on stage! Also playing their first gig for us were Rydell, David Gamage's new band from Tunbridge Wells. They'd morphed out of the Couch Potatoes and had more of a Texas Is The Reason or Sense Field sound than earlier. From Vienna came the fast hardcore of Konstrukt, the first Austrian band we'd put on since Target of Demand seven years earlier. They'd done a split 7" with Kito and were good guys. Can't remember who booked this tour, but the flyer backdrop artwork was from Penetration's 'Moving Targets' classic debut."

It was cool to play at Minute Manifesto's first gig, especially in their hometown and so early on with Rydell too. They were really good guys, and we became mates, playing quite a few shows together and even releasing our first vinyl records around the same time too. Konstruckt were technically great, but oh so heavy, and the vocalist was just insane. On the way back from the show, Adam suggested that to recreate the vocal style of the mighty Konstruckt in the privacy of your own home you could simply hammer nails through your nuts, screaming KKKKonstruckttt, aaarrrrggggghhhh!

3/6/97 Cardinal Fink, Homogenius and Rydell
Gravity, Dionysus Club, Kingston

We had a call from Mark, the promoter who set up Gravity shows at the Dionysus underground club up in Kingston, asking if we wanted to play one of his indie showcase nights for new bands. We agreed and were on a bill about a week later with Homogenius and Cardinal Fink. I knew Homogenius as they'd been on an Abstract Sounds compilation with Joeyfat. Their singer used two microphones, each with a different effect for his voice. They were a bit weird and very arty, even for a mid-Nineties indie band. Cardinal Fink was comprised of three rockstars who really didn't want to share their equipment with us. That was never a good sign and made for an awkward soundcheck and gig as we'd turned up with just amp-heads and a snare drum, as we were told this would be ok. The Finks would eventually release a single orange-coloured four track EP called 'Ginge' on Osmosis Records before deciding they'd irritated enough people and calling it a day. This show was reviewed in one of the local music zines afterwards, which kindly said; "Rydell were as cool as hell." The gig posters, one of which I grabbed, announced that Rydell were an "Ace new UK emo-core combo," and likened us to Texas is the Reason, Fugazi and The Promise Ring.

Recording the `Switched On´ demo

The next week we were down at Wilbury Road studios in Hove, to record a demo with Chris Priestly. We'd worked with him before, way back on the early Couch Potatoes recordings, and by now he'd worked with the BBMFs, Sleep, M.T.A., Red Letter Day and The Levellers, to name just a few. It worked out that we could get in there to record fairly cheaply and see how some of the new songs sounded. The session was mid-week though and, as Milo was working at a school, he couldn't get any holiday at short notice during term time so would have to bunk off, which he did, with some ridiculously unbelievable excuse that I still can't believe they fell for. Chris was there to engineer the session, but he also had two other guys with him, trainee sound engineers, but neither of them seemed to have much of a clue and just got in the way. We had two days and wanted to get six tracks down. We just cracked on with it, playing the songs through, pretty much as we would live, and then listening back to see if they needed changing or embellishing in some way. It was weird, the room was still covered in carpet and smelled of mothballs, as it had done for years. Once you'd gone in through those heavy, bank vault-like doors, time just seemed to disappear.

Duncan's drumming and Milo's guitar work took a couple of goes on most tracks, but we got there, and even added a spontaneous new track from an idea we developed in the studio too. This recording was just a demo so lacked the power a properly finished record might have, but you could see the intent and where we were heading with it. The off-timing was on purpose, the stop-starts and jazzy drumbeats we wanted were all there, as was the texture, if not quite the tightness.

The basslines were strong and Milo's introverted lyrics and occasional tambourine additions kept it interesting throughout. The guitar sound was very clean, certainly the least distorted on anything I'd recorded up to this point, and we built up textures with chugging, stops and starts, and adding extra vocals and guitars where needed. We had to be able to recreate it all live at a gig of course, so the tracks were recorded with as few overdubs as possible. This cleaner guitar sound was unforgiving though, so when we went from some quieter moments into noisier parts it could be more jangly than powerful, but it all still worked ok.

We jammed on and were gradually getting better so, by the second evening, we'd recorded 'Switched On', Rydell's very first demo, featuring seven tracks, which were 'Switched On', 'Streetlight Orange', 'Empty', 'Honeywell Shirt', 'Across Three Parks', 'Don't Mean A Thing' and 'Lost Under Your Sky'.

These were the six songs we'd played at our first five gigs, plus 'Honeywell Shirt', an instrumental idea we developed in the studio and named after the work-shirt Adam was wearing, one of those I'd brought back from the US with me. None of these tracks were really intended to see the light of day or be heard beyond ourselves, but we were so stoked to have new recordings that we duplicated a few cassettes and CDs for mates. Later, we'd even create a cover for it, working with Fleece Napier, whose real name was Graeme Noble, but was called Fleece as he always wore woolly jumpers and Napier as for some reason no-one could remember Noble! Graeme was a friend and a good designer, who was keen to sort some artwork for us. We used night-time shots of Brooklyn in the rain as the cover art, with streetlights, car headlamps and a few shadows of people walking around, all blurred in an attempt to give it some atmosphere. This had our oval white on black Rydell logo on top of it, and a little David S. Blanco cartoon artwork panel inside on the CD label itself.

WED. MAY 28TH.

KONSTRUKT AUSTRIA

STE 120

RYDELL

MINUTE MANIFESTO

TUNBRIDGE WELLS

SOUTHAMPTON

THE JOINERS **ST MARYS ST.**

SOUTHAMPTON 8pm

£3.00/2.50

Access One Step

Sparkmarker

13/6/97 Sparkmarker, Beacon and Rydell
The Albert, Brighton

That Friday we had another show down in Brighton opening for Sparkmarker and Beacon. As a new band we were opening a lot of shows and we were fine with that. It meant we could soundcheck last, so knew it'd sound just how we wanted it when we went on stage. Then we could do our thing early, relax and enjoy the rest of the evening.

We'd played with Beacon before, at one of their first gigs up at the St John's Tavern in London, but by then they'd signed to Subjugation and put out a three track 7" called 'Weakness Change' and then followed it with two more tracks on a split 7" with Tribute, out on Spread Records and recorded by Rob Coleman of Understand at his new studio. It turned out that these two would be their only records before they imploded, but right then they were riding a wave in the scene and were very popular. I liked the three-piece musically. Dan, Dan and Martin sounded like a heavier version of a lot of the bands I was into, but they always came over just a little too arty for me. Dan Carter would wear sandals on stage and paint his toenails black. Stuff like that at a hardcore show just put me off.

Sparkmarker were happy to let us use all their gear and played a great set. A really good band, a lot like Quicksand but hailing from Vancouver in Canada, so you knew they'd be friendly guys, eh. They had a great album called 'Products & Accessories' on Final Notice Records, but this tour was for their second album, on Crisis Records, entitled '500wattburneratseven', a great name and still a good record, but it didn't hit me in quite the same way as their first. All three bands rocked it and Rigsby, a local Brighton hardcore zine, were at the show to report on it, their review said;

Sparkmarker, Beacon & Rydell. Friday 13th June, The Albert, Brighton.

"Look, I'm not one of those superstitious types but come kick-off only one band had turned up, so you do kinda wonder if some dark force is out there you're doing battle with. All fell into place though and localised band Rydell got the gig underway. Ex-members of Couch Potatoes and frontman Miles had promised us something new. Well sure enough, big departure from the pop tuneage of the Couchettes and now they're rocking out in the same lane as some better-known American bands like Sense Field or Farside, and have adopted the same slow burning and big on emotive melodies that's become characteristic with the Revelation label of late. Beacon go for that pummelling Helmet style big riff attack.

Sparkmarker looked knackered after some serious road time. Hard to put your finger on where they're coming from, but similar to Quicksand."

Just a few days after this show I managed to burn myself pretty badly. I was clearing some ground near my house to make a parking space and we were having a fire to burn off some of the rubbish. The petrol can we'd used to get it going was a long way from the blaze but still managed to explode just as I was walking past it, engulfing me in huge fireball and catching my hair and shirt on fire. That was a shock I can tell you and certainly cut short whatever song I was humming to myself at the time. I started rolling around and remembered to breathe out, basically screaming like a girl, rather than inhale the flames. My friends managed to get a hose on me quickly, which must have been hilarious fun for them, but I was taken to the burns unit at East Grinstead where they started going on about skin grafts and all that horrendous stuff. I was treated to a morphine drip and fell asleep. When I woke up, I had no idea where I was and didn't recognise myself, jumping out of my skin when I looked in a mirror to see some crackle glazed horror movie monster. Luckily, I heal fast as I'm used to such hijinks, having been shot, stabbed, bottled and all sorts of other silliness too. My advice to you though is to avoid petrol explosions if at all possible. This one meant I couldn't play the guitar for a few weeks, so no change there then, some might say.

9/8/97 Stroppy, Rydell and Soil
The Forum, Tunbridge Wells
11/8/97 Month of Birthdays, Imbiss and Rydell
The Albert, Brighton

Soon after we recorded the 'Switched On' demo and played that Sparkmarker gig our jazz-styling drummer, Duncan 'Legs' Morris, decided to clear off travelling for a while. He'd be coming back but would be gone for about three months as he was off to India. In the meantime, we wanted to keep on writing songs and sending out demos. I remember sending tapes of those early songs to John Peel, hoping for a slot on his radio show, and Alan McGee at Creation Records too, at Milo's insistence.

In July, Dan Kingdon came back from uni in Cardiff and stood in at practises for Dunc so we could keep writing. This led to most of the tracks speeding up to twice their normal tempo, but also gave us some new ideas for songs. Additionally, it meant that we could play a couple more shows in August while we waited for Dunc to return.

The first was another trip to our local, The Forum in Tunbridge Wells, where we played with two more three-chord Green Day style pop-punk bands again. Stroppy, who were pretty damn good and were celebrating releasing a track on an 'Indie Breakers' compilation album, and Soil, who weren't bad either, but we couldn't get over their name. "Good evening, we are Soil!" It was a busy show, with lots of dancing and quite a few inebriated girls at the front shouting for Adam, our bassist, which he was loving and acting up to. We had a lot of mates there and I remember it being a fun evening, with no-one spontaneously combusting.

A day or two later, we all headed down to Brighton to play at the graffiti-covered (Prince) Albert again, this time with Month of Birthdays and Imbiss, both Subjugation Records bands but fairly new to the scene.

Imbiss had a two track 7" with the songs 'Brain food' and 'Consequences' on it and Month of Birthdays had their great debut album, 'These things that we do are not good for the self' to promote. They each had a few copies with them, and I bought the MoB album before they'd even played. It had tracks with such great names as 'Actions of the irrationally disappointed' and 'Repeated discrepancies'. As far as I am aware, that was Imbiss only single, but MoB later had an EP called 'Heightened' and another album, 'Lost in Translation', both released by Subjugations Records too.

This was when Month of Birthdays had their original singer and were musically more upbeat. Also, Rob Holden(previously of Baby Harp Seal)'s shorts were so baggy you could see, if you were unfortunate enough to look, half of his arse hanging out. There was much mutual back slapping going on between the bands that evening, and it was a really good-natured gig. It was one of the few early Rydell shows I have photos from our roadie Nick (Burning Picks Photography) Wilkinson took a few snapshots and they've survived, with the venue looking as colourful as I remember it. The Albert's blue logo on a bright orange drape, standing out at the back of the stage amidst all that black.

These summer shows would be the last we played with the ever energetic and reliable Dan Kingdon drumming for us. He stuck it out at UWIC and ended up completing a Master's degree. Despite being a total punk rocker at heart he went to work in manufacturing and retail for several big corporations. He's had a bunch of cute kids and worked all over the world. He's never returned to band life but still has the famous Couchies golden drum kit and occasionally knocks out a fast punk beat to upset everyone in the street. He's the same guy, doing everything enthusiastically, but of late has worked to find that zen balance between work and life. We stay in touch through Facebook and LinkedIn, and he assures me we never knew how good we had it back then.

We went to see a bunch more shows throughout the month. Millencolin, Samiam, 59 Times The Pain and Shutdown at the Astoria 2 on the 21st, all for just £7.50, I was a big fan of Samiam but thought that the UK band, Shutdown, were probably the best of the evening. Then another £7 was well spent on seeing the Descendents at The Garage on the 25th and then we saw Dweeb, Kris Wact's new band, at the Union Bar on the 29th for about three quid. Generally, I think musicians should be paid much more. Not the talentless shite you'll often see on tv or hear on the radio, but the actually good musicians that write their own music, play their own instruments and work hard, gigging all the time. They should earn much more. But that said, I just can't get my head around how much gigs cost now. I spent so long seeing great bands for a fiver or a tenner, I just can't be doing with re-mortgaging my house or having to sell a kidney to see some holier than thou dots on a stage in the far distance. I've been spoilt, I guess.

5/9/97 Lever and Rydell
Cardinal's Cap, Canterbury

It wasn't until Duncan came back and we had a couple of refresher rehearsals that we played another gig, on 5th September at the Cardinal's Cap with Lever. The Cap could be hit or miss. We'd seen some bands play there to just their roadies and girlfriends (and did that ourselves at a few shows too, of course) but this gig would be packed with metallers and punks, lots of colourful mohicans and much spilt beer. It was very hot that night, and stuffy as hell in the Cap, but they had to keep the windows and doors closed so they didn't get complaints about the noise. Mal had brought his strobe light and was jumping around, screaming his lungs out in front of it. It was like a free sauna in there and this was the gig at which he fainted mid-song. He was fine, but of course, we all took the piss. I reminded him of that a few years later when I bumped into him working at the Hugo Boss store in Bluewater.

About a week later, we saw Dweeb play again, this time at the TW Forum (12/9) and hung out with Kris and Lara afterwards. Their band was starting to get noticed beyond the pop-punk scene and in the indie disco world. They'd made a series of 7"s and split EPs of great, fun, catchy pop punk, with the guitar lines augmented by keyboards and a drum machine. They added shouty, slogan-heavy lyrics which definitely gave them a far broader crossover appeal. Many of these tracks had started life as Wact songs, some co-written by Adam, and more guitar-heavy versions of them can be found on the Wact 'Anthology' CD. There were inevitable comparisons to Bis, also comprised of two guys and a girl with guitar, keyboards and drum machine, in the music press and Dweeb definitely belonged to a little scene that was going on in tandem with the Britpop of the time, and included the likes of Bis, Kenickie, Tiger, Disco Pistol and a host of other long forgotten underground heroes. They ticked all the boxes for an up-and-coming indie band with singles on the highly respected Damaged Goods and Fierce Panda labels and a split with Mogwai, which seems unfathomable now. Even at the time of its release it seemed like a curious pairing of bands who were stylistically worlds apart, but the split has of course gone on to be a highly sought-after holy grail amongst Mogwai record collectors.

Dweeb soon signed to a major label, the Geoff Travis (formerly head of Rough Trade) helmed Warners subsidiary Blanco Y Negro, which on paper at least certainly sounded good as they were immediately labelmates with artists as diverse as Dinosaur Jr, the Jesus and Mary Chain and Everything But The Girl. Their debut major label single still sounded like they had on the indie releases, although the track 'Scooby Doo' was actually a re-recording of the B-side of their Fierce Panda single. They followed this with 'Oh Yeah Baby' which clearly someone at the label saw as having club potential and commissioned remixes by dance world luminaries including the Beatmasters and Tony De Vit, which allegedly cost several thousand pounds each. Unfortunately, their next single 'IOU Everything' was a bit cheesy and just pop nonsense, so flopped with their indie fan-base. I can only imagine that someone at the label said, "You need to write a top 20 pop hit or you're dropped," and this was the result. This CD EP was aimed at the charts and came out in various versions, with sales of all adding towards the count. In its defence, one of the versions, CD2, has no less than three Descendents covers as B-sides. 'Clean Sheets', 'Cheer' and 'Silly Girl', so is worth checking out just for that. Presumably because this latest single wasn't a hit, the album essentially went unpromoted by the label and copies of it are rare. After that, Dweeb soon called it a day and disbanded. As far as I'm aware, Kris, the once prolific pop-punk songwriter, hasn't written a song since. As a side note though, John Stanley, the third member of the band, went on to remix countless dance tracks under his DJ Downfall pseudonym, as well as playing in Marine Research and Tender Trap, alongside former members of Talulah Gosh and Heavenly. None of which I'm into, but just saying.

Also, late in September '97, the Get Up Kids released their brilliant debut album, 'Four minute mile' on Doghouse Records. I managed to get a copy early on through the Lumberjack distro, so it had the launch postcard and some other promo merchandise with it. I was listening to this record non-stop for the next few months and it certainly influenced Rydell's song-writing. We were all listening to this when we drove up to London for our next recording session.

Recording the `Rhythm Kings´ demo

I'd booked us into Recent Studios in Leyton with Charlie Mackintosh. This was the guy I'd worked with to record the God EP with Joeyfat and knew he'd do a decent job for us, so long as he could capture the tracks between the trains rolling overhead or the mixing desk clicking in and out, that was. We liked a challenge and were looking forward to recording with him. This session would become our second demo, 'Rhythm Kings'.

We went up to London for two consecutive weekends, one to record and another to mix, and spent them in a claustrophobic and sweaty railway arch, recording our new songs. The live area at Recent studios was a long, damp room with a drum riser in the middle of a small stage at the far end. There was a control room at the opposite end behind a sliding glass door. Above us, the trains rattled by every five minutes or so and below us there was a brick corridor with several band rehearsal rooms coming off it. The sound of the bands practising below us would drift through between songs as we tuned up or discussed what to record next. During these sessions, I remember one band playing a cover of Jefferson Airplane's 'White Rabbit' for the entire day one Saturday, and then again the following Saturday too! They were essentially playing a carbon copy of the original and doing it well too, so why on earth they needed to keep banging on at it we just didn't know. Maybe they only knew one song. I really should have gone down to ask them.

Milo played even more guitar on these tracks so concentrated on that and his singing, with no tambourine or percussive additions. I sung a lot more back-up vocals, even sharing vocal duties on a couple of tracks so wanted to spend a bit more time on the mix after we'd recorded the music, trying to bury my vocals well within it. It took us two weekends, but by the end of it we'd recorded and mixed eight tracks. They were 'Hey Neve Campbell', 'Home', 'You Take Forever', 'Across Three Parks', 'Try 17', 'Time Of Our Time', 'An Event' and 'Don't Mean A Thing'.

The new versions of 'Across Three Parks' and 'Don't Mean A Thing' were way better than the originals and all of these tracks had a far more developed sound, tighter and much more powerful than the first demo, signalling more or less how Rydell would sound going forward from then on. With this demo we were soon starting to get asked about releases, offered tracks on compilations, split EPs, all sorts of good things, so these tracks would all see the light of day quickly.

For now though, this was just another demo and we simply burned a few CDs and sent them out, more widely this time to labels, promoters, reviewers and radio stations. There was a 'white label' version going out initially, but for our friends copies we soon turned to our designer mate Graeme Noble / Fleece Napier for the artwork and layout again. We had a few photos of the band that Fleece added big afros and beards to, and we also had another piece of Dave Blanco cartoon art for the CD label. The photoshop work on the images was purposefully unsubtle and Adam's massive '70s pimp hair was particularly amusing. Although we were resolutely a 'post-punk' band now, even an early emo band, and we intended for our songs and music to speak for themselves, we still didn't take everything else too seriously.

I also invited another friend, 'Beerlight' author Steve Aylett, to write a humorous story for the CD insert, to go with Fleece's art. Steve was writing his awesome 'Slaughtermatic' novel at the time but a took a moment out to scribble a rant for the insert sheet, taking on the story of us being some Cuban salsa rhythm band. It went together well with Fleece's purposely b-grade artwork and told a story that made us all chuckle at the time. Because of this, the demo became known as 'Rhythm Kings'.

For anyone that was lucky enough to receive a copy of the demo and could be bothered to read them, Steve Aylett's inner sleeve notes for the CD read; "Rydell have come a long way since the early fusion of Cuban salsa, thrash lethargy and onstage penis extension which launched them into the public eye. Their beginnings in the Kingston revolutionary cell 'The Belchers' led them to frame this philosophy in music and their first release as the 'Rydell Castro Sunshine Love Band' stated it in plain terms with 'Arses on fire'. Their stage act became legendary after a firecracker flew at the bass player, igniting his bullet belt. 'We are a grenade in the Sacred Heart of Jesus," Miles 'energy maggot' Booker told the Cuban activist. 'Follow us into the flames of death. How can you do anything less?' On stage he bit the head off a small wren, shouting that the bird had been 'a threat to us all'. Urging the audience to pay close attention to their eyelids, throwing artificially swollen lizards into the uncomprehending crowd and grandiosely stamping on snails at the climax of 'Eat the fin', the band were paid in tinder dry handfuls of straw. Dogs will speak, they warned in the song 'Dogs will speak'. When all four were interrupted naked in a trout hatchery, 'Rydell Zapatistas in undersea death romp' was the headline, and the photograph shows Dave 'destruction' Gamage in the Cuban embassy being slapped in the face with his own passport. This still was used on the cover of the 'Belting the nun' album.

Now simply Rydell, the band were becoming increasingly experimental, a trend which began with a misguided attempt at amplified whispering on the 'We are uncertain' EP. Drumming with seaweed and sucking on the squid which were hung to dry by the restaurant opposite the studio, the band began to hallucinate and weep openly, braying like pathetic beasts of burden. Gripped by paranoia, they torched twelve police cars and set off in a high-speed pursuit which ended with the Rydell van being buried in eight tons of nutty slack. In the police cell, Gamage went on a hunger strike which lasted 32 minutes before he broke down and demanded 'cakes and understanding'. Some claim the guitarist was killed by covert operatives and replaced with a motorised lard sculpture. Theorists state that a reverse message on the 'Kelp bomb' album says 'Dave is in god's kennel'. What is certain is that Rydell fled to Europe wearing flame retardant dungarees. 'We warm our hands on the fruit machine of the west,' says Adam 'barrier method' French. 'For recognition we must pretend to be south England honky white boys. We spit on this nasty state of affairs.' But the spit lands on their own capitalist swollen bellies. Dogged by success, they languish in splendour and riches, practising unnatural lusts and presenting each other with bizarre trophies made of frozen snot. Rumours of a solo album 'I snog horses' from drummer Duncan 'legs' Morris, and a new album, '97 fractures', suggest they have only just begun. You hold in your dead hands their latest assault on western capitalism. Rydell, the Rhythm Kings."

We were pretty stoked with how these tracks came out and sent two of the very first CD packages going out to Dennis and Emre, our buddies at Scene Police Records, who helped us out with all the early Rydell releases. It would be this version of 'An event' that was used on our first vinyl release, the Revolution Inside 'Food not bombs' benefit 7" and also this version of 'Try 17' that was used on the split 7" with Hot Water Music, which would go on to sell out and be repressed six times. All eight of these tracks would soon appear on releases in their own right, and I have to say that overall we got pretty good value out of this recording session.

Scene Police ads

Revolution Inside, Food Not Bombs 7" cover

27, Far from Home

4/10/97 Rydell, No Legs and Unbelievables
The Albert, Brighton
12/10/97 Samiam, Shades Apart and Rydell
The Forum, Tunbridge Wells
18/10/97 Platform, Rydell and Parma Violets
The Cardinal's Cap, Canterbury
21/10/97 Blue Tip, Kerosene 454 and Rydell
The Freebutt, Brighton

We started gigging again in October and just became busier and busier from then on. On Saturday the 4th we played what was still only our tenth show as Rydell. It was an anti-jobseekers-allowance benefit gig. Now who says we weren't punk rock?!

JSA or Jobseekers Allowance had been brought in by the government late the previous year to replace the unemployment benefit that had been in place since 1911. It was ostensibly to ensure that benefit claimants were actively looking for work, but the new rules were stringent to say the least and caused a lot of hardship and arguments. This benefit from the welfare state has since been changed again and is part of the current JSA, ESA, Universal Credit shambles.

Anyway, Rydell headlined this gig at The Albert in Brighton with two local indie-punk bands, No Legs and The Unbelievables, supporting us. We'd played at The Albert a couple of times recently, with Sparkmarker in June and Month Of Birthdays in August, and we'd play there many times again. The solid old boozer was built in 1848 and stood on a corner in The Lanes area of Brighton. It had become well known as an alternative music venue and was plastered with flyers and posters for punk, rock and ska gigs, as well as having Banksy style graffiti art painted on the walls outside. Now, The Prince Albert, is known as 'the home of the free' by its local regulars and is still a popular music venue, with the entire building painted in bright colours and covered in caricatures and portraits of famous musicians from Jimi Hendrix to Lemmy, Prince to Sid Vicious, and James Brown to John Lennon. Visitors regularly stop there to take a photo against that wall.

The vocalist of the Unbelievables was a local character called Tony Green, and you'd know if he was standing next to you at any gig as the old leather tobacco pouch he permanently had hanging from his belt absolutely reeked. He'd usually sport a pair of old para boots, so worn down that he walked a bit funny in them, compensating for the fact there was no left heel hanging onto the sole anymore. We'd see him at the Brighton Record fair, running his stall, always with the same old stock, and he eventually set up his own record store in Sydney Street in Brighton's north lanes at the shop that is now Across The Tracks Records. The Unbelievables had recorded a live four-track EP in the Lewes Scout Hut and released it as a one-sided 12" with a silk-screened b-side on their own Jaguar Ride record label. Soon after, they broke up and Tony would eventually resurface in a new psyche rock band that included former members of The Damned and Johnny Moped.

No Legs had a few tracks on various punk and indie compilations, most notably two tracks on the 'Adopt this baby' EP alongside Spanking Herman labelmates Anal Beard. They were kind of comedy punks. One of No Legs more comedy tracks was called 'If I was hard I'd kick your ass'. The Spanking Herman label they were on would also release 'How to bomb everything' by The Propagumbhis, another ska-punk band we played a few shows with.

The show was fun and, as all the bands played for free, it raised a few pounds for the anti-JSA benefit too, although I've no idea what they then did with that money to help the situation.

Then on the 12th, an otherwise boring Sunday, we got to share the stage with some of our musical heroes. Samiam were playing the Forum, along with Shades Apart as their touring partners, and as I'd booked them in, we'd also managed to wangle the support slot. This really ought to have been an awesome show for such a small town as Tunbridge Wells, and I was stoked that we'd been in touch and managed to get them to come and play our local venue on their tour.

Maybe because it was a Sunday night in school term, but nowhere near as many kids came out as we thought would do. I reckon I knew pretty much everyone at the gig and there were certainly less than a hundred people in the club. This doubly sucked as Samiam had played at the Forum only a year before, on a Friday or Saturday night to a packed crowd, and we thought that most of those punters would take the opportunity to come out again. They didn't and we took that as an indication that most local people didn't give enough of a shit about good music. That didn't enhance the mood of any of the bands. Luckily a lot of our mates were there, and a bunch of kids came up from Brighton and the south coast too, but it was still a poor turn out for such a great line-up.

Worse still, Samiam and Shades Apart had hired a drum kit for the tour so weren't at all keen on us using it. This was a major pain in the arse as we'd only brought a snare and cymbals, our guitars and amp heads, as was usual as support. As the conversations went on, their tour manager got involved and it became more unpleasant and really pissed me off. There was very little hardcore camaraderie on display that night, and I just didn't expect it from these bands. Luckily for us, the day was saved by Simon from Tartan / Odd Most Odd. He lived nearby and raced home to grab his kit for us to borrow. Cheers buddy! For all that though, once things got started this was still a great gig, with the California Samiam (certainly my favourite Samiam) playing songs from 'Clumsy', 'Billy' and 'Soar', as well as their new album 'You are freaking me out', and Shades Apart playing their rocking Revelation Records tracks from 'Save it' and 'Seeing things'. The few people that saw the gig had a real treat.

Next up, on the following Saturday, was a return trip to The Cardinal's Cap in Canterbury, where Milo's girlfriend, Michelle, was now going to uni. I don't remember if Michelle had hooked the gig up for us or if it was another promoter, but she'd brought along a bunch of her uni friends and they seemed to know all the words to our new songs. They even sung along to 'Lost under your sky', an early track from the 'Switched on' demo, that I believe Milo wrote about meeting Michelle, so Milo was grinning ear to ear while we were playing that.

That night, Rydell were playing in between two indie bands, The Parma Violets and Platform, neither of which were very good on the night, but that's just my opinion of course and what do I know. After the gig, Michelle and her girlfriends took us all back to their place to continue the party.

After that came another goodie, a Just One Life show put on by Buz at The Freebutt in Brighton, on Tuesday 21st, with Rydell supporting Blue Tip and Kerosene 454, both over from Washington D.C. on tour. This was one of the early shows at the Freebutt when the stage was still in the front half of the pub, and the place was easily filled up and crowded. These two bands were good and already well known in the close-knit hardcore scene, but as can be the case with some American bands when they get to tour in Europe, they were a little bit up themselves and acting like rockstars. Tonight this meant they didn't want to share equipment either, but that's fair enough I guess if you are on tour and don't know the support bands. This time we'd brought all our own gear just in case and set up in front on theirs, right at the very front of the small stage, so that Milo and I were practically falling off in every song and couldn't really jump around. Eventually we moved our mic stands down onto the pub floor and just started wandering around the front of the crowd as we played.

These two US bands had a split record out together on green vinyl for the tour, with one track each on it, which was selling well, along with a few shirts, from their merch table at the side of the stage. Bluetip were headlining and were really good, they played tracks from 'Dischord no 101' and a few early songs that would've been on 'Join Us', both releases coming out on Dischord Records. Kerosene 454 went on before them and I noticed that their drummer wore those massive ear-defender headphones that people who drill holes

Kerosene 454

Samiam

Blue Tip

Shades Apart

Rydell at The Cooperage

Travis Cut

Hooton 3 Car

The Cooperage, Plymouth

The Prince Albert, Brighton

384

in the street with Kango hammers wear. They played tracks from 'Situation at hand' (Art Monk Construction) and 'Came by to kill me' (Dischord), and also a couple of new tracks from 'At zero' (Slowdime) in advance of its release too. It was awesome to see bands like this playing in such an intimate venue. Another good night and after the show we all piled around the back of the block to the all-night diner to get a slap-up feed.

Towards the end of the month, Rydell supplied our first tracks for a couple of compilation CDs and then heard from Dennis at Scene Police that he'd managed to get one of our songs, 'An event?', onto a Food Not Bombs benefit 7" that was being planned for the new year by his German distribution partners and fellow record label, Revolution Inside. We were chuffed with this and celebrated in style as it also happened to be one of our crew, Johnny Hotwing's, birthday on the 27th and our bassist, Adam's birthday on the 29th. So, we'd arranged a big joint bash on the 28th in Tunbridge Wells, booking out the largest part of a local Mexican restaurant called Zapatas for the evening. This Mexican was in the Pantiles area of Tunbridge Wells and was one of Adam's favourites. Outwardly it seemed authentic enough, but it was actually run by a Scottish couple who, over time, kept reducing the portion sizes and putting the costs up, so eventually the restaurant ran out of customers and had to close. At that point though the food was still good and the service friendly, so we all liked going there.

Johnny Hotwings, real name John Christoforou, but known as 'Hotwings' due to his rapacious appetite and success in one of our many over-eating competitions, was on good form that evening. His particularly renowned scoffing victory had come with thirty spicy chicken hot wings devoured in less than fifteen minutes, a feat he'd repeat and continue to see off all challengers over the following years. On that evening he was playing it a bit cooler though and disappeared at one point to successfully chat up a young Amanda Lamb, the girl from the Scottish Widows TV ads at the time. He went on to date her for several months, a birthday present I definitely think Adam would have preferred to the baseball cap and new set of bass strings we'd bought him.

19/11/97 Hooton 3 Car, Travis Cut and Rydell
The Joiners, Southampton
20/11/97 Rydell, Lever and Minute Manifesto
The Railway Inn, Winchester
21/11/97 Rydell and Echofiend
The Cavern, Exeter
22/11/97 Rydell and Echofiend
The Parrot, Torquay
23/11/97 Rydell, Lever, Natural Disasters and Terminal Virgins
The Cooperage, Plymouth

I had some travelling planned and was arsing around over in Malaysia and Singapore for the first half of November, but came back to the UK on the 17th in time for my girlfriend's, a rather lovely air-stewardess named Bernice, birthday party and to play another run of gigs we had booked from the 19th to the 23rd.

We were heading west again, along the south coast, for this run of five shows. We'd been planning it for a while with some good promoters who we'd already played shows for. The first was Rich and the STE guys down at The Joiners in Southampton. This was a favourite venue of ours and like a home from home for any punk or hardcore band. The fact that it was a Wednesday night, mid-week on a school night, wouldn't make much difference there as everyone came out and this show would be with Hooton 3 Car and Travis Cut, two massively underrated bands.

It would be the S.T.E.'s 134th show and there were flyers going around for the gig with the Resin / Still Life split LP cover as the background artwork. Rydell would go on first and we were quite happy with that, to rock out and then sit back and enjoy the show.

Travis Cut were from Harlow in Essex and they peddled a very catchy form of pop-punk that you couldn't help but enjoy. They had absolutely loads of great vinyl out, including one 7" on Southampton's own Suspect Device label, and an album called 'Serial Incompetence' on Damaged Goods records. They were already in the process of writing their brilliant 'Seventh Inning Stretch' album whilst on that tour and every song they played was a corker.

Hooton 3 Car had come all the way down from Sunderland for these gigs. They'd played some support slots on the recent Samiam / Shades Apart tour and their tuneful, melodic hardcore, packed with memorable hooks, was getting them noticed. They too had a load of 7"s and EPs out already, and had released two albums in quick succession, 'Cramp like a fox' on Out Of Step Records and 'Monkey mayor' on Rumblestrip Records. They'd soon release their third album, 'By means of maybe' in '98 and just kept getting better and better. This was a good gig and a very positive start to the tourette.

The next evening, we were at another favourite venue of ours, The Railway Inn in Winchester, where a few of the Joiners regulars came up to see us play again, a better and longer set tonight, alongside our Maidstone mates Lever and local punkers Minute Manifesto. The promoter and sound guys at the Railway were always cool and the bands sounded really great, but not enough people were there to see it really. Very few. But despite that, all the bands absolutely went for it. You gotta be committed to play any sort of hardcore, and that's one of the things I loved about it. There were no half-assed half-measures. Lever always brought a good heavy show and Mal didn't faint this time, but they weren't too keen on the thin crowd. Minute Manifesto brought the most energy though; "This one's called 'Colonisation of the America's'. It's about the genocide of a whole fucking race... 1.2.3. AAAAAARRRRGGGHHHH!!!" over what sounded like the

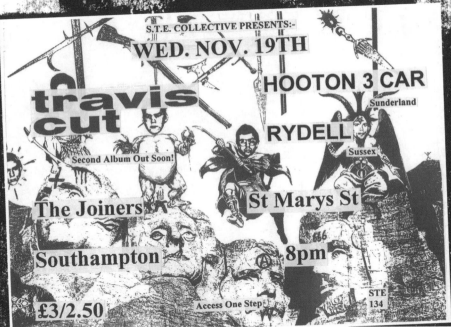

Travis Cut, Hooton 3 Car and Rydell pop-punkathon flyer

Goober Patrol

The Red Eye, Copenhagen St, London

Milo and Adam

Dennis at the Scene Police HQ

band's tour van hitting a wall. Then about one minute later, barely stopping to draw breath, "OK, Thanks. This song's called 'Macho Prick', Go!" and so on. It was great fun. A good-natured live practise, I guess.

The next two evenings were a little calmer but far better attended. Also, a lot more professionally organised, with Rydell headlining and an upcoming indie rock band called Echofiend as support. First we played at The Cavern in Exeter, and then at The Parrot in Torquay, booked courtesy of our mate Sam who we met on the last tour and would stay with while we were down in the west country. The show at The Parrot was particularly memorable as it was absolutely packed, mainly with hundreds of young heavy metal types, boys and girls alike with big perms and little clothing. It reminded me of the show Couch Potatoes had played with Annalise at Panama Jax in Paignton, just along the coast, and when the soundman came over, just after soundcheck as the club was filling up, and said "They don' ged many rock bandz in this part o' the country," I could've sworn he was the guy on the sound desk at that club too.

The Echofiend guys were friendly enough, but all looked like Shaggy out of Scooby Doo, and they insisted on playing what seemed to me like a two hour long set of mostly Blur covers. It was pretty dull fare, so by the time we got on, tuned up and turned up, ready to rock with a thumbs-up to the familiar sound guy (probably the only one who could work a mixing desk in the entire west country) the crowd were already very drunk and ready to enjoy themselves no matter how we played. We gave a big shout out to Sam 'the man' Hamer and his endless supply of lady-friends for putting us on and putting us up, and in return he took us to an after-show party and woke us the next day for late breakfasts at some run-down transport cafe where the Prodigy had supposedly been hanging out the day before.

We had another show that evening, at The Cooperage in Plymouth, but as we left Torquay to head along the coast it started raining hard and this soon developed into a serious thunderstorm. The roads were flooding so we aquaplaned along, narrowly avoiding trees, kerbs and other cars, as lightning struck all around us. I wasn't sure we were going to make it, but of course we did, and then I wasn't sure if that was a good thing or not. The Cooperage seemed like a decent venue, and we would be playing with Lever again, as well as two local supports, The Natural Disasters and The Terminal Virgins. They'd all brought a few people along, but it seemed to me that we'd ended up playing to a bunch of farmers and sailors in a pissing gale, and worse, as Milo has chosen this gig to wear his new bright orange shirt, he spent most of the evening being dissed and heckled by the local yokels. God knows what would happen when he put down his guitar and picked up the tambourine he was now playing again in a couple of the mellower songs. I swear I could hear them building a wicker man outside whilst they waited for the gig and the rain to stop.

16/12/97 Rydell, Jetpak and Muchasgaluchas
Gravity, Kingston, London
22/12/97 Rydell, TipaGore and Fiction
The Forum, Tunbridge Wells

Safely back home I was sending off more tracks for the various benefits and compilations we'd been asked to be on. Concrete Parachutes was one of them and there were several others from Germany too. I'd been chasing up promoters again too, sending off demos and booking gigs as best I could. I'd also been chatting with Dennis and Emre at Scene Police and was heading over to Germany early in December to spend a few days with Dennis, working on Scene Police and checking out the local record stores. When I came back from that I heard from Mark, the promoter at the Gravity club in Kingston, asking if we wanted to come and play with Jetpak and Muchasgaluchas on the 16th. We certainly did and I booked that in, as well as another local show at The Forum in Tunbridge Wells to act as our big Christmas party.

Gravity was a great venue and Jetpak were a great band. They'd just played some shows with A and recorded a new three track 7" that would come out on a small label called Gravitate in the new year. The EP had cool imagery of a guy riding a jetpack through the sky. They were always a bit different, trying to be original whilst still playing heartfelt hardcore. They reminded me a little of Joeyfat, or Tribute, or even Understand, who they'd later have a split release with. They'd have sudden handclaps and breakdowns, interesting backing vocals and quirky parts you didn't expect, then power off again with a catchy full-on riff. I liked that, and the good sound at the venue did it all justice. There was a good crowd tonight, and all three bands got them bouncing and rocking the place. Muchasgaluchas were really good too. I hadn't heard of them before the show and haven't heard much since, which was a real shame as we'd have loved to have played more shows with them.

Over the next week there were a lot of parties, a couple of which turned into impromptu jams, but our next proper show was the Christmas party we had booked at our local venue, The Forum. This was the old brass rubbing centre and public toilet on the common in sunny tunny, now turned into a great music venue by some old school friends and ex-bandmates of mine, where we'd played many times. This time we'd have support from two other local bands; our friends Fiction, who were on particularly jangly indie form that evening, and the new heavy irregulars known as TipaGore.

TipaGore were, of course, named after Tipper Gore, the US political activist who founded the PMRC back in '85, the Parents Music Resource Centre, that successfully campaigned for those ugly black and white 'Parental Advisory' warning labels to go on all recordings that contained swearing or anything they deemed inappropriate or less than ideal at the time. This, of course, spawned outrage in the alternative music scene and many bands adopted that name, including one dumb-ass drunk-rock band previously called Unholy Swill, who changed their name to Tipper Gore's Anal Retentive Love Children. There were also songs about her by well-known bands including The Ramones, Jello Biafra (of the Dead Kennedys), Alice Donut, Warrant, and of course, Fudge Tunnel, the Nottingham-based punkers.

This TipaGore, writing it all as one word, were Tunbridge Well's own metal, punk, indie crossover band and they had some good songs. My favourite was called 'Goat', and it appeared on the Unlabel Two compilation. They had their own demo CD out too, called 'Fig. 4, Ideal Boot', with a drawing of a boot on the cover and five tracks on the CD, including 'Ingredients' which would appear on the Blip2 compilation, alongside bands like Cardinal Fink, The Ugly Boys, Barbie's Evil Twins and TV Guru.

They played some pretty good shows and were the only local band taking on the Korn-inspired down-tuning and slap bass style. Their frontman, Paul Cheese, just known as Cheese when they played, would often paint himself silver and blue for gigs and jump around screaming and bashing his guitar entertainingly. TipaGore appeared briefly on the Johnny Vaughan TV show but unfortunately had most of their footage cut out of the final airing. They eventually split up when the bassist, Tim, shagged Cheese's girlfriend, as when he found out they beat each other to a pulp. Now that's the sort of Christmas party I wanted to be at every year.

6/1/98 Knuckledust, Rydell and Mouthwash
The Red Eye, London
22/1/98 Rydell, Maudib and Alphawave
The Freebutt, Brighton

The year started with an early reminder for us all that a mellower band like Rydell were just never going to be hardcore enough for a large part of the scene. A friendly label owner and gig promoter named Lil had called me up about playing some shows and he had one coming up at The Red Eye in town with two London bands, Knuckledust and Mouthwash.

Mouthwash were a ska-core band, the sort of stuff Lil really liked, and they had a new 7" out on Hot Wok Records, amusingly entitled 'Music for the average ninja'. They went on to sign to Hellcat Records and record a couple of albums. But Knuckledust were a heavy, heavy HC band. Noisy, fast, extreme hardcore. I liked some of this stuff, but preferred it with some melody thrown in, a la Gorilla Biscuits. This would be Rydell's first proper show in central London and we wanted to play it. The Red Eye was a good venue and in fact we ended up playing there many times, but going on in the middle of these two bands may not have been our wisest choice.

Lil and Kafren ran Household Name Records and they were going to put out a 7" for Knuckledust called 'In Yer Boat' as the band were really kicking off in the London scene at the time. Knuckledust already had a split 7" out with Area Effect on Rucktion Records and a mini album called 'London Hardcore' on Days of Fury Records too. It was all tough-guy hardcore stuff, finger pointing, metallic old-school style. I quite liked it, but the London scene then could be narrow-minded and mouthy with it. I remember being engaged by hecklers from the crowd more or less throughout our set. Dumb shit like, "You sound like Oasis," was the best they could muster, and I'd do my best to correct them at the time, but you can't really win an argument with an idiot. It all seemed a bit macho to me.

Later that month, at the other end of the scale, we played a very indie gig at The Freebutt in Brighton with Maudib and Alphawave. The Freebutt was normally a punk venue, but this was for a different promoter, Darren, not Buz, and we were happy to play it. Adjusting our set accordingly to suit the audience, with the more indie style of hardcore we were playing we could go down pretty well with a wide range of rock genres.

Muadib were good, and quite original for an indie band at the time. They changed their name to Hicks soon after this show and Jess, their singer, went on to do something on TV called Pier Pressure. Alphawave were a more standard indie pop band, and the guitarists did these weird funky dances during their songs, then they'd all swap instruments over and start again. It was odd. At the end of our set, definitely heavier than either of the other bands even at our mellowest, the promoter said we sounded like The Black Crowes. Smashing.

28/2/98 Recording 'Home' with Charlie at Recent Studios, Leyton, London.
The year had started very busily, as apart from those two early hardcore and indie gigs, I'd also had lengthy trips to Canada and Italy, all whilst trying to sort out Rydell's next recording session and hopefully a few European gigs, or even a tour over there soon.

First, I spoke with Andy Sneap, the Sabbat guitarist who then ran Backstage Studios. I'd seen his band play enough times and had heard several bands he'd recorded since. I'd gotten his contact off the Schema and Tribute guys after they'd recorded with him. I forget why exactly, I think the dates he had available were no good for us to make, but the recording session didn't work out there. Andy has gone on to record everyone from Kreator to Exodus, Saxon to Megadeth, Amon Amarth to Cradle of Filth, Killswitch Engage to Soulfly, As I Lay Dying to Bullet For My Valentine, Testament to Trivium, the list gets boring and I get envious. He also ended up playing guitar in Judas Priest.

So then I called Charlie Mackintosh again at Recent Studios in London, where we'd recorded the Rhythm Kings demo and booked us back in for another session. This recording would become 'Home', Rydell's third demo, of mainly acoustic tracks. We were all available when I'd booked the dates, but I think something came up for Duncan, maybe work, maybe travelling again, but he didn't make it. So Milo, Adam and I ended up recording mellow versions of 'Home', 'Red Light Runner', 'Stars Break Free', 'Instro', 'Post College Rock' and 'Gilsenan' at Recent with Charlie. He gave it a simple mix and those six tracks soon became available as the 'Home' demo CD and cassette, as well as a 7" vinyl EP on Firewalk With Me Records, out of Austria. Both the demo and 7" covers featured some photos of general redneckery that I'd taken on a trip around the southern states in the USA, and were put together with some nifty Fleece Napier design work.

28, Just don't say you lost it!

March started busily with another round of gigs for us in Tunbridge Wells, Brighton, Maidstone and London, followed by a couple of days mailing out the new Rydell tracks to promoters, labels, fanzines, radio stations and the like. Some of the labels came back asking for tracks on compilations again, including the new local start-up called Unlabel. I also heard back from Dennis in Germany about the European shows we'd been trying to hook up and they were starting to come together too.

On the 26th we went up to London to see the Bosstones at the LA2 and the very next morning we were all on our way to Germany, for a couple of shows Dennis had arranged for us through his Scene Police contacts. These would be Rydell's first gigs abroad.

27/3/98, 999 and Rydell
Jugendkulturcafe, Troisdorf, Germany
28/3/98 Canal Terror, Rydell and others (Kurdish benefit gig)
Jugendkulturcafe, Siegburg, Germany
We'd all crammed into one car for this trip, the four of us with our basic equipment; guitars, amp heads, snare, cymbals, pedals and a load of demo CDs to dish out too. We turned up the music and hammered across France and Belgium on the E40, crossing the border into Germany near Aachen, and meeting up with our good friend Dennis Merklinghaus, the main man of Scene Police Records, in Bonn where he lived. Dennis had a few mates with him and they'd agreed to lead us to the venue for tonight's gig, just to the north over the Rhine and Sieg rivers, in Troisdorf at the Jugendkulturcafe, or Youth Club, there. First, we all went to Jam Records to buy a load of CDs and drink a lot of root beer, and then we went on to the venue for the show, where we'd be playing with one of the most long-lived and prolific original UK '77 punk bands, 999. We couldn't really believe it.

Milo and I had been here before, when Couch Potatoes played with the X-men on our tour through the area in '94. The youth club still looked exactly the same, a big bland prefabricated building standing just off the main road, looking like a school or council office, but with lots of glass between the graffitied plastered panels and a huge JKC spray painted above the door by a semi-talented youth. The youth clubs here doubled as community centres, cafes, music venues, all sorts, so there were plenty people hanging around already. We noticed a big tour van parked just up the road and sure enough, as we piled in, we could see 999 already onstage sound-checking. They were jamming a track I'd heard before, 'Lust, power and money' I believe it's called. It sounded OK, but was frankly way too loud whilst people were still sitting there eating and hanging out. Kids were playing pool and table football a couple of feet from the stage and the constantly feedbacking speaker stacks. They didn't seem to care. We waved over to them at the end of the song, just to let them know we had arrived, but no reaction. They went into another one, a new track I think called 'No prisoners', that they kept on messing up and starting again. I remember seeing the covers of some of their early albums from back in the day; 'Separates', 'High Energy Plan' and '999', where they wore colourful clothes and dressed in a similar bright and stylish way as The Buzzcocks did, but now they had leather jackets, cut-down band t-shirts and tartan bondage trousers. They looked just like every other ageing punk rocker.

The ever-friendly German promoters came over and Dennis introduced us all. It seemed like 999 would be a while, so they took us upstairs where there was a room we could relax and get ready for the show. They offered us veggie stew and pizza, and as much beer or soft drinks as we wanted. We sat around up there for about an hour, Adam and I playing pool on a table with fishing rods for cues and balls the size of grapefruits. Time was passing and it looked like we wouldn't get a soundcheck.

A few minutes later and someone was running up the stairs towards us. "Ain't you gone on yet!?" shouted Nick (real name Keith), the singer of 999, in some over-emphasised chirpy Cockney accent. He was half joking but half being serious, as he wandered back across the room and started drinking the pile of beer set aside for the bands. "Ain't you dead yet?" mumbled Adam back at him, just loud enough for me to hear as I took my next shot with the ridiculous excuse for a pool cue. It made me laugh and miss, so now Nick / Keith was poking fun at that as his bandmates joined us and wanted to play. He was clearly loving being on tour and hamming it right up. Can't blame him, I suppose, but I hoped the band's music would be more original than this guy's humour. Milo and Duncan gamely tried to engage them in conversation, noticing that their bass player had a giraffe tattooed on his arm and wondering what that was all about. But that query got rebutted with some sarky bullshit too, so before it all kicked off over the pool table and people got battered with grapefruit-sized balls and fishing rods, we said fuck it and headed back downstairs to find some more intelligent conversation.

By now the place was heaving, and we were indeed due onstage in less than half an hour. We set up our gear, using their drums and backline as had been agreed with the promoters, and just got levels about right for when it was time to start. We had a pretty tight, nailed-on set by now and were well ready for these shows, playing mainly 'Rhythm Kings' tracks; 'Don't mean a thing', 'Across three parks', 'Try 17', 'Home' and trying out a couple of newer songs too. It all went down well and we warmed the crowd up for what I felt might be a bit of a disappointment coming their way next. The only one of 999 to come down to watch any of our set was the drummer, Arty I think his name was, who wandered over during our last couple of songs to 'see if we were done yet', but then hung around and said he actually enjoyed it.

Dennis took a few photos during our set and most of the people I spoke with afterwards seemed to really enjoy it, but I guess they'd tell me that, wouldn't they? We loaded out quickly and after watching a few 999 songs, featuring a surprising amount of swearing and voluminous spitting, we couldn't see much point in hanging around so followed Dennis and his convoy of mate's cars back into Bonn, where they knew a good late night Chinese restaurant that served veggie food.

We all crashed at the Scene Police HQ in Bonn that night, basically Dennis' apartment, that was absolutely filled with records and comic books and covered in sci fi models and posters. I loved hanging out at that place and we'd stay there many times, meeting all sorts of cool punk rock characters. It was a large apartment in a big old period building, well made with high ceilings and large windows. If we were in the UK, I'd guess it would be Georgian or maybe Victorian. It had survived the war and architecturally speaking this was clearly one of the nicer streets in town. As impressive as this was, Dennis had managed to turn every inch of it over to punk rock and hardcore, and even the hallway outside was full of his mate's bikes and skateboards.

We stayed in late, eating a leisurely breakfast and showering, whilst everyone went through Dennis' endless record collection, playing a few they hadn't heard yet. Then we headed into the city to visit more record stores, comic shops and a very well-stocked bakery. The gig we had booked for tonight wasn't far away either, in Siegburg, again just over the river to the northeast, another suburb town of the main city. Milo and I had played shows in Siegburg before and made good friends there that we hoped would come to the show tonight, so we were quite keen to get rolling, but Dennis had to wait for a couple of his friends to show up and also make some calls to ensure that the main band tonight, Canal Terror, brought enough gear and were ok with us using it.

Canal Terror were a local band and had been around for ages. A full-on hardcore punk band, they'd broken up and reformed a couple of times in the Eighties and Nineties and were coming out of retirement to play tonight's show, along with several other local punk rock supports, as it was a benefit gig, raising funds for the war-torn Kurdish people. Although the German bands seemed far more political than their UK counterparts, they never seemed to take it all too seriously on stage. So, despite the serious nature of the benefit, I had a feeling the gig would be fun too. I noticed that some wit had been going around with a marker pen, scribbling out the 'C' in Canal Terror on all the posters, and that's when I wondered where Duncan and Milo were, they were meant to be writing out a setlist for us, using the Sharpies we'd brought along just for that purpose.

First pressing cover of HWM / Rydell split

hot water music
just don't say you lost it

★ ★ ★

rydell
try seventeen

scene police
distributed by REVELATION INSIDE

rydell
try seventeen

hot water music
just don't say you lost it

take a ride out of the city, not, yet on empty • singing to myself like I've done so many times • cause you're not around to ride with me; I'll ride the ride anyway • you're not around at all and I feel sick • wide awake, heaven's sake, I'm sunk and breaking up • this time who's signing off? who's had enough this time? you're done and we're breaking up • so don't think trust is flowing easy, now is when to question the questions • when I used to trust you like I trust myself • and what is trust when it's not sacred? and so what will you say when it's time to cut me loose from your new life? don't say... • just don't say you lost the feeling, I'll bring it

she said do you like my shoes as she tripped • "well I'll see you saturday at two..." • she said do you like my face as it hit • "...unless I meet someone else before you" • all these signs add up to nothing • every bump knocks out the bass • last time I was here I was twenty two • you were twenty three • she said do you think I'm cool as she slipped • "well he says that he'll marry me..." • she said do you like these clothes as they split • "...unless this is not really pregnancy • all these signs add up to something • every tree has two kids under it • last time we were here we were twenty two • try seventeen • now tell me, what's too far? would you go out in a car? would you do, what's too near? now tell me, what to do here?

Inside notes for HWM / Rydell 7"

Broccoli, on tour with
Hooton 3 Car

Broccoli supporting MTX
at Drouthy's, Dundee

The Garage,
Highbury, London

The Jugendkulturcafe,
Siegburg

The Jugendkulturcafe,
Troisdorf

Karate

Voorhees at The
Duchess, Leeds

The Jugendkulturcafe in Siegburg was even newer and nicer than those we'd seen before. It had the usual pool and kicker tables, but also automated darts boards and all sorts of new vending machines for anything from nuts to yoghurt. They clearly had clubs running there for kids, and a large part of the young community had turned out for the show. I'd never seen so many kids just sitting around drinking beer or cider, and listening to NOFX or Spermbirds, Hot Water Music or Lifetime, and when Green Day or Blink 182 came on they all knew every word and sung along. It was like Dashboard Confessional for punks. We made ourselves at home and again didn't bother to soundcheck, figuring we'd just let the other bands do that and get levels when we went on. It was a good evening, but a long one, and by the time we played, the stage was swimming in spilt beer. We were practically up to our ankles in it and had to be very careful where we put the electric cables.

After the gig, there was a late-night party back at Dennis' apartment, and I got the feeling he was warming to Rydell's music now. I knew he was a big fan of the pop-punk hardcore of Couch Potatoes, but he was getting into Rydell now too, and said he'd hook us up with some more gigs, hopefully some bigger ones for this summer. We couldn't wait.

2/4/98 Karate, Broccoli and Rydell
The Garage, Highbury, London

Soon after our German weekend, we were all headed up to London again, this time to play at The Garage, supporting Karate, a jazz-core band out of Boston, USA. We'd be playing with them alongside the Dundee-bred, but now London-based, pop-punkers Broccoli. We figured this should be a good show as it was being talked about by everyone, and I'd seen it listed three times in the same issue of the NME that week; once in the gig listings, once as part of the Garage's listings and again as a small ad for the gig itself. All the bands had their own style and were good at it, but as a show it ought to work well. Sure enough, the gig was packed, and it seemed to me that every HC kid in the greater London area was there that night.

The Garage is one of London's better music venues, holding up to 600 people and playing host to all sorts of indie and alternative acts. The last show I'd seen there was the Descendents, but over time they also had Green Day, Hot Water Music, Jimmy Eat World, Paramore, My Chemical Romance, Piebald, The Satellite Year and many more. It had been converted from an old-time billiards hall, but now had a great stage and sound system and made an ideal venue for mid-sized indie rock gigs. We played there quite a few times so I can tell you with annoying certainty that parking in the area wasn't ideal, but by means of making up for it, there was a great chip shop along the road if you got peckish.

Broccoli turned out to be very friendly guys, and we spent much of the evening chatting with them, Milo blagging copies of their albums and EPs. They were prolific and had a whole bunch of split 7"s and EPs out on various labels, but had now signed to Rugger Bugger Discs, the record label run by big Sean of Wat Tyler, that was known for quality pop-punk in the late Nineties. Broccoli had two full albums out, their self-titled first, and the new 'Home', annoyingly the same name as our current demo that we were pushing that very evening. We'd have to change that for a proper release.

Broccoli were at their peak at that point and played a storming set. We played a blinder too as I recall, coming off stage very pleased with ourselves and the crowd's reaction. We promptly and profusely thanked the promoter, Kita, for the gig as we hoped to book a few more together.

The reaction to Karate was mixed. They were the band most people had come to see, but also seemed to be Marmite for the hardcore kids. Some were loving it. I know Dunky and Macca were really into them. But from where I was standing, they seemed to bore the pants off most of the crowd with their minimal, jazzy noodling. I wanted them to be good. I knew a lot of people who had their albums on Southern Records and really rated them, but maybe the minimal style they played was better suited to recordings than the live environment. They were a rock band and I wanted them to turn it up, and maybe speed it up. Maybe after all the adrenaline of playing it just seemed a little dull. At one point during their set, I turned to Milo and Adam to give them the Fast Show, Jazz Club 'Nice' impression. I can appreciate them a bit more now.

They went on to sell a lot of records, certainly more than us, and on later listens to their first three Southern albums, 'Karate', 'In place of real insight' and 'The bed is in the ocean', I had to admire some of their gentle twisting rhythms. Definitely a grower for home listening. I know if I'd still been in Joeyfat or was writing a review for NME I'd have said they were giving the instruments beautiful room to breathe, letting it all simmer and strip-down, or some arty shite like that. Karate went on to produce nine albums and six EPs, some as a three-piece and some as a four-piece. The EPs are rare now and sell for insane prices on Discogs and other record collector sites. The band's main man, Geoff Farina, played in Glorytellers too and had several solo releases, but eventually had to wind things up as he was suffering from bad tinnitus. I can't think of much worse for a musician so was glad to read an interview with him in Guitar World magazine, published during the pandemic, saying that he was still playing guitar and evolving his sound even now.

4/4 & 5/4/98 Back at Recent Studios, Leyton, London.

Just two days later we were back under the railway arches at Recent Studios with Charlie. He was a great engineer, and as Duncan was now available again for this recording, we got down some of the newer songs properly for the releases we hoped were coming soon. This session went pretty well overall, although the passing trains did cut out the

Rydell at The Albert, Brighton

just one life d.i.y + spanking herman present

THE BRIGHTON PUNK-A-THON '98
19 BANDS OVER TWO DAYS

SATURDAY

FROM CROYDON. PUNK/SOUL NUTTERS
FLYING MEDALLIONS
+ CHIRPY, CHEEKY, COCKNEY PUNKERS
(WITH A DELICATE HINT OF SKA)
LOOPHOLE
+ BE AFRAID. BE VERY AFRAID.
+ LOCAL SAD-CORE NUTJOBS
VULVA ESPRIT
+ FROM WASHINGTON, U.S.A.
+ FURIOUS + MELODIC SKA -DAG NASTY]
THE MARSHES
+ RESPECTED AND PROLIFIC POP-PUNKERS
TRAVIS CUT
+ LOCAL BASS-HEAVY SURREALISTS
NO LEGS
+ PUNK TEEN DRAG QUEENS
ANAL BEARD
+ ENGLISH INDIECORE JANGLERS
RYDELL
+ FROM CANADA VIA LONDON
TEEN C THIRTYSOMETHINGS
CHESTER
+ LOCAL POP-ECCENTRICS
NOT A BIT OF WOOD
+ LOCAL KIDS GONE FAT
PENFOLD
+ LOCAL RP4228D OUT THRASHERS
UNSLUG

SATURDAY/SUNDAY 23rd/24th MAY

£3.50 ONE DAY ADVANCE TICKET
or £4 ON THE DOOR

TWO DAY ADVANCE TICKET ONLY £6
FROM EDGEWORLD RECORDS, KENSINGTON GARDENS.
BRIGHTON

SATURDAY DOORS @ 3PM FIRST BAND @ 3.30 10pm

SATURDAY BAR AND BANDS TILL MIDNIGHT
SUNDAY DOORS 6.30PM FIRST BAND @ 7.00
SUNDAY BAR AND BANDS TILL ELEVEN

@ THE ALBERT, TRAFALGAR st. UNDER
BRIGHTON STATION, PHONE (01273) 730499.
JUST ONE LIFE INFO (01273) 275304 or 737045
or http://www.olf-brighton.com

RUNNING ORDER TO BE CONFIRMED ON THE DAY

SUNDAY

FROM GRIMSBY, OLD SCHOOL
HARDCORE PUNK ROCK]
IMBALENCE
+ FROM LONDON. HARSH CONTEMPORARY HC
KNUCKLEDUST
+ FROM TELFORD. BRUTAL POLITICAL HC
ASSERT
+ FROM THE MIDLANDS
W.O.R.M
+ ALSO FROM THE MIDLANDS
COMBAT SHOCK
+ FROM SOUTHAMPTON. SPEED THRASH HC
MINUTE MANIFESTO

TWO BARS,
POOL ROOM,
FOOD AVAILABLE

Flyer for The Brighton Punkathon '98

Thommy Almdudler sharing a beer with Kitty Sunset, Jeff Rowe and Christian Tollner

Thommy Reitmayer rememberance patch

The T.U. Club, Vienna

sound to Charlie's mixing desk occasionally mid-song, leaving clicks in the recording so we'd have to go through the track again. That's all rock 'n' roll I guess, but maybe we should have asked for a discount.

We were getting cassettes duplicated, about a hundred or so at a time by a guy called Rob up in Birmingham, and CDs pressed anything from 200 to 500 at a time at a couple of places where we'd found good deals. They'd arrive at the Rydell clubhouse, basically my home, and we'd send some out to anyone remotely interested through the post and take the rest along to our next gigs, trying to sell them for a couple of quid each, but still happy to give them away if needs be to anyone who'd enjoyed the show. Such was the nature of being an unsigned hardcore band at the time. We just wanted people to hear our music.

We were developing a few ideas for release artwork and t-shirts too, supremely confident in the knowledge that record labels would be knocking down the door to put out our records any day. We'd chase up any and all gigs, and travel far and wide to play wherever we needed to in order to find new audiences. Such was the case with our next gig, and it's entirely possible that I was getting a little bit carried away with it all.

19/4/98 Oi Polloi, Voorhees, Month of Birthdays, Rydell, Imbiss, Withdrawn, Hard to Swallow, Scalplock, Iron Monkey, Active Minds and more
1 in 12 Club, Bradford (Two day festival)

I'd been speaking with Ian from Subjugation and he invited us up to play at the weekend-long hardcore festival in the 1 in 12 Club in Bradford. I'd played the club before, when Couch Potatoes supported Bob Tilton and UnderClass and was up for it, but had kind of forgotten what a long way it was to play one show. The Saturday, the first day, was always heavy and packed, with the Sunday being slightly mellower as everyone had stayed overnight, crashed out around the various rooms in the club. With that in mind, we were due on midway through the second day's bill but were running late getting there, even on a Sunday, due to rain and bad traffic.

The previous night had seen Voorhees, Durham's heavy hardcore horror merchants, as well as Nottingham's doom-lords Iron Monkey, and also Hard To Swallow, who'd just released their gloriously-named new album, 'Protected by the ejaculation of serpents' on Household Name Records. This title, I'm reliably informed, is a quote from The Wicker Man. All of that would have been bone-crushingly heavy and hard going for everyone there. That probably explained the downbeat atmosphere that seemed to prevail the next day. The mellower Sunday headliners were meant to be Oi Polloi, an anarcho punk band from Scotland with seemingly hundreds of members, but I'm not sure if they even turned up. The place was full though, so they may well have been there, passed out in a pile in one of the corners. We saw Urko, and Rauschen, and I think Scalplock and Imbiss too, but when we went on, early Sunday evening, we knew we had to punk it up - so launched into our opener, 'Try 17' with even more vigour than normal and almost immediately Milo fell off the stage. That was our intro song and that was how the day was going.

We soldiered through the set with good sound and maybe half of the crowd paying attention, the other half either asleep or fighting. It's true we may well not have been at our very best that day. At some point Dunc messed up a drum fill, causing him to miss a few beats. This threw us and I remember one of the more awake members of the audience piping up with, "Tighten those guy ropes," to which I shouted back, "Thank you, Mozart." It was as witty a repost as I could muster at the moment, but the guy was right, this wasn't one of our best gigs. We hung around for a while, picking up a few zines and buying a bag of chips up the road, but knowing how long it took to get home, decided to leave by around 9pm. I hate not watching the other bands we are playing with. I know it's rude and rockstar and self-centred and hardly supports the scene, but this was a day-long festival, 250 miles and a good four hours away from home on a cold rainy Sunday night. We thanked the promoters, grabbed some cans of Coke and headed back south.

I spent most of the end of April and the start of May over in the Far East, travelling around Malaysia and Singapore again, partly on holiday and partly for work. I made it mainly holiday, so it was brilliant fun. I arrived back home just in time to pick up my tickets for the European Cup Winners Cup Final, where my beloved Chelsea were playing VfB Stuttgart. I flew out with my brother and a couple of mates and we had a right old crack, staying on an ostrich farm in the middle of a forest, but with a well-stocked bar. There was football, and singing, and fighting in the railway station, then travelling back to the airport in limos. For those that give a shit, Chelsea won, when the brilliant Gianfranco Zola came on for Torre Andre Flo in the 71st minute and immediately ran up the wing and stuck it straight in the net. The place went Dambusters crazy and Chelsea did the double that year. I got back from that trip to find some copies of the new Food Not Bombs 7" waiting for me at home. The idea and intent behind this release was certainly a sobering thought compared to what I'd been used to for the last three weeks, but the record itself came as a very welcome surprise, containing as it did, Rydell's very first track on vinyl.

This Food Not Bombs benefit 7" EP was released by Revolution Inside Records in Germany. It had cool graphics on the cover featuring a '50s comic book style FNB carrot as a rocket ship, blasting off in red and orange over a black and white planet, and the FNB logo, a fist holding a carrot, on the back cover as well as on the vinyl centre labels too, with editorial pieces on the charity and each of the bands inside. We'd set it up with the help of Dennis and Scene Police as they worked closely with Revolution Inside, one of the label's distributors. Those guys knew Couch Potatoes from our gigs and the 'Outweighed' album, and now were getting into Rydell too. I'd sent them the 'Rhythm Kings' demo saying they could use any track they liked, and they'd chosen 'An Event' for the EP. I think Milo was over in Germany, staying with Dennis, when the actual meeting took place with the Revolution Inside guys to decide which bands should go on the release, so that was very handy and worked out well for us. This vinyl 7" would be Revolution Inside's thirty-ninth release and the other three bands featured on it would all be from Germany. It had tracks by Superfan, Bhang Dextro and Free Yourself, as well as Rydell. They pressed a thousand copies and must have promoted it very well, as it sold out quickly and they made a good donation. I still have a cherished copy gathering dust somewhere in my nerdy record collection.

Soon after that I called Dennis to thank him again for all his help. He told me that he and Emre had discussed it and decided that they wanted to put a Rydell release out. In fact, they had come up with the ideal thing. As Dennis and his friends put on a lot of shows they had a tour for Hot Water Music coming up. The Scene Police guys thought this would suit us well and were going to get us on the shows as main support. That would be awesome. As well as this, they wanted to do a limited release single, with a track by each band, which would be the ideal thing to sell on the tour. I was absolutely stoked with that idea and we got to work on it straight away. I roped in Davey Blanco for the artwork and design again, and he came up with an awesome and colourful montage for the front cover, featuring his girlfriend of the time smoking a cigarette in a London street scene for the front, with an old-school New York fire truck on the back. There'd be live band shots and lyrics on the inside, and it would be a good-looking release. I still have an original bromide proof of the cover art on the wall in my office. It looks cool as hell. Dennis contacted HWM and their record label at the time, Doghouse, and they sent over an unreleased version of a great track called 'Just don't say you lost it'.

Now to say I am a big fan of Hot Water Music would be a huge understatement. But at that time, I didn't know them as people and hadn't been into their music for that long. I'd recently got hold of copies of their first two albums on No Idea Records, 'Finding the rhythms' and 'Fuel for the hate game', from Var Thelin himself (the guy who owned and ran No Idea) and I was getting into them. The gruff dual vocals, the complex but powerful rhythms, the instant riffs that stuck in your head. But when 'Forever and counting' came out on Doghouse Records, that quickly became my favourite, and on an album comprised of ten more or less perfect hardcore gems, 'Just don't say you lost it' was the pick of the bunch. That perfectly measured chugging riff, then the drums and bass roll in, then the second guitar line over the top of it all, and then those lyrics. Those lyrics. They just ripped my heart out. Chuck and Chris screaming each line... "Take a ride out of the city, not yet on empty. Singing to myself, like I've done so many times... Don't say you lost the feeling. I'll bring it." It's just an incredible song. The version they had sent for the split was different to the album track, in some ways even better, as it was not as heavily produced, a sort of heartfelt demo version. If you haven't yet, trust me, you just gotta hear it. I knew we couldn't come close to that with our track, but 'Try 17' was probably our best bet at the time. It's an angst-ridden song, musically inspired by another great band, Split Lip / Chamberlain, and although it only lasts about two and half minutes, it has a great guitar line that I am proud of and that would have to do for our side. But what an opportunity. I wouldn't believe it until I held this record in my hands. It was late April by then, and we needed these singles for shows coming up in late May. We'd better get cracking...

Sat 23/5/98 The Marshes, Rydell, Unslug and others The Albert, Brighton.

We'd been invited down to Brighton to play at the Prince Albert again, this time with Colin Sear's new band, The Marshes, and local punksters, Unslug. We'd arrived early, about 6pm, for a 6.30 soundcheck as we'd been asked to by the promoters. This was all part of a two day long punk fest with about twenty bands, so it all had to be timed just right. As we loaded in our gear and greeted the people that we knew there, I was stoked to notice that the Couch Potatoes 'Outweighed' CD was blasting out of the p.a. I'm not sure who we had to thank for that, possibly the local Penfold boys who'd played earlier in the day and knew we were coming, but it was cool to see people enjoying it, quite a few singing and foot-tapping along as we set up our gear onstage and then headed to the bar.

Unslug played before us and they were insane. Milo's pal Darren was on vocals and Tim from Manchester punk legends Kitchener was on guitar, they'd only played a handful of shows, and never did many as far as I know, but they were great. Bringing a real energy for sure, so people were really into it and well warmed-up for us. As all the bands playing that evening were sharing our equipment, it was great to hear such a powerful sound mix coming through the speakers too. We were up next and played a storming set, though I do say so myself, getting a decent crowd reaction. And then it was time for The Marshes.

The Marshes were from the Washington DC area of the US, and although their main man, Colin Sears, had been the drummer in Dag Nasty and Alloy, they weren't signed to Dischord, but instead were on Dr Strange Records. I'd met Colin before, when Joeyfat toured with Alloy, but the two front men of The Marshes, Emil (bass and vocals) and Steve (guitar), were both new guys, and this band was much more of a pop-punk thing. They were a lot more straightforward, just three people, playing three chords, simple stuff. It was good though, catchy as hell and well played, with some faster punky songs and some slower rockier numbers, but up until now I hadn't heard any of their records so didn't know the tracks or what to expect. I recognised a Psychedelic Furs cover thrown in there, towards the end of their set, and apparently that later came out on a limited run split 7" with UK band Travis Cut. You could pick up a brown marbled vinyl version from Speedowax, a UK label that loved their limited-edition wax and put out some really good releases in the late Nineties and early Noughties, including records for Gameface, Discount, Douglas, Broccoli and more for Travis Cut too.

I was late to the party getting to know The Marshes as they already had three albums out, as well as several EPs and split 7"s. This tour was in support of their 'Pox on the tracks' album on Dr Strange, a Californian distro that had morphed into a record label and brought out releases by bands like Guttermouth, Face to Face, Rhythm Collision, Voodoo Glow Skulls, Schleprock, Gameface, Zoinks and Brown Lobster Tank.

Sun 24/5/98 Rudedog, Rydell, Flex, Mong, TipaGore and Stroppy The Forum, Tunbridge Wells

The next day we were back in Tunbridge Wells at The Forum for a six band all-dayer. We'd opted to go on in the middle of the line-up as we had to get rolling to the port early in the morning and get over to Europe for some shows through the week with Hot Water Music. We had one eye on that, as you can imagine, so this wasn't our best show at The Forum. It was part of a weekend-long three-day event for the launch of the first Unlabel compilation CD. This collection featured the Rydell track 'Try 17' as well as 'Give it away' by our good friends Rudedog (basically Macca's band, The BBMFs, but with a new name), 'Deleted' by Stroppy, 'Par Avion' by Unhome (featuring ex-Joeyfat members Jason and Jim), 'Learning Curve' by Flex, and thirteen other local rockers. The compilation was Unlabel's first CD, but their second release, the first being a Joeyfat 7", so it was simply called 'Two'. Anyway, we picked up a few copies of the new CD, thanking Phil and Jason for them, dropped off some of our demos and 7"s, played our set and then headed off to load up the car and catch the late ferry, so we could go on tour.

Mon 25/5/98 Hot Water Music and Rydell T.U. Club, Vienna, Austria.

We'd crammed the car with our guitars, snare and cymbals, and as much Rydell merchandise as possible. Also, some spare clothes and a few snacks, so then we were ready for an adventure. The Hot Water Music / Rydell split 7" had arrived from the pressing plant to Scene Police HQ in Bonn about a few days earlier, but Dennis wasn't sure where he'd be able to meet up with us on the tour so had sent a couple of hundred copies over in advance so we had plenty in the UK, including a few boxes to take with us for the first shows which were starting tomorrow in Vienna. Yes. Vienna, in bloody Austria. That's a long drive for a gig, I can tell you. It's about 750 miles from the port at Hoek van Holland in The Netherlands to the TU Club in the centre of Vienna and even hurtling along at well above the speed limits most of the way, it would still take us about twelve hours.

First, we had to catch the late ferry from Harwich in Essex and take the night crossing to Hoek van Holland, when we arrived, we'd have the usual buttock-clenched moment getting through customs while bored men in uniform, on both sides of the channel, scrutinised a vehicle full of rock 'n' roll youth clearly intent on getting up to no good. But when through, released, relieved, and grinning wildly, we'd hurtle past the tulip fields and windmills of Holland and across much of Germany's beautiful countryside, dotted as it is with heavy industry, without even a second glance. We stopped for petrol somewhere between Frankfurt and Wurzburg, squinting in the morning sun, whilst Milo and Dunc changed over the travel music from Pegboy and Sugar, to Lifetime and Hot Water Music, and Adam and I restocked our supplies of crisps and chocolate milkshake. Then on we went. Zooming along the autobahns in southeast Germany and crossing the border into Austria somewhere between Passau and Salzburg.

The countryside around there really is beautiful. I'd been a few times before and wanted to slow down and enjoy it, but we were on a strict schedule. It was well into the afternoon already as we approached Linz and we still had to cross the northern plains along the Danube yet, with Vienna over a hundred miles away and notoriously hard to drive around and find things, especially if you are a bit of a muppet like me. I was glad I'd managed to talk my work into getting me a new Audi as a company car. The old van was great for space, but not fast and dying on its wheels. This thing was like lightning, and although a little cramped, we'd devised ways to store all the gear, like a game of Jenga in the boot, and Milo was the master of that. He'd be at the car five minutes early after every show to load things in properly, and it made all the difference.

I'd driven around Europe a lot so wasn't fazed at all by the subtle nuances of their road rules, let alone driving on the right, but I had been warned about Vienna. Respect the trams. No, worship the trams. And be very careful at tram stops. Also, be wary at any roundabouts, and there are hundreds of them, and always look out for cyclists, as there are hundreds of them too. There are many cobbled streets, odd signs, sudden bus lanes and traffic lights. People jump out with a coffee or a cake just when you are admiring some amazing architecture. Just don't expect any special treatment because you are a stupid foreigner. I'd got us this far and with nearly an hour to spare, now we were looking for Karlsplatz and the massive technical university building. It couldn't be that hard to find and get parked surely. The clock was ticking, and typically, I needed a piss. Where the bloody hell was this place?

When we eventually found it, we could hardly believe it. A huge ornate building, like a giant four-storey cake, made of carved white stone rather than sponge. Built in the early 1800s, I guess it was typical Viennese renaissance revival style, it was bloody impressive and, frankly, the last place I'd expect to be playing a hardcore gig! There were three archways at the front with large doors welcoming us inside. Already loads of student types and alternative-looking people were milling about, wandering in and out. We

Hot Water Music in Italy

Chuck skateboarding at the Leon Cavallo

grabbed our guitars and headed in. Once inside, the building was huge and full of light through the many windows, but we were led downstairs into the basement, or TU Club. Even this was massive, easily able to hold hundreds of people. The big bar was at one end, and a high stage at the other, where we could already see the Hot Water Music guys setting up. George was tapping on his drums, tightening things up and waiting for the others, Chuck and Chris were pissing around with mic stands and duelling with their guitars, whilst Jason was plugging into the biggest bass amps I'd seen for some time, and all of it was linked into a very impressive sound system. This was clearly all at a different level to what we'd been used to. We hadn't even played yet, but I could easily get used to this. I have no idea how or why larger touring bands ever stop. We were no-ones, the lucky support act, but as we put down our guitars and boxes of merch, people were already offering us drinks and seeing what we needed. This was mad.

One of the guys from Doghouse Records was on the tour with HWM and he came over to greet us. He was a huge guy, bearded but balding, in a stripey shirt that had no chance of containing all of him. His name was Tom Husman, and he was like an amiable bear. He shook our hands and introduced us to everyone. The friendly German tour driver, Stefaan, who was travelling with them so hung out and helped Tom with merch at all the shows, and the ultra-friendly Austrian promoters who were putting this show on at the Technical University for the students. Damn, I wish I could remember all their names. We wandered over to the stage to drop our gear and greet the HWM guys, and it was apparent that they were as blown away by this place as we were. None of us were expecting this venue, but now it was time for soundchecks.

After you've played a few gigs, and by that I mean a few hundred, you get bored of soundchecks and are just happy to show up and plug in, save all the hassle. But that's smaller gigs in pubs and clubs. For larger venues though, it's more important and you have to get it right. This is when I admired the American bands on tour. We'd played with quite a few of them by now and it was always more or less the same. They wander on in a very unassuming way, often wearing shoes with shorts, or comfortable jumpers and non-descript shirts, looking a million miles away from the accomplished musicians and rockstars that they actually were. They'd shuffle about moving equipment, trying to understand the language and layout, and find where to plug in, but then they'd come alive. They'd take over, and you could see the confidence grow and the talent start to flood out. They'd take time with each piece of the drum kit, then the massively booming bass, so you could feel it through the floor, but it was still nice and punchy. Then the guitars. My first love. In HWM's case both Gibson Les Pauls, and the screams and growls they could produce. Adjusting the amps and pedals to get the sound just how they wanted it, the levels right, the ideal amount of distortion. Then silence and a few moments of "one two, one two, check," into the mics. Maybe the drummer hits a few snare beats in impatience. Then, "OK, let's try one," and off they go. All those separate constituent parts get blended into a beautiful powerful one, and suddenly a song you recognise appears that makes you want to jump up and down and join in singing along, and that's just the bloody soundcheck. Man, it is no exaggeration to say that I absolutely lived for this shit. As tired as we all were, we were immediately re-energised. At that moment, in that space, there was nowhere else in the world I would have rather been than with my mates watching Hot Water Music soundcheck.

We were treated to large sections of 'Translocation', 'Better Sense' and 'Minno' whilst we sat drinking orange Fanta and the lighting guys played around with different colours. When HWM were done, Rydell sound-checked too, clambering up on that stage and looking back across the big hall. We were all using the same gear, so just plugged our guitars in and were good to go. We waited a moment, first checking our tuning and then getting a feel for the stage space we had to move around in, while Dunky changed over the snare, bass drum pedal, and a couple of his hilariously cracked and taped cymbals. One was so worn out you could only just about read the Z of Zildjian on it. We jammed through a song, 'Try 17' I think, and it sounded amazing. I really wanted to play another, so made up some excuse about monitor levels and went through half of 'Across Three Parks' too, as I loved that riff and wanted to hear it boom around the hall. The sound was massive, but everything was as clear as a bell. This was going to be awesome.

Now we had an hour or two to kill before the actual show. We'd already had a drink and there were plenty of sandwiches and pizza for the bands and uni staff, but the HWM guys wanted to go for a walk and check the place out. So about twelve of us headed out across the square to a small park we'd seen, where the local kids were skateboarding. We soon got chatting, we had Germans and Austrians with us, but all the locals spoke more or less perfect English, and it turned out that quite a few of the skaters were students and were coming along to the show tonight.

After a while, we headed back to the TU Club and it was heaving. You have to picture it. The previous two nights we'd played in a pub and then a club, and both times to maybe a hundred people at most. This place must have easily had 400 or 500 people in it already and there was still room for more, and despite them all being alternative types, punks, rockers, coloured-haired students, it was all good natured and friendly. There was a buzz of conversation over the background music. Everyone was drinking, a lot, but no-one was smashing anything. The atmosphere was one of good-natured expectation. They were there to have fun and enjoy the music.

The architecture of the venue may have helped too. This place was built to last, nearly 200 years ago, and although the stiff Austrian information notice about it said, "The TU Club in Vienna's Paniglgasse is a non-commercial communication centre and pub. It has been in existence for 20 years now and is operated by a grass-roots self-governing association. In 1978, the former auditorium in the basement (the club's current event room) was dedicated by the academic senate of the Vienna University of

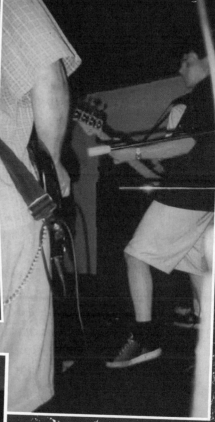

Rydell in Italy

A day off to be tourists

Technology (HTU), which commissioned the association to set up a communication centre." It was basically a massive student union / music venue.

As I mentioned, the HWM guys were as blown away by this place as we were. You have to remember that although they were getting big in America, very few people had heard of them yet in the UK or Europe. Hot Water Music were an unknown quantity to all apart from a few clued-in scene kids, and this tour wasn't even going to the UK. That wouldn't happen for nearly another two years.

While we were waiting, several zines turned up who wanted interviews so both bands were being kept busy. Dunk and Milo were interviewed by a fanzine guy whose every question seemed to centre around abortion or sexuality. This was a new and interesting tactic, but as usual, Dunk slayed them with his knowledge and personal / political trivia. The zine guy had a dictaphone on the table and was recording all Duncan's answers so he could write it all up later. Christ knows how that tape came out. We never did see a copy of the zine.

I was hoping to meet a penpal friend of mine called Thomas Reitmayer at this show. I'd been writing to him for a while now as he ran a little punk zine and distro out of Vienna called Yummy, and we'd exchanged a lot of good music, also punk zines, alternative ideas, and even local food and drink. He would send me Almdudler, the tasty alpine lemonade that I'd loved ever since going to Austria on a school skiing trip as a boy. This wasn't cheap to ship, and you could only get it in Austria and Germany, so I'd gratefully send him back crates of records for his trouble, and he must have thought I was mad. We got on well and I called him Thommy Almdudler, which he didn't mind. In fact, I think he rather quite liked it. We hadn't actually met in person yet, but I'd let him know about the show as I knew he lived in Vienna and hoped he'd show up. I'm glad to say he did come along and turned out to be just as much of a great guy as I'd expected, and a serious drinker too, dealing with most of our rider by himself. Thommy was clearly excited to be at the show and meet everyone, and had brought a few mates with him too. They were telling us that the University and students had been arguing about the venue and having shows here anymore, so this could be one of the last gigs they put on there and we were lucky to be playing it. Man, that would suck, this place was a great venue. They finished our beers and went off to enjoy the show.

(Sure enough, the University decided the TU Club had become far too 'Counter-Concept' and tried to close it down later that year. The disgruntled students occupied it, saying there were far too few independent political and cultural centres in Vienna, but the collective was eventually evicted, and the last day on which the TU Club was open was December 31, 1998. Just seven months after our gig).

The show that night was absolutely incredible. We rose to the occasion and played out of our skins, and Hot Water Music just blew everyone away. They were astoundingly good, without doubt one of the best live acts I've ever seen, and I've seen many. But looking back on this show is particularly bittersweet for me. When I was scrawling down my notes for this book I wrote to Thommy again, asking him about what he remembered about the gig, and if / how the venue closed. He emailed me back the following.

"Hey David, Just for the record, your show that night made me write you a letter and start a record label!

I have been dusting off the cobwebs in the darkest corners of my brain for memories, but most details about that particular night seem lost. We are talking about pre-internet days in a metropolis that has always felt like a small town to me. Shows happened far less frequently and promotion was scarce. If you saw a poster in one of the three, maybe four record stores in town on your weekly round, you were lucky. Chances were that those posters were replaced by other posters within a few hours. But if you knew, you knew. It was like a secret society in much simpler times, like an engine running on word of mouth... and that was half the fun of it. Ironically enough, I do remember how I found out about this show: Green Hell from Germany had printed the HWM tour dates in one of their mailorder catalogues – whether or not they had a hand in organizing the tour at all escapes me though – and the description referenced Fugazi. That was it. I was going there. And I did, as you know.

Both bands were incredible that night, in their very own unique ways. And while I have fond memories of the HWM set that night, it was Rydell who made a lasting impression on me.

I had never heard of them before (and I don't think anyone in the crowd did, for that matter), but they were impressive. A skinny and a chubby guy with string instruments controlled the band like conductors and every time I thought they would lose their way through whatever song they played, they fucking nailed it. And then they did it again. And again.

I bought the split 7" at the merch table (that was back when touring bands could have split 7"s and actually sell them!) and when I had sobered up the next morning, I put it on the turntable and read the insert... and there it was, in a very unfortunate font, black on blurry gray: a name that I was familiar with: David Gamage. Could it be...? Yes. It could. I had known this gentleman for quite a while. I bought his zine and tapes of his music back in the day, and – fun fact! - traded with him for bottles of an Austrian soft drink called Almdudler that he was particularly fond of. A couple of days later, I sat down at my desk, wrote a letter to the band address and reconnected with an old friend. Next thing I knew, I was putting out a Rydell 7", but that's another story for another time..."

I was stoked to receive this response from Thommy. He had drunk a lot that night so maybe didn't remember it all, and I'm not sure about 'a skinny guy and chubby guy', ha ha, clearly Milo and me, but it's always good to get other people's perspectives on things, and I'm sure my ego liked being stroked by someone who really enjoyed a Rydell gig too. He also told me a little about the new Black Candle zine he was writing, and also about a new film he was producing, all about the punk and hardcore scene in Vienna and how great it was. He sent me over the rough cuts of the film to check out, saying it needed more editing. But I could clearly see how it inspired him and how vital a part of the punk community he had become. I was interested in what he would do with the film and if there would be an English language version too. Maybe we could help in some way and work together on PR for it over here? I knew it'd be great. I also wanted to get some more notes from him for this book about his excellent record label, Firewalk With Me, as not only did he put out a Rydell 7" but twelve other great releases too. The Rydell EP was Flame One, his first release, and I was stoked that we'd inspired him, but I needed to know more about Flame Two through Thirteen too, so I emailed him back. About two days later I heard back from Judith Moser, his girlfriend, or I should say fiancée as they were engaged to get married. Thommy had died from a heart attack, aged just forty-six.

Thommy and Judith have a daughter, Olive, and by all accounts Thommy was a great dad. I know for sure that he was a friend to all punks, and he'll be skating around, drinking beer and rocking out wherever he is now. Rest in peace Mr Almdudler. I'm honoured to have known you.

Wed 27/5/98 Hot Water Music and Rydell
Plan 9 Club, Limena, Padua, Italy

The show at the TU Club finished late. We were knackered and more than a bit sweaty, so we stayed with one of the promoters at his apartment nearby and were hoping for showers, everyone really needed one, but for some bizarre reason the apartment didn't seem to have one, our host explaining that it was his grandmother's place and she never put one in. Worse still, he had to be up at 6am and out the door to go to work at Subway, so we couldn't stay after that. Bloody hell. We'd all been up 48 hours already and would be lucky to grab three or four hours sleep now on the floor or couch here. We'd drawn the short straw on which of the promoters to stay with tonight, but there you go. The ups and downs of the touring rollercoaster. We were still having fun, just a bit 'on the nose' as the Aussies say.

Tuesday would be a day off for us so we drove out of Vienna and south across Austria towards Italy, where our next gigs would be. Passing by Graz and then Klagenfurt, and crossing over the far end of the Alps, into Italy. We headed towards Venice as, well why not, and stopped often in the beautiful scenery to take photos or buy coffee and cake. It was a trip of 360 miles or so, but we did it at a leisurely pace and found ourselves walking around Piazza San Marco late that afternoon, looking at the Basilica and Campanile whilst drinking slush puppies. We had time to kill and I knew a good place to stay over by Verona that I'd been to before, so we headed there, booked in for the night and finally got those showers.

In the morning, after a decent and much needed night's sleep, we wandered around town for a while, making time to see Juliet's balcony and the amphitheatre, and spill gelati all down my shirt. Then we headed over to Sirmione on Lake Garda and when we got there, decided to take a boat out on the lake, just for the hell of it. I took a few photos and we definitely behaved more like tourists than a band on tour. We made the most of it. By late afternoon we were heading to the Plan 9 Club in Limena, just outside Padua, a heavy metal club slapped down in the middle of an industrial area. We were told that we'd find it by looking for all the motorbikes parked outside. It wasn't far away, maybe an hour and a half, but much of the journey was spent sitting in a traffic jam that had been caused by a trucker a few cars ahead of us crashing into a bollard as he letched at some whores by the roadside, an often seen occurrence in Italy, apparently.

The Club was called Plan 9 and was situated on the first floor of a very run-down and mundane looking building in the middle of a very run-down and mundane looking industrial estate. There was a gym on the ground floor beneath us, so we heard dodgy Eighties music pumping out the windows for quite some time and then saw the occasional sweaty vest-wearing punter sticking his head in the club door to see what was going on, and then promptly leaving a few moments later. This went on for quite some time, much to our amusement.

This show was more like what we were expecting, a small to mid-size rock club with graffiti on every wall and no doors on the toilets. The Hot Water Music guys were there already and had set all the gear up, so we just wandered in, said Hi to everyone, and sound-checked. We were told by the promoter that they were expecting maybe 150 people to turn up for the show, but it was hard to know. In the end I'd have said it was closer to 60, maybe 80, including the bands and crew if we were lucky. Right now, the audience consisted of four blokes that Milo was chatting to, all wearing baseball caps and New York hardcore shirts. They were from a local straight edge band called Product who said they mainly played covers, but did have a release of their own coming out soon on Genet Records. They said they were going to hang around and had invited all their mates too, but none had turned up yet. Possibly because of the distracted truck driver crash I mentioned before, or maybe they'd just gone to the beach on their mopeds instead.

While we waited some of us got fed and some didn't, but looking at what was on offer, that may not have been a bad thing. We all sat around chatting together. Hot Water Music were really easy-going guys, cracking gags at Tom, the Doghouse guy, and

Stefaan, their German driver / tour guide, who were both as friendly and likeable blokes as you'd ever want to meet. I'm assuming that anyone bothering to read this far through the book probably already knows a bit about most of the bands I'm talking about, but for those of you that don't, a quick potted history of Hot Water Music:

Chris Wollard, Jason Black and George Rebelo all played together in a band called Thread. They'd moved to the university town of Gainsville (in Florida) to be able to play more gigs, but their singer hadn't come along with them. Initially, when Chuck Ragan moved into the same apartments, he had his own band called Fossil, but they had no singer either, so very soon Hot Water Music was formed with both Chuck and Chris taking turns at singing, and Jason and George keeping the rhythms tight. They were influenced by punk and hardcore bands, but George was also into free-form jazz drumming and the guitarists were all self-taught so came up with barre chords and ideas as they went along. The band's first song, soon after Chuck joined, was 'Us and Chuck'. This style definitely influenced Rydell too, we'd play power chords, often with bending strings or higher melodies over the top, and had pretty much jazz style drumming going on underneath, certainly an unusual mix for a hardcore band at that time.

The band's name came from a book, a collection of Charles Bukowski short stories. They played a few early gigs at the Hardback Café in Gainesville where they'd later record a brilliant live album. Their first demo was a four-track cassette called 'Push for coin' that eventually came out as a 7" on Happy Days Records out of New Jersey. All the band wrote music and lyrics, and they all moved around a lot on stage. Both Chuck and Chris would sing/shout, sometimes in key and sometimes not, but clearly always from the heart. Early in '95 they recorded 'Eating the filler' and 'Recliner' for a new 7" on Toybox Records from Florida. It was soon after this they met Var Thelin of No Idea Records and had the chance to put a full album out.

Var was a skateboarder from Gainesville whose friend, Ken Collet, ran a comics fanzine called Rats. Seeing this and realising he could do something similar himself, he started No Idea, first of all as a fanzine when he was just fifteen, then only starting the record label when he released a 7" for local Florida band the Doldrums with issue six of the zine. He was into the hardcore scene and the whole friendly, community vibe that HWM seemed to have too, so they soon started to work together. Right from the start, No Idea produced great-looking records on multi-coloured vinyl. Whenever I wrote to Var he'd always come straight back and we'd talk about new bands and releases. When Engineer Records set up a distro, he was one of the first labels to work with us and regularly supply us stock.

Hot Water Music's first record for No Idea was 'Finding the rhythms', a collection of demos and recordings to make up a full album as they needed something to sell on tour and were keen to get out there. Around that time, they also met another scene buddy, an art student called Scott 'Sinc' Sinclair, who was playing in a band called Vent. The artwork style on HWM Records has always struck me as unique and well suited for them, and that came from Sinc. He did all the paintings for the HWM covers and has done ever since.

By the time they recorded 'Fuel for the hate game' in '96, with Assuck guitarist Steve Heritage engineering it at a studio in Tampa that specialised in heavy metal, they'd really found their style. This release took a while to come out even though the band needed records to sell on tour, they were playing shows with Avail, Promise Ring, Discount, Strife and starting to do their own small tours now. They wanted to do more and travel further afield, so when Dirk Hemsath of Doghouse Records offered them a European tour with The Get Up Kids late in '96, as well as $5k upfront so that they could record a new album, they went for it and recorded what became their absolute classic 'Forever and counting' release that came out early in '97. This album had so many great tracks on it, including my favourite, 'Just don't say you lost it' which later came out on a split 7" vinyl with Rydell, of course, on Scene Police Records in Germany, partly for sale on our tours together in '98.

NB. The 'Forever and counting' album on Doghouse originally came out with HWM using the name 'The Hot Water Music Band' as some new group that had just signed to one of the major labels and was trying to sue them and steal the name. HWM fought this and won fairly easily, proving they had been releasing records under their band name for some time already. My copy and all the early presses on Doghouse had this temporary band name on the cover, but the later versions, from No Idea, Defiance and now Rise Records, all came out with the correct name on them again.

The album on Doghouse did however cause a few problems with Var at No Idea, who was understandably feeling let down by them moving labels. The band came back to Europe for another tour but by then were considering breaking up. That was the tour we were playing gigs on. This later led to the 'Live at the Hardback' gig, which was meant to be their last, but instead came out as a live album on No Idea as they patched things up with Var. The band did work on their own side projects around that time too, to get some space. Blacktop Cadence, Unitas and Rumbleseat, but also produced two more HWM 7"s for No Idea Records which also came out as the 'Moonpies for Misfits' CD EP too.

When Hot Water Music got back together later in '98 it was to record the awesome 'No Division' album for Some Records, a new label started up by Walter Schriefels of Gorilla Biscuits, Quicksand and at that time, Rival Schools. (At the time of writing, Walter was playing in Walking Concert, but he has now reformed Quicksand). HWM recorded at sessions in Gainsville and Richmond as it had backing vocals from Walter and also Tim

Barry and Erik Larsson of Avail, with the brilliant call and response in 'It's hard to know' where they all shout 'Live your heart and never follow'. The album was released in '99 alongside several other compilations and splits, including the great BYO-released split with Leatherface, which led to more shows in Europe, where Rydell would again be lucky enough to play a few more gigs with them.

After this it was the Warped tour and more widespread growth for the band as they signed with Epitaph and recorded 'A Flight and a Crash', then 'Caution' and then 'The New What Next'. Brett and Var did a deal so that the new HWM CDs would come out on Epitaph whilst the coloured vinyl LPs would continue to be released by No Idea. There were quite a few more great split releases too, including a 7" on Second Nature Recordings with The Casket Lottery, and a great CD and picture disc 12" on Jade Tree with Alkaline Trio where the bands cover each other's songs. After this the band took another, longer break and concentrated mainly on solo projects, but also a new band called The Draft, involving three of the four members of HWM. Eventually they'd get back together properly and when they played the 2011 Fest in Chicago a double album live recording of the gig came out on No Idea Records. The band then signed with Rise Records and released 'Exister', followed by a twentieth anniversary four-LP collection, and then the 'Light It Up' album. To bring you more or less up to date, the band have just recorded their eighth studio album, titled 'Feel the void' and released via End Hits Records in Europe and Equal Vision Records in the USA. It is an absolute return to form with twelve impassioned and energetic tracks seeing them push through personal darkness and global uncertainty by using the band to bring them strength together.

Chuck Ragan, one of their two singer / guitarists, said about it, "This is so much more than just a band. A lot of people understood a long time ago that we used Hot Water Music as a vehicle for our own therapy, to help get over barriers and be able to continue when we're feeling at our lowest or feeling like the rest of the world is against us. Years ago, that was the choice that we made as a band. It's not about being popular or making money or seeing your name on a marquee. This is a way for us to release all this angst and inspiration and positivity and share music that drives us to become better people, better friends, and better communities. It literally started with four of us, and over the years it became so much more than just a band. I'm just so incredibly honoured to be a piece of this puzzle."

Back on the tour though they were clearly out of sorts, having hassles at home between No Idea and Some, as well as personal issues to deal with. They were trying to make light of it and get on, but at one point Chuck took a call from home to hear that his dog had been beaten up by a neighbour, and he was clearly upset and distraught from the news. I never once saw any of them argue or have raised words between each other, so they seemed to be dealing with whatever the problems were very well. And it certainly didn't affect their playing. Tonight's show was another cracker, despite the smaller crowd. The HWM guys performed with black lines under their eyes made from strips of gaffa tape, in American football player / 7-Seconds style. I'm not sure why, I think they were cracking up a bit, but it looked cool and I have a few photos from the gig.

After the show, we all stayed at the promoter's house. This guy's home was pitch black, it just didn't seem to have any working lights, and when Duncan got up for a piss and thought he was pushing the door open, it was actually a wide screen TV, that went crashing to the floor. After that the guy found some lamps and we noticed that there were a lot of weird things in the room with us, pith helmets and animal skins, and in one corner a small bar, which was soon emptied. In the morning, the guy, whose parents house it actually was, told us he played in a band too and they had a new demo out called 'Vasectomy prevents abortion'. He produced a copy to give to Adam who asked him to describe their style of music and he said, "Oh, you know, noise." We then asked why they hadn't played with us as support the previous night and his reply was, "Ah, well, no-one can be bothered really." We gave up.

Thurs 28/5/98 Hot Water Music, Rydell and Suburban Noise C.S.A.O. Pesaro, Italy

In the morning, we drove in convoy with the HWM guys down the coast towards Pesaro, as that's where the next gig was. The sun was shining and the journey was long, so we pulled into a petrol station and all agreed to detour into Rimini and spend some time on the beach. While we were there discussing this, three very dodgy tracksuit-wearing mafia types turned up and tried to sell us some cameras, no doubt stolen, right there on the forecourt. They wanted 100,000 lira, about fifty quid, but were willing to barter. This was still a year before the euro was introduced. They'd turned around and put something camera shaped in a bag, but glued the zip shut, and were trying to pull some kind of clumsy switcheroo on us. We politely declined their offer, and they became a bit lairy, shouting and gesturing. I thought it was going to kick off right there. There were ten of us big hairy bastards and just three of them, so I figured either they had a gun, or knives, or were totally insane, or a mixture of all three, so thinking the better of it, we ushered everyone back into the vehicles and got the hell out of there.

The beach at Rimini was a bit odd, it reminded me of a previous trip when Couch Potatoes visited Sylt Island, although this place was much sunnier, everywhere was expensive and closed off to the public unless you wanted to pay for it. Seats on the beach cost money, the cafes were very expensive and clearly didn't want a bunch of smelly punkers just hanging around. This wasn't really a good place for us to relax after all. The Americans wanted to keep on and try it out, as we still had hours to kill, but I could see this wasn't going to go well so decided to visit San Marino instead. The world's smallest republic was literally only twelve miles inland from where we were, and I'd always wanted to go.

The Most Serene Republic of San Marino is a European microstate, entirely landlocked and surrounded by Italy. It covers a land area of just 24 square miles but has a population of over 33,500 who enjoy a high GDP per capita, making them one of the richest countries, per person, in the world. Also, they recently became the smallest country in the world to win an Olympic medal, when their women's trap shooter (sounds bad!) managed a bronze. I didn't know about any of that, but wanted to visit San Marino City at the top of Mount Titan, as let's face it, that sounds cool. There could be monsters, or transformers, or aliens, maybe all three lurking up there. It took us a while to traverse the narrow single lane roads in and out, up and down, following diesel-blowing trucks and shuddering, struggling three-wheeled Piaggio Apes trying to climb up that hill. But it was well worth it. The place was beautiful. Modern day amenities in medieval castles atop steep hills with views that went on forever, and what seemed like half the population wearing smart uniforms of green and red, or blue and gold, replete with brass and feathers, and guns and swords. This town was cool. We grabbed some ice-creams and went to sit on the highest wall we could find, peering over the edge at the bone-shattering drop below. We accosted some fellow tourists to take a few 'band photos' up there, well why not? And then headed back down the hill towards punkville and the reality of our next show.

We eventually found the CSAO Club in Pesaro and, of course, Hot Water Music were already there. They'd set up, sound-checked, and were now sitting around bored out of their heads. We told them they really should have come with us. This club seemed to have a lot of football memorabilia on the walls, so I'm pretty sure it was a football supporters club as well as a music venue. There was a sign saying Cucaracha painted on the wall above the door with a large cockroach next to it, and near to that another bright painting, this one of Che Guevara, the Cuban communist and guerrilla leader, in black and red, holding his fist up in defiance. It was the entire size of the wall. Duncan liked that mural and we took a few pics of him in front of it re-creating the pose.

This would be a similar show to the previous night, but maybe 150 people came along this time, so a few more, but still not packed. It was a good job really as there seemed to be no air-conditioning in the club and it was boiling. The first band on, Suburban Noise, really rocked out and the place became even hotter. I loved the Descendents and All, and they had a bit of that going on in their style, short sharp blasts of punk, but with plenty of clever riffs and timings. They were clearly accomplished musicians. There was just the three of them in Suburban Noise; Luca, Luigi and Stefano, but they all sang and played, and sweated a lot whilst making quite a lot of noise. Rydell followed them and sweated a lot too. Then HWM went on and were amazing as usual. The HC kids that were there went crazy and this became a very sweaty show all around.

Later, someone came over and bizarrely, apropos of nothing, wanted a photo of Duncan's tooth fillings. Milo was chatting with Chris Wollard about his new side project band, Blacktop Cadence, comparing it to bands like Seam. Chris already had a tape of some new tracks and lent it to us to check out.

That night we all slept in the club, on the floor, or across chairs and tables. Let's just say that it wasn't comfortable, so we were up most of the night, partly due to Tom's constant burping and farting. We were comparing English and American jokes and draining whatever we found behind the bar. A typical dodgy American joke seemed to start like this "Three Hispanics walk into McDonalds..." and end with "Big Mac please!" No, we didn't get it either. By now Tom Husman, the Doghouse guy, who'd been telling us that he was the original singer of Majority of One from way back in the day in Toledo, and that he'd taken the photos of the band for their first EP, 'Decisions Made', had now climbed up onto the stage and was lying next to Milo. He fell asleep and was snoring like a chainsaw. It woke Milo up and he would definitely have rolled him right off the stage if he could have moved him. I may have been losing it, due to lack of sleep, but I swear in the morning we were woken up by nuns coming in to clean the place and shifting us all out of their way.

Fri 29/5/98 Hot Water Music, Rydell and Kenza Neke
Leon Cavallo, Milan, Italy

After being chucked out of the cockroach club by over-zealous nuns we looked for some swimming baths or anywhere to wash and then get breakfast. The gigs on this trip were great but the comfort levels left a little to be desired. We had to get back up to the north of Italy as our next show was in Milan at a massive squat called the Leon Cavallo. It was about 275 miles from Pesaro to Milan, probably a four-hour drive right up the spine of the country so we figured we'd better get rolling. Our light-speed mobile travelled a lot faster than the big black tour van Hot Water Music were in, so we agreed to meet them there and wished them a safe journey. We headed northwest past Bologna, Modena, Reggio Emilia, Parma, Piacenza, and lots of places that just made me feel even hungrier. We stopped to get food.

Driving around Italian cities isn't easy, especially when you haven't slept in the last week or so, but despite plenty of honking, gesturing and near misses, we eventually found the Leon Cavallo Social Centre in Via Watteau, in the industrial area near the centre of Milan. I was glad we were there without having to resort to any serious road rage. This place was huge. It used to be a paper mill with its own warehouses, but it had been taken over as a punk and socialist squat. The entire building was covered in colourful graffiti, but good stuff that had been put there with care and a reason. It was like an art gallery. The venue was surrounded by towering blocks of brutalist flats and a few more run-down warehouses and factories. But it seemed to be the only one with any signs of life and was clearly in an area the council would like to develop, if they could just move the punks on. We drove into the main courtyard where a few trees and some raised vegetable beds greeted us, and pulled up in front of a cafe with lots of

The Leon Cavallo Social Centre in Milan

A scrapbook page of photos from the Euro tour showing
Hot Water Music, Rydell and El Guapo Stunt Team

plastic tables and chairs outside. The HWM van was nowhere to be seen, but there were a few other bangers abandoned there that looked like they could barely drive. I'd parked next to them, suddenly overtly aware that I'd driven an almost new Audi to a punk squat, and was now feeling a bit self-conscious about our choice of tour vehicle. We climbed out and stretched our legs, noticing immediately that the main crop for the café wasn't fruit or vegetables, but seemed to be hemp plants. We wandered up a ramp to the right of the café into the main warehouse building and looked inside. We were just in awe.

This was possibly the biggest venue we had ever played. An absolutely enormous stage stood at one end of the cavernous hall, with a full-size skate ramp off to one side, a sound mixing tower in the middle with bars and a restaurant at the other end. It was Milan's official anarchist centre and squat. It was just so well organised and full of people. This place was impressive. This would be the 1 in 12 Club on steroids if there were any space left in the UK for such things. The warehouse covered nearly 10,000 square metres and as we walked around, we could see art and photography areas, a bicycle repair shop, a printing press, and even their own radio station. One of the guys told me that they fed the local homeless in the community kitchen and ran language courses for immigrants too. It was a hell of a place.

These shows were being promoted by Green Hell Records all over Europe, but the locals had obviously done a good job too. This was way bigger than the TU Club in Vienna and they regularly had audiences of up to 1000 people at shows, although they weren't sure what it'd be tonight, but hoped for a good one. A couple more of the squat's main guys came over to say ciao and Milo was transfixed by one of the promoters with incredibly manky teeth, that he just kept sucking on. We had to turn away, and luckily, saw the Hot Water Music tour van arrive. They piled in and were greeted by the promoters too. Chuck saw the ramp and borrowed a deck. Before long he was off, skateboarding on the vert ramp in a pretty accomplished manner, with those black lines of gaffa tape under his eyes again. He still didn't look too happy though, maybe the call about his dog, maybe he was just tired, maybe something else, so we ventured over to chat with him and see if a couple of dopey English kids could cheer him up. He wasn't keen and this was not like him. Chuck Ragan was normally the most positive and friendly guy you could ever meet. Duncan wanted to have a go on the ramp, he was the best skater amongst us and pretty adept, but he was also our drummer and he'd already broken both his wrists before, stagediving at a Gang Green gig in London with me. I think that was partly why he played with such an odd jazz style. But nevertheless, we weren't about to let him skate just before a gig, so we dragged him and Chuck off to the café to see what was cooking.

The UK Subs, Youth of Today and Sick Of It All had played here shortly before us and Fugazi, Rocket From The Crypt and Boy Sets Fire would all play here soon after us too, so this venue was clearly no stranger to good hardcore shows. Tonight's gig would be opened by an Italian folk-rock band called Kenza Neke, who turned out to be Italy's answer to The Levellers. They had a new album out called 'Equal Freedoms' which was sure to appeal to this crowd. By the time we went on after them the place was absolutely heaving, and that crowd would have enjoyed themselves and danced along no matter who was onstage. Good for us, and we rocked out, playing the longest set possible with a couple of new tracks we'd been working on. It was brilliant fun, although at one point, Milo broke a string and the re-invigorated Chuck was there immediately, loaning him his black Les Paul. Now that was a decent guitar, but incredibly heavy if you weren't used to it, and Milo was very careful with it for the last couple of songs. We packed up our gear and moved it to the back of the stage, then waited for Hot Water Music to come on and blow the roof off the place. As we stood waiting, one of the sound guys came over and handed us a soundboard recording of our set. That was unexpected and we thanked him. Unfortunately, it turned out to be pretty bad quality mix-wise, as it was for stage levels, but it was still exciting to listen to on the way back later, so we could hear how the newer songs sounded live.

Then Hot Water Music came on and opened up with 'Better Sense'. The whole place went crazy and started bouncing around. HWM were amazing and by now we knew all the new songs so could singalong too. They just seemed to get better each night, mixing up the set a little, but playing with just as much commitment to the smaller crowds as the larger ones. It was a joy to watch. When they'd finished, after two encores demanded by the crowd, we went over to congratulate them and help move the equipment back out to the van. We thanked them for the shows this week and reminded them that we'd back for more gigs next weekend with them in Germany. We honestly couldn't wait. By that stage we only had a couple of copies of the split single left, so we gave them to Tom to sell on the merch table, as he'd been doing such a good job of it, selling all our Food Not Bombs 7"s, all our Unlabel CDs, all our demos, and all but about eight copies of the new split single so far too – the release we had by far the most of. Luckily Dennis had many more and had promised to bring them along next week for the German part of the tour. For now though, HWM were off to France and Spain, and we were off home to the UK. We wished them all the best for their next shows, and they wished us a safe trip and looked forward to seeing us in Cologne.

We headed out of Italy, driving north like speed demons up to Switzerland, taking the Gotthard Tunnel under the Alps, one of the longest road tunnels in Europe at over 10 miles long, and zooming on through parts of France, Luxembourg, Belgium and Holland until we finally reached the ferry port. Yet another 675 miles and about eleven hours of driving behind us. We took shifts on this last leg of the journey though, with Adam having a go and then Milo too, but Milo drives like Postman Pat and terrified us all, so that didn't last too long. I couldn't sleep so took over again, wary of police and cameras, but driving flat-out, pedal to the metal for as long as I

Dennis with a recently shaved Chuck

Tom Husman (RIP)

could. How we didn't crash and die on that trip is a miracle really. I guess it was just a good job I'd had all that sleep.

The Milan gig was on Friday night, but we had to be back home at some point on Saturday as it was Adam's mum's birthday and he'd told her he'd take her out for a Chinese with his brother, Paul. Believe me, Mrs French was not to be crossed when she'd been promised an outing with her boys, so we made it back and dropped him off in plenty of time for their meal. Then we headed the last few miles down the A21 home for a well-earned night's sleep in a comfortable bed.

As it happens, I had to be at Gatwick airport the next day to catch a flight to Helsinki as I had some work stuff to do in Finland that week. I also wanted to see my friend Nick, the guy I mentioned way back in the first chapter, who was one of the very first to jam on guitars with me. We wanted to catch up and go visit the tractor bar. I had a busy week in Scandinavia then flew back to the UK on Friday, giving me a few hours to sort things out before our next trip. We would be leaving early in the morning to catch the Eurotunnel car shuttle from Folkestone to Calais and head on into Germany where we had a couple more gigs booked with Hot Water Music over the weekend. I couldn't wait.

Hot Water Music and Rydell tour party outside the Leon Cavallo in Milan

29, Time of our times

Sat 6/6/98 Hot Water Music and Rydell
Between Club, Cologne, Germany.
Sun 7/6/98 Hot Water Music and Rydell
Subkultur, Hannover, Germany.

We headed straight to the Scene Police headquarters in Bonn where we met up with Dennis, his girlfriend Elke, and a couple of their friends, to help fold and stuff a load more of the Hot Water Music / Rydell split 7"s into their sleeves and take them with us to the shows. The covers looked so cool with Blanco's artwork, and we were stoked to have this record for the gigs. Dennis pointed out the band photo inside was one he'd taken of us playing with 999 at the youth club in Troisdorf less than three months before. It was blurry but you could just see the 999 backdrop lurking behind me and Milo. This had all been arranged so quickly, both the tour and the record, and we were grateful to Dennis and enjoying every moment of it. We loaded up all we could and followed Elke's car in convoy over to Cologne, where tonight's show would be.

Heading into the venue, we immediately saw Tom Husman and Stefaan, laying out the merch table at the side, so we gave them a load of split 7"s to restock with, and then went over to the HWM guys, setting up on stage. We put down our guitars and greeted them, but something looked odd. They'd all cut their hair short and shaved. Chuck in particular had gone extreme, totally shaving his head and face. With all that usual hair gone it looked like a young skinhead kid was standing in his place. He was grinning away though and Dennis and Elke took him outside to take a few photos. We spoke briefly with all the HWM guys about what they'd been up to through the week, and it sounded like they'd had a tough time with some low turn-out shows. Germany would be better we hoped, usually by far the best crowds for hardcore gigs in Europe.

Both the shows we had coming up were in smaller rock clubs, the Between in Cologne and the Subkultur in Hannover, both known for their heavy and alternative music, and both regular tour stops for hardcore bands. Each could hold a couple of hundred people and were pretty much full on these nights as word about Hot Water Music was starting to spread. As the bands played, people in the audience were ripping up tickets, flyers, and any posters they could find, then throwing them like confetti at the band. In Hannover some guy was trying to film the show and was getting really annoyed as the pieces kept landing on his video camera lens.

These shows were great fun. There were a lot of people at the Cologne show who we already knew so that gave us even more confidence. Plus, we were staying in Bonn with Dennis, so we'd get some sleep too. It all helps. In Hannover, Hot Water Music opened with 'Better Sense' as they always seemed to. It had such impact. They followed it with a fast version of 'Just don't say you lost it' and mentioned the split single, which was already flying out. Then, going into 'Rest Assured' they were bouncing around like mad things. They'd set the mic stands up high and were stretching to reach them, shouting at them from a distance as the crowd joined in. It was raucous and great. Everyone was involved. Chris and Chuck's voices were very hoarse, even more than normal. Chuck had almost totally lost his and it was cracking in every song now. They seemed to be enjoying themselves onstage, but the tour was definitely taking a toll on them.

Then it was that beautiful gentle guitar line and Chris shouting "Prepare Yourself!" as they went into 'Position'. Hot Water Music were basically rocking their way through all of 'Forever and Counting'. As they jumped around, Jason seemed to be the only one staying in tune, so they stopped briefly to tune up before launching into 'Alachua'. "This one's for Thorsten," said Chris, pointing out the grinning promoter, and off they went again. A rolling, rumbling wall of noise, but with melody and control woven all the way through. It was all played at a much higher speed and intensity than the recorded album. Both Chuck and Chris hammered away on their Les Pauls, while Jason played the bass with his fingers on what looked like a Fender Precision, he played everything so fast but never missed a note, and George sat behind them all, smiling to himself and keeping a tight beat. It was a joy to watch, and boy these gigs were fun. I didn't want them to end. But it was hot and sweaty in there, the venue had drapes hung behind the stage and along each side of the hall, so the humidity just seemed to hang there, trapped in the room. There was sweat running down the walls. It reminded me of the old Rumble Club back in Tunbridge Wells. Chris took off his shirt to wring it out and showed off his flames over water HWM tramp stamp tattoo, so everyone threw the paper confetti at him, and it stuck to him. Chuck's guitar had gone out of tune again now and it took him a while to sort it out, so Jason tried to get Tom up on stage to tell a few of his terrible jokes. When he wouldn't, George played some jazzy drumbeats while we all waited, but before long they were ready again and the chaos ensued.

They played a couple of newer songs too, the frantic 'Moments Pass' was followed soon after by a mellower moment in the set and another new track, 'Moonpies for Misfits'. This calm was followed by 'Where We Belong' and the great riffing and shout-a-long choruses were back again. (These crackers would later come out on 7"s and then on a four-track 'Moonpies for Misfits' CD, all in '99 on No Idea Records). Hot Water Music played for about fifty minutes, but when they finished their set, they just walked off stage. They just wouldn't play any more even with the crowd doing a slow handclap. It was a strange way to end such a great gig, and there was clearly something up in the HWM camp.

Rydell in Germany

El Guapo Stunt Team

Belting it out!

Hot Water Music in Germany

Rydell soundcheck

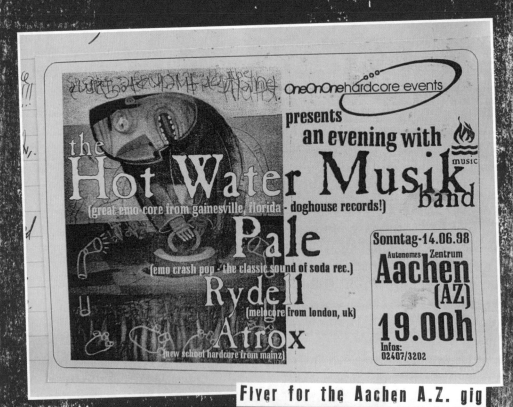

OneOnOne hardcore events

presents
an evening with

the Hot Water Musik band

(great emo-core from gainesville, florida - doghouse records!)

Pale

(emo crash pop - the classic sound of soda rec.)

Rydell

(melocore from london, uk)

Atrox

(new school hardcore from mainz)

Sonntag-14.06.98
Autonomes Zentrum
Aachen (AZ)
19.00h

Infos:
02407/3202

Flyer for the Aachen A.Z. gig

We had to get rolling and drive back through the night as we all had work on Monday. We hugged and thanked everyone, saying our goodbyes, and then hammered off westwards along autobahn no. 2 leaving the HWM guys to head further east into Germany.

During the week we were home, the Promise Ring toured the UK so we all went to see them. It was a tricky one, as on the same day, Wednesday 10/6, Rancid were playing at The Astoria in London and that would have been good too, but we opted for the Promise Ring. Typically, they then came back to the UK a week or so later, so we got to see them again, on 17/6, at The Garage too. Anyway, they were another favourite band of mine and I'd been to see them on their previous tour too, both in Brighton and London, but neither of those gigs went very well.

Brighton was their first ever UK show, and it seemed that they were unaware that gigs in pubs had to end by 11pm so they went off exploring the town. Their support act, a very Quicksand-esque German band called Water Breaks Stone were doing their best to entertain everyone, but it was getting a little heated. When the Promise Ring finally arrived back at the venue about 10.45 there wasn't much to be done. In their defence, they grabbed their guitars and absolutely belted out five songs for the few of us who had stuck around to see them.

The London show was at The Hope and Anchor in Islington, a terrible little basement venue that was usually a pay-to-play sort of place. It was a matinee show and really badly run because the posters weren't clear on the starting time. I have no idea who the promoters were or what they were up to. Despite the room only being about half full, the venue also had some kind of strict capacity rule, so when many people arrived late, including our good friends Dan, Syd and Rachel who we'd agreed to meet there, they just wouldn't let them in.

Sat 13/6/98 Rydell and El Guapo Stunt Team
`t Skut, Aalbeke, Belgium
Also Sat 13/6/98 Rydell, Tumult and Logical Nonsense
Between Club, Cologne, Germany
Sun 14/6/98 Hot Water Music, Rydell, Pale and Atrox
Jugendculture, Aachen, Germany

Rydell were back again the next weekend for more shows in Europe, where we were getting popular because of our releases there, and finding it easier to get good shows. We started with an all-dayer at 't Skut in Aalbeke, Belgium. 't Skut meant The Shot and it was another café come youth club that was used as a music venue. It was busy when we arrived and looked like a good show was underway, with people already inside and spilling outside too. T' Skut had friendly bar staff who offered us beers the second we walked in the door, then pointed us towards the low stage with a shooting gun backdrop and walls covered, as always, in graffiti, but this time in an Eighties gangster rap style.

This venue wasn't far from the famous Vort 'n' Vis in Ieper (Ypres) and is also very near where the big Alcatraz heavy metal festival is held each year now, so definitely a good area to draw a crowd from. We'd been booked to play late in the afternoon, going on after a bunch of nutters called The El Guapo Stunt Team. These guys dressed in capes and masks like those worn by Mexican wrestlers. They had about four guitarists who all tried to sing, a drummer in a crash helmet and a girl in her underwear breathing fire on stage. They came up with various theatrics and plenty of crazy guitar surfing dances, so were a very hard act to follow.

We watched their set and soon realised that the lead singer only spoke between songs in Elvis quotes, saying things like; "Love me tender, love me true", "Take my hand, take my whole life too. I can't help falling in love with you", his favourite, "Lord almighty, I feel my temperature rising" and at the end of every song, "Thankyou. Thank you very much". That was funny enough, but they introduced songs about Evel Knievel, Betty Crocker, King Fatso, and the Duke of Danger too. These guys clearly lived in their own crazy garage rock world and ought to have been huge, if only for the sheer entertainment value they provided. Duncan took some great photos of them, saying they reminded him of a European BBMFs.

So Rydell followed that. No problem. Afterwards we went outside, where everyone was now sitting down to watch a football match and having a BBQ. This place was great. The phone rang and it was Dennis. He said that Hot Water Music had basically split up a couple of days before and gone off in various directions. He thought a couple of them had headed to Amsterdam and they certainly wouldn't be joining us at the show in Belgium today. Now that sucked. There was, however, another show going on in Germany that evening which we could play if we could get there in time. It was in Cologne with the local power-violence band, Tumult. Well, that was only about two hundred miles / three hours away, we could be there by 9pm easy. Let's go.

We sped along the E40 and A4 at breakneck speed and made it into Cologne around 9.30pm. We headed downstairs at the Between Club, where we'd played with HWM the week before, and were back onstage before 10pm, sandwiched between two heavy grind-core bands, Logical Nonsense from the USA and Tumult, the German locals. The show was brilliant fun, a spontaneous extra bonus gig. We couldn't really keep up with the technical thrash racket all around us, but we rocked out anyway and had a right old time of it.

Logical Nonsense had just signed with Alternative Tentacles. They absolutely filled the stage and bounced all around it, playing an aggressive and heavy fast-paced hardcore that reminded me of early hardcore / metal crossover bands like Extreme Noise Terror, Heresy, Carcass, Napalm Death, Electro Hippies and Bolt Thrower. It was noisy and sweaty, and an interesting way to be welcomed into a small basement.

Tumult were a bunch of utter maniacs who played insanely fast all the time too. Their album on Per Koro Records had 22 songs on it and clocked in at about 15 minutes. It was mad. They made Napalm Death look like real slouches. Tumult were all lovely, funny guys though. One of their guitarists, Dirk, a slick-looking dude with a quiff who we all called the Diggler, had a good line in Hawaiian shirts, and seemed to have a new one every time he came along to a Rydell gig. Milo had met him when he stayed with Dennis earlier in the year and met the Revolution Inside guys too. He told us to ask Dirk about his special briefcase, as this was where he kept his favourite porno mags, with 666 as the combination code, which he'd proudly open up and show anyone who asked. Their singer, Marco Andree, went on to be a labelmate of ours on Scene Police Records in a band called April. Another noisy gang of speed-merchants. While they played, we'd shout at them; "Come on, don't you guys know any fast ones?" and stupid shit like that, to which they'd just laugh and blast out another 30 second explosion of mayhem. All the time Marco would encourage perfect strangers in the crowd to "Fucken Mosh!" about an inch from their face. It was another crazy night of fun and afterwards we all went for veggie falafel.

We stayed with Dennis at SPHQ that night and took it easy the next day, playing records and reading comics, then later visiting a few record shops, and trying to make calls to find out if Hot Water Music were coming back for tonight's show. I'm very glad to say that it looked like they were, so later in the afternoon we headed west on the A4, back past the big Haribo sweets factory, towards the border and Aachen.

The venue for tonight's show was another Jugendculture, or youth club, but this one in Aachen was a huge bomb shelter near the railway station with massive iron doors and colourful graffiti all over the thick concrete walls. It was clearly left-over from the second world war, but the venue had been modernised inside and had ideal sound-proofing so could put on noisy punk and metal bands right in the centre of a very well-to-do town. I'd visited before with Couch Potatoes on tour and was glad to be back. I was also looking forward to meeting up with the other band that were playing with us this evening, called Pale.

Pale were a great rock band, post-punk before their time really, sounding like a cool mix of The Jam or The Who meets The Promise Ring or The Get Up Kids. At this point I'd only heard their 'Drop Pants For Food' album on Soda Records after Dennis or Emre had sent me a copy, but soon we'd have a split single out with them, called 'Today Stopped Counting', with two versions, one on black and one on white vinyl, on Soda Records. They'd later have great albums out on Defiance Records, 'Another Smart Move', 'Razzmatazz (The Arts at the Sands)', and 'How to Survive Chance'. It helped that Holger, Christian, Hilly and Stephan were really good guys and easy to hang out with, so this would be the first of many great gigs we'd play with them all around Germany and the UK.

(Pale would later add a fifth member, Jost, on keyboards and sign to an even bigger German indie label called Grand Hotel Van Cleef, who released records for US bands like Maritime and Death Cab For Cutie, as well as great German bands like Kettcar and Muff Potter. Pale's album for them, 'Brother, Sister, Bores!', is often overlooked but well worth checking out as it essentially continues the creative progression they made through the Defiance releases).

There were flyers all over town with cool Sinc / HWM style artwork on them announcing 'One On One hardcore events presents an evening with; The Hot Water Music Band (great emo-core from Gainesville, Florida on Doghouse Records), Pale (emo crash pop, the classic sound of Soda Records), Rydell (Melo-core from London, UK) and Atrox (new school hardcore from Mainz), Sunday 14th June at the Aachen Autonomes Zentrum all kicking off at 7pm'. It had a contact telephone number but no door price or age of admission. It was an invitation for an evening out, a free for all, and it looked good.

Anyway, there was a fourth band on the bill, going on first, called Atrox. These guys were another German punk group, a five-piece and a lot noisier and more hardcore than Pale, with a new EP out on Underground Records entitled 'Who is free to choose?' They turned out to be a very good band too and went on to sign with Rockstar Records for a couple of releases. This gig had a hell of a line-up.

The most important thing were the headliners of course. Hot Water Music were coming back and when their rumbling black tour van rounded the corner and mounted the pavement outside the main doors, we all gave a cheer. Tom, Stefaan, and the four HWM guys all seemed glad to see us. They piled out of the van, and we started to unload the equipment and catch up. Jason told us they'd decided to take a couple of days off to rest and chill out but were back at it now. Fair enough. I was glad they were here, especially as I knew this would be our last show with them on this trip and we all had to head home again after tonight. Let's all make it a good one.

Sure enough, this was an amazing show. Here we were, playing in a huge underground bomb shelter, with our friends Hot Water Music and Pale. It was really good fun, made all the better by loads of free food and drink, and the crowd joining in throughout the show. Milo did manage to break a lot of strings jumping around during our set, and went through three different guitars, so thanks to Chuck and Stefaan for sorting him out the replacements. Special thanks to Dennis, the Scene Police booking deity, for hooking all this up and getting us on the gigs. Also, for giving us loads of extra copies of the HWM/Rydell split 7" to take back to the UK with us and for general all around coolness, we were very glad have him on our side and hoped for a few more mini-tours like this one. We spoke with Hot Water Music and Pale and arranged more gigs in the future, those with Pale coming up soon, but said our goodbyes for now.

Home

Home

Red light runner

Stars break free

Gilsenan

Rydell are: Miles, David, Adam & Duncan.
Recorded by Rydell and Charlie at Recent Studios in London.
Cover Design: Fleece Napier, photo: David
Contact: 3 Underhill Lane, Maresfield, Sussex, TN22 3AY. UK

flame one

firewalk with me

flame one * nineteenninetynine * the sound of noise to come

Thomas Reitmayer
Lerystr. 54/1/21
1110 Wien * Austria
firewalkwithyummy@yahoo.de
Fax: [+43/1] 595 36 12

fear is the only enemy that i know

...sometimes i wonder how many hours of my life i have spent in dirty basements so far, listening to screams and whispers and noises of rage and alienation created by people who had the same goal as me: that this one moment could last forever. because there was nowhere else to go. because i didn't want to be anywhere else anyway. because it was worth it. to the big bad world out there it might seem ridiculous, but at the end of the day i still don't give a fuck. because these are my memories, all mine, and no one in the world can take them away from me. all my collected flyers and stickers might slowly be yellowing from age, the tapes i have stacked under my bed have not been played for years, some tattoos have faded a bit, but they're still there and that's what counts. they're still there, just like my memories. and they won't go away, they can't. because if they do, then it was really nothing more than a phase after all. but all the people that i met along the way, all the conversations that made me think that could change the world, all the letters in my mailbox that saved my day and all that energy was real. and how could i possibly describe it to someone who hasn't been there? even if i put myself at the risk of sounding cheesy, those are the best of times. and this is my attempt to make them last forever.

thank you beaucoup.

Artwork for Thommy's first Firewalk With Me release, the Rydell 'Home' 7"

It was Tom who caught up with us as we were climbing into the car to leave and said what fun it had been, "Remember guys, it's all rock 'n' roll, just enjoy it. Oh, and a Big Mac Please!" That joke still wasn't funny, but that guy was, and he was great to have on tour running the merchandise and managing things, helping everyone out. Tom went on to tour manage loads of great bands, ending up on the road with the Warped Tour, Pixies and Pearl Jam until he succumbed to cancer in 2020, aged just 51. A friendly soul and a superhero HC merch guy. May his legend never die.

Fri 19/6 Hasselt, Sat 20th Nuremberg, Sun 21st Munich. Rydell and Pale 4/7/98 Rydell at Shake Some Action, Croydon, London 18/7/98 Pale, Rydell and Fiction at The Forum, Tunbridge Wells 21/7/98 Rydell, Shaft and Lymph at Fat Pauly's Noisebox, Norwich 30/7/98 Rydell and others at Cairo Jacks, Soho, London

We were back over in Belgium and Germany for three more gigs the next weekend with Pale. Starting on Friday 19/6 in Hasselt, the Belgian city near the borders with Holland and Germany, where those El Guapo Stunt Team lunatics we met in Aalbeke came from. Then heading southeast and far into Germany, playing on Saturday 20th in Nuremberg, a city of rallies and big brass goat balls, but also a lot of punks, and then Sunday 21st in Munich, a city of neo-gothic architecture, friendly people and great beer. Pale were fast developing their great rock meets dance sound, with guitar lines similar to Cross My Heart or Promise Ring, but with lots of clever touches and samples thrown in. We were discussing a split release with them, ideally using our track 'Home' and they would take the idea to their label, Soda Records, and see what could be done.

Soon after this long weekend adventure we played back in the UK again, all through July, first at Shake Some Action, the cool indie record shop in Croydon, where James had made a little more space for bands to play and wanted Rydell to christen it. This would be a Saturday matinee show, of course, so we had to be there by 1pm to sort out and set up, then we played at 2pm, to 20 or 30 baseball-capped and back-packed emo kids crammed into the shop and a handful of passing chavs gawping through the window at us, whilst we rocked around with a slightly mellower set and tried to avoid that column that was still right in the middle of the playing area. That was an intimate show, and we bought a few new records as well as dropping off copies of our split 7" with HWM while we were there. This new release was proving very popular and flying out, mainly because of Hot Water Music, of course, but so much so that I was already speaking with Dennis and Emre about a repress as we'd definitely need more for our upcoming gigs.

The next weekend we were all at our friend Dan's housewarming party and ended up in an impromptu jam there. We had proper practises mid-week too as we were writing more new songs now, developing our style, inspired a lot by HWM and the bands we were playing with. We'd invited Pale over to play in the UK and had a few shows booked with them. Starting with a local opener coming up on Saturday 18th with our buddies

Fiction at the Forum in Tunbridge Wells. The Fiction guys were all local lads. One of them, Graham 'Fleece' Noble, was the designer who worked on the Rydell record covers, another was the manager of the local Our Price record shop, and they played quirky mellow indie. They worked really well as an opener for us, and they brought loads of their friends along too. Both Rydell and Pale had been developing our style along the lines of Samiam meets Texas is the Reason, but our German chums were starting to throw in a few samples now too, pre-recorded electronics from sound effects to dance beats. We stuck with our guitars as traditionalists, but I think Milo still got his tambourine out in a couple of songs, probably for the last time. This was a great gig, the best we'd played at The Forum for a while, and it was good to see all our friends there.

This was the first of a few shows with Pale around the UK and the trip went very well, giving them a great introduction to the scene. They came back over to play several times more and in 2000 Milo booked them a show in Margate, at the Ambulance Station Social Club of all places, as it was the only venue you could book a show in Thanet on a night that wasn't a Friday or Saturday, and importantly, it was free to hire! Margate had a really good hardcore scene, and you could guarantee a decent crowd, so it wasn't as mad as it sounds. Pale also played at The Peel in Kingston on that tour where they opened for Juno, a great indie rock band from Seattle who had singles out on Sub Pop, Jade Tree and Mag Wheel Records, as well as a split EP with the great Dismemberment Plan and two albums on DeSoto Records that are well worth checking out too.

Later in the month Rydell made a mid-week trip up to Norwich to play at Fat Pauly's. This was a snooker club that doubled as an alternative music venue and it had become quite a well-known stop-off on the indie tour circuit, where we'd seen All and Goober Patrol play before. They were calling the Tuesday night slot the Noisebox club and had booked us to headline with two hilariously bad indie grunge bands, Shaft and Lymph, as support. The soundman had a Samiam shirt on and was mad keen on melodic hardcore. He was really into the sort of thing we were playing and just kept on turning us up. I was fine with that, as were the hordes of seventeen-year-old Nirvana wannabees that had turned up too, and we were all jumping around enjoying ourselves without a care in the world. I was having a few tuning problems towards the end of the set and had possibly managed to crack the neck of my guitar, as moments later, wham! I got bashed into by an over-zealous dancer and tripping backwards, somehow managed to catch my beloved black Gibson SG guitar between my amp and the wall, snapping the headstock clean off its neck! I was not impressed. I managed to borrow a guitar to finish up the set and then took mine to be repaired. I thought it was a goner, but the guitar workshop fixed it quickly and it looked seamless. That said, my old SG never quite played right or stayed in tune after that.

The last gig I can remember from that month saw us up in town playing one of those terrible indie band showcase nights that Alan McGee, the founder of Creation Records, had started putting on. Creation had put out some good bands in the early Nineties, including Swervedriver, The Boo Radleys, Sugar and Slowdive. They'd even produced releases for The Cramps and Glen Matlock to turn a few pennies, but now they were peddling some real shite and looking to sell out to Sony as soon as they could. Everyone figured they needed to find the next big thing and we were pretty sure it wasn't lurking, out of tune, in the dark corners of this club. The show was held in the basement of Cairo Jacks, a dodgy pub hidden somewhere between Carnaby Street and the Soho red-light district. The girl setting up the shows said she was providing A&R for various labels and they wanted five 'up and coming' indie acts to perform for Mr McGee and all his industry mates, plus anyone else who could blag a ticket, to sit in judgment on. I don't remember how we got onto this bill, but we didn't mind being called 'up and coming' in the indie scene and we'd play pretty much any show.

We had to wait around for ages, but this wasn't too bad as Davey Blanco had come along and we all got to meet his girlfriend, who'd been on the cover of our new release with Hot Water Music. Duncan had brought along his new lady too, who I believe he called Miss Peabody for some reason. We never saw her again and I still don't know who she was. I didn't think we were that bad. Getting bored, Milo, Dan Pullin and I were hanging around outside when some smooth operator in a silk suit walked past us with a page three girl on his arm, he paused and looked over, saying with a cheesy grin, "Hey guys, what do you think, sexy or what?" gesturing to his date, who clearly embarrassed, hurried off. The dude followed her but as he left Dan P, in a very out of character moment, yelled after him "I dunno mate, I never see her face coz I always fuck her from behind!"

When we finally got to play, Rydell went on well after midnight and between two terrible grunge wannabee bands, like an early morning emo sandwich. We gave it our best shot, but were limited in time to five or six tracks. We relied on Adam and Dunk to keep it tight, with me noodling around on a borrowed guitar and Milo's voice breaking regularly whenever he tried to hold a note. Being hardcore kids just back from tour we quite liked that, but I'm not sure anyone else did. Suffice to say, we didn't get a call to join the major label sell-out party just yet, but they did ask us to come back and play again sometime.

By now the Hot Water Music / Rydell split 7" on Scene Police Records had been out for about two months and Dennis, Emre and I had all been busy sending copies of it to as many magazines and fanzines as possible, asking for reviews. We were also sending them to promoters and radio stations and anyone else we thought might help with PR or promotion. And of course, we were trading them with other record labels, selling them through distros, mail-order and at gigs, as well as giving a load to HWM to take with them back to the US too. The first pressing of 1000 singles was just about gone, so the second pressing was already underway, and this would be followed by four more pressings, each of around 1000 copies, adding up to around 6000 copies with six different covers over a period of two years or so. During that time, we played a lot more shows with Hot Water Music and it was great fun! It surprised us how popular the release was, all due to HWM of course, but each time we ran out of singles and had more requests in, we considered another pressing. Each release would have a different cover and apart from the classic original first pressing with the full colour David S Blanco artwork, my favourite version was the sixth, pressed on clear transparent vinyl with mistletoe on the front cover and a great photo taken of us all standing on the ramp outside the Leon Cavallo show in Milan. The first four presses were Scene Police only, the last two presses came out later when I'd started Ignition / Engineer Records and were jointly between both labels.

Rydell / Hot Water Music split 7″ reviews

Anvil #3 – Emo is what is on offer here, the real thing. On this new release Hot Water Music, from Gainesville, deliver a song that is sharper and yet rougher than most of the genre. Rydell from London's song 'Try Seventeen' explodes and then hits you with a familiarity, then the guitars sit quiet and sober as the drums roll and the vocals uncover themselves. These guys are coming on tour so we may meet, and what new products they may bring after we can only dream. (Amboss zine, Germany)

HeartattaCk #20 – Melodic and rockin' Hot Water Music and Rydell each offer up one tune. HWM are what you would expect from a melodic high energy band that still maintains some edge in their sound. I assume most have heard of their countless releases by now. Rydell are less edgy with sort of moody back woods feel to the vocal delivery. In a vague way they remind me a bit of Lungfish, though this is the one and only Rydell song I have heard so it is hard to make much of a comparison. (KM).

Only A Phase #3 – At the moment HWM are one of the best bands out there for me, but this song was already on the 'Forever and counting' album so I guess once is enough. Rydell used to be called Couch Potatoes and still play a kind of Dischord version of older Samiam, which is very beautiful in this case. Musically there's nothing wrong with this record, and furthermore it has a nice cover.

WorldWidePunk – You need to hear Rydell, they are a powerful and original emo-punk band from the UK.

Spread – HWM are the toast of many with their mixed sound, Lifetime meets Fuel. Rydell are the UKs Chamberlain, and it shows on this song.

Yummy - The usual high class driving emotional hardcore from Hot Water Music together with an almost brit-pop-ish song from Rydell that gets the Yummy top hit award.

Flying Revolving Blade #18 - Just a quick mention of this new release from Scene Police Records through Revolution Inside as it will be commented on more next time. So here we have a song from each band, both are emocore with the A side first having noisy impact, and then not much different on the other side, but it is a bit slower, more tearful and poppier.

Blurr #17 – The new release from Scene Police for the English band Rydell, who used to be the Couch Potatoes, and this time on vinyl. On side one, the musicians from HWM bring nice heartachey melancholic emo with a lot of feeling. Nice. On the flip side the islanders already mentioned above. It is a little more difficult for me to get into it, but I think that after a few listens this will grow dear to my heart. Emo again and very successful. I am looking forward to hearing more.

Collective zine - First up on the review pile is this 7″. I'm shocked because Scene Police have somehow managed to put this out for a very reasonable price (I paid a quid for it). Sure, it's only two tracks (one by each band) but a full colour, glossy gatefold sleeve as well?!? And when the two bands in question are of such a high calibre it's pretty much the all-round perfect package.

Rydell are from the UK and have a penchant for emo-rock in the vein of bands like Chamberlain. I apologise if that's the third review in a row that we mention Rydell and Chamberlain in the same sentence, but I'll be the first to admit that my knowledge of emo-rock is limited, and the two bands do sound similar. 'Try Seventeen' is driving and powerful, a myriad blur of guitars and passionate vocals. Its compares very favourably with other tracks I've heard from this band.

Hot Water Music are from across the other side of the pond and contribute 'Just Don't Say You Lost It'. Infectious drums and gruff vocals ahoy. They strike me as a hardcore band where the rest of the band have been replaced with, say a group of emo minded musicians, except no one told the lead singer and he still believes that his band is a hardcore band, only playing a little more slowly. While Rydell steal the show with this 7″ I'm really looking forward to hearing some more HWM.
One very nice 7″ and a very nice price. (Ian Cavell).

Room Thirteen - Rydell's first release is a split 7″ with HOT WATER MUSIC, released to coincide with a European tour the two bands did together. This tour did not include the UK, however, when HOT WATER MUSIC came to the UK the following year the two bands played together again, and have continued to do so.

Rydell's sound has evolved over the years but comparisons are often drawn with the likes of older GET UP KIDS for the pop element, CAP'N JAZZ for the chaos, BRAID for the indie-rock, SPLIT LIP for the darker moments and CHRISTIE FRONT DRIVE for the epic emotional feel.

MRR #200 - Rydell shared a split with Hot Water Music a few months ago and it looks like that did some lasting damage. Very melodic, theatrical, dramatic and some 'Soar' era Samiam vocals.

Interpunk - The 5th press of this 7" which is hardly surprising as it's a great little slab of vinyl that everyone should own! Literally back by popular demand it seems that all the kids love this split record between awesome hardcore favourites Hot Water Music and UK emo boys Rydell. It really works as a split with Hot Water Music delivering their reliable up front rockin' hardcore and Rydell grooving with their familiar throaty emo. This is a great record in two main ways. Firstly, it's a chance to own an exclusive version of one of Hot Water Music's best ever songs. Secondly, it's a chance to get to know Rydell, who play addictive, heartfelt, rocking music and have been proving to us for a while that we can expect more from the UK. If not for those reasons it's just a great record to spin and lift your spirits, all you have to do now is decide which side to play again coz you'll be playing this one all the time - guaranteed!

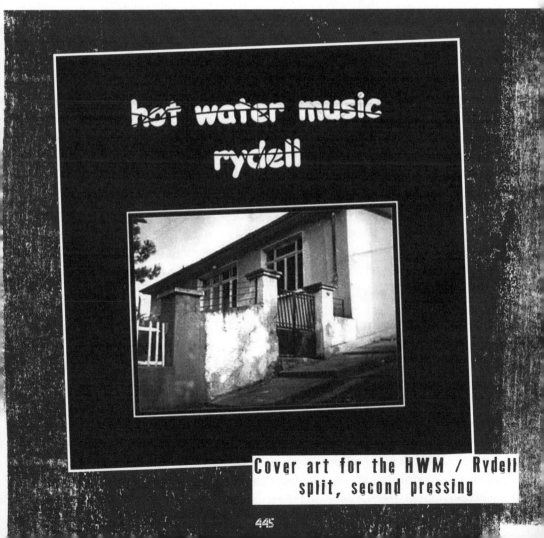

Cover art for the HWM / Rydell split, second pressing

30, Emotion Sickness

7/8 to 9/8/98 Recording at Chuckalumba studios

Rydell kept busy pretty much throughout the rest of the year, sending out demos and singles, and chasing up more releases whilst playing as many shows as possible. We were developing our sound and writing new songs all the time, trying out new things, some of which worked better than others.

We had a long weekend, from the 7th to the 9th of August '98, booked in the studio. We headed down to Chuckalumba recording studios, in a quiet and leafy little place called Bransgore, right in the middle of the New Forest, between Lyndhurst and Christchurch. It was absolutely in the middle of nowhere really and I don't remember exactly why we went there instead of Recent, Metway or Whitehouse studios. I think we'd met John, the studio engineer, at one of our gigs and I know we'd been given his contacts by the Minute Manifesto guys as they'd recorded there and said it was pretty cool and easy going. It was certainly easy going with nothing to do other than record, or chill out in the gardens, or maybe walk to the pub a few miles away. The guys who ran the studio were very friendly and it was like being on holiday, provided you liked your weekend breaks to involve staying in a hippy B&B with loads of guitars and drums lying around.

The studio was wood-lined with very little sound-proofing and was boiling hot at this time of year. There were windows looking out into the garden providing constant distractions, plenty of analogue gear to play with, and for some reason, piles of rice sacks stacked against one wall. John's wife seemed very fond of rice. He told us that rice, lentils and cider formed the bulk of their diet, and I think they were even calling the studio 'The Rice Garage' at the time.

John Stevens was the main man at Chuckalumba and he would engineer and mix the recording for us. We'd all be jamming in the same room, John with headphones on nodding along, and us playing the new songs, or trying to, whilst his small kids ran around hitting us with plastic hammers. That was up until the point I became bored of it and booted one out into the garden, landing it deep into a forest of nettles. One of the hammers that was, not one of the kids. John's favourite phrases seemed to be, "Ok, shall we try that one again?" in the studio, and "Why won't you guys try the lentil soup?" in the kitchen. As well as being the Chuckalumba recording engineer, John was also the drummer in a band called Humans The Size Of Microphones. This was the same band Pete Osmond, the guy who ran the great Land of Treason distro, played guitar for too. It was Pete's Orange head and cab that Milo would be playing through for this session. Although John had recorded more folk and indie bands, stuff like The Huckleberries, he still knew punk and rock pretty well and seemed to get where we were coming from. Unsurprisingly, the tracks from this session turned out quite mellow, semi-acoustic in fact, but were still pretty good. They included three new songs; 'Bring the lights down', 'Dreams and lines' and 'All my neighbours have moved'. These would be used on a split release we had coming up with a US band called Hunter Gatherer.

19/8/98 Rydell, Hicks and Chief Wiggum at The Freebutt, Brighton
10/9/98 Abhinanda, One Fine Day and Rydell at The Lift, Brighton
23/9/98 Rydell, Fiction and Resolve at The Forum, Tunbridge Wells
6/10/98 Rydell and others at Cairo Jacks, London

We were playing all sorts of shows too, lots of pubs and clubs with indie bands and punk bands alike, all over the UK but mainly in the southeast and around the home counties so we could get back to our own beds. The next gig I remember was soon after the Chuckalumba session when we played the very first show at the newly refurbished and reopened Freebutt in Brighton. They'd moved the stage and vastly improved the venue so that more people could get in to see the bands and still be served at the bar. Posters for the re-opening had been up everywhere and it was a packed indie night, full of happy Brighton indie boys and girls watching the alternative bands. Jess, the TV personality singer of Hicks, had invited us to play with her band, who were getting really good and a lot heavier now. (I say Jess was a TV personality, she was actually the presenter of a youth TV arts show that was on very late at night in the southeast region and only a few people I know ever saw it, but still, that's a celebrity compared to most). As she'd been busy on other stuff some of the Hicks guys were also playing in a new band called Psil. They played much heavier stuff, kind of like Helmet, and not knowing any better, I like to think that their name stands for 'People stuck in lift' or "Problem solving idiot list' or something fun like that.

Another band, called Chief Wiggum, also played that night. They were named after the police chief in The Simpsons, obviously, and hailed from Lewes, a small but historical town nearby, where some angry barons beat the King's army back in 1264 and the place has been a little bit rebellious ever since. They haven't done enough with that though, apart from a raucous annual fireworks party and the occasional punk gig. The town's most famous resident is currently Piers Morgan, an opinionated TV pundit, and there aren't many good bands from there either, but it is home to Mark Chadwick, the singer of The Levellers, as well as quite a few dog-on-a-string crusties, usually to be found begging or doped out somewhere near the Harvey's brewery on the river. But anyway, Chief Wiggum were great, a powerful and original sounding indie rock band. The problem was that they had no records out that I knew of, and they rarely came out to play gigs either. I'm glad they did venture out for this one though, as it was a very good evening.

We'd be back in Brighton a couple of weeks later for a full-on hardcore gig with Abhinanda and One Fine Day at The Lift in Queens Road. This was a great venue that often put on alternative shows, holding about 150 punters upstairs in front of the small stage, with even more in the bar downstairs listening to the heavy metal and new wave jukebox. We'd brought our guitars and amp heads, as usual, but Milo's amplifier was playing up so he had to share the One Fine Day equipment. Their set up was really harsh and loud, and they didn't want it changed. We weren't used to it as around then we'd been playing quite few indie shows, so our set became something of a wall of noise, with plenty of feedback. We bounced our way through the evening and the Abhinanda guys in particular seemed to be really into it. This was supposed to be their last ever show, they were splitting up after the tour and heading back to Sweden, so they played a blinder.

Abhinanda were a straight-edge hardcore band out of Umea in Sweden. They had a couple of albums out on Desperate Fight Records and were well-known in the European hardcore scene, having toured with their countrymates Refused. Their current UK / European tour was with One Fine Day, who were XXX straight-edgers too, but hailed from Novarra in Italy. They played heavy hardcore and had a new album out on Impression Records called 'Tough Guy Anthems'. They were so chaotic and noisy that the p.a. had to be 'fixed' when they'd finished before Abhinanda could go on.

We played a bunch more shows throughout September, and late in the month my good friend and ex-next-door-neighbour Nick came over from Finland to visit his family for a few days. We knew he was coming and wanted to see Rydell play so we'd managed to set up another local gig at the Forum. It was a homeless benefit, so we were glad to play it and our mates Fiction were on the bill too, along with another indie band called Resolve. Loads of people came out for that and we finished with a heavy cover version of Tears for Fear's 'Mad World'. This sort of song wouldn't be our normal choice, but Milo really liked the lyrics and was sure there was an emo gem hidden in there somewhere if we just hammered it out right. Lyrically I think he was right and a couple of years later an American singer-songwriter called Gary Jules had a number one for weeks in the UK with an acoustic cover of the same song. But for now, this was a story waiting to be realised, as no-one else was covering '80s pop bands in the hardcore scene, with the exception perhaps of Cap'N Jazz's version of A-ha's 'Take On Me'.

The next month we'd been booked on another of those talent scout shows in London at Cairo Jacks, but this one was even more ridiculous than the first. The girl who was setting them up reminded us they were for Alan McGee and Creation Records, but she was the booker and seemed to have eclectic tastes to say the least. I really wasn't sure what we were doing there at all. This was an industry show full of hilarious wannabees and very odd characters. There was a middle-aged Goth woman singing opera, a banker playing the keyboards, a Marilyn Manson lookalike on his expensive guitar and oh my god, worst of all, an incredibly shite hair-rock band who couldn't play for toffee and looked like a bunch of estate agents stumbling around in their suits and mirrored shades. It was bad. A waste of time. I had a flight to New York booked for the next day and couldn't wait to get out of there.

Luckily, I spent much of the next few weeks either in the US or Italy, but came back to the UK in time to help mix some of our recent recordings and then send them off to a few labels we were speaking with about releases. The Scene Police guys were working on another pressing of the Hot Water Music / Rydell split 7" as well as a possible new release for us and a new US band called Hunter Gatherer. This would be a split CD release and could involve a tour too, although that would take some time to arrange. We were also speaking with The Babies Three and Sunfactor about a possible tour and joint release, as well as chasing up tracks on various compilations too.

21/11/98 Rydell, Rauschen, Symbiosis, Vorhees and others
Royal Park Hotel, Leeds

Now this was a brilliant show. We'd travelled all the way up to Leeds for an all-dayer but it was well worthwhile, with so many good hardcore bands on the bill, and really well organised with a great turn-out. The promoters had a strict no smoking policy on the door and I was into that, sick of coming home stinking from all the club and pub gigs we were playing and still being straight-edge at the time. This club's policy was voluntary and more to do with the straight-edge clean-living ethic than any legislation or rule. The government ban on smoking in pubs and clubs wouldn't come into effect throughout the UK until July 2007.

The venue was a big old hotel and the bands played in the cellar bar underneath with its own entrance and a great p.a. There were loads of chatty, friendly people, quite commonplace up north, and everyone was upfront for the gig, dancing around and getting into it, instead of lurking in the dark at the back. Rydell were on form, though I do say so myself, and soon after we'd finished our set, I was already asking the promoters if we could play here again. I remember Milo thanking Leo and Jim for the show, but then getting the evil eye from the Voorhees guitarist for some reason. This was Richard 'Arms' Armitage, who had previously been the singer for Ironside and then joined Voorhees on second guitar. Rich was quite an imposing presence and for some reason during our set he sat on an amp about three feet away from Milo for the whole show. Milo took off his guitar for our final song, 'Across Three Parks', which at this point we had revived into a much snappier version and were all jumping around playing it. The guitar fell over right in front of Rich during the song and he didn't even pick it up, he just sat there staring at it. This was all a bit odd as Milo and I had spoken with him briefly a few years earlier when Ironside played their first London show and he seemed like a nice enough chap. Maybe he was having a bad day.

Voorhees could be scary bastards though, so maybe this was part of their thing. They'd only had to come down the road from Bradford for this show, as Lecky their vocalist had moved, but they always seemed angry about something. Milo reminded me about their first London show, a real eye-opener for all of us soft as shite southern shandy drinkers. We'd taken the train up as they were opening for Slapshot. Lecky came out with a padlocked chain for a belt holding his trousers up and two of the band were wearing Newcastle United football shirts. I don't think I'd ever seen a hardcore band wearing football shirts up to that point, let alone two of them. Every song was about killing cops or killing innocent people from the point of view of a murderer, and I think Lecky called the crowd a bunch of posers more than once. Then Slapshot came on and Choke was wearing a full Manchester United football kit, complete with shorts and socks. This seemed odd and they were terrible. But Understand had opened the gig that night and they rocked as always, making the trip worthwhile. Rob, one of the Understand guitarists, was still working full time in an office job then, so played in his suit and tie, and was probably the best dressed at the show.

Voorhees early releases on Armed With Anger, and their Stalingrad split, had all sold out by now, but they had new records out in the US. 'What you see is what you get' 7" on Crust Records and 'Fireproof' 7" on Chainsaw Safety Records. They also had a raging new album on the way and a scorching split release with Kill Your Idols on the cards soon too. I read a review, in Fracture fanzine, of the 'What you see...' 7" that made me chuckle, it said; "Eight fast as fuck, raging scorchers that will definitely make you want to kick the fuck out of some copper walking up the street. Anti-conformist lyrics mingled with fighting type stuff." Brilliant. HardFuckingCore. We'd played with them and Rauschen before, at the 1 in 12 Club, but despite all the attitude this show just seemed way better. A real cracker.

23/11/98 Discount, The Tone, Rydell and The Duvalls The Red Eye, London

We followed that with another absolutely packed goody, back down in soft-as-shite London. Lil and Kafren of Household Name Records had brought Discount over from Florida and with the help of Sean Rugger Bugger and a ska-core band called The Tone, they'd booked a tour all around the UK. Rydell got the support slot in town, along with another band called The Duvalls. This was a Monday night in November but Household Name and Rugger Bugger had done such a good job of promoting the gig that The Red Eye was rammed.

The Duvalls were a melodic pop-punk band, playing that Bay Area style, kind of like The Mr T Experience, and they warmed things up brilliantly. Their singer had to catch a National Express coach to get to the gig, but didn't seem at all put out by this, happily telling us about being pleasured by a young lady, under his coat, during the journey.

The Tone were a ska band who'd really like to be the Clash, but they were good and had a hell of a stage presence, although many of their lyrics seemed to me like "So then I ad

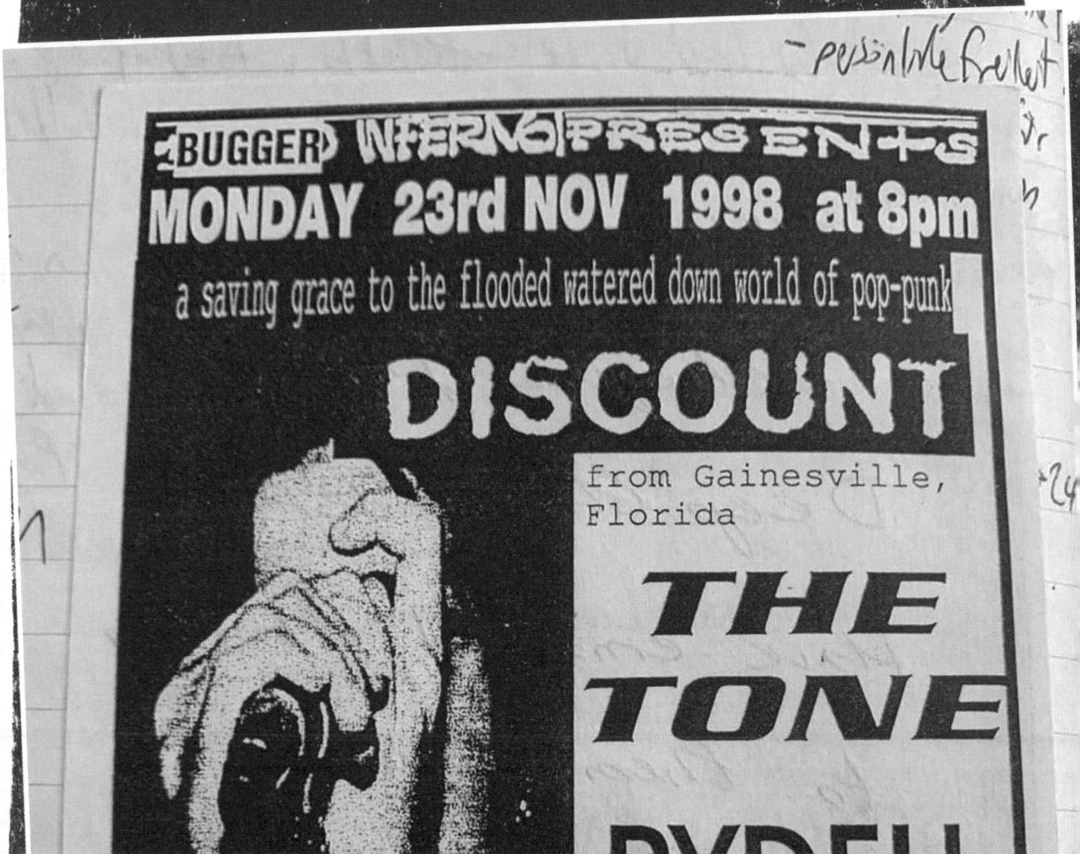

(BUGGER) INFERNO PRESENTS

MONDAY 23rd NOV 1998 at 8pm

a saving grace to the flooded watered down world of pop-punk

DISCOUNT

from Gainesville, Florida

THE TONE

RYDELL

THE DUVALLS

£3 for all

THE RED EYE

105 Copenhagen Street

London N1: 0171 387 4422

Flyer for Discount, The Tone, Rydell and The Duvalls at The Red Eye

rydell sunfactor thebabiesthree
rydell sunfactor thebabiesthree

rydell
sunfactor
thebabiesthree

scene police

dts

time of our time
hey nieve campbell
you fake forever
like the angel you are
fall in new england
the rain that fell today
eleven
pepsi lite
untitled number one

scene police
auf dem
stefansberg 58
53340
germany

scene police
2 church meadow
tarlxton
surrey
kt6 5rw
uk

http://cube.jdcastorm.com/scenepolice

rydell consists of david,miles,duncan and
adam, they're songs can be located in blue
you should write to them at
3 underhill lane maresfield in east sussex
tn22 3ay.

thank you.

sunfactor consists of andy,nic,graham and
james
they're songs can be located in brown and was
recorded by ben tufft and rob blackham at backline studios in surrey
guilford.
you may also like to write to them@
25 harts grdns guilford,surrey gu2 6qb
http://surf.to/sunfactor
thankyou again

the babies three consists of
russell,jim,alex,daniel and paul
you can contact them@
4 cuthbert road,westgate on sea,kent,ct8 8nr
they're songs were recorded between the calender days of the 26th
and the 28th of february in the year 1999 by a rob tufft altheide

thank you once more

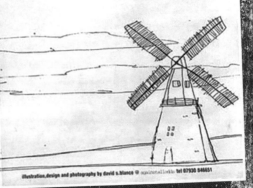

illustration,design and photography by david s.blanco @ aquirerailierklo tel 07930 846651

Rydell, Sunfactor & The Babies Three split CD artwork

452

anufa drink and I kicked er in de ead, la la la," but there you go. The Tone featured Ben Corrigan sharing vocals and guitar duties (with Dan Bernstein), and formerly of Thatcher on Acid, who went on to be in Hard Skin under the moniker Johnny Takeaway, and also Scott Stewart on drums, previously of Broccoli and also later in Hard Skin too. They already had a bunch of 7" EPs out on Sean Forbe's Rugger Bugger Discs (Sean played in Wat Tyler and now helps run Rough Trade) and would soon release a split with our buddies Annalise on Tony and Gaz's Suspect Device Records too, before signing with No Idea Records for their 'Here's another reason to believe in rock 'n' roll' album. But the band of the night by a long way were Discount.

Discount were a young band, but they already had at least three albums out and a bunch of great EPs, including splits with J Church and As Friends Rust. They came from Vero Beach but had managed to become part of the Gainsville scene, home of Hot Water Music, about 200 miles north, in Florida. This had set them in good stead, and as well as being good at what they did, they also had Alison Mosshart singing for them. A very cool female vocalist in a very male dominated scene. Alison had talent and style and deservedly went on to continued success in the music industry, forming The Kills with British guitarist Jamie Hince (who married the supermodel Kate Moss in 2011) and then The Dead Weather with Jack White (of the White Stripes) amongst others, recording at his Nashville studio. Discount stood out. They were a cracking band, and luckily, we'd get to play with them quite a few times more. The flyers for the show that evening said it well; "Discount – a saving grace to the flooded, watered-down world of pop-punk".

5/12/98 Rydell, Spy Versus Spy, Minute Manifesto and others Guinan's, Liverpool

We had another long journey but a great show at a punk benefit festival organised by Tom and the Wounded Knee Collective. We'd had a decent drive up and arrived early, so wandered around Liverpool town centre checking out the Cavern Club before returning to Guinan's to watch the other bands. We saw Minute Manifesto rock the house and noticed quite a few familiar faces from the Leeds show a couple of weeks before. Rydell played earlier on in the evening, because quite a few people had arrived but only parts of some of the other bands had made it. We had a good show despite a few tuning problems and shifted loads of copies of the third pressing of the HWM/Rydell split. This would be the first time we'd played with Spy Versus Spy and I was blown away by their original emo-hardcore sound. They'd only just recorded their self-titled six-track mini-album for Subjugation Records, and I hadn't even seen a copy of that yet, but already they were causing a buzz in the scene. Spy Versus Spy hadn't quite hit their stride live yet but seeing them overcome a few sound issues to belt out those early songs, clearly from the heart, showed exactly why they would become so influential in the UK post-punk scene. We'd play with them quite a few more times after this and I picked up all their releases. Two albums on Subjugation and a collection on Gravity DIP.

20/2/99 JetPak, Rydell and Spy Versus Spy
The Forum, Tunbridge Wells

I'd spent a lot of time on the phone with Paul Waller of The Babies Three, a Margate based hardcore band, talking about a tour and split CD we were setting up with them and Sunfactor, another new emocore band from Guildford. It was all coming together well, and we'd already been talking about artwork ideas with Davey Blanco and how soon the release might be ready with Emre and Dennis at Scene Police. We were sending demos to the promoters at venues we wanted to play, but would need the new CDs for the gigs late in March.

I was also working on the beginnings of Engineer Records, then called Ignition, a name we all liked and I think Milo came up with, inspired by the DC band of the same name. As that was underway now, I was speaking with Southern about possible distribution for the new label and our releases.

We also had a local gig to look forward to that I hoped would be a good one. Jetpak were coming over from Kingston in southwest London, and Spy Versus Spy were travelling all the way down from Stoke-on-Trent to play with us at The Forum in Tunbridge Wells. We'd been telling all our mates it would be a good one and putting up posters all around town. Sure enough, loads of our friends turned up to the club, shouting, singing along, dancing and enjoying themselves. They all loved Spy Versus Spy and Jetpak too, and afterwards a bunch of us piled around Adam's house to watch 'The Evil Dead' and a couple of new surfing videos Rydell had tracks on.

I'd noticed a few of the Anti-Nowhere League guys in the crowd that night and got chatting with them. A little while later, JB, their drummer, asked me if I'd play guitar for them at a few shows and maybe join the reformed band for a tour in Japan. That was a cool offer and I thought seriously about it, especially keen on the touring Japan part of it, but eventually declined. We had more Rydell gigs coming up and I had other commitments too. Plus, as much as I was into it, I really wanted to try to create some new music rather than rehash old punk songs. I knew I could've done it and it would have been an adventure, especially with their increased fame after the Metallica 'Garage Days Inc' EP and gigs, but there you go. I was focused on what I was already doing with Rydell.

26/3/99 Babies Three, Sunfactor and Rydell
The Cardinal's Cap, Canterbury
27/3/99 Babies Three, Sunfactor and Rydell
The Forum, Tunbridge Wells
28/3/99 Rydell, Babies Three and Sunfactor
The Old Railway Inn, Winchester
29/3/99 Babies Three, Rydell and Sunfactor
Skate and Ride, Bristol

30/3/99 Rydell, Babies Three and Grand Central
The Packhorse, Leeds
31/3/99 Inside Right, Pylon, Rydell, Babies Three and
Propagumbhis
Star and Garter, Manchester
1/4/99 Rydell, Babies Three, Month of Birthdays and others
1 in 12 Club, Bradford
3/4/99 Babies Three, Sunfactor and Rydell
Fat Pauly's, Norwich
4/4/99 Rydell, Babies Three, Sunfactor and Imbalance
The Freebutt, Brighton

In March I went on another trip to the USA, originally for work, but I managed to turn it into a decent holiday and still get back in time to head down to The Freebutt in Brighton with Milo to see a great Bluetip, Farewell Bend and Babies Three gig on the 22nd. Then I had to go over to France for a couple of days, so arranged to pick up the brand new Rydell / Sunfactor / Babies Three split CDs from Dennis and Stefan, who'd driven from the Scene Police HQ in Bonn, Germany to meet me while I was over there. I drove all the way home from the south of France to get to the first show of the tour, on time and with the new release.

The Rydell / Sunfactor / Babies Three split CD would be SCP007, Scene Police's seventh release, and the pressing was limited to just 500 copies for the tour. All three of the bands came from the southeast of England and weren't that well-known, so we figured that'd probably be enough for the tour. David S. Blanco had created the artwork for us again. It made use of clever photography of a bench by a lake, but arranged and designed with some illustrations and band photos, all colour coded in the layout too. There were nine tracks on the CD, three by each band. The Rydell tracks are 'Time of our time', 'Hey Neve Campbell' & 'You take forever', all taken from the Rhythm Kings session at Recent Studios in London. The Sunfactor tracks are 'Like the angel you are', 'Fall in New England' & 'The rain that fell today' recorded at Backline studios in Guildford. The Babies Three tracks are 'Eleven', 'Pepsi Lite' & 'Untitled number one', all recorded that February by Zak Williams.

The first show of this three-band mini-tour would be at the Cardinal's Cap in Canterbury. We'd played gigs at The Cap many times before and knew that it didn't hold many people, so filled up fast and became very hot. Sure enough, the place was soon packed, and the atmosphere was electric. It was insane how many people had crowded into this tiny venue. It was like the great photos you see of classic hardcore shows, with kids surrounding all sides of the stage and packed in right in front of the bands too. It was rare to experience this and a great thing to see and be part of. This was helped by the fact that Babies Three had brought a good crew over from Margate with them and we had a decent following too. Everyone seemed to be really into what these three bands were doing. Rydell kicked off with 'Stars Break Free' and rocked our way through a fun set. Sunfactor and Babies Three both rocked out too and everyone was sweating bullets. There were clouds of smoke and steam pouring out of the door when anyone opened it to get some air.

The next night we were back at the Forum again for our local release show. Some nights at this venue really rocked, and some sucked. This one wasn't the best and even the soundchecks didn't go well, but it was saved from disaster by loads of our mates turning up, led by Dan P and the local skull posse. It was good to see so many friendly faces. Rydell played several new songs, we thought we may as well give them a go in front of a home crowd. Sunfactor played their mellow emo-core very well, and were comparable to bands like Mineral, Sunny Day Real Estate, Pop Unknown and Promise Ring in places. The Babies Three had so much energy when they performed live, always bouncing around, playing screaming hardcore that just made you want to move, like Fugazi or Boy Sets Fire. None of us had far to go home either, which was good, because as we loaded out it was so cold that Milo was complaining that he couldn't feel his feet. The Sunfactor guys headed home for the night, but The Babies Three guys stayed with Adam and Milo in Rusthall, some sleeping in their van and others on the living room floor.

The next show was originally booked at the Joiners in Southampton, but there was some problem at the last minute so the STE guys and the Winchester guys got together to put us all on at The Railway Inn. I'm really glad they did, as this was a brilliant show. Moonrip fanzine later described it as; "The Babies Three were comparable to Boy Sets Fire and Kill Holiday, Sunfactor were emo that went down well and Rydell brought the Texas is the Reason type shenanigans." After the show we drove from Winchester down to Southampton where we were billeted with one of the promoters. He let us crash downstairs and disappeared off to bed. We made ourselves comfortable on couches and the floor. Adam, Dunc and I all around the TV, and Milo wrapped in a blanket under the dining table.

From Southampton, we headed west over to the big Skate and Ride in Bristol. This venue was awesome, with massive skate ramps, a café and pool room, all run by the local kids. It reminded us of some of the venues we'd played in Germany, but unfortunately it'd become a bit neglected and the guy who was meant to be promoting the show turned out to be some kind of fuckwit, turning up late and saying, "I thought you were playing tomorrow!" There had been no proper promotion at all, even though we'd arranged it with them and sent posters ahead nearly a month before. Bloody nightmare. But we did get to check out Bristol, buying a few records and chilling in a coffee shop with a view. When we eventually headed back to the Skate and Ride to meet the other bands again and play, it was to about twenty-five people, mainly each other. Such a cock-up on the local promotion, and totally wasted potential of what could have been a great gig. Shows how important the local promoters were. Just a few kids were there to skate so they

Sunfactor

THE S.T.E COLLECTIVE PRESENTS

AN EVENING OF PUNK ROCK, EMO, POP AND TAMBOURINES.

MOONRIP

THE BABIES THREE

COMPARED TO THE SOUNDS OF BOY SETS FIRE AND KILL HOLIDAY.

SUNFACTOR

EMOTIVE SOUNDS.

RYDELL

TEXAS IS THE REASON AND TAMBOURINES.

DOOR OPEN AT 7.30   DISABLED ACCESS AVAILABLE

£3 / 2.50

SUN 28th MARCH 1999   one year till .....

RECORD STALLS,

DISCO   BOOZE,   THE RAILWAY INN, ST PAUL'S HILL, WINCHESTER (3 MINS FROM TRAIN STATION)

The Babies Three

Poster (top right):

SLASH N BURN Promotions **Friday 16th April**

The final Date of their UK tour

BABIES 3

Pretty much a pure surfust band - Mad Monks

Blistering The Babies3 steal back US Punk and force it down their throat - Oragazine

Rydell

African Whigs with a bit more crunch - Fangzine

One of the most promising bands to emerge from the UK scene - Hi! Parader

Sun Factor

One of the best emo-rock bands around - Feature

Reclaimed emo Kings - Punk scene

£3 ON DOOR   **Lido Cliff Bar** Cliftonville Margate   £2.50 WITH THIS FLYER

8pm - 12pm

Aural Penetration + Eardrum Perforation GUARANTEED!
OR NONE OF YOUR MONEY BACK!

MORE DATES - appril 30th- 3d house of beef, deadbolt, labrat - may 7th: assert, snub, glueball - may 21st: nerger, shnikar erik Ted.

Rydell

Manchester Hunt Sabs/
Food not Bombs Benefit

Featuring

RYDELL

Emotional H/C from Sussex. Split out with Hot Water Music.

INSIDE RIGHT

Don't have a fucking clue what these guys sound like, but it should be good though! (hopefully!)
I think I met the singer at a gig in Leeds once and he seemed like a nice guy!

BABIES 3

Intelligent modern Hardcore from down south.

PYLON

Poppier Hooton;Car, Ex-Chopper from Wakefield.

MORE BANDS T.B.C.

Wednesday, 31st

March, 7.30pm sharp!

Manchester
Hunt Saboteurs

£4.00/£3.50 w/ Tin of
Veggie Food.
@Star 'n' Garter,
Fairfield St. behind
Piccadilly Station.

just one life d.i.y presents
An Evening of Hardcore and Emo Featuring
From Grimsby the Old School Hardcore Gymnastics of-

IMBALANCE

+ From Margate, Emotive Boy Sets Fire Style Hardcore-

BABIES 3

+ Semi-local Jangle-core

RYDEL

+ Acclaimed New Emo Outfit

SUNFACTOR

SUNDAY 4TH APRIL
£3   7.30pm

@ the Free Butt, Albion st, behind the Phoenix Gallery, opp. St.Peters church,
BRIGHTON,
Phone (01273) 603974
or just one life info on (01273) 249114 or www.alt-brighton.co.uk

---

LIVE ON TOUR AT EASTER
THE INFAMOUS MARGATE POST EMO HARDCORE QUINTET

THE BABIES THREE

MARCH:
22ND - BRIGHTON FREEBUT W/ BLUETIP + FAREWELL BEND
26TH - CANTERBURY. CARDINALS CAP
27TH - TUNBRIDGE WELLS. FORUM
28TH - WINCHESTER. THE OLD RAILWAY
29TH - BRISTOL. SKATE AND RIDE
30TH - LEEDS. PACKHORSE W/ RYDELL + GRAND CENTRAL
31ST - MANCHESTER. STAR + GARTER W/ RYDELL
APRIL
1ST - BRADFORD. 1 IN 12 W/ RYDELL - MONTH OF BIRTHDAYS
2ND - BOSTON. AXE + CLEAVER W/ VIOLET ULTRA
3RD - NORWICH. FAT PAULYS
4TH - BRIGHTON. THE ALBERT W/ SUNFACTOR. RYDELL + IMBALANCE
(ALL SHOWS WITH SUNFACTOR + RYDELL UNLESS STATED)

SLENDER MEANS PRESENTS AN EIGHTH
BENEFIT FESTIVAL

Friday 4th July (7.30pm)
HARD TO SWALLOW (Notts)
CANVAS (Leeds)
IMBIS (Leeds)
FACEACHE (Lincs)
YEAST (London)

Saturday 5th July (6pm)
SEKTOR (Belgium)
AREA EFFECT (Manchester)
MONTH OF BIRTHDAYS (North East)
BOB TILT...
KNI... (London)
... (Grimsby)
... (Glasgow)
...NS OF PRESLEY (Notts)
RYDELL (Sussex)

Sunday 6th July (1pm)
FACEDOWN (Belgium)
POLARIS (Leeds)
UNBORN (everywhere)
BEACON (London)
DEADFALL (Middlesbrough)
...

Where...1in12 Club, Albion St, Bradford, West Yorkshire. Easy access from Bradford city centre. Ask for Morrisons supermarket should you have problems. The club is a community based thing, please don't abuse it.
Prices...the final price has not been set as we haven't costed exact expenses for all the bands yet. The Friday night show is to be treated as seperate, and will be cheap. Thereafter tickets will be available for the two remaining days or for Saturday and Sunday individually. We will require a tin of vegetarian food from everyone who attends (bands included). We are trying to provide for the Bradford Soup Run and the Manchester Runway Protestors, so we need as much food as we can get.
Food...provided by the 1in12 cafe, also plenty of beverages.
Sleeping...there will be places to stay at the 1in12 Club on the Friday and Saturday nights, please let them know in advance. (01274) 734160.
Information...phone Jan (01325) 352207, or Helene (0161) 4450287, for further information.

Slender Means formed in 1993 as a collaboration between Armed With Anger, How We Rock and Subjugation, to raise benefit for organisations/activists, such as Rape Crisis, Anti Facist Action, Hunt Sabs, and many others, whilst providing bands with shows. Thank you all for past support.

1in12 Club Albion Street Bradford

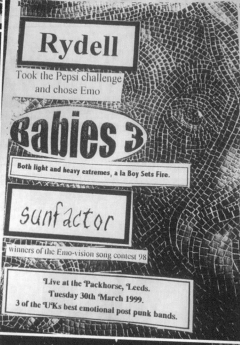

Rydell
Took the Pepsi challenge and chose Emo

Babies 3

Both light and heavy extremes, a la Boy Sets Fire.

sunfactor

winners of the Emo-vision song contest 98

Live at the Packhorse, Leeds.
Tuesday 30th March 1999.
3 of the UKs best emotional post punk bands.

Flyers from the Rydell, Sunfactor & Babies Three tour

hung around, but that was about it. I guess it was still worth it though, just to see Babies Three play a crazy cover of 'Great Cop' by Fugazi with everyone singing along, "You got a lot of questions for me. You'd make a great cop, you pig!"

On Tuesday, the Sunfactor guys had to head home for a couple of days but Rydell and Babies Three continued on up to Leeds to play at The Packhorse, a big pub venue near the university that often put on alternative shows. It wasn't an easy trip as by now The Babies Three van had started falling apart, so it took a while to get there. On top of that, it was the end of term so we couldn't be sure what the audience would be like. We knew we had good support coming from Grand Central, great guys whose band sounded a lot like Dag Nasty, but who'd travelled up there themselves all the way from Croydon in south London.

Grand Central were friends of Sunfactor's and had been on a recent Speedowax compilation with them. They'd also have a couple of tracks on the 'Emotion Sickness' collection that came out on Memory Man Records soon after this tour. Rydell, Babies Three, Sunfactor and several other great UKHC bands were on this compilation CD too, so I'll come back to that in a moment.

At The Packhorse we met the promoter Alex, who thankfully had it all sorted and was pretty sure that a good crowd would turn up. He showed us a poster that had been made for the show which said on it, 'Three of the UK's best emotional post-punk bands,' which seemed a comment way ahead of its time in 1999 Yorkshire, and then added amusingly about each band, 'Rydell – Took the Pepsi challenge and chose emo, Sunfactor – Winners of the emo-vision song contest '98 and Babies Three – both light and heavy extremes, a la Boy Sets Fire', perhaps running out of humour when they got to this last one. Sunfactor didn't make it to this show, so it would be Rydell and The Babies Three with very able support from Grand Central. So, no locals playing at all, but luckily, still a good turnout and great show to an appreciative crowd, with Milo joining The Babies Three onstage to sing 'Great Cop' with Paul as the finale.

We all managed to get some sleep that night and even have a wash too, luxury. In the morning, Alex, and a very pretty girl from the show whose name I can't remember but was covered in tattoos, led us out of the maze of red brick terraced houses that seemed to fill that part of Leeds, to get breakfast. It was like a scene from a down on its luck Coronation Street. We wandered through the boarded-up tenements, several of which were being squatted in by students we'd seen at the gig the night before, to get a big veggie fry-up in one of Leed's many greasy spoons. It turned out that Alex ran Zandor Records and would later release In the Clear's great 'Leave this city in flames' album, as well as records for Walk The Plank, Self Destruct, and Voorhees, all of which we'd sell loads of through the Engineer Records distro.

Later that day, we crossed the Pennines over to Manchester for a Hunt Sabs / Food Not Bombs benefit show at the Star and Garter that was absolutely packed. The promoters, M14, had pasted flyers everywhere. We'd be playing with Inside Right and Pylon who were both northern melodic punk bands and brought a lot of support with them.

Inside Right would have a split release with Sunfactor on Speedowax Records, and then their own album, 'Superman Toolbelt', on Slendermeans Records.

Pylon featured ex-members of the pop-punk band Chopper and had now gone more post-punk / emo, writing songs that The Promise Ring would have been proud of. They'd be even more prolific with releases on Subjugation, Jealous Records and Gravity DIP. But for now, both bands were starting out and this would be one of their first gigs.

First up though was a ska-core band who called themselves The Propagumbhis. They all crammed onto the small stage and fell about into each other, there seemed to be at least seven or eight of them up there at once. Despite the chaos, they were way better than most of the ska bands I'd heard, not too polished, but still blasting out hardcore punk with political lyrics that really kicked things off. They had a new EP out on Fuxony Records called 'How to bomb everything' and would follow it up with split releases with Imbalance and Caeser Soze, as well as a great album on Hermit Records called 'The rise and fall of nothing much at all'.

Almost everyone in the pub was dancing or nodding along and there was a superb atmosphere. Only broken momentarily when, during Inside Right's set, some muppet threw a pint pot at the wall behind the band and glass rained down on them. Inside Right stopped playing and Paul, their singer, asked the crowd, "Has someone got a problem here?" but there was silence. They carried on playing and there were thankfully, no more projectiles. The punk united atmosphere soon came back so both Rydell and Babies Three were right at home at this gig and played our socks off, with Milo joining the Babies onstage again for another 'Great Cop' sing-a-long. We ended up staying in a house where a couple of the guys from Spy Vs Spy lived. Both Leeds and Manchester had great hardcore scenes in the late Nineties and these had been memorable shows.

The Geek Essay fanzine guys were at the Manchester gig and they reported on it in their next issue, saying; "This was a benefit for the Manchester Hunt Sabs and they certainly got a good line up to support the cause. Rydell, on tour with The Babies 3 and Sunfactor, another new band for me and another one I really liked. An emo band, reminiscent of Braid in some ways. Some of the songs are a bit quirky and the vocals are all kinda breathless and urgent. Only problem with their set was that it was too short! A good night all around, especially grand to see so many people turn out to see the bands and support a good cause. It's what punk's all about, man."

Rydell, Sunfactor and
Babies Three tour party

The Star and Garter, Manchester

Milo

The Pack Horse, Leeds

The Babies Three rocking out

The Royal Park Hotel, Leeds

We didn't really want to leave Manchester but the next day we had another show over in Bradford at the 1 in 12 Club. This was a venue that depended a lot on the atmosphere on the night and could be a grim place if it didn't go well. There didn't seem to be any posters up in town for the show so we made a few and started sticking them around. We went into Lecky's skate shop and he didn't even know the gig was on. Not a good sign. Month of Birthdays were meant to be playing, but I don't think they showed up and a lot of people disappeared over to Leeds to see an Oi Polloi show there instead. All this meant the turn-out was low and not a great night. Both Rydell and Babies Three played jazzy, improvised sets that night, Rydell's partly caused through Duncan's drumming. The few people that were there seemed to enjoy it well enough, and the 1 in 12 sound man, who was also the Stalingrad guitarist, was almost crying with happiness when Babies Three blasted through a cover of a Melvins track.

As soon as we'd packed away after the show, we headed home for a much-needed day off. The Babies Three went on to The Axe in Boston, Lincs for a show with Cleaver and Ultraviolet, but I'm not sure how that gig went. We were all meant to meet up again on Saturday, with Rydell and Sunfactor joining the Babies Three to play at Fat Pauly's in Norwich. This show was being put on by Andy Malcolm of Collective zine, but he ended up having to move it at the last minute to the upstairs of a pub. It was all becoming a bit of a shambles.

For the final show of this tour, we were playing close to home again at the Freebutt in Brighton. The gig was being put on by Buz and the Just One Life promotions crew so should be ok. Because it was close to home, we had loads of our mates coming along too. Buz had Imbalance originally booked to come down from Grimsby on that day, but he piled us onto the bill too and all the bands got to play to an absolutely packed venue. Imbalance brought their mix of fast crossover hardcore, keeping it just the right side of metal for the punk rock kids. They'd signed with Household Name Records and were on tour promoting their new 'Spouting Rhetoric' album, as well as their 'March of the yes man' 7". We'd just about sold out of the Rydell / Sunfactor / Babies Three split CD and most of our demo CDs and 7"s too. It was a great way to finish the trip, and now I needed my bed.

Emotion Sickness CD

The Emotion Sickness compilation featured sixteen tracks from Rydell, Babies Three, Sunfactor, Month of Birthdays, Spy versus Spy, Jetpak, Yeast, Soeza, Inside Right, Grand Central and Coag. It was arranged by James of Yeast and released on his Memory Man record label, then distributed widely by Southern Record Distributors, a London-based distributor who'd push everything from Crass to Fugazi and represent loads of cool labels, becoming one of the biggest indie distros of the time. Partly thanks to that, Memory Man managed to shift all one thousand copies of the CD, either direct from them at just £5 post-paid, or through independent record stores.

The CD was a collection of all the early UK emo / post-hardcore bands on one release. The Rydell tracks on this compilation were 'Across Three Parks' and 'Home' (acoustic version) and there were plenty of good tracks by new bands to check out. The artwork had band photos taken at gigs with direct home contacts underneath. The green-tinged, cut and paste style cover art was by Matilda Saxow, and even back then, in '99, she and James had thought to add the following caveat to the inside cover notes;

"This compilation of music from various parts of the UK is a document of bands that have emerged unscathed from our punk and hardcore scenes. It's called 'Emotion Sickness' for tenuous reasons. The main reason is that some of the bands on this record may well have been tagged with the 'emo' label, and that while this term might give a general idea, it can never encapsulate all the styles on show here. Secondly, the term suggests a formula and is the sort of tag that people who don't like the music would use as a weapon against it. And regardless of everything else, isn't emotion a fairly common element of all good music?"

The CD did well, and we certainly shifted a lot of copies, so there was a lot of press coverage kicking around. Here's a couple of zine reviews from soon after the compilation first came out:

ENZK fanzine - V/A - Emotion Sickness (Memory Man)
If you're into the whole emo, indie rock thing you should get hold of this comp and check out some of the UK's finest in the field. You get 70 minutes from the likes of Sunfactor, Spy vs Spy, Grand Central and Rydell and it's all pretty high-quality stuff. 'Home' by Rydell is definitely the best track in my opinion, it just has that heart wrenching vibe to it. (GE)

Scanner #7 fanzine - Emotion Sickness comp
A massive 70-minute comp of emo kinda sounds from bands all over the UK. It gets underway with the best of the bunch too, Rydell, with the great 'Across Three Parks'. Other highlights are the two Grand Central tracks, Inside Right's slightly more rocking song, Sunfactor and Spy vs Spy. Gotta fess up and say that I didn't realise there were so many UK bands doing this stuff so well. Only the tuneless caterwauling of Month of Birthdays turned my stomach. Good packaging too with contact addresses and photos. I think Rydell have some copies so drop them a line.

Collective zine (Andy Malcolm) - Emotion Sickness CD
We need more of these things. Compilations of a bunch of UK bands who hang around in the punk scene, yet don't get much 'word'. Despite the title, this is not necessarily bands who immediately would get classified by reviewer goons like myself as emo. But some of them are.

(By the way, saw a cool new UK emo band playing with the rocking Bluetip last night. Cortina (ex-members of Tribute) playing awesome collegey indie rock a la Beezewax, with added Christie FD and TITR influences. Splendid).
Ok. Listofun...

Rydell: Two tracks, the first one "Across 3 Parks", I don't think I've got anywhere else so must remember it from the live show. It's short, pacey, melodic emocore with their trademarked strain vocals. You know the score, Rydell = UKs Split Lip / Chamberlain. They also do "Home" which I have a demo version of. It's done in a stripped down, almost acoustic fashion and is really rather impressive. Vocalists take turns, both hoarse & sung. Great.

Yeast: I saw these guys about a year ago, supporting Braid and paid scant attention. I wanted to see Braid! And anyways, Yeast were playing some sort of post-hardcore style or something which I didn't really understand at the time. So it came as a surprise when I first heard the song "Eyebrows" here, as it's total emo rock reminding of a lot of the Deep Elm stuff. Fairly mid paced and melodic, solid but nothing out of the ordinary. "Drown" on the other hand, is more what I was expecting. Quirky, discordant post-hardcore with stops and starts and spoken vocals, breaking into bursts of noisy energy and screaming. Hoover? A little Native Nod? Heading that way. I like this a lot more than the other song.

Grand Central: One song from the demo / cd and one newbie. "Never Say Goodbye" kicks in with totally cool rumbling bass and builds into a great little emocore / rock track along the lines of Sense Field mixed with a bit of Dag Nasty. This song has so many subtle and clever touches to hook you in, it's unreal. "White Paper Delay" is yeah, Sense Field + TITR goodness, slower and more miserable sounding than the other song here. GC have great vocals and by all accounts are an awesome live band.

Soeza: First up is "Grease the Receiver" which is some groovy, jazzy booty shaking fun. I really don't know what the fuck this is to be honest, it's not way out and weird, just different. Not as whacked as Get Hustle, but maybe moving towards that. Trumpet and piano. "Chronic Wrongdoing" is herky-jerky and kinda sounds like you're stumbling home at 3am. It's the loping basslines that do it. There's some excellent and very strong girl vocals going on here. Heh, liable to confuse the heck out a ya, I guess this is just so out of place on this comp, but it's not too bad at all!

The Babies 3: Two songs that don't appear to be from the new album (which rocks!), which is kinda weird because the "Target Practise" has the lyrics from which the album title was taken. Anyways, it's also got a lot of pretty twinkles duelling it out with the more rumbling guitar and distinctive vocals. Sounds like a big TITR influence to me on this track, but they're making more out of it than most. Spirals into a great big epic emo end of the world finale. Just how I like 'em. "Feint Ruled" is punkier, catchy and all around fine. Has a pretty original sound and once more the duelling guitars are top notch.

Inside Right: These guys are getting a lot of 'props' from the scene, and while they have a great song title: "Four Fingered BMX Rider", I am having trouble doing anything more than making yet another Texas Is The Reason comparison here (TITR's faster songs). Even the vocals have a bit of a Garrett edge to them at times! Still, it's very well done and is another prime example of UK emo rock done good. Split 7″ with Sunfactor soon, hopefully it'll see them developing their own sound a little, but it'll be worth a look anyway.

Month of Birthdays: "Heightened" is taken from their last 7″, and is that gloomy, dark post-hardcore that was their prevailing style back then. It's ok, but really their new album absolutely walks all over it in every way conceivable. Subjugation should have donated an LP track and maybe that would help shift a few more copies.

Jetpak: They coulda bin a contenduh! Man, these guys were just so good and it's a shame they had to split. No band in the UK punk scene harmonises as well as Jetpak do, sorry did. "The Bowling Song" is absolutely lovely, upbeat poppy emo rock which will have you bobbing your head and then convulsing to the groove when it all gets noisy and RAWK! later on. I dunno who they sound like, there's a small bit of Promise Ring, and some other bands. But it's all good, and those harmonies will kill you. Why did you have to split up, you bastards?

Sunfactor: "Like The Angel You Are". I have this track 94 times now, and so do you. You know the score, mid-paced TITR style emo with passionate vocals and twinkly parts. Bonus points for still featuring the excellent "beeoow" sound fuck-up near the start.

Coag: Sounds like it's going to be something special at the start, slow building and twinkly with kind of semi-gravelly vocals like Grant Broccoli didn't have a car in his throat. Then it fires up into a pretty nice indie / emo song. Geez, Boilermaker? Stuff like that. I wouldn't mind hearing more because I don't know who the hell these guys are.

Spy versus Spy: An acoustic demo track where for extra fun value, they leave in the part where someone gives them a phone call. If you didn't know, you'd never guess this was the Spys. Nicely sung vocals over slow guitars. Gets more upbeat in places. Fine stuff, dunno how new this is though.

A very competent comp, missing one or two bands (probably those that haven't recorded yet – i.e. Pylon, Carver, Cortina and Jay Schraeder), and well worth your

emotionn
sickness
ness

*A compilation
of bands from the UK*

rydellsunfactorthebabiesthree
rydellsunfactorthebabiesthree

Blanco´s fold out artwork for the three band tour split

moolah. Maybe this'll become a series of releases in future once more these bands start springing up as they surely will.

After the tour the few remaining copies of the three-band split CD found their way to reviewers at punk fanzines and magazines, so here's a few reviews and comments on that.

Rydell / Sunfactor / Babies Three split CD — Reviews:

Collective (Ian Cavell) - This gets this month's award for most stunning record. Glorious artwork and great music. Nine songs, three by each band and not a clanger among them - sounds like a good deal to me. You may have had the fortune to pick this up at one of the recent shows that these three did. If not, then make one almighty effort to get your grubby paws on a copy. Believe me when I say that these are three of the most exciting bands to have surfaced in these shores for quite some time.

First up, Rydell. Think Chamberlain, think heartfelt emo-rock, grating vocals and powerful songs. Think, fucking excellent! I can't emphasise strongly enough how good these three songs are. I think a Rydell album is going to be a very great thing indeed.

And on to Sunfactor. Fracture showered adulation on this band when they reviewed their demo tape. I now see why. 'Like The Angel You Are' and 'Fall In New England' are two classic examples of how to do emo-rock well. The former bursts into life with sporadic bursts of guitar noise and is home to some great vocal work. The latter is nice and melodic. What more can you ask?

Which leaves the Babies Three to hurtle off in a new direction and astound me all over again. In a small, upstairs room above a pub in Leicester, the Babies Three played a mix of noisy emo/hardcore with an intensity that was second to none. The three songs here capture that ferocity remarkably well. Everyone should get a chance to hear the chilling emo-like guitar and the wonderful vocals of 'Pepsi Lite'. Likewise, prepare to be astounded by the subsequent degeneration of the Babies Three into a screaming gem of a song called 'untitled number one'. I don't think my jaw can drop much lower.

I have a great deal of trouble deciding which band I like best of this CD. It changes pretty much every day - all three are just too incredible to choose one over the other. So yeah, this is pretty much an essential purchase.

Only A Phase - Rydell are the winner in this competition - which isn't actually supposed to be one. They managed to create an all own style during the years and I really like it. In the last reviews I always wrote something like 'If Samiam were from DC'. That's not the case anymore, but it's still there. You can still hear it. They got calmer and the two singers make it very interesting.

Fracture #8 - A record with the recurring number three. Three bands (one which even has three in its name), three songs each, and here's three reasons to buy it: It's great, great, great.

Rydell are first up with a cool emo-rock sound and vocals that are reminiscent of Split Lip (before they went country rock) with that same confidence and emotion. They're definitely a rock band but have spliced in heavy doses of poppy hooks, emotive choruses and rhythms that flow both powerfully and subtly at the same time. Great stuff and I can't wait to hear more. The three Sunfactor tracks are their demo reviewed a couple of issues ago and well, you all know how good it was then and it sounds even better on CD. After hearing these three tracks repeated on a few different formats now I'm positively gagging to hear more stuff by this amazing band. And lastly, The Babies Three are a band who are making progress in gigantic leaps. Their album was fine but a little schizophrenic at times, but with these three new songs it sounds as though they've found their natural sound, mid-paced melodic rock mixed with forceful and passionate hardcore that can display itself with some excellent thick riffs and screamed vocals. All three bands on this are different but complement each other beautifully, swinging the mood back and forth. Don't miss it.

Yummy - OK, you all should know how g-r-e-a-t Rydell are by now, so no more comments needed about them. Sunfactor are somewhere along the same lines and the Babies Three remind me a bit of Boy Sets Fire and they even do some serious screaming on one of their songs. Amazing stuff. 100 / 100.

The Last Resort - A compilation CD, showcasing three bands from the Southeast of Britain who recently toured together, and featuring three tracks from each. If the CD is anything to go by, it would have been a good tour to see. The common theme running across all three bands is that they seem to be coming from the restrained, melodic side of hardcore, basically, passionate music with a certain lo-fi chic. The first of the three, Rydell, are perhaps the most distinctive, with a unique sound that twists and turns from pounding grooves to delicate guitars, and from staccato vocals to powerful melodies. 'Hey Neve Campbell', in particular, showcases their distinctive mix of the beautiful and heavy.

Next up, Sunfactor, come across as more organic and, indeed, epic, and are perhaps the most melodic of the three... 'Like The Angel You Are', with its breezy verse and driving chorus, is particularly impressive.

And last, but not least, The Babies Three up the tempo with three bursts of melodic vitriol. All in all, a worthwhile purchase for anyone wanting to sample something a little different, and if that doesn't convince you, perhaps the price tag of around £5 will.

Trust #77 (Jorg) - This split CD was created for the English tour of these three bands. Three songs are offered by each band, all of which can be assigned to the emo area, but the emo varies from rock to hardcore. All in all, a very successful compilation that I will listen to more often.

Ox #35 (DH) - The CD came about because the three bands were touring England together for two weeks and also come from this country. So, they got along so well, and bang, the CD is in my player. I have nothing against it, well-made emocore can always hope for open CD slots. All three bands can't quite keep up with the greats from overseas, but that doesn't mean that they had to hide behind them.
Above all, Rydell and Sunfactor are quite skilful and routine. If the production is a little thicker and the songs a little more mature, they will probably be everybody's darlings. The CD rounds off with The Babies Three, who then scream aloud to wake us up, even if the tendency is towards more worn-out song structures and the brakes are loosened in between.

NME - I also wanted to add a piece from the NME that Alex of The Babies Three wrote several years later as part of an article about the mainstream latching onto the emo tag where he mentions the tour we all played, as I think it helps give a more overall picture not just of the record or the tour, but of the feeling around the scene at that particular moment...

"Having been into music since I was a kid in the '80s, to being a long-haired grunger in my early teens to then falling in love with punk, pop punk, indie, post hardcore etc from the mid '90s, music held a lot of importance in my life. In 1998 the band I was in (The Babies Three) were making the transition from playing throwaway pop-punk into something more substantial. We would spend hours listening to Mineral, Sunny Day Real Estate, Beezewax, Fugazi, The Promise Ring and so on, and our music reflected this. We started to feel like we were part of something, bands were coming to play our small seaside town. Our singer, Paul, put on Harriet The Spy in his living room and Appleseed Cast at our local Friday night hangout. Come Easter of 1999, we were going out on a UK tour with two bands, Rydell and Sunfactor, with whom we had just put out a three-way split CD. In all honesty, some of the shows were terrible but some were the most amazing I've ever played, the whole time though it really felt like we were part of something that was happening there and then. Up until that point anything I'd been into I was either too young to be a proper part of or had already happened. But this was happening, we were a tiny part of it, and it was fucking exciting, we didn't want or need the mainstream music press to get involved."

31, Today stopped counting

After the Babies Three and Sunfactor tour I spent a lot of time working on my new Ignition (Engineer Records) label and trying to create a website for it with the help of my friend Ian Sims, who worked at a new-fangled web-agency in Tunbridge Wells called Webscript. This wasn't as easy as you'd think and back then websites took ages. In the meantime, Milo, Dan Pullin and Stephen 'Syd' Franklin were helping me get stock together for the distro, whilst Dennis and Emre were helping me with the first couple of pressings to get the label going. These were basically Scene Police re-releases on Ignition for the Hot Water Music / Rydell split 7", already on its fourth pressing, and the excellent new Hunter Gatherer CD called 'Low Standards For High Fives'. All this took a while, so at the same time Syd and I started speaking with loads more great bands about sending us tracks for a sampler compilation we wanted to put out, to be called 'Firework Anatomy'. The hardcore scene was still quite small and close knit back then, so this put me in touch with so many great bands that I formed good friendships with and would eventually put releases out for.

The 'Firework Anatomy' compilation probably took the best part of a year to get together and turned out to be Ignition's third release with twenty bands on it, every one of them a killer. We had tracks by Grade, Penfold, Red Animal War, Speedwell, Kevlar, San Geronimo (ex-Lifetime), A Rocket Sent To You, Crosstide, Ashen, Slowride and The Casket Lottery, supplying an exclusive cover of Shudder To Think's 'Red House'. Also, Hillside, Mock Orange, That Very Time I Saw, My Spacecoaster, Dira, Two Weeks from Tomorrow, Five Cent Hero, Hunter Gatherer and of course, Rydell. These were all great bands, both from Europe and the US, many of whom we'd work with on full releases for over the next couple of years, and all seemed to represent the flavour of the scene to me at that moment.

I did clear off to Chicago for a few days to pick up a load of records and second-hand workwear shirts to bring back for the distro, like you do, and when I came home, I was speaking with distributors like Cargo, Green Hell and Southern about their help getting the new releases we had planned into stores. I have to say, they didn't seem keen until the label had already built-up a following and had at least ten releases in its catalogue. A bit of a chicken and egg situation there that didn't help matters in the label's early stages. But undaunted and determined, we pressed on.

Through the previous labels I'd helped run, and all the contacts I had through my fanzine and band, I knew a lot of good people. I wanted to trade records with other independent labels and help get our band's releases out there, both through partners in the UK and world-wide. We started putting Ignition flyers in with every Rydell demo we sent or record we sold, always adding extra releases to any orders as free samples wherever possible and posting them out to every contact we had. Having been on both sides of several record releases now, both in the band and as part of the label, I had a pretty good understanding of what each party was looking for and needed, and I wanted to add value to that. I wanted to over-deliver for the bands, but keep it credible, in as punk and underground a way as possible. This would mean a lot of hard work. Of course, we needed quality bands, but they still needed good artwork and packaging, then plenty of support for the release, with lots of PR, promotion, merchandise, gigs / tours and distribution. Pressing the record was the easy part. The hard work was in all the marketing and distribution that came afterwards. It still is.

While all this was going on we were still writing new songs for Rydell too, and exchanging letters with as many alternative record labels as possible. We loved having the split releases and compilations out but were dreaming of releasing our own EPs, and maybe the holy grail of an album. Hell, maybe several albums! We were prolific songwriters and getting better as a band all the time. Who knew what would happen next? Well, as it goes, I did. I'd been speaking with Stefan at Soda Records in Germany and our next shows would be for the release of a vinyl 7" split with our buddies Pale.

1/5/99 Rydell, Pale and Reno Kid at the A.Z. Aachen
2/5/99 Rydell, Reno Kid and Losome at the A.Z. Mainz
3/5/99 Rydell, Painted Thin and Kurt at the Bla Club, Bonn

For our next gigs we headed over to Germany again, zooming along the autobahns, blasting out The Get Up Kids with the four of us singing along, and all the equipment we could cram in rattling around the back of my car. For the first night we headed straight to the A.Z. youth club, or the Autonomous Centre in Aachen, as they so snappily named it. This venue wasn't far across the German border, but it was like going back in time, buried as it was under metres of concrete in the big bomb shelter where we'd played with Hot Water Music, Pale and Atrox almost a year earlier. This would be the launch party for the 'Today stopped counting' Rydell and Pale split single on Soda Records. It had been hooked up for us by Stefan from Soda Records, and of course, Dennis and Emre, our great friends at Scene Police.

There were flyers for the gig all around, showing a cartoon boy with headphones on saying 'Downtown, waiting for you tonight!' and the list of bands that would be playing. The local punkers had come out in good numbers and Stefan had set up a merch stand to make the most of it, bringing boxes of the new 7" vinyl along with him. There were 1000 copies on regular black vinyl with an extra 100 or so on opaque white. These

RYDELL.PALE

A SODA RECORDS RELEASE. SPLITSINGLE. 45 RPM. 8.41 MINUTES
TODAY STOPPED COUNTING

ECORDS 62039
STEREO

Rydell / Pale split 7"

The Bla Club, Bonn

The A.Z., Aachen

Do 18.3. BLA

20 UHR
BONN
BORNHEIMERSTR. 20

Caffè a la **RYDELL**

(CAF-AY' A-MER-I-CAH'-NO)

03.05. BONN BLA
mit KURT &
Painted Thin

INFO's: Mo-Fri 14-19k
0228/9637800

SCENE POLICE COFFEE

Hot Water
Fresh water, specially purified, is heated to the ideal temperature, then added to the espresso. The result is a cup of full-flavored coffee, as mild as it is satisfying.

Espresso
The pure essence of espresso, full, intense, and slightly sweet with a distinctive aroma and toasty finish brood of

Beginn: 19.30 pünktlich!!

Gig flyer for Rydell,
Kurt and Painted
Thin at the Bonn Bla

AUTONOMES ZENTRUM
Vereinsstr.25, 52062 Aachen, Tel.:0241-38468

APRIL/MAI 1999

Dienstag 20.4.	**ONE FINE DAY** "Emo SXE" + special guest
Donnerstag 22.4.	BALTHASAR (OH) the new work
Samstag 24.4.	**CHEESE-BACK** "Psycho-Industrial-Rock"
Freitag 30.4.	PUNKROCK - ABEND mit **THE PIG MUST DIE** **PLEEBOYS** **HONEY HONEY**
Samstag 1.5.	"EMO CORE" **RYDELL** **PALE** **RENO KID**

Messing around at
the Ruhrpark

A.Z. Aachen gig flyer

474

records looked beautiful and went really well with the striking black on white cover design. The artwork had Rydell and Pale in bold black type on the front cover, with a thin line drawn illustration of what I'd guess is a satellite of some kind and text saying; 'Today stopped counting. A Soda records release split single. 45rpm. 8.41 minutes'. That tickled me. The Rydell track, 'Home' went on for three minutes and thirty-two seconds. Not bad for a hardcore song. But the Pale track, 'Home is lost' well, that was over five minutes long. A very lengthy anthem. This was practically a two-track album for some hardcore bands. What value the kids were getting.

On the back cover there was a black and white photo of some bored looking people, possibly Afghans or maybe Pakistanis, waiting around in some non-descript room, maybe at an airport or stale government immigration building. But there was a boy running or dancing through the middle of them, just happily doing his own thing. Next to that there was a note typed under the title 'Who the hell needs vinyl?' and it read as follows.

"How was I supposed to know that vinyl will have its great comeback? Well, how am I supposed to explain to you? There is no great comeback, it has always been there. I guess most of you experienced a similar situation, a certain desperation, which never meant anything to you. So what? Another type that died by its existence, by just being there. I mean it's great to have an overwhelming digital sound, but it's also distant. I hope we share the feeling of a lack of nearness."

Forgive the Germanglish grammar, but this was 1999 remember, not 2020 and here they are talking about the first resurgence of vinyl and its tactile qualities. Analogue over digital. What comes around goes around. The writer went on.

"Listening to a song or a band means feeling it. Fortunately, there are bands and songs which are able to transfer waves of emotions. Fortunately, I know some of them."

Ah, now it's getting emo. Now he's talking about the impact of talented people's creativity. And why not, the note writer was Christian Dang, one of the vocalists and guitarists in Pale. He went on, generously trying to explain to the uninitiated the urgent and extreme need that many of us felt for these obscure little cuts of post-punk noise. This hardcore record we held in our sweaty hands.

"It sometimes takes just one chord, one beat, one single tune to unlock the doors to tears, melancholy, happiness and sunshine. Isn't that great? It simply means that you can decide whether you fall into something warm and sad or you rise above all doubts. But the most important thing about music is honesty. This is the base of the little chords and breaks that try to take you away. Being honest is the basic virtue to persuade somebody or something, even if you are the somebody yourself. (Who you are in the first place)"

It's not easy to explain the emotions good music can bring. We all felt it but rarely spoke about it. I'd say that it's quite possibly even harder to explain if you are writing in English when that isn't your first language. So, Christian went back to the vinyl aesthetic.

"Now the question arises, is digital honest? Well, to be honest, I don't know. It's not that easy to answer this, but the fact is, vinyl has always been there and always will. But to prove all this and much more, let Pale and Rydell persuade you and may vinyl be a true emphasis."

Being honest was a basic virtue and a vital part of good music. He'd nailed that. The emotions that this sort of music could bring up were strong and hard to explain, not only for adolescent teenagers, but for twenty something young adults too, who wanted nothing more than to see positives in the world around them, but in failing that, often ended up introverted and creating music that meant something to them. There was much more bound up in all this than just a few punk rock songs and we all knew it. Tonight, we'd travelled another three hundred miles or so just to share it.

Pale and Reno Kid had already set up and sound-checked and, as we were using most of their gear, it was a quick process for us too. Well, sort of, I was having a few initial struggles with a constantly wandering G string on my SG, but eventually managed to tame the beast. Knowing most of these guys would have only heard the Hot Water Music split we jammed through 'Try 17' first and it sounded massive. As it was on the new split and I wanted to check the levels of our dual vocals, we ran through 'Home' too. I always made sure that the sound guy turned my mic down, quite a bit lower than Milo, so I could get all worked up and really belt it out without my screaming ever being too loud or drowning out Milo. I didn't want it too loud. I knew I couldn't really sing so concentrated on the guitar playing, but we all liked the effect dual vocals had in the live situation and it was fun to sing along. I'd do it with or without the mic, we all would. I have to say that this venue had amazing sound, or we thought so at least, especially considering the fact that we were all in a huge underground bomb shelter next to a busy railway line.

As the place filled up, I wandered back over to Dennis, Emre and Elke, who had now set up a Scene Police merch table next to Stefan's. They were looking at the new singles too and Dennis was trading a few for his mail order. Emre was showing Adam the great photo of him on the record insert – he was flying through the air with his Fender Precision bass, a good few feet above the ground, almost hitting his head on a low ceiling at one of our gigs. It was a great pic. And next to that there was some more bumpf about the band, peppered with mini reviews, saying.

'From the ashes of Couch Potatoes (more experienced sense of melody than most bands playing their game. In some vague sense it reminds me of Les Thugs. Top notch –

Heartattack #19) rise Rydell! Rydell from the UK play that mid-tempo emo that y'all been missing since Jawbreaker broke up. (Mellow yet intensive melodies with a raunchy Jawbreakerish vocalist. Fuck, buy this! Trust #72) consisting of ex-members of Couch Potatoes (of course), Pseudo Hippies and Wact, they've been playing in the UK for almost friggin forever and are now expanding into Europe... after their highly successful tour with Hot Water Music (with whom they also have a split 7") and some German gigs for the Food Not Bombs benefit, they are ready for their 4th release (might we say 5th if you wanna include the Couchies CD) with them German emo-rockers Pale. After playing some highly successful gigs in the UK with them, this release was inevitable!'

Crikey, these guys were hyping us up, and I started to feel the rare and unwanted sensation of pre-gig nerves creeping up on me. I just wanted to get on stage and get on with it now.

Reno Kid went on first and they were great. They played melodic emo with big jangly guitars and introspective lyrics, very much like Pop Unknown or Cross My Heart, or even a more upbeat Mineral. They already had their 'Hearts pounding everywhere' split with Soulmate out on Soda Records, and this was the launch show for their split with Drifts Get Deeper; the 7" on black and white vinyl with Soda in Germany, and the CD EP on Nerd Rock Records in the US. They would very soon have their brilliant album, 'Sun you've got to hurry', out on Defiance Records too. They should have been massive, and this would be the first of quite a few shows we'd play with them.

Pale had continued to develop their own style of hardcore in a very quirky and clever direction. They were even better now than when we'd last played together, and far more confident of themselves. Holger, Christian, Hilly and Stephan filled the stage, and I couldn't help but think that Holger and Christian harmonised way better than me and Milo ever could. They reminded me of Braid, around the time of 'Frame & Canvas', by far their best record, but with a very homespun European style too. It was hard to put your finger on exactly what made these guys so great. They had the Get Up Kids and Promise Ring influences we all loved, but threw in electronic gadgetry and little original touches that just kept you guessing throughout their set. This was a hometown show for them and the crowd loved it.

There were loads of people there we knew from our last visit, and everyone seemed to be having great fun. At the end of the night, we didn't really want to leave, but Elke, Dennis' long suffering but ever friendly girlfriend, had said we could all stay at her flat and the chance of a shower and some sleep persuaded us out of the door and back on the road.

The next day we headed in convoy southeast along the Rhine valley for about a hundred miles, passing Remagen (with its famous bridge), Koblenz (with its famous castle) and Wiesbaden (twin town of Tunbridge Wells) on the way to Mainz and its A.Z. or Autonomous Centre where the next gig would take place. I'd noticed the bigger venues were called AZ now instead of JZ, or Jugendzentrum. We were playing art centres instead of youth clubs.

Mainz was a big old city, known to most people as the home of Johannes Gutenberg, the inventor of the printing press (actually the moveable metal-type printing press, or letterpress) but remembered by me now as the first place I'd see Jimmy Eat World play a gig in Europe when I was there for the show they filmed the 'Salt, Sweat, Sugar' video at, about two years after the show we were about to play.

A band called Dear Diary were meant to be playing with us tonight, but they'd had to pull out for some reason, so the Reno Kid guys had jumped on it and came along with us too. This was a decent-sized venue where Hot Water Music, Pop Unknown and Boy Sets Fire had all recently played. We met the promoters, Mark and the Atrox guys, and they showed us around, taking us to a backroom where we could rest and just hang out before the show. Every inch of it was covered in graffiti, and some hippy fucker with the widest flares I'd ever seen was sitting on the couch in there smoking a huge bong throughout the entire show.

Losome opened up for us and blasted out some seriously heavy hardcore. They were good and surprisingly easy to sing along to as all their choruses were just, 'Yeeaaahhhhhhhh'. Emre was filming this trip and took some cool footage of the show, with us and Reno Kid rocking out, singing into microphones with pop-covers that looked like giant oranges, and dedicating the whole set to my brother, Steve, who'd just been in a car crash again, sticking his beautiful Datsun Fairlady through someone's hedge whilst out racing around in it. He was fine, I'm glad to say, but his classic car didn't fare so well, and nor did the hedge.

The next day we were back in Bonn for the big 'Caffe a la Rydell' gig that had been promoted not only by Dennis and Scene Police, but also by the Revolution Inside guys, the label that put the Food Not Bombs EP out and ran a great local record shop. All the flyers had a big coffee cup on them, with the Starbucks logo changed to a Scene Police logo and Caffe a la Rydell written across the top. All the information was there, bands (Rydell, Kurt and Painted Thin), time, place, and I particularly like the part where it suggested the gig would be 'full-flavoured and satisfying'.

It seemed to us that every punk in Bonn had turned out. Rydell opened this one to a crowded house that just got hotter and hotter. Everyone was jumping about, and the sound was great. Kurt brought a noisy brand of punk rock 'n' roll straight out of the Black Forest and were pushing a new album out on X-Mist Records. Painted Thin had come all the way from Winnipeg in Canada to play their melodic pop-punk. They had a new album out, called 'Clear, Plausible Stories' on a record label I'd never heard of with the bizarre name, The Company With The Golden Arm Records. The band featured Stephen Carroll and Jason Tait of The Weakerthans, another Canadian pop-punk band, and seemed to be very well respected. It turned out to be a really fun show, so big thanks to Painted Thin for letting us use all their gear and thanks also to our No.1 fans Mark and Rene for turning up yet again to cheer us on. They'd been to every gig that weekend. We hung out for a while with Dennis and Dirk, the Diggler from Tumult, then thanked everyone profusely, especially Elke for putting up with us all weekend, and hammered off towards the ferry and home. It had been a great weekend.

11/5/99 One Day Elliott, Rydell and Changeling at The Union Bar, Maidstone
12/6/99 Rudedog and Rydell at The Albert, Brighton
25/6 and 10/7 Rydell and others at The Union Bar, Maidstone
6/8/99 Babies Three, Rydell and Cut Your Own Head Off at The Lido, Margate

Over the next months we played loads more gigs and started to see even more reviews of the new releases we'd been sending out. These in turn seemed to help us get even more gigs, or the good ones did at least. We kept on writing new songs and improving the ones we had, and that meant we wanted to record again too and then chase up more labels for releases. We kept busy and kept on getting our songs out there.

A new local pop punk band called One Day Elliott invited us to play a show with them in their hometown of Maidstone. They told us that the gig would be a metal night at a new club, and we'd be the support acts. That was fine by us, it sounded like a good night out. When we arrived the headlining heavy metal band were still sound-checking, so we went over and greeted the promoters and other band, as you do, then went to get some drinks, leaving our guitars by the stage. We were chatting with the One Day Elliott guys and swapping some demo tapes, looking forward to seeing each other play, but half an hour later, Changeling, the metal band, were still bloody sound-checking! It was all hair and galloping horses riffs and double bass drumming, and I didn't mind a bit of this, but thought maybe they'd save something for the actual show and let us have a quick levels check on our gear too. This was becoming an onstage practise. We waited a while longer and it was now well past the time the doors should've been open and the club filling up. Even the sound guys were getting impatient, playing with lights and a smoke-machine instead of paying attention, one of them saying, "Yep, that'll do. I think we got it," over and over, but to no avail. The metalling went on for what seemed like an age, and the promoters, Steve, Simon and James, decided they'd just open the doors. A few kids started to filter in but instead of going to the bar or finding a table in one of the dark corners, they went and stood in front of the stage, nodding along, thinking the show had already begun. This just encouraged the metallers to noodle around even more. I tell you, there was no easy way this band could have spent any longer sound-checking. They just didn't give a shit. I think at this stage they were working on the perfect sound level for their cow-bell or something like that. It was now over an hour since we arrived, and they still sucked.

We did get to play eventually, but had to cut our set short, and so did One Day Elliott, which was a shame as even at this early stage, ODE displayed a talent for writing great pop punk songs with catchy choruses and well-harmonised vocals. They are still going strong now, one of the longest running bands I know, with hundreds of gigs under their belts and many records out, including one of their best, an EP called 'Triple A Side', on Engineer Records. The promoters liked what they'd heard of Rydell though and invited us back so we could play a longer set. We revisited the Union Bar on 25th June and again on 10th July, playing to bigger crowds each time.

At another of our shows, down in Brighton at The Albert on 12th June, we supported our mates Rudedog again. This was basically still the BBMFs, but a more polished and 'chart-friendly' version. They'd had interest from some big management companies, including some of the people involved with Take That, but for some reason it just hadn't worked out. They could write a great song and had even moved with the times, taking on a new guy, Jez, formerly of Shelley Arms mainstays The Lawnmower Men, who'd be scratching on turntables and adding samples and effects to their set. It was still a fun show with the guys jumping around, bumping into each other and spilling beer over everything, but it was a million miles away from the antics of their Shelley Arms heyday, and I couldn't help but wish they had a more 'alternative' band as well. They hardly ever played and this was around the time that we started speaking with Macca, their bassist, about joining Rydell on second guitar, so Milo could concentrate on vocals. We'd all been friends for years and Macca was into the idea from the start. He wasn't unhappy with Rudedog, but he was really into what Rydell were doing and wanted to be in a band that played a lot of gigs. Rudedog only played a few times each year at this point, and we played all the time and wanted to do even more. Macca and Duncan went back an especially long way, growing up minutes from each other and going to the same school. It would take a while for him to join and get up to speed, but that would be a good thing all around when it came and massively improve us as a band. For now though, we forged ahead as a four-piece.

Rydell played shows all through the summer and were looking forward to some more gigs supporting Hot Water Music in August. As a warm-up for those, we booked a weekend of local shows, with the Friday in Margate, Saturday in Tunbridge Wells and Sunday in Eastbourne. The best and most memorable of these was the Margate show at The Lido with Babies Three and Cut Your Own Head Off.

The Lido was a great venue. Small enough to have atmosphere, but big enough to hold maybe 250 people at a push. Situated right on Margate's seafront with its cliffside bar housed underneath a 1920's art-deco swimming pool, it was full of plush red cloth seats and dark corners for dirty deeds. Although very run down in the late Nineties it was the ideal venue for hardcore shows and would soon become the main location for 'Geekscene' promotions nights, set up by Paul Waller from Babies Three with a bunch of his friends. They'd put on gigs and bring bands to the town as often as they could. We supported their efforts, by both playing and promoting, and saw so many great and intimate shows there. This would be our first gig at the Lido.

As we rolled into Margate past Dreamland, travelling along its ageing seafront, all we could smell was rotting seaweed and the only gig posters we could see were for Chas 'n' Dave. That didn't bode well, but as we rounded the corner past the clocktower and casino, heading towards the lido, we soon saw lots of alternative kids walking that way and hanging around. We'd found the venue. We knew The Babies Three well and spotted Dan and Russ hanging around outside. They were looking forward to the show and had invited all their friends. Jim, one of The Babies guitarists, was also playing drums for a new band, CYOHO, and they would play tonight too.

CYOHO stood for Cut Your Own Head Off, an interesting name as well as a clear and friendly instruction for anyone they didn't like. They'd played their first show just a week or two before, supporting End of the Century Party, a hardcore band from Tampa in Florida, and part of the whole HWM / Gainsville scene. EOTCP had a great album out on Belladonna Records called 'Isn't it perfectly fucking delightful to be so goddamn certain' which featured tracks with excellent and endearing names like 'Always on the outskirts of enthusiastically missing the point', 'Ask my exorcist or my school psychiatrist', 'People ain't no damn good and shit' and 'The only reason you say you're a vampire is because werewolves and Frankenstein don't get laid'. Anyway, that gig was down the road at The Ship and CYOHO had called themselves Power Violence then, but now had clearly matured and figured out that Cut Your Own Head Off was a far classier moniker. Another friend of ours, Dan Docwra, was on bass and they boasted a couple of singers, one of whom was a guy Milo knew well called Chris Bress. Chris had come along on the Rydell, Babies Three, Sunfactor tour as a roadie and merch guy.

The Lido was full, and we all thanked Habib, the promoter, for letting us play. We tried out heavier versions of 'Dreams and lines', 'Bring the lights down' and 'All my neighbours have moved' live for the first time that evening and rocked our way through most of the 'Rhythm Kings' demo too. We had a cracking evening and The Babies Three were on fire too, rousing a full-on stage invasion of crowd singers to join in with their cover of 'Great Cop'.

14/8/99 Hot Water Music, Discount and Rydell at Stars and Stripes Bar, Brighton
15/8/99 Hot Water Music, Discount, Rydell, Sunfactor, Spy Versus Spy, Annalise, The Autumn Year, Travis Cut and The Tone (All dayer) at The Garage, Islington, London
16/8/99 Hot Water Music, Discount, Rydell and Southport at The Joiners, Southampton
25/8/99 Rydell and Kneejerk at The Red Eye, London

A few days later we were back in Brighton at a new venue called The Stars & Stripes to support Hot Water Music and Discount at one of Buz's 'Just One Life' shows. Buz told us he had real trouble getting a venue for the show on this night so in the end he'd had to settle on a very small and odd little venue behind Western Road, the main shopping street through Brighton. This place was essentially in the car park of the Waitrose supermarket. We had never heard of this venue before, and it was never used again for a gig that I knew of. The Stars and Stripes held no more than sixty or seventy people and the flyer for the show warned people they should arrive at the venue early. When you think how big both Hot Water Music and Discount became later, and were getting even then, it's astonishing they played in somewhere so small! Anyway, it was great to see HWM again and hang out with them. I'm glad to say that they seemed back on top form. Discount headlined the show and predictably enough, it was as packed as it could be and superb fun, even with Milo trying to break every guitar string he touched.

The next day we headed up to London for a Household Name all-dayer with loads of great bands, and it seemed to me that every hardcore kid in town had come out of the woodwork for this one. We were given our furry blue access all areas passes by Lil and wandered around The Garage bumping into loads of people we knew, including a young Frank Turner, then playing in a new hardcore band called Kneejerk, who was there with X's on his shoes and was clearly loving the show.

Rich Levene was there too with most of the S.T.E. crew and asked us if we wanted to play the following night in Southampton, which at this point we were not on the bill for. Of course, we jumped at the chance so ended up playing three of the four UK shows on the HWM and Discount tour.

Chuck Ragan (HWM guitarist and singer) had his wife, Samantha, with him for these shows and she was massively enjoying the trip, taking photos from the side of the stage as each band played. Rydell went on quite late in the day, just before Discount and HWM, and were on good form I'm glad to say. I couldn't remember when I last had so much fun!

At the London show Milo had managed to break his high E string just before we played the last song of our set, but decided he didn't need it for 'All my neighbours have moved' as he essentially just picked the middle four strings the whole way through in a very chiming sort of way. However, something must have been wrong with the tuning peg for that string, as the small screws in the back of the headstock came out and during the song, he remembers catching a glint of something out of the corner of his eye that later turned out to be the tuning peg flying off into the crowd. We couldn't find it when packing up but luckily my brother Steve had an old Westone, the same guitar as Milo, so on the drive home we called him and arranged to pick it up and swap over the tuning peg before the next gig. We really needed some better equipment.

We saw a review of the gig in Dragg fanzine a little while later that said, "The next band that caused my ears to prick up were Rydell, who peddled a nice line in emotional sounding hardcore. The singer looked like someone was repeatedly stamping on his foot. They played some stuff I'd heard before and some stuff I hadn't heard before and just one life d.i.y proudly presents.........................

AN AWESOME DOUBLE HEADER FROM
FLORIDA U.S of A

The angst fueled pop stylings of-

DISCOUNT

AND Leatherface inspired Emo-core Heavyweights-

HOTWATER MUSIC

Plus, your warm up for this evening, local jangle-core types

RYDELL

Saturday 14th August

@ the Stars and Stripes bar,

Western rd, BRIGHTON, behind Waitrose car park,
12 mins walk from Brighton station.

Show ends before last trains. Further info- (01273) 249114

£4-/£3.50cons   Doors open 8pm

PLEASE NOTE: THIS VENUE HAS LIMITED CAPACITY,
SO COME EARLY TO AVOID DISAPPOINTMENT.
THIS IS ONE OF ONLY FOUR SHOWS THESE BANDS
ARE PLAYING IN THE U.K.

Brighton gig flyer

Garage pass

the garage
access
all areas
photo

date 15/8/99

band RYDELL

HOTWATERMUSIC

RYDELL

hwm: just don`t say you lost it
rydell: try seventeen

Ignition PO Box 333, Margate Kent, CT9 2FU, UK

www.scenepolice.de !!! www.ignitiononline.co.uk
distributed in the us by Stickfigure, PO BOX 55462, Atlanta, GA 30308

Fourth pressing HWM /
Rydell split cover

483

it all kicked my ass. Definitely a band to look out for." Well, it was quite a big stage at The Garage but I am pretty clumsy so it may well have been me stamping on Milo's foot!

On Monday we all headed over to Southampton for what was possibly the best gig I'd seen Hot Water Music play yet. This was their first show for the S.T.E. and the set up at The Joiners suited HWM very well. Chuck, Chris, Jason and George had really hit their stride and there were plenty of happy, friendly people dancing around, singing along and having a great time.

Southport also played this Joiners gig with us. They were a noisy mod-punk three-piece with Simon Wells, a talented ex-member of Snuff and Your Mum, singing and playing guitar for them. They rocked along in a raw but melodic punky way, instantly catchy and likeable, kind of a mix of The Jam meets Jawbreaker. It was a great show, with all four bands playing out of their skin, and not bad value either at just £4 on the door.

Emre, from Scene Police, had come down from London for this show too, and the HWM guys were going to drop him back in town the next day on their way up to the next show, at The Duchess in Leeds. But tonight, they all needed a place to stay, so Cov John invited both the travelling bands and all their entourage, about twenty people in all, back to stay at his two-bedroom flat. That must've been a party.

Next week we were back in London at the Red Eye, where we'd supported Discount on their first UK tour in '98, to play at a new alternative club night with Kneejerk, but only a handful of people came out for two more or less unknown bands on a Wednesday night. We made the most of it, as we always did, and it was cool getting to know Kneejerk, agreeing to play more shows with them.

Kneejerk were a three-piece band, with Chris Lucas on guitar and vocals, Frank Turner on bass and vocals, and Ben Dawson on drums. They were determinedly post-punk and heartfelt in style, and we dug that. At this time, they had a self-released CD on their own Now We Must label, called 'Helpless I Cry' and they'd get better and better with Frank taking on more of the vocal duties as they went on to release two more records, a split with Abjure on Skipworth Records called 'Don't clap it startles me', and then an album on Sakari Empire Records called 'The Half Life of Kissing'. This was a fair distance from the tuneful hit-meister Frank Turner that everyone now knows and loves, even from Million Dead, his post-punk band that came after this, but you could see the beginnings glimmering and growing.

More Rydell releases...
'Home' EP, HWM split 4th & 5th presses, Hunter Gatherer split CD
The autumn that year was all about releases for us. First, we had the new semi-acoustic 'Home' EP from Thommy Almdudler at Firewalk With Me Records in Austria. He'd

pressed 1000 copies on black vinyl, and 100 more on blue, and sent a load over to us. He'd then set up promotions and distribution all around Europe through various distros and websites, so that you could buy the EP for a maximum of postpaid. He'd even settle for a good trade through his own Yummy distro. It was proper punk rock, making full use of D.I.Y., underground network distribution, and it worked well. The 7" EP had 'Home' and 'Red Light Runner' on the A-side, with the lyric, "Someone understand me please" written in the run-out grooves, then 'Stars Break Free' and 'Gilsenan' on the B-side with "Constellations are only maps" in the run-out there. The cover photos were taken by me on one of my US trips, and the layout was by Graham 'Fleece' Noble. The record itself had Thommy's very HWM style heart and flame logo for Firewalk With Me on one side, and the Rydell logo with '50s style Cadillac fins and rocket tail-lights on the other. As this was Flame One, his first release, he'd written a note inside too, under the title 'Fear is the only enemy that I know' saying:

"Sometimes I wonder how many hours of my life I have spent in dirty basements so far, listening to screams and whispers and noises of rage and alienation created by people who had the same goal as me: That this one moment could last forever. Because there was nowhere else to go. Because I didn't want to be anywhere else anyway, because it was worth it. To the big bad world out there it might seem ridiculous, but at the end of the day I still don't give a fuck, because these are my memories, all mine, and no one in the world can take them away from me. All my collected flyers and stickers might slowly be yellowing from age, the tapes I have stacked under my bed have not been played for years, some tattoos have faded a bit, but they're still there and that's what counts. They're still there, just like my memories and they won't go away. They can't, because if they do then it was really nothing more than a phase after all. But all the people I met along the way, all the conversations that made me think that I could change the world, all the letters in my mailbox that saved my day, and all that energy was real. And how could I possibly describe it to someone who hasn't been there? Even if I put myself at the risk of sounding cheesy, those are the best of times, and this is my attempt to make them last forever."

Then we'd have the fourth pressing of the Hot Water Music / Rydell split 7" too, although we didn't get too many copies in the UK; most went straight from Germany to supply US distros like Stickfigure, Interpunk, Saul Goodman, Choke, Lumberjack and Very. That meant a fifth pressing very soon too, involving Green Hell, Flight 13 and Cargo distribution in Germany. This version had another new cover, a black and white stripey affair that I wasn't too keen on. I loved the first pressing artwork by Davey Blanco, it was colourful and beautiful. The second pressing was a black and white version of that, and then the third press had a photo of our friend and Scene Police comrade Emre's house in Turkey on the cover. This one just had black and white stripes on it and seemed a little dull to me. But it did contain some more Scene Police info on the inside, as the label had grown considerably since we started, and also a great photo of Hot Water Music and Rydell hanging out together outside the Leon Cavallo show we played in Milan. It also had the new Ignition online details on it too, as our own label and store (the beginnings of Engineer Records) was just picking up then.

Soon we'd see the new Hunter Gatherer / Rydell split CD released by Scene Police Records. It was SCP010, the tenth release on Scene Police already, and featured three tracks from each band and amazing cover artwork by the German artist Lars Renkel. Even before the CD came out, Dennis had been teasing the original artwork on the Scene Police HQ website and using it in ads, and you could see why. It was awesome. The packaging and artwork for all the Scene Police releases was usually pretty damn good, and this one folded out to reveal more original artwork alongside all the song lyrics. We really should have made posters and even more of it. (Later, when we toured with Hunter Gatherer, we did).

The Hunter Gatherer tracks are the powerful but quirky 'Laughing Tiger', 'Train hopping without you' and 'In stained glass waiting'. I loved that band and was stoked to be on a release with them. They were definitely doing things a little different to most and their style took a while to get used to. That's a good thing I guess, but it made them 'Marmite' in the scene. The slightly more straight-forward emo-pop tracks from Rydell were 'Bring the lights down', 'Dreams and lines' and 'All my neighbours have moved'. All those songs were previously unreleased but would be flying out now. The CD's first press was limited to 1500, but that's pretty good for two independent punk bands. It was distributed in Europe by Dennis at Scene Police, with the help of Flight 13, Green Hell, Revolution Inside, etc and in America by Gav at Stickfigure. The CD would be available for just £4 postpaid and had all our home addresses and emails on it. Including Lars, the artists, in case more people wanted to make use of his great talent.

As well as these main releases, we still had plenty of demos to send out, plus a few copies left of the Pale split, the Babies Three / Sunfactor split and various compilations. I'd also managed to get Rydell songs onto the soundtracks of some new skateboarding, surfing and BMXing videos too. The Keg Farmers, Strange Daze and Surf Nation videos, all filmed by Tim Nunn at Nunn Too Sharp productions and promoted by British Sponger, a popular surfing magazine, all contained Rydell tracks. They were decent quality videos and filmed worldwide (tough job for someone, eh Tim?), and gave us great PR throughout the alternative sports scene. Tim had sent us a few copies of each video to dish out to our friends, so along with all the records, we were keeping the postie busy.

More Reviews...

I realise that old reviews may not be the most riveting things to read, unless you are really into the band in question, but I can hardly say good or bad things about my own band, so I'm taking a few reviews from the alternative press at the time to let other people judge and see what they had to say about Rydell. Of course, we had our fair share

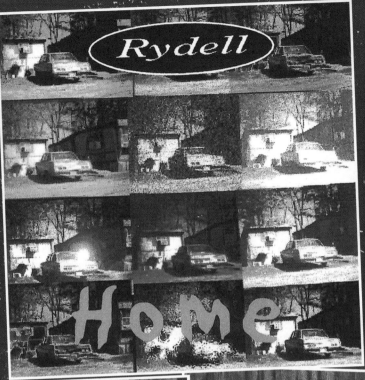

1. Home
2. Red light runner
3. Stars break free
4. Instro
5. Post college rock
6. Gilsenan

Recorded by Rydell and Charlie at Recent Studios in London.
Rydell are: Miles, David, Adam & Duncan.
Cover Design: Fleece Napier. photo: David
Contact: 3 Underhill Lane, Maresfield, Sussex,
TN22 3AY. UK

Rydell `Home´ CD and cassette covers

1. Home
2. Red light runner
3. Stars break free
4. Instro
5. Post college rock
6. Gilsenan

Home

Rydell

DEMO 4 Home

Rydell
3 UNDERHILL
MARESFIELD
SUSSEX
TN22 3AY
01825 767254

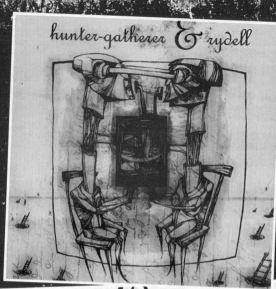

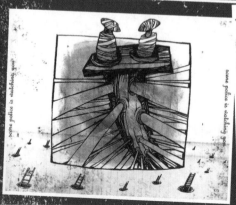

Rydell / Hunter Gatherer split CD artwork

of both shining and stinking reviews, and we took them all with a pinch of salt, knowing that what we were doing was mainly for ourselves. But if you are in band, it's still good to get press, and for the purpose of this book it helps show the development of the band and how we were finding more and more contacts through, and gaining interest from, the all-important grapevine of fanzines. As well as, of course, giving you an idea of how our releases were being received in the scene...

Rydell / Pale split 7" reviews

Collective - What's up with Rydell? All three releases come on European labels, first Scene Police, now Soda from Germany and they have an acoustic 7" lined up on an Austrian one. Some UK label really ought to give these guys a chance as they are rather good. 'Home' starts off rather confusingly with its shouty vocals and drumbeat. Hey, it's a hip-hop record! No, hang on a second, it goes all jangly and laid back, slow building into an enormous indie rock chorus. This song won't help them shake that 'England's (pre-country rock) Chamberlain' tag, although the vocals might engender some Jawbreaker comparisons this time around. Kind of. 'Home' is great, a real indie emo anthem for the masses. With bands like Rydell and Sunfactor, the UK is showing those tired-ass American bands how to do this thing good.

Pale are German and they back up the 'Dell here with a five-minute effort called 'Home is lost (When I'll be back in your heart)' Ooh, listen to that pretty chiming guitar intro and that drum sound. Definite Christie Front Drive, in comes the vocalist and oh, he's American. Or at least sounds like it. Now it sounds like all those bands on Emo Diaries 3 and I am bored. Gee-neric. It has a fast chorus. This sounds like every other emo band ever and that means that although it does sound nice and good, it's not particularly inspired. You have this song already if you own anything by Sunny Day, or Mineral, or CFD, or goddamn anybody. The band they sound most like is Waxwing, who also sound like everyone else.

Pale - Need to bring something new to the indie emo table.
Rydell - Lay a banquet on the whole damn thing.

Only A Phase - I'm out of new ways to describe Rydell's music. This time it has some Hot Water Music influences, especially the use of two vocalists. This song is really cool. I dare to say the best Rydell song ever.

Yummy - One singalong emo rock anthem from Pale that just has to make you feel good and the electric version of 'Home' from Rydell's acoustic record. For lovers of Samiam and the classic DC sound, but not only for those.

Second Nature – Rydell demo 2 (Rhythm Kings)
This could just possibly be the third best demo I've ever gotten for review. Any band

that has done a split with Hot Water Music is most likely worthy of a good review. Extremely Fuel influenced melodic punk emo. Good catchy riffs and good scratchy vocals. I need to hear more!

The Last Resort – Rydell demo 3 - Hmmm. An intriguing one this. Jangly guitars working over a punishing rhythm section, punctuated by passionate yet somehow understated vocals. I can't really put my finger on why it's so damn fantastic... I just know that it is! Maybe it's because it sounds so unlike anything I've ever heard before... or because they've written some classic musical moments, where they manage to be both breathtakingly beautiful and incredibly heavy, while not being obvious about either! The nearest comparisons I can draw are the likes of Bob Tilton, but something about Rydell elevates them onto another plain. I can't wait to hear what they come up with next. The only thing I can say about Rydell with any certainty is that you really should hear this tape.

Scanner – Rydell demo 3 - Just after we got the last issue out Rydell sent us this, their latest five-track demo and the production alone left me gobsmacked! It's really crisp, everything is clearly audible, even the toms for Christ's sake, which is a total rarity for a demo, and it's loud. I get CDs that sound a lot worse than this. It all kicks off with the excellent 'Hey Neve Campbell' from the recent split CD and carries on through the jangly 'You take forever', and then pretty much rocks out on the closing two tracks. If your thing is Split Lip / Samiam kinda tuneage, complete with really strong vocals, then you need this!

Collective – Rydell demo 3 - Another demo tape, another good 'un. Rydell have a 7" out with Hot Water Music, which hints at the area of music they inhabit. Yup, emo rock. But Rydell aren't as gruff or hardcore influenced as HWM. Think Chamberlain (before they went country). Definitely think Chamberlain. There are five songs on here, and as soon as the singing on opener, 'Hey Neve Campbell', starts up you've got the comparison to go with their hardcore influenced indie rock sound. Shouty sung vocals, with that emotional edge that the guy out of Chamberlain has.

'Home' starts off like hip-hop in a bizarre way. I guess it's just the drumbeats and shouting that makes me think that. Anyway, it's soon back into emo rock territory. Kinda minimal at times, guitars aren't doing too much, and vocals and drumming dominates it, but that may just be production. 'You Take Forever' opens up with the chiming pretty guitars that I always love, and then continues in the style of the first couple of songs. Doesn't quite work as well though for some reason, feels a bit messy.

I was most impressed with the final two songs. 'Across Three Parks' is really rocking. Faster, louder, poppier, not too far from what Jetpak did on their Understand split CD.

Cool indeed. Wish it was longer! They finish up on 'Don't Mean A Thing', which again has a bigger, poppier more upbeat sound. Very fine indeed.

They'll complement Sunfactor perfectly on their upcoming tour, so go see them. Especially in Leicester. In fact, I think everyone should come to the Leicester show, even if you live in, say, Cleveland, Ohio.

The Last Resort – Rydell demo 4 (Home, acoustic)
Opening with a reworking of older song 'Home', this six-song tape is something of a departure from Rydell's previous demos. Gone are the pounding electric guitar grooves... this time the band have stripped their sound down to something far more minimalistic, with delicate acoustic guitars to the fore... Rydell unplugged, if you like. But the vocals are as raw and passionate, and the melodies as involved and moving, as before, and the overall effect is, if anything, even more captivating. Rydell are a band who are not afraid to refine their sound and have always mutated from one demo to the next, without ever sounding like anyone else, which is what makes them such an exciting proposition.

The Exclusive – Rydell, Home, demo.
Sort of epic punk, if there is such a thing. I doubt it, but this sounds something like that. Screaming vocals and heavy, almost rock, guitars make this sound a little like pop punk played at the wrong speed, but a lot more tuneful than that sounds.

Rydell `Home´ 7″ EP reviews:

Collective - I want to give this 7" a 10/10 purely on the basis of a little slip of photocopied paper that I found inside the sleeve. The slip of paper contains a truly honest and sincere message that I'm not going to describe here (you'll have to buy the 7" if you're really that bothered); suffice to say that it really touched a chord with me.

For those who don't know, Rydell basically play emo-rock, in a similar vain to Chamberlain. Except on this release, they've gone for the unplugged effect and recorded four acoustic songs. It seems a little odd listening to a song such as 'Home' in such a stripped-down format, but it actually works quite well. And it's definitely the best song out of the four. Although that's not to say that the other three don't cut because they all have a certain charm too. And while I still don't think this is Rydell at their very best you could do a lot worse than picking up this 7". Rating 7/10.

Fates Got A Driver - Rydell doesn't only mean the name of the High School in Grease, but also great poppy, melodic hardcore. Think The Get Up Kids, Cap'n Jazz, Chamberlain with more abrasive vocals.

Cracked #9 - If you should plan a romantic evening in with your lover but don't know where to get the flickering fire from, simply put on this single. So many emotions with hardly any electric distortion is something we're not used to anymore. But exactly this immense honesty surprised me. These four songs are not what everyone had been expecting, but only people without any feelings will be disappointed. But even those could melt...

Scanner #6 - Don't know what it is about these guys outta Sussex but not many bands would get a good review for an acoustic four-track 7". Somehow Rydell have made a great record here. There are some good twists to the songs, the chord progressions keep everything flowing, and then you've got that great vocal over the top of everything. 'Stars break free' features some smart drum loops, but the title track steals the show for me with its arrangement and inventive backing vocals. Right now, we can't get enough of this band and can only urge you to hunt out anything you can by these guys. Come on fellas, we really need an album, and we need it soon!

Silent child, crying soul (Belgian HC zine) - Four sugar sweet acoustic songs from Rydell. I think this is great although it doesn't have to get sweeter than it is now for me to enjoy it. Also, the lyrics (not included!) deal with love and feelings and on the inside of the seven inch is the inscription 'someone understand me please'. It's good boys, but don't take it further, please... The main voice reminds me of Hot Water Music, and furthermore the acoustic sound is awesome. Certainly a must-have for people who are tired of hearing the hard stuff or another Deep Elm styled band.

Dragg - This seemed like a weird idea at first, and I was kinda apprehensive before I listened to it. Rydell play four acoustic songs. Now, they rocked like a mofo when I saw them at the Garage but most of that was down to all the energy they created, and somehow I couldn't picture it being the same with them all sitting round a campfire with two acoustic guitars and a tambourine. Well, it turns out I was wrong. Just as they do live, Rydell shows off all their intense moments; this shows off their jangly introspective side, and what a side it is. The vocals are still just as passionate and sound incredibly powerful and confident, whilst the flowing rhythms set them off nicely. Would have liked to hear one electric track maybe, but for what it is this works perfectly. They have a web page at www.rydell.co.uk. Yeah, this is really rather cool, and you should all try and pick up a copy.

Yummy - Four new mellow, semi-acoustic songs from UK's emo heroes, somewhere in between the Van Pelt, Schema, Fuel or Lungfish. A true emo beauty that will break your heart and will make you fall in love, kid. Coloured vinyl available only through Fire Walk With Me.

Rydell / Hunter Gatherer split CD, reviews:

Scanner #7 - Three tracks from each of these well-matched bands, with Georgia (USA) Hunter Gatherer up first. They do something similar to Hot Water Music I guess, maybe a bit more sparse, but in a similar ball park. A few of the tracks feature some real inventive dual vocals that are layered over each other and get nice and shouty in parts. Scanner favourites Rydell should be familiar to regular readers. After the acoustic 'Home' 7", the guys are back to their electrics for yet more captivating and exquisite tuneage. 'Dreams & Lines' could be the band's best tune yet, with a really infectious lead guitar riff and some deftly understated and addictive lead guitar lines. Of course, all over that you have that great voice that just lifts this band into another league. I really hope Rydell release a shit record soon, because I am running out of positive things to say about them!

Law Of Inertia #8 – Hunter Gatherer, a pretty novel name for a band, do the dual vocal emo thing pretty well, 'weak and touchy' alongside 'hard and gruff'. Sounding more like a deliberate, less rushed Hot Water Music at times and a decent pop band at others, weak n touchy's voice is seriously off when not balanced out by hard n gruff. Maybe it's a Spy vs Spy type of thing, or perhaps they should try to inbreed one singer with more well-rounded vocal chords. The UK-based Rydell shows more polish from the get-go, with pretty guitar work that's just enough to grace the surface of simple rhythm arrangements. The vocals retain the slight edge of raspiness to make one envision a coffee-house poet ranting in the best possible way. Great emo. The Brits win by far. Three tracks each.

Original Sin - Long live the underground. This is a split single between an American hardcore noise band and an English noise-slowcore-emocoreband. Sure, I know, this is perhaps the 1233657th split single, but it's still cool that bands who got rejected by majors get a chance this way. But now comes the most difficult part. Who's best? Well, for me it's undoubtedly the British Rydell (...and it's not cos I'm in touch with them!) but this was something like Girls Against Boys before they discovered the electronics! A band that surely would be loved for anyone who's plugging Org Records. And as for Hunter-Gatherer, well, it was good, but just hardcore noise (...although it's very listenable), but sorry, I prefer Rydell. Every band appears with three songs on here. (Didier, Original Sin, Belgian hardcore zine).

Fracture #12 – Three songs from each band, starting off with America's Hunter Gatherer who are new to me and impressed a lot. They have a fine blend of rock and emo going on... almost constant dual vocals. Rydell seem to be getting gradually more stripped down each time I hear them. 'Dreams and lines' has a neat Promise Ring style riff and a nice poppy feel to it, but the upfront vocals eclipse the catchy riffs.

Collective - It seems as though Rydell have a million and one releases out at the moment. This particular one is a split CD put out by the Scene Police label (you know, the one that seems to coexist in two different countries). And while the whole package looks beautiful, I can't say that I'm totally blown away by the music contained inside. For starters, I'm sure Rydell have written better songs than these. There are three tracks included here, and none of them are a patch on, say, 'Try 17' or any of the songs from the earlier Tour CD. Yes, they are jangly, melodic, nice etc, but for me emo-rock has to have a little more drive, and on this CD Rydell seem to be stuck in first gear. They've also made the mistake of messing up the vocals BIG TIME on 'Dreams and lines' by switching vocalists on the last word of every line. It's hard to describe it but trust me – it does not work.

Hunter Gatherer have three songs which are a little more interesting, although the Hot Water Music aspirations are obvious. Imagine the emo-rock of the 'Music with the emo in the driving seat and the rock providing the directions. Anyway, the first song is fairly solid, the second is pretty good, but the third song, 'in stained-glass waiting', is fucking excellent. Starting off with the mellowest of mellow parts, the whole thing just glides along blissfully until a neat vocal-only part. Which in turn gives way to big, crunching guitar blasts and leaves me with a satisfied grin. Yeah!

OX #38 - Design follows style, one would like to say in view of this split CD, which looks so much like 'Emo' that any other style of music on this CD would have surprised me. Hunter Gatherer, who wrote the first three songs, are from Atlanta*, Georgia and it may sound cheap to compare them to The Get Up Kids, but that's just the way it is. If you like the latter and have a taste for it, you will definitely not be disappointed.

Rydell, who have already published on Scene Police, come from England and are a bit rougher. They have something of an acoustic version of Samiam about them.

(*Hunter Gatherer are actually from Athens, Georgia, the same town as R.E.M., about seventy miles east of Atlanta, and although this was the home of the University of Georgia, these guys were all hairy mountain-men, living in the wooded foothills of the Blue Ridge Mountains. We were surprised they ever came out for shows, but are glad they did!)

ENZK - I'm not one that cares for packaging, but I have to say I really like the artwork on this CD, a sort of wood-cut print style with ink washes. The music from the two bands is great stuff as well. HG steal into your brain with subdued and sparse melodies with strained vocals, and once there give you intense bursts of guitar-laden emotion before lulling you back to calmness and through to energy again, a ride you shouldn't miss. Last issue I said I'd have to be in the right mood for Rydell, but in the more convenient CD format they have become a regular player here. 'Dreams and lines' is so good it hurts, the slightly out of time back-ups work so well, I just love it. They have a sparse and melancholic sound that sounds both sad yet hopeful, and I can sit for ages with this on repeat play, it's just beautiful. (GE)

Anvil #4 – Two bands, six songs and a layout with really intriguing artwork. This CD starts out with Hunter Gatherer's unique and refreshing use of interesting lyrics, which I keep finding myself singing in the shower, and a steady rocking beat. At times I am reminded of Leatherface, by their powerful riffs and personal harmonizing vocals. Rydell picks up where HG left off and keeps the second half of the split rocking with their English tunes. I'm not sure if a comparison to Tomorrow is fair, but it's not too far off. In all, I really liked this split a lot, and with each additional listen I grew more of a liking for each band.

Yummy - So, we really can't help you if don't know Rydell by now. They're the UK's finest and cutest emo poppers at the moment, and still sound as if Washington DC was a British colony. Hunter Gatherer on the other hand are said to sound like a rawer version of Hot Water Music, but that doesn't really matter as long as there is Rydell ;-) 100.

32, Speed kills

Much of the autumn was spent answering fanzine interviews and sending out demos and records. We'd constantly get sent interviews and tried to make time to answer them as thoroughly as possible, sending them back with band photos and current releases so the editors could illustrate them as best they could. The internet was becoming much more prevalent then, but zines were still massively important in the scene, and we worked with as many as possible. Of course, we also made time to gig, as well as write new songs and practise, which was vital. And personally, I did quite a bit of travelling too, mainly around Europe, when the opportunities arose.

I also worked hard on getting my new label, Ignition, going with a couple of early releases and a lot of distro stalls at gigs. Ignition Records was the original name of Engineer Records, until some heavy-handed bullying letters about our name were sent to us by an oxygen-thieving music management agency of the same name, who apparently represented the whining talent-vacuum known as Oasis. We'd been using the name for a couple of years and were the only record label doing so at the time, but they were clearly going to be dicks about it and had much more money, time, solicitors, and inclination to be assholes about it than we did, or would ever want to. Sometimes you just think fuck it, you know? We'd done quite a bit of branding for Ignition early on, and as well as the releases were spending a lot of our time and effort on getting hold of loads of great records for the distro, to sell at gigs. We had better things to do than get into a costly court battle. As the saying goes, you can't win an argument with an idiot. And especially an idiot with money and nothing better to do. So, after some deliberation I decided against wasting time and money arguing with them. As much as a bunch of monied posers trying to push us around annoyed the hell out of me, and I may have reacted differently now, I think it was a name change for the best anyway.

Although angry about it, as you can probably tell, maybe in retrospect we should have more thoroughly explored all angles at the time we decided on the name, beyond making sure there were no other punk or hardcore labels named that. I guess calmer minds should have prevailed, but we were just enthusiastic kids really. Punks starting our own D.I.Y. record label. It was never about big business or competition. Milo was working closely with me throughout the early years of the label, so I asked him for his memories of this event.

"Right around the time we were forced to change the name from Ignition, an identity was becoming established for not only releasing records, but as a mail-order, distro and for putting gigs on. We had actually only just made our first pin badges with the logo on (two designs which also featured Betty Page who we, and seemingly every HC kid around, were all very into at the time) and had just had a great T-shirt design drawn for us by Thomas Hooper, who went on to become one of the world's most respected tattoo artists. Which sadly, because of this debacle, was never able to be used.

"I was answering emails and received one from a guy asking if he could buy the recently released 'Ride OX4: The Best of Ride' CD. I replied to him that we only sold hardcore type stuff and Ride was not really our thing. I was polite and thought nothing more of it. As I recall, it was a couple of days after this email exchange that we received a letter in the post, several pages long, from a lawyer's office saying that we needed to cease and desist using the name Ignition. To this day, I wonder if the person who emailed me asking about the Ride release, which was released on the 'other' Ignition records we didn't know about, had gone away, found the other Ignition and messaged them, telling them they had come across us. This random person could have been the catalyst for us spending weeks having to reinvent ourselves, not only costing us financially, but all the time we had spent working hard to establish the name.

"At the time it seemed that a management company called Ignition, who managed the band Oasis, had at some point in the past taken out the copyright on everything to do with the name Ignition, even though they were not, at the time, actively using any of them. It turned out they had Ignition Books, Ignition Publishing and Ignition Records. My understanding of this, being charitable years later, is that Oasis's Noel Gallagher was a huge fan of the band Ride and wanted to reissue their catalogue at some point, which had been out of print since their original label Creation Records had gone under in 1999. I'm assuming he went to his management with this idea and they were like, 'No problem, we already have a record label name copyrighted, we can use that.' However, if modern internet sources (not always reliable) such as Discogs are to be believed, the other Ignition records were actually occasionally releasing stuff in the late '90s, so it seems they did beat us to the name. I can only put our ignorance of their existence down to the internet still being in its relative infancy. Not everything on earth had an online presence at that time, but I guess even as punks trying to start a business, we could have checked harder.

"My initial thought was that the letter was a joke, but on showing it to David, we figured it was real. It was very specific about what we needed to do, including not using a website called Ignition Records or anything similar; we had to destroy all product with the name Ignition on it (we opted to cover the name / logo with some stickers we had made), and we had to provide a large box (dimensions were given, and it was big) with product bearing our Ignition name and logo 'for destruction'. This last point seems designed simply as a power move and ultimately pointless, as they were likely to simply drop it in a dustbin rather than actually destroy it by burning or something. We actually had something of a laugh with this in the end - more on that in a moment.

"So, we hastily decided on the new name Engineer, I think in part inspired by the first song that Couch Potatoes Mk2 wrote. Back then having a dot.com was expensive. We had to go through a whole process of setting that up again and then getting the guy who basically built our website to move everything over. I ought to point out that by that point Syd had left the label, and much of the day-to-day running was by me and David, and this guy Ian (Sims) who worked in IT and knew about websites, so ran that side of things for us. He had his own part-time label putting out mostly dance music, but we could adapt the framework from that, and then he was basically our go-to for anything to do with the website. We had to ask him to fix / move / change / edit anything pretty much, so those kinds of changes were always a huge effort. I seem to recall we were also paying him a percentage of any revenue we made from online sales in return for using his online pay set up (this was pre PayPal, Venmo, Easy Pay, Shopify, etc where you needed some kind of account with a company like WorldPay that could charge credit cards).

"We had several rolls of stickers printed quickly with the new label name, that were the perfect size to cover the old logo on pretty much all the releases we had out. They were quite expensive too, but necessary, as we didn't want to waste stock.

"I remember calling up Plastic Head Distribution (PHD), who were Ignition's mainstream distributors, although from what I could tell did very little to promote the label, but I guess at least we had an option to potentially get the releases into record stores all over the country. PHD held at least fifty copies of each Ignition release to date, and by that point there were about twenty releases out there. I told them that for legal reasons we had to sticker every copy they held with a new label name. This was going to be painstaking task which would have involved removing the shrink wrap, popping open the CD jewel case, taking out the back cover art, stickering over the old logo then putting the whole thing back together again (without shrink-wrap) for 100s of CDs, plus numerous 7"s and 12"s. I arranged a day to go, rounded up a couple of guys to help me and set off on what was one of the hottest days I can remember. PHD's warehouse was on an industrial estate in the middle of nowhere, down some country lanes somewhere near Oxford. We arrived there after two hours in a car like an oven to be told that they had decided to rearrange their warehouse on that day, and we would not be able to get to our releases. No one had mentioned this to me the day before when I arranged what I needed to do. The girl on reception said that they would be able to do the re-brand for us, and told me to leave a roll of stickers. I stressed to her the importance of this from a legal point of view, and she assured me they would take care of it. I fully expect that they did absolutely nothing and probably lost the stickers, but who knows?

"The final part of the 'other' Ignition lawyer's decree was that we deliver a box to a local solicitor's office in Tunbridge Wells (not the actual legal firm that had contacted us, but a local one affiliated with them) that contained all the items bearing the Ignition logo 'for destruction'. The box dimensions they provided were huge, in the end we managed to get one from a supermarket that was the type they ship toilet rolls in, it was big enough for two people to have climbed into! We filled it with crap for them. We had 1000 Speedwell CDs that had a tiny glitch on the disc making them jump. The pressing plant had sent us 1000 replacement discs which we had switched over into the cases, but for some reason we'd decided to keep the old discs as they could be promos or giveaways. So, I threw those 1000 CDs on spindles in. We also had 1000 covers each for the Dead Red Sea and Rydell / HWM (2nd pressing) 7"s that had both come out really badly so we had to get them re-printed. For some reason, we had kept the bad covers in our storeroom, so I threw them in too. Early on, we had produced an eight-page paper catalogue that was A5 fanzine size as a promo to post out and give away at gigs. Obviously, it dated very quickly so was already redundant, but for some reason our printer had made an insane amount of them, so they went in the box too. Basically, I filled a box with useless rubbish, drove it down to this fancy law firm office, dumped the box at reception, explained what it was to a bewildered receptionist and left.

"The slightly curious end to this saga is that we never heard from these guys again which convinces me that once they had sent that cease-and-desist letter they never gave us another thought and seemingly never checked up with any of the things we spent time and effort changing to please them. The whole process cost us a few thousand pounds and essentially put the identity we had been cultivating back to square one."

That is why all Engineer Records releases, of which there are well over three hundred now, all have catalogue numbers that start with IGN. The releases between '99 and '02 were initially on Ignition, and those included great records from Chamberlain, Speedwell, Crosstide, Planes Mistaken For Stars, Dead Red Sea, Flyswatter, Elemae, Last Year's Diary, San Geronimo, Hot Water Music, Rydell, Winter in June, Urotsukidoji, Steel Rules Die, Eden Maine, Canaan and many more. Crikey, we had some good bands, and we kept on that way, but by IGN030 and Sometimes Why's album, 'To: All Loose Ends' late in '02, we'd changed the label's name to Engineer records. The label has been rolling along as Engineer Records ever since, for over twenty years, with about three hundred and fifty releases now, so one day I may have to write a book about that too!

Anyway, when I was wasn't distracted by that, Rydell played loads more shows too. We were out there rocking it constantly. I remember a great gig for Adam's birthday at The Ship in Margate, with our buddies The Babies Three and a new band called I Said Something. I Said Something were a four-piece with Phil Buch, later of Eden Maine, on vocals and guitar. I'd seen their very first gig, with Appleseed Cast, Babies Three and Unruh at the Lido in Margate just a few weeks before, and they were quickly developing a good sound. They needed a better frontman though, to develop in more of a Far, Sunny Day Real Estate, Sense Field kind of way, and our very own Milo joined them on vocals for a new demo and a few shows, the first at Christmas followed by a few more early the next year. Milo also met his new girlfriend, Clare, over in Margate and ended up moving to the area. We didn't hold it against him at all, the Margate scene was really good around that time, full of friendly kids who wanted to be an active part of things, so it was always a pleasure to head over there and party. Milo continued to run a big part of the Ignition distro there too, so we were all at loads of shows. There was plenty going on and our singer living in a different town didn't slow Rydell down at all. In fact, it probably helped get us even more gigs. It may have helped develop his vocal style too, as I Said Something played three gigs with Milo as their vocalist and recorded a demo, which was very well received by fanzines at the time. But by the summer he bowed out to concentrate on Rydell, and recording our new album.

Not long after the Ship gig, I was down in Taunton, Somerset, for a friend's birthday party, but got nicked for speeding on the way back. I was rushing up the motorway to catch a flight, so it was my own stupid fault. I'd been drinking at the party so luckily had decided to stay the night, but was then running late. I was headed out to the Far East, for a visit to Singapore and Malaysia, from 6th to 21st November and needed to get to Heathrow in time for the flight, so was hammering it a bit, although in good weather and on fairly clear roads. This didn't help though as the cops had obviously seen me coming. Nor did the fact that the pig, lurking beside the road with a radar gun, had clocked me at 112mph either. I'd seen them just in time and slowed down from about 128mph at the last minute, but it was still too late. I used my car constantly, for work and gigs, so now had some serious explaining to do, although the case wouldn't come to court for a while yet.

Good job too, as when I arrived back in the UK, we had a few shows booked with the German bands, Tupamaros and Creuztfeldt. Dennis 'Scene Police' Merklinghaus came to the UK with them, and over a long weekend from 26th to 28th November we played gigs in Birmingham, Bradford and Margate. The best show again being in Margate, kind of an end of tour party with local bands The Babies Three, I Said Something, Neckbreak and Ear Shot all playing too. It was another busy one. I guess no one had anything better to do on a Sunday! Babies Three and Tupamaros were particularly good, with the latter really going for it in a Boy Sets Fire kind of way, and we did a brisk trade on the merch / distro stall too, shifting a lot of copies of the new Hunter Gatherer / Rydell split CD.

Then, from the 11th to 19th December, we headed back to Europe with Dennis and the Tupamaros guys, to play gigs in France, Belgium and Germany. After that we were back home, practising hard and writing new songs, vastly improving the breadth of our set with Mark 'Macca' Wilkinson joining on second guitar. This was something we'd considered before, as Duncan had mentioned Macca was keen to join, but hadn't yet acted upon as we knew Macca as a bassist, and that he was already in Rudedog (The BBMFs new band name, since '94), plus Milo was happy enough playing rhythm guitar and singing too. We were ready now though, and so was Macca. We already knew him as a good friend so just had a few jams with him to see how it would go. Macca turned up with Toby from Rudedog's beautiful old Gordon Smith guitar and we started playing together, showing him the basic second guitar lines that he almost instantly improved. It just worked. Really well.

Milo came over from Margate and met us all at Monster Studio in Hove, where we reworked his guitar parts. Milo could now concentrate on vocals and rabble-rousing, and Macca fitted in perfectly, developing the guitar lines and making them his own very quickly. We were all pleased with the options the new line-up gave us, and we started working on new songs immediately.

It seemed like such a natural progression for the band, and a definite improvement, so looking back now I wonder why we didn't make this change sooner. I asked Macca about what led to him joining us, and he explained a bit more of the history.

"Although I'd played the bass in bands since I was fifteen, I used to hack around on the guitar too, and always had a hankering to have a go at playing six-strings in a band. I was good friends with Duncan in my late teens, and sometime at the turn of the '90s I'd managed to cadge my way into a pre-Angus Bagpipe (they were originally called Cellar Dweller) band practise with Dunc and my brother Nick. I played one chord for about an hour and that was it. Over the years I bothered Duncan to join his band twice more. The next was Angus Bagpipe for their final tour. Joining bands for gigs or tours seemed to be a trend. I also managed to join local hardcore luminaries Strength Alone for their final ever gig, and then for the third time, Rydell some nine or ten years later."

But back to the BBMFs. "When we were in our teens (and for several years after that), we used to play a game called Swing Back and Shoot. It was a fake numbers / drinking game where we'd make the rules up as we went along. The ultimate plan was to get people to join in who didn't know what was going on and get them playing. It was one big in-joke. We found it hilarious, making up increasingly stupid rules, and truly wonderful when people joined in and thought they'd figured out how to play. Anyway, Swing Back and Shoot was a perfect analogy for the BBMFs. One long in-joke that lasted fifteen years. Funny to us, very annoying to anyone else.

"By '94, we were no longer really part of the scene. The BBMFs daft brand of neo-Stupids hardcore had slowed down to a daft brand of shouty rap pop-punk with occasional epic indie aspirations. Not edgy or loud enough for the punk kids, but too loud for anyone else. We didn't really fit in with any other bands, which always made gigs hard to come by, but we kept plugging away and found our own niche. As we got older, it was an easy decision to drop the Big Bastard Mother Fuckers moniker, and we became the Beebs, briefly Easy, and finally Rudedog.

"Through a strange turn of events we ended up with management around that time. With Tim Byrne, who went on to put together and manage Steps, and Alex Kadis, who ran the Take That official magazine and would later manage Mark Owen. They had plans for us, big plans, but unfortunately for them they'd backed a piss-taking, self-deprecating, immature horse, who always managed to self-sabotage any opportunity that came their way.

"We found ourselves on the periphery of the far edge of the mid-90s UK boy band scene. Still the BBMFs at heart, but now subject to 'pec checks', wearing 'band clothes' for gigs and special occasions only, and role-playing interviews for when we made it (we were told 'don't mention the girl friends'). We sat at tables next to Let Loose, Worlds Apart, 911 (literally, at the launch party for Mark Owen's solo album) and were as annoying as we could possibly be.

"A few key moments crystallised both the ridiculousness of the situation and ultimately our ability to torpedo any opportunity presented to us. Epic Records (then part of Sony Music) put us in a studio for a week to see what we could do. The studio (Foel Studios) was halfway up a Welsh mountain and run by Dave Anderson from Hawkwind (before he got bumped by a certain Ian Fraser Kilmister, aka Lemmy). We got to stay there for a week which was a dream, ship in whatever equipment we liked, and drink away our per diems on beer. We got on brilliantly with Dave and a great time was had by all. I used to play a lot of chords on my bass which was great fun for me, but a bugger to record. Dave indulged me and I think we spent at least half our allotted time getting the bass sounding just right, probably leaving only an afternoon for vocals.

"Instead of recording the songs that Epic liked, we chose a new pop-punk number about a mythical Belgian detective duo and a dreary sub-Oasis number called 'Bloke' (about a bloke down the pub). Tim and Alex joined us at some point, and they realised that somewhere between our song choices, delivery and late nights playing pool we weren't going to land the Epic deal. I still remember the penultimate night; we were getting a bollocking for our lack of focus, when there was a knock at the door. Dave Anderson had turned up with his copy of 'Animal Farm' (not the George Orwell version) to lend to us, needless to say, it was more fuel for the fire. We finished recording and mixing on the Sunday and Rob Stringer, the MD of Epic, turned up in his red open-top sports car to collect the cassette by hand. He must have driven a couple of hundred miles. He screeched off with it playing on his tape deck, but I can only imagine he'd popped it out and flung it in a Welsh field somewhere before he'd reached the bottom of the mountain.

"We also got to visit Abbey Road. It was an incredible experience. We got to look around the legendary studios, and I even had a piss next to Gavin Rossdale from Bush, who were recording their second album there with Steve Albini. Unfortunately, we were there to listen to one of the first playthroughs of Mark Owen's solo album, 'Green Man'. There we were, in one of the control rooms at Abbey Road, listening back to Mark Owen's Britpop-inspired album at extra loud volume. Needless to say, it was terrible, we got the giggles and I think we ended up pretty much laughing in the poor man's face.

"We thought we were going to be popstars, but it became increasingly clear as the Nineties wore on that was not going to happen. People use the phrase 'right place right time' and we absolutely were, but we couldn't quite manage to take ourselves seriously enough to do what we needed to do to succeed. We rolled on for a few more years, and indeed ended up playing some of our most coherent well-put together music towards the end, during our 'punk / nu-metal' phase in the early Noughties (unfortunately we were a couple of years too late...)

"Anyway, I liked to keep busy. Rudedog were never a busy band and it meant I had time to play elsewhere. I loved the Rydell tracks Duncan was playing me. 'Try 17' and 'Hey Neve Campbell' sounded amazing to my ears, and I started talking to him about whether Rydell could do with another guitar player. I'd known the other guys in the band for years and it felt like the perfect opportunity. I'm not sure what conversations were had at the other end, but I got the thumbs up and before I knew it, I was stood in Monster Studios in Brighton clutching a borrowed Gordon Smith guitar ready to add my own layer of made-up chords to that Rydell sound. We never looked back."

In the New Year, now as a five-piece, Rydell were booked to play the Emolution evening at the Goldsmiths in London. We were also chasing dates on the upcoming Elliott and Promise Ring tours. Keener than ever now, we would chase gigs with any good bands we knew, and still spent a lot of time hassling every promoter we met.

15/2/2000 Leiah, Rydell and Babies Three at The Ship, Margate (Macca's first show)
19/2/2000 Rydell, Kneejerk, Abdure and Hythe at Goldsmiths Tavern, London

Rydell's first show as a five-piece was on a rainy Tuesday night back at The Ship in Margate. The superb Babies Three kicked things off in their usual energetic style, getting everyone going, and then we rocked out with Milo enjoying only having to worry about his vocals, and Mark really adding to the songs with his great extra guitar lines. This would be the way forward for us and inspired, we'd already written some new tracks and added a couple of songs to the set tonight that went down really well. The headline act for the evening was Sweden's Leiah. More-or-less unknown at the time, they brought a set of massively accomplished, and unexpectedly catchy, emo indie pop-core and blew us all away.

Leiah were a gothic-looking four-piece from a small Swedish coastal town called Gavle and their music could be both mellow or powerful, upbeat or melancholy, but always beautiful. They were soon labelled emo but were an awesome rock band, and great to see playing live. At that point they had just one album out, on Bruno Vandeyvere and Kathy Dejongh's Belgian hardcore label, Genet Records, suitably called 'Mood Shifting Tones'. But over the next months and years they'd have several more; 'The Tigra Songs', 'Surrounded by Sensations' and 'Sound and Diversity' all being rockers, and they'd tour around Europe prolifically, supporting everyone from The Get Up Kids, Hot Water Music, As Friends Rust, Grade and At The Drive-In, as well as Pale and even the El Guapo Stunt Team too! They had a couple of line-up changes, with Gunnar replacing Anders on drums, due to his drugs problems, but made a lot of great music, and when they eventually broke up early in 2004, their main man David Lehnberg, would continue with his solo project, Ariel Kill Him, and later go on to form a new band called The Deer Tracks. Then, in 2018, Leiah reformed to release 'Surrender'.

I asked Milo what he remembered of the Rydell gig with Leiah and he told me, "Apart from it being our first show as a five-piece with Macca having joined us, there are two things that stick in my mind from that show.

"Leiah's frontman David Lehnberg looked unlike anyone I had ever seen fronting a band that operated within the hardcore / punk scene. He had fully embraced the idea that punk allowed you to become anything you wanted to be, and this was true of both his appearance, with make-up, backcombed hair and jewellery, as well as the ambition of the music. It's unsurprising that he went on to become, and continues to be, a highly respected musician in his native Sweden, as both Ariel Kill Him and part of the Deer Tracks.

"Also, nearly everyone I knew who was at that show bought the EP they were selling but was disappointed with it, having witnessed a much more dynamic live set. Sadly, the 'Mood Shifting Tones' EP was made by a band still finding their sound, and a much better debut album, 'The Tigra Songs', most of which was their live set that night, was not released until later that year. I'd highly recommend that anyone who likes the '90s emo sound listen to 'Fleur D'interdit', a track from 'The Tigra Songs', particularly for the honesty of the lyrics and the wild abandon of the playing. I'd like to think that at every Leiah live show, at least one person had their life changed."

A few days later, we'd be up at Tom and Laura's Emolution show at the Goldsmiths in New Cross, London. It was a busy gig, and I couldn't remember when I'd had so much fun at a show in the capital for ages. It was full of friendly people, with four decent bands playing,

Rydell

Leiah

The Babies Three at The Ship, Margate

Kneejerk

Rydell

Goldsmith's Tavern, London

record stalls and plenty of food being collected for the local refugee charity. Much of the hardcore scene had a real emo flavour to the shows around that time. Rydell headlined and rocked our way through the newly re-vamped set. Frank Turner's Kneejerk went on before us and were superb. Still just a three-piece but by then they'd developed their style, adding in Boy Sets Fire-style chaotic hardcore parts, and even a few techno samples to their melodic emo meanderings. Frank was definitely the main man and feeling it. At one point towards the end of their set, he was rolling around on the floor, crying and screaming, and it all seemed to go down very well with the emo crowd.

For that gig Kneejerk and Abjure had a brand-new split CD out on Skipworth Records called 'Don't clap it startles me'. This release contained five songs by each band and, despite its plain parchment cover and handwritten artwork, the CD seemed to be flying off the merch table. Those two bands were gigging together a lot, and we'd join them for a few more shows. Kneejerk would record their excellent but practically unheard-of album, 'The half-life of kissing' that autumn, engineered by Dave Chang at Backstage Studios (Stampin' Ground, Knuckledust, Canvas, etc) which would be released by Sakari Empire Records early in 2001. But unfortunately, late in 2000, Kneejerk called it a day after a terrible all-dayer show up in Nottingham, with xCanaanx and a lot of full-on hardcore bands. Kneejerk were the headline act but rather than play the songs that everyone had come to hear they decided, in truly experimental emo-punk style, to play a thirty-minute-long improvised piece about the plight of the inner cities. For this, they were joined on stage by Franks girlfriend at the time, who wailed away over the unexpected mess of music. The crowd practically bottled them off, so they left, travelled all the way back to London, and the next day announced online that they no longer wanted anything to do with the hardcore scene and broke up.

That was a shame because when they were good, and especially on their new album, they absolutely killed it. Kneejerk had a million ideas crammed into every song, much like Refused's 'Shape of punk to come'. Frank clearly had the bug though and would come back with his new post-punk band, Million Dead, within just a few months. They'd push a self-released demo CD for a while, before signing to Integrity and Xtra Mile Records for a slew of EPs and two albums. Frank Turner's massively successful career as a solo-artist* would start with a bunch of demos released as the 'Campfire Punkrock' EP by Xtra Mile recordings in 2005, and since then he's never looked back. Even with the ever-growing popularity of his well-loved albums full of catchy as hell sing-a-long anthems, I know Frank would be the first to admit that he cut his teeth in the London hardcore scene.

*Although Frank Turner is ostensibly a folk-punk solo-artist he is usually / often ably backed by his brilliant long-term band The Sleeping Souls, named after a line from his song 'I Am Disappeared' and also has a side project hardcore band with the moniker Mongol Horde.

Signing with Cargo Music / Headhunter Records

We'd been keeping incredibly busy for months as a band and for me, the enthusiasm, confidence and excitement from the best days with Couch Potatoes or Joeyfat had returned, and even been surpassed. I was loving writing music with Rydell and really believed in what we were doing. As well as re-working our entire set for two lead guitars now Macca had joined, we were all writing and practising new songs, desperately wanting to record an album. Also, we couldn't wait for each gig. I'd been chasing promoters and labels again. There were big tours coming up that we were trying get gigs on; Hot Water Music in May, Promise Ring in June and Elliott in August. All favourite bands of ours. We had copies of the Hunter Gatherer and Hot Water Music splits, as well as our own singles and demos to send out, and we were speaking with lots of new labels. I was dreaming of a Rydell album, and we all needed this to become a reality.

On the 21st February 2000, I received an email from an A&R* guy called Gubby Szvoboda at Headhunter Records in San Diego, USA. (*A&R meaning 'artists and repertoire', basically a music talent scout for a larger record label). It said:

"Hello Rydell folk. My name is Gubby and I work for Cargo music, with Headhunter as one of the labels under our umbrella.

Headhunter has released records for Rocket From The Crypt, Deadbolts, Thingey, 7 Seconds, Overwhelming Colourfast, Black Heart Procession, Smile, Armchair Martian, 3 Mile Pilot, Garden Variety, My Complex, Boys Life, Big Drill Car, Drive Like Jehu, Uniform Choice, Slap of Reality, The Smears and many more.

We are always interested in who is doing what out there and I have read nothing but great things about you guys.

If you are interested you can send us some material to Cargo music, care of Headhunter Records, Dept 209, Attn Gubby Szvoboda, 4901-906 Morena Blvd, San Diego, CA 92117, USA. You can also email me at this address.

Thanks for your time and I do hope we will be hearing something from you guys soon.

Take care and best of luck in 2000. Sincerely, Gubby".

Bloody hell! It was as simple as that then. A decent sized record label had heard of Rydell, all the way over in America, and were now chasing us. This could be very interesting. This could be the album we wanted to get out there.

I think I'd sent him some info on Rydell and a demo the previous year. He'd clearly liked it and maybe done some research on us. We had a band website up now with a load of news on it, but I don't think there were any tracks streaming on it and certainly no videos yet. This was well before MySpace had started (2003) or even Facebook (2004) or YouTube (2005) so you have to remember the only way labels could hear bands was from demos and releases, or going to see them at a gig. Luckily, we had quite a few tracks on split releases and compilations, as well as being played on various alternative punk and rock radio shows around the world, and reviews in zines throughout the scene, but still, this was very cool and totally unexpected.

I had the feeling, and still do, that sending demos to labels was usually unproductive. They liked to hear of a band organically, through the scene, and have that band be doing good things and building a following before they even get involved. A bit of a chicken and egg situation for new bands, frustratingly, and probably why many of the demos I'd sent out in the past were either ignored, or just received standard issue brush-off letters back from the larger labels. What did we expect? But we'd been focusing on more 'alternative' labels, and these guys actually seemed into it.

I emailed Gubby back and we chatted a little. He was clearly serious. He'd been checking out our releases up to that point and liked what he'd heard. He was therefore a man of taste in my opinion, so I liked the guy already. We spoke about a few other bands we were into, on and off the label, including Chris Broach of Braid's new project, The Firebird Band, who I had heard, and they were speaking with, and also Blink 182, a pop-punk band that I'd never heard of before, but they had signed and were working with already, that Gubby thought I might like.

I told him straight out that we wanted to record a new album, which would be way better than any of the EPs or tracks he'd heard from Rydell so far, but we needed a good label to work with us. I wasn't holding out much hope, to be honest, as I'd been here before about a hundred times, usually with smaller labels, so was just chatting with him about all sorts of stuff and trying my luck. They'd asked, after all, so why not? I posted him some more demos to check out and, although flattered and hopeful, I was glad we had Scene Police, Soda, Firewalk With Me and even Ignition to fall back on, if need be. But a few days later, he emailed back.

"Hello David, Gubby here. For sure we are interested in doing something with you guys. Who is doing this album you are speaking of in your email to me? Scene Police?

Are you signed to anybody? If you are committed to doing an album with Scene Police or someone else, maybe Headhunter could license that record for North America and in turn sign the band to Headhunter? How does that sound?

I would also like to do a singles compilation with you guys too.

Let me know what's up with this new album in regard to who is doing it and of course how you guys feel about signing to Headhunter.

Regardless of what it is, we want to do something with the band, so please get back to me."

Bloody hell. My jaw hit the floor. This could actually be real. I was stoked and wanted to tell the rest of the guys right away. I wrote back though, excitedly, with a few more questions about signing us for an album, and maybe some touring support too. I was getting carried away now. I also mentioned that our US buddies Hunter Gatherer were great and were also looking for a larger label to support them. They'd toured with us in the UK, and I wondered if we could set up a US tour with them, maybe booking it ourselves but with some US label support. I hoped that maybe Gubby could suggest some tour / gig bookers he might know and help us that way too, as he was definitely into the band. Then maybe he'd get to see us live and really see where we were coming from. But that said, he already seemed to get it. He came back saying that he'd ask the guys from Hunter Gatherer to send him some material, as I'd suggested, and maybe if the other guys there at Cargo liked them too, they could help with a tour, or even a release. He came back to me on that in his next email:

"I am really surprised that you guys are booking yourselves. An old friend of mine runs CNL bookings over here, Jon Barry. He books a lot of the Touch And Go and Dischord bands over here. Man, that would be great if you guys could come over and play some shows. Anyway, please get back to me and let me know how we should proceed. Take care of yourself. Sincerely, Gubby."

Bloody hell, again. I wanted to simply send back, "Mate, we should proceed with you signing us and putting out a new album whilst setting up a US tour!" but I considered my response more carefully. Up to that point, we'd never had a record out in the USA. We had some releases being distributed over there, mainly by friends and helpful scene guys, like Gav at Stickfigure and Var at No Idea. And they had also suggested a possible summer tour for us over there, either with Hot Water Music or Panthro UK United 13, but nothing had come of it yet. We didn't have a manager or anything like that. We were far too punk rock so just did it all ourselves.

We did have some very good friends in the scene though, and it'd be fair to say that by now quite a few people with respected taste were getting into what Rydell was doing. We'd had an offer from the ex-manager of Braid about supporting us in the US if we could get over, this was who I'd heard of Chris Broach's new band from, and we had another indie showcase gig coming up in London, in front of Creation and some of the bigger indie labels, but we knew that would be a waste of time. I never really expected them to 'get it' and we didn't hold out much hope that they'd see where we were coming from. Gubby, and now his boss Eric Goodis, the owner of the label, and several of the other top guys at Cargo / Headhunter clearly did 'get it'.

We could just soldier on doing our own thing, of course. I knew Dennis and Emre at Scene Police would probably put out an album for us if we asked them, and they'd do a good job of it too. But the promotion would be mainly in Europe, and they certainly couldn't pay us to record it. Also, it would be very cool if we could go over and tour in the USA. Imagine that. We'd have a riot and get our records out to loads more people too. This was good timing, Milo, Adam, Duncan and I having just roped in Macca to join the band on second guitar, we were sounding better than ever live, and we were confident that the new songs all had extra nuances to them which would sound great when we finally made it back into a recording studio.

I wrote back to Gubby the next morning, finding it hard to conceal how chuffed I was, but wanting to make sure this was the real deal and getting them to send something over for us to look at and sign, so I could discuss with all the guys.

"Hello Gubby, good to hear from you again. I was having a fairly crummy morning and you have cheered me up. We are still working on the new album, and have not yet agreed which label will be putting it out. We would love it to be Headhunter though, maybe both in the USA and Europe, that would be great.

Scene Police have said they will do it and they are good friends of ours, and No Idea might put it out in the USA, but Cargo/Headhunter would be a better choice for us overall, for distribution and promotion. You guys would be our first choice.

"Also, all the songs we have released so far have been on smaller independent labels, so all the song rights are still ours and we have signed nothing. If you guys are into doing a singles compilation or something like that before the new album, then that'd be cool and fine by us too. There should be no problems with any of this, and we would be absolutely stoked to sign to Headhunter and get all our music to an even bigger audience.

"About show bookings, we know loads of people, many UK promoters and labels in Europe, so shows over here never seem to be a problem. We'd love to play in North America though. I have never spoken with Jon Barry, and any good booking contacts are always very useful. Thank you.

"Anyway, let me know what the situation would be regarding you guys releasing our album or whatever. Also, if Headhunter would pay for the recording or just the release. I only ask because the new songs are almost there, but we will have to wait a while to save enough money for the studio.

Talk with you again soon I hope, Cheers. David / Rydell."

That was it, I was off to see The Promise Ring and Burning Airlines play in London that night, so tried not to think about it too much more. An impossible task. The next day I heard back from Gubby, who it turned out was their main designer as well as A&R man and was actually based in Cargo's Montreal office. Then I heard from Eric Goodis, the label boss, based in the San Diego head office, who told me he'd been listening to our demos in his car and absolutely loved them. And then I heard from Jim MacPherson, their tour booking and promo guy, who wanted to get started on booking US gigs for us as soon as possible. Christ on a bike! This was nothing short of bloody awesome and would surely step things up another gear for Rydell. To say we were stoked would be an understatement. I exchanged a few more emails with them, and a couple of days later a hefty document arrived in the post. It was Rydell's recording artist agreement with Headhunter Records / Cargo Music, and it was for three albums, with promotion and touring support.

The agreement seemed a bit wordy and contained a lot of US legal jargon, but I read through it with interest, nonetheless. It was to be signed by all of us and then countersigned by Eric Goodis on behalf of Cargo Records.

There's no doubt these were the golden words we wanted to hear from a larger record label, and ideally a US label so we could go and tour there too. Part of me felt bad for wanting this instead of being happy with all the cool little indie labels we already worked with, and another part of me still didn't really believe it, and wouldn't until we had a new record in our hands. But the larger part of me was over the moon and couldn't wait to get this rolling.

At the next practise, we all discussed the agreement and, not seeing any downside, signed. What the hell. We scribbled our signatures on the contract, resting on the bonnet of my car outside the practise studios in Kemptown, Brighton, next to the old public toilets! Then we sent it back, recorded airmail, and waited.

We were excited about the whole thing so started looking for a good recording studio straight away, whilst working even harder on the new songs for what would soon become Rydell's 'Per Ardua Ad Astra' album. We were on our way to a larger audience and even more gigs, or so we thought, as for some reason this piece of paper and the few promised dollars behind it made us all feel a bit more like a proper band. A real rock band who would soon have our albums displayed on shelves in high street chain stores while we toured around the US living the high life. Haha. We couldn't wait.

In the meantime, I exchanged more emails with Eric, where he confirmed that this would be a three album deal if we wanted it, and they'd cover the recording costs, pr and promo costs, distribution, etc. Jim, who was keen on the gigging and touring ideas, suggested we started with an east coast trip when the first record was ready and he'd book it. And we could bring Hunter Gatherer along too if we wanted – that way we could borrow their backline. And the Gubster too, who discussed artwork and layout ideas with me, but was more keen on chatting about our gigs and all the other bands we were into in the UK and Europe.

Back in the real world, we had more shows coming up, the next being a local gig at The Forum with two indie bands, Absolute and Trilogy. But before that I had another work trip to Italy, and then afterwards, just enough time for a couple more practise jams before decent gigs in Brighton and London. I'd then follow that with another trip to the Far East, but by then we had already secured a ten-day slot at the Metway Recording Studios in Brighton, from the 1st to the 10th of July, to record our new album as soon as I was back.

Macca had recommended the Metway as Rudedog had recorded there. We knew this would be a quality studio as it was owned and kitted out by The Levellers, a massively popular folk-rock band who had progressed from dog-on-a-string crustiness to chart-topping pop albums in the early Nineties, so must've had plenty of dosh to spend on the place. This would be way easier for us than going up to London, and Headhunter had agreed to pick up the £200 per day bill too, sending over a £2k advance. The session we'd booked would be the longest we'd ever spent in the studio on one record and, although we didn't think we'd need that long really, we couldn't wait to have the luxury of finding out.

6/5/2000 Hot Water Music, Rydell and Trophy Girls at The Solent Health & Sports Club, Southampton
26/5/2000 King Adora, Rydell and One Day Elliott at The Forum, Tunbridge Wells

While all this was going on, Rydell played a bunch of good shows. We were booked at The Cartoon in Croydon, South London, with a great indie rock band called The Junket. I had their single on Deceptive Records called 'You're the same' and was really into it, so was looking forward to the gig. But then I received a call from Ross, one of the S.T.E. collective promoters saying that they were putting on a Hot Water Music show in Southampton on the same day, 6th May, and we could come and play that if we wanted to. Damn, it was HWM, of course we wanted to play! I hoped we'd get to play with The Junket another time, but decided to call and cancel the show at the Cartoon. I hated doing that. Cancelling any gig was something we very rarely did, and despite most promoters being pretty cool about it and easily finding replacements for us, of course, we still felt bad about letting them down.

I didn't feel bad for too long though, as this was Hot Water Music after all, good guys to a man and one of the most absolutely rocking bands to ever grace a stage. This was now around the time HWM were playing their 'No Division' and 'Live at the Hardback' set, so they were absolutely at the peak of their powers too. The Joiners wasn't available, so this show had been moved three times to different venues for various reasons, and because of that we were a little worried about the turnout. We needn't have been. Ross, Rich and the S.T.E. guys had done a great job as usual, working with Scott Stewart, the tour promoter, and the place was packed. The place in question being a big sweaty gym called the Solent Health and Sports Club in Southampton. We'd set the gear up in what seemed to be the club's lounge as there were sofas all around the walls. This venue had clearly never seen anything like what was about to hit them, and the place was soon a massive sweaty sauna, filled with happy, bouncing, shouting punkers.

There was one incident, early on during the Trophy Girls set, relayed to us later by the S.T.E. guys on the door. A couple of lads paid to get in, but soon decided it wasn't for them and asked for their money back, saying it just wasn't 'rowdy enough' for them. The guys on the door tried to explain that the headliners, Hot Water Music, would be a bit more straight-forward punk than the Slint stylings of Trophy Girls, but they were having none of it and insisted on a refund. This was reluctantly agreed to, but about fifteen minutes later they were back and agitated, saying they'd lost some hash in the venue and had it been handed in? Barely restraining mockery, the S.T.E. guys advised them they didn't have their weed and when they became annoyed by this, told them to do one! Then ironically, the hash was later found and given to a member of Hot Water Music's party. This incident aside, the gig went swimmingly and although the club manager said he didn't want the S.T.E. to put on any more shows there, he admitted that the punks were friendlier and more polite than most of his regulars.

This was Rydell's third gig for the S.T.E. in Southampton, and my eleventh, and possibly the best so far. We played practically a whole new set, much of it for the first time, and had a hell of an evening, rocking out to HWM and enjoying the free danceroom sauna. That gig was just £3.50 on the door to get in, or three quid for concessions, and although it was actually their 184th gig, the posters said 'STE183 - Gig of the year!' and that may well have been right!

Our next show was still fun, but nowhere near as sweaty, sandwiched between our pop-punk buddies from Maidstone, One Day Elliott, and the NME's latest 'ones to watch in the indie scene', King Adora. This gig was back at The Forum in Tunbridge Wells, where it was very easy for us to play, but we were starting to overdo the local shows. That said, it is a cool little venue, and all our friends could come along, so we ended up playing more or less any shows offered to us there. This one we weren't so sure about but ended up doing it anyway. We always had fun with ODE, but King Adora were overrated rubbish and didn't make it an easy gig. They'd just been signed by a label called Superior Quality Recordings, basically an A&M Records offshoot masquerading as a cool indie, having previously signed The Bluetones, Hell is for Heroes, Mover and The Rocking Horses. But now they'd made a bit of a mistake with these glam punks from Birmingham who strutted around on the stage, acting like they owned it, but just couldn't play very well at all. They were regularly

STE Collective Presents: **From Gainsville, Florida USA**
The Gig Of The Year!

Hot Water Music

PLUS RYDELL AND TROPHY GIRLS
Saturday 6th May
New Venue: Solent Health & Sports Club
Lodge Road, Southampton

£3.50/£3   Access: One Step   STE 183

info: 023 80 771 354

Flyer for The Gig Of The Year!

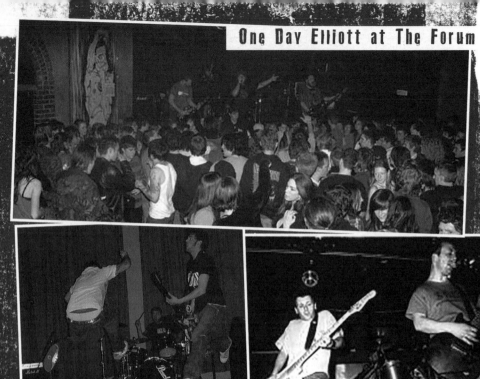

One Day Elliott at The Forum

One Day Elliott

Leatherface

The Underground, Cologne

Sojus 7, Monheim

Dismemberment Plan

Burning Airlines

being compared to The Smiths or The Manics or even the New York Dolls in indie magazines at the time, but I just couldn't see it. Watching them pout and pose in their Oxfam glamour-chic, it all seemed a very thin veneer of punk over a thick dollop of whiny wannabee chart-focused sleaze-pop to me, and I'd sooner see Motley Crue!

Always keen to support worthy causes, Rydell became involved with a couple more benefit compilations released around that time. The first was the Yojimbo benefit on Moonrip Records in aid of the RASAC (Rape and Sexual Abuse Counselling), offering free counselling and helplines for victims. The Rydell song they chose was 'Time of our time', and this twenty-track release also featured tracks by Submission Hold, Serpico, Citizen Fish, Anal Beard, The Tone, Bus Station Loonies, Travis Cut and Portiswood.

The next was Erdata Ishee on Chiggeryellem Records, a twenty-two track compilation raising money for charities supporting homeless children in Ethiopia. The Rydell track on that one was 'Bring the lights down', and the CD also featured songs by Southport, The Duvals, Dina, Lunasuit, Annalise, Wat Tyler, CarCrashDrama, The Know It Alls and Blocko.

8/6/2000 Leatherface and Rydell at The Underground, Cologne
9/6/2000 Errortype 11, Dismemberment Plan and Rydell at The Blackout, Bochum
10/6/2000 Burning Airlines, Rydell and Nothing in Common at Sojus 7, Monheim

Next up, Rydell had another brief trip to Germany planned where we would play three nights in a row, starting Thursday 8/6 with Leatherface at the Underground in Cologne, followed by Friday 9/6 at the Blackout in Bochum with Errortype 11 and The Dismemberment Plan, and finishing on Saturday 10/6 with Burning Airlines and The Promise Ring, at the Sojus 7 in Monheim. What a great trip this would be! Playing some excellent support slots, then all back home to Blighty in time for Sunday lunch in the pub. That sounded like a plan. We'd also be picking up some copies of the latest (fifth) pressing of our 'Try 17' split with Hot Water Music from Dennis at Scene Police while we were over there too.

The Leatherface show was at a very friendly and superbly well organised club in Cologne called The Underground. Although I'd played a gig with HDQ back in the day, and we were occasionally likened to them, this would be the first time we'd played a show with Leatherface, and the prospect was a little daunting as they were one of the most-respected bands in the UK hardcore scene. The band were named after the murderous villain in The Texas Chainsaw Massacre but of course, all turned out to be really friendly guys (for Sunderland fans). Straight off the bat they were happy for us to use all their gear, which made load-in and soundchecks very easy. Frankie Stubbs was like an elder statesman of the hardcore scene, even back then, but he was sitting around with us, just chatting, drinking whisky, wearing an old pair of slippers. Dennis was there, our German fixer and label guy, so was Elke, who was letting us spend the weekend at hers, so we didn't have to crash on beer-soaked club floors every night. Hoffee, the promoter, was hanging out with us too, and so was Jenny 'The Boots', a lovely girl and one of Elke's mates who'd be helping drive us all around.

There must have been 500 people packed into The Underground by the time we hit the stage. It was raucous, rocking and sweaty. We busted through a lot of the new songs for 'Per Ardua' as well as a few older favourites, and the Leatherface guys were hanging out at the side of the stage, tapping their feet and clapping along. Even Frankie had shuffled over, half-drunk by now and still in his slippers. Mark busted a string jumping around in one song, and Frankie handed him his Gordon Smith guitar to use while he restrung and tuned Macca's for him. It was a great atmosphere and so many people sung along to the Leatherface set, knowing the old classics from the 'Mush' and 'Minx' albums, but particularly getting into the new tracks from their split with Hot Water Music on BYO (Better Youth Organisation), their first release since reforming and the lead-up to their great new album, 'Horsebox'. Everyone was just enjoying themselves and clearly not wanting it to end. That ecstatic feeling of one-ness you only really get at an awesome live gig was all pervading. Up close and personal, you could really see why these grizzled northern hardcore martyrs had become as popular and well-respected as they were.

Macca remembers this gig very well too, recounting that, "Rydell were overseas for the first time as a five-piece and playing with the legendary Leatherface! I was still pretty new to the guitar, playing it very much like I played my bass, with lots of chords we'd made up. I was already infamous for breaking bass strings at gigs, so you can imagine what happened when I was faced with weedy little guitar strings. Sure enough, halfway through one of our songs I broke a string, but as I desperately looked around for my bag, hoping there'd be a G in there somewhere, Frankie Stubbs popped up with his guitar for me to use for the rest of the set. This was both amazing and daunting at the same time, as Frankie had a fearsome reputation and he'd just handed me his pride and joy. As you can imagine, I was desperately focused on finishing the set without clunking his guitar or snapping anymore strings. Fortunately, it all went without a hitch. But following our set, Dunk and I somehow managed to get ourselves locked backstage. I can't recall exactly how this happened, but I do remember the backstage area was crammed full of beer, so whilst we missed Leatherface, we managed to drink our way through a huge pile of German pilsner!"

We were lucky enough to play a few more shows with Leatherface as they continued to gig and release records prolifically, right up to their cracking album for Var Thelin and No Idea Records (as well as on their own Big Ugly Fish label) called 'The Stormy Petrel', after the birds they often saw being buffeted in the wind on the coast of their beloved Sunderland. There were Leatherface tracks on punk compilations for the best part of twenty years, and deservedly so. When one collection came out, a discography on Rejected Records in Ireland, the reviewer for Fracture fanzine, clearly a footie fan himself, commented that, "A punk record collection without a Leatherface section is as incomplete as Columbia will be without Carlos Valderama," and I'd say that was about right.

The next night was awesome too. It had to be really; it was Milo's birthday! We'd spent the day hanging out with Dennis in Bonn, then headed over to a small club in Bochum, a mining town in the Ruhr valley. The venue was a small drinking bar called The Blackout that didn't really look like it could hold a hardcore show. But sure enough, the two American bands we'd be supporting were already inside, setting up and sound-checking. They were quiet guys, even a bit grumpy when they realised we'd be sharing their gear, and looked like college kids in button-down shirts, chinos and brogue type shoes (Dismemberment Plan), or blue-collar workers in Carhartt workwear (Errortype 11). These were guys that you'd just walk by on the street, and didn't look punk at all. They were very quiet for Americans too. Non-confrontational and not at all showy. They'd just let their music do the talking, as we were about to find out.

Errortype 11 were very good in a melodic and clever sort of way, very much like Sense Field or Samiam. We'd heard of them from the releases they had out on Some and Crank! Records, so knew roughly what to expect and weren't disappointed. Arty Shepherd, one of their two vocalists and guitarists, had also been in NY's Bad Trip, and would go on to join Gay For Johnny Depp. These days he helps run and book bands at the Brooklyn rock venue, Saint Vitus.

The Dismemberment Plan were an entirely different kettle of fish. Totally new to us and unexpected when they kicked off their quirky, energetic, almost math-rock madness. This tour was to promote their brilliant 'Emergency & I' album on DeSoto Records, and I eagerly picked up a copy, noticing the big names involved in recording this great little band I'd never heard of before. J. Robbins of Government Issue, Jawbox and Burning Airlines fame had mixed it. Don Zientara, who'd engineered most of the early Dischord releases, including Minor Threat and Dag Nasty, seemed to be the main sound engineer. But there was also help in the mix from Alan Douches (Poison the Well, Dillinger Escape Plan, etc), Chad Clark and Roy Grenoble. Up until now, I'd never heard anything of this band. They were a real discovery!

You just didn't know what the other bands were going to be like. Duncan remembers this gig as being with, "The grumpy Americans," but then he had to ask about borrowing their drum kit. Whereas Macca remembers, "Turning up at the venue and inwardly groaning when I saw The Dismemberment Plan on the bill. Having no idea who they were, I assumed from the name that they were probably a local death metal band. How wrong I was! They were utterly incredible live. I'd never seen anything like it, and I was lucky enough to see them again at the Free Butt in Brighton, a year or two later."

This was a great show for Rydell too. Partly buoyed by the occasion of Milo's birthday, we absolutely rocked the Blackout Club that night, then still on a high, went on with a few of the friendlier guys and girls in the audience to a nearby nightclub called the Carpe Noctum, to continue the party until very late. I don't remember how we made it back to Elke's, but when she woke us late in the morning, almost at midday, we were worse for wear, and in no rush to head over to Monheim for the next show.

Luckily, Monheim was not too far away, just about forty miles north up the Rhine valley, past Cologne again, and near to the A46 motorway, which we needed to head home on afterwards. The Sojus 7 Club we would be playing at turned out to be a top-notch venue. Another of those easy-going German social and cultural meeting points, with a stage, café, and both inside and outside areas perfect for hosting any sort of event, but particularly ideal for noisy young punkers to let off their energy. The club and surrounding area were all covered in colourful graffiti, with Sojus 7 painted in large white letters high up on the main brick chimney, so you could see it from far off. The club was named after the Russian Soyuz 7 space rocket, and may well have been modern back in 1969 but was looking well-worn by then. We piled in, enthusiastic as ever to get going, with Dennis, Elke, Jenny and Cello alongside us, but we seemed to be the first ones there, so we all sat, drinking and waiting, enjoying the bonhomie of the talkative promoters.

Soon Michael, Jorg, Rene and Sascha turned up; these guys were in band called Nothing In Common and came from Neuss, just to the west, across the river. They were as affable as it is possible to be, something we'd come to expect from all the German alternative kids we met, and they happily moved all the gear in to set up for soundcheck. I got chatting with Jorg, their guitarist, and exchanged a couple of demo CDs with him. Theirs was self-titled and looked professional in a jewel case, with a printed green cover and containing five powerful but melodic tracks that blew me away on the very first listen. It reminded me of the Couch Potatoes 'Outweighed' album, and it turned out that they sounded like a more polished emo version of that when they played live too. I instantly liked them.

We spent a while jamming together and getting the onstage sound as good as possible, and then went back to waiting while the club started to fill up and the promoters worriedly called the American bands to ask where the hell they were. While we marked time, waiting for more news, we set up the merchandise stall, with the few remaining copies of our demo CDs and all the Rydell/HWM 7"s we had left. Having sold over a hundred at the Leatherface show, and probably fifty more at the Errortype 11 show, that wasn't too many now. We'd sell more tonight too, but wanted to have some left to take back to the UK with us!

Erdata Ishee

A PUNK BENEFIT COMPILATION FOR
HOMELESS CHILDREN IN ETHIOPIA

`Erdata Ishee` comp CD cover

David and Macca, Rydell

Adam and Milo, Rydell

(Scene Police had pressed 720 copies of this fifth version of the split single, but I'd chipped in too, so Dennis gave us 250 copies. He wanted some more to send to Gav at Stickfigure for distribution in the USA, and needed the rest for sale in Germany through his contacts at shops and distros. Thanks to HWM this single was shifting very fast, so would soon lead to a sixth and final pressing of 1000 more, on clear vinyl with a handsome new cover).

Burning Airlines tour van eventually showed up and five guys jumped out, the three in the band, J. Robbins, Bill Barbot and Peter Moffett, as well as their tour manager from DeSoto Records and their ever-busy German driver / roadie / merch guy. The news was bad. The Promise Ring would not make it to tonight's show. Damn! I wanted to see them play again. I thought they were an exceptional band, so that put a downer on things for a while.

Nevertheless, we enjoyed the Nothing in Common set, then thrashed through our own with gay abandon, all lurching around the stage, with Adam and I shouting the backing vocals into the air, Macca now tight as hell on second guitar and playing the tracks like he'd always known them, and Milo conducting things and then cheerfully encouraging the crowd to buy our new records. And soon it was time for Burning Airlines to go on and rock out. Their 'Mission: Control!' album had been out for quite a while, but this was way before the 'Identikit' album and around the time they released a split picture disc 7" with At The Drive-In on Thick Records. They were certainly an accomplished live band. If I'd have known the tracks better, I'd probably have loved them. I know Milo did, and he picked up a copy of the Burning Airlines / Braid split 7" from their merch guy. It was a real shame to be going back already, but it was getting very late, so as soon as they finished playing, we thanked everyone, said our goodbyes, then loaded out and headed home as fast as we could.

33, Per Ardua Ad Astra

1/7 to 10/7/2000 Recording at Metway Studios, Brighton

We headed into The Metway Studio on a gloriously sunny day, early in July. It almost seemed a shame to be going inside on a day like that, but we were on a mission. Since we'd been back in the UK, we'd played a couple more gigs and sent off some older tracks for compilations, but by far our main focus had been practising hard and finishing writing what would soon become the 'Per Ardua Ad Astra' album. We figured we were ready to rock, and couldn't wait to get started.

The Metway was basically The Leveller's studio. They'd had some hugely successful albums in the early Nineties; 'A weapon called the word', 'Levelling the land' and 'Levellers', all of which had hung around in the album charts for quite some time, allowing them a certain artistic altruism. Part of which was to fund their own recording studio, which they'd set up in an old warehouse in Canning Street, within the stylish Kemptown area of Brighton, sandwiched between the pier and lanes on one side and the marina and racecourse on the other. It was right at the end of the road, at number 55, so it had a big red 55 painted above the huge wooden double doors that led into the courtyard, and Metway, painted in red on the warehouse walls. This studio was way easier for all of us to get to than London; it was near to home but, in the sun, felt almost like being on holiday, and importantly, it had a lot more space and far better equipment for us to make use of too.

There was nothing wrong with Charlie Mackintosh and Recent Studios in London, apart from the desk cutting out when trains went past, but we just wanted to try something different with the new songs. We'd been up to Recent just a couple of months before to record the semi-acoustic 'Home' demo, and then again for an EP on the Austrian record label, Firewalk With Me. We were satisfied with those, and still had some unreleased tracks coming out on a split CD with our mates Hunter Gatherer on Scene Police Records too. We'd been keeping busy, sending off demos all over and offering tracks for upcoming Southern, Cargo and Deep Elm compilation CDs, but what we really needed were better tracks and better recordings. We knew it, and that was what we were here to do. Plus, this studio had a pool table and kitchen, so we might just move in.

For our part, we thought that we had some cracking new songs that deserved a better recording. We had the added guitar lines from Macca, and our songs were definitely getting stronger as we were influenced by all the great bands we'd been lucky enough to be playing gigs with too. We asked Charlie if he'd come down from London for a holiday on the coast to produce the recording and luckily, we also met Jake Rousham, the endlessly patient studio engineer at Metway, who definitely knew his way around the mixing desk. At the time I didn't realise it, but Jake was formerly in the Brighton psyche rock band Hooflung, who had a track on the 'Ingrown Toejam' compilation LP a few years earlier, famous in our local scene for featuring the only BBMFs track to ever make it onto vinyl. Anyway, between the two of them, Charlie and Jake were a huge help. They really seemed to understand where we were coming from and what sort of sound we were after, and they helped us get those ideas onto tape.

Looking back now, I will say that having two engineers / producers for the record was problematic from a practical point of view. We hadn't really considered this and unfortunately, it led to a few complications. We liked Charlie and how he had made the earlier demos sound, so wanted him around I guess as a safety net, but it was Jake's studio and he seemed to think he was going to 'produce' us as well as record us. In the end, Charlie only came down for the mixing, but I think Jake took some issue with this and I noticed several times when Charlie would adjust something in the mix that, as soon as he walked away, Jake would adjust it back to exactly where it had been previously. Also, Jake smoked weed constantly so several of us must have been indirectly stoned for the whole week, just from being in the same room with him for ten hours a day.

Like any band going into the recording studio, we were excited about our new tracks and had plenty of new ideas. We also wanted to re-work and re-record four older songs, three of which had only been recorded semi-acoustically before, and we had eight brand new songs, as yet unrecorded, plus a ninth idea we were working on. We were still a scruffy punk band, but our gigs and practises lately were getting much tighter. As a five-piece our songs were sounding fuller too, and most were overflowing with melodies or crammed with riffs. We did okay before, but time in this studio just allowed us more scope so the record would sound way more complete. Macca was a brilliant bassist, but we already had a great bassist in Adam, so having him on second guitar now allowed us to add extra hooks where they were needed, and gave us much more power live too. It was definitely the way forward for Rydell, and this recording would define our sound from then on.

We'd all upgraded our equipment, restrung and cleaned our guitars. They'd seen a lot of sweaty use recently, after all. I had my battered but trusty old Gibson SG, and Macca had his new Epiphone SG. Adam had new strings and a new strap on his Fender Precision bass. Milo had scribbled all his lyrics down in a scruffy notepad, and even Duncan had bought himself a new cymbal and a bunch of drumsticks. More than you'd imagine he'd need in fact, but he went through them fast, turning the hickory into wood chips at a rapid pace. We were eager to get started but confident we had plenty of time, so planned on adding some acoustic guitar parts and effects on this record too. When we went into the main sound room, we found it had all sorts of goodies there, including a Steinway grand piano in one corner, that Dunc decided to have a go on. That sounded amazing, so we all agreed to add some keys from that in too, if they fitted. It was a musician's playground really, so easy to get distracted, but very creative.

We were messing around for quite a while, but Jake soon brought us back into focus with, "OK, let's get this show on the road," as he started putting microphones all around the drum kit. We wanted to record the basis of the songs more or less live, as if it were a gig, as we usually did. Then only adding in what was needed, and hoping not to need many retakes. This was what we were used to, and the studio equipment was still analogue, not digital yet, so drop-ins or fixes weren't easy. To do that we had to get the initial sounds we recorded as close to what we finally wanted as possible. This can be hardest with the drums, so Dunc spent what seemed like ages getting his kit sounding just right, with the liberal addition of gaffa tape and sponges, and all sorts of nonsense. Adam and I took this as a chance to go out and get supplies of Coke and ice-cream.

Things sound different in a studio than live, so it can take a while to get everything set up and sounding just how you want it. The drums are always first and take a while, then the bass, then guitars, and we jammed through the music a lot over the first days. Macca and I were like duelling banjos on the guitars and improved most of the melody lines as we went along. Musically we found the sound we were happy with and started recording. This could be very dull for the singer though, and on top of that I think Milo was feeling some anxiety about the recording, so decided to join us after the first couple of days, when something had actually been recorded. His initial intention was to record the vocals for each track as the music was finished, rather than waiting until last as was normal, and recording all the vocals at the end in a day. This seemed sensible enough and he arrived just as we completed one of the first songs. This track, 'The plot is lost', has a number of shouted 'Yeahs' in it, which are held notes, and Jake kept on getting him to sing them again and again, looking for the perfect version. Milo should have said he'd come back to those and fix any lines later when he'd warmed up, but obviously had it in his head that this was some kind of proper record we were making here, with a professional engineer, and he had to give it everything there and then. Dammit. The combination of singing the same (slightly too high for his range) vocal, probably combined with the stress he was feeling about it all, basically destroyed his voice and he needed a break. We wanted to do the songs justice so agreed he should come back later, ironically meaning that he'd have to do what he had been trying to avoid all along.

I thought the vocals went well, but I know Milo doesn't think they're as good as he could have done, especially considering how strong his voice had been at the gigs in the run up to that recording. He'd been regularly singing with two bands for the first half of the year and developing his unique style. He'd even been drinking a lot of coffee and trying to relax, so as not to push it too hard. I've asked him about it since as I've always been very proud of this album, and I'd like to think he is too. He told me; "In the long run it took my voice a couple of years to fully recover. We had a few months where I could not even finish a set without losing my voice; on one occasion, I had to leave the stage mid-set and you bravely sung the rest of the songs on your own. I'll always remember watching from the crowd, feeling like a total failure for letting the band down." I know, I've told him that's ridiculous and he rocks! But stress and anxiety suck, and can get to any of us. We all agreed that Milo's singing voice was great and definitely part of Rydell's unique character. On reflection, talking about unique character, I'm off to have a word with Duncan about his jazz-drumming style now!

Despite all this, over the next five or six days we recorded thirteen songs, and listening back to the mixes we could already hear a huge step up in the quality of the recordings. New tracks always sounded great blasted through huge studio quality speakers via the mixing desk, but we'd take them outside to the car too, and listen on the way home, checking the levels and considering what might be needed. We still had time, but by the end of the week we'd only need to add or adjust very few parts. 'Per Ardua Ad Astra' is a very genuine record.

At this point our new, and first, full-length album was still untitled. We were breaking the recording session up with quick trips to the beach and veggie-burger bars, and discussing things like the album name and artwork, and what order the tracks should run in. I think we came up with the name for the record sitting on the beach in Brighton one evening. I thought 'Per Ardua Ad Astra' sounded cool, and we all liked the encouraging message of 'through hardship to the stars', at some point later finding out that it was the RAF's motto too. If we'd have simply named the album that in English, it would have been way too dull and seem far too much like hard work, but in Latin we thought it sounded interesting, even slightly mysterious, so went with that. We didn't over-think it or feel it was pretentious in any way, just that it sounded quite cool and was a bit different to what people might expect. You have to remember that although our music and lyrics were certainly heartfelt and earnest enough, we were really just a bunch of young guys messing about and having fun. Our focus was on writing music, playing gigs and getting the record out. Even the band's name, Rydell, although inspired by the high school in 'Grease', was more a statement about cliques of kids hanging out and exploring relationships. Milo was really into this sort of teen angst symbolism, and we were all fine with that. It was all very John Hughes (the '80s American film-maker) and as much about the mundane and everyday as it was any form of art. We did feel like we were on a journey though, with all its ups and downs and twists and turns, and we definitely wanted to encourage others to take their own journeys, in some kind of positive, alternative

Per Ardua Ad Astra

`Per Ardua Ad Astra`
CD artwork

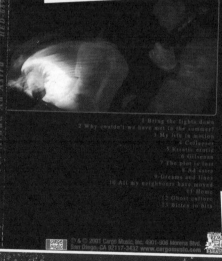

1 Bring the lights down
2 Why couldn't we have met in the summer?
3 My life in motion
4 Collapser
5 Erratic erotic
6 Gilsenan
7 The plot is lost
8 Ad astra
9 Dreams and lines
10 All my neighbours have moved
11 Home
12 Ghost culture
13 Bitten in bits

Metway Studios

Rydell at The Forum
photos by Paul French

and creative way. We saw that as punk. Also, it's simply harder than you'd think to name something that you've worked on for so long and poured so much into. Albums, books, and even every song all mean so much. They all have a story behind them, but they all need names. You can glean a lot of the back-stories from the lyrics, but you'd have to check the finer details with Milo.

We were playing through the tracks, and then listening back to them properly for the first time now. The jump around lead line of 'Why couldn't we have met in the summer?', the urgent riff or 'Erratic erotic' with the drums rolling in, the gentle chug of 'My life in motion' slowly building, and the beautiful intertwining guitars of 'The plot is lost' with Milo singing, "I'd like something simple, like love." We had something powerful here, maybe not the most accomplished musicianship you'd ever hear, but certainly some atmosphere and texture. There were real emotions caught up in those simple songs, and the music ebbed and flowed, like an indie tide, rather than being smashed by the wave of a hardcore onslaught. A few days later, we had the power chords of 'Ghost culture' ringing out over its almost piano-like melody, and the haunting guitar lines of 'Bitten to bits' (written entirely in the studio during this recording session) safely in the bag too. All that was left now was to record the grand piano for 'Ad astra' and add some final backing vocals. Charlie and Jake were mixing as we went along, so although there was still some polishing to do, we had a pretty good idea of how this album was going to sound. Maybe we should have spent more time on the record at that stage, producing it with even more care, but we were pleased with it overall and just excited to get it to the label. By the end of the session, we had the album burned onto a few CDs and I sent the audio masters off to Eric at Cargo / Headhunter Records in San Diego, along with a copy for Gubby and a few artwork ideas too. We burnt copies for ourselves to play in our cars for our friends and girlfriends, of course, but also to send off to a few key reviewers later. We waited to see what the record label thought of it.

The guys at Cargo / Headhunter loved it and wanted to start work on the artwork ideas immediately, so they could get the CD pressed and underway as soon as possible. That was great news, as I'd figured this part might take a while. I gave our logo, photos and imagery ideas to Gubby, as he was a designer as well as label A&R, and he started to work on the art. We wanted a cityscape at night, brooding but electric, seemingly empty of people outside, but with streetlamps lit and lights on in the buildings' windows. Quite a similar concept to our first ever demo, 'Switched On'. I think in my mind the city would be London, or Brighton, or maybe New York, but it didn't really matter. As it happens, it ended up being Montreal as Gubby had a suitable skyline image and that was the city where he lived. We had some great live shots from our recent gigs, particularly a blurred one of Milo and Macca, which looked cool in black and white. In the artwork, they'd be outlined in gold against the brown and black backgrounds we'd chosen to look suitably low key and emo.

Maybe this part of the record was a little rushed. Gubby was dealing with it for us, and we were so keen to get the album out, we gave him carte blanche to just get on with it. I don't remember ever seeing proofs and, looking at the artwork now, I notice there are quite a few typos in the lyric sheet, and the background should have been lighter, so the words are easier to read. There are some blurry live shots too, taken from whatever photos we had available at the time, as remember this was before most digital cameras too. Although the photo of us sitting in the Pantiles, opposite the Forum in Tunbridge Wells, seems sharp enough. We all look young, as this was over twenty years ago now.

Despite our enthusiasm and Gubby's best intentions with the art, Eric reminded us that it'd take a while to see the final CD ready for shops. Marketing had to be done first and radio airplay booked to achieve sales. We were pretty much unheard of in the USA, and they needed to know how many CDs to press at first. So, a long time before the full album was ready, we were sent a few demo copies to send out to radio stations and reviewers around the UK and Europe. These demo CDs had a properly pressed disc inside, but no front cover, just an insert with a brief review of the release and a picture of the cover art on one side, with the album tracklist and all the Cargo marketing, publicity and sales distributor information and contacts on the other. This was the music business after all, and they wanted to build up some pre-orders at stores. We were always eager just to get new tracks out there, but maybe they were right.

To their credit, Eric, Gubby, Jim and another guy called Bruce, who was also working on the album marketing, all suggested a US tour as soon as possible, to support the album launch, which we were delighted to let them start working on and arrange. We reminded them about taking our mates Hunter Gatherer out with us, and suggested maybe The Firebird Band too. (Chris Broach from Braid's new group). They were looking at that as a possibility, but had some other bands in mind for support slots too. As well as this, and ever greedy for gigs, we also asked about supporting larger bands on their tours, as that would probably do us more good. For now, they were thinking we'd headline an east coast tour of rock clubs and colleges, to introduce us to the USA, and then work on more gigs that side of the Atlantic too. I was often chatting with Jim and Bruce about the tour, what dates we could make, which venues, equipment, etc and it all started to take shape.

Soon after he had the masters for 'Per ardua ad astra', Eric Goodis, the Headhunter boss, also suggested that we gather the second album, made up as a collection of our tracks on previous releases, and work on art for that too. I guess he figured they may as well promote two albums as one, and have everything available in the US. Being a record nerd and completist, I was totally into that idea but wanted to just check that Dennis and Emre at Scene Police, and all the guys at the other labels we'd released tracks with up to then, were all cool about that. I started calling and emailing them to discuss it, and then put a tracklist together for what would eventually become Rydell's 'Always remember everything' album. This was all going on while we continued gigging, promoting the new album, and even working on tracks for a third record too. Cargo were keen on more records and willing to cover any costs. Gubby told me that they had over 2000 copies of the 'Per ardua ad astra' CD already on order for US stores, and were working on adding to that number, so it was all very encouraging.

We'd have promo copies of the album late in the autumn of 2000, but it would be officially released on Headhunter Records early in 2001. Rydell's 'Per Ardua Ad Astra' album would be HED089. And just out of interest, they'd also release The Firebird Band's 'The setting sun and its satellites' as HED094, Kevin Seconds (of seminal USHC band 7 Seconds) 'Heaven's near wherever you are' as HED095, and later Rydell's 'Always Remember Everything', as HED105, one of their very last releases.

When we finally received copies of the full CD, early in 2001, it would have a cool-looking but dark cover, with eight-page fold-out lyric sheet containing live band photos, release notes and a thanks list. The CD itself was printed black with the oval Rydell logo in gold on it, and behind the CD there was a photo of us sitting on the steps in The Pantiles, just over the road from The Forum in Tunbridge Wells, all looking very 'emo'.

Around this time, 'emo' was starting to become a bigger thing in the UK media, and there was a popular new website called 4emo.com. The guy who ran this blog, Owen Humphreys, was already a bit of a fan from our previous releases, so we sent him a pre-release copy of the new album to check out and this was his review...

4emo.com - Rydell ´Per Ardua Ad Astra´ (Headhunter/Cargo)

'The British melodic hardcore / indie rock has been relatively untapped, only a few bands seem to have broken into the main scene, will this all change with the release of the debut album from Rydell?

Track one, 'Bring the lights down', starts with guitars and the other instruments slowly coming in. The slight tapping of a cymbal and then the plodding bass hitting high notes. Then the vocals come in sounding a little like a harder Van Pelt. You initially feel this is going to be a normal indie rock record, but the melodies hit highs that really 'feel good' and they combine harmony and power so expertly. This record isn't going to be 'run of the mill'.

Track two, 'Why couldn't we have met in the summer?', starts with the guitars but then the power of the drums and bass is colossal. The vocals are also different, melodic but with more power. The energy of the song is fantastic and the way, three-quarters of the way through, the song breaks down is so nice. The bass reverberating and the Samiam-esque guitar lines.

It is quite apparent that Rydell have a unique sound. They combine elements of the likes of The Get Up Kids, Cap'n Jazz and Christie Front Drive, but add their own originality. They are very melodic, the way Cap'n Jazz were, but seem to have even more energy and also have tremendous power in their music. If you like the power and originality of Four Hundred Years, mixed with the melody of Cap'n Jazz and The Get Up Kids, then you are going to love Rydell.

The guitars are always strikingly melodic. It would appear that most songs are hard to listen to without developing goose bumps. The drums and bass are always very good, working extremely well together.

The harsher style vocals are pitched in the Hot Water Music, Jawbreaker and early Split Lip area. They take a short while to get used to, but you soon realise that they are very tuneful, without losing the power or compromising with inane harmony.

'Per Ardua Ad Astra' combines so many elements. It can be very powerful and hard-out, then suddenly soft and gentle. Tracks four and eight are absolutely awesome. Piano and effected organ sound. A completely new edge that depicts their versatility and imagination.

This is a band who enjoy their music, and it comes across to the listener. You may initially feel that the vocals are too abrasive, but after a couple of songs, they work really well and compliment the music with a fresh edge. The songs are catchy without resorting to hackneyed tunes; instead, they introduce novel breakdowns and interesting melody.

With a lot of bands becoming too rock and trite, Rydell are breaking the stereotype of an indie rock band. Britain doesn't just produce Britpop, they also create awesome melodic hardcore. Just witness Rydell.'

28/7/2000 Rydell and The Junket at The Forum, Tunbridge Wells
2/9/2000 Rydell and others at Worthing Green Festival, Worthing

We were pretty stoked with how things were going, and I was even more pleased, when late in July, we eventually got to play that gig with The Junket too. This time it would be at The Forum in Tunbridge Wells, instead of The Cartoon in Croydon, but that did mean that all our local chums could come along and see us play through 'Per ardua' for the first time. It was a lucky booking; Milo had heard The Junket's 'Engine Man' on Steve Lamacq's evening session and loved it, then he'd happened to be in the Forum in sunny tunny asking Jason (the Joeyfat bassist and main promoter there) about what gigs were coming up that we could get onto. Jason mentioned The Junket and he jumped on it, asking if we could support them.

This gig was a riot, and I believe it may have been where the photos we used on the 'Per Ardua' album cover came from. The Junket rocked it too. They were one of the best indie bands around at the time, with a kind of hard-edged DC-esque post HC element to their sound. We were so glad we'd managed to play together. I only knew the tracks on the 'You're the same' 7" on Deceptive, but they also had a new album out, 'Lux Safari' on Lime Street Records and it was packed with metallic-edged indie tracks that oozed real character. They made a lot of noise for a three-piece from Kettering. The Junket's early singles were all later compiled on the 'Stamina' CD, out on Deceptive Records, and frontman Rik Flynn went on to form Captain, who released an LP on EMI, but despite rave reviews and various festival appearances, they never really took off. These days he's the editor of Classic Pop magazine.

Rydell carried on sending out our old demos and playing gigs all throughout the summer, hoping to get a support slot on the Elliott tour in late August. We were on a bit of a high, but it didn't take long to bring us back down to earth. We were booked to play the Worthing Green Festival on Saturday 2nd September, and found ourselves tuning up in front of a load of dreadlocked hippies and seaside holidaymakers around teatime. The festival was entirely green, a well-intended but not entirely thought through early attempt at sustainability, and the electricity for our electricity sucking amps and the big p.a. system would be bicycle powered, provided by volunteers pedalling as fast as they could on bikes at the side and behind the stage, all hooked up to generators and batteries. It had worked okay for most of the afternoon, but they hadn't had any heavy bands on yet and you could see the hippies on the bikes tire almost as soon as we started. The sound was not great to begin with, but now the amps kept cutting out. We gave up after about four songs, and left the stage in a huff. The conversation on the way back was not a happy one. We'd already been stuck in a traffic jam to get there, and I remember a lot of comments like, "Well that was the biggest waste of time ever," and, "So bloody embarrassing, just glad there weren't many people there to see us," and, "Seriously, is this only gig we can get?" and simply, "That shit was beyond a joke!". It was not one of the band's most celebrated moments, even though we were all getting used to the rollercoaster of ups and down that is band life.

You'll forgive me then if I cheer myself up with a few early reviews of the 'Per Ardua Ad Astra' album from the press when they received the CDs to check out...

Kerrang – Rydell, Per Ardua Ad Astra (Cargo/Headhunter HED089)
KKKK - One of the best British emo albums ever made
The smoky atmospherics of Afghan Whigs, the twin vocal attack of Hot Water Music, gorgeous melodic arrangements a la Braid. Frankly, this is a quite fantastic collection of influences, and a suitably fantastic album.

The band is made up of former members of such UK bands as Couch Potatoes, Joeyfat, Wact and Rudedog. Their collective experience enables them to embrace both the upbeat, poppier side of the emo genre - 'Why Couldn't We Have Met In The Summer?'

is Get Up Kids-meets-Promise Ring, and the less instant, more thoughtful side too - witness 'The Plot Is Lost', a laid-back, passionate beauty.

There are a lot of good British post-punk bands around, but few reach the heights of their American forefathers. Rydell do. And occasionally they go beyond them. Utterly brilliant.
(Ashley Bird)

Rocksound - Rydell - 'Per Ardua Ad Astra' (Headhunter)
Rydell's line-up has one hell of a c.v. Having played over 800 shows between them (including supporting some band called Green Day), they combined forces to form this melodic hardcore / emo band and plan on taking the world by storm. With the rising popularity in that scene, it appears that they couldn't have picked a better time to unleash 'Per Ardua Ad Astra' on their following. Songs like 'Why couldn't we have met in the summer?' are dripping with power and melody, while also possessing that abrasive edge that the emo scene is well known for. While not possessing the catchiness or instantly memorable hooks in their songs that some bands have, Rydell offer up emotional journeys like 'Ghost culture' ,making this another interesting addition to their impressive resume.
(Graham Finney)

Big Cheese - Rydell - 'Per Ardua Ad Astra' (Headhunter)
Let me start by saying that this is truly great. All the essential elements necessary for a remarkable album are here. There are a few really tasty English bands doing the rounds, and playing very good and similar music, but this is the best I have heard for a while. This said, they take their lead from US and European bands / labels that I like. They are at the Deep Elm end of the genre. I still feel this is selling Rydell short. Lovely and intricate guitar work underpins the music, allowing the bass and rhythm section to explore new ground and bring in elements alien to a lot of bog-standard emotive guitar rock. The vocals sound natural and hence are more powerful for it. Combining with seemingly confessional lyrics (I didn't get the lyrics in the pack), the voice almost doubles up as another instrument.

The album is recorded relatively sparsely, allowing the instruments and the voice to lead the listener where the band want them to go. Too often bands rely on the production of the record to do this. This means that the record can sound more fragile, and it allows the musicians to take it to the next level when they play live, which incidentally they do. I recommend this record.

Ox (Germany) - Rydell - 'Per Ardua Ad Astra' (Headhunter)
Once again, I'm surprised in a positive way by RYDELL, who have released their best album yet. Ok, ok, they are dealt as 'emo', but since they are not rookies in this

B/W photos taken at The
Forum for album artwork

Live shots from three more Rydell gigs

business and not suspicious in any way to have jumped onto a trend-train, it's allowed to title them like that. But it makes even more sense to give a choice of several bands RYDELL toured with: HOT WATER MUSIC, SAMIAM, BURNING AIRLINES, KARATE, BLUETIP... this is the circle RYDELL move in. Most of all, the first two bands have been the best teachers in drive, aggression and angry melancholy, although RYDELL have already proved with their first releases that they play in the same league as the bands named above. Great band, and I hope to see them on a stage in my area soon. 8/10.

Reason To Believe - Rydell - 'Per Ardua Ad Astra' (Headhunter)
This is how I think emo should be... not half-baked, indie-rock, cry baby, pretty boy, fashion victim kak with self-indulgent, useless, apathetic lyrics... but full-on, inventive, powerful, heartfelt, intelligent, mid '90s-esque, still wears Foundation skate flannels, inspirational word spewing stuff like this. These fellas are one of the most underrated bands in the UK. And why? Because they don't act like fuckwit rockstars or ponce about trying to get the ladies. (Well, I'm sure Dave does, but obviously nothing's ever going to happen in that department). I've always been into these guys, and I respect them whole-heartedly for their great attitude and musical ability. They're even better now they've made Miles stop pretending to play guitar and get in a new lad who actually knows what he's doing. Ah yes, Rydell, you rock! (LH).

Drowned In Sound - Rydell - 'Per Ardua Ad Astra' (Headhunter)
In amidst dissing most of the newer punk / rock bands around today, I remember Gubby from Cargo Music raving on about this bunch, saying how much they stand out from the pack as musicians and songwriters. And I've gotta say, I haven't heard anything quite like them.

Each song is an emotional yearning or reminiscence, with song titles like 'Why Couldn't We Have Met In The Summer?' and 'My Life In Motion'. Fiddley, twiddly dual guitars dance around a supportive bass line, while powerfully delivered vocals speak melancholic words of what could and should have been.

In fact, on first listening it could be the vocals that put you off, but I think it's this uniqueness that I like about Rydell. When he does muster the energy to sing, it does sort of verge on the out-of-tune, but 'Gilsenan' sees this husky vocal style mix strangely well with those twiddley emo guitars.

If you're looking for something with power and drive, but also relaxingly different to chill out to then I'd check these guys out. (As well as label mates The Firebird Band).
(Mat Hocking)

UK Base – Rydell – 'Per Ardua Ad Astra' (Headhunter)

I had not heard much about Rydell until I did their page (on UK Base), but now I will definitely be keeping an eye on them.

There are 13 songs on this CD, and they vary between 'Home' which at times is almost hardcore, to the atmospheric structure of 'Ad Astra'. Most people write this band off as emo and there is something in that, but listening to it, you can definitely hear an early DC sound, especially bands like Rites of Spring. This comes over to a large extent in 'Bring The Lights Down', 'Why Couldn't We Have Meet In The Summer?' and 'Erratic Erotic', the latter sounds a little like Sink as well. There are songs on this CD that do take influences from Hot Water Music, ie 'Dreams & Lines', which is no big surprise seeing as Rydell have shared a release and a tour with Hot Water Music.

Having mentioned all these different influences, Rydell still manage to bring a style in all of their own. Miles' vocals are great, a little like Leatherface but not so growly (though at times on 'Collapser' they did sound a bit too much like some indie Manchester band), and the way David and Mark play off each other with their guitar work is outstanding, not forgetting the rhythm section's underlying power. The varied styles on this release also stops the CD becoming monotonous, as some emo albums can be.

If you're an emo fan, get this release – it's that simple.

If you're like me and like all genres of punk, hardcore, emo, etc. Then this release is well worth spending your hard-earned cash on.

If you hate emo still check out the mp3s on their page, as this band may change your mind.

Summary: Probably the best emo release ever by a UK band.

Rhythm and Booze – Rydell – 'Per Ardua Ad Astra' (Headhunter)

Over in America, emocore or melodic hardcore if you prefer is becoming big news. Dischord Records has certainly helped the scene with releases by the likes of Bluetip, and other acts like Samiam and Hot Water Music are getting much deserved praise. Here in England, it looks like we're starting to understand it, and there are now a number of home-grown bands that are easily competing with their American counterparts. Rydell are one of the best of them.

This is Rydell's third(?) album and having toured with Hot Water Music, Bluetip and Samiam amongst others, they know exactly what emo fans are looking for. Rydell have written an album that is packed with shimmering guitars and vocals that are both powerful and full of emotion; to class this under hardcore is somewhat misleading, it has nothing in common with the likes of Tribute to Nothing or Knuckledust. For a start, the music is so much more restrained. Yes, it is really powerful in places but with emotion rather than brutality. The vocals aren't grunted or growled, they're sung with passion; okay they might be slightly snarled, but still clear and hook-laden.

'Collapser' is about someone collapsing and possibly dying, and it's handled with such melody that it's truly heart-breaking. 'Erratic Erotic' is somewhat punkier, it motors away but you could still imagine it being played on Radio One. There is even an amazingly subtle instrumental called 'Ad Astra', that is just so quiet that you have to alter the volume to hear its shimmering beauty. All in all, this is an album that deserves to be heard. It's charged with emotion and holds your attention from start to finish, a truly mesmerising album of emo/melodic hardcore.

Splendid - Rydell - 'Per Ardua Ad Astra' (Headhunter)
Oh my god, the British do emo?! Just kidding. Comprised of ex-members of some well-known UK hardcore bands, Rydell's members have collectively played over 800 hardcore shows, making them something of an English emo supergroup. And they feel things deeply and poignantly. This is as obvious from wistful song titles like 'All My Neighbours Have Moved' and 'Why Couldn't We Have Met In Summer' as it is from the trademark mournful hardcore scream of the lead singer (whose name I don't know because, surprisingly, the band members' names aren't listed anywhere, not even on the label website!)

Sometimes it seems that if you've heard one emo band, you've heard them all. But putting my emo cynicism aside, Rydell is an interesting listen. They have a musical diversity in the same vein as Hot Water Music, with moments of intelligent yet melodic aggression which call to mind Leatherface, but without the Oi! overtones. 'Ghost Culture' is the strongest track on the album, making good use of layered vocals (something they also attempt on the final track, 'Bitten to Bits') and shifts from sweet melodies to abrupt riffs and back again. There is a definite hooky, indie-rock feel to Rydell's flavour of emo.

While some have compared Rydell to The Get Up Kids because of their poppier side, I really just don't hear it; the music is more aggressive, the vocal style too traditionally hardcore. I like this album for the same reason I like other emo albums - the energy and raw emotion - but Rydell's sound has more depth and variety, making 'Per Ardua Ad Astra' more compelling than most of the competition. (Alex Zorn).

PennyBlackMusic - Rydell - 'Per Ardua Ad Astra' (Headhunter)
When I think of hardcore punk, I think of loud, fast and simplistic music from labels such as Epitaph and Fat Wreck Chords. A lot of people hate this stuff and, despite being

a fan of NOFX, Terrorgruppe and The Get Up Kids, I can see that they might have a point. It is great, therefore, to have discovered two magnificent punk bands on the same label (MyComplex and now Rydell) who don't conform to this simplistic approach. This record is both melodic and fast, but is also far from lacking in genuine musical thrills. Rydell are great musicians, and they make a wonderful noise.

Rydell are comprised of ex-members of bands such as Couch Potatoes, Joeyfat, Wact and Rudedog. They have managed to play collectively over 800 shows on their various projects, and next on their list is a tour of America. To be honest, such is the American influence on their sound, I wouldn't have known they were British. The band I feel they most sound like is ....And You Will Know Us By The Trail Of Dead, and the vocal styles of these two groups appear very similar. The voice is not the focus of the sound, nor are the vocals technically strong, but they don't resort to pointless shouting.

The most striking thing about Rydell is the guitar sound. Unlike so many punk groups it is clear and distinctive, not tuned low in that stereotypical nu-metal / grunge way, and not resorting to power chords and noise for noise's sake. Added to this is the combination of two guitars in tandem with the rhythm section. It provides a tight rhythmic sound far different from the sloppy style often associated with punk. Rydell are perhaps at their best when they abandon the vocals entirely on the slow reflective instrumental track 'Ad Astra'.

The (US) press info makes some snooty remark about how they prove that England doesn't only do Britpop. That Britpop went out of fashion in '96 has clearly escaped their attention! They do have a point in some ways because Rydell prove that punk rock isn't a distinctly American forte nowadays. In fact, they take a distinctly American template and improve it immensely. I'd go as far tas o say that this is the best thing I've heard so far this year.
Good luck in America, guys! (Ben Howarth)

Some of these reviews were of the pre-release promo CD, sent out with a standard press sheet by the label in the US, mainly for marketing and without much band information. Others were of the full album with its final artwork, when it came out about six months after we'd recorded it. That's not too bad for a record label to turn an album launch around in that time. All of these reviewers were pretty kind to us, but of course, art is in the eye of the beholder, or the ear of the listener in this case, so we had some bad reviews too, of course. But what we loved seeing was that some of these muso reporters could actually see where we were coming from, and get what it was about. This was hardcore, but from the soul. We wanted to be different, but we would never be fake.

Another great thing about the band and album becoming better known abroad was that even more of our tracks were getting picked up for benefits and compilations now, even more gigs were getting booked for us, and some fans were even creating their own videos to go with our songs and posting them online. Rydell had never produced a video for any of our songs at that point. This was all new and very welcome.

We were still supporting any benefit releases we could and working with as many independent fanzines as possible, not just for reviews but articles and interviews too, if they wanted them. We even suggested CD and t-shirt giveaways and sent out free stuff. Milo and I were always busy posting things off and answering any questions. While he caught up with Mike at Conditioned for an interview, I took a call from Owen at 4emo about the release of 'Per ardua' and he posted the resulting conversation as another short interview on his blog. It makes for relevant reading at this point, and shows how everything was starting to go online around then, even us.

4emo.com – Rydell interview on the release of 'Per ardua ad astra'
I was lucky enough to get an interview with the awesome UK melodic hardcore / emo band Rydell. They have their debut album coming out on Headhunter / Cargo in the next few months. I caught up with guitarist David.

1. Introduce us to the band and your respective backgrounds?
Rydell are Miles Booker (Vocals), Adam French (Bass), David Gamage (Guitar), Duncan Morris (Drums) and Mark Wilkinson (Guitar).

We have all been close friends and playing in hardcore bands for a while. We're ex-members of Couch Potatoes, BBMFs, Wact, Joeyfat, Angus Bagpipe, etc so we all kind of know where we're coming from musically.

The music we make now is powerful melodic indie rock. Emo music with a great deal of passion, and, we like to think, quite original too.

2. Where are you guys from and what is the local music scene like there?
Rydell are all from the Southeast of England. Mainly the Brighton and Tunbridge Wells areas. The scene is ok; that is, it is what you make of it. There are a couple of good venues and some really good bands, Babies Three, Sporting Heroes, etc. Any underground thing that's worthwhile always takes a lot of effort. We're always trying to get more publicity and more kids along to shows.

3. Your debut album comes out on Headhunter / Cargo in a few month's time, how did the deal with Cargo come about?
Yeah, Rydell's first full-length album, 'Per ardua ad astra', will be out in a month or so on Headhunter Records. We are really stoked about this! We have a bunch of releases out on various great European labels, but really wanted something out on a US hardcore label, as that seems to be what people listen to.

We put out the last couple of releases with our very good friends at Scene Police records, and they were doing a superb job, but we are skint as a band and Headhunter offered us some money towards recording and better distribution in the USA, so we thought why not?

(Scene Police may still be releasing the vinyl in Europe).

The deal came about because the guys at Headhunter heard a couple of our tracks, either from the Hot Water Music and Hunter Gatherer splits, or the Firewalk With Me acoustic EP and then went onto our new website, at www.rydell.co.uk to check out more. I guess they liked us!

4. What are the main influences behind your music?
Rydell have many influences. Musically as a band we listen to a wide variety of stuff, but mainly hardcore / emo bands I guess. Stuff like Get Up Kids, Hot Water Music, Braid, Mineral, Chamberlain, that sort of thing. I think lyrically we are more influenced by events around us, girlfriends, friends, observations, thoughts. You'd have to ask Milo.

5. You've been playing music, particularly melodic hardcore for many years now, what drives you?
We love it! All of Rydell really enjoy creating and playing new music and being in the band. We travel and make many new friends through the band. We are driven because we enjoy what we do, and we believe in it. There's a lot of depth and passion in Rydell's music.

6. Explain the Rydell sound?
Hmm. The Rydell sound has developed. We have all played in pretty heavy hardcore bands before, and with Rydell we set out to do something slightly different. Not really indie, or rock, or emo, or hardcore, but somewhere in between. Our sound or style is constant, despite very different tracks. It may be Miles' singing, or whatever. On the new record there are heavy songs, mellow songs, even a piano piece, but it's all definitely Rydell.

7. You've toured extensively around the UK and Europe. Any plans to go to the States?
Yes, we have toured quite a bit, but we would love to do even more. We have European tour plans with Elliott and Hunter Gatherer coming up, and maybe a few other things too. We would love to get to tour in America, and maybe Headhunter can help us do that fairly soon.

I know Adam also fancies a trip to Japan sometime, so if anyone can help...

8. What does the future hold for Rydell?

The future for Rydell is looking pretty good at the moment. We have a couple of good shows booked and are looking forward to promoting the new album when it is released. We have tracks on various compilations coming out soon too - one on Starlette with Penfold, one on Scene Police with HWM, another on Firewalk featuring the unreleased track 'Post college rock' and several other benefits.

We are also working on the new website, www.rydell.co.uk and also starting some promotions on our MP3 site at www.mp3.com/rydell

There should even be new t-shirts and stuff available soon.

Just get in touch if you want us to play!

Let's just hope people like the new record. Order it now from Rydell or Headhunter-Cargo.

Check out the Rydell website at http://www.rydell.co.uk/. Alternatively go to Cargo Music at http://www.cargomusic.com/

34, Nothing by morning

6/10/2000 Rydell and The Get Up and Go-Ers at The Lido, Margate
27/12/2000 Rydell and The Babies Three at The Swan, Ashford
17/1/2001 Rydell, San Quentin and Yeast at The Garage, London

Things carried on pretty much as normal through the autumn, corresponding with labels, playing gigs and going to see gigs. I remember lots of Just One Life shows put on by Buz at the Freebutt in Brighton, the best of which was Pop Unknown, they were amazing, and also another good gig over at the Lido in Margate, a Friday night which would normally have been a 'Geekscene' special, but we'd started putting on Ignition shows too.

For that one, Milo had booked Winchester 73 to headline. They were one of our German Scene Police labelmates from Bonn, but for some reason they cancelled on us so it ended up with just two bands playing, Rydell and The Get Up and Go-Ers. The Get Up and Go-Ers were a Swedish rockabilly trio who had a couple of albums and EPs out on Euphony Records. They later had a split with Dead End, another Swedish hardcore band, that came out jointly on four labels, one of which was Armed With Anger, and it turned out to be that label's last release.

I went off on a few more trips abroad, first to Italy, then Greece with Adam and a few friends, then another visit to Dennis in Germany, which occasioned a great veggie Thai dinner in Bonn with a load of the Scene Police bands, but also a car crash as we were leaving the city. I managed to get t-boned by some idiot on a roundabout, and it may have been partly my own fault, as my lovely girlfriend Loui had been drinking all night at the party and was throwing up out of the window at the time of the collision. It's entirely possible that I was a bit distracted looking after her, so probably wasn't taking as much care and attention as a busy road like that demanded. Luckily, no serious harm was done to anything other than my car, but it did cost us a few hours of hassle with the cops, who cheerfully extorted a fine from me before allowing us back on our way again. My battered car was still rolling along, and the trunk was now filled with Almdudler from the Guter Getrankesupermarkt. The bottles clinked to the tunes of Sugar and The Get Up Kids as the autobahns sailed by.

By our standards, it'd been a quiet couple of months for the band so we put a post in the message board on the Rydell website, just before Christmas, that pretty much summed it up:

Hello everyone and sorry we've been away for a while,
Rydell have been writing new songs and working on various other stuff, not all of it totally band related.

We'll start touring again early next year and have gigs already lined up with Hunter Gatherer, Elliott, Babies 3, Sunfactor, Sporting Heroes and a few other good friends. Let us know if you'd like us to come play in your area.

There is a new EP out on 'Firewalk with me' records from Austria, featuring the track 'Post college rock' and there's several other unreleased tracks on compilations here in Europe and in the USA being released soon. There will also be Rydell t-shirts available at the shows in the new year!

Also, most importantly, the first (and long awaited) Rydell full length album will be released early next year! Entitled 'Per Ardua Ad Astra' on Headhunter Records, it will be available worldwide through Cargo distribution, at shows from us and found in any cool record shops from February. Please rush out and buy it!

The thirteen tracks were recorded at Metway Studios in Brighton, with the help of Jake Rousham and Charlie McIntosh. The track-listing is below...

Rydell - Per ardua ad astra
1, Bring the lights down
2, Why couldn't we have met in the summer?
3, My life in motion
4, Collapser
5, Erratic erotic
6, Gilsenan
7, The plot is lost
8, Ad astra
9, Dreams and lines
10, All my neighbours have moved
11, Home
12, Ghost culture
13, Bitten to bits

Thanks and hope to see you all soon. Rydell.

PS, Congratulations to our friends Hot Water Music on signing with Epitaph. A truly great band that even more people are going to hear now. The Scene Police released Rydell / HWM split is sold out again, so hopefully there may be just one last repress, with a new cover, to celebrate this.

Just after Christmas, we met up with The Babies Three at The Swan in Ashford for a holiday party gig, to save anyone from being trapped at home with crabby relatives and bored out of their minds. It was a much-needed show, and we all worked off some of the Xmas 'excess all areas' as we bounced around that old pub.

We also had another gig early in the New Year, up in London at The Garage with San Quentin and Yeast. Both those bands were great, but I was particularly blown away by Yeast, a three-piece with some mighty impressive riffage that veered from the distinctly catchy emo pop of Braid to the heavier grooving styles of Understand. They had a couple of records out on Household Name and Memory Man Records, including an album called 'History Equals Fog', but this was the first time I'd seen them play. Their vocalist / guitarist James had a job at one of the big record distributors in town, and they had another album out in a year or so called 'Expander' on Golf Records. For that record, Yeast had recruited Stuart Mills on vocals. He'd been in Grand Central, one of the bands on the 'Emotion Sickness' compilation CD with us, and they came on in leaps and bounds as a four-piece, really finding their sound. Yeast were another band who were lucky enough to record with John Hannon at Mushroom Studios in Essex too.

Rydell played at The Garage quite a few times, both upstairs and downstairs, and we were back there again soon after, supporting a Czech band called Sunshine. They were signed to Day After Records, another label we were in conversations with for releases at the time. We chased pretty much everyone!

It says in my diary that there was an Elliott tour of the UK for their 'False Cathedrals' album late in January too, with shows at The Grapes in Sheffield, Josephs Well in Leeds, The Victoria Inn in Derby, The Underworld in London and The Lift in Brighton, but for a band I loved so much, I'm damned if I can remember these gigs. That probably means we didn't get to play at any of them after all, and it may have been as I headed off to Canada from the 27th, where I skilfully managed to crash a snowmobile into a tree.

Milo took the Ignition distro to the London and Brighton shows, and said it was a weird tour for Elliott as they'd lost their original guitarist and bass player, not long before the tour began, and had drafted in new band members. This gave the songs a very different feel, so all the kids who flocked to the shows expecting to hear the epic and majestic 'False Cathedrals' album as they knew it had a shock when the songs were performed with a dreamier, slightly shoegaze / psychedelic vibe. This was something that would work well for them on their next album, 'Song in the Air', but not something people particularly wanted to hear right then. People were leaving in droves at the London show and spending more time browsing the distro, oddly making it a very good night for Ignition. The following night in Brighton was apparently a similar story too, with people leaving throughout their set, and when Elliott had finished some asshole yelled out, "That sounded like fucking Marillion!" at them.

In February, we had an in-store show at Shake Some Action as part of the new album promotions. James was always happy to stock our records and we wanted to play these tracks in intimate venues if possible. It's not like we had much choice! This turned out to be the last time we played at the store, as it closed down soon after. I hope that wasn't our fault. James McCabe went on to do some extras work in films and TV, including a walk-on in 'Spy Game' with Robert Redford and Brad Pitt. Not sure what he does now, but I hope it's fun.

Later that February, I went to see The Babies Three play at a tiny venue called The Studio in Canterbury, supported by xCanaanx and DeadLifePortrait. This place was basically the café at the back of a laser tag venue called Planet Laser, and couldn't hold many people. The gig was £3.50 in advance, with tickets from Richards Records in Canterbury high street, or £4 on the door. The show was put on by Pureland promotions as an Integrity event. These new promoters intended to showcase three HC bands every Tuesday night. It was a busy gig and a real eye-opener for many of the locals. A hard-moshing, finger-pointing old-school style hardcore gig, with loads of kids packed into that tiny venue. I was particularly blown away by the power and avid following of the local straight-edge band, xCanaanx. I spoke with their singer / screamer Nate and promptly offered to put out releases for them on Ignition / Engineer Records. This soon led to their awesome six-track CD, 'Gehenna made flesh' (originally out on Abstraction Communications from Manchester, but that label disappeared with the band only ever receiving a very few copies), and later two more tracks on their split 7" with Thirty Seconds Until Armageddon. These guys meant business and for a while deservedly became incredibly popular.

Nathan 'Nate' Bean also created the XXX hardcore zine 'Harder they fall' and worked with a great artist, Richard Shiner. Richard had been helping the band with most of their artwork and sent us along some ideas. As well as pressing the xCanaanx records, we printed a few t-shirts for them too, including the macabre but stylish, blood-dripping razor blade design for xCanaanx's 'Sometimes death is better' shirt. Richard would later join xCanaanx, first on bass when Charlie Warren left, and then moving to guitar. He started working with us on Ignition / Engineer Records artwork too, and would be responsible for the artwork and cover design of several releases, including Rydell's 'Always Remember Everything' album.

Milo and Clare were running the Ignition distro at that show but, as space inside the venue became so tight, they'd later move it outside and were selling records and CDs out of the boot of Milo's car. This was where he met Tom Hooper, a great tattoo artist, and arranged to get a load of ink done. Tom also designed a very cool Ignition t-shirt for us, but unfortunately we never got to use it, as this wasn't long before the label's name change debacle.

A short while after that gig, I was back to the tiny Studio café venue again to see The Babies Three, always prolifically busy, supporting Swedish noisecore heroes J R Ewing, in another packed gig alongside North by Northwest and the brilliant, and soon to be signed to Ignition / Engineer Records, Urotsukidoji.

10/3/2001 Hunter Gatherer, Rydell and Tupamaros at The Swan, Tottenham, London.
11/3/2001 Hunter Gatherer, Rydell, Tupamaros and Bob Hope at The Lido, Margate
17/3/2001 Wimpfest – Rydell, Babies Three, Autumn Year, Summer Book Club, Spy vs Spy, Sunfactor, Stapleton and others at The Freebutt, Brighton
30/3/2001 Rydell, The Evil Pantano and Fadeout at The Horseshoe, Portsmouth

In March, we were preparing for our run of gigs with Hunter Gatherer. Rydell were well-practised and tight enough, but didn't have much merchandise to leave behind after the shows. We didn't have any stickers or t-shirts, as Cargo had said they'd print some for us and we were still waiting for those, so we went and bought a few shirts online that were for the 'Grease' musical taking place in London at that time. They simply had Rydell printed in red on grey shirts and looked pretty cool, so that would have to do. We had a few vinyl singles left, as well as the split CD with Hunter Gatherer on Scene Police, but now we had copies of the new 'Per Ardua Ad Astra' CD on Headhunter to sell at gigs too. There was also a new benefit compilation, kind of a low-end punk-rock Live-Aid thing for homeless children in Ethiopia, it was called 'Erdata Ishee' and had just been released by Chiggeryellem / Boss Tuneage records. The compilation featured tracks by twenty-two UK hardcore bands including Annalise, Blocko, The Duvals, Wat Tyler, Southport, The Tone and CarCrashDrama, as well as Rydell of course, with 'Bring the lights down'. This CD was available, very inexpensively, direct from Ben at Chiggeryellem in Croydon, and he had ads running in all the good punk zines. Any profits were set to go to charities involved in housing homeless children in Ethiopia, and there were a couple of benefit shows planned to support the release too. I'd bought a bunch of copies from Ben and Aston for the distro, so we were good to go.

It was Dennis and Emre of Scene Police who helped us out again and brought Hunter Gatherer over. They'd meet them in the UK, on the way to Europe, to make the most of their visit. Rydell couldn't play all the tour, so our Scene Police labelmates the Tupamaros, from Solingen in Germany, would bring the equipment and be the support act at all the shows, with us just playing those we could. There were four or five UK gigs to start things off, and I remember Hunter Gatherer being incredible to watch live. They were friendly, but very quiet, like a bunch of bearded mountain men that hadn't been out much; they seemed spooked by civilised society and liked to stay in the shadows. They'd amble on stage and tune up, and only then come alive, bursting into beautiful, quirky, stop-start songs with intricate guitars and drums, and gravelly dual-vocals, that seemed like a stripped-down version of Hot Water Music or Small Brown Bike. They were doing something different, and it sucked that the audiences at those shows weren't a lot bigger to see it.

The London show was at The Swan in Tottenham, a big Victorian boozer on the corner of two busy roads, often packed with locals playing dominoes and bus drivers from the depot opposite. It was busy enough, but only half the people there had come to see the bands and when the Tupamaros started up their noisy Boy Sets Fire-style hardcore, it sent a load of them scurrying to the other bar. This created a bit more space for all the backpack-wearing hardcore kids that had turned up to rock backwards and forwards in, and it was still a good show, but maybe not quite the atmosphere we'd all hoped for. The gig was made much worse by the fact that Milo really blew his voice out trying to shout over the crappy p.a. and suffered from that for what seemed like months afterwards.

The gig at The Lido in Margate the next night was busy and a lot friendlier. Bob Hope, who would soon change their name to North by Northwest, went on first. They'd developed their sound along the lines of Explosions In The Sky, Godpseed You Black Emperor or early Mogwai and were always good to watch live. Then Tupamaros rocked out, technically awesome and a great band, but sometimes annoyingly derisive of ours and other bands musical abilities, and although they may well have been right, that's not really in the spirit of things. Rydell busted through our setlist of favourites, but Milo had to bow out before the end due to his destroyed throat. It was sounding like he'd been gargling glass, and I was worried for him. So, after we'd apologised to the crowd, I finished up the set by singing 'All My Neighbours...' and 'Dreams and Lines' by myself. This was far from ideal, but we made the most of it; we had to, it was my birthday, and I was intent on a party.

The Hunter Gatherer boys were brilliant, bearded, blasting and beautiful, playing the songs they'd crafted in the woods around Athens, Georgia (also the hometown of R.E.M.) to everyone gathered by the seaside in Kent. All their tracks had something clever about them, like a very hairy jazz band playing hardcore, but never losing their intensity. The slow build of 'Laughing tiger' with its shouted chorus of "I will stand by your side", the bass and drums intro of 'Train hopping without you' and the rising and falling guitars of 'In stained glass waiting', before the acapella break and crashing craziness that followed. "I cannot wait, it's something with pressure, leading me back, trying to capture." These tracks, taken from the split CD with us, were pretty special. It was a great show to behold, and we were certain they were the guys we wanted on tour with us when we visited the US later that year. When the Lido finally kicked us all out, early in the morning, it was all back to Milo's, where the Hunter Gatherer boys found a copy of the Viz Profanisaurus and spent the next couple of hours rolling around on the floor, pissing themselves with laughter.

It was annoying we couldn't join Hunter Gatherer for their shows up north, but we hoped we'd be seeing them again soon. Our next gig would be the Wimpfest emo all-dayer at the Freebutt in Brighton. This turned out to be a great get-together, with loads of good bands playing and plenty of friendly faces from the south coast scene. Our old friends and tour buddies The Babies Three and Sunfactor were all there, so were the superb Spy vs Spy, down from the potteries*, and with them another great band on Subjugation Records called Stapleton. These guys had come all the way from Glasgow to play the gig. I'd heard their 'Rebuild the pier' album out on Year 3 Thousand, Sunfactor's label, and now they had a new record on Subjugation called 'On the enjoyment of unpleasant places' and were clearly putting that title to the test at The Freebutt.

(*The Potteries is the slang name for the area of six towns that make up Stoke-on-Trent. As well as post-punk heroes Spy Vs Spy, this area had spawned the massively influential punk / metal crossover band Discharge, also Broken Bones, Lemmy from Motorhead and Slash from GnFnR. Clay Records was also based in Stoke. This label had developed out of Mike Stone's independent record shop and was home to Discharge, GBH, English Dogs and The Lurkers. There was definitely something in the polluted water up there!)

The Autumn Year were at Wimpfest with us too, a great band with a self-titled CDEP out on Karl Fieldhouse's Leeds-based label, Contrition. Karl played guitar in Canvas, and then Thirty Seconds Until Armageddon, who The Autumn Year would soon have a split CD with too. They featured the multi-talented Steve Byrne on bass, who has gone on to become one of the most respected tattoo artists in the world. He, and Tom Hooper, who as well as that Ignition shirt design, inked several of Milo's tattoos, both worked together for a while in Steve's Rock of Ages tattoo shop in Austin, Texas. In 2002, The Autumn Year would put out the brilliant and prophetically-titled mini-album, 'It's better to leave something while you still love it, than to leave something because you hate it' on Santos Records, before calling it quits.

Another Santos Records band called Summer Book Club were at this gig too. They were more or less unheard of at the time and would release their only record, a great mini-

A NIGHT OF
GLOBAL HARDCORE

GEEK
SCENE

PRESENTS

The Babies Three

TUPA MOROS

CReut ZFeLDT

RYDELL

cut your own head off

I SAID SOMETHING

TWO MORE BANDS

BE THERE EARLY

At The Ship Inn

SUN 28th
November

Margate sea front

FREE ENTRY

FIVE Pm START

Geek Scene gig flyer

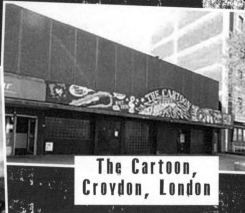

The Cartoon,
Croydon, London

The Ferryboat, Norwich

The Horseshoe, Portsmouth

The Portland Arms,
Cambridge

The Shed, Leicester

The Swan, Tottenham

The Underworld, Camden, London

album entitled 'The Unabridged Edition', later in 2001. There were a few other local bands who'd played before we got there, but all seemed to have gone down well. We really enjoyed the great atmosphere of the gig, and Milo croaked his way through our set with me singing as many of the shouty parts as possible. I'm not sure we were quite at our best, but we certainly enjoyed the show, and I remember it fondly. The Babies Three enjoyed the show too, and even named a song after it, 'Wimpfest', on their brilliant 'File Under Retaliation' album.

We decided to take a couple of weeks for Milo to rest and repair his voice before our next shows and another studio session. We all hoped he'd get right back on form, but he'd only partially recovered before our next gig, at The Horseshoe in Portsmouth. This show was being promoted by a friend of ours called Joe Watson. We'd met Joe at The Joiners many times, at various S.T.E. gigs, and he was trying to get a better scene going in his hometown of Portsmouth. We agreed to come along and play anytime, and after a chat at the sweaty HWM show in the gym in Southampton, he told us he was putting on the gig and booked us. Although I'd been to see Sugar at The Pyramid and Shelter at the Wedgewood Rooms, I'd never seen any smaller hardcore shows in Portsmouth before, but Joe was trying to make it happen and we didn't want to let him down.

Macca recalls this gig fondly, saying that, "Although this was a tiny little venue and one of those shows where you felt that there were more people onstage than in the audience, it was still great fun. Rydell were always about heart, soul and passion before musicianship, and this was one of those gigs where everything clicked."

I wish I could remember more about the two local support bands Joe had booked. They were Fadeout and The Evil Pantano, and both were good, but we were all focused on Milo's straining vocal chords and how he'd do, especially as we were back in the recording studio very soon. Milo's voice was always gravelly, so it just seemed even more that way to me. He soldiered through with a few breaks in the screamo parts, where Macca, Adam and I filled in the gaps with plenty of shouty backing vocals. There was a lot of croakiness, but the music was tight, and everyone got into it. I think Joe was pleased that the show had gone so well. Milo wasn't so happy with it though, and after some discussion we decided to move the recording session back from April to June.

Joe had his camera with him and took some great live shots at the Horseshoe, many of which we used on our upcoming records. In fact, most of the photos on the lyric sheet of 'Hard on the trail' (Rydell's third album) were taken by him. He also got involved in a new label called Cat N Cakey Records, who put out the first releases for his band, Jets Vs Sharks. The multi-talented Joe is a great vocalist too, just check out the Jets Vs Sharks releases, 'From your first cigarette to your last dying day',

'Our bodies our anchors' and 'These tired monuments', all on Cat N Cakey. Also, his next band, the Attack! Vipers! and their albums, 'The mirror and the destroyer' on Rat Patrol Records, straight outta the Rhondda Valleys, that came out soon after their great 'Four short hymns to the patron of bare-knuckle boxing' 7", and 'Deadweight revival' on Specialist Subject Records, the label run by Andrew Horne and Kay Stanley, based in The Exchange in Bristol.

We eased off shows for a couple of months to give Milo's voice a chance to recuperate, but honoured the few we had booked, and slowly built things back up again before the recording session which was now moved to June. The 'Per ardua ad astra' album was going well and Headhunter seemed pleased, getting good airplay on college radio in the US ahead of the tour they were planning for us. We'd been collecting together tracks for what would become 'Always Remember Everything', our second album on Headhunter, and sending them off too. Now we were writing new music for the songs that would appear on our 'Memo demo' and a split release we had planned with San Geronimo and A Rocket Sent To You, that was to come out on Ignition / Engineer Records. To design the artwork for this, we were speaking with Richard Shiner, one of the xCanaanx guitarists. He'd helped us with the redesign of a cover for the Planes Mistaken For Stars 'Fucking Fight' EP we'd put out on Ignition / Engineer Records and that'd looked awesome, with the original cut and paste art from the band on the cover and a skull design on the CD itself. Now we were getting together images of fifties cars with huge chrome bumpers, and all five of us piled into a photo booth to take an impromptu new band photo.

I was in touch with so any great musicians around that time, both through the band and now the record label too. With the help of Syd in particular, but Dan and Rachel too, we'd put together a compilation release for Ignition called 'Firework Anatomy' and it had twenty of the most incredible bands around on it. Some of which, like Grade, Penfold, Red Animal War and The Casket Lottery you may well know, but all of whom were amazing and many of them would later have full releases on the label too. These new and lesser-known bands included Speedwell, Crosstide, That Very Time I Saw, Hunter Gatherer, and now San Geronimo and A Rocket Sent To You.

I had been chasing up Pete Martin, one of the original guitarists of New Jersey's best dancers, Lifetime, for some unreleased recordings by his new band, San Geronimo. I was initially in awe of the guy and just hopeful, but he'd turned out to be really friendly and keen to be on the label. Pete soon sent over some great tracks, and first of all we agreed to put a song called 'My Friend James' on the 'Firework Anatomy' comp CD. Then we'd release a five track EP, self-titled as the 'SG EP' by San Geronimo. This CD featured the tracks 'Here I go Ohio', 'If I had a shovel', 'My friend James', 'Face like a janitor' and 'I'm gonna be famous'. Those releases went really well and, soon after their next studio session, he'd send three more brand new tracks for a split with Rydell.

I was excited about this, as Lifetime were one of my favourite bands, and their guitar style had massively influenced my own so I couldn't wait to get working on the record.

I was also corresponding with Ron Price, a guy I'd first gotten in touch with through John Szuch at Deep Elm Records. He was in a band called Epstein, who had appeared on the third 'Emo Diaries' compilation 'The moment of truth', alongside other emo luminaries such as Last Days of April, Planes Mistaken For Stars, Cross My Heart, Penfold and Speedwell, not to mention the UK's very own Schema. Ron, Mike Borlik and Dave Forman from Epstein had formed a new band, called A Rocket Sent To You, and they'd sent me their new demo. It was amazing. First, we chose a track called 'Chesapeake, America' to go on the 'Firework Anatomy' compilation, and soon we'd have four amazing new tracks from ARSTY to join us on the split release too.

All three of the bands had their own distinctive style but complimented each other well, and I figured this would make a great release, promoting us all in the same way our tour split with The Babies Three and Sunfactor had done on Scene Police a couple of years earlier. My chief concern was that Rydell's songs would be good enough and Milo would be OK to sing them.

30/4/2001 Sunshine, Cars As Weapons and Rydell at The Garage, Islington, London
2/5/2001 Rydell, Like Herod and North by Northwest at The Studio, Canterbury
7/5/2001 Blocko, Rydell, Southport, W.O.R.M, Lunasuit, Know It Alls and Vehicle Derek at The Cartoon, Croydon, London
26/5/2001 British Sea Power, Rydell and WHYDWYD at The Lift, Brighton
6/6/2001 Rydell, The Babies Three, Copperpot Journals and Summer Book Club at The Airlock, Canterbury

Before that though, we were going to warm up again, first playing a show I mentioned earlier, upstairs at The Garage in London, with Sunshine from Prague in the Czech Republic.

These guys were mainly known for a split release they'd done with At The Drive-In on Big Wheel Recreation, but they signed to Day After Records, the most prolific indie label in eastern Europe, and we had been selling loads of copies of their second album, 'Hysterical stereo loops, beats and bloody lips' through the Ignition distro. Milo had just bought a copy of their new album, 'Necromance', and was really into it. He thought they'd be big on the back of it and, sure enough, they later signed to Universal and played loads of big festivals around Europe.

The other support band for this gig was Cars As Weapons, another band touted to hit the bigtime and the current darlings of Kerrang! magazine, who were running pieces describing them as "Forward thinking rockers with added crack cocaine," or "Led Zeppelin with rucksacks." As always, the coverage fizzled out after a while, and as far as I'm aware they only had two releases, an EP called 'Bigger pictures' on Freakscene Records (home of a later Spy Vs Spy release) and a mini-album on Bravestar Records called 'Dear Strutter'. Bravestar also put out releases for Copeland and My Awesome Compilation. Anyway, it was a strong line-up at the Garage that night but I just wish more people had heard the hype about all three bands, as we ended up playing to no more than fifty people.

The next week we headed over to Canterbury to play at The Studio, where we'd seen the absolutely rammed show with The Babies Three, xCanaanx and DeadLifePortrait. This was a very small venue, basically just one end of a bar that served a laser tag venue, and we'd be going on after two Margate-based bands. Our noisy buddies North By Northwest and a new band called Like Herod, featuring Nate from xCanaanx on vocals, Tom from North By Northwest on guitar, Anton of the BreakXin on drums, and sounding like they were playing a bunch of Slayer covers.

We followed this up with an all-dayer at The Cartoon Club in Croydon, but the big-name headline act had pulled out a few days before, which meant that the locals, Blocko, a south London trio on Boss Tuneage, would step-up and become the headliners. As good as they were, Blocko were maybe not well enough known yet outside of the local punk scene to bring in many new punters, and that was a big venue to play to a relatively small audience. Despite that, they rocked out and blew us all away, playing the sort of melodic pop-punk UK bands do so well. All Gordon Smith guitars and emotional vocals, following in the footsteps of bands like Snuff, Drive, Hooton 3 Car, Broccoli and Chopper.

I heard the terrible news since that Marc 'Mates' Maitland, Blocko's drummer, took his own life, back in 2019. He seemed a good guy, so by some small way of tribute, I'd just urge you to check out any of their records on Boss Tuneage and listen to his superb drumming.

Southport played at that Cartoon club all-dayer and were very good too, featuring Simon of the OG Snuff line-up, and later Your Mum; they were a bit harder-edged than the other pop-punk bands playing that day, but still melodic, with touches of ska thrown in. They had an album out on Golf Records called 'Nothing is easy', and would soon have a split EP on Lil and Kafren's label, Household Name Records, with Capdown and Hard Skin.

Lunasuit were good too, kind of a poppier version of Bikini Kill, Huggy Bear or Sleater Kinney, and I liked the fact that they gave themselves stage names like Headache, Hammer, Fallout and Spideyfingers. They had a track on the 'Erdata Ishee' compilation with us, called 'Apology'.

Saturday 26th May

The Lift, 11-12 Queens Road, Brighton

CLUB SEA POWER

The indie-rock bear market at its most brash and ebullient

Featuring:

British Sea Power

"Like a storm on the peak of Scafell Pike," say the press. But can the
huddled quartet survive with just a bail of twine and 1000 watts of rock music?

Rydell

Includes Latin lessons with the RAF, brutish American leanings and sounds
resonating somewhere between The Get-up Kids and The Trail of Dead. Splendid!

What Have You Done With Your Daughters

All the way from the Hong Kong meat-packing district, they
leap and jump like Sonic Youth fleeing from the football crowd.

DJs Domestic 4 and 'Old Sarge'

Brighton's Krautrock bubble-bath kru occasionally troubled by
an elderly gent in search of tea and a night out with Françoise Hardy.

Dresscode: The princess and the gemütlich, stein-quaffing peasant
Entrance: £4 / £3 with flyer
8pm-11pm

British Sea Power gig flyer

Rydell

David and Adam

Macca

Probably my fave band of the day though was Vehicle Derek. They were a bunch of jump-around clowns who had a split release with our buddies Goober Patrol back in the day. They'd now reformed and had a new album out on Aston Stephen's Boss Tuneage record label, so were playing a few shows to promote it. These guys were incredibly entertaining and injected us all with the energy we needed. That, along with about five cans of Coke I'd foolishly drunk, that meant I was bursting for a piss by the time Rydell hit the stage. Dammit.

Our next show was back down in Brighton, and the pubs and shops all around town there were plastered with cool little flyers for the gig, which would be at The Lift with a new band called British Sea Power. They said:

'Saturday, the 26th of May, at The Lift, Queens Road Brighton. Club Seapower. The indie rock bear market at its most brash and ebullient!

Featuring; British Sea Power - like a storm on the peak of Scafell Pike said the press, can the saddle quartet survive with just a bail of twine and 1000 watts of rock music?

Rydell - Includes Latin lessons with the RAF, British American leanings and sounds resonating somewhere between the Get Up Kids and the Trail of Dead. Splendid!

What have you done with your daughters, all the way from the Hong Kong meatpacking district, they leap and jump like Sonic Youth fleeing from the football crowd.

DJs Domestic 4 and Old Sarge. Brighton's Kraut rock bubble-bath crew occasionally troubled by an elderly gent in search of tea and a night out with Françoise Hardy.

Dress code; the Princess and the gemutlich, stein quaffing peasant.
Entrance; £4 / £3 with this flyer. 8pm – 11pm.'

The Lift was a popular music venue in Queens Road in Brighton, and put on regular gigs upstairs in the large room above the bar for crowds of up to 150. We played there a bunch of times and I'm glad to say that the venue still exists, although is now known as the Hope and Ruin, serving veggie food and plenty of beer downstairs whilst putting on indie bands upstairs.

This time we were supporting British Sea Power, an indie band from Reading that had just moved down to Brighton and were starting to get a lot of radio airplay and press interest. Our drummer Dunky had met their guitarist Martin whilst they were both working in a depressing call centre job in Brighton. Realising they were both in bands, they chatted about music to kill time and soon decided to play a show together, booking us in. This was one of their early gigs, but already they were pretty damn good live with a great stage presence. It was a slightly gentler, more indie show for us, but it made a for a good evening and brought us a bunch of new local fans. The four of them seemed intent on putting on regular shows and running an indie club night, so the gig was well-attended and it all seemed to be going quite well for them. Their singer was called Yan, the same as the old Couch Potatoes singer, and he seemed a friendly enough bloke. British Sea Power went on to sign to Rough Trade Records and then Golden Chariot Records, releasing loads of albums and EPs. They have been touring and releasing records for about twenty years now; having recently dropped the 'British' from their name, they are now known as just Sea Power. They were solid and determined right from the get-go, and have now even managed to set up their own festival, called Krankenhaus. I'm stoked to see they are all still doing what they love.

We were offered a slot on the big Wigan punk all-dayer that went on over the bank holiday weekend, but decided to skip it to protect Milo's voice and instead just have one more local warm-up show before the recording session. This would be at The Airlock Club, back at The Studio in Canterbury with our noisy hardcore chums The Babies Three, and one of the new emo bands we'd met at Wimpfest, Summer Book Club. Also playing were another new band called The Copperpot Journals, who turned out to be great. Very melodic and clever emo-core in the style of Tribute or Schema. This was the first time I'd seen them play and they were handing out demo CDs, self-titled five track EPs in a simple blue card sleeve, on their own Blind Bear Records. Within a year, they'd be recording with Understand's John Hannon at his Mushroom Studios near Southend and signing to Firefly Recordings, the new West London label that was home to Kids Near Water, Scuttle, Otherwise, Beezewax and Travis Cut. Hardly anyone outside of the UK emo scene seems to have heard of them, but they were brilliant. They released two superb albums, 'Plotting to kill your friends' and 'Pilots', both on Firefly Recordings.

9/6 & 10/6/2001 Recording at Metway Studios, Brighton

We went back down to the Metway Studios in sunny Brighton the next weekend to finally record the new tracks for the split we had planned with San Geronimo and A Rocket Sent To You. Headhunter were keen on the idea of this release too, and said they'd co-release it with Ignition / Engineer Records and distribute it through Cargo (they agreed to do this with 'Always Remember Everything' too). That was great as, although we intended to record these songs quickly, we now had the option of taking an extra day or two to mix them if we needed it. We'd arranged to have Jake Rousham engineer the recording again, and he'd been able to get the drums and backline set up and ready for us, so it was pretty much just plug in and play when we arrived.

Working with Jake again was great. He made it efficient and easy, and we all had a good laugh. He managed to make the mix of this record slightly more powerful, but still beautiful, and he finished the mix and sent the masters back to us quickly. Clearly, we didn't put him off engineering for bands, as he still works at Metway Studios even now, and has helped make recordings there for Roger Daltrey, Nick Cave, Wilko Johnson, Royal Blood, Snow Patrol and, of course, The Levellers, amongst many others.

The first day saw us get 'Nothing by morning', 'Margin for ever' and a new version of 'The plot is lost' all recorded. These were the three Rydell originals we'd come to record for the split CD with San Geronimo and ARSTY, although we also had a new idea for a Shudder to Think cover we wanted to work on, and we had to get all the vocals down the next day as well as finishing the music. To give Milo some breaks if need be, we'd invited our friend Rachel Waller down too, as she was a great singer and fronted a local hardcore band called Sporting Heroes. She also helped out at Ignition Records and lived in the same house as me, Milo, Syd and Dan at the time (Syd and Dan were both Sporting Heroes guitarists, Dan having been in the second iteration of Couch Potatoes with me and Milo, and both worked on Ignition with me too). We figured that the new mellower version of 'The Plot is Lost' needed some female vocals, and she added them brilliantly and beautifully, fitting her lines in between Milo's and allowing him any breaks he needed. This meant I had fewer backing vocals to sing / shout too, always a good thing, and we had time to add some acoustic guitar and piano to the track too, giving us a very different version to the original on 'Per Ardua Ad Astra'.

We also recorded a second, shorter version of 'Nothing by morning', for a video we had planned and a German compilation CD release, adding a short radio station scrolling sample to the start of the song. Then we moved on to a track we called 'Heaven Ditty'. It was a re-imagined cover, a mixture of two Shudder to Think songs, 'Heaven Here' and 'Day Ditty', that we'd put together with pretty much the music from one ('Day Ditty') accompanied by the lyrics from the other ('Heaven Here'). This would be for a Shudder to Think tribute CD that was coming up on Ignition. Maybe we were being a bit too clever and arty for our own good, but the recording of this track came out really well too. Very textured and powerful, just how we wanted it.

All these tracks would see official release, as well as forming our new 'Memo demo' to send out to reviewers, promoters and radio stations while we waited for the proper pressings. We were always in a rush to get new tracks out there, and I kept the posties busy with these new tracks too.

An early review of these new tracks, on the 'Memo demo', came from Graeme at ENZK punk fanzine. This is what he generously had to say about it:

ENZK – Rydell 'Memo Demo' 5 - I've had this for about three hours so far and it's just been playing constantly. Rydell are one of those rare bands that can really pull of that melancholy yet totally uplifting sound. 4 songs (well 5, you get a second version of 'Nothing By Morning') all quite mellow, soft guitars and some keys. Great vocals, there's something heart wrenching about them, and the female vocals on 'The Plot Is Lost' work so well as a contrast. These songs are going to be on splits with San Geronimo and A Rocket Sent To You, two bands who'll have their work cut out for them to get their sides listened to. (GE)

With 'Per ardua ad astra' now on general release pretty much everywhere, and this new recording in the pipeline, we had some decent stuff out there. You could pick up our new CD, alongside loads of other cool stuff, through most of the good hardcore distros, including Revelation, Insound, Green Hell, Cargo, Saul Goodman, Very, Interpunk, Flight 13, Stickfigure and of course, Ignition. We were featured on several new compilation CDs, including releases on Household Name, Five Point Limey and Big Scary Monsters. There'd also be new Rydell tracks appearing on several Sponge Nation surfing and skateboarding videos, as well as soundtrack songs on the upcoming Clicked, Compzine and Props BMX DVDs.

We were getting onto so many cool alternative sports and BMX soundtracks through my friend Steev Bartholomew. He ran CVM BMX and was a big alternative music fan. He'd asked to use some of our music when he first heard Rydell, and we've been working together ever since. I asked him how he got into BMX riding and producing videos, and if he thought the music was a big part of it. He told me, "In 1993, I was 13 years old, and I grew up in a town called Wallington that is wedged between Sutton and Croydon in Greater London. At that time, there didn't seem to be any obvious influences that really resonated with me. The local surroundings were dominated with football culture and crappy chart music. There were no shortage of Adidas tracksuit bottoms and Reebok classics sported along the high street. It was almost a dress code! Needless to say, I felt like an outsider.

"American wrestling was the only thing I was a fan of. Although it's cheesy and fun, there's a lot of similarities between American wrestling and freestyle BMX. There are flamboyant and colourful expressions in both, along with immense individuality, style, signature moves and tricks etc. Upon discovering BMX, I quickly left the wrestling behind and became obsessed with BMX. Every car boot sale had an abundance of BMX bikes and parts, discarded from the '80s boom. Before I knew it, I had a shed full of parts and was building, trading and swapping bikes around daily. Freestyle BMX was culturally pretty much dead at that time and no one was really doing it. There were a few scenes dotted around, but there was probably only a couple of thousand riders left in the entire country.

Rydell San Geronimo A Rocket Sent To You

Rydell, San Geronimo & A Rocket Sent To You split CD

Recording again at Metway Studios

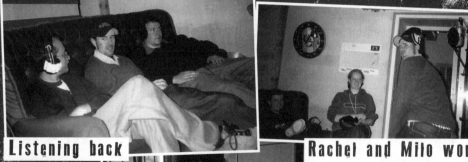

Listening back

Rachel and Milo working on their vocals

Jake and Charlie mixing mayhem

hot water music & rydell
a split seveninch record brought to you by ignition and scene police.

Sixth pressing HWM / Rydell 7" artwork

hot water music
rydell

ignition

SCENE POLICE

c/o Dennis-P. Merklinghaus
Humboldtstr. 15
53115 Bonn - Germany
www.scenepolice.de

"Thankfully though, freestyle BMX was reignited for a lot of people when American freestyle legend Mat Hoffman decided to build a huge quarter pipe ramp and proceeded to do an air twenty-five feet above the top of it. He was assisted by a motorcycle which towed him up to speed. MTV and other mainstream media companies covered the 'big air' event, and media started to filter through to UK television. With this event, a new era of freestyle was born, which is now referred to as Mid School BMX.

"A few months later, a TV show called Hi-5 aired on Channel 4, and it covered the Mat Hoffman event and his life story. This show changed everything; it was my first real exposure to freestyle BMX, highlighting all of the diversity. I recorded it off the TV and watched that VHS tape thousands of times! Many riders owe a lot to that show. The next few years were spent 'doing my time' in the completely pointless senior school system, and simply daydreaming about BMX, all day, every day. After I was freed from the 'school prison', I just rode my bike, progressed my tricks and went to as many jams and events as possible.

"By eighteen the worldly pressures of getting a job and 'thinking about one's future' were mounting up, but then an American video dropped called 'Props Road Fools One'. This video showcased the latest trend in BMX freestyle, which was more street-based opposed to ramp-based. The riders were ditching the full-face helmets and elbow pads and refining their styles, in the streets. It was the most influential content I'd ever seen; everything about the video, from the music, bikes and characters, literally formed me into who I was then, and who I am today. I won't even attempt to express the power of this influence in words, however I will list some of the bands they featured: Archers of Loaf, Trans Am, The Get Up Kids. So you get the idea!

"Overall, I knew that all I wanted to do was ride, travel and document BMX. For a life, for a job, without any exceptions. So, that's exactly what I did. Without sounding too 'Oprah', I really 'found myself'. Throughout the process of BMX video-making, I quickly felt that 'stealing' music for a soundtrack wasn't really fair or right. So, by my second video, I was sourcing soundtracks by communicating with bands and labels directly. The soundtrack of a video plays a massive part in how the video feels and how influential it can become. To this day, I still get messages from people expressing how much a certain video meant to them, how inspiring it was, or how it altered their perspective in some way. I feel that the soundtrack is equally as responsible for these reflections as the visuals are.

"I soon found David. I'm not sure if it was through contacting his label, Ignition Records, or from finding his band at the time, Rydell. Either way, we've been connected since the late '90s. It's now 2022, and I'm still making BMX videos with David's help!

"Throughout the years, bands under Ignition and Engineer Records have moulded my editing style and given the videos a distinctive feel. In the present, these videos will hopefully inspire and motivate. Nostalgically, these videos will hopefully be historically and emotionally valuable. I'm eternally thankful for the connection to David and the bands he's in and represents."

Clicked 07, BMX DVD
The seventh in the excellent series of BMX videos by Steev at Clicked. Loads of great bands on the soundtrack including The Jazz June, Hunter Gatherer, The Enkindels and Dugong, with Rydell providing 'Why couldn't we have met in the summer?'.
The DVD was packed with awesome stunts and street riding, with over 40 rider sections and hardcore bands from the UK and USA.

Compzine One, BMX DVD
The latest BMX competition video zine from the guys at Clicked. Featuring footage from Dallas B3, Urban Games, Redditch, Weymouth, Romford, Barcelona X games and King of Concrete meetings, with a soundtrack by Elliott, Rydell, Casket Lottery, A Rocket Sent To You, The White Octave, Annalise, Vanilla Pod, Metroshifter and The Stereo. The Rydell track on this one was 'Nothing by morning'.

Rumours, Ridicule and the Profit Motive, comp CD, Household Name Records
A great new compilation CD from Kafren and Lil's London-based Household Name Records showcasing Hundred Reasons, Canvas, Assert, Yeast, Anthem of the Century and twelve other audio tracks, with a Capdown video tagged on the end too. The Rydell track was 'Erratic erotic'. Kafren designed the great packaging, with a black skull and crossbones on a red background, and with the help of plenty of positive zine reviews this CD quickly went onto a second pressing.

In the Limelight, comp CD, Five Point Limey Records
Point Five Limey Records of America brought out a twelve band, fifteen track sampler CD, including tracks by Rydell, Spengler, Choking on Progress, Premier League, Fall Out, Stuck Zipper, Alien 101 and Damn the Man.

Ox 44 compilation CD
There were thirty-two bands crammed onto this sampler CD from the famous German punk and hardcore magazine. The Rydell track is 'Nothing by morning' and other bands featured included Strike Anywhere, Grade, Converge, Scared of Chaka, White Flag, Down and Away, Always Outnumbered, Tiger Army, Scorefor and the Nerve Agents.

You Do Know What This Means Don't You? comp CD, Big Scary Monsters Records
Another big sampler we were on, with twenty-four UK-based alternative bands and a

clicked.07

compzinevideoone

Dilite 80
Urban Games
Redditch Relax
King of Concrete
Barcelona X-Games
Weymouth Comp
Romford Comp

ignition

HOUSEHOLD RECO

SHUDDER
TO
THINK

a

tribute

Compilation CDs

FIREWORK

Anatomy

SUPER LOUD

MAXIMUM POWER

A TWENTY BAND COMPILATION

RYDELL
memo; demo

1. Nothing by morning
2. Margin for ever
3. The plot is lost
4. Heaven ditty
5. Nothing by morning (v2)

www.rydell.co.uk

Another demo

running time of over seventy minutes. This release included tracks by Annalise, Vanilla Pod, Cleatus, Fishtake, Shootin' Goon, Capdown, Eighty Six and Rydell.

Big Scary Monsters was Kevin Douch's Oxford-based label and over time it would develop into one of the best and most prolific alternative labels in the country, with releases for Jamie Lenman and Reuben, Walter Schreifels, Kevin Devine, Matt Pryor and The Get Up Kids, La Dispute, Gnarwolves, Into it Over it, Pulled Apart By Horses, Jairus, Minus the Bear, Hell is for Heroes, American Football, Cursive, Pedro the Lion, Owen, The Casket Lottery, The Gloria Record, My Favourite Co-Pilot and We Were Promised Jetpacks. This sampler was one of the first releases they ever did, and we were dead chuffed to be on it.

Firework Anatomy, comp CD, Ignition (Engineer Records) / Cargo
Our own labels new twenty band compilation album, featuring Kevlar, Hunter Gatherer, Slowride, Casket Lottery, Grade, San Geronimo, ARSTY, Speedwell, Mock Orange, Crosstide, Penfold, Ashen, etc. The Rydell track was 'The plot is lost' from 'Per ardua'.

There was also a bootleg ten track MP3 CD sampler of earlier Rydell tracks called 'Noise Annoys' doing the rounds, and we soon had more discussions with Dennis and Emre at Scene Police about Ignition pressing a sixth and final version of the popular Hot Water Music split 7" featuring 'Try Seventeen' and 'Just don't say you lost it'.

We didn't play any more shows in June, but did see our buddies Hot Water Music and Leatherface play a packed show on the 15th at The Garage in London. Lil of Household Name had put the show on, so had a load of his label's bands supporting them, but we spent the evening hanging out with the HWM guys and still got to see a great show.

Then on the 27th, whilst over in Germany on yet another trip there to drop off and pick up records for the Ignition distro, I went to see Jimmy Eat World and Ash at The Capitol in Mannheim. The Capitol was a massive theatre in the centre of town, and there were hundreds of kids dodging the trams and traffic to get inside. I'd heard J.E.W. were coming to Europe for the first time and picked up some tickets weeks before, knowing I'd be in Germany. Ash were supporting, and this was when they were a four-piece as Charlotte had joined Tim on guitar and vocal duties, and they'd just released 'Free All Angels' on Infectious Records. They weren't bad, but everyone was there to see Jimmy Eat World. 'Clarity' had been a hugely popular album with those in the more indie side of the scene, and I loved it. 'Bleed American' was just being launched and hitting big all over. The J.E.W. roadies had been handing out a limited-edition CD for the first hundred or so people into the show as a keepsake, and telling people there might be some filming tonight. This CD had a red and white cover and contained a couple of new demo tracks. I still have my copy. This was the show where they filmed their video for the track, 'Salt Sweat Sugar' (originally titled 'Bleed American') It was a great gig with plenty of sweaty dancing and a very happy crowd. I went back home wanting to play hot, happy, crowded shows like that.

1/7/2001 Anthem of the Century, Rydell, Stars Rain Down, No Comply, Sixty Seventh Morning and others. All-dayer at The Shed, Leicester
2/7/2001 Rydell, Vanilla Pod and Vehicle Derek at The Portland Arms, Cambridge
24/7/2001 Rydell, That Very Time I Saw, Hillside and Words May Fail at The Swan, Tottenham, London
27/7/2001 HHH, Deadweight, Rydell, Incoherence and others at the Fuck America Festival, Boston, Lincolnshire
28/7/2001 Green Acre, The Autumn Year, Rydell, Stars Rain Down and others at Mikefest, The Ferryboat, Norwich
2/8/2001 OneLineDrawing and Rydell at The Lift, Brighton
3/8/2001 OneLineDrawing, Rydell and The Babies Three at The Underworld, Camden, London
18/8/2001 The Backyard Federation, Rydell and Fishtake at The Portland Arms, Cambridge

The next Sunday we all piled into the van and drove up to Leicester for an all-dayer at The Shed. I hadn't been here since Couch Potatoes played with Tribute and Schema at The Charlotte, but we knew there was a really good local hardcore scene growing in Leicester, and The Shed was now the place to play. It was a hot, crowded, happy show. Just what I'd hoped for.

The Shed was a cool venue too, with a big but low stage, a large dancefloor and a long bar. The p.a. was quality and at certain points the sound guy would play with the lights too, and bathe the whole place in a red glow, like we were on a trip to Amsterdam. It's a rare thing, but this great venue is still going strong and putting on shows today.

JR Ewing were meant to headline but didn't make it for some reason, so Anthem of the Century became the headliners. They were great and reminded me of Majority of One, playing very positive upbeat hardcore. They had a six-track mini-album called 'The Enduring Vision' out on Germany's Join The Team Player Records. A great independent label, run by Marco Walzel and Ivonne Kreye out of Munich, who provided Ignition with loads of stock for our distro and were home to other seriously heavy hardcore contenders like Dawncore, Himsa, Darkest Hour and My Hero Died Today, as well as putting out European re-releases for Boy Sets Fire, Ensign and

Sheer Terror. Several of the Anthem Of The Century guys would form Steel Rules Die about a year or so later and sign with Ignition for a blasting split CD release with Winter In June, before more releases on In At The Deep End ('Nostalgia For Beginners') and Reflections Records ('The Hemingway Solution').

Pretty much all the bands rocked it that day. No Comply stood out with their female fronted ska-core, but it was all good and showed the range of musical styles all covered within the one scene. That was good to see, the message and intent going beyond the genre of music.

On Monday we played with Vanilla Pod and Vehicle Derek again, up at the Portland Arms in Cambridge. This was a lively venue pub that held about 200 punters, solid red brick outside with lots of wood panelling and fireplaces inside. I'm glad to say that it's still going strong now and still putting on rock bands. Tonight, it was hot and crowded, and turned out to be another great show, the other two bands really reminding me of the Goobers, playing tight, catchy, melodic hardcore and messing around, cracking gags between every song. A really fun gig followed by a raucous late-night drive back.

We'd bought expensive tickets, seven pounds each, for the Jimmy Eat World gig being put on by Mean Fiddler promotions at The Garage in London on the Friday. At that point, Jimmy Eat World were just on the cusp of taking off. 'Clarity' was out and popular in the scene with the kids who knew, but not yet the huge album it would be for them. 'Bleed American' would be the one that really blew J.E.W. up in the mainstream. They were over in the UK opening for Weezer at larger venues, and this show was booked on what would otherwise have been a night off for them. I remember Jim Adkins (singer / guitarist) having a few problems with his amp that night, but considering how popular they soon became, I was just glad we got to see them at a relatively small venue.

Rydell didn't have another show booked until a run at the end of the month. That started with another cracker, this time to a packed house at the Swan in Tottenham, where we'd played a few months earlier with Hunter Gatherer to a mix of bus drivers and punks. I'm glad to say that they'd improved the p.a. and it was a different sound guy working that night too. We had some more of our German mates over to play in London with us, That Very Time I Saw and Hillside, both brilliant bands but practically unheard of in the UK. I'd been listening to their demos and managed to get them both to supply tracks for the 'Firework Anatomy' compilation CD out on Ignition. Hillside's track was the poppy J Church, Seam or Superchunk style 'Counting time' and TVTIS's track was the powerful chuggy Grade style 'Don Quixote', also later to appear on their brilliant debut album, 'Observing life through rose coloured glass', co-released on Redfield Records in Germany and Ignition in the UK. Both these bands could deliver the goods live, and along with Words May Fail, we gave everyone an interesting Wednesday night in town.

Vanilla Pod

OneLineDrawing

the get up kids

Get Up Kids
postcard

xCanaanx

Vehicle Derek

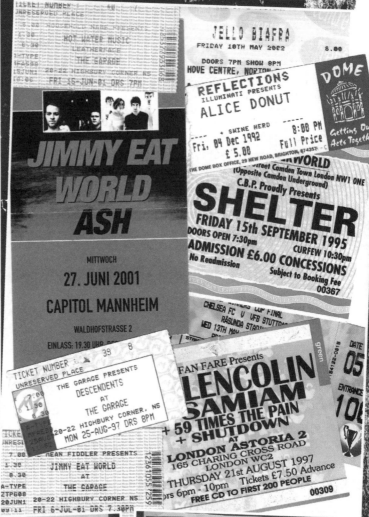

JIMMY EAT WORLD
ASH

MITTWOCH
27. JUNI 2001
CAPITOL MANNHEIM
WALDHOFSTRASSE 2
EINLASS: 19.30 UHR

JELLO BIAFRA
FRIDAY 10TH MAY 2002   8.00
DOORS 7PM SHOW 8PM
HOVE CENTRE, NORTON

REFLECTIONS
ILLUMINATI PRESENTS
ALICE DONUT
+ SWINE HERD
Fri. 04 Dec 1992   8:00 PM
£5.00   Full Price
THE DOME BOX OFFICE, 29 NEW ROAD, BRIGHTON

C.B.P. Proudly Presents
SHELTER
FRIDAY 15th SEPTEMBER 1995
DOORS OPEN 7:30pm   CURFEW 10:30pm
ADMISSION £6.00 CONCESSIONS
No Readmission   Subject to Booking Fee
00367

TICKET NUMBER
UNRESERVED PLACE
THE GARAGE PRESENTS
DESCENDENTS
AT
THE GARAGE
20-22 HIGHBURY CORNER, N5
MON 25-AUG-97 DRS 8PM

MEAN FIDDLER PRESENTS
JIMMY EAT WORLD
AT
THE GARAGE
20-22 HIGHBURY CORNER N5
FRI 6-JUL-01 DRS 7.30PM

FAN FARE Presents
LENCOLIN
SAMIAM
+ 59 TIMES THE PAIN
+ SHUTDOWN
AT
LONDON ASTORIA 2
165 CHARING CROSS ROAD
LONDON WC2
THURSDAY 21st AUGUST 1997   Tickets £7.50 Advance
Drs 6pm - 10pm
FREE CD TO FIRST 200 PEOPLE   00309

XCROSSBONESX
PRESENTS
THE BABIES THREE
UNREAL EMOTIONAL HARDCORE

XCANAANX
CANTERBURYS STRAIGHT EDGE MOSH MACHINE

UROTSUKIDOJI
CHAOTIC HARDCORE/METAL

ALL AGES SHOW
SATURDAY MARCH 16TH
JUBILEE HALL, WINCHEAP ROAD

FIRST RIGHT AFTER THE ESSO GARAGE
IF COMING FROM CANTERBURY, 5 MINUTES

CANTERBURY EAST

£3.00 ON THE DOOR

DOORS OPEN AT 7:00
FIRST BAND AT 7:30
SHOW FINISHES AT 10:30

INFO: JENKINSS77@AOL.COM

3 Live Bands every Tuesday Night
INTEGRITY
Tuesday 20th February 2001
Pureland Promotions proudly presents
in no particular order...

The Babies Three
emo hardcore
+
X canaan X
metallic hardcore
+
deadlifeportrait
noise metal

Live on stage from 8.45pm
Tickets £3.50 in advance - from Richards Records
no admission or re-admission after 11.45pm

Venue: 'The Studio' - planet lazer entrance
41 st georges place , Canterbury
Time: 8.30pm - 12.30am, Late bar until 1am.
Price: £4 with flyer, £3.50 members.
Info: 07802 523 926
Email: pureland@bigfoot.com

www.thewell.co.uk/integrity

Flyers & tickets

That weekend we had two festivals to play in the east of the country, the rather unsportingly titled Fuck America Fest in Boston, Lincolnshire, alongside some serious hardcore bands including Deadweight, Incoherence and HHH, and then the much more friendly MikeFest, another all-dayer at The Ferryboat in Norwich, this time a more indie / emo-core affair with The Autumn Year, Green Acre, Stars Rain Down and others.

This led to a pair of shows that exemplified the sort of wild ups and downs that only a struggling rock band can empathise with. Two shows with OneLineDrawing, the solo music project of Jonah Matranga, the singer of Far and New End Original. Jonah was a bit of a favourite of mine and Milo's, we both had his 'Sketchy' EPs, 1 and 2, and more recently his OneLineDrawing split with Sense Field, another favourite band of mine, so we were excited about these shows and figured they would be great.

The first gig was at The Lift in Brighton, a decent enough venue where we'd played a few times before, and seen plenty of good bands there too. Tonight though, seemed to be some club night and the first band, dragging their set on for what seemed like forever, sounded like the bloody M People. They sucked, the sound sucked, and the audience was not at all what we'd hoped for, with many people coming in, figuring they'd made a mistake and leaving again. It dragged on and on, so both Rydell and OneLineDrawing had to cut our sets very short and play to practically no-one. Jonah was clearly not impressed and hardly said two words to us all night, other than to complain or borrow my amp. We didn't see him again until the next night, but thankfully that was for a packed house at The Underworld in Camden, London, where everyone was treated to a range of emotional hardcore going from the extremely heavy to the beautifully soft.

The Babies Three played the London show with us and had clearly decided that because they were opening for a solo acoustic guy, they would play the heaviest, loudest set they possibly could, just to be contrary. I don't know if they were deliberately trying to make a point, but they screamed their heads off and were crushingly noisy. There's no doubting that they were absolutely on top of their game at this point, but that was far from subtle. One could argue that punk thrives on defying expectations and creating confrontation, but this seemed more like they were embarrassed to be playing with mellower bands.

I loved playing that gig as it was quite possibly the best onstage sound we ever had. You could hear all the subtleties, the riffs, the melodies, the rhythms, every word of Milo's vocals; it all came across as if we were back in the studio, but if anything, with even more feeling, thanks to the great live atmosphere at the Underworld.

There were mags and zines there interviewing both Jonah / OneLineDrawing and Rydell before and after the show, and we managed a decent chat and a few drinks afterwards too, staying in touch and eventually (about ten years later) bringing him back to do another solo tour in the UK. For that, we also put out a release on Engineer Records, a great four-track split CD for Jonah Matranga and Mikee J Reds (of Call Off The Search), called 'Countrysides'.

We finished off that run of warm-up shows for our upcoming US tour with a Saturday night return to the Portland Arms in Cambridge, where we'd been booked to support a skate-rock band called The Backyard Federation and some pop-punkers from Cardiff called Fishtake. This turned into another evening of swelteringly hot hardcore mayhem, basically a noisy dance and sauna thrown in. Fishtake kept having their name spelt incorrectly on gig posters as Fishtank, or Fishcake, and eventually changed it to The Take, going on to put out releases on Household Name, Good Clean Fun, Detournement and Bombed Out Records.

Rydell were all ready to become fully-fledged rockstars now and get on with our dream trip to the States. We'd booked our flights and were looking forward to spending three weeks touring colleges and rock clubs up and down the east coast with our buddies Hunter Gatherer, promoting our new 'Per Ardua Ad Astra' album. We couldn't wait.

A little while before that, Milo and I had got together with Ben Howarth of PennyBlackMusic magazine, to answer an interview. We met up in a Chinese restaurant in Maidstone (dunno where Adam was, he loves Chinese!) and although it wasn't our most interesting interview ever, it was fun. It turned out to be Ben's first face to face band interview, when he was just seventeen, and he enjoyed it so much that he is still working as a music journalist now. Partly because of that, and the fact his magazine made us their 'band of the year', I've added it here for context.

Rydell Interview with PennyBlackMusic magazine. (Ben Howarth)

The reason why I was so keen to interview Rydell is because they have released my favourite record of the year, their debut album 'Per Ardua Ad Astra' (which means 'Through hardship to the stars' by the way) on Headhunter Records. The album is, I think, essential listening to anyone interested in melodic indie-rock or punk.

Rydell are a hardcore band, and I know that puts some people off - although it shouldn't - but Rydell actually have a guitar sound closer to Johnny Marr than Fugazi, and the atmosphere of the record is similar to that achieved by REM in the early days.

Rydell are Miles Booker / Milo (vocals), David Gamage (Guitar and backing vocals), Adam French (Bass), Duncan Morris (Drums) and new recruit Mark Wilkinson (Guitar).

David & Adam

Macca

Milo

Duncan

Rydell

They formed in 1997 after the break-up of Couch Potatoes, the hardcore band formed in 1990 that had featured, across several line-ups, Milo, Dave and Adam.

Rydell are key figures in the south-east's 'emo' hardcore scene and have released a variety of records on many small hardcore labels, before Headhunter stepped in with an album deal. Their most successful release is a split single with Hot Water Music on the Scene Police label, which is now on its fifth reprint after selling over 4000 copies. Other than that, Rydell have released splits with Hunter Gatherer, Pale, The Babies 3 and Sunfactor.

They have also recorded the brilliant acoustic EP 'Home' (on Firewalk With Me Records) and have several tracks on compilations, benefits and extreme sports videos. This includes the 'Emotion Sickness' compilation, a collection of British emo bands, highly recommended, which includes two Rydell songs, 'Across Three Parks' and the acoustic version of 'Home'.

For most of these records, Rydell had been a four-piece but opted to add a fifth member, Mark Wilkinson, for the recording of their debut album. Before that, Milo had been playing rhythm guitar. So, I began by asking why they decided to increase to a five piece...

Milo: "Basically because I was really shit at playing the guitar and it got to the point where I was breaking more strings than I was playing. Mark wanted to join, he was pestering us and we thought 'Ah, give it a go!' It's worked really well."

Dave: "To be fair, Miles is pretty good at playing the guitar, but if we've got two people who can concentrate on playing the guitar when we're playing live, and one person who concentrates on singing and jumping around it gives the whole thing a better dynamic. Our songs aren't exactly difficult, but for him to sing and play guitar at the same time was getting a bit complicated. And Mark is a good friend of ours so it seemed like the right way to go."

Why did you decide to change from being Couch Potatoes to Rydell?

Dave: "We didn't really change from Couch Potatoes to Rydell. Our bassist went to University, our drummer went to Chile, and it just kind of stopped."

Milo: "There was a gap of three months in-between."

Were you getting bored with being in Couch Potatoes, because Rydell are very different?

Dave: "Not really, no. Couch Potatoes were more your straight-forward hardcore band like Jawbreaker or The Descendants. We were really into that at the time. Our old guitarist Dan (Pullin) has got a new band, Sporting Heroes, who absolutely rock, and they are more hardcore-based. We wanted to do something more emo, a slightly different thing, basically."

Milo: "It could have gone either way though. At the time it could have gone much heavier as opposed to much softer. Fortunately, we took the softer approach, but we did talk about becoming a very heavy band."

Dave: "But Rydell's style wasn't planned. We were actually a lot more like an indie band when we started."

Milo: "Very mellow"

Dave: "We've still got soft tracks but a lot of heavier ones now. We wouldn't say we were an 'emo' band or a 'hardcore' band. We're just a band!"

Has being in Couch Potatoes changed what you do with Rydell at all?

Dave: "Yeah, for example, with Couch Potatoes we played hundreds of shows, so we know what shows are worth doing and which ones aren't."

Why did you decide to make the 'Home' EP acoustic?

Milo: "Can I tell him the real reason? Well, we can laugh about it now, but at the time we were very annoyed. We did want to do an acoustic EP at some stage, but hadn't planned to do it when we did. But we had studio time booked, and our drummer was going to come back from holiday the day before. He worked it out wrong and got back the day after. So, very rushed, we did an acoustic EP. It was basically a jam the night before to work the songs out!"

Dave: "The record we did before the acoustic EP was the split single with Hot Water Music, which was quite heavy. A lot of people were saying, "Bloody Hell, what are Rydell doing?" We got reviews calling it "romantic, campfire music," which I was really pleased with when it came out."

Milo: "I wish we could have had more time. Then we could have really gone to town and got a cello or piano in."

The hardcore scene is very tightly knit, it seems, with bands keen to help each other out, touring together, releasing split singles and generally being part of the scene. Musically, perhaps, it has moved on from '70s punk, but it annoys me when people criticise it as being fake-punk or just a poor alternative. Musically it takes its roots from the American underground of the '80s, but in spirit it is still true to punk rock and has a right to call itself punk. Rydell have over time lent their names to a number of causes, including a show for the Manchester Hunt Saboteurs. However, they wouldn't call themselves a 'political' band.

Milo: "Doing benefits is just the nature of the scene we're in really. It's good to be playing benefits but they've probably been the most poorly attended shows that we've played, which isn't good. As a band we don't have any shared political beliefs, and we certainly don't have any political songs."

Dave: "Punk is more social politics than, like, party politics. That kind of thing is part of the punk scene, definitely. You could ask any band and they would have cool opinions but, at the same time, they wouldn't call themselves a political band."

Milo: "At some time or other, we've been into bands like Conflict and old-school punk, so we've got nothing against them."

However, when Rydell signed with Headhunter Records, an American label linked to the worldwide Cargo distribution, they took a step outside this hardcore scene. How did you get in contact with Headhunter?

Dave: "Well, they got in contact with us actually. We were on a German label, Scene Police, and we were happy with them. But on Scene Police we had to pay for our own recordings and stuff. Our drummer is a student and two of the band are unemployed. They emailed us, after hearing some of our demos and said, 'We'll pay you to record the album for us!'"

Milo: "Headhunter is a cool label; they've got 7 Seconds, Rocket From The Crypt, 3 Mile Pilot - good bands. And they are owned by Cargo - a worldwide distributor. We had nothing to lose, and we'd already written the songs."

And it means that Rydell are now in a position to tour America, something, despite having played over 800 shows in various projects, they'd never done.

Dave: "We're touring in September. In three week's time! We're really looking forward to that. We've toured in Europe quite a few times now, and around the UK as well, but we've never been to America, and we all wanted to go."

The hardcore scene is much bigger over there, isn't it?

Dave: "Yeah, its massive. But, unless you're an American band, it's very hard to crack. But we just want to go and have the experience of touring America."

Milo: "I'll be interested to see what sort of crowd turns up. I'm not sure whether Headhunter have marketed us towards a hardcore crowd or a college rock crowd. It would be nice to play to a mix of both. But we're touring with Hunter Gatherer, who are a hardcore band. We're also playing the CMJ music festival in New York, which should be amazing."

It's a bonus crowd as well, so long as you get the British sales.

Dave: "Yeah, but we actually sell most of our records in Europe, in places like Germany. Germany is an amazing place to tour, there is such a big hardcore scene."

The record has a good flow to it but features quite a few songs Rydell had released before; the three songs on the Hunter Gatherer split and a fourth version of the track 'Home'. Was the record conceived or was it a case of sticking your thirteen strongest songs on a record?

Milo: "We wrote nine songs for it, and the remainder were old songs. But with Mark joining they could have an intricate second guitar line, rather than just me bashing a power chord."

Dave: "After writing eight or nine new songs we wanted just to get the album done quickly. But, saying that, once Mark joined, we were just bashing out songs at a phenomenal rate."

Milo: "I don't have any problem with reworking older songs, because for the fans it's just like a remix. Also, a lot of the earlier versions were on limited editions, so more people can hear them now."

Dave: "Also there is a financial element to it. We just can't afford to go into the studio every time someone asks us for a track to go on a compilation. So, most tracks we actually record end up on at least two releases."

The album has quite a polished sound. Was this your intention?

Dave: "It is polished, but we were actually trying to make it quite raw. We recorded it practically live. But the drums sound better. The drums on the album sound really good."

Milo: "I had terrible problems with my voice tuning, and we had to have quite a few breaks. Then they went and mixed it with the vocals very loud! But I think it works well, and quite a few people have commented about the vocals."

Dave: "We are, don't forget, just a wimp-out indie-rock band, and to be a wimp-out indie rock band, you have to have quite a polished sound!"

Do you envy in any way the success and coverage of bands you've toured with, such as Green Day?

Dave: "No, we don't envy them. We wish them luck."

Milo: "What bothers me is the way people will go ape over some 'latest thing out of America', people in Britain that is, but won't give five minutes to a band who is playing down the road. If you're playing with an American band, nobody cares about the support group. But when we started going to hardcore shows, years ago, it would be like, three bands playing - wow, look at this great, varied line-up. We'd go ape over every band."

Dave: "It would just be about enjoying yourself."

Milo: "I'm jealous of the response foreign bands, no I'll take that back - American bands - get over here. 'Cos we played recently with a band from the Czech republic who were great, but no one turned out to see them and this was their London show, which was really annoying. Unless bands are from California, it seems like no one cares. It's like in the NME, they will mega-hype Burning Airlines, and, yeah, they're a good band but they don't even put a Rydell review in."

Dave: "Yeah, we supported Burning Airlines. We don't begrudge the bands themselves, Green Day or whoever, because they are very good bands and nice blokes as well, so you feel good for them, not bad. But it would be nice if people were a bit more open minded and listened to European hardcore bands as well as the American ones. Often though, there just aren't enough good gigs to go around."

You often get compared to Hot Water Music and Chamberlain, in particular. A lot of bands find these sorts of comparisons annoying, but do you?

Milo: "People will always draw comparisons like that. It's one of those things."

Dave: "Chamberlain and Hot Water Music are two of the best bands ever. They are excellent. So if somebody says a band sounds like one of them then go see them. Unless it's Rydell, of course, and then don't bother!"

Who influenced Rydell's sound?

Dave: "Revolver, definitely. A lot of British indie bands. We started Rydell before this whole 'emo' thing kicked off, but there were bands like Split Lip, Braid, Get Up Kids and Promise Ring who were doing a similar thing to us."

Milo: "Suede, lyrically and musically."

Dave: "Everyone in Rydell likes different music. But we all commonly like hardcore. But as we like a diverse set of bands, we tend not to do the obvious thing when writing songs. But there a lot of indie influences, especially early on, like Suede, Revolver, Radiohead maybe."

What are your overall aims for the band?

Dave: "We're in a band because we're all friends, and we all like doing it. Touring America was something I really wanted to do, and now we're doing that. I know Adam is keen to go to Japan, so we'll try to sort that out. But I really enjoy just recording and writing songs. It would be great if more people got to hear us. Not really from an ego point of view. It would be great if we could make a living out of it and do it all the time. People who say that punk groups who sign to major labels are corporate whores are arseholes, basically. If somebody said that I could be in a band and play gigs all the time, and earn a living, I'd bite their arm off!"

In the short term however, Rydell have a number of exciting plans. The second album could be recorded in the New Year, and the songs, in Dave's opinion, are "blistering, really fun to play." They predict that the second Rydell album will be a marked improvement on the first, a stunning prospect to say the least! But before that there is the aforementioned US tour, a new split release with San Geronimo and A Rocket Sent To You, and also a single from the album with older B-Sides on a Canadian label. Hopefully, there will also be a full tour of the UK in the near future.

Rydell have been successful so far, the album is fantastic, and they have received encouraging press (despite the absence of Rydell from the NME), none more so than from Kerrang!, which called 'Per Ardua Ad Astra', "One of the best British emo albums ever."

35, Copper and Stars

Rydell's first US tour was booked by our new label, Headhunter / Cargo, to cover the east coast colleges and clubs. It'd be a flying visit really, a quick adventure for us to test reactions, but then if all went well, we'd soon be back for more. We were flying out on the twelfth and back on the twenty third of September, so just twelve days in the country, but during that time we'd fit in ten shows, along with numerous radio station visits and magazine interviews. Eric and Bruce at the label had arranged it all and sent out plenty of posters and CDs in advance. They'd kept back some for us too, and we couldn't wait to see them. Originally, Gubby was bringing them down from Montreal and meeting us in Boston or New York, but as the first gig had now been moved to Baltimore, he wasn't sure if it'd be him, Eric, Jon or Bruce that met us, or even if it'd be the first or second show. Because of this, they eventually decided to mail a bunch of shirts and stickers to the Hunter Gatherer guys, so they could bring them along in their van with all the backline and we'd at least have some merchandise at the first show. We'd seen images of the posters, and of course had CDs we were sending out too, so it didn't really matter we wouldn't see the shirts or stickers until the first show. We'd packed our guitars and a few other releases to take with us, and now just wanted to get over and play the gigs as soon as possible.

There would be six of us going. Milo, Macca, Adam, Duncan and myself, of course, but also our good buddy Dan Pullin, who'd be driving us and helping out with merch. I'd booked the tickets a while ago, and was given booking ref 7Y03RI, with us all on a 10.30am flight out of London Gatwick, arriving into New York, JFK at 1.30pm EST. These return flights cost just £329 each then, and we'd hired a spacious seven-seater Chevy Astrovan from Alamo to pick up from JFK too. We'd booked unlimited mileage on that, and made sure it had air conditioning and a good, loud stereo system. Being a bit OCD, I'd noted it all down in the back of my 2001 diary, and checked everyone's passports too. We were all good to go. It may as well have been set in stone.

We'd drive from New York down to Baltimore, where we had a radio interview booked and then the first gig at the University of Maryland. From then on, we had a fairly straightforward itinerary to follow all around the east coast, with us and Hunter Gatherer travelling in two vans, until the final show at the Engine Room in their hometown of Athens. That should be a party. The next day we'd drop off the van and fly back from Atlanta Hartsfield-Jackson airport to home. We'd be departing at 6.20pm on 23/9 and arriving back in good ol' blighty at 7.30am on 24/9. I can't tell you how excited we were about all this. We'd arranged to meet up with a few of our US mates on the way, and we all figured it'd be great fun.

We had a fairly new website at that time, still quite a rare thing for bands back then, and although it was basic and simplistic by today's standards, we could still add gig dates and news, so were able to update our 'fans' or anyone who gave a shit, with positive, upbeat stuff.

Our latest post was:

"Rydell leave next week for a short tour of the US East Coast. Starting on 12/9 in New York and finishing in Atlanta on 23/9, we'll have Hunter Gatherer and other friends along with us for the ride. The dates and venues are in the gig guide, and there'll be new shirts, stickers and posters for the tour. Maybe we'll see you there!"

The stickers had been made by an American company called StickerGuy who often advertised in MRR, HeartattaCk and all the bigger US zines. They had the oval Rydell logo on them and were die-cut to this oval shape too. They were sent to Hunter Gatherer along with the new t-shirts. I'm not sure where Headhunter had the shirts printed, but they said there would be plenty of them in a few different sizes. My biggest concern at the time was if my guitar would make it through the airport luggage system and come out in one piece at the other end!

There was another post on the website before this, announcing proudly that, "The new album is out on Headhunter Records. You need to own this. Kerrang! says, "Utterly brilliant" and "One of the best British emo albums ever made". Big Cheese says, "Truly great" and "Essential... remarkable album". Rocksound says, "Dripping with power and melody". Check it out for yourself. Thirteen tracks recorded at Metway Studios in Brighton to rock your world. Fold out, full colour packaging with lyrics. Available now from this website or most good distros, including Revelation, Insound, Green Hell, etc." That seems a bit smug now, but we were excited. We didn't realise we were asking for it.

We also had an image of the tour poster on the website, showing all the gigs that were booked, along with our logo and the CD cover artwork on there. Of course, it had Headhunter / Cargo's logos and contacts as well, and most of the venues too. I was determined to grab a few copies of the real thing when we got there to bring back home and display on a wall somewhere.

Headhunter had booked some of their other acts to support at these gigs, and these mainly seemed to be new bands they wanted to check out live, so most weren't listed on the poster. This included a screamo band called Oman Ra, from Olean in New York state about six hours / 350 miles west of New York City, who had booked one of the shows so were playing on it. We'd also managed to get a few of our US friends, mainly bands from the 'Firework Anatomy' compilation, onto some of the shows as support acts too. So, as well as Hunter Gatherer, we had A Rocket Sent To You playing with us in Baltimore, then Two Weeks From Tomorrow and Five Cent Hero at one of the shows in New York, as well as other surprise guests we were hoping to confirm further south too. We wanted to make every show a party.

The gigs and bands listed on the poster were:
13/9/2001 WMUC, College Park Radio Station, University of Maryland (Baltimore)
Rydell with A Rocket Sent To You, Hunter Gatherer and Velvet

14/9/2001 Cobra, La Olean, New York
Rydell with Hunter Gatherer, Ben Davis and Oman Ra

15/9/2001 Hotel Mold, New Brunswick, New Jersey
Rydell with Hunter Gatherer

16/9/2001 Acme Underground, New York, New York
Rydell with Two Weeks From Tomorrow, Five Cent Hero and Hunter Gatherer

17/9/2001 PRC, Richmond, Virginia
Rydell with Hunter Gatherer

18/9/2001 Pontiac Grille, Philadelphia, Pennsylvania
Rydell with Hunter Gatherer

19/9/2001VFW, Huntingdon, West Virginia
Rydell with Hunter Gatherer

20/9/2001 Club 123, Morgantown, West Virginia
Rydell with Hunter Gatherer

21/9/2001 Backdoor Club, Greenville, North Carolina
Rydell with Hunter Gatherer

22/9/2001 The Engine Room, Athens, Georgia
Hunter Gatherer with Rydell & local supports tba. (HG's hometown).

As we all know now, there was some considerable disruption to a lot of people's plans the day before we were due to leave on 11th September 2001, or what is more commonly known as 9/11 now. The terrible suicide attacks involving four aeroplanes on that day killed nearly 3,000 people, and the chaos that ensued went on for weeks, with the repercussions lasting years. Receiving calls from my bandmates and then watching it all unfold, live on TV in the UK, it was just unbelievable. It seemed unreal. My heart sank, mainly for those poor innocent souls on the planes and in the buildings, of course, but right then, just a little for us too. Very soon, my work called and asked if I'd be able to come in for the next couple of weeks after all. Rub it in, for fuck's sake.

Faced with this, what can you say? What can you do? Obviously, things like bands and tours really don't matter much when confronted with a terrible and horrifying situation like that. The more the reality of things unfurled and what had happened became clear, it just sickened me. It still does to this day, especially when I see the footage or visit the memorials. What a truly ghastly thing, and from our own selfish point of view, what shitty timing! There were other people involved in the tour as well as the bands, plenty of promoters, the audiences who'd bought tickets and our record label too, of course. But the shows started in and around New York and all flights to the US were grounded anyway. Even after that, people weren't going out. Was this good or bad luck for us, a day earlier we could have been on one of those aeroplanes. No-one felt like playing any gigs.

9/11 became a huge turning point in American culture as the shock and horror of those days led to repercussions that are still felt now, not only the war against terror and increased anti-muslim violence, but also the passing of the Patriot Act involving a huge increase in government surveillance and the transformation of air travel. With all that has passed in the twenty years since, most people still remember exactly what they were doing that day and how it made them feel at the time.

I asked Milo and he recalled, "I was at home on the 11th, actually packing my bag, when Rob, one of my housemates, called me from work and said that I might want to turn on the TV, which I did and immediately saw the Twin Towers with smoke coming from the tops where the planes had hit. I was frozen. My gut knotted. I can still picture that moment now.

"For several days afterwards, we were calling the airport every day, asking when flights were going to start again. At this point the magnitude of the situation, (which ultimately led to the Second Gulf War etc), had not really sunk in and I think we all thought that flights would start again soon, so maybe we could pick the tour up down the line somewhere. Every day, I would check in with you (David) to see if we were still going. I think flights into NYC did not actually start again for about a month." (Although flights were grounded on the days directly following 9/11 and disrupted for ages after that, civilian air traffic did begin again as early as 13th September).

"There was also the question of whether people would come out to shows after something like that happening. Certainly, it affected people in New York and the way they socialised for years to come; people I know still talk about it now, and it's true to say that to some degree, the city was never the same again. (NB. Milo now lives in New York).

"These weren't easy decisions to make at the time, and I think Hunter Gatherer split up over it because half the band wanted to continue touring despite what had happened, and half the band thought they should stay home because no one was going to want to come out to shows that soon after 9/11. I can well believe this was the case for a lot of bands. The US is so big that even a lesser-known punk band could easily tour for nine months of the year, but post 9/11 that circuit was not what it had been, and I know a lot of smaller bands were really badly affected."

I also asked Adam later about the impacts of that disastrous day too, and his comments were, "It was always a bucket list item of mine to be seen walking through an airport with a guitar case. The trip would have been just before my wedding to Liz. I was at work that day when someone said a plane had hit the World Trade Centre. I couldn't believe what I was seeing and sat there knowing my ambition was slipping away, but couldn't feel sad because of the awful events affecting others much more than any insignificant ambition I had.

"I knew immediately the world had changed, and any thought of an American tour were gone, most likely for good, which turned out to be correct. I'm not sure the band was ever the same after that day. I still think about it sometimes, and wonder if we had toured the US then perhaps we would have achieved more."

A couple of weeks later, on the 28th we posted on the Rydell website, "Sorry we've been offline for a while. The US tour was due to start on 12/9/01 so things were really disrupted. Our feelings of being the UK's most unlucky band pale in comparison to the victims of this disaster. Our thoughts are with all those affected. We have many close friends in America. We would like to thank the bands, labels and promoters involved for all their patience, and we hope to see you next year instead."

On the 30th, trying to move on from it all, we posted, "On a more positive note, the new Rydell tracks should be available any day now on a split CD release with San Geronimo and A Rocket Sent To You. Also, the 'Per Ardua Ad Astra' CD is back in stock at Cargo and most distros. The German zine Ox features a new Rydell track, 'Nothing By Morning', on the cover CD of its latest edition, and the new Compzine BMX/Skate video also features Rydell tracks.

We'll be looking for new gigs/tours. Any place, any time, anywhere. Everyone get in touch and let's get things rolling again."

I know we had a gig booked in Eastbourne at Strummers Club that evening too, on the 30th. The promoter Daz was a big fan and he'd booked us again, hoping it'd be a fun 'after tour' party. We didn't want to cancel on him, but it was a pretty half-assed event after all these heart-sinking happenings, and I don't even remember who else played or if many people turned up.

Moving on, inevitably as we have to, the next show Rydell had booked was with the aptly named bands, The Unfinished Sympathy and The Mercy Suite. This was over at The Lido in Margate, on the seaweed-stinking Kent coast, for our friends at Geekscene promotions. Paul and Dan always put on great shows and this would be their 21st, costing just £3 on the door, on Monday 22nd October.

The Unfinished Sympathy from Barcelona were headlining. A great rock band who'd signed with Jordi's Bcore Records and had a similar powerful sound to the Foo Fighters, but with far more arty lyrics. One track on their self-titled debut album was called 'The charming beauty of the things we never had', another 'Elderly mermaid' and yet another 'Slept with the dead girl'. This was their first ever tour, but whilst they were in the UK they managed to record a Peel Session in the BBC studios, the first Spanish band ever to do so. The Unfinished Sympathy would go on to record six albums, mainly for Bcore and Subterfuge Records, as well as many EPs and singles, and kept playing right up until 2017.

Knowing Rydell would be supporting them, some wheeze had written on the flyer, "rockin' guys collapsing their little lungs" as that was a reference to our song 'Collapser', one of Milo's most sincere emo style lyrics at the time. The wheeze in question was Paul Waller of The Babies Three and Geekscene promotions, who always had something amusing to write on the flyers as descriptions of any bands they put on, hoping it'd attract a few more kids to come along to the gig. He'd make up quotes like, "Mineral wish they were this good" or "Like Sunny Day Real Estate but better," even if it was just some random noise band from Bradford playing.

Also playing that evening were The Mercy Suite, an up-tempo melodic hardcore band from Leeds, a city that had a great alternative music scene and was churning out some superb bands. They later signed to Bombed Out Records, a fast-growing local label founded by Steve Jackson (no, not the Fighting Fantasy guy) and Alex Hurworth, responsible for putting out great releases from Dugong, Joe 90, The Leif Ericsson and The Dauntless Elite, amongst others. The Mercy Suite's releases with them included a six-track EP called 'Credis Quod Habes Et Habes' (meaning 'It is fraud to conceal a fraud') and their great fourteen-track album, 'Crestfallen'.

We were all still unsettled by the events of the previous month. Up to that point, it had seemed that things had all been going quite well for Rydell, but now I occasionally found myself wondering about the point of it all, and certainly not sure what to do next. We'd been writing new songs and on fire with ideas before, but that seemed to be drying up for now. And the label, although obviously not blaming us for not being able to make it over for the tour, had no plans to arrange another one just yet, and had lost a lot of time and money on the promotion of the 'Per ardua ad astra' release that was far less likely to be recouped now.

We needed a change so moved our regular practise sessions from Forest Row over to a muddy farm in the middle of Ashdown Forest. Friar's Gate Farm was about half-way between between Tunbridge Wells and Brighton, so easy enough for all of us to get to, and had the added bonus that we could store our gear there quite securely too. But even so, it took a while to get our usual motivation and inspiration back. We were additionally hampered as this new practise place was turning out to be comedy gold. We would often be distracted from bouncing power chords around the cow-shit covered concrete walls by Dudley, the friendly but incredibly hairy guy who ran the farm. Dudders, as we all called him, would charge around the farm in his shit-covered green wellies, wearing shorts and a t-shirt in all weather, and stopping by to chip in hilarious comments about his never-ending work, or our progress as a band compared to his '70s rock idols. One day, he had thoughtfully decided to include a fridge full of beers in the rehearsal room, where we could take whatever we wanted and simply leave our money in a bowl. Every single week after that, Duncan would get a beer out to drink on the drive back to Brighton with Macca, and every week Adam would vigorously shake the bottle while Duncan was out loading up his car. I have no doubt that, on a weekly basis, the beer would explode all over him and Macca while they were driving home. This was an endless source of amusement for Adam, Milo and me, but Dunc never once mentioned it.

It was around this time that Jonathan 'JB' Birch, the current drummer of Anti-Nowhere League, asked me if I wanted to join the band and play guitar for them. The ANL had a bit of a reputation in my hometown of Tunbridge Wells, after managing to get themselves arrested at their first ever gig there, in a park near where I lived. The PR resulting from this mayhem got them onto gigs with The Damned, The Exploited and Discharge and, after releasing a couple of ridiculously offensive punk rock songs, they never looked back. By then though, their original guitarist, Chris 'Magoo' Exall had quit, but ever since Metallica had covered 'So What' on their 'Garage Days Revisited' release they'd been getting more and more offers. Animal, their singer, whose real name was Nick Culmer, used to work on the door at the old Rumble Club with me. He'd been over to the US to sing onstage with Metallica while they played the cover to tens of thousands of screaming fans, and he had definitely got the taste for gigging again. The League had recently had an offer to tour Japan, and JB knew I loved playing so thought I might be up for it. It was good of him to ask, and I was grateful for the offer. I considered it for a while but decided to turn it down. I'd tried being in two bands at once before, and it just hadn't worked out. Plus, I still believed in Rydell, and we had plenty more to offer yet.

At the end of October, on the 27th at Tonbridge Castle, to be precise, Adam, our bassmaster general, married his sweetheart, Liz. They'd walked in to 'Friday I'm in love' by The Cure, mixed in some Ramones and Dead Kennedys between the romantic stuff, and at one point even blasted out 'Erratic Erotic' (from the 'Per Ardua' album) for us all to bop around to. After far too much beer and a slap-up fish 'n' chips supper, we all bounced around to some more punk songs before they cleared off on their honeymoon to Florida. As a band, we now took some downtime, and needing something positive to do, Milo and I, with help from Dan Pullin, Stephen 'Syd' Franklin and Rachel Waller, worked hard on improving and expanding Ignition (Engineer Records) and its distro.

We had loads of good stock coming in, some records we traded for our own Ignition releases, others we bought in wholesale from labels we knew. Ever optimistic, I still believed punk rock could change the world for the better and wanted to spread the message. I don't know if the other guys agreed, or just wanted to go to lots of gigs. We certainly went to loads of them! By then, I'd saved up almost £10k and really wanted to do things properly with the new label. I'd bought a new computer to run our stock and promos, and launched a new website store, at IgnitionOnline.co.uk so anyone could get in touch at any time.

I'd started out buying in stock from friend's labels we were already close with and whose releases we all loved. Ignition distro's first order was nearly $1000 worth of stock from Var Thelin at No Idea Records, which included many of our current favourites plus anything he had that was new in, of course. The second order was about $1000 again, from John Szuch at Deep Elm (who we'd later run the Deep Elm UK amazon account for, and represent over here for a few years), and the third was about $500 from Vique Martin (ex-Simba zine), then at Revelation Records.

We also bought direct from smaller labels and bands too, and traded releases wherever we could. Which definitely became easier as the label grew and people saw the quality of what we were doing. In late October, we bought a bunch of Bane's 'Holding this moment' 7" and Fall Silent's 'Life, beautiful but heartless' 7", and also started work with another new UK label, Year3Thousand Records, on their upcoming compilation. We advertised our releases in as many punk and alternative zines as possible, sometimes paying for the ads with copies of Ignition releases. From early on, we'd decided that we wanted to trade with other small independent HC labels, so we set up a contact list and quickly started offering trades and cheap wholesale rates for extra stock to everyone we could. Day After (CZ), Doghouse (US), DimMak (US), Mag Wheel (Can), Subjugation (UK), Redfield (Ger), Rugger Bugger (UK), Rise (Can), Funtime (Bel), Household Name (UK), Vacation House (IT), Lifeforce (Ger), Per Koro (Ger), Nova (Ger), Incendiary (Ger), Bastardized (Ger), X-Mist (Ger), Prawda (CZ), Reflections (Ned), Winter (Ger), Let It Burn (Ger) and Crank (US) were some of the first record labels to take us up on this.

As I already mentioned, the first releases on Ignition (later Engineer Records) were represses of a couple of the records I'd already helped put out with Dennis and Emre on the Scene Police label. The Hunter Gatherer album on CD, and the Rydell / Hot Water Music split on 7" vinyl. Additionally, by November I'd bought up well over 3000 deutschmarks (about £1k) of Dennis and Emre's spare Scene Police stock too, and brought it back to the UK as we were now running stalls at all the shows we went to, and couldn't sell the new HC releases here fast enough. We also added Kent Mclard's Ebullition Records to our partner labels and, alongside No Idea, Deep Elm and Revelation, they would provide the bulk of our distro stock over the next months and years.

The first Ignition distro sales came in from friends coming around to check out the new records pretty much straightaway as they came out. Being an OCD nerd, I still have notes on most of those initial orders and sales, originally kept for accounts and so that I knew what to re-order. Those early sales included the 'World Hardcore' compilation CD and zine at £3, the Rydell / Pale split 7" on white vinyl at £2, Couch Potatoes 'Outweighed' CD at £3, plus a popular package deal on the 'Emotion Sickness' compilation CD, Rydell / Hot Water Music split 7", Rydell / Hunter Gatherer split CD, and Rydell 'Home' 7" all for £15. We also shifted a lot of Appleseed Cast, mainly their brilliant 'Mare Vitalis' CD, and also quite a few copies of the 'Music for the working class' comp CD from Deep Elm too, for just £7 and £2.50 respectively, as the latter was a sampler compilation.

Very soon, we had our own releases out on Ignition for San Geronimo, Dead Red Sea, One Last Thing, Crosstide, Last Year's Diary, Planes Mistaken For Stars and Speedwell, as well as a great Shudder To Think tribute CD. This would be followed by Chamberlain, Elemae, Tidal, Flyswatter, xCanaanx, Urotsukidoji, Winter in June, Eden Maine, and more Rydell releases. The label and distro were both going well.

We did most of our business at shows though, direct with kids at the gigs. The first of these had been back in October 2000, at a Bane gig at The Swan in Ashford, where we'd started with a small box of mainly Deep Elm CDs and a few vinyl singles, but seeing our idea work so well, built up the stock fast. Since then, we'd expanded rapidly and were having Ignition distro stalls at as many gigs as possible. It was a great way to share the new music with our friends, and get the hardcore message out there at the same time. The really great thing was that for every bigger US label release we were selling, we were also selling and trading three or four of our Ignition releases, and other smaller UK and European labels records as well. Helping to get previously unheard-of bands far better known.

GeekScene put on their 22nd show, with a little help from the Slash 'n' Burn guys, on Friday 2nd November, 2001. It was Planes Mistaken For Stars at the Margate Lido, and that gig would be sweaty, noisy and become a thing of local legend. Of course, Ignition had a distro stall there. PMFS were incredibly popular in the underground scene at that time, and already had great releases out on Deep Elm, Dim Mak, No Idea

geek scene presents show #21

the unfinished sympathy
Spanish rock music with a similar vibe
to the foo fighters in a hardcore stylee.

RYDELL
sorta local rockin' guys collapsing their little lungs.

mercy suite
uptempo punkyemo from leeds. killer stuff.

monday 22nd october 2001
margate lido cliff bar
£3 entry . doors 8pm.
22 the avenue, that's the place that we all go...

The Mercy Suite

The Unfinished Sympathy

and even Ignition. We'd put out a cool skull-shaped CD version of their 'Fucking Fight' 7", which was a mad idea really for less than four minutes of music, but everyone suddenly wanted CDs. John at Deep Elm and Gared of Planes Mistaken For Stars just said go for it and sent us the masters, so with a little design help from Richard Shiner of xCanaanx, we made it look as cool as possible.

PMFS were supported by three bands; Brighton's Scuttle, who had a split 7" with Vanilla Pod on Mother Stoat Recordings, as well as a CD called 'Testing the strength of the surface' on Firefly Records; Third Season, an old school rock band from Belgium, and Ashford's killer hardcore outfit Urotsukidoji, who would soon have their first release out with us on Ignition / Engineer Records, a split CD with Winter in June.

Planes Mistaken For Stars were such a great band, and almost everybody I knew had their self-titled eight-track mini-album when it came out on Deep Elm Records. Originally, it had been released by the band themselves on their own Desperate Acts label, but John Szuch at Deep Elm signed them and tidied up the record, releasing it on CD as well as both black and white vinyl versions in '99. They quickly followed that with a split CD with Deep Elm labelmates, The Appleseed Cast and Race Car Riot, and then the 'Fucking Fight' 7" on Steve Aoki's Dim Mak Records and CD on Ignition Records. They'd also release another mini-album, this time with seven tracks, called 'Knife in the Marathon', on Dim Mak Records in '99.

The band then moved from Peoria, Illinois to Denver, Colorado, so they could tour more easily, and left Deep Elm to sign with Var Thelin at No Idea Records. This resulted in their 2001 album, 'Fuck with Fire', and the 2002 release, 'Spearheading the sin movement', seeing the band get progressively heavier. PMFS toured constantly and later released 'Up in them guts' on No Idea, 'Mercy' on Abacus Recordings, 'We ride to fight', a collection of early EPs on No Idea, and then much later 'Prey' on Deathwish Records. They decided to call it quits in 2008, bowing out at the Marquis Theatre in their adopted hometown of Denver, but got bored and reformed in 2010, going back out on tour.

Their main man, singer and guitarist was Gared O'Donnell, and he'd been the guy I was speaking with who'd been kind enough to agree to the early release on Ignition. A massive character in the scene, he sadly succumbed to oesophageal cancer and died in 2021, aged just 44.

"I don't want to say that I wasted my days chasing, instead of catching. Keeping wasting wishes on copper and stars. I'm wanting you to save me and I'm not only asking because I can face this falling, it's just the taking that I fell. I'm breaking down." – PMFS.

Planes Mistaken For Stars

PLANESMISTAKENFORSTARS

fucking fight

GEEK SCENE PRESENTS SHOW #22
in conjunction with SLASH N' BURN

PLANES MISTAKEN FOR STARS
One of America's most exciting
hardcore bands. A must see.

SCUTTLE
Emo-punk from 'round Brighton way.

THIRD SEASON
Old school hardcore from Belgium.

UROTSUKIDOJI
Canterbury killer hardcore. RAAWWK!

Friday 2nd November 2001
Lido cliff bar, Margate
Doors open at 7.30 pm

☆ Planes Mistaken for Stars ☆

**Planes Mistaken
For Stars**

36, Always Remember Everything

There was an As Friends Rust and Strike Anywhere show on the 16th November at the Camden Underworld that Ignition had a very busy stall at. This was the gig they filmed for the 'Live at Camden Underworld' video and DVD on Punkervision. The Underworld shows were usually excellent, both to play or run distros at. In fact, the most money we ever made from the distro at one show, well over a grand, was when Elliott played the Underworld. But of course, not all the London venues were so accommodating. Milo did most of the distro shows I couldn't make, and reminded me about one of the Appleseed Cast gigs, right around the time of the 'Low Level Owl' albums.

"The promoter who'd been offered the gig had, for some bizarre reason, chosen to put it on at the Dublin Castle, a venue that could be described accurately as follows; miserable old locals-only bar at the front, full of dirty old men talking shit, toilets were among some of the worst ever with no paper, no locks, no working taps and an inch of water on the floor. Most nights there were shitty pay-to-play events where they'd just round up any three bands who needed a gig and hoped they bring a crowd.

"I was distroing there and I went up with Sam The Man and set up the stall in a corner across two of those small, round pub tables. We had to slim the distro right down as we didn't have much table space. On the way in, I'd noticed a scruffy old bloke sat at the bar in a filthy suit covered with stains, sporting a comb-over and long at the back thin grey hair. He had skin so pale he barely looked alive. Kind of a zombie crossed with the character from the Fast Show who always said, "Hardest game in the world, thirty years man and boy.

"Anyway, at some point soon after Appleseed Cast had started playing, he walked up to the distro table, leans over and yells (loudly, over the noise of the band playing just metres away) "Fuck Off!" I roll my eyes at Sam and think to myself, "Here we go, local nutter", but he leans in again and says, now in an Irish accent, "You're taking up the space of ten people, fuck off out of it!" It occurred to me that this guy might be the landlord, but regardless of his extreme rudeness, there's no way I was taking up that much space, the tables would have been there anyway and, as far I could see, there wasn't a line of people trying to get in the door.

"I was enjoying the band so asked Sam to find the promoter, who came over, but the old wanker started yelling in his ear. I couldn't hear what was said, but the kid caved in and came over to tell me I had to leave, or the show would be over. FFS, the gig was good, the distro was going well, and the room was packed now, so carrying out boxes of vinyl and CDs through that crowd was going to be tough. Soon enough though, we had to exit. I started to take boxes out to my car, which conveniently was parked just across the road from the venue. I took my time so that Sam could continue selling from the remaining boxes. As predicted, as soon as I exit the live room the rest of the pub is just locals, not packed and certainly no line to get in so proof, if it were needed, that the old bastard just didn't like people spending money on anything other than his bar, but there it was.

"We hung around and, as the crowd was leaving the gig, Sam and I did a roaring trade out of the boot of my car. A lot of kids were saying they were going to come and buy stuff after the bands anyway. That's what usually happened. The promoter kid must have felt guilty too, as he came over and spent at least £50!"

On a more positive note, Milo added, "I also remember the legendary Beach Fest in Westgate (Kent) though, for being really friendly and crazy busy. I had to drive home to Margate twice for restocks!" He'd moved down to Margate by that time, to be with his girlfriend Clare, and did a ridiculous amount of driving in this busted-up old Toyota Corolla he had. It was a real workhorse that he'd bought from our housemate Syd, and it became Ignition distro's road wagon. It'd done well over 100,000 miles but never missed a beat. Milo would hammer back and forth to Southampton, London, Leicester, Margate, Canterbury, Basingstoke, Brighton, anywhere a gig was on, with it stuffed full of records and CDs, several nights a week, every week, for a few years. By then, we were pretty much a full-time label and actually brought in a few quid to cover costs and pay us a bit. It was genuinely great.

Milo added, about the house we all shared at 1 Chandos Road in Tunbridge Wells, running the label and playing in bands together; "I always feel I was very lucky to have had the opportunity to run the distro and label full time for a while, and live in such a cool house whilst doing it."

In the New Year, we'd all decided to pick our gigs more carefully and concentrate on recording new songs for releases, hopefully a new album. We were still getting together to jam every week, but playing far fewer shows. This was more due to the growth of other commitments, such as work and travel, rather than any lack of love for the band, but we wanted what we did to be good and special. Headhunter Cargo were just now starting to ask about a possible tour again, and agreed to put out a 'collection of singles and EPs' as our second album, while we worked on the new tracks for a third.

Rydell appeared on the new Compzine BMX video from Clicked, alongside tracks from Elliott, Casket Lottery, San Geronimo and A Rocket Sent To You. We had a few copies on both VHS PAL and NTSC turn up for the distro, and promptly found them all good homes.

Then, Mag Wheel Records of Canada agreed to release a Rydell / Elemae split CD in March with three tracks by each band. The main Rydell track would be 'Why couldn't we have met in the summer?' from our 'Per Ardua Ad Astra' album, with two other as yet unreleased tracks. The Elemae tracks would be remixed from their 'A life to be defined' album. Elemae had a sound like Sense Field, or Seaweed, or maybe Texas is the Reason, but even more radio friendly. This release would be MAG036 and the label's other records included singles for Juno and New Sweet Breath. There was even a chance they could help us book a few shows over in Canada, so we were pretty excited about it.

12/1/2002 Arcaine, Rydell and Last Year's Diary at The Mermaid, Folkestone.
12/2/2002 Piebald, Rydell at TJ's, Newport
13/2/2002 Piebald, Rydell and Pylon and The Retro Bar, Manchester
14/2/2002 Piebald, Rydell and The Day I Snapped at The 13th Note, Glasgow
15/2/2002 Piebald, Rydell and Pylon at The Fenton, Leeds
16/2/2002 Arcaine, Rydell and Jester at The Leas Cliff Hall, Folkestone

Rydell's first gig of 2002 would be in Folkestone, Kent, a town we played in very often. This is a town with plenty of venues and that proudly proclaims it has been 'made in music' and is now, in fact, the world's first official Music Town! This show was originally booked at the Stripes Club, but had to be moved at the very last minute due to a massive fight at the venue the previous night that had wrecked the place. The promoters, Steve and Simon, managed to arrange the new sea front venue at short notice and hook up a mini-bus to bring people from one to the other. Despite all that, the show turned out to be great fun, with the new venue, The Mermaid, looking out over the gardens and cliffs to the sea beyond.

Buses were soon arriving, and the smaller venue was filled with people sitting inside and outside, as one of our talented German friends, Alex Erich, calling his own beautiful solo music Last Year's Diary (very much in the style of Kevin Devine or an early Dashboard Confessional) went on to warm things up and played a heartfelt set, singing, playing guitar and harmonica. Then Rydell turned things up another level and rocked out, blasting through a bunch of new songs we wanted to try out, that all seemed to go down pretty well. Finally, Arcaine played, showing how they were fast becoming one of the best new bands in the UK. They had a four-track demo called 'The Best Advice', and were handing out tapes as fast as they could duplicate them. It really was a superb night and an encouraging way to start the year.

Our next gigs would be a tour around the UK with Piebald. These guys were from Boston, Massachusetts and sounded a little like a rockier Weezer or Promise Ring. Up to that point I didn't really know of them, although they had two albums out, 'When life hands you lemons' on Hydra Head and 'If it weren't for venetian blinds, it'd be curtains for us all' on Big Wheel Recreation, as well as loads of EPs and singles. This tour was for their brilliant new album, 'We are the only friends we have', which soon became a favourite of mine. The tour posters had us advertised as playing all the dates; Newport, Manchester, Glasgow, Leeds and London, but we had already given our word to Arcaine and their promoters, Steve and Simon of Stay Press Records, that we would play the Leas Cliff Hall in Folkestone with them on the 16th, so we would be there instead. We didn't know what equipment Piebald were bringing with them so hired a van for this tour. It only cost us £45, but they wanted another £12 per day insurance too, obviously having experienced rock bands on tour before, and not relishing the thought of cleaning up afterwards. We were clean living kids, didn't they know? We filled it with all our gear and hit the road.

I still have flyers for most of those gigs, and remember a few ups and downs from them. The weather was terrible, almost constantly, and the audiences were not huge. I guess, like me, most people didn't really know about Piebald yet so didn't come out. I don't even remember the TJ's show, but The Retro Bar in Manchester was a cool little club, a small room with no stage, but we didn't mind that so much. Despite the promoter's best efforts, Jo and Lee of Quarantined zine, it was more or less empty. We played to maybe twenty people, even though Wakefield's wonderful Pylon were also on the bill. A band who just two years later, would headline the Out of Spite Festival in Leeds to absolute mania from the crowd; clearly their star was still on the ascent in 2002.

After the show, we stayed in a truly bizarre flat, somewhere in Moss Side, in Manchester's inner-city, where the kitchen was actually in the middle of the living room, as if someone had designed the flat, but forgotten that it needed a kitchen. So then just built a room with four walls and windows, right in the centre of the largest room. I'm not sure I can do the absolute peculiarity of this architecture justice. Suffice to say, it was odd. That night, while we tried to get some sleep, one of the kids who lived there regaled us with tales of how many times he had been stabbed and robbed in the neighbourhood.

For the next show, we drove up to Glasgow in Scotland where it never stops raining. Never. The 13th Note was a big venue with large hardened-glass windows facing onto Kings Street, under one of those huge red/brown stone buildings you see in the big Scottish cities, built solidly to keep the dreich out. We said hello to Paul and Richie, the promoters, and set up the gear ready to soundcheck, but one of the Piebald guys had a new keyboard that he wanted to fiddle around with, so just spent hours playing on that. After a while, we left them to it and went out for some food, twice having to dodge into the street to avoid zombie-esque drug casualties stumbling towards us along the pavement, like an angry mix of Rab C. Nesbitt and the junkie from 'Trainspotting'. We ended up in a curry house and proceeded to try to finish the hottest Madras I've ever had, whilst a punch-up kicked off right there in the restaurant over seemingly nothing. Glasgow could be a mad place.

Back at the venue, the Piebald guys had finally worked out the keyboard and had now finished sound-checking, so we could have a go. They were still a bit grumpy about the poor weather and even poorer turnouts at the gigs so far. They were clearly not enjoying their first trip to the UK. When we finally started to play, the sound was pretty good and the friendly p.a. guys there seemed to know exactly what they were doing. We banged through 'Nothing by morning', and it sounded great.

A few people actually turned up to this gig, possibly brought along by the local support band, The Day I Snapped, who rocked out in a very Get Up Kids sort of way that I appreciated. We were getting to know the Piebald songs now, even one that sounded like a Van Halen cover, and they ours, so were both now hanging around during each other's sets and starting to enjoy them more. There was a lot of sweating, screaming and cheering; it turned out to be a very worthwhile show. This cheered us all up no end. The 13th Note is another one of the few venues we visited that is still putting on gigs to this day.

Loading out the equipment in the wind and rain after the gig, the key for our hire-van decided to break in two, meaning that the electronic code in the handle of the key was separated from the regular metal piece. This meant that the only way to open and start the van now was by gripping both key parts together in a pair of pliers and turning them together, using the pliers, and twisting your arm around like something from 'The Exorcist'. This had all the makings of becoming a serious inconvenience. Partly because of this, Adam and I decided to stay in the van, possibly not a wise choice as it was freezing. Macca, Milo and Duncan headed off to stay with a guy called Alan in his flat. They came back in the morning after breakfast telling us how warm it was, the bastards. Adam and Milo then went off in search of a hardware store, to get some mole-grips that we could use to turn the broken shaft of the key in the van door and ignition properly. They eventually found a junk shop that sold used tools, so Adam forked out for a rusted old pair and we managed to get rolling on our way again.

The next show was in Leeds, at The Fenton, an old-fashioned pub and music venue, with beer and graffiti in equal measures, and a stage that had clearly seen a few heavy metal bands collapse on it in a pool of their own piss. I have to say though, that it still stands out to me as one of the most fun shows Rydell ever played in the UK, for the simple reason that there were a lot of like-minded hardcore kids there and they all seemed to be really into what we were doing. I wish all our shows were like that. There was another local support band on first, and they were good, but I just can't remember their name, sorry. Then Pylon, who were great, then Rydell and then Piebald, replete with keyboards, Van Halen covers and now, at last, broad smiles too. It had even

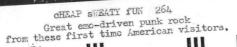

CHEAP SWEATY FUN 264
Great emo-driven punk rock
from these first time American visitors.

piebald

Hot U.K. punk.

RYDELL

FATHEAD

TUES. FEB 12th
Tickets : £5.00 (Rockaway)

● TJ'S NIGHTCLUB CLARENCE PLACE, NEWPORT SOUTH WALES, NP9 0AE TEL: 01633 216608	**TJ'S** www.tjs-newport.demon.co.uk	Tickets from: ROCKAWAY RECORDS PROVISIONS MARKET NEWPORT, NP9 1DD

Rydell

on
wednesday 13th
february

PIEBALD

fantastic emorock with catchy tunes and witty lyrics ... have toured
the US with everyone from new found glory to cave-in

PYLON
wakefield indie rock

RYDELL
southern emo types

LITTLE GIRL WITH CHERRIES
largely instrumental emorock with occaisional female vocals

8PM

@ the retro bar, sackville street, near UMIST.. email for directions
quarantinednine@hotmail.com ... blame_the_parents_collective@hotmail.com

£4

Piebald

stopped raining outside, and maybe that's why we had a decent crowd. Or maybe the cool AKA promoters had arranged that for us. If so, thanks guys.

We said goodbye to Piebald and drove home after the Leeds show, as the next day, instead of playing with Piebald at The Garage in London, quite probably to a bunch of too-cool-for-school seen-it-all-before scenesters (that honour fell to Sunfactor), we played to hundreds of amped up teenage skateboarders in Folkestone, along with our pals Arcaine.

And as for Piebald, for a bunch of dudes who had such wacky, Weezer-esque schtick on stage, they were the total opposite off-stage and barely said five words to any of us all week. That seemed a shame, but does happen sometimes. It's entirely possible this could have been down to 'European tour blues', which many American bands seem to suffer from. The weather was bad, the crowds weren't great, and if you're not used to it, everyone gets sick and tired after spending too much time together in the back of a van. I guess they could have just thought we were dicks. Who knows what their deal was? I hope The Garage gig was good for them and made it all worthwhile, but I kind of wish they'd come with us to the Leas Cliff Hall that Saturday instead, as they would definitely have enjoyed that.

I have never seen so many little punk, metal and indie kids at a show in Kent. The venue is a huge old theatre on the Leas promenade, right on the cliff edge. It's part of the Ambassador Theatre Group and had seen everyone from Thin Lizzy to Motorhead, Jimi Hendrix to the Rolling Stones play there. It easily holds 1500 people, and they'd sold hundreds of tickets, each at the princely sum of a fiver each. Everyone who had one seemed to rush to the front of the stage as soon as they came in, and it still didn't even look half full.

We'd booked Sam Washington, a film student who'd just started working for Sky TV, to come along and make a video for 'Nothing by morning' for us. This was one of the Rydell tracks on the new split CD with San Geronimo and ARSTY. He'd film it at the gig and then edit the image with our studio audio, so it could be shown on Kerrang, Rocksound, Scuzz, and all those other rock channels of the time. He was a good guy and ended up shooting a load of footage of us just hanging out backstage and looking over the cliffs, but he did get enough of the gig and that particular track, played somewhere in the middle of our set, to make a decent job of it, even though it seemed to take him months to come up with a final edit for us.

We went on between Jester, an old-style punk band who really did a good job of getting the kids going, and Arcaine, the popular local pop-punk kids. It was a huge stage, with plenty of space to really move around. You felt that you should be running up and down, playing guitar solos like you were in Iron Maiden or something. I managed to contain myself, but only just, as it seemed for a moment at least, a long way removed from the previous few nights. I guess it all amounts to the same when you finish your forty-five-minute set. At least it allowed us to get home to our own beds afterwards. We had a wholesome evening of alternative music mayhem and mini-bike riding. I particularly enjoying watching Macca ride his miniature bicycle, like a clown or trained chimp might have, all the way across the stage and back again in a figure of eight between the band. Christ alone knows why he'd brought it with him, but Macca successfully weaved this bike in-between the Arcaine guys during their set, making it right across to the other side of stage and back, before falling off the edge to much applause. Now I wish that had been in the video!

6/4/2002 Arcaine, Rydell, Crane and Seed at The Sound Club, London
27/4/2002 Always Outnumbered, Kids Near Water and Rydell at The Lanterns, Folkestone
15/5/2002 Rydell, The Beat Collective, Enola and Derek at The Railway Inn, Winchester
8/6/2002 Urotsukidoji, Winter in June, Jairus and Rydell at Jubilee Hall, Canterbury
28/6/2002 Rydell, The Splitters, The Idiots and The Flying Marrows at The Forum, Tunbridge Wells

A few weeks later, we were up in London playing with Arcaine again at some massively overpriced nightclub alongside two grungy indie bands. I don't remember much about it apart from going to Chinatown for some good food. Our next show was back in Folkestone, at The Lanterns Club, in the big function room above the snooker and pool hall where we'd played many times before. This time would be with Always Outnumbered and Kids Near Water, and it was a great show.

Always Outnumbered were a melodic hardcore band from Canada who had been signed by Two Friends Records in Germany. They had an album and two EPs out with the label, and Adam had their 'When potential outweighs ability' EP and was really into it. TFR had brought them over to tour in Europe, and Kids Near Water were supporting them on the UK dates.

Kids Near Water were a catchy as hell pop-punk four-piece from Exeter. They'd recorded their first demo, five tracks they called 'Extended Player One', with John Hannon of Understand at his Mushroom Studios in Essex, and it caused quite a stir in the UK HC scene. Chris from Travis Cut had set up a new label called Firefly and he released it on CD as the label's debut. This was closely followed by releases for Otherwise, Scuttle, and loads of great UKHC bands. The EP received great reviews, and there was talk of Kids Near Water signing to Drive Thru Records in the US, the big pop-punk label that put out New Found Glory, The Starting Line, Midtown, Finch, The Movielife, Dashboard Confessional and RxBandits, amongst others. They stayed with

Rydell at The Leas Cliff Hall, Folkestone

staypress records **PRESENTS**

JESTER ARCAINE RYDELL

JESTER ARCAINE RYDELL

EMO-PUNK

PLAYING LIVE @

LEAS SAT. 16TH FEB. 7.30-12.00
CLIFF HALL THE LEAS CLIFF HALL FOLKESTONE
TICKETS £5.00 IN ADVANCE. £6.00 ON DOOR
AVAILABLE FROM BOX OFFICE TEL 01303 253193
LIVE VIDEO SHOOT ON THE NIGHT

Excellent crowd for The Leas Cliff Hall show, Piebald would have loved it!

Firefly though for all five of their CD releases, but their first album, 'Hey Zeus!' was co-released with Abstract in the USA, and distributed over there by Lumberjack, a huge distro run by our old friend Dirk Hemsath (Majority Of One, Doghouse Records), making it pretty much omnipresent in the scene for a while.

I'd been hassling the Illuminanti and Just One Life promoters for more Rydell shows in Brighton around that time, and I asked them again when we met at the Jello Biafra spoken word show at the Hove Centre in Norton Road. Macca and I went, and it was just £8 a ticket, but there wasn't much else going on in Brighton at the time. We played a bunch of non-descript gigs that I don't really remember many details about then, but we did visit the Railway Inn in Winchester again, one of our favourite venues, to play at one of their big indie rock nights. These regular nights are still going strong at The Railway, and this one was with Enola, Derek and The Beat Collective, which was fun, but looking back now sounds like a bad evening at a swinger's club.

We were also booked to play at one of the new hardcore nights that were happening regularly in a scout hut / community centre building over in Canterbury. It would be absolutely packed with the local youth all sweating and screaming. Milo and Clare were helping to promote this one, so I know we wanted it to be good, but I remember a night of broken strings and very little finesse on our part unfortunately. The bands we played with there were all awesome though. Urotsukidoji and Winter in June, both of whom blasted out intense angry hardcore with underlying melody and message. You couldn't help but love them, and I had signed both for a split release on Ignition which turned out to be a roaring success. Winter In June were soon working with us again on a second split release with Steel Rules Die.

Also playing their first gig ever that night were Jairus, another brand-new Kentish band, whose sonic influences may well have come from HC acts such as Hopesfall, Poison The Well and At the Drive-In, but they added their own flavour to things and were soon being touted as one of the best new rock bands in the UK. They played for ages and, when Milo went over to tell them they could only do one more, everyone hissed and tutted at him. Their speedy rise in popularity was doubly impressive as they did most of their initial promotion and pr themselves, with self-released demos, before signing to Skipworth Records, a cool and hard-working indie label, who'd later release their debut album, 'The Need To Change The Mapmaker'. Jairus would play the Goodlife Summer Festival in Belgium, sharing the stage with bands like Shai Hulud and Naiad, and then release a record in Japan, a split with The Stiff on Alliance Traxx, before later signing with Kevin Douch's great Oxford-based indie label, Big Scary Monsters, for their next release, a self-titled four-track EP.

We rounded this run of shows off with a hometown special for me, another visit to The Forum in Tunbridge Wells where we'd be playing an evening of ska-punk alongside

The Splitters, The Idiots and The Flying Marrows. This sort of booking made we wonder if Jason and the Forum promoters were still holding a grudge, as Rydell with three ska bands wasn't really a good fit. But as much as it might not have seemed our normal style, it was a packed show, and we had the kids circle moshing and diving off the stage after the first song. It was like being back in the early Nineties, good fun and quick to get home.

All this time we'd been writing a whole new set of songs and getting ready to record a new album. I'd been chasing Eric Goodis at Cargo Headhunter about it again, trying to get commitment from him for the new recording, but he seemed to want to push 'Per Ardua Ad Astra' more and then see 'Always Remember Everything' come out too. Fair enough, I guess. It was great to have any support, and they were still keen on pushing us in the States and trying to get us out there again. So, at the same time as writing new tracks for a new album, we were working on getting the various releases we had in the pipeline actually out and available.

The three-way split CD with our friends San Geronimo and A Rocket Sent To You was out then on Ignition, with support from Cargo in the USA, who were distributing and promoting it over there. Scene Police had cooled on the idea when they heard Cargo were involved, something to do with different distributors in Germany. We just wanted the record to come out now. We'd needed a new band photo for that, so all five of us had crammed into a tiny photo booth and I sent that over to Gubby at Headhunter, along with a couple of pieces of art I thought would be suitable. He spent ages dithering on it though, saying he was busy on other jobs, so instead we roped in Richard Shiner again to sort the layout. We had a violin and cogs for the inside page, and the big old curvy Cadillac, with all the chrome, for the front. Each band had provided their own art, alongside their own tracks. The outcome was a well-packaged ten-track CD that I know all three bands were very pleased with. We sold loads of them through Ignition.

There was also the sixth and final pressing of the Hot Water Music / Rydell 7", this time on clear vinyl. This single was always popular, thanks to HWM's continuing greatness and constant touring, but we had better new tracks that we wanted to concentrate on now.

One of these was 'Nothing By Morning', and the video for it featured an edited three minute ten second version of the song, cut down from the full four minute fifty eight second epic. We'd used footage filmed at the Leas Cliff Hall gig in Folkestone by Sam Washington, and it would be out any day now. This video would later appear on Engineer Record's first DVD compilation too, 'Building on sight and sound', alongside Chamberlain, We're All Broken, Kover, The Fire Still Burns, Elemae, AndTheWinnerIs, Nine Days To No One, Son Of The Mourning, Cornflames, Red Car Burns, Catalyst, Sometimes Why, Cashless, Six Second Hero, Worlds Between Us, Cohesion, The No One,

Nathaniel Sutton and Losing Six Seconds. This DVD would be available on both sides of the pond in VHS PAL and NTSC formats, still required in the early days of DVDs.

Rydell's second full length CD, 'Always Remember Everything', a collection of fourteen unreleased, older and compilation tracks from many of our pre-'Per Ardua Ad Astra' recordings, would be out very soon too. We'd sent over the masters to Headhunter / Cargo and they'd more or less decided the tracklist. We'd also sent along the artwork, put together by Richard Shiner (now in xCanaanx), with new imagery based on the concepts and photos I'd taken in Georgia and Tennessee for the 'Home' EP. The CD came out quickly and we were sent a load of them. It looked great, with the packaging and layout heavily influenced in style by The Promise Ring's 'Nothing Feels Good' album.

We were still waiting for the Mag Wheel split CD with Elemae, and had sent off tracks for that a while ago. We were told it'd be out after their current release, for The Fearless Freep, a band named after the Bugs Bunny character. Unfortunately, the label had a few issues, and that release never saw the light of day. I loved Elemae's 'A Life to be Defined' CD and was very keen for this release, having just signed the New Jersey rockers for their great 'Sleeping with adrenaline' 7" on Ignition. Instead though, we went on to release their 'Popular Misconceptions of Happiness' CD, and many more over the following years.

Rydell did however have a track on the upcoming Shudder To Think tribute on Ignition. Shudder To Think were such a great and influential band, on Dischord in the nineties, so we knew that would do well and find us new fans. The album featured great bands such as Casket Lottery, Joshua, Tomorrow, Speedwell and the Firebird Band. Rydell's track was called 'Heaven Ditty', as it had the lyrics to 'Heaven Here' sung over a re-worked version of the 'Day Ditty' music. We were so arty - two tracks in one!

We were well pleased with the track and this release, so sent a few out for review. One of the editors of Fracture, the biggest UK punk fanzine of the time, agreed to write about the compilation. Dave Stuart started the review by saying what a huge fan of Shudder To Think he was and how happy he was to be reviewing the CD, but then passed right by our track in his write-up, simply saying he was not familiar with it. Surely a 'huge fan' could spot that the music at least was 'Day Ditty' with some different lyrics? Milo never liked the lyrics to that one, but bizarrely found that the words to 'Heaven Here' fitted very well, so thought it would make for a more interesting version. The comp didn't seem to get mentioned in Dischord circles very much either so was overlooked by most Shudder To Think fans. However, Adam Wade, the original drummer with Jawbox, who joined Shudder when they signed to Epic records, did contact Ignition to ask for a copy, which Milo happily sent him. It's a superb record though, and I may now, twenty years later, have to re-release it and try again to introduce new people to this great band.

Rydell's 'Heaven Here / Day Ditty' track also made it onto another compilation CD, 'A tribute to Dischord Records', put out by Millipede Records in Germany. That one seemed to fare a bit better throughout the scene. It featured twenty-two covers of Dischord band classics, including The Robocop Kraus ('Filler', Minor Threat), Amen 81 ('I Can't Forgive', Embrace), The Nationale Blue ('Double Edged Knife', Slant 6), The European Translation Of ('Blueprint', Fugazi), Sky Promises Rain ('The Godfather', Dag Nasty), Squarewell ('Promises', Fugazi) and Phonetics ('Little Sparkee', Q And Not U).

We also had the track 'Margin Forever' on the new Starecase Records compilation CD, called 'This way to rocket city'. Starecase was a new label out of Kentucky, USA, who'd put together a great tracklist for the release, including Kissing Chaos (ex-Pop Unknown), Someday I, Retisonic (ex-Swiz / Bluetip / Garden Variety), Elevator Division, The Casket Lottery, Pilot to Gunner, Mock Orange, The Honor System, Fireside (Sweden), Colt (Germany), Irwin, Time Spent Driving, Heros Severum (a new band produced by J Robbins), Cadillac Blindside, Attention (ex-The Stereo), Jack Potential (ex-Burning Airlines) and San Geronimo (ex-Lifetime / Jets to Brazil).

Rydell had a lot going on again, and plenty of releases to send out to fanzines, magazines and websites for reviews. So that's exactly what we did.

Rydell / San Geronimo / A Rocket Sent To You - split CD Reviews

PunkNews.Org - Three emo bands on one cd, and you can't argue with that. UK hopefuls Rydell mixing it with two Yank bands and coming out of it smelling of roses is another reason to be chauvinistic (okay, maybe not.). And while it probably seems like I'm being as one-eyed as Gerard Houllier, after a blatant penalty isn't given in front of the Kop, Rydell give a really good account of themselves. Not a bit as sickly-sweet-like-too-many-Chupa-Chubs, like so many emo bands in it for the cool, Rydell are unscrubbed enough to sound honest with a great sense of melody. 'Nothing by morning' and 'Margin Forever' are the two better tracks of their three, with the final one, the re-worked 'The Plot is Lost', giving you the uncomfortable feeling that you've heard it done before, but you can't remember who did it. Rydell are not a million miles from Jawbreaker circa '24 hour...', and elicit the same feelings of intimacy and fondness I get when I listen to that album. There is also a detectable Britishness to their music, which always gets brownie points from me. On to the other two American bands, who I feel deserve a mention as well. ARSTY are slightly more impressive than SG, showing more of a Dischord influence. And while SG tend to draw things out a little more than necessary after the promise of 'Better if you didn't', ARSTY mix riffage and delicacy as well as Jamie Oliver whips up a korma... Larrrrvelleeyyy. So, if you fall out with your missus you can always fall in love with these bands.

Unfit for consumption #6 - Three-way emo rock split spanning from the UK across the Atlantic to the US. The UK's Rydell (three tracks) kick things off, and it comes as no surprise that they have had a split release with Hot Water Music, such is their quality. It is emocore, but in the honest emo sense as opposed to the 'crying into their soup'-type stuff. They sound quite like HWM in fact, but the vocals are a lot smoother. I found myself singing the chorus to 'Nothing By Morning' constantly. Easily one of the more accomplished bands I've heard from the UK. I'm off to track down more by this band.

San Geronimo (three tracks) are the first of the two US bands to step to the plate. Featuring ex-members of Lifetime, Drowningman and Jets to Brazil (wow!), they manage not to sound like any of those bands while still delivering powerful emo-core. Their songwriting is solid, and their experiences in the aforementioned bands shine through on their sparkling offering. A Rocket Sent To You (four tracks) finish things off rather magnificently with a sound steeped in the Deep Elm crew, Garrison and Jawbox. They're emotional and melodic, but with plenty of bite and crunch; the guitar work and riffs are interesting stuff, and their four-song contribution is really strong. Three bands and ten songs equals one fantastic split!

Inside knowledge #5 - This three-way split perfectly summarises the talent Ignition has in stock. Three marvellous bands on one CD. Rydell has the honour to open with rocking emo. I was very excited about San Geronimo, when I read it features ex-members of Lifetime, Drowningman and Jets To Brazil. You clearly hear the influences of those bands. San Geronimo is definitely the top of this split album. The closing credits go to A Rocket Sent To You, who perfectly take this album to an end. A must-have for fans of Texas is the Reason, Jimmy Eat World, the Get Up Kids and Saves the Day.

Scanner #12 - Highly enjoyable three-way split here, featuring the bands in the title and totalling 10 tracks. The UK's own RYDELL kick things off. All three of their tracks were on the recent 'Memo demo' release, including what would be their best track yet 'Nothing By Morning'. Great impassioned vocals as ever, backed by those expertly executed guitars. As usual, good stuff. SAN GERONIMO feature ex-LIFETIME members and as you may expect, they are the heaviest band on here. Their three tracks of tumultuous post-HC include 'Rolling Blackouts' which is catchy while retaining a HC edge. Finally, A ROCKET SENT TO YOU finish things off. They're from Maryland and do, musically at least, a very TEXAS IS THE REASON kinda deal. They do it well ('The Law of Entropy' in particular) but lack that amazing 'X' factor that TEXAS... had in bucket loads. They're very able and can create large, post-HC, sweeping soundscapes mixed with subtle melodies. Three bands who really complement each other making a most welcome release.

Suburban Voice - Okay, so split CDs are a pain, that's a given. Usually at least one of the bands reeks, leaving the better bands in a weird state of release limbo. Not only do the three bands on this split all sound good, but they are also almost equally enjoyable, which means none of them are punished by trigger-happy CD listeners. Rydell have improved by leaps and bounds since their Headhunter full-length, adding maturity and elegance to their Samiam-sounding emo rock. San Geronimo (ex-members of Lifetime/Jets to Brazil/Drowningman) aren't up to the level of their previous bands, but do manage to put an interesting spin on the basic emo formula. At best this is a more energetic Mineral. A Rocket Sent to You round things up with competent, driving emo in the vein of Garrison or Burning Airlines. Ignition definitely have their shit together to get three bands this good on one CD. Emo rock fans should put some lenses in those goofy horn-rimmed glasses and write down this address...

UK Base - This offering has been a long time in the making considering that Ignition are now on their 21st release and this is catalogued as number five, but for the Hot Water Music, Small Brown Bike to Joshua fans out there, this is worth the wait and has probably been on your want list for quite a while. Rydell kick things of with three tracks that show that these guys are developing their own sound a little more than their last CD. The first track 'Nothing By Morning' is a great fusion of Hot Water Music (especially as the vocals sound similar), mid-season Fugazi and later Grade, as there is a slight metallic edge to parts of this song, and to Rydell's credit I think this is the best track on here. The next track by them isn't so uplifting, and plods on in an indie rock meets emo way in comparison to the first track. Their third offering 'The Plot Is Lost' is very novel as it has female backing vocals and the gruff vocals of the lead singer and the sweet melodies of the backing vocals really work together, though this song is slightly tainted when she sings on her own as she can't carry it off. This track is a slow track but has a pissed-off feel to it, and I think we'll see a lot more people following the female backing vocals route.

Now to San Geronimo offering. I've got their first release which sounds great, well it would - members of this band used to be in the mighty Lifetime, and their 'Hello Bastards' CD is one of my favourite releases. Their first song 'Better if you didn't' gives this release an injection of pace and this song has a feel of Lifetime about it though more on the emo side of things, with lighter, thoughtful breaks. 'Rolling blackouts' has a wonderfully catchy chorus that just makes you rock, whilst 'Stars and anchors' is an emo rock track but with the bass player calling the shots, and the whole song is based around the bass riffs supplied, which really works well; I've never heard anybody else do this before but I'm sure I will in the future. Three great tracks but only what you come to expect.

I've never heard of A Rocket Sent To You, but from the name you know their emo/indie rock title, the four tracks supplied by this band are cool but it's not anything you haven't heard before, but credit where credit's due, they write good songs and that's all that counts. Oh yeah, they play them well, though I did find myself wanting to put the CD back to the more passionate San Geronimo or Rydell, and that's the only criticism I would give this band; the singer either doesn't sound like he means what he's singing, or he just doesn't have a wide vocal range. 'The law of entropy' is probably their best song on here as it has a varied feel to it, heavier and light moments. These are good songs and worth checking out.

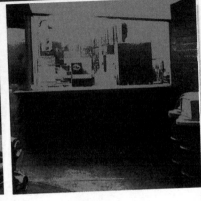

rydell

always remember everything

a collection

TRY 17 TIME OF OUR TIME AN EVENT HEY NEVE CAMPBELL HOME
YOU TAKE FOREVER ACROSS THREE PARKS DON'T MEAN A THING
HOME (ACOUSTIC) RED LIGHT RUNNER STARS BREAK FREE
INSTRO POST COLLEGE ROCK GILSENAN

'Always Remember
Everything' CD
artwork

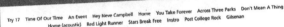

Try 17   Time Of Our Time   An Event   Hey Neve Campbell   Home   You Take Forever   Across Three Parks   Don't Mean A Thing
Home (acoustic)   Red Light Runner   Stars Break Free   Instro   Post College Rock   Gilsenan

®& © 2002 Cargo Music, 4901-906 Morena Blvd, San Diego, CA 92117-3432 www.cargomusic.com
IGNITION   IGN029 - 1 Chandos Road - Tunbridge Wells - Kent - TN1 2NY - England - www.ignitiononline.co.uk

RYDELL   ALWAYS REMEMBER EVERYTHING

HED-105

The 13th Note, Glasgow

The Fenton, Leeds

The Retro Bar, Manchester

The Lanterns, Folkestone

The Leas Cliff Hall, Folkestone

Very - A three way split between three melodic emo / indie bands. You may remember Rydell (three songs) from their split with Hot Water Music or their recent full-length on Cargo. San Geronimo (three songs) feature ex-Lifetime and Drowningman members and have released two other EPs. Newcomers A.R.S.T.Y. play four songs of pleasant, upbeat, mid-paced emo / indie rock with nice vocal harmonies.

Suspect Device – I like the idea behind this, it's like your normal two band split, but one better, freaking genius! All three bands tread a similar path, the post hardcore / indie rock / emo one, a well-trodden path I know, but a good path. First up are those fine English chaps Rydell with three tracks, who are sounding better than ever, I reckon. Two new tracks off the 'Memo: demo' CDEP, and a re-recorded version of 'The plot is lost' off the album, with cool female vocals added to great effect. All three tracks are really strong. Next up is San Geronimo, a band who were good but never quite fulfilled their potential and who have now split up. I think maybe having Pete (ex-Lifetime) Martin on guitar built my hopes up a bit too high. Three good songs though, but they could've been great. Last up is A Rocket Sent To You; never heard of these chaps before but, daft name aside, they are good, and they also get an extra track, they do four. Like I said though, all three bands sound quite similar and though they're good, it all seems to blend together a bit much, and maybe having a bit of variation in the sound would have made this CD a blooming stormer.

Drowned in Sound - A three-way split CD, this disc showcases three of post-hardcore-emo's top of the class hopefuls. Opening up the proceedings are the UK's very own rough-hewn Rydell. It's taken me a while to adapt to their brand of emo-rock, but maybe that's just their vocalist's tendencies to verge on the out-of-tune on occasions. Well, whatever. No-one can deny that the three tracks offered here show a healthy proficiency for emo noodling, one of which is a re-working of 'The Plot is Lost', the addition of echoing female vocals working really well.

Although San Geronimo contain an old member of Drowningman, don't for a minute think that he's brought one ounce of their crazed ferocity, or indeed that this is a band that's arisen from their untimely demise (caused by vocalist Simon Brody's escalating drug problems). Instead, San Geronimo (also containing ex-members of Lifetime and Jets To Brazil) follow on nicely from Rydell, with an emo mesh that hooks nicely onto early Jimmy Eat World in parts of their fuzzed-up song structures. Nice.

Finishing off this release are A Rocket Sent to You who continue the emo thread with cleverly syncopated rhythms and catchy vocal lines (although nervously delivered), with 'Silencer' being one of the stand-out tracks on here.

This is a good split, compiling material from three of the scene's more talented acts. But with not much to separate their sounds from each other, their impact is sadly reduced somewhat. Utterly recommended, nonetheless.

Rydell `Always Remember Everything` CD Reviews

ENZK - This is a collection of songs from Rydell's past releases, a summary, the story so far, pulling together stuff from various 7"s, splits, demos and compilations into one handy CD. This has some of my favourite Rydell stuff on it, 'Try 17', 'Home' plus the acoustic version, which I like even better, 'Post College Rock', 'Gilsenan'... it's all great. They have quite an open and sparse sound and with mostly clean guitars and Miles' raspy vocals, it's laid back yet still intense, lovelorn and hopeful' and as I keep saying about this band, they pull off the whole uplifting melancholy thing brilliantly.

Alt UK - This is a collection of earlier Rydell stuff and you can hear the band as they were before the release of the album. There are 14 tracks here of emotional Punk Rock. The band still sound very Hot Water Music but on this CD they sound much more emotional, and there are no more aggressive hardcore tracks like on the album. This is a good CD to chill out to, as it is extremely mellow and so emotional that at times you want to cry, but you just can't because at the same time it is so strong that it is unbelievable. You hear the band as they progress through and become better musicians, and then you see how they arrived at the sort of style that they have now. It is quite amazing to see how much they have improved since they started out, and a band that started off great have become legendary!

If you look at the discography for this band then you can see that it is extremely impressive, so this is not just a change that has happened over night; the sound of the band has been refined over a series of years and CDs. All of these songs are awesome in their own right, and I feel that they have really managed to create their own unique style in the time that they have been around. Yes, it may draw many different influences but in taking these influences they have put them all together and added their own secret ingredient to spice it up a bit, and they have emerged far greater for it and have the most original and unique take on emo that I have ever heard in my life. I think that they are definitely the best in the UK at what they do, and they deserve to be a famous band as by the number of CDs and shows that they have done you can tell that they are not a lazy band, and what they have achieved so far has been through sheer determination and hard work.

Look out for this band in the future, and look out for their next album as I am sure that it will be a cracker, with many nice little twists to take you by surprise!

Check out their site at Rydell.co.uk

UK Base - This is a collection of tracks from 7"s (including their split with Hot Water Music), unreleased and acoustic numbers. Fourteen in all, the lot of them good tracks. Rydell are similar to early Hot Water Music, but not as aggressive and with a lighter kind of folky edge to their music, or kind of a softer version of HMW's side project

Unitas. The vocals are nice and gravelly, and the songs are well structured and recorded. I would have liked to see on the inlay a description of where each of the tracks came from and when they were recorded, so you can judge the growth in the band over the years before their full-length came out, but the inlay is pretty substantial with lyrics and a discography with cover images. If you're a fan of this style of mid-paced punk with a emo rock edge and a folk influence then check this out, it's calming but full of strength. Look out for their full-length of new material later in the year.

Collective Zine - I got this through for review just the week after I picked up Rydell's debut 'Per Ardua Ad Astra', so I was feeling pretty won over by this band already by the time I gave this a spin. And fortunately, this is more of the same feel-good, vocally-gruff indie-rock, collecting together tracks from all the band's pre-'Ad Astra' releases. I love this band, and whilst it may sound very simple, I find myself wanting to listen to their music all the time and as a result, the new CD hasn't been far from the nearest pile for the last couple of weeks. Maybe it's the fact this is so accessible, yet not in a trite and banal way; sometimes the guitars give me fleeting reminders of the poppier moments of the Get Up Kids, the Promise Ring and Chamberlain, whilst somehow remaining fresh-sounding and original. The conclusion I've come to, is that Rydell, for all their '90s indie-rock/pop sensibilities, just sound inescapably English in their songs: there's something about the lyrics, the non-American accents, and just the sound of the songs that ultimately endears enormously to them.

This CD is worthwhile if you enjoyed 'Ad Astra' and don't have any of the other tracks on other releases. Opener 'Try 17' is catchy as anything, with a type of rhetorical style to the lyrics, the kind of which I can't help but smile when hearing. The next few tracks are equally as fun and infectious, with those familiar vocals and super-melodic guitar lines. 'Home' then appears twice on the record, meaning I now own three versions of it. Not that I mind all that much, the first version on here is by far my favourite, with a quieter, twinkly-er verse, still with that big chorus but slightly more restrained this time.

'Across three parks' has to be up there as one of Rydell's best songs. The guitar line is a great hook, the vocals come in, then the band crashes in and it hits the 'feel good' level instantly. Fun. Some tracks on here don't quite match those on the album proper, the two unreleased songs only hinting at Rydell's best songwriting, but 'Always remember everything' is a quality package all the same. The entire acoustic 7" is included, and just reiterates the talent on show really. I'm quite amazed that 'Home' and 'Post College Rock' work so well. I'd love to hear more of that acoustic guitar in their songs in the future because it really does sound quite unique with the raw-sounding vocals.

So, to summarise, a CD that works perfectly in that it's more Rydell and saves tracking down various old vinyl and comps.

I realised the other day that I've been buying much of my indie rock over the last two years from these guy's distro, and for what it's worth, they seem like really great and friendly guys as well. Looking forward to the new album.

David

Milo

Macca

Messing about in band practise at Dudley's farm

37, Hard on the trail

I'd been speaking with my old friend John Hannon, the ex-guitarist of Understand, who was now playing in a band called Woe and running his own recording studio over in Rayleigh, near Southend in Essex. I wanted Rydell to go over and record with him, but he was already getting very busy, having recently recorded Hundred Reasons, Hell Is For Heroes, Capdown and Kids Near Water, to name just a few. He was keen to record us, and we originally booked in a session in July, six days from 19th to 24th, to get some new tracks down. We agreed that if we needed more time, we'd book in again later when he had another gap in his diary.

It was a swelteringly hot summer and the drives over to studio with all our gear were just sweat fests. We had a lot of fun when we were there though, jamming through the new tracks and trying out a few new ideas. Mushroom studios weren't large, but John had it all set up comfortably and we could sit outside with a drink if it got too hot or we needed inspiration. The studio was situated out of town, on the edge of fields and a farmyard, and I remember one day a goat wandered into the lounge area, stood on the sofa and just had a piss. John immediately shooed it away and threw the whole couch out!

Over the course of that hot sweaty week, Macca, Adam, Dunc and I recorded pretty much all of the music for the ten new original tracks, and one sped-up cover version, that would become Rydell's third album, entitled 'Hard on the trail'. We'd have to come back, from 28/10 to 1/11, for the next session he had available, where Milo would record his vocals and add a few subtle overdubs. John played his trumpet for us on the opening track, 'Know now', and Milo added some subtle keys, samples and guitar feedback too. We were getting close to it now, but the record still needed to be mixed.

In the meantime, I'd been speaking with Eric Goodis at Headhunter Records in San Diego again, about what to do with this release, if they could set up a new tour for us, ideally in the US for longer and maybe in Japan too, through their partners. I also asked about an advance payment to cover the recording costs of the album and how we would promote it. I was in contact with Gubby much less frequently now, and it seemed to me that Eric was starting to dodge my questions too. I thought maybe they were still pissed at us about the tour we couldn't make, or maybe not happy with record sales, but it seemed they had bigger problems and just didn't want to say. Something was definitely up. Sure enough, over the next weeks, we found out that Headhunter had run into some serious financial issues and the record label in San Diego would be closing, although Cargo would continue as a distributor.

I tried to get hold of Gubby, Eric and all the guys again, I wanted to thank them for what they had done for us, or tried to, at least. But unfortunately, I didn't hear from them again. The label had been getting into psychobilly and surf rock towards the end and, as far as I know, their last release was HED108 for San Diego locals Deadbolt. (Rydell's 'Per Ardua Ad Astra' was HED089 and 'Always Remember Everything' was HED105).

For many reasons, this was not good news. The main ones being that we'd never seen a dime for the first two albums, and even more importantly hadn't got around to re-booking a US tour. Now the record label we'd signed to was closing. More bad luck for Rydell. We never did get to see any of the Rydell t-shirts or play in the US. But we couldn't complain really; we'd had the recording advance for the first album and some copies of both albums for the band to sell, so I guess good support there and we counted our blessings and moved on.

John Hannon was only charging us £120 per day for the new recording, so I wrote him out a cheque and we got on with it. Actually, I made the cheque out to his sister, as she had loaned him some of the money to start up the studio, and he was still in the process of paying her back. We'd need to come back again to finish the mix of the album, but that would have to be in the New Year now. It ended up taking ages to finish the album, with us finally mixing and mastering 'Hard on the Trail' with John quite a while later, from 28th June to 1st July 2003. He was just so busy. It took nearly a year to record the final Rydell album, on and off in those three sessions, with him. By which time we'd lost a lot of the heart for it.

'Hard on the trail' eventually came out on our own Engineer Records as a CD, catalogue number IGN035, late in 2003. It would have beautiful cover photography and layout by our friend Verity Keniger, who used photos taken out of the aeroplane window from one of her holidays, plus great live photos from our gigs along the South Coast, taken by Joe Watson, in the artwork. By this time, we'd improved our logo, adding in a curve of stars, and we really liked the packaging design, with the mainly red text over blue-grey images on a white background. The record would feature ten new up-tempo rockers of our own, with the second half of the album, after 'Shifter (girls with skulls)', getting slightly slower and mellower, and then finishing with an absolute blast through Don Henley's 'Boys of Summer' just for the hell of it.

The tracklist was on the back cover with band photos, a thanks list and credits inside on the fold-out lyrics sheet. The initial pressing of 1000 CDs sold out fast so we went straight to a second pressing, but they hung around a while longer as Rydell had massively slowed down on gigs by then.

Rydell - Hard on the trail CD track-listing:
Know now
Darkness before home
Born witness
Awkward times
Cut to end
Shifter (Girls with skulls)
Analysis of the evidence
Fire at the end of the street
Ground never held me
Team building exercise
Boys of summer* (Don Henley *cover)

Rydell would like to thank everyone who has supported and helped us, particularly our families and friends, Louise, Liz, Mel, Martina and Kim. All the great bands we have played and toured with, all the promoters that put us on, all the radios that play our tracks and all the zines that write about us. Thanks to Jon at Mushroom Studios for the recording, mixing and trumpet playing. Thanks to Joe and Tom for the photos and special artistic thanks to Verity for the cover design. Thanks most of all to our fans. Hard on the trail. Always stay true.

Rydell is: Miles Booker – vocals, Adam French – bass, David Gamage -guitar, Duncan Morris – drums and Mark Wilkinson – guitar.
Cover design and photography by Verity Keniger
Live photography by Joe Watson
An engineer release IGN035.

15/11/2002 Rydell, Final Thought and Placid Storm at The Richard Aldworth School, Basingstoke
19/12/2002 One Time Champion, Rydell and The Photobook Stories at The Lanterns, Folkestone
20/12/2002 One Time Champion, Rydell, The Guillaume Seam and Dead Memento at The King Alfred, Southampton

Although our main focus in the second half of 2002 was recording the 'Hard on the trail' album, we did still play quite a few more gigs too. I don't remember them all, but the last three that year were all good and worth mentioning. Starting with a show at a big grammar school in Basingstoke where the kids had decided to put some noisy rock bands on and, amazingly, the teachers had agreed to it. Winter in June were meant to be playing but pulled out for some reason, so Rydell stepped in and headlined with two local bands in support. Final Thought were a '77 style punk band with a lot of anti-war songs and energy, and Placid Storm were a chuggy skatecore band who appeared on several south coast hardcore compilations, including one called 'Southern Comfort' that also featured 'Know now' by Rydell, as well as new tracks by Chillerton, Pilger, Jets vs Sharks and others. It turned out to be a great party with the school kids going nuts in a well-behaved sort of way. It was often the shows you thought might not be good that turned out to be the best ones.

The next two gigs were with our mates Arcaine, who by now had changed their name to One Time Champion and recruited a new singer in Chris Pritchard, who brought with him even more pop sensibilities. Chris had worked in both Richard's Records and Sound's Records in Canterbury, and obviously listened to a lot of pop-punk. He'd been in a band called Dead Life Portrait too, and we knew him from quite a few gigs. He's been in the scene for a while and is now one of the guys putting on bands and helping to run The Forum in Tunbridge Wells. One Time Champion had so many catchy sing-along songs, and were such a polished unit live, that it was always a pleasure to play gigs with them. They had a great new demo called 'Five weeks gone' and you can still find it on Bandcamp, alongside their later 'We love audio' EP too.

The first show was at The Lanterns in Folkestone, an old haunt of ours, but with a brand new band, called The Photobook Stories. These guys were emo in the same beautiful, delicate way as Cross My Heart, Mineral, Penfold or Pop Unknown were, and although live they seemed to take it easy and be the masters of understated minimalism (honestly, I've seen Hootie rock harder!), they soon started producing these beautiful demo CDs with hand-made covers and gorgeous tracks that everyone got into. The Photobook's mellowness was even more unexpected when we realised they featured Ross from Urotsukidoji, the crushingly brutal hardcore band who'd been on Ignition, and who'd later briefly be in The Luzhin Defence too.

The second date of our mini-tour with the One Time Champion guys had a smaller turnout but was still a cool show. It was in a pub in Southampton that seemed to be the local sports bar for all the Saints fans, as well as a music venue and heavy drinking establishment. It's long closed now, of course, but it was a great place to play. Dead Memento went on first and ripped through some very Planes Mistaken For Stars inspired hardcore, then The Guillaume Seam went on and immediately went absolutely mental, jumping around, shouting, playing just four very loud songs and then leaving the stage and splitting up! Rydell gave it a moment and then had to follow that, so banged through most of 'Hard on the trail' and finished with a 'Boys of summer' sing-along in the cold depths of winter. One Time Champion rounded things off and rocked as ever, and that was a good way to prepare for a Christmas break.

The New Year started with a few more foreign trips for me, one to Germany to pick up more stock for the distro, another to Canada for a much-needed holiday and a third to Spain, supposedly for work, but it soon turned into a tapas eating expedition. Because of this there weren't many early gigs, but in the middle of February our local paper, the

rydell

HARD ON THE TRAIL

an engineer release
IGN_035

rydell ★

HARD ON THE TRAIL

KNOW NOW 02.00 DARKNESS BEFORE HOME 03.14
BORN WITNESS 04.03 AWKWARD TIMES 03.17 CUT TO END 02.42
SHIFTER (GIRLS WITH SKULLS) 03.30 ANALYSIS OF THE EVIDENCE 04.38
FIRE AT THE END OF THE STREET 04.35 GROUND NEVER HELD ME 03.28
TEAM BUILDING EXERCISE 04.32 BOYS OF SUMMER' 03.35

rydell

HARD ON THE TRAIL

Rydell at The Horseshoe, Portsmouth
photos by Joe Watson

Kent and Sussex Courier, came around to Chandos Towers, the Ignition HQ, to interview me and Milo. Their piece appeared in the next week's paper, under the heading 'Ignition takes off at home', with a dodgy photo of me in my favourite quicksand t-shirt, standing in front of shelves and shelves of CDs and records, but blocking most of them out, above a caption that read; "Passionate – David Gamage who set up his record label Ignition from his storeroom at home". The article continued in that slightly inaccurate way local paper pieces always seem to, but here it is, for your interest and humour...

"Tunbridge Well's rock credentials are somewhat less fine than its reputation as the home of disgusted, but it has a secret. Major rock bands such as Coldplay, Oasis and Muse, who could now sell-out stadiums, have all played gigs in the town in their infancy. In light of this hidden history, there should be no surprise that a punk rock record label has been set up in a quiet suburban road.

"Sitting in their home from which they run the label, David Gamage and Miles Booker, who form half of the team, are surrounded by framed artwork, collected from years of devotion to the hardcore punk sound. The house encompasses a bizarrely synergetic mix of domesticity and rock 'n' roll. A ginger cat called Tom leaves its sleeping place, next to a large pile of 12-inch records, before resentfully meowing for attention. And on the dining table a bunch of plastic daffodils lies; 'Someone is going to a fancy-dress party as Morrissey', David hurriedly explains.

"Formed by a group of friends, Ignition was born out of the punk D.I.Y. attitude. 'D.I.Y. is about believing that if something is not getting done and you want it done, then don't complain about it, get up and do something,' David said.

"The group wanted to give people the opportunity to hear the kind of music and bands that they loved, so they set up Ignition, originally as a distribution label, and sold records made by their friends mainly to other friends.

"The first release was Hunter Gatherer, 'Low standards for high fives', a split release with German label Scene Police. From there, D.I.Y. became more than just doing it yourself.

Their first signed act was San Geronimo from San Francisco. They usually only sign a band for one release at a time, but have a release list as long as the hair of some of their bands. Ignition has really, well... ignited.

"As well as a regular newsletter they now have a website at ignitiononline.co.uk which has generated a lot of interest from music fans all over the world, to their obvious delight.

"Some people come to the house from nearby, Maidstone, Tonbridge and local towns, others email us from all over the world," Milo enthused.

"David explained why this makes them so pleased, 'This is why we set this up. People come from all over because you cannot really get this music in record shops. Also, unless you're willing to order it in dollars and wait weeks for it to arrive from America, it's tricky to order'. We can get them at better prices too. In most shops you'd have to pay about £15 for a CD, whereas we sell them for between a fiver up to about £8. We want to tell people about the music. Share it. It's great that a lot of hardcore bands have got to become bigger now, but there's thousands of really cool bands out there that are just as good, but no-one has ever heard of'

"And as if just to prove a point, one of Ignition's bands, Eden Maine, has been picking up growing acclaim from the music press. But the band's growing popularity means that the label could be faced with criticism from the underground scene, which often views success as selling out. The two of them are phlegmatic. Milo says, 'A lot of people talk about having to maintain credibility, but we don't have to answer to anyone. It's most important that this is on our terms. While we may not be seen as keeping it underground, we are certainly keeping it D.I.Y.'

"David added, 'We don't want to limit our bands. We want to give them the best coverage possible. Sometimes punk politics get in the way. There's nothing wrong with wanting to say to your mates, 'check this out'. What would you rather see in the charts, Britney Spears or bands like NOFX? At least hardcore bands have something to say. Parents should be happy that their kids are listening to punk.'

"David has to get back to his day job in publishing now, having run over his lunch hour quite considerably. It's a fitting symbol of the town's well discoloured rock underground. On the surface mild-mannered, be-suited and respectable, but underneath the future sound of rock music is alive and kicking."

28/2/2003 Rydell, Chillerton, 107 Debutantes and Awkward Silence at The Horseshoe, Portsmouth
27/5/2003 Rydell, Jets Vs Sharks, Placid Storm and Mullet at The Railway Inn, Winchester
4/6/2003 The Killerest Expression, Hitechjet, Rydell, Otherwise and Kids Near Water at The Verge, Kentish Town, London
8/6/2003 Day Of The Fight, Jets Vs Sharks, Rydell, Chillerton and Odd-Man-Out at The Wedgewood Rooms, Portsmouth

The South Coast hardcore scene seemed to be picking up again with some great new bands, and we wanted to get back out there gigging. Our next show was one of the best I can remember from that later period, absolutely packed with friendly people, making us feel very welcome and singing along to the songs they knew. I can only put this down to the fact that this gig was Joe, the promoter's birthday party and he was a big Rydell fan. This was the gig from which the live photos for the 'Hard on the trail' CD artwork came. All three support bands were good, but Chillerton were great. They had that gruff vocal over Samiam-esque guitar sound we all loved, but the male screaming was tempered by a female vocal too, and some slower parts that made it sound like Leatherface on speed, or a tightly wound-up version of our own 'Plot is lost' track being played by a bunch of angry kids. We loved it, and good support bands always encourage you to raise your game.

At that point, Chillerton didn't have any releases out yet, but they'd soon be working with both Aston Stephen's brilliant pop-punk label Boss Tuneage, as well as Joe Watson's own new label, Cat N Cakey, on some great new records. These included a split CD with When All Else Fails, and a brilliant self-titled five-track 7" EP, on beautiful clear vinyl with pink and blue splashes, inside a sleeve with a nuke going off on the front and a hand grenade on the back. Subtle it wasn't, but damn good it was.

I headed over to Paris in May, to hang out with Fred Brasselet for his 30th birthday party. This was the guy from N.F.L. who'd put Joeyfat on at the New Moon Club back in '93, and had helped me with Gotham Tapes and BHP zine. He wanted us to play but only I could make it. It turned into a very messy party with lots of French punk bands, and far too many substances.

I came back from that in time to head over to the Railway Inn in Winchester again and play a show with Joe Watson's new band, Jets vs Sharks. Placid Storm would play again too, and another bunch of pop-punk loons calling themselves Mullet, but the highlight was definitely Jets vs Sharks. They had a brand-new CD out on Cat N Cakey called 'From your first cigarette to your last dying day', and although it only contained their first five tracks, it had lit a touch-paper. Even the cover was a thing of beauty, with imagery of a dove taking off from a wire above their calligraphy logo, all in blood red, over a black background. It looked cool. It sounded cool. A lot like Hot Water Music and our favourite No Idea style US bands, but with a distinctly UK sound and that underlying enthusiasm and passion. They'd go on to refine this even more with their next record, 'Our bodies our anchors', and would become a mainstay of the south coast hardcore scene.

A week later, Rydell would be heading up to London to play a mid-week post-punk special at The Verge in Kentish Town. This was another big and beautiful Victorian-era corner boozer, that regularly saw indie music nights. Adam and I had been up the previous autumn to see a ten-band Boss Tuneage all-dayer there, headlined by The Pavers, and were looking forward to playing there. Of course, this venue has joined the

6   GO!, February 14, 2003

XTPWESCU

Ignition takes off at home

PASSIONATE: David Gammage who set up record label Ignition in his store room at home

By **James Drury**

TUNBRIDGE WELLS' rock credentials are somewhat less famed than its reputation as the home of Disgusted, but it has a secret.

Major rock bands such as Coldplay, Oasis and Muse, which could now sell out stadia, have played gigs in the town in their infancy.

In light of this hidden history it should be no surprise that a punk record label has been set up in a quiet suburban road.

Sitting in their home, from which they run the label, Milo Booker and David Gammage, who form half of the team, are surrounded by framed artwork collected from years of devotion to the Hardcore punk sound.

The house encompasses a bizarrely synergetic mix of domesticity and rock 'n' roll.

A ginger cat called Tom leaves his sleeping place next to a large pile of 12-inch records before resentfully miaowing for attention.

And on the dining table, a bunch of plastic daffodils lies (someone's going to a fancy dress party as Morrisey), David hurriedly explains.

Formed by a group of friends, Ignition was born out of the punk

DIY attitude: "DIY is about believing that if something is not getting done that you want done, don't complain about it, do something," David said.

The group wanted to give people the opportunity to hear the kind of music and bands they loved, so set up Ignition, originally as a distribution label, and sold records made by their friends – mainly to other friends.

The first release was Hunter Gatherer – Low Standards For High Fives, a split release with German

> **'What would you rather see in the charts – Britney Spears or NOFX?'**

label Scene Police.

And from there DIY became more than just doing it yourself.

Their first signed act was San Geronimo from San Francisco.

They usually only "sign" a band for one release but have a release list as long as the hair of some of their bands.

Ignition has really, well ... ignited. As well as a regular

newsletter they now have a website: www.ignitiononline.co.uk which has generated a lot of interest from music fans all over the world – to their obvious delight.

Some people come to the house from Maidstone, Tonbridge and so on and others e-mail us from all over the world," Milo enthused.

David explained why this makes them so pleased: "It's why we set this up. People come from all over because you cannot really get this music in record shops as a lot of it is obscure.

"Also unless you are willing to order it in dollars and wait weeks for it to arrive you cannot get them at the prices we sell them at.

"In the shops you would have to pay about £15 for a CD whereas we sell them for between a fiver and £8.

"We want to tell people about music.

"It's great that a lot of hardcore bands got big, but there's thousands of really cool bands that are just as good."

And as if to prove a point, one of Ignition's bands, Eden Maine, has been picking up growing acclaim from the music press.

But the band's growing popularity means the label could be faced with criticism from the underground scene, which often

views success as "selling out".

But the two are phlegmatic. Milo said: "A lot of people talk about having to maintain credibility, but we don't have to answer to anyone.

"It's most important that its on our terms. While we may not be seen as keeping it underground, we are keeping it DIY."

David added: "We don't want to limit our bands, we want to give them the best coverage.

"Sometimes punk politics get in the way. There's nothing wrong with wanting to say to your mate – 'check this out'.

"What would you rather see in the charts – Britney Spears or bands like NOFX?

"At least hardcore bands have something to say. Parents should be happy their kids are listening to punk because the lyrics tend to be morally very strong and the bands have something to say. "

And it's at this point that David, dressed in a suit, has to get back to his day job in publishing, having run over his lunch hour quite considerably.

It's a fitting symbol of the town's well-disguised rock underground.

On the surface, mild-mannered besuited and respectable. Underneath, the future sound of rock music is alive and kicking.

DIY/TWR PRESENT STAY TRUE V

DAY OF THE FIGHT

JETS VS SHARKS

Rydell
Odd-man-out
chillerton

Portsmouth Wedgewood Rooms
Sunday 8th June
Doors 8pm

023 9286 3911
BOOK ONLINE tickets@wedgewood-rooms.co.uk

Wedgewood Rooms HC gig flyer

Rydell

The King Alfred, Southampton

The Wedgewood Rooms, Portsmouth

long list of those bull-dozed now to make way for rabbit-hutch flats or Pizza Expresses, but it was quite cool back then, with the matt black and blue exterior facing out onto Kentish Town Road.

This show would be headlined by The Killerest Expression, a melodic pop-punk band that had come down from Birmingham to play a few shows in support of their new mini-album, 'Four days that shook the world', out on In At The Deep End Records. They'd brought with them another Midlands-based IATDE band, called Hitechjet, as main support, and then there'd be Rydell, Otherwise and Kids Near Water too. Quite a line up really, and for those five bands I think it was just a fiver on the door!

That weekend, we'd head back over to Portsmouth to play with Jets vs Sharks and Chillerton again, but this time it was at the much bigger Wedgewood Rooms, that could hold up to 400 people and had seen everyone play there from The Buzzcocks and Joe Strummer to Shelter, Coheed and Cambria, Hell is for Heroes and Taking Back Sunday. As well as Rydell, Jets vs Sharks and Chillerton, two more bands had been shoehorned onto the bill. Day Of The Fight, another fairly new local emo band that had a split CD with a band called Weiser (not Weezer) on Red Crayon Records, and Odd-Man-Out, an indie skatecore band down from Milton Keynes, with a self-released CDEP called 'The Landfill' that they were dishing out to anyone who'd take one. This was a good show and I wish I had photos of the crowd going off on one, but of course, I was playing my guitar at the time!

Soon after this, we'd be back in the studio with John Hannon to finish mixing Rydell's third album, 'Hard on the trail', and then get to work on releasing it as soon as possible. That autumn there didn't seem to be many shows worth mentioning, and unfortunately things were winding down for Rydell as a band. Adam, Macca and I all had busy day jobs, and Duncan was looking to go travelling again soon. Milo had moved up to London in the summer, and although he'd still been commuting down three days a week, to work on the label and then join the regular Rydell rehearsals, he'd also got another job working at a Music and Video Exchange and joined a new band called Point Counterpoint based over in Thanet, with some of his mates from Margate. There was no particular catalyst, but I think we all felt it was coming to an end, even before the new album had come out.

I went down to Cardiff one weekend late in September, to attend Dan Kingdon's wedding. Dan was the manic drummer of the second incarnation of Couch Potatoes and a good friend. We were sat drinking in the Big Sleep Hotel, discussing bands, girlfriends, and life in general, when it struck me. I remember feeling I really wanted to play one last gig with my Rydell buddies, and I also wanted to get back home and see Louise, my girlfriend, who I would marry the next year.

12/12/2003 Mustard Plug, Rydell, Howard's Alias and Kenisia at The Forum, Tunbridge Wells

So, Rydell bowed out just before Christmas 2003, at The Forum in Tunbridge Wells, opening for an American ska-core band called Mustard Plug. We all realised, without ever really discussing it, that it was over and decided to play a final show. The 'Hard on the trail' album had finally been pressed and we had quite a few copies of the CD to send out. I took one of them down to my old hometown mates at The Forum, and asked if we could get on a show. They looked in the booking diary to see what they could offer us, and there it was, a Friday night, but bottom of the bill to a bunch of past their sell-by-date ska-punkers, still flogging a dead horse to grunge kids on the weekends.

We actually ended up going on in the middle, playing most of the new 'Hard on the trail' album to a bunch of die-hard local friends, who'd come to see us off amongst a bunch of bemused teenagers. Kenisia went on first; they were on their third UK tour that year, and getting very popular in the ska-core scene, with a new record entitled 'Nothing to say' out on Household Name Records. Then it was Howard's Alias, a quintet from Southampton who were currently on Good Clean Fun Records but would soon join Kenisia on Household Name too. They boasted a constantly bouncing guitarist / singer, a trombonist and trumpeter who also provided backing vocals, and a rock-solid bassist and drummer.

We went on before the headliners, and squeezed an eleven-track 'best of' set into about forty raucous and energetic minutes, before Mustard Plug went on. They were a six-piece ska punk band from Grand Rapids, Michigan. They were actually pretty good and knew how to bring the energy live, similar to Voodoo Glow Skulls or Less Than Jake. They were over on tour promoting their fifth album, entitled 'Yellow #5', out on Louis Posen's big California-based label, Hopeless Records. This was a follow-up to their big hit record, 'Evil Doers Beware', which had sold more than 90,000 copies, partly because it was engineered and produced by Bill Stevenson and Stephen Egerton, of All and Descendents, at their Blasting Room studios.

As it goes, I remember us playing an absolute blinder and there are some great photos kicking around to remind me of that night, taken by Macca's brother Nick. There's even a video of the gig that Macca's dad filmed for us. These things never quite capture it, but in 'Home', our very last track, it shows a few kids with their backs to the stage, clearly knackered, with us lot still going for it, whilst party poppers are going off all around and most people are dancing and singing along, really enjoying themselves. Macca was so busy jumping around throughout the show that he did his knee in. He'd had a cruciate ligament injury playing football ages ago and it didn't normally bother him, but during a particularly hearty stomp along for 'Across Three Parks', you can actually hear his knee twist and pop. It makes we wince even now thinking of it. He went a bit green and was clearly in agony, but gamely carried on playing the song. What a man!

Rydell´s last gig
photos by Nick Wilkinson

At the end of 'Home', in the final crescendo, we all got a bit carried away. Macca stuck his guitar headstock into the stage next to his amp and leaned on it, letting out a long noisy drone of feedback that covered up a lot of the guitar jangles, but it didn't matter, we were sad knowing it was over, but elated, nevertheless. I know we were all knackered, but you can see me grinning and flicking my plectrum into the audience in real 'rock n roll' style at the end (Loui caught it), and Duncan throwing his drumsticks in too, as Milo and Adam wave to the crowd, and Macca tries to hobble off.

I'm proud to say we rocked that last show hard, and definitely brought the feeling. We always did. We never lost that. Rydell were a decent band with a solid set of songs, and we'd left it all on the stage. It makes me smile when I think of the hundreds of party poppers Milo threw into the crowd for those last songs, and I expect the Forum guys were cursing us for ages as they were clearing up all the mess afterwards.

Rydell
The Forum 12/12/2003 setlist

Darkness Before Home
Born Witness
Know Now
Awkward Times
Cut to End
Team Building Exercise
Ground Never Held Me
Shifter (Girls with Skulls)
The Boys of Summer
Across Three Parks
Home

Rydell `Hard On The Trail´ CD reviews:

Punk News - Rydell have always been a band that had to work hard for the good reputation they've gained these days. The five British guys toured their asses off, released split CDs with many bands, including a quite popular Gainesville band, but somehow Rydell never seemed to get the recognition they deserved. They definitely play honest music, with honest melodies and honest lyrics. They've been part of the scene for a long time now, and there's definitely no reason to question the band's integrity.

'Hard On The Trail' is the new release of these five musicians. The singer knows how to express the mood of the songs with his well-known voice. What's typical, at least on every Rydell release, is the particular sadness and melancholy in the songs, although they can be quite punky on the one hand and quite catchy pop-like on the other. The guitars are distorted in certain parts, but clean and full of harmony in other parts. Rydell also play fantastic pop parts, a trademark of this band. One can read 'always stay true' in the credits and I know that the band itself has always been the best example in realising that. With 'Hard On The Trail', Rydell play the music they always did and do what they were always best at.

It's quite understandable that Rydell are called the British Hot Water Music. 'Hard On The Trail' does not kick in directly after the first listening. One first has to cope with some quite tricky rhythms and unexpected and surprising melodies. But after doing this, Rydell are a man's best friend and songs like 'Awkward Times', 'Born Witness' and 'Analysis Of The Evidence' become so familiar it's clear that they have the potential to become personal top-hits. 'Hard On The Trail' contains eleven songs, which are an ideal fix for every Hot Water Music and Samiam nerd. Song no. 11 is a cover of 'The Boys Of Summer' that we already know from bands like The Ataris, but Rydell's version is better by far. It shows the courage of these musicians too, as Rydell did not try to make it sound original or too catchy, but more in the style of their own rocking band.

And it seems this band will always be England's un-crowned kings of the melodic hardcore genre. To the people out there wanting to listen to honest, passionate music with lots of energy, I can say Rydell are the perfect deal. 'Hard On The Trail' is definitely one of the most important indie records so far in 2004.
4/5, reviewed by Dennis Grenzel

Room Thirteen - Deservedly 'Hard on the trail' of success.
Rydell are here with their third full-length album and, for once, it opens with a style of punk that I actually scarily enjoy. The 11 tracks here are all packed with the tuneful-Sex-Pistols-yelp of Miles Booker, which aggressively, yet emotively, dances around the dual guitar-work fuelled melodies inherent in every song.

Considering the lyrics of the songs, Rydell seem to rely on a small amount of words, coupled with a lot of repetition. For instance, 'Darkness Before Home', whilst lasting over three minutes, only has eight lines to its name, and repeats them all at least three times. Not that this is bad - I've never been much of a lyrics listener anyway, but judge for yourself.

The drumming in most of the songs provides a thought-provoking rhythm, rarely relying on simply using one constant beat - it leaps around like a monkey and keeps you on your toes, which is good, I assure you.

Miles Booker's vocals are really powerful, although his tendency to shout may put many off, whilst others might not enjoy his husky, untrained singing voice. Despite these flaws, this is seriously one of the finest examples of emo bands. Similar to Joshua, it's nice to see a band present 'emo' music without the down-tuned guitars and explosive riffs. It's always nice to have a change from the normal, and Rydell provide music that is both loud yet quiet - the music is powerful, yet doesn't entirely dominate your ears, which can become annoying.

The real standout tracks come towards the middle of the album, mainly as the album swings into the second half. Such examples are 'Analysis of the Evidence' and 'Fire at the End of the Street', the second song providing a strange kind of script through its vocals: 'first boy to the second boy; "where do you think I am? how do you think it's gone tonight?" This is generally the quieter side of the album, where the punk elements of the band are removed, and the juicy talent is exposed for your listening pleasure.

Providing a very un-Rydell heavy-emo cover of 'Boys of Summer' by Don Henley for the final song, Rydell finish with a bang and justify their fanbase. This CD would have scored far higher if it weren't for the punk-style tracks at the beginning of the album, which weaken the LP as a whole; the first few tracks aren't bad, but they pale in comparison to what appears as you continue to listen.
8/10, reviewed by Stephen Kyle

Drowned In Sound - I'm guilty of judging upon first impressions more often than not, and when I first encountered Rydell, some years ago now, at some hardcore / punk gig or other, I was distinctly unimpressed. A mixture of predictable influences, I thought, with no real identity of their own. I forgot them and got on with whatever it is I've been doing since.

Of course, such behaviour regularly results in a metaphysical slap about the face when the band in question re-emerges a few years later and blows one's socks off.

Well, sorta – Rydell are a mixture of predictable influences (tick off Hot Water Music, The Get Up Kids and Braid on the 'We really like US emo' wallchart; no socks blown off here), but 'Hard On The Trail' is an entertaining and consistently upbeat listen that eclipses current scene darlings like The Holiday Plan with considerable ease. It bounces in all the right places, and on standout tracks like 'Shifter (Girls with Skulls)' you're left wondering exactly how Rydell were overlooked for so long. As it happens this is their third and final album, which is a shame, as it's unquestionably their best work, a dodgy hardcore cover of Don Henley's 'The Boys of Summer' aside. Nothing mind-bendingly original then, but 'Hard On The Trail' is a solid, respectable epitaph that Rydell can be proud of, and is a worthy addition to any punk rock kid's collection.
7/10, reviewed by Mike Diver

Scanner - I've long championed this band in the pages of Scanner, although I seem to have lost touch with the band's progression a little over the last year or so. Little has changed though - the songs are still strong and, if anything, the band seems somewhat more aggressive on this, the second full album. Some of the tracks have a distinct mid-period Hot Water Music vitality, if mixed with the contours of Braid and the smooth fluidity of Sense Field. There is some impressive - as ever - guitar interplay going on here, as 'Darkness Before Home' and album highlight 'Shifter' prove. Singer Miles appears to have been snacking on broken glass too, as his already distinctive and effective vocal now has a gruff attack about it, without losing any of its subtleties. Hopefully this release will finally bring the band the recognition some of us have been demanding for many a year - it's certainly a strong enough record to justify it.

Selfish - Rydell is the name of those five gentlemen from the island who, like their fellow countrymen from Steel Rules Die, combine rough punk, devoted emo-rock and a pinch of hardcore. It is not surprising that the (somewhat moderately produced) result is reminiscent of Hot Water Music - especially since you already started a split 7" with the heroes from Gainesville. Nevertheless, or precisely because of this, the eleven songs have their own charm. Maybe this is because 'Hard on the trail' is miles away from the smoothly produced high-gloss products of some colleagues. Since their early days, the band has added a couple of brackets in terms of hardening their technical ability, so that the new work is a whole lot more compelling than the (also okay) singles compilation, 'Always remember everything'. In addition, with pieces like 'Cut to end' or the intense 'Analysis of the evidence', Rydell have a few really great pieces in their repertoire that won't let go of you quickly. Only with the 'The boys of summer' cover at the end is it possible at all - even if the included screamo version is at least a hundred percent better than the unspeakable Ataris copy of this wonderful Don Henley composition. These British guys deserve your attention; as do Engineer Records, a label worth supporting in the background. Just beautiful.

Past & Present - Musically Rydell is pretty predictable, I'd say. I mean, they sound a lot like many of the bands that are popular right now within modern hardcore, emo and punk music, but I still like this album. Not because it has anything new, but because it's more memorable than a lot of what's being released within this genre at the moment. And where else are you going to get a full-blown hardcore cover of Don Henley's 'The Boys of Summer' anyway?

Blueprint - Rydell, a band that has somehow passed me by in the last few years, should now sound through my home speakers again. A few years ago, the split 7" with Hot Water Music brought Rydell to our attention. Maybe in between too, we should have listened, but I didn't, so enough of the senseless gibberish. Rydell delight us with nice snotty punk rock, as you are used to from them, and parallels to the above mentioned HWM are also not to be dismissed. The opener 'Know now' is extremely catchy, the melodies and enthusiasm spread. Associations with Samiam or early Get Up Kids are also not far away. 'Hard on the Trail' offers a loosely flaky mix of emo and punk, a horny

drunk voice from singer Miles Booker, and convinces you with good guitar work, varied tracks and great song writing. On top of it all, you will hear several potential hits. OK, the production is not the best, but who cares? Finally, there is the Don Henley classic 'The Boys of Summer'. Yes, I know, that's what the Ataris did - but here the song is turned through the meat grinder and pressed onto the record, plate like, with a lot of shouting and snot. That's how it should be. Let's hear it again.
Rating: 7.5 / 10.

Derry High School Killing Team Zine – Rydell - Hard On The Trail (Engineer records)
I'd never heard these guys before but on first listen, to me it sounds very similar to Hot Water Music, quite catchy and up-beat stuff. It slows down a bit mid-album, but this helps to show the depth and song writing skills of the band. This isn't something I would normally buy, but it's a nice album to relax to. The vocals don't have much of a range; I mean they sound good when the guy screams a little, but he doesn't really have a 'singing' voice, which would definitely add more to the band if he did, but the cool guitar work makes up for that. Two guitars always playing differently to each other like Fireside do it. What's the point of having two guitars if they're just going to play the same thing? So that adds a lot to the album, and the drums sound good too, but you can't hear too much of the bass. Rydell seem like a band that would do well to have more bass solos and I don't mean like Rancid or anything, but just something to add more to the quiet bits in the songs, so they're more interesting. A good, enjoyable album that shows the potential of the band off well.

Fans of Fireside, Rival Schools and Hot Water Music would appreciate this album.

Vampster - Impeccable and officially rocking fodder for the emo disciples.
I am relieved. The way singer Miles Booker looks in the picture, you'd think the poor guy hasn't had anything fresh to wear in five weeks because he's looking so sad. The third album by the British emo stars isn't as sad and bitter as the sensitive boys look on the photos: Power, joie de vivre and, here and there ,a few off-key tones rule here.

Nevertheless, it wouldn't be an emo record if the sensitive hooligans weren't a little more melancholic at times. 'Cut to End', for example, shows why Rydell are simply necessary in this musical area: a powerful song with beautiful melodies and a lot of character, thanks to Miles Booker's rough voice. Rydell aren't violent for a second, but the rock part is considerable. Rydell sometimes spit around nicely, but don't forget the melodies. Sometimes fast, sometimes slow, sometimes sad, sometimes happy; the quintet from the island is versatile and actually convinces in all areas, even if 'Analysis of the Evidence' is a bit long-winded and the guitars are mixed too thinly. Otherwise, 'Hard on the Trail' is perfect and officially rocking fodder for the emo fans, which is really successful in its own way, not too smooth ironed and, above all, very original. Anyone who likes Hot Water Music and Jimmy Eat will definitely have a lot of fun with the third album by the Brits.

Penny Black - Excellent farewell album from the underacknowledged and unique Rydell, who were one of the early champions of the emo movement.

Nearly three years ago, an album arrived on my doormat that simply changed the foundations of my musical tastes and left me utterly committed to underground music. Since then, emo has gone mainstream and been subsequently ridiculed, despite the passion and brilliance of the likes of Jimmy Eat World, Rival Schools and Hundred Reasons.

The world Rydell's album opened up for me, however, went a long way beyond mainstream emo, to a scene that may only have small audiences comparatively, but whose audiences are passionately devoted to this music, and whose bands really are completely unique and breathtakingly good. Without Rydell's album, I would never have sought out the bands that influenced them, like Chamberlain – who I interviewed last year and whose 'The Moon My Saddle' is an all-time favourite, or Elliott, or the Appleseed Cast, or the completely ignored but brilliant Crosstide, or the legion of Deep Elm Records bands, in particular Brandtson.

I say this in all my reviews, but if you like indie rock, then you will like these bands. If I had to choose between these and the far more celebrated records I own, these win every time. Despite all the praise lavished on so many art-rock bands, these bands – who get criminally small coverage – outstrip them in all areas. Not just in passion and songwriting, but in experimentation and adventurousness and recklessness as well.

But when it comes down to it, Rydell's 'Per Ardua Ad Astra' was the first, and I'll always love it. No wonder it was my album of the year in 2001. If I could vote for it every year, I probably would. Age has not decreased its power. Last year, Rydell put out a compilation of early and rare tracks, including some acoustic interpretations, but finally a full follow-up has emerged. Tragically, it is the last act in the Rydell story, as the band has been forced to break up. Like so many great bands before them, the lack of commercial recognition had meant that other commitments have had to take precedence over the music. Like Chamberlain and Elliott, they have broken up despite being on a creative roll.

'Hard On The Trail' is a more diverse collection than 'Per Ardua Ad Astra', which was very immediate. This takes more time, but the melodies are always there and the arrangements always unique. The band is, however, slightly more adventurous on this album. 'Per Ardua Ad Astra' was very much an emo album, but there are certainly nods here to the band's hardcore roots, especially on their likeable cover of 'The Boys Of Summer'. The band doesn't hide their influences, but they don't allow these bands to dictate their direction either. The gruff hardcore of Hot Water Music is seemingly incompatible with the pop rock of the Get Up Kids, or the introspection of

Chamberlain or indeed the mysteriousness of early REM, but all are part of the Rydell package. There are even hints of a hidden admiration for the Strokes in the jangly but propulsive guitar lines.

If you are already a Rydell fan, and anyone with sense is, rest assured that just because this is the final offering it is not below par. 'Team Building Exercise' is by far and away the best thing they've done, 'Know Now' is Rydell at their most intense and 'Cut To End' their most catchy. Frontman Milo's vocals veer from sweet and melodic to full-on intensity, whilst the interaction between the instrumentalists allows them to do pretty much the same. The production is top notch. I can't decide if it's a better album as a whole than 'Per Ardua Ad Astra', so if you're new to Rydell then just get both! Then check out their label's website and order some Chamberlain and Elliott records. It'll make sense to you! The only question that remains is, album of the year? Almost certainly! Rydell may not be famous, but they will be missed.

38, You could call it an outro, but it's really just feedback

So that was the end of Rydell. Although of course it wasn't. We didn't play any more gigs together after that, but we did continue to promote the records and sell loads of CDs, with hundreds of thousands of downloads and streams nowadays. There were many more compilations and benefits, and there was a collection of twenty-two of our best songs, entitled 'Anchors & Parachutes', out on an Italian hardcore label, Chorus of One. This took a while to come out, the CD seeing the light of day early in 2007, but these guys were big fans, based in Turin, and did a really good job of promoting the release. They put out albums for other alternative rock bands, including Kover, The Chuck Norris Experiment, Against The World and Fire At Will, before selling the label's catalogue to a distro of the same name, based out of Indiana, USA.

To celebrate the twenty-fifth anniversaries of the 'Per Ardua Ad Astra' and 'Hard On The Trail' albums there will be vinyl re-releases. With the massive resurgence in vinyl and record collecting, we figured that we may as well have our own silver jubilee for the few post-punk nerds who give a shit, like us. This way we get to re-master the tracks and re-work the album artwork too, safely in the hands of Ian Sadler at Emeline Studios as the best sound engineer I know, and Craig Cirinelli of HouseWithoutWalls Design as the best designer I know. Both of whom have been long time Rydell fans, and both of whom have played in great alt-rock bands themselves, so totally get it.

Although it was an end for Rydell, it was the start of many new things. Milo would eventually move to New York to be with his wife and work in alternative record stores there, spreading the indie scene gospel. Duncan would move to South Korea, to teach English and marry, and drum in a post-punk band over there. Adam moved down to Somerset, and Macca stayed in Brighton, both building new businesses and having lovely families to fill their time. I was lucky and married my soulmate, Louise. We did loads of travelling, moved house, set up another business and have two wonderful boys. This all kept us pretty busy. But there was still that D.I.Y. bug. That punk rock spirit of the underground that just encourages you to get up and do something else creative. I'd kept my guitars and kept on writing music, and I was always in touch with the UKHC scene through Engineer Records (which I'd started back in '99 and is still going strong now, with over 350 releases to date), as well as fanzines, websites, gigs and the alternative scene grapevine.

I'm still in touch with all the guys and had been speaking with Macca Wilkinson (ex Rydell and BBMFs), Jamie Donbroski (ex BBMFs and Strength Alone) and Simon Goodrick (ex Strength Alone) about forming a new band. Sometime in 2012, we decided to do just that and called ourselves Come The Spring. We intended to get together in Brighton once a week to jam, and then go for a few beers. It was meant to be just for the hell of it, but we all really clicked, and it was such fun that soon enough we were playing gigs again and then heading into the studio to record our songs. We move slower now though, partly out of necessity, only playing the gigs we want to and fitting band things in between other commitments. Even so, between 2013 and 2018, we put out three good CD EPs, entitled 'Seven For A Secret' with Vic Payne of My So Called Life singing, and then 'Revive' and 'Echoes' both with Sam Craddock of Hands Shaped Like Hearts singing. In 2021, we released 'Echoes Revived' as a full album and that CD has already had three represses, but this was now well into the Covid lockdowns, so the gigs had stopped.

We'd also written a fourth EP as Come The Spring around this time, but wanted our American friend Craig Cirinelli (ex Elemae, Damn This Desert Air, World Concave, Hidden Cabins, etc) to sing on it. We recorded the music at Emeline Studios in Whitstable with Ian, then sent the tapes over to Craig to work on the lyrics and vocals in New Jersey. He recorded his tracks at home in Boonton and sent them back to us, for mixing and mastering here. We decided to call this cross-channel collaboration The Atlantic Union Project and would release the '3,482 Miles' EP, representing the distance between Brighton, UK and Boonton, NJ, in 2022 on Sell The Heart Records in the USA, Shield Recordings in Europe and my own Engineer Records here in the UK. Our latest musical venture would be available on digital, CD and gatefold coloured vinyl formats, and is distributed worldwide. Another creative idea brought to fruition through the D.I.Y. alternative scene.

It was also during these long days of Covid lockdown that I started work on this book. I'd been chatting about a few shows we'd played, with bands like Hot Water Music and Green Day, with my boys, Carl and Jake. They were intrigued, more interested than I expected, and laughing at some of the stories, so encouraged me to scribble down some more notes. These lockdown notes, alongside my gig booking diaries and general hardcore scene nerdiness have developed into this book. But, like any good album cover, I have a thanks list too. Obviously, I owe this story to everyone involved in the '90s UKHC scene and I've mentioned and spoken about as many as possible. Certainly not all the gigs we played or people we met, but as many of them as I could remember positive things to say about them. All the bands, venues, fanzine editors, gig promoters and record labels, and of course, all the people who came to shows and bought records too. You're in this book and this book is about you. A D.I.Y. scene could be created then, and it can be created now. And it can be about whatever you are into. So, what's stopping you?

'Anchors and Parachutes'
CD cover and layout

`Per Ardua Ad Astra´ new cover and layout

New `Hard On The Trail´ LP cover

COME

THE

SPRING

THE DEBUT
SEVEN FOR A SECRET
OUT 25.03.13

COMETHESPRING   COMETHESPRING

ENGINEER
RECORDS
EngineerRecords.com

`Seven For A Secret´ release poster

Come The Spring
`Seven For A Secret`

COME THE SPRING // REVIVE

Come The Spring
`Revive`

Come The Spring
outside Bar42,
Worthing

Come The Spring
at The Quadrant,
Brighton

COME THE SPRING
ECHOES

COME THE SPRING
ECHOES

Sam Craddock-Caing - Vocals
Simon Goodrick - Guitar
David Gamage - Guitar
Mark Wilkinson - Bass
Jamie Denbrooks - Drums

Recorded at Emeline Studios 2018
Engineered and produced by Ian Sadler
All songs written and performed by Come The Spring except Boys of Summer (Don Henley)
Photography by Sofia Wåhlin

Live in the feedback
Die in the velvet

Come The Spring `Echoes´

**Come The Spring
`Echoes Revived`**

THE ATLANTIC UNION PROJECT
3,482 mi.

| THE ACTUARY | TRUSTWORTHY | SOON TO END | CHEAP SEATS | STRINGS ATTACHED | WAIT INDOORS |

The Atlantic
Union Project
`3,482 Miles`

Cast and crew –

Where are they now?

Yan – Still 'The Man', lives with his family in Epping Forest, somewhere near the Kelvedon Hatch bunker.

Jim – Disappeared abroad for so long I thought he was either dead or had become a spy, but recently back in the UK and occasionally drumming for Unhome.

Jason – Married Isabel and has a family that all live for music. Still runs The Forum in Tunbridge Wells, which was awarded Britain's Best Small Venue by NME in 2012 and Best Grassroots Venue by Music Week in 2020.

Matt – Works for Radio Kent and can often be heard commentating on Gillingham FC games and county cricket.

Aidan – Often found at Leyton Orient or Walthamstow FC matches when he's not helping people at the hospital.

Dan P – Rocks the guitar in a band called Superstructures.

Paul – Lives in Maidstone and plays fingerbass in Superstructures.

Dan K – Works far too hard for such a punk rocker and occasionally bangs around on his golden Ludwig drum kit until his kids or neighbours tell him to stop.

Duncan – Moved to Busan in South Korea where he teaches English at the university, a job which he describes as 'ridiculous' on account of having five months of vacation a year. He drummed for an expat band there, called Jake and the Slut, who appeared on Canadian morning TV after being involved in a horror movie soundtrack. Dunc married Soryeong and they have two sons, who all come and visit for vegetarian summer BBQs and Rydell reminiscences.

Adam – Moved down to Somerset to get away from it all and lead an easier life. But then had three sons with his wife Liz and started his own locksmith's business, so still doesn't get much rest.

Milo – Bounced around for a while and ended up living in New York. Still totally obsessed with music and works in two record stores there. The last photo he sent me was of him in one of the stores chatting with Ian MacKaye!

Macca – Lives in Portslade, Brighton with his lovely family, working from home as an IT Project Manager, going to see The Seagulls when they play at home and still living and breathing music. He plays the bass for The Evening Sons and The Atlantic Union Project.

Nik N – Runs a hipster barber shop in Helsinki, Finland and blasts heavy rock at all his customers.

Omen – Worshipping Satan whilst getting truck drivers out of parking tickets.

Bill S – Runs The Blasting Room recording studio in Fort Collins, Colorado and still drums in All and the Descendents.

Mark D – The co-founder of Tunbridge Wells Forum and founder/CEO of Music Venue Trust.

Warren – Bartending in heaven (RIP).

Al W – Writes excellent comedy books, probably while wearing silly hats.

Toby D – Last I heard he was locked in an asylum somewhere.

Jamie D – Lives in Worthing and works in IT, still drums for The Evening Sons and The Atlantic Union Project.

Simon G – Lives in Brighton, repairs guitars and occasionally edits films. Plays guitar for The Evening Sons and The Atlantic Union Project.

Johnny Deathshead – Lurking somewhere in Brighton and I worry about him.

Billie-Joe – Carried on playing with Mike and Tre in his little band and had some success.

Christy C – Went back to the US and helped create the documentary, 'Turn It Around: The Story of East Bay Punk'.

Nick W – Attends every gig in the Southeast and runs Burning Picks Photography.

Vique Simba – Moved to the US to work for Revelation Records and now works for Pirates Press Records.

Buz – One of the godfathers of the Brighton punk scene. Continues to put on shows and run his Punker Bunker store. Just One Life. The rise and fall of nothing much at all.

Dave B – Still writes the odd song with fellow Strookas, John and Tony, under the name Tonota 80.

Kris B – Lives in London with his Swedish wife Bex and their skateboarding mad kids.

Tom W – Unbelievably, works as a very sensible lawyer now, a criminal barrister in fact.

Dan M – Still lives in London, drinks and hits things a lot.

Rich L – Part of the S.T.E crew and puts up bands in Eastleigh.

Martin N – Soldiering on with blasted ears at The White House studios.

Simon L – Rides his bike around Uckfield and has seen more Rydell shows than anyone else alive

Rich M – Works as a sports journalist and still found time to manage some bands. Now runs Lonestar Comedy.

Paul W – Sings for sludge metal band OHHMS and runs the Different Times podcast with fellow Babies Three compadre Dan S.

Syd F – Lives in Crawley and plays guitar in Superstructures with Dan P and Paul.

Rachel W - Lives in Brighton and tries to help people with their mental health whilst being covered in tattoos.

Dennis M – Still lives in Bonn, just down the road from the old Scene Police HQ, and works in PR and journalism, but spends all his money on vinyl records.

Emre A – Lives in London with his music-publisher wife and is currently enjoying a mid-life gap year. Worked for a while in catastrophe reinsurance but realised how silly that was, so is now plotting a return to the alt-music scene, possibly with a new record label.

Chuck R – Often to be found down the riverbank or at a BBQ, but still sings and plays guitar in HWM with Chris, Jason, George and the new guy Chris C. They are just as awesome as ever. Check out 'Feel The Void' on Equal Vision Records.

Eric G – Came back to London to work at Cargo Records UK record distribution.

Gubby S – Last seen scoffing poutines with his headphones on at PouzzaFest in Montreal.

Charlie M – Blew his ears out recording Rydell and Blaggers I.T.A. and now resides in a darkened room insisting that all music should be mezzopiano.

Jake R – Still produces music at his Tan Rallt Studio in deepest Sussex.

Steev CVM – Runs CVM BMX Media and creates great videos.

Ben H – Lives in Bexleyheath and still writes about music. Occasionally books gigs at The Water Rats in Kings Cross, London and likes to celebrate unrecognised figures.

Frank T - Continues gigging, both solo acoustic sets and with his band, The Sleeping Souls, and has now played quite a few shows, both in and out of the HC scene. A big supporter of the Music Venue Trust and runs his own Lost Evenings Festival.

John H – Playing the guitar and trumpet and mixing records in heaven (RIP)

The obligatory Thanks list...

Thanks to: All the bands we shared a stage with, especially; The BBMFs, HDQ, Drive, Sleep, Alice Donut, Active Response, Jailcell Recipes, Angus Bagpipe, Strength Alone, Majority Of One, NOFX, Green Day, Pseudo Hippies, Juice, Understand, Spermbirds, Rorschach, Blaggers ITA, The Strookas, Sonar Nation, Sofahead, Goober Patrol, Alloy, Artless, Guns N Wankers, Your Mum, Funbug, Down By Law, N.F.L., China Drum, Dipsomaniacs, 18th Dye, Torque, Broken Toys, Harries, Iconoclast, Bob Tilton, Above All, Tequila Girls, X-Men, Travis Cut, Another Fine Mess, Toast, M-80s, Policy Of 3, Malva, Beacon, Unfold, Tribute, Schema, Annalise, Wact, Chocolate, Underclass, Tartan, Lever, Konstrukt, Minute Manifesto, Sparkmarker, Month Of Birthdays, Imbiss, Samiam, Shades Apart, Blue Tip, Kerosene 454, Hooton 3 Car, Jetpak, Fiction, Knuckledust, Karate, Broccoli, Voorhees, The Marshes, Rudedog, Hot Water Music, Pale, Tumult, El Guapo Stunt Team, Abhinanda, Discount, The Tone, Spy Versus Spy, The Babies Three, Sunfactor, Grand Central, Pylon, Inside Right, Imbalance, Reno Kid, Losome, Painted Thin, Kurt, One Day Elliott, Autumn Year, Kneejerk, Southport, Leiah, Leatherface, Errortype 11, Dismemberment Plan, Burning Airlines, Nothing In Common, The Junket, The Get Up and Go-Ers, San Quentin, Yeast, Hunter Gatherer, Tupamaros, Stapleton, Summer Book Club, Sunshine, Cars As Weapons, Like Herod, North By Northwest, Blocko, Vehicle Derek, British Sea Power, Copperpot Journals, Anthem Of The Century, Stars Rain Down, No Comply, Vanilla Pod, That Very Time I Saw, Hillside, Green Acre, OneLineDrawing, Arcaine, Last Year's Diary, The Day I Snapped, Piebald, Always Outnumbered, Kids Near Water, Urotsukidoji, Winter In June, Jairus, One Time Champion, Photobook Stories, Guillaume Seam, Chillerton, Jets Vs Sharks, Hitechject, The Killerest Expression, Otherwise, Day Of The Fight, Odd Man Out, Mustard Plug, Howards Alias and Kenisia.

And those we didn't, but who inspired us; Dead Kennedys, Conflict, Minor Threat, SNFU, 7 Seconds, Dag Nasty, OP IV, Crimpshrine, Mr T Experience, Pegboy, Gorilla Biscuits, Libido Boyz, Descendents, All, Jawbreaker, Sugar, Split Lip / Chamberlain, Sense Field, Quicksand, The Get Up Kids, Promise Ring, Braid, Lifetime, Elliott, Shudder To Think, Texas Is The Reason, San Geronimo, A Rocket Sent To You, Mineral, Cross My Heart, Pop Unknown, Appleseed Cast, Planes Mistaken For Stars, Last Days Of April, Crosstide, Jimmy Eat World, Speedwell, Joshua, Elemae and many, many more.

All the venues and promoters, records labels, fanzines, radio stations and recording studios along the way. And most of all, to anyone who came to a gig or bought a record, and allowed us this fun trip.

Special thanks to Miles Booker and Louise Gamage for helping me compile my notes for this book. Jenni Brindley and Ian Glasper for proof-reading my scribblings. Steve Crawley for laying out the book. Craig Cirinelli for designing the cover. And you, for bothering to read it.

D.I.Y. UKHC 4EVER.

Also available at

Nimrod
by Ryan Roberts

Combat Ready
by Tim Satchwell

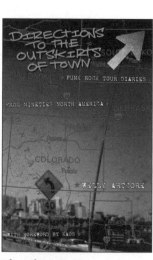

Worst Eurovision Ever
by Roy D. Hacksaw

**Terrorized: The Collected
Interviews. Volume One & Two**
by Ian Glasper

We Can Be The New Wind
by Alexandros Anesiadis

**Directions To The
Outskirts Of Town**
by Welly Artcore

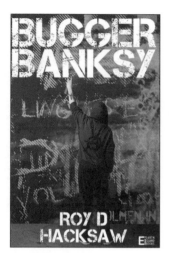

Bugger Banksy
by Roy D Hacksaw

Mass Movement Volume 1 & 2
by Tim Cundle

The Scene That Would Not Die
by Ian Glasper

What Would Garry Gygax Do?
by Tim Cundle

Punk Faction BHP '91 to '95
by David Gamage

Compression
by Tim Cundle

earthislandbooks.com